Peasants and Peasant Societies

To Nancy, quarrelsomely . . .

Peasants and Peasant Societies

SELECTED READINGS

Edited by

Teodor Shanin

Second Edition

Basil Blackwell

Selection, introduction and notes copyright © Teodor Shanin 1971 and 1987

Second edition published 1987 by
Basil Blackwell Ltd
108 Cowley Road, Oxford OX4 1JF, UK
Reprinted 1989

Basil Blackwell Inc.
432 Park Avenue South, Suite 1503
New York, NY 10016, USA

in association with
Penguin Books Ltd, Harmondsworth,
Middlesex, England

First published 1971 by Penguin Books Ltd

British Library Cataloguing in Publication Data

Peasants and peasant societies: selected
  readings. – 2nd ed.
  1. Peasantry
  I. Shanin, Teodor
  305.5' 63   HD1521
  ISBN 0–631–15212–1

Library of Congress Cataloging in Publication Data

Peasants and peasant societies.
  Bibliography: p.
  Includes index.
  1. Peasantry.   2. Rural conditions.   I.
Shanin,
Teodor.
  HD1521.P42   1987   305.5' 63   87-775
  ISBN 0–631–15212–1
  ISBN 0–631–15619–4 (pbk)

Typeset in 10 on 11½pt Ehrhardt
by Joshua Associates Limited, Oxford
Printed in Great Britain by
Billing and Sons Ltd, Worcester

Contents

Contents

V 'THEM' – PEASANTS AS OBJECTS OF POLICIES AND STUDIES

Acknowledgements

The editor and the publishers are grateful to the following for permission to reproduce material previously published elsewhere: Dover Publications Inc. (item 1); Macmillan Publishers Ltd and Yale University Press (item 2); Beacon Press (item 4); Weidenfeld & Nicolson Ltd and John Wiley and Sons Inc. (item 5); American Anthropological Association and Eric R. Wolf (item 6); University of Chicago Press (items 7 and 8); Mouton and Co. (item 9); Andrew Pearse (item 10); John S. Saul (item 11); Latin American Center for Research in the Social Sciences and Ernest Feder (item 12); Polish Academy of Sciences and Boguslaw Galeski (item 18); Associated Book Publishers Ltd (item 19); Van Gorcum (item 21); Macmillan Publishers Ltd (item 22); Penguin Books Ltd (item 24); Basile Kerblay (item 25); University of Texas Press and Manning Nash (item 27); International Labour Office (item 29, copyright © International Labour Organization, Geneva); Polish Academy of Sciences (item 33); The British Association for the Advancement of Science and Frederick G. Bailey (item 35); Sutti Ortiz (item 36); Yale University Press (item 37); Lawrence and Wishart Ltd 1979 (item 39); Manchester University Press (item 40); *Peasant Studies* (item 41); Yale University Press (item 42): Frank Cass and Co. Ltd (item 43, reprinted by permission of Frank Cass and Co. Ltd); Penguin Books Ltd and Beacon Press (item 45); UNESCO (item 46); Alfred A. Knopf Inc. (item 47); Granada Publishing Ltd and Grove Press Inc. (item 48b); Oxford University Press (item 48c); Chatto & Windus and Oxford University Press Inc. (item 48d); Clarendon Press (item 50); Routledge and Kegan Paul (item 51); Asian Economic Research Institute and R. P. Dore (item 52); Robert S. McNamara (item 53); Penguin Books Ltd (item 54); Macmillan Publishers Ltd (item 55); UNESCO (item 57, copyright © UNESCO 1985, reproduced by permission of UNESCO); Hutchinson Books Ltd (item 60); Alfred A. Knopf (item 61).

Introduction: Peasantry as
a Concept

One can seldom speak of inventions in social sciences, yet time and again a social issue strikes the scholar's eye with all the dramatic force of the apple which fell at Newton's feet. The late 1960s/early 1970s have seen the somewhat paradoxical rediscovery of peasants. In a rapidly expanding world the character, livelihood and fate of massive rural populations of the world's poorest and potentially most explosive areas have come to be seen as one of the most crucial issues of our time. Suddenly, behind the newsmen's headings about glib politicians, vicious generals, pushy foreigners, and fiery revolutionaries, a great unknown of the peasantry was detected as one of the major structural determinants which make the so-called 'developing societies' into what they are. After a quarter of a century in obscurity the 'peasant problem' came back with a bang – as a dominant issue of Vietnam battlefields and India's poverty, Latin American guerrillas, Africa's stagnation and China's 'Great Leap'. For the English-speaking core of Western academic culture of the post-war years it was discovered rather than rediscovered – the first extensive encounter with this social phenomenon expressed as a conceptual issue and even with the term 'peasant' in contemporaneity. Next came a virtual flood of publications specifically devoted to peasants, from few and far between to hundreds and then thousands, as the word 'peasant' moved right to the top of sociological fashions and publishers' popularity charts. The proof of this is close to hand. The 1971 first edition of *Peasants and Peasant Societies* went through seven reprints to sell more than 50,000 copies.

A number of questions follow. Why the surprise? – after all, peasants have existed for millennia as the massive majority of mankind and were still its majority when their recognition so forcefully struck social scientists. Secondly, what has the surprise been about? – i.e. what are peasants as an analytical concept rather than a loose descriptive term? Also, what were the theoretical tools available to consider this issue when it dawned on the analysts? Finally, what was the heuristic result of 'bringing into focus' and accentuating peasant studies, that is, what have we learned and in what direction is the field advancing?

Of these questions we shall begin with the second one, that is, with defining peasants. The possibility to do so realistically has been in itself a matter of fundamental controversy and an analytical issue and, should it fail, our book would turn into a ghost story. The content of the volume will then be considered. The other questions suggested and in particular the 1960s/1970s wave of peasant studies and its analytical results will be discussed in the book's last section (item 62).

Defining Peasants: a General Type

The reasons why the validity of peasantry as a concept has been put into doubt belong to three categories. Firstly, the extensive diversity between peasantries (or what was designated as such) in different regions and communities, as well as within most of the rural communities, seems to militate against generalization. Secondly, peasants must be considered in their change and transformation, as a process. Yet, how does one delimit an entity involved in mutations evident to all? Finally, contemporary peasants form part of a broader society. If so, why single them out at all: why not treat them simply through the general categories of social analysis (along quantitative scales signifying, for example, that some peasants are poorer, or less educated or more 'traditional', etc.)? It is the testing of these doubts which will guide us in the defining of qualitative particularity underlying the use of the term peasantry as a valid generalization and a theoretical concept.

As against the initial charge of heterogeneity, the existence of peasantry as a realistic rather than semantic notion can be claimed on grounds of epistemology, comparative evidence and application. First, any tendency to treat peasantry as a bodiless notion is countered by the essential point of the methodology of the social sciences – the trivial but often forgotten truth that a sociological generalization does not imply a claim of homogeneity or an attempt at uniformity. Quite to the contrary, comparative studies assume the existence of both similarities and differences, without which a generalization would, of course, be pointless. In pursuing a 'generalizing science' sociologists lay themselves open to outrage of the adherents of methods and of disciplines to which the study of uniqueness is central, and has easily developed into a canon of faith. Much of this is based on misunderstanding; some of it simply illustrates the difficulties of grasping theoretically the uniqueness of social reality. As often, it was Max Weber who put this issue in words at its clearest: 'The abstract character of sociology is responsible for the fact that compared with actual historical reality they [i.e. sociological concepts] are relatively lacking in fullness of concrete content' but, consequently, 'sociological analysis both abstracts from reality and, at the same time, helps us to understand it' (Weber, 1925, pp. 109–12).

Secondly, it is sufficient to read concurrently a sequence of peasant studies originating in countries as far removed in their physical and social conditions as Russia, Hungary, Turkey, China, Tanzania, Colombia and so on, or better still to study them synchronically, to note substantive similarities. There are, of course, important differences, to be expected in view of the varied conditions and experience. What strikes one, however, is, to quote some views, 'the persistence of certain peasant attributes in societies far removed' (Erasmus, 1967, p. 150), 'something generic about it . . . [a] type without localization' (Redfield, 1956, pp. 25, 23). The widespread conclusion of the practitioners of research that we face a 'recurrent syndrome' (Wolf, 1977) has been central to the acceptability of a generalization and to its increasing use. It also led to efforts to establish it as a particular unit of theoretical thought.

Finally, and still referring to the issue of heterogeneity, the massive empirical and analytical work of the last decade concerning rural societies and economies has demonstrated the usefulness and illumination of transferring methodologies and concepts applied by students of peasantry from one particular setting to another, cross-cutting countries and continents. Shcherbina's methodology of Budget Studies (Shanin, 1972, chapter 3), Wolf's 'power brokers' (p. 55 below) or Marx's discussions of peasant land property's communal base and of family farms as 'potatoes' in a sack (see item 39 below), right or wrong, are still fresh in shaping debate and offering illumination in places thousands of miles apart and a century afar from their objects. It goes without saying that mindless re-use of notions, methods and conclusions is fools' preserve. Regional and historical particularities call for both adjustment and sophisticated use of any comparison and/or method drawn from elsewhere. But, significantly, there is no need to begin each time from square one, the experience of peasant studies has been, in part, cumulative.

As a first approximation we can distinguish peasants as *small agricultural producers, who, with the help of simple equipment and the labour of their families, produce mostly for their own consumption, direct or indirect, and for the fulfilment of obligations to holders of political and economic power*. Sociological definitions and types resemble two-dimensional sketches of multi-dimensional reality, each reflects only part of the characterized phenomena. A further step would be to establish a more developed general type expressed in four interdependent facets: the family farm, the agriculture, the village and its culture, and the plebeian slot within the systems of social domination. Definitions of peasantry by one single determining factor are 'neater' but too limiting for our purpose.

Peasant family farm as the basic multi-dimensional unit of social organization. The family and mostly the family provides the labour on the farm. The farm and mostly the farm provides for the consumption needs of the family and the payments of its dues. It is not autarkic: peasants are involved in daily exchange of goods and in labour markets. Their economic action is, however, closely interwoven with family relations. Family division of labour and the consumption needs of the family give rise to particular strategies of survival and use of the resources. The family farm operates as the major unit of peasant property, production, consumption, welfare, social reproduction, identity, prestige, sociability and welfare. In it, the individual tends to submit to a formalized family role-behaviour and patriarchal authority.

Land husbandry as the main means of livelihood. Peasant farming includes a specific, traditionally defined, combination of tasks on a relatively low level of specialization. (Another way to put it is to say that different occupations are 'telescoped' into peasant productive activities.) Related to this is the informal and family-based vocational training. Self-employment and food production result in particular mini-ecological 'packages'. The impact of nature is particularly important for the livelihood of small production units with limited resources, defining its rhythms: seasonal cyclicity deeply influences the life of the family, family events are reflected in the dynamics of the farm, while a crop failure may lead to its total extinction. Of the forces/factors of production, land and family labour are central – a 'licence' to enter the occupation and a major way the local status of the families is defined.

Specific cultural patterns linked to the way of life of a small rural community. Life of a small community within which most of the peasant needs of social living and social reproduction can be met offers a characteristic context to the life of peasants. Particularities of residence, social network and consciousness link and interdepend. Peasantries' cultural features, in the sense of socially determined norms and cognitions, show typical tendencies, such as, for example, the pre-eminence of traditional and conformist attitudes (i.e. the justification of action in terms of past experience and the will of the community), particular norms of property inheritance, of solidarity, exclusion, etc. Peasant culture both reflects and reinforces the characteristics and life experience of a small village community, e.g. lack of anonymity and face-to-face relations, *vis-à-vis* strong normative controls or the common experience of growing up in similar physical and social environment *vis-à-vis* the attitudes to 'outsiders'.

The 'underdog' position — the domination of peasantry by outsiders. Peasants as a rule have been kept at arm's length from the social sources of power. Their political subjugation interlinks with cultural subordination and economic exploitation through tax, rent, corvée, interest and terms of trade unfavourable to the peasant. Subordination has entailed repeated attempts at self-defence through the extensive use of the 'weapons of the weak' such as economic sabotage, avoidance, boycott, etc., and in some conditions, of revolts which turned peasants into a major revolutionary force of our century.

The four 'facets' suggested mean not only a sequence of characteristics but their interdependence, which must be treated as a *Gestalt*, the elements of which reinforce each other. When any one of the major characteristics from the set is removed, the nature of each of its further components changes.

Different schools of thought concerning peasantry have often expressed their diversity by the accentuation of one characteristic treated as the core of the *differentia specifica* of peasanthood and as the cutting edge of its definition. In a limited sense such a hierarchy of significance can be claimed also for the present definition. In the views of a majority of contemporary analysts who accept peasantry as a valid concept, it is the family farm which is the most significant characteristic of peasantry.

Defining Peasants: Margins and Changes, Insertion and Particularity

The next step to unfold and explore the typification suggested, as well as to meet the doubts concerning peasantry's existence as a valid concept in the face of heterogeneity, changeability and social 'embedment', is to consider its analytical 'margins' or 'hedges', i.e. to look at social groups which share with the peasants, as defined, most but not all of their main characteristics. Discrepancy between the clear-cut frontiers of theoretical concepts and the finer graded and often ambivalent divisions within social phenomena itself is, of course, part and parcel of the practice of the social sciences. We can do somewhat better than simply to note it by proceeding to categorize the marginal groups and to put such taxonomy to use in defining characteristics and changes of different rural societies. A few points should here be kept in mind. First, analytical marginality does not imply numerical insignificance or particular instability. Second, their representatives share rural environments with the 'hard-core' peasants and may be supplementing them or be supplemented by them within a historical process. Finally, many of them are colloquially referred to as peasants, a usage which reflects rural actuality and can be validly accepted in analysis as long as the difference between peasantry in its strict and its broad sense is kept clear.

The analytical marginal groups can be classified most directly by the basic *characteristics which they do not share* with the proposed general type, e.g. labourer lacking a fully fledged farm but engaged in agriculture, resident in a village and lowly in social status, or a rural craftsman holding little land, etc. The most significant of these groups today are:

1 The agricultural labourers, but also the worker-peasants who often adopt a 'man in town, rest of the family on the land' division of labour. The same applies to members of fully fledged production cooperatives holding most of production capacity (be it the Soviet *Kolkhoz* or the considerably different Hungarian, Chinese, African or Latin American variations of such an organization).

2   Family farmers who engage in production which differs substantively from peasant land husbandry based mostly on land and labour. Significant here are the semi-nomadic populations as well as fishermen and some hunters involved mainly in the direct use of natural resources, usually combining this with some subsistence farming. The capitalist family farmers who use capital-intensive equipment, transforming thereby the nature of the agriculture they engage in would also belong here. We shall return to this category presently while considering issues of social change. (For discussion of this major analytical issue see also items 16, 19 and 21 below.)

3   The village-less peasants (who often lack also the associated patterns of collective cognition), like, for example, some of the squatters at the Latin American agricultural frontiers, its 'gauchos' or the peasant farmers inhabiting the outskirts of large cities.

4   The 'uncaptured' peasants, i.e. peasant communities penetrated and controlled to a limited degree only by the 'national' networks of state bureaucracy, market economy and acculturation, e.g. contemporary shift cultivators of East Africa or highland Kurds and the armed peasants who in the past escaped political submission along frontiers or in the mountains (e.g. the Swiss cantons or the Cossacks). Revolutionary peasantries in periods of popular armed struggle often display similar characteristics.

Analytical typologies are at times regarded statically, i.e. as an implicit declaration of social stability/stagnation. Like every social entity, peasantry exists in fact only as a process. Its sociology must be seen as 'history of the present' – Paul Sweezy's rightly celebrated phrase. The typology suggested can be used, also, as a yardstick in a historical analysis, i.e. to 'measure' the extent of peasantization or depeasantization. One should beware, however, of forcing complex and often multi-directional changes into any schemes which pre-suppose a one-track, necessary development of peasantries in every period, area or nation. Indeed, the considerable regional differences among peasants reflect to a large extent their diverse histories.

In so far as the broad social dynamics is concerned one must keep in mind social reproduction and other cyclical rhythms which do not lead to changes of social structure but rather reinforce its stability. In such processes quantitative changes and changes of personnel leave the basic patterns of social interaction essentially intact. The attention of scholars has been particularly drawn, however, to structural changes, especially those leading to the increasing integration of peasants into national and world-wide society. These have occurred at each of the dimensions singled out as the fundamental components of the concept. Capital investment and the 'deepening' of market relations (whose characteristics change thereby) have been transforming peasant *family farms* into enterprises more akin to capitalist. Professionalization reflected an increasing division of labour which changed the character of *agriculture* and led to the occupational narrowing of the functions of a peasant. Advance of urban/ rural continua decreased the particularities of the *village communities and culture*, transforming the peasant *placement/subsumption* within society.

As to the main generic patterns of peasantry-related change in the contemporary world, these can be ordered into five categories which, while analytically diverse, are often parallel or interrelated in actuality.

1   Socio-economic differentiation, i.e. cumulative polarization of rural wealth and means of production followed by mutation of some peasants into the rich farmers who adopt entrepreneurial strategies based on the employment of wage labour while the poor become the rural wage labour, emigrate or else die out.

2   Pauperization, when the increase of rural population/land rates, without alternative sources of income and/or new productive investments, leads to a cycle of poverty and to an aggregate economic decline with ecological consequences for the mass of peasants. Agricultural surpluses, if any, are syphoned off from the rural production cycle. A quarter of a century ago a senior anthropologist named it 'agricultural involution' (Geertz, 1963). It is still the fact of life to many peasant societies.

3   'Farmerization'/marginalization, usually when the family farm proceeds as the major unit of agricultural production while its character changes. Such 'peasant-into-farmer' development is linked to massive investment which ties the family farmer into capitalist economy via credit, supplies and sales, often organized by agro-business. The capital-intensive family farmer becomes more productive but also finds himself subsumed thereby under Big Business dynamics and controls. Declining significance of agriculture as a national branch of production and employment usually parallels these developments. In terms of further typology one may consider such farmers and peasants as the sub-categories of the general species of family farming species (see items 16, 17 and 32 below).

4   Collectivization/statization, when the state takes over responsibility for agriculture, structuring it into large production units open to governmental control (but often operating formally as cooperatives of production, the membership in which is nominally free). One should not overstate here the exceptionality, the socialist character or the uniformity of this form of rural organization. State intervention in agriculture is nowadays global, be it control of prices, subsidies, credits or monopolies over the smallholder inputs. The difference between collectivization and the monopoly of state-controlled Boards of Trade over the smallholders' produce is often only one of degree. Second, *Kolkhoz*-like enterprises were promoted and set up not only in USSR but in Iran under the Shah. Finally, collectivizations differ extensively in form, e.g. in the ways the family farming and the collective farming are mixed, etc.

5   Peasantization by an egalitarian land reform, and, at times the re-peasantization as peasants' sons return to farm because of state inducement, political pressure or else because of new opportunities to do so profitably (e.g. Venezuela's recent upswing of smallholders' vegetable production for towns by 'returnees' to lands previously abandoned). Numerous rural migrants who succeeded in using a period of work elsewhere, possibly abroad, to save enough to establish a viable family farm back home belong in part to this category.

One more analytical warning is called for here. The identifying of factors of social change does not necessarily mean that such a change does take place. If simultaneously operating social mechanisms resist it or side-track it, the actual rural change (and 'development programmes') can reverse or change beyond recognition.

As to the last of the initial queries concerning the validity of peasantry as a concept and a particular field of studies, any images of peasant household or a peasant community with no 'external' ties are conceptual constructs, exceptions, miscomprehensions or caricatures. Peasants form parts of broader societies and of their histories. The massive extension in intensity of those ties during the last decade made them more central than ever to any effort at the understanding of peasantry. The issue has been referred to often as one of 'insertion' or of 'subsumption' of peasants when controlled by powerful external forces which put them to use, i.e. make them into resource and object of schemes and plans designed elsewhere and of profits drawn mostly by others. No plot against the peasants is necessarily assumed here: it is mostly the way the political economy and the political systems of societies operate which results in conditions in which the peasants (as well as, usually, other family smallholders) face hardship and risk without usually reaping their benefits.

The issue of how to define peasantry subsumed under large-scale economy and controlled by national and international forces, and yet with its particularity not fully eroded thereby, is too complex to be discussed in a short introduction. It is sufficient to note the issue of which further elucidation and discussion appear in this book (especially its parts I, II and V) and elsewhere (see Shanin, 1982). Peasants are part of broader structures and flows but their particularity does not reside simply in what they 'are' as against the pressures of 'change' or 'society', 'capitalism' or 'development plans'. Most importantly, it is expressed in the ways peasants respond to those forces, potentials and impacts which form the crucial characteristics of their particularity. It was this particularity of characteristics and responses which brought forward particularity of methods and modes of analysis.

The many definitions of peasantry which view it as representing an aspect of and a bridge to the past are valid but should be treated gingerly. Past retained in the present is not the same thing as simply 'the dead past'. A peasant linked into agro-industry differs structurally from his predecessors, yet his similarities with them do not disappear entirely and one must learn from it *on par* with considering the changes which occurred. Even in our 'dynamic' times we live not in the future but in the present, rooted in the past, and that is where our future is shaped. It is therefore worth remembering that – as in the past, so in the present – peasants and peasants' sons are the majority of mankind and, be that what it may, will remain so until the end of the century and beyond.

Scope and Organization of This Book

This Reader focuses upon the generic characteristics of peasant societies viewed as a qualitatively distinct type of social organization. Such an approach seems particularly important for Western readers unfamiliar with peasantry, but experience shows how much the same can also be said of the urbanites of countries in which peasants form a substantial majority. Consideration of the diversity of peasant societies, 'subsumptions' and their transformations are equally necessary, and an attempt has been made to keep this clearly in sight. Major scholarly controversy which seems to traverse each of the possible subdivisions in the field is between those who tend to concentrate on the specific features of peasant social characteristics (and consequently consider specific theoretical constructs and methodologies necessary), and those who tend to support the opposite view. Views differ on many scores and place in the texts was given, accordingly, not only to analysis but to the dispute.

The internal division of the Reader is arranged according to topic and not geographical regions, relating to the outlined typology of peasant societies. Such division of articles is somewhat arbitrary; many of them could appear in more than one part. These should therefore be viewed as analytical focuses rather than as watertight compartments. In order to avoid a conservative sociological tradition in which sections about 'social structure' are followed by a section on 'social change' (and an implicit image of some non-changing social structures), all sections treat structural and dynamic analyses as different sides of one coin.

In the selection of contributions an attempt has been made to draw the reader's attention to the classical roots of the relevant sociological traditions and to break linguistic divisions. The selection also – and rightly so – violated interdisciplinary barriers.

While the basic structure of the first edition of the volume was kept, numerous new items have been introduced and others replaced or shortened. More than half of the text is new. The new itinerary reflects the directions in which the field has developed since its late 1960s/early 1970s 'explosion'.

Section A of part I focuses on the basic units of peasant social organization: the family farm, the village community, peasant regional groups and market networks as well as their internal differentiation, mobility and structural change. The new itinerary accentuates ethnography, culture and history as ways to define peasantry and has added also some issues of gender in rural social structuration. Section B presents major 'analytically marginal groups' of peasants and a categorization of lines along which rural forms transform. The new items centre on different forms of collectivization and on family farming within the industrial capitalist societies of today.

Part II is devoted mostly to production and exchange characteristic of peasant societies. Its section A carries new contributions concerning agriculture, peasant labour and peasant credit. A specific discussion of the Marxist theoretical paradigm was added to the one concerning Chayanov and a whole new section B devoted to 'extra-village' context of rural political economy, i.e. markets, capitalism, landed property, social causes of starvation and international food regimes. Part III brings together contributions concerning peasant culture. The new items include an original piece about peasant aesthetic sense by John Berger, an item on peasant 'subsistence ethics' and a paper concerning collective cognition and transformation of political consciousness. Part IV is devoted to the political sociology of peasants and was expanded by contributions concerning peasant resistance, village factions and an alternative regime set up in Mexico's Morelos by peasant rebels.

The fifth and last part is devoted to attitudes and policies towards peasantry in the contemporary world. Item 48 serves as an introduction to the texts by exemplifying the diversity and the emotions which underline contemporary intellectual attitudes towards peasantry. An item of introspection by a leading socialist intellectual, Raymond Williams, was added to it. The other contributions added to part V include a major study of the state–capitalism–peasants triangle of social determination, a newly discovered Marx in contradistinction with a broadly accepted view of what is seen as Marxist orthodoxy, some items concerning contemporary issues of 'development planning' where peasants are concerned and others which see 'development policies' as a threat, as they 'take the peasants' side'. The part ends with a new consideration of the changing paradigms of peasant studies.

Inevitable limitations imposed on the size of a publication of this sort formed, no doubt, the most frustrating part of the editing process. After all, Znaniecki's 2000 pages reflect not verbosity, but the 'richness' of the issue (Thomas and Znaniecki, 1918). For example, 'Peasantry as History' could only be cursorily treated, no place could be assigned where the peasant voices could be heard directly – a 'Peasant Speak' section. And so on. The reading list should partially rectify this. Another partial remedy has been the use of 'snippets', that is short excerpts of one or two pages which do not 'cover' an issue but accentuate it, calling attention to the need to study it in more depth. A full solution might be found, however, only in a further increase in the number and variety of relevant publications: an increase large enough to match the complexity and the importance of the issue.

References

Erasmus, C. (1967) 'The upper limits of peasantry and agrarian reform: Bolivia, Venezuela and Mexico compared', *Ethnology*, vol. 6, no. 4.

Geertz, C. (1963) *Agricultural Involution*, University of California Press.

Marx, K. (1964) *Pre-Capitalist Economic Formations*, Lawrence & Wishart.

Redfield, R. (1956) *Peasant Society and Culture*, University of Chicago Press.

Shanin, Teodor (1972) *The Awkward Class*, Clarendon Press.

Shanin, Teodor (1983) 'Defining peasants: conceptualizations and deconceptualizations', *Sociological Review*, vol. 30, no. 1.

Thomas, W. I. and Znaniecki, F. (1958) *The Polish Peasant in Europe and America*, Dover Publications. First published in 1918.

Weber, M. (1964) *The Theory of Social and Economic Organization*, Free Press .

Wolf, E. (1977) *Is the Peasant a Class Category Separate from Bourgeois and Proletarian?* – (notes for a talk), Binghampton.

Part I

Peasant Societies

Part I presents peasantry as social structure, that is, considers those aspects of patterned social interaction which are characterized as peasant and define peasantry as a recognizable entity. There are several ways to approach such a task. One is to look at the major units of social organization and social reproduction in which the particularities of peasantry are expressed. The second is to look at peasant societies as an analytical category reflected in particular stages of social history. The third is to focus on a multi-faceted general type following the definition suggested in the book's Introduction, and to use it as an analytical yardstick for the consideration of different rural inhabitants and communities. Such a view centres attention as much on the generic as on the diversities from the type assumed, both synchronically and diachronically, i.e. on the analytically marginal categories which carry some but not all of the characteristics adopted as well as on the relevant processes of social change. Consideration of change refers here to major transformations, that is, on peasantization and depeasantization as well as some lesser changes of content and context, those linking it to the issues of social reproduction.

Part IA commences with contributions representing the two most significant units of peasant social organization, namely the family farm and the village community. A combined picture of the peasant family household and of the village is drawn from the classical study of Thomas and Znaniecki, followed by the works of Shanin and Stirling (see also Galeski, Taylor and Dobrowolski, items 13, 23 and 33). It is critically supplemented by discussion of the place of women in contemporary rural Franconia, of the diversity between the peasant communities of Mexico and by 'snippets' concerning rural neighbourhoods, coming from Inhetveen and Blasche, Wolf and Ayrout respectively, items 3, 6 and 4 (see also Nash, Barbara Harriss, J. Harriss, Alavi, *Factions* and Kandyoti, items 27, 28, 31, 43 and 57). Two 'snippets' from classical studies by Fei and Redfield (items 7 and 8) introduce ethnography and the debate about the defining of peasants as a particular social and/or cultural structure (see also the book's Introduction, Saul and Woods, Figes and Galeski, items 11, 16 and 18). Thorner's consideration of peasant economy as an analytical category linked to a historical stage (item 9) offers a different approach to this matter. It is followed by Pearse's discussion of urbanization and industrialization as major transforming forces restructuring the contemporary peasantry (see also Hann, Figes, Galeski, Kerblay, Alavi and de Janvry, items 15, 16, 13, 25, 26 and 49).

Part IB looks at a number of 'analytically marginal groups' or conceptual 'hedges' of peasantry, i.e. at social entities which, while similar in a number of ways, lack at least one of the major peasant characteristics suggested in the Introduction. They share rural environments with the 'fully fledged' peasants and also, at times, may replace peasants or be replaced by them. As stated, analytical marginality does not imply numerical insignificance or lesser stability than that of the other social categories.

The section begins with Saul and Wood's discussion of African peasantries – their formation, sedantarization and the colonial impact upon them. It also tests the realism of the definition of peasantry drawn from extra-African experiences *vis-à-vis* East Africa's ruralities. Agricultural labourers on the Latin American *latifundios*, past and present, are considered next in a paper by Feder. Galeski's analysis presents a taxonomy of farming enterprises and of the patterns of their contemporary transformation including a short discussion of collectivization of the Soviet type. It is followed by a short rejoinder about a contemporary Hungarian version of collectivization which took a different turn and produced different results. Part I is brought to a close by three items representing major dimensions of contemporary rural change. In item 15 Hann discusses workers, peasants and rural emigration within different environments (see also Taylor, item 23). Figes proceeds with presentation of an original reconceptualization of the 'peasant into farmer' sequence by V. Danilov (see also Alavi, Friedmann and de Janvry, items 26, 32 and 49). Last, Djurfeld relates the analytical anticipations of the beginning of the century to the actual experience of transformation of the Western rural economies and societies, and then draws some lessons from it concerning the ruralities of contemporary 'Developing Societies'.

Part IA

Units and Structure

1

A Polish Peasant Family

W. I. Thomas and F. Znaniecki

The family is a very complex group, with limits only approximately determined and with very various kinds and degrees of relationship between its members. But the fundamental familial connection is one and irreducible; it cannot be converted into any other type of group-relationship nor reduced to a personal relation between otherwise isolated individuals. It may be termed *familial solidarity*, and it manifests itself both in assistance rendered to, and in control exerted over, any member of the group by any other member representing the group as a whole. It is totally different from territorial, religious, economic or national solidarity, though evidently these are additional bonds promoting familial solidarity, and we shall see that any dissolution of them certainly exerts a dissolving influence upon the family. And again, the familial solidarity and the degree of assistance and of control involved should not depend upon the personal character of the members, but only upon the kind and degree of their relationship; the familial relation between two members admits no gradation, as does love or friendship.

In this light all the familial relations in their ideal form, that is, as they would be if there were no progressive disintegration of the family, become perfectly plain.

The relation of husband and wife is controlled by both the united families, and husband and wife are not individuals more or less closely connected according to their personal sentiments, but group-members connected absolutely in a single way. Therefore the marriage norm is not love, but 'respect', as the relation which can be controlled and reinforced by the family, and which corresponds also exactly to the situation of the other party as member of a group and representing the dignity of that group. The norm of respect from wife to husband includes obedience, fidelity, care for the husband's comfort and health; from husband to wife, good treatment, fidelity,

Excerpts from William I. Thomas and Florian Znaniecki, *The Polish Peasant in Europe and America*, Dover Publications, 1958, pp. 89–112. First published in 1918.

not letting the wife do hired work if it is not indispensable. In general, neither husband nor wife ought to do anything which could lower the social standing of the other, since this would lead to a lowering of the social standing of the other's family. Affection is not explicitly included in the norm of respect, but is desirable. As to sexual love, it is a purely personal matter, is not and ought not to be socialized in any form; the family purposely ignores it, and the slightest indecency or indiscreetness with regard to sexual relations in marriage is viewed with disgust and is morally condemned.

The familial assistance to the young married people is given in the form of the dowry, which they both receive. Though the parents usually give the dowry, a grandfather or grandmother, brother, or uncle may just as well endow the boy or the girl or help to do so. This shows the familial character of the institution, and this character is still more manifest if we recognize that the dowry is not in the full sense the property of the married couple. It remains a part of the general familial property to the extent that the married couple remains a part of the family. The fact that, not the future husband and wife, but their families, represented by their parents and by the matchmakers, come to an understanding on this point is another proof of this relative community of property. The assistance must assume the form of dowry simply because the married couple, composed of members of two different families, must to some extent isolate itself from one or the other of these families; but the isolation is not an individualization, it is only an addition of some new familial ties to the old ones, a beginning of a new nucleus.

The relation of parents to children is also determined by the familial organization. The parental authority is complex. It is, first, the right of control which they exercise as members of the group over other members, but naturally the control is unusually strong in this case because of the particularly intimate relationship. But it is more than this. The parents are privileged representatives of the group as a whole, backed by every other member in the exertion of their authority, but also responsible before the group for their actions. The power of this authority is really great; a rebellious child finds nowhere any help, not even in the younger generation, for every member of the family will side with the child's parents if he considers them right, and everyone will feel the familial will behind him and will play the part of a representative of the group. On the other hand, the responsibility of the parents to the familial group is very clear in every case of undue severity or of too great leniency on their part. . . .

The Polish peasant family, as we have seen, is organized as a plurality of interrelated marriage-groups which are so many nuclei of familial life and whose importance is various and changing. The process of constitution and evolution of these nuclei is therefore the essential phenomenon of familial life. But at the same time there culminate in marriage many other interests of the peasant life, and we must take the role of these into consideration.

The whole familial system of attitudes involves absolutely the postulate of marriage for every member of the young generation. The family is a dynamic organization, and changes brought by birth, growth, marriage and death have nothing of the incidental or unexpected, but are included as normal in the organization itself, continually accounted for and foreseen, and the whole practical life of the family is adapted to them. A person who does not marry within a certain time, as well as an old man who does not die at a certain age, provokes in the family-group an attitude of unfavourable astonishment; they seem to have stopped in the midst of a continuous movement, and they are passed by and left alone. There are, indeed, exceptions. A boy (or girl) with some physical or intellectual defect is not supposed to marry, and in his early childhood a corresponding attitude is adopted by the family and a place for him is provided beforehand. His eventual marriage will then provoke the same unfavourable astonishment as the bachelorship of others. . . .

The family not only requires its members to be married, but directs their choice. This is neither tyranny nor self-interest on the part of the parents nor solicitude for the future of the child, but a logical consequence of the individual's situation in the familial group. The individual is a match only as a member of the group and owing to the social standing of the family within the community and to the protection and help in social and economic matters given by the family. He has therefore corresponding responsibilities; in marrying he must take, not only his own, but also the family's interests into consideration. These latter interests condition the choice of the partner in three respects.

1   The partner in marriage is an outsider who through marriage becomes a member of the family. The family therefore requires in this individual a personality which will fit easily into the group and be assimilated to the group with as little effort as possible. Not only a good character, but a set of habits similar to those prevailing in the family to be entered, is important. Sometimes the prospective partner is unknown to the family, sometimes even unknown to the marrying member of the family, and in this case social guarantees are demanded. The boy or girl ought to come at least from a good family, belonging to the same class as the family to be entered, and settled if possible in the same district, since customs and habits differ from locality to locality. The occupation of a boy ought to be of such a kind as not to develop any undesirable, that is, unassimilable, traits. A girl should have lived at home and should not have done hired work habitually. A man should never have an occupation against which a prejudice exists in the community. In this matter there is still another motive of selection, that is, vanity. Finally, a widow or a widower is an undesirable partner, because more difficult to assimilate than a young girl or boy. If not only the future partner, but even his family, is unknown, the parents, or someone in their place, will try to get acquainted personally with some of his relatives, in order to inspect the general type of their character and behaviour. Thence comes the frequent custom of arranging marriages through friends and relatives. This form of matchmaking is

intermediary between the one in which the starting-point is personal acquaintance and the other in which the connection with a certain family is sought first
through the *swaty* (professional matchmaker) and personal acquaintance
comes later. In this intermediary form the starting-point is the friendship with
relatives of the boy or the girl. It is supposed that the future partner resembles
his relatives in character, and at the same time that the family to which those
relatives belong is worth being connected with. But this leads us to the second
aspect of the familial control of marriage.

2   The candidate for marriage belongs himself to a family, which through
marriage will become connected with that of his wife. The familial group
therefore assumes the right to control the choice of its member, not only with
regard to the personal qualities of the future partner, but also with regard to the
nature of the group with which it will be allied. The standing of the group
within the community is here the basis of selection. This standing itself is
conditioned by various factors – wealth, morality, intelligence, instruction,
religiousness, political and social influence, connection with higher classes,
solidarity between the family members, kind of occupation, numerousness of
the family, its more or less ancient residence in the locality, etc. Every family
naturally tries not to lower its own dignity by risking a refusal or by accepting at
once even the best match and thereby showing too great eagerness. Thence the
long selection and hesitation, real or pretended, on both sides, while the
problem is not to discourage any possible match, for the range of possibilities
open to an individual is proof of the high standing of the family. Thence also
such institutions as that of the matchmaker, whose task is to shorten the
ceremonial of choosing without apparently lowering the dignity of the families
involved. The relative freedom given to the individuals themselves, the
apparent yielding to individual love, has in many cases its source in the desire
to shorten the process of selection by shifting the responsibility from the group
to the individual. In the traditional formal *swaty* is embodied this familial
control of marriage. The young man, accompanied by the matchmaker, visits
the families with which his family has judged it desirable to be allied, and only
among these can he select a girl. He is received by the parents of the girl, who
first learn everything about him and his family and then encourage him to call
further or reject him at once. And the girl can select a suitor only among those
encouraged by her family.

3   A particular situation is created when a widow or widower with children
from the first marriage is involved. Here assimilation is very difficult, because
no longer an individual, but a part of a strange marriage-group, has to be
assimilated. At the same time the connection with the widow's or widower's
family will be incomplete, because the family of the first husband or wife also
has some claims. Therefore such a marriage is not viewed favourably, and there
must be some real social superiority of the future partner and his or her family
in order to counterbalance the inferiority caused by the peculiar familial

situation. A second marriage is thus usually one which, if it were the first, would be a misalliance.

With the disintegration of the familial life there must come, of course, a certain liberation from the familial claims in matters of marriage. But this liberation itself may assume various forms. With regard to the personal qualities of his future wife, the man may neglect to consult his family and still apply the same principles of appreciation which his family would apply – select a person whose character and habits resemble the type prevailing in his own family, a person whose relatives he knows, who comes perhaps from the same locality, etc. Therefore, for example, immigrants in America whose individualization has only begun always try to marry boys or girls fresh from the old country, if possible from their own native village.

A second degree of individualization manifests itself in a more reasoned selection of such qualities as the individual wishes his future mate to possess in view of his own personal happiness and regardless of the family's desire. This type of selection prevails, for example, in most of the second marriages, when the individual has become fully conscious of what he desires from his eventual partner and when the feeling of his own importance, increasing with age, teaches him to neglect the possible protests of his family. It is also a frequent type in towns, where the individual associates with persons of various origins and habits. The typical and universal argument opposed here against any familial protests has the content: 'I shall live with this person, not you, so it is none of your business.'

Finally, the highest form of individualization is found in the real love-marriage. While a reasoned determination of the qualities which the individual wishes to find in his future mate permits of some discussion, some familial control, and some influence of tradition, in the love-marriage every possibility of control is rejected *a priori*. Here, under the influence of the moment, the largest opportunity is given for matches between individuals whose social determinism differs most widely, though this difference is after all usually not very great, since the feeling of love requires a certain community of social traditions.

| Related Items |

2, 3, 4, 6, 7, 13, 23, 25, 28, 33, 42, 57, 62.

2

A Peasant Household: Russia at the Turn of the Century

Teodor Shanin

Peasant households form the nuclei of peasant society. The nature of the peasant household constitutes the most significant single characteristic of the peasantry as a specific social phenomenon and gives rise to the generic features displayed by peasantries all over the world. A peasant household is characterized by the extent of integration of the peasant family's life with its farming enterprise. The family provides the essential work team of the farm, while the farm's activities are geared mainly to production of the basic needs of the family and the dues enforced by the holders of political and economic power. The vast diversities between and within the peasantries do not obliterate the insights of this classification.

The Russian peasant household (*dvor*) at the turn of the century corresponded very closely to the general type depicted. 'The family and the farm appear as almost synonymous', testified Mukhin in his compilation on peasant legal customs at the end of the nineteenth century (Mukhin, 1881, p. 151). A volume of a Russian encyclopaedia published in 1913 described the bulk of peasant households as 'consumer–labour enterprises, with the consumer needs of the family as their main aim and the labour force of the family as their means, with no or very little use of wage labour' (*Novyi entsiklopedicheskii slovar'*, vol. 18, p. 519).

A Russian peasant household consisted typically of blood relatives spanning two or three generations and their spouses. However, the basic determinant of household membership was not actual kinship but the total participation in the life of the household or, as the Russian peasants put it, 'eating from the common pot'. This unity implied living together under the authority of a patriarchal head, close cooperation in day-to-day labour, a 'common purse', and the basic identification of a member with the household. Consequently, one who joined the household through marriage or adoption (*primaka, vlazen'*)

Excerpt from Teodor Shanin, *Russia as a 'Developing Society'*, Macmillan/Yale University Press, 1986, pp. 66–72.

was considered its full member, inclusive of all property rights, while a son of the family who set up a household on his own was viewed as an outsider (*otrezannyi lomot'*).

The peasant household operated as a highly cohesive unit of social organization, with basic divisions of labour, authority and prestige along traditionally prescribed family lines. Generally, the head of the household was the father of the family or its oldest male member. His authority over other members and over household affairs implied both autocratic rights and extensive duties of care and protection. The household was the basic unit of production, consumption, ownership, political alliances, socialization, sociability, moral support and mutual help. The social prestige and the self-esteem of a peasant within his community were defined by the social standing of the household he belonged to and his position in it, as were his loyalties and self-identification.

Women, in spite of their heavy burden of labour (both housework and fieldwork), and their functional importance in a peasant household, were considered second-class members of it, and nearly always placed under the authority of a male. The exceptions were represented mainly by widows with small children to sustain (these could usually head a household and hold land directly). Even the full rights of the male members should be considered, however, in the framework of a patriarchal structure involving extensive powers of the head over his household. The cohesion of the family and the way family property operated meant submission and lack of tangible property for its junior male members. The policy of the Russian state before 1906 (and to a lesser degree, later on) supported the stability and cohesion of the peasant household by imposing collective family responsibility for the payment of dues and for the 'good behaviour' of its members. Up to 1906, it also legally confirmed the head of the household's wide disciplinary powers over its members.

'The life of a family is the life of a farm' (Makarov, 1917, p. 71). A typical peasant farm in Russia in the period under consideration was a small agricultural enterprise based on centuries-old agricultural techniques and types of equipment, communal crop rotation, family labour and the horse-drawn wooden *sokha*, slowly being replaced by an iron plough. Grain dominated peasant field production and diet (Den, 1925; Parker, 1968). Peasant family life and labour offered the main form of occupational training for the younger generation, while tradition acted as the main occupational guide. The scope of market and money relations was limited by the extent of the consumption-determined production, low rates of surplus, and a low level of professional specialization and diversification of the rural population. It was, on the other hand, gradually enhanced by the pressure of taxes and rents, the penetration of industrial produce into the countryside, and the supplementary employment in crafts and trades (*promysly*), made increasingly necessary as additional or alternative sources of peasant income. Growth of production and markets of the agricultural goods led to similar results (Anfimov, 1980).

The household's production activities and plans consisted primarily of strenuous efforts to make ends meet – that is, to feed the family and to pay dues and taxes. Heavy rural underemployment, both total and seasonal, was partly tempered by peasants' supplementary employment. Competition with growing industry and with the use of machinery was made possible by desperately low rural earnings.[1] The Russian peasant usage of the term *promysly*, which puzzled economists and led their figures astray, was indicative of the way such tasks integrated into the peasant economy. As used by the peasants, it comprised a single category of activities that could appear as quite diverse: domestic industry, off-farm wage work in agriculture, off-farm non-agricultural work (at times as part of a traditional cooperative – the *artel'*). The logic of such an all-embracing term was simple enough to the peasants, for these activities formed the residuum of their occupations over and above the peasants' 'proper' task, that is, family farming on their own farms. The main occupation of Russian peasants consisted both ideally (i.e. in normative terms of preference) and in reality, of performing a wide variety of tasks combined to make a coherent whole of land and animal husbandry. Yet the *promysly* formed an important and increasingly necessary part of their occupation and income, especially so in the poorer strata.

The massive use of family labour, the high levels of home consumption, the 'traditional' methods of production, the relatively low marketability and the lack of bookkeeping in generalized money terms made the peasant household into a production unit very different from a capitalist enterprise. Production strategies and economic solutions differed consistently and considerably – for example, the 'non-profitable' land renting that made excellent economic sense within the specifically peasant economy.[2] Also, the influence of nature upon the peasant economy was powerful and direct; the smallness of peasant resources magnified its impact. The difference between a good agricultural year and a very bad one was the difference between prosperity and famine, if not death and the extinction of a family. The demographic cycles of family history determined to a considerable extent the functioning of the farms, while the needs and seasons of traditional farming prescribed the patterns of everyday life. Nature and the typical family history made for a peculiarly deep-rooted cyclical rhythm of daily, annual and multi-annual stages of life on the peasant family farms which were often of more immediate significance than the grand flows of national and international markets of goods and labour.

The longest of the cycles was usually biographical in its major determinants. Within the established division of labour only a male–female team could make the farm fully functional and effective. The dominance of the male has defined typical family-farm histories in essentially masculine terms. A peasant male normally proceeded through the prescribed stages: childhood, premarital adolescence, marriage, a headship of his own household and, eventually, retirement and death. Only by becoming the head of a household could he rise to the full status of a man within the peasant community. (The only alternative road to self-emancipation involved his leaving the peasant community altogether.) Marriage was thereby 'an absolute postulate' – a crucial precondition of social maturity necessitated by the character of farming. The second parallel condition was the availability of a farm, that is, a holding of land and equipment. Its passing from one generation into the next was a decisive issue of peasant life.

Family property was a major legal reflection of the character of the Russian peasant household (Shanin, 1972, Appendix B). So far as peasants were concerned, Russian legislation since 1861 had left these matters to the customs of the locality as understood by its elected magistrates. The latter codifications have shown that peasant customs concerning property were remarkably uniform all over Russia, despite the fact that until 1921 no unifying legislation was passed on that matter. Unlike *private property* defined in the Legal Code of the Russian empire by which the non-peasant Russians lived, *family property* limited to a considerable degree the rights of the formal 'owner' (*khozyain*); he acted as the administrator of the property (*bol'shak*) rather than its exclusive proprietor in the sense current outside peasant society. (An extreme expression of this feature was the legal possibility and actual practice of removing the head of a household from his position by an order of the peasant commune in some cases of 'mismanagement' or 'wastefulness' and of the appointment of another member of the household in his place.) On the other hand, and in contrast to *collective property*, that is, a partnership or a shareholding company, the participation in family property did not entail any specific and definable share in the property or the profits that an individual member could claim at his choice, except of the general right of each to share in the collective consumption.

Within the legal customary framework of 'family property', the very notion of *inheritance*, as developed and enacted in non-peasant Russia, failed to appear. The passing of property from generation to generation did not usually await the death of a parent and was legally treated as *partitioning* of family property between its members. Partitioning (or apportionment, to set up a junior male) corresponded to a considerable extent with the growth of nuclear families and their requests for independence. The head of the household took the decision (partly defined by custom) as to when exactly to partition his farm or when to make apportionment to a son, and when to retire. His refusal to do so could be, and at times was, challenged before the communal assembly or peasant magistrates. The whole issue was treated not just as a problem of economic expedience but also one of social living and 'maturation' in its broadest sense.

Partitioning meant, on the whole, equal division of household property between all its male members. A somewhat larger share was at times granted to the son who was to look after the aged parents or the unmarried sisters. The peasant customary law made an exception of 'female property', which included cutlery, cloth, etc. The 'female's property' was within the peasant household the only private property in the 'urban' sense and could consequently be left by will and/or unequally divided. In cases of the death of all members of a household (*vymorochnost'*), the property was generally taken over by the peasant commune.

A typical new household would begin as a young couple with a few young children on a smallholding. Such a farm would usually consist of a limited amount of land, little equipment and possibly one or two horses shared out from the original unit in the process of partitioning. It would benefit also from some communal rights – for example, to grazing land. The growing children provided additional labour on the farm but also created new consumption needs and problems of employment. Children also posed the problem of providing a dowry for daughters and equipment for setting up new farms for sons, which required apportionment.

In the times of serfdom, the peasant family often consisted of several nuclear families, that is, family couples and their children. The decline of the squire's control over the day-to-day life of the peasants once serfdom came to an end legally in 1861 led to 'nuclearization' of the peasant households – when left to themselves, the Russian peasants tended to synchronize the nuclear family and the farm while the number of households grew accordingly. Government 'educational efforts' and decrees that attempted to preach and to legislate some minimal size for an 'efficient' farm, were consistently defeated by the peasant way of living – the patterns of social reproduction and customs of social 'maturing' prevalent within the Russian countryside.

Budget Studies – a major Russian contribution to the advanced methodology of peasant studies – came into their own at the turn of the century and provided a store of additional knowledge concerning the ways peasant household economies operated (Shanin, 1972, chapter 3). The essence of this methodology lay in the detailed presentation and analysis of input/output relations within selected peasant households during a whole agricultural cycle/year. The Budget Studies have presented and quantified with increasing clarity the complex yet closely knit picture of production patterns involving husbandry (of land and animals), gathering and manufacturing on the farm, as well as wage labour elsewhere. Their findings have consistently substantiated the massive reliance on family labour within the peasant economy and a strong tendency for actual physical division of the sources of income into consumption-directed farming versus the cash-directed activities that were specific to each region (e.g. rye for home consumption and wheat or hemp for sale in the Black-earth area, flax and, alternatively, engagement in crafts to secure the necessary money income in the northern areas, etc.). The relation between wealth differentiation and the economic strategy of the households was explicated as a *u* curve, expressing a tendency for a higher share of the extra-farming income to come from wage employment for the poorest, the concentration of one's own farm by the majority at the middle range, the higher extra-farming (mostly 'entrepreneurial') income of the well-to-do. Monetization followed a similar distribution, but less than half the average peasant income came from wages or sale of produce (Prokopovich, 1918). The consumption side of these accounts showed a large share of food (especially grain and potatoes), a small share of expenses on textiles, tea or oil, practically nothing for 'culture' (e.g. books), and very little investment in equipment. It also showed an extensive similarity of the types of goods used by the different strata of peasants.

The Budget Studies and the parallel investigations of rural migration have indicated also how often the seasonal and even permanent jobs in town fitted closely into the operation of the Russian peasant household and were determined by its needs. The same man could be a farmer in spring and autumn, an urban carpenter in summer and a lumberjack elsewhere in winter. Russia, however, knew much less flexibility of rural labour than, say, Latin America of today. The majority of its peasants were farmers only and consistently so.

Of those who left the village, quite a number were peasants' sons collecting money to facilitate the setting up of a household of their own, or else poor householders attempting to save money for a horse or an urgent due – an emigration aimed at underpinning of the peasant economy and/or re-peasantization. Male and female workers coming directly from the villages provided much of the permanent labour engaged in the urban construction, industry and services. Even when settled in town, many of them returned seasonally to the village and 'kept their roots' there, that is, contributed financially to the upkeep of their farming household, held on to their rights within it and often left their children, wives and elderly in its care. The significance of the peasant-workers in Russian towns was very considerable, both actually and potentially (one should remember that even one extra peasant per village per annum could swamp the urban labour markets).

The studies of the Russian peasant households have specified, beside structural similarities, some major dimensions of difference and discontinuity, without which any generalization about 'the peasants' would easily mislead and mystify. Two of these discontinuities were particularly pertinent to the life of the peasants, that is, the socio-economic and the regional diversities. Both meant systematic differences in the livelihood, in typical productive 'packages' and strategies, etc., both between the peasant communities and in each of them. Also, the character of the peasant households can be fully understood only in its broader societal setting.

Notes

1 See part IIA below for a relevant snippet by G. T. Robinson (item 22).
2 See the contribution by Kerblay in part IIA below for discussion (item 25).

References

Anfimov, A. (1980) *Krest'yanskoe khozyaistvo europeiscoi rossii*, Moscow.
Den, V. (1925) *Kurs ekonomicheskoi geografii*, Leningrad.
Makarov, N. (1917) *Krest'yanskoe khozyaistvo i ego interesy*, Moscow.
Mukhin, V. (1888) *Obychnyi poryadok nasledovaniya krest'yan*, St Petersburg.
Novyi entsiklopedicheski slovar', Brokganz and Efron (1913), St Petersburg.
Parker, W. H. (1968) *An Historical Geography of Russia*, Chicago.
Prokopovich, S. (1918) *Opyt izncheniya narodnogo doklode*, Moscow.
Shanin, T. (1972) *The Awkward Class*, Oxford.

Related Items

1, 3, 6, 7, 9, 13, 15, 17, 18, 21, 23, 25, 26, 32, 37, 44, 52, 56, 57, 60, 62.

3

Women in the Smallholder Economy

H. Inhetveen and M. Blasche

The Peasant Family – an Indivisible Whole?

Literature on the peasant economy or family farming describes the peasant family as a 'complex' but 'indivisible', 'irreducible', 'totally integrated whole'.[1] This means that on account of joint property, labour and consumption the family is a quasi-symbiotic unit. In this context patriarchy becomes the psychological cement of internal power structures. The economically active farmer as paterfamilias subjects the thoughts, actions, emotions and intentions of all family members to his own will and represents the family in public village life. Given such a perspective, the farmer's wife is presumed to be only a secondary member within this hierarchy. The village microcosm is perceived in a similar vein. It appears as a series of patriarchal family units and the predominance of the male sector of village society over the female half is the projection of power relations in each family.

The peasant world has not always been viewed in this light. The agrarian literature at the beginning of the modern age often drew a sharp distinction between the male and the female domains within family farming.[2] Each of them was treated separately and extensively as was their interrelationship.

It was not until the paradigmatic change of agricultural theory from a holistic 'art of husbandry' to a modern 'theory of rational farming', with a bent toward production management, market orientation and the natural sciences, that the farm came to be perceived as a male-directed business enterprise.[3] Women and their economic domains receded into the background. Since then an andro-centric orientation has been characteristic of the conceptualization of agricultural sciences. Even the theory of family farming developed by Chayanov did not take into account the female sections of the economy, in spite of being focused on the reproductive and consumptive characteristics of the

An original paper.

peasant household. There are, therefore, gaps and distortions in its portrayal of the peasant family and its economy.[4]

On the other hand, since the turn of the century there has been some interesting empirical research on the conditions of life and work among country women mostly by female researchers engaged in social politics and often motivated by their own experiences.[5] In Germany these studies have been prompted by problems of the female labour market in the urban centres and by population policies which provoked an interest in the question of the relationship between the increasing workload of female farmers and the migration from the land or decreasing birth rates.

In recent years research into the role of women has again turned its attention to the countryside. For example, in the past few years the difficulties young farmers have had in finding a wife exacerbated the problem of the survival of small farms and drew public attention to the fundamental role of women in smallhold farming.

Women in Family Farming

The pattern of a woman's life on a small farm depends on numerous factors: the financial state of the family enterprise, the number, age and characters of the members of the family, the general social climate, her own physical and mental state of health, and so on. Therefore, the concrete forms of a woman's life vary greatly from farm to farm. Nevertheless, there are astonishing similarities in the situations of female farmers even if they live at great temporal or geographical distance. This is due to, firstly, the object of production that all of them share, secondly, the conditions of commodity production, to which all have to adapt, and, last but not least – for this is our subject in what follows – the family economy as the basic structure of traditional farm holdings.[6]

1   The basis of smallholders' existence is the farm. It meets material needs, is a source of certain employment and guarantees relative independence and self-determination. It is the basis of status and standing, a mirror of past achievements or neglect and the source of future promise. Although, as a rule (in about 85 per cent of all cases), women had to leave their farm of origin upon marriage to face the often difficult process of reorientation on the husband's farm, the wives of smallholders identify extraordinarily strongly with 'their' farm. In our questionnaire on the future of farms 80 per cent of the female respondents wanted to retain the farm for the rest of their life; only 4 per cent wanted to give up the farm after retirement. As reasons, the women mentioned the guaranteed existence provided by farming, the duty towards previous and future generations, the importance of farming in providing for the needs of the whole population, their love of farming and their attachment to the farm, as well as the almost total lack of other employment opportunities for women in rural areas.

Women fight particularly strongly for the survival of the farm in times of general crisis or a particular emergency. Their interest lies in keeping the farm in the family, preventing it from falling into the hands of 'strangers'. Besides these traditional attitudes, they have a thoroughly realistic approach. Nowadays the children are given a solid basis for further existence in the form of education (preferably agricultural) and a site for a house, if one is not already available. At the same time all efforts are made to keep the children on the land as potential farmers and future owners of the family farm. They should learn most of the farmwork involved by helping in it, but should not be overworked. This modern dual strategy of smallholder survival requires additional physical and mental effort, particularly on the part of the women, who are held, and also feel themselves, primarily responsible for the well-being of the family.

2   The smallholdings of Franconia are mixed economies, both subsistence- and market-oriented, despite the predominance of the latter. The economic role of female farmers is greater than seems at first sight. They know the farm's financial situation, administer the housekeeping funds and have access to the family bank account, through which large transactions are conducted. They have a voice in decisions on investments, new purchases or changes in production; they are in charge of farmyard sales and, as has always been the case, the 'sphere of subsistence': the home and garden economy, including in some regions the market-gardening still practised. Especially in times of need or under particularly adverse conditions 'qualitative budgeting', a characteristic of agricultural economic practice, may become 'matriarchal budgeting'. The female farmers' economic concepts are a mixture of traditional, conservative norms (thrift, 'recycling' and re-use of as much material as possible on the farm, utility orientation, etc.), and of modern, dynamic methods (calculation, bookkeeping and flexible reactions to external pressures). This continually gives rise to problems and contradictions, which the female farmer tries to reconcile or balance. Her tactic is facilitated by her experience in almost all the different areas of the farm economy.

An example of flexible reactions to a crisis situation, and, as a consequence, of additional burdens for the women, are the milk quotas set by the state. The reduction in the quota for which the 'normal' milk price is paid and the 'unjust price' for 'overproduction' has resulted in many small farmers slowly reducing their dairy herds (which means less work for the women). But it has also resulted in an increase in subsistence production: butter, quark and yoghurt are once again being produced from the milk surpluses. Women welcome the return to former practices, although there can be little question that it involves extra work for them.

There can be no doubt that through their economic competence female farmers exercise actual power and influence on what happens on the farm. But this power is never openly demonstrated; such behaviour would be contrary to the values of the farming community. The farm is presented to the outside world as an integrated enterprise, and the joint bank account is, as it were, a symbol of this. For this reason most farmers' wives flatly reject the idea of holding a separate bank account and their own personal interest.

3 Family farming is characterized by a specific labour situation:

Production, especially in small enterprises, is highly diversified, which creates a broad spectrum of activity. This is true of women in particular; they are traditionally responsible for the housework and the care of the children and – in contrast to the men – in principle prepared 'to do everything'.[7]

Small farming enterprises have been under permanent pressure to adapt and reorientate production. The consequence was a continual reorganizing of agricultural processes. Fundamental changes included the shift from farming as a full-time occupation to a part-time one, or a supplementary income only, and involved structural changes, mechanization and chemicalization. Such developments have relaxed practices of the traditional division of labour (once again, increasing rather than reducing the women's workload). Since it is usually the men who seek employment in the non-agricultural sectors, the transition to new forms of work has produced a noticeable 'feminization' of farming as the women have to take over new spheres. Women are also becoming more experienced with farm machinery, despite their non-technical socialization plus the rather 'masculine' conception of modern farming methods.

The nature of agricultural production requires continual change in place, rhythm and the amount of effort as well as in the social constellation.

For women all this has involved a challenging variety and continual move between effort and relaxation, which they regard as an advantage of their situation in comparison with the existence of ordinary housewives or female workers. This is all the more true for despite all the pressures they feel independent and responsible in their work. On the other hand, they are not always successful in organizing their numerous activities so that a balance between effort and relaxation can be achieved. Frequently, their work demands are just too much for them, their working hours very long. This was borne out by statistics: the working hours of women are considerably longer than those of men, especially so on the small farms. The high demands women place on their own ability to work, internalized in their socialization and their enthusiasm for continual occupation, often clash with physical possibilities. In trying to resolve this some women drive themselves to utter exhaustion and illness.

Women in the Village Community

The importance of a woman in family farming becomes clear when we observe her in her various domains. Likewise, we only get a proper impression of her role in the village community by focusing on the female networks in village life. Some ethnological studies have stressed the fact of gender segregation and, hence, a duality in village public life, each with specific forms, rules and themes.[8] The worlds of men and women in the traditional village appear as separate territories, connected by special rituals and regulations of communication.

Men congregate in public places, such as the village centre or the pub; even at the village cooperative, while buying and selling farm goods, they prefer to present themselves as leisured rather than busy. Their topics of conversation tend to be more general, technical and abstract: agriculture, politics, the weather. The topic of kinship is dealt with, if at all, in a matter-of-fact manner and tends to be objectified in terms of land ownership. Men usually relate to one another as colleagues rather than as members of particular families.

By contrast, the world of women is more extensively oriented towards family affairs and relationships.[9] In everyday village life women customarily met at the places of collective family labour: the village wash-house and fountains, the baking-house and the milk depot, the garden fence, the shops, the common village refrigeration plant. The disappearance of such institutions has put an end to many of these traditional forms of female communication. Women's chat is always combined with some form of work for the family; it is neither acceptable to the women themselves, nor to the village, that they have nothing to do. The topics of their communication centre on the family and the village: they talk mostly about the family's daily routine, housework, the menfolk and the children, the making and breaking of families, problems and crises, sickness and health, life and death. Girls are initiated into this perspective at an early age. They learn the history of the village as a history of its families, their own and others.

Apart from this social network of families and neighbours, the women's competence includes other important forms of village communal life, e.g. the exchange of goods and ideas. Women not only help each other to prepare family or village feasts, either by assisting in the preparations or exchanging implements and products from the female domains of the household; they also apportion food in the event of certain feasts or large-scale home production (e.g. when animals are slaughtered) according to custom, which must nevertheless be applied to the concrete situation. Especially in times of misfortune or accident, illness or death, there is a network of material help or spiritual involvement across the boundaries of farm and even long-standing village enmities, which is forged mainly by women.

Finally, mention should be made of another female form of exchange: talking and gossiping about others. This form of communication is extremely effective, especially in small farming communities, as repeatedly emphasized in the literature.[10] Although gossiping is formally disreputable, it is an important part of village life and a never-ending source of informal influence. Talking about everybody and everything is mainly the business of women. It defines the honour of families and farms, establishing the reputation of the villagers, making or breaking them.

Although we lack extensive empirical studies of different forms of male and female power, an almost invisible and usually indirect form of family and village female politics has as much influence on village life as the more spectacular and demonstrative open-air politics of the men. As long as there is anything left at all to be decided in villages, women will engage in it also in their own way. Moreover, men and women alike are interested in maintaining this form of sharing and exercising power.

We have treated the world of women separately. To acquaint oneself with the specific structures of the female domains on the farm and in the village this analytical divide is useful so as not to fall into an androcentric bias. But this can form only an analytical step to be followed by the reintegrating of this picture, that is by synthesis of the workings and of the various social mechanisms regulating the dynamic interaction between the two gender worlds of the rural community. To do so would call forth further and comprehensive empirical work.

Notes

1 German agricultural sociologists speak of the 'Ganzes Haus', referring to Otto Brunner's characterization of traditional European economy.

2 See the 'Hausväterliteratur' and the 'Predigten zum christlichen Hausstand', those widely read German texts of the seventeenth and eighteenth centuries on 'art of husbandry'.

3 In this connection special mention must be made of Thaer, who applied English agricultural concepts to the German situation.

4 Cf. Inhetveen, 1986.

5 Cf. Inhetveen and Blasche, 1983, p. 60.

6 We refer below to the results of an empirical study on smallholder female farmers conducted at the end of 1970s in Franconia, southern Germany.

7 Cf. Y. Verdier, 1982, pp. 335 ff.

8 Cf. S. Harding, 1975 and R. R. Reiter, 1975.

9 On the forms and continuity of kinship orientation in transition from family farming to industrial forms of living and work cf. J. W. Scott and L. A. Tilly, 1975, pp. 59 ff.

10 Cf. R. Schulte, 1985; Ch. Benard and E. Schlaffer, 1981.

References

Benard, Ch. and Schlaffer, E. (1981) 'Männerdiskurs und Frauentratsch: Zum Doppelstandard in der Soziologie', *Soziale Welt 32*, Göttingen, Otto Schwarz & Co., pp. 119-36.

Harding, S. (1975) 'Women and Words in a Spanish village', in R. R. Reiter (ed.), *Toward an Anthropology of Women*, New York, Monthly Review Press, pp. 283–308.

Inhetveen, H. (1986) 'Von der "Hausmutter" zur "mithelfenden Familienangehörigen. Zur Stellung der Frau in Agrartheorien', in K. Bedal and H. Heidrich, *Freilichtmuseum und Sozialgeschichte*, Bad Windsheim, Verlag Junge und Sohn, pp. 109-21.

Inhetveen, H. and Blasche, M. (1983) *Frauen in der kleinbäuerlichen Landwirtschaft*, Opladen, Westdeutscher Verlag.

Reiter, R. R. (1975) 'Men and women in the south of France: public and private domains', in R. R. Reiter (ed.), *Toward an Anthropology of Women*, New York, Monthly Review Press, pp. 252–82.

Schulte, R. (1985) 'Bevor das Gerede zum Tratsch wird. Das Sagen der Frauen in der bäuerlich-dörflichen Welt Bayerns im 19. Jahrhundert', *Journal für Geschichte*, 2, Weinheim, Beltz-Verlag, pp. 16-21.

Scott, J. W. and Tilly, L. A. (1975) 'Women's work and the family in nineteenth-century Europe', *Comparative Studies in Society and History*, 17, pp. 36–64, Cambridge University Press.

Related Items

1, 2, 4, 5, 7, 9, 15, 18, 20, 25, 28, 33, 37, 42, 55, 57, 62.

4

Peasanthood as Neighbourhood
Henry Habib Ayrout

The fellah should really be referred to in the plural, for he lives as the member of a group, if not of a crowd. In the fields, as tenant or owner, he toils with his family; as a day labourer he works in a gang.

Within the limited confines of the village, he lives and works more in the open than in his house. Nowhere is there privacy. The women fetch water in groups, children swarm everywhere; the daily life is collective and communal. The village or its quarter, not the house, makes up the entity, a community more important in many ways than the family or clan. It happened that the author once drew on the blackboard of one of our village schools the outline of a hut, as a test for observation, and asked:

'Now, my children, what must we add to make a real home?'

'A door!' 'Windows!' 'Stairs!' they began to call.

We thought the house complete, and were ready to erase it, when a little girl cried: 'No, it needs something more.'

'And what is that?'

'The neighbours!' (*al-giran*).

Related Items

5, 6, 7, 11, 13, 18, 27, 28, 33, 34, 35, 37, 47, 59, 61.

Excerpt from Henry Habib Ayrout, *The Egyptian Peasant*, translated by John Alden Williams, Beacon Press, 1963, p. 87. First published in 1938.

5

A Turkish Village

Paul Stirling

One major problem in giving or following any ethnographic description is the order of presentation, since an adequate understanding of any one institution presumes a knowledge of other institutions in the same society. I hope I have overcome this difficulty by offering my summary here instead of at the end.

The village itself is the most striking group. No village forms part of any larger indigenous organization. All the villages in the area, and indeed in most of Turkey, are self-contained clusters of buildings, separated from each other by stretches of unfenced land. To walk from one to the next may take half an hour or two or more hours. There were two villages within half an hour of Sakaltutan, and another nine within one and a half hours.

Each village is composed of distinct patrilineal, patrilocal households. Although several households often occupy one block of buildings, the physical and social boundaries between them are never vague. Village and household are the main social units. Newly married women apart, everyone must belong at one time to one and only one village, and to one and only one household.

Every village is divided into a number of quarters or wards (*mahalle*). These have no clear boundaries and are not corporate. People acknowledge loyalty to their quarters, and may speak of fights in the village as fights between quarters. Because close neighbours often intermarry, and close agnates and sometimes other close kin live near each other, these quarters often have some kinship unity as well. In Elbaşı, several quarters were actually called after lineages. Close neighbours, whether kin or not, will tend to form informal groups for recreation and conversation.

Last of the important groups in the village is the lineage. This group consists of a number of households, the heads of which are descended patrilineally, i.e. strictly through males only, from a common ancestor generally three or four generations back. These households normally form local clusters. The rights and duties of membership are not precisely defined, and the degree to which

Excerpts from Paul Stirling, *A Turkish Village*, Weidenfeld & Nicolson, 1965, pp. 26–35, 290–3.

members are committed varies greatly between individuals. The main function of the lineage is the protection of members from aggression by supporting them in quarrels. Yet not all household heads are members of lineages, nor do all lineages that could be defined genealogically constitute significant social groups. Most of those who are not committed lineage members are among the poorer and less powerful strata of village society.

Apart from membership of these groups, a person's position in the network of interpersonal relationships is mainly determined by the obvious factors – sex and age, kinship, occupation and wealth; and to a lesser degree by piety and learning, by personal honour and, for a man, by the range and strength of his urban contacts.

The sexual distinction is, as one would expect in an Islamic society, strongly emphasized, and for most normal social life the sexes are sharply segregated. Age is not a criterion for any formal groups, but it carries respect and authority.

Kinship relations are both the most intimate and intense and the commonest type of social relations. The personal kin ties of men through men form the core of the lineage groups. Extra lineage kin ties form strong and numerous relationships between both households and individuals. This kinship network extends from village to village and provides vital channels for all sorts of activities – economic, political, religious – and for the arranging of marriages which will in turn forge new kin ties.

Distinctions of wealth are not conspicuous. All households in both villages appear at first sight to live in much the same way. All who can, work. There are no permanent *rentier* households, though one or two elderly men are supported largely by their sons, womenfolk and share-croppers. The wealthiest and most urbanized households have a comfortable sufficiency, while the poor are badly housed and clothed, and underfed in all but good years. But though differences in wealth are not conspicuous in the way of life, they are of great social importance. The rich are the leaders of the village; they receive deference, carry weight in village counsels, employ their neighbours, and are able, by gifts and loans, to exercise influence and even direct control, especially among their own kin.

Religious learning carries high prestige in the villages. Many village boys receive some kind of special religious training either informally from kinsmen, or from special schools in the towns. A few of these may become village *imams*; others live a normal agricultural life, but with a special reputation for learning and piety. How far a man succeeds in exploiting this prestige for gaining power and wealth seems to depend on personality and circumstances.

Other non-agricultural occupations and skills are structurally of minor importance. Most specialists are part-time, owning or at least wishing to own land; there are no social groups based on occupations such as the castes of Indian society, nor are craftsmen treated as outsiders.

Urban contacts have probably always conferred great influence and prestige in the villages, chiefly, of course, because they imply influence with officials, an influence often overestimated by villagers. Traditionally, it is likely that the main channels for social promotion lay through the official religious hierarchy. Nowadays, in a village like Elbaşı, and even in many poorer ones, people have sons, brothers or affines who are traders or officials, sometimes of fairly high standing, in the urban world. These links give great prestige in the village. Where they exist in numbers as in Elbaşı, they seem to be leading to the beginning of a class structure in the village.

But only the merest beginnings. Village society seems in the past to have had a highly mobile ranking system, with a marked absence of inherited rank. In every generation, each household split, dividing its land at least among the sons, sometimes among both sons and daughters. The richer a man, the more wives and therefore the more heirs he would be likely to have, so that in general there was a tendency for each young married man to find himself on his father's death with a fairly modest amount of land and thus bound to start building up afresh on his own account. In a situation so open, one would expect that occasionally a particular man by skill and luck would establish considerable personal pre-eminence, and stories about the great villagers of the past are current in most villages. But it seems equally true that the successful men did not found dynasties. Their sons normally began again with, at the most, a short lead over rivals.

Village Solidarity

People belong to their village in a way they belong to no other social group. On any definition of community, the village is a community – a social group with many functions, not all of them explicit, and to which people are committed by birth or marriage, and bound by many ties.

None of the geographical or administrative units larger than a village is in any way comparable. The villagers do, of course, see themselves as belonging to a vaguely defined district, and to the Province of Kayseri. Men in the army or working away in the cities often form friendships and groups along the lines of locality of origin, but the actual units of administration, *nahiye*, *kaza* and *vilayet* as such have no social relevance outside their administrative functions.

The virtues of the village are an eternal topic of conversation with outsiders, and of banter between men of different villages. Every village has the best drinking water, and the best climate. One village, which stored winter snow in large deep wells, and drank all through the summer the stagnant water which resulted, pleaded the superiority of their water as an argument for my moving in at once. Every village is more hospitable, more honourable, more virile, more peaceable, gives better weddings, than any of its neighbours. Other villages are savage, mean, dishonourable, lying, lazy, cowardly. Neither Sakaltutan nor Elbaşı found my choice of themselves surprising, but everyone else found it quite incredible.

Each village possesses a territory, recognized by the state as its administrative area, over which it exercises *de facto* pasture rights. Villages normally own common land, and sometimes meadow or crop land which can be let; but in the Civil Code it has no rights to land within its territory owned by individuals, and unoccupied land belongs to the state.

For the village, this territory is much more than an administrative area – it is a symbol of village identity (de Planhol, 1958, p. 340). If any other village attempts to use land lying within the village boundaries, people mobilize rapidly and are quite prepared to fight, with firearms if necessary. Even incursions by other villages' flocks or herds cause at the very least militant indignation. On one occasion, Sakaltutan animals crossed the frontier to Süleymanli, and the Süleymanli headman, who happened to be passing on a horse, struck the shepherd in charge with his whip. Many Sakaltutan men talked of immediate armed attack. However, they were restrained by wiser counsel. I never witnessed mobilization of this kind, but it is clear that all members are expected to defend the village regardless of the quarrels which constantly divide them. Not even lineages cross village frontiers, so that the village from the outside presents a solid front of loyalty. Its members are ready at all times to defend both its reputation and its territories.

This outward solidarity is matched by what one might call internal intensity. Village populations are highly stable. Almost all men and more than half the adult women in a village were born there. If we could measure the intensity of social relationships in terms of emotional strength, of the number of rights and duties involved, and of the frequency of contact, we would find that all residents except the more newly arrived wives had their more intense social relationships almost exclusively inside the village. Of course, many indispensable and controlling economic and political relationships lie outside, but these are not intense in the same way. Even beyond their immediate circle, all the villagers belong to one another. Even enemies inside the village are intimate enemies.

Village Organization

Since the village is a community – a group with a multitude of functions and involvements for its members – it is not surprising that a number of offices and corporate rights and duties are attached to it. Roughly, these are of two kinds, the formal institutions laid down by the state, and the informal institutions run by the village for its own purposes to meet the actual needs of its members. . . .

Administratively and legally, the village is ruled by a headman, elected every four years up to 1950, now every two, nominated by secret ballot; all persons over eighteen can vote. He is expected to receive all public visitors, especially officials; to help keep order and bring criminals to justice; to take care of public property – for example the school; to draw up electoral lists; to countersign all official applications for government seed, bank loans and such; to see to the registration of births, deaths and marriages; to report the arrival of strangers, the occurrence of epidemics, and other untoward events, and so on. He is in short the agent, guarantor and communication channel for all village business with government. This post is not sought after.

The council of elders is elected with the headman, and its size depends on the number of the inhabitants. Sakaltutan had four councillors, Elbaşı six. Each council is covered by a like number of reserves, also elected, who take the place of the full members if they are unable to attend meetings. The elder who receives most votes in the election is automatically deputy headman, and so on down the list. The council is supposed to meet at least every month and to discuss all village business.

It would be rash to state that these councils ever meet. The council in Sakaltutan did not meet during my stay, and the only function attributed to it by villagers was the supervision of the assessment of contributions to the village chest. People said the Elbaşı council did meet, but did not do so regularly, and it did not to my knowledge supervise assessment. Certainly the councils did not function as the main decision-making body of the villages. No one took the slightest interest in their election, or attached any importance to their activities. Instead, when something called for corporate action in a matter which the villagers considered important, the senior heads of households and lineage segments assembled either spontaneously, or on the initiative of any leading villager with sufficient prestige. Such a meeting has no formal standing, no constitution, no procedures, and no responsibilities. It can only occur if the matter is important enough to draw together important people. It serves as a means of thrashing out public issues, and letting the headman know what people think, but the interpretation of what is said and the tactical assessment of what is possible and desirable remains in his hands.

Every village is compelled by law to levy a local tax, *Köy Salması*, and to raise a fund, the village chest, *Köy Sandığı*. Out of this, the headman draws a small allowance for entertaining visitors, and meets other expenses, such as keeping school equipment and other village property in order, and clothing and sometimes paying the village watchman. The village households are divided into four tax assessment classes. This assessment is mainly based on the amount of land held, but other circumstances – the number of animals owned, the number of grown working men and the number of mouths to feed – are also taken into account. The poorest households are excluded altogether.

In Sakaltutan the assessment of the four classes were T.L.15, T.L.12, T.L.8 and T.L.5 per annum respectively, in Elbaşı T.L.15, T.L.11, T.L.7 and T.L.4. This fund is the only officially imposed institution which arouses real interest, and, with the offices of headman and watchman, comprises the only area of genuine overlap between village institutions and state-imposed ones. It is the subject of continual argument and accusation, and very difficult to collect. In 1953, many headmen were still not literate, so that even those who wished could hardly keep adequate records. Accusations of cheating the village chest are therefore inevitable, universal, impossible to disprove, but undoubtedly wildly exaggerated, and probably often unfounded.

Villagers claimed that even if the council of elders did nothing else, at least it met to assess the contributions to the chest. Obviously, where the assessing authority, the headman, is a neighbour of no particular eminence or authority except for his temporary office, individuals who feel over-assessed are likely to argue, and any obvious anomaly will arouse jealousy and protest. But I have a strong impression that, once established, the assessment was changed little from year to year, and that changes were normally left to the headman. In general, the headman consults members of the elected council if they are friends of his, if they can actively assist him, or if they represent sections of the village capable of making trouble if not consulted. But very much the same applies to any leading villagers, whether council members or not.

In almost all cases I came across, headman and elders were young or middle-aged men. Senior and outstanding men did not hold office themselves, though very often their sons and younger brothers might.

All villagers must also by law appoint a watchman, a *bekci*; he is a sort of policeman, supposed to act under the orders of the headman. He is also expected by the authorities to act as a messenger, and is continually going back and forth between the District Office and his village. He is chosen by the headman, for a year at a time, on so lowly a salary (T.L.300-100, £37 10s. downwards, in 1949–52) that only the poorest and most incompetent villagers will normally take on the office. The watchman in most villages acts as a servant to the headman, and is often to be found making his coffee, running his errands or even chopping his wood. The Sakaltutan watchman collected his dues in kind himself, household by household.

Apart from this legally required set of institutions, every village has a number of its own officers and servants to meet the needs of a farming community, mostly herdsmen. Two or more special watchmen are usually appointed to guard the harvest for the village as a whole. These are expected to, and do, run foul of the herders, whose animals frequently maraud the standing crops. Elbaşı also appointed two men to supervise the allocation of water during the months of June and July when demand is high and supplies are low. Most of these are chosen by village elders, among whom the current headman has the most say. But the shepherds are appointed by leading sheep-owners. All are paid directly in cash or kind, household by household.

The village is then a corporation, with both official and unofficial servants, and an official and in a sense an unofficial income. The state-imposed general village fund is clearly alien, and so far the traditional arrangements for traditional village servants have not been brought into the new scheme. The traditional method has the advantages that village servants are responsible for collecting their own dues, and that people pay in proportion to their use of the services.

People still regard themselves as dependent politically on the village for defence against other villages, although the vastly increased efficiency of the national maintenance of order has largely rendered this dependence obsolete. But if political dependence is minimal, economic dependence on the village is still very real. Shepherds and watchmen and common pastures are indispensable. Refusal to allow a man to use them would cripple him. Moreover, the annual switch from one side of the village territory to the other ties all the villagers to the alternate year of fallow. The introduction, for example, of a revolutionary crop cycle is impossible without disrupting the whole village farming system. Meanwhile, the legal freehold of land is subject to the *de facto* common right of the village to pasture flocks and herds on it every other year. . . .

Other Villages

Differences of prestige among neighbouring villages did not prevent a great deal of social intercourse. People visit, hire craftsmen, seek advice on religious or technical problems, commission magical services, borrow money or food, search for oxen to buy, buy up animals for market, take grain to be milled. In the past, before the petrol engine, longer journeys, especially journeys to town, compelled the traveller to put up for the night with kinsmen or friends on the road. Now people congregate in the villages which serve as boarding points for lorries and buses to Kayseri, gossiping and often visiting as they pass through. The villages are too similar in production for intense economic exchange between them, but social contact is nevertheless constant and lively.

Beyond the occasional conflict over territory, and some traditional enmities, political relations between villages as groups are unimportant. In this area, all the villages were Sunni- and Turkish-speaking, so that the issue of ethnic or language differences did not arise. No one village nowadays has the slightest hope of dominating others, whatever may have been the case in the past. Fighting is rapidly suppressed by the gendarmerie. Feuds did not seem ever to be pursued between whole villages. . . .

Pressures and Change

Peasants are proverbially conservative. The reasons for this are plain. They live normally in societies in which many of their main contacts are with people like themselves who share their values. They are bound to put more weight upon the good opinion of their kin and neighbours with whom they are in daily relations, and on whom they depend for essential help in times of stress or crisis, than upon the values of people superior in standing but remote from the village.

In these Turkish villages the social controls are as strong as one would expect. Any signs of unusual conduct will immediately lead to detailed and widespread discussion. If people take, as they are almost certain to do, the view that the innovation is malicious, pretentious, dangerous, impious or absurd, the innovator, if he persists, has to face criticism, ridicule or even ostracism.

The importance of this conservatism is twofold. First, it slows down directly the acceptance of most, but not all, technical improvements such as hygienic habits, improved agricultural techniques, and so on. Secondly, in so far as people's ideas about the behaviour appropriate to the various roles in village society is reinforced, the traditional social structure is prevented from adapting itself to changes in the larger world of which it is a part. Traditional relationships persist in social situations to which they are no longer appropriate.

But the forces for change are stronger still. The very great increase in communications with the outside world is at the root of the changes. Increase in law and order makes it possible for anyone to go to town for political or economic purposes with no danger of physical attack. Lorries and buses make possible much cheaper and more rapid transport between town and village not only of people but also of goods in quantity. The vast new market for casual labour draws a constant stream of men out of the rural area, sending them back armed with much information and some new ideas. At the same time the national government is concerned for national reasons with village productivity and welfare, and sends an increasing stream of officials to the village to impose unfamiliar rules of conduct for a host of different purposes.

The villages I visited were tightly knit communities. But once they must have been a great deal tighter. Not long ago, individual villagers only approached officialdom with the special protection of their village superiors, or in the company of the headman. The village rulers ruled largely by a monopoly of contact with state sources of power, which both conferred and depended on a dominant position inside the village. Almost every man in those days was dependent on his father's land for his daily food, and if people did leave the village to seek their fortunes, they did not write, nor send money through the post office, nor turn up in person at frequent intervals. It was possible for the village to lead a much more isolated and autonomous life, and virtually to ignore its obvious inferiority to the town.

The effect of the vastly increased contact between town and village which I have just described is twofold. By greatly increasing the range of social relations even the poorer villagers have with people outside the village, it has decreased the solidarity of the village, weakening the strength of the social controls on which village conservatism is founded. The villagers are no longer necessarily dependent on their leaders. At the same time they come to depend on the goodwill of a host of other people outside the village with different assumptions and ideas. The village community is pulled apart by multiplying relations between its members and the outside world. This process so far is no more than begun, but it has already brought the village into the nation in a much more definite and inescapable way. Even if he pays his taxes without argument and keeps out of the way when involved in violence, the villager can no longer hope to ignore the authorities. He is constantly, through the radio, reminded that he and his village are part of a much larger social unit, the nation. He has become aware also that the village is despised by townsmen, and that most villagers have a vastly lower standard of living than the urban educated. The village is all too clearly at the bottom of the national hierarchy. Once the village was a social foothill to the distant urban peaks, proud in its semi-autonomy and more or less able to ignore them by looking the other way. Its social world was centred on itself. Now it is acutely aware that it is only the peripheral lower slopes, uncomfortably forced to face or evade the constant stream of interference and scorn which pours down from the urban peaks of national power.

The old attitudes are not gone. The village is still proud; each village still knows itself to be the best of all communities and, like most rural communities, at times writes town society off as corrupt and decadent. But contradictions are a normal part of any society, and the opposite is heard even more often – that the village is backward, uncouth, poor, dirty and violent. Such contradictions can, of course, live more or less permanently in a society. But though I have no empirical first-hand evidence of the village attitudes two generations ago, I am confident that its pride and independent spirit are declining and its diffidence and sense of inferiority increasing.

Changes in this direction are inevitable, and serve humanitarian as well as national ends. A higher standard of living can only come with more technical efficiency, more controls, more education, more taxes, more intervention by national organizations in local politics, and so on. Eventually the full weight of all this may narrow the gap, and by destroying the tightness of the local community, integrate its members more effectively in the nation. But the initial effect of attempts at reform and betterment, by their more or less unintended transformation of the social structure, is likely to be an increase of tension between the villagers and their urban rulers, both local and national.

Reference

Planhol, X. de (1958) *De la plaine pampaglienne aux lacs pisidiens*, Paris.

Related Items

3, 4, 6, 8, 10, 23, 27, 28, 30, 33, 35, 37, 38, 42, 43, 52, 57, 59, 61.

6

Group Relations in a Complex Society: Rural Mexico

Eric R. Wolf

If the communities of a complex system such as Mexico represent but the local termini of group relationships which go beyond the community level, we cannot hope to construct a model of how the larger society operates by simply adding more community studies. Mexico – or any complex system – is more than the arithmetic sum of its constituent communities. It is also more than the sum of its national-level institutions, or the sum of all the communities and national-level institutions taken together. From the point of view of this paper, it is rather the web of group relationships which connect localities and national-level institutions. The focus of study is not communities or institutions, but groups of people.

In dealing with the group relationships of a complex society, we cannot neglect to underline the fact that the exercise of power by some people over others enters into all of them, on all levels of integration. Certain economic and political relationships are crucial to the functioning of any complex society. No matter what other functions such a society may contain or elaborate, it must both produce surpluses and exercise power to transfer a part of these surpluses from the producing communities to people other than the producers. No matter what combination of cultural forms such a society may utilize, it must also wield power to limit the autonomy of its constituent communities and to interfere in their affairs. This means that all interpersonal and intergroup relationships of such a society must at some point conform to the dictates of economic or political power. Let it be said again, however, that these dictates of power are but aspects of group relationships, mediated in this case through the forms of an economic or political apparatus.

Finally, we must be aware that a web of group relationships implies a historical dimension. Group relationships involve conflict and accommodation, integration and disintegration, processes which take place over time. And

A shortened version of Eric R. Wolf, 'Aspects of group relations in a complex society: Mexico', *American Anthropologist*, vol. 58, 1956, no. 6, pp. 1065–78.

just as Mexico in its synchronic aspect is a web of group relationships with termini in both communities and national-level institutions, so it is also more in its diachronic aspect than a sum of the histories of these termini. Local histories are important, as are the histories of national-level institutions, but they are not enough. They are but local or institutional manifestations of group relations in continuous change.

In this paper, then, we shall deal with the relations of community-oriented and nation-oriented groups which characterize Mexico as a whole. We shall emphasize the economic and political aspects of these relationships, and we shall stress their historical dimension, their present as a rearrangement of their past, and their past as a determinant of their present.

From the beginning of Spanish rule in Mexico, we confront a society riven by group conflicts for economic and political control. The Spanish Crown sought to limit the economic and political autonomy of the military entrepreneurs who had conquered the country in its name. It hoped to convert the *conquistadores* into town dwellers, not directly involved in the process of production on the community level but dependent rather on carefully graded hand-outs by the Crown. They were to have no roots in local communities, but to depend directly on a group of officials operating at the level of the nation. The strategic cultural form selected for this purpose was the *encomienda*, in which the recipient received rights to a specified amount of Indian tribute and services, but was not permitted to organize his own labour force nor to settle in Indian towns. Both control of Indian labour and the allocation of tribute payments were to remain in the hands of royal bureaucrats.

To this end, the Crown encouraged the organization of the Indian population into compact communities with self-rule over their own affairs, subject to supervision and interference at the hands of royal officials. Many of the cultural forms of this community organization are pre-Hispanic in origin, but they were generally re-patterned and charged with new functions. We must remember that the Indian sector of society underwent a serious reduction in social complexity during the sixteenth and seventeenth centuries. The Indians lost some of their best lands and water supply, as well as the larger part of their population. As a result of this social cataclysm, as well as of government policy, the re-patterned Indian community emerged as something qualitatively new: a corporate organization of a local group inhabited by peasants (Wolf, 1955a, pp. 456–61). Each community was granted a legal charter and communal lands; equipped with a communal treasury (Chávez Orozco, 1943, pp. 23–4; Zavala and Miranda, 1954, pp. 87–8) and administrative centre (Zavala and Miranda, 1954, pp. 80–2); and connected with one of the newly established churches. It was charged with the autonomous enforcement of social control, and with the payment of dues (Zavala and Miranda, 1954, p. 82).

Thus equipped to function in terms of their own resources, these communities became in the centuries after the Conquest veritable redoubts of cultural homeostasis. Communal jurisdiction over land, obligations to expend surplus funds in religious ceremonies, negative attitudes toward personal display of wealth and self-assertion, strong defences against deviant behaviour, all served to emphasize social and cultural homogeneity and to reduce tendencies toward the development of internal class differences and heterogeneity in behaviour and interests. The taboo on sales of land to outsiders and the tendency toward endogamy made it difficult for outsiders to gain footholds in these villages (Redfield and Tax, 1952; Wolf, 1955a, pp. 457–61).

At the same time, the Crown failed in its attempt to change the Spanish conquerors into passive dependents on royal favours. Supported by large retinues of clients (such as *criados*, *deudos*, *allegados*, *paniaguados*, cf. Chevalier, 1952, pp. 33–8), the colonists increasingly wrested control of the crucial economic and political relationships from the hands of the royal bureaucracy. Most significantly, they developed their own labour force, in contravention of royal command and independently of the Indian communities. They bought Indian and Negro slaves; they attracted to their embryonic enterprises poor whites who had come off second best in the distribution of conquered riches; and they furnished asylum to Indians who were willing to pay the price of acculturation and personal obligation to a Spanish entrepreneur for freedom from the increasingly narrow life of the encysting Indian communities. By the end of the eighteenth century, the colonist enterprises had achieved substantial independence of the Crown in most economic, political, legal, and even military matters. Power thus passed from the hands of the Crown into the hands of local rulers who interposed themselves effectively between nation and community. Effective power to enforce political and economic decisions contrary to the interest of these power-holders was not returned to the national level until the victory of the Mexican Revolution of 1910 (Wolf, 1955b, pp. 193–5).

Alongside the Indian villages and the entrepreneurial communities located near *haciendas*, mines or mills, there developed loosely structured settlements of casual farmers and workers, middlemen and 'lumpenproletarians' who had no legal place in the colonial order. Colonial records tended to ignore them except when they came into overt conflict with the law. Their symbol in Mexican literature is *El Periquillo Sarniento*, the man who lives by his wits. 'Conceived in violence and without joy, born into the world in sorrow', the very marginality of their original and social position forced them to develop patterns of behaviour adapted to a life unstructured by formal law. They were thus well fitted to take charge of the crucial economic and political relationships of the society at a time when social and cultural change began to break down the barriers between statuses and put a premium on individuals and groups able to rise above their traditional stations through manipulation of social ties and improvization upon them.

The transfer of power from the national level to the intermediate power-holders, and the abolition of laws protecting the Indian communities – both accomplished when Mexico gained its independence from Spain (Chávez Orozco, 1943, pp. 35–47) – produced a new constellation of relationships among Indian communities, colonist entrepreneurs and 'marginals'. The colonists' enterprises, and chief among them the *hacienda*, began to encroach more and more heavily on the Indian communities. At the same time, the Indian communities increasingly faced the twin threats of internal differentiation and of invasion from the outside by the 'marginals' of colonial times.

Despite the transcendent importance of the *hacienda* in Mexican life, anthropologists have paid little attention to this cultural form. To date we do not have a single anthropological or sociological study of a Mexican *hacienda* or *hacienda* community. Recent historical research has shown that the *hacienda* is not an offspring of the *encomienda*. The *encomienda* always remained a form of royal control. The *hacienda*, however, proved admirably adapted to the purposes of the colonists who strove for greater autonomy. Unlike the *encomienda*, it granted direct ownership of land to a manager-owner, and permitted direct control of a resident labour force. From the beginning, it served commercial ends. Its principal function was to convert community-oriented peasants into a disciplined labour force able to produce cash crops for a supracommunity market. The social relationships through which this was accomplished involved a series of voluntary or forced transactions in which the worker abdicated much personal autonomy in exchange for heightened social and economic security.

Many observers have stressed the voracity of the *hacienda* for land and labour. Its appetite for these two factors of production was great indeed, and yet ultimately limited by its very structure. First, the *hacienda* always lacked capital. It thus tended to farm only the best land (Tannenbaum, 1929, pp. 121–2), and relied heavily on the traditional technology of its labour force. *Hacienda* owners also curtailed production in order to raise land rent and prices, and to keep down wages. Thus 'Mexico has been a land of large estates, but not a nation of large-scale agriculture'. Second, the *hacienda* was always limited by available demand (Chávez Orozco, 1950, p. 19), which in a country with a largely self-sufficient population was always small. What the *hacienda* owner lacked in capital, however, he made up in the exercise of power over people. He tended to 'monopolize land that he might monopolize labour'. But here again the *hacienda* encountered limits to its expansion. Even with intensive farming of its core lands and lavish use of gardeners and torch bearers, it reached a point where its mechanisms of control could no longer cope with the surplus of population nominally under its domination. At this point the *haciendas* ceased to grow, allowing Indian communities like Tepoztlán or the Sierra and Lake Tarascan villages to survive on their fringes. Most *hacienda* workers did not live on the *hacienda*; they were generally residents of nearby communities who had lost their land, and exchanged their labour for the right to farm a subsistence plot on *hacienda* lands (Aguirre and Pozas, 1954, pp. 202–3). Similarly, only in the arid and sparsely populated north did large *haciendas* predominate. In the heavily populated central region, Mexico's core area, large *haciendas* were the exception and the 'medium-size' *hacienda* of about 3000 hectares was the norm (Aguirre and Pozas, 1954, p. 201).

I should even go so far as to assert that once the *haciendas* reached the apex of their growth within a given area, they began to add to the defensive capacity of the corporately organized communities of Indian peasantry rather than to detract from it. Their major innovation lay in the field of labour organization and not in the field of technology. Their tenants continued to farm substantial land areas by traditional means (Aguirre and Pozas, 1954, p. 201; Whetten, 1948, p. 105) and the *hacienda* did not generally interfere in village affairs except when these came into conflict with its interests. The very threat of a *hacienda's* presence unified the villagers on its fringes in ways which would have been impossible in its absence. A *hacienda* owner also resented outside interference with 'his' Indians, whether these lived inside or outside his property, and outsiders were allowed to operate in the communities only 'by his leave'. He thus often acted as a buffer between the Indian communities and nation-oriented groups, a role similar to that played by the *hacienda* owner in the Northern Highlands of Peru (Mangin, 1955). Periodic work on the *haciendas* further provided the villagers with opportunities, however small, to maintain aspects of their lives which required small outlays of cash and goods, such as their festive patterns, and thus tended to preserve traditional cultural forms and functions which might otherwise have fallen into disuse (Aguirre and Pozas, 1954, p. 221; Wolf, 1953, p. 161).

Where corporate peasant communities were ultimately able to establish relations of hostile symbiosis with the *haciendas*, they confronted other pressures towards dissolution. These pressures came both from within and without the villages, and aimed at the abolition of communal jurisdiction over land. They sought to replace communal jurisdiction with private property in land, that is, to convert village land into a commodity. Like any commodity, land was to become an object to be bought, sold, and used not according to the common understanding of community-oriented groups, but according to the interests of nation-oriented groups outside the community. In some corporate communities outsiders were able to become landowners by buying land or taking land as security on unpaid loans, e.g. in the Tarascan area (Carrasco, 1952, p. 17). Typically, these outsiders belonged to the strata of the population which during colonial times had occupied a marginal position, but which exerted increased pressure for wealth, mobility and social recognition during the nineteenth century. Unable to break the monopoly which the *haciendas* exercised over the best land, they followed the line of least resistance and established beachheads in the Indian communities. They were aided in their endeavours by laws designed to break up the holdings of so-called corporations, which included the lands of the Church and the communal holdings of the Indians.

But even where outsiders were barred from acquiring village lands, the best land of the communities tended to pass into private ownership, this time of members of the community itself. Important in this change seems to have been the spread of plough culture and oxen which required some capital investment, coupled with the development of wage labour on such holdings and increasing production for a supra-community market. As Oscar Lewis has so well shown for Tepoztlán, once private ownership in land allied to plough culture is established in at least part of the community, the community tends to differentiate into a series of social groups, with different technologies, patterns of work, interests, and thus with different supra-community relationships. This tendency has proceeded at different rates in different parts of Mexico. It has not yet run its course where land constitutes a poor investment risk, or where a favourable man–land ratio makes private property in land nonfunctional, as among the Popoluca of Sayula in Veracruz. Elsewhere it was complete at the end of the nineteenth century.

The Mexican Revolution of 1910 destroyed both the cultural form of the *hacienda* and the social relationships which were mediated through it. It did so in part because the *hacienda* was a self-limiting economic system, incapable of further expansion. It did so in part because the *hacienda* prevented the geographic mobility of a large part of Mexico's population. The end of debt bondage, for example, has permitted or forced large numbers of people to leave their local communities and to seek new opportunities elsewhere. It did so, finally, because the *hacienda* blocked the channels of social and cultural mobility and communication from nation to community, and tended to atomize the power of the central government. By destroying its power, the Revolution reopened channels of relationship from the communities to the national level, and permitted new circulation of individuals and groups through the various levels (Iturriaga, 1951, p. 66).

The new power-holders have moved upwards mainly through political channels, and the major means of consolidating and obtaining power on the regional and national level in Mexico today appear to be political. Moreover – and due perhaps in part to the lack of capital in the Mexican economy as a whole – political advantages are necessary to obtain economic advantages. Both economic and political interests must aim at the establishment of monopolistic positions within defined areas of crucial economic and political relationships. Thus political and economic power-seekers tend to meet in alliances and cliques on all levels of the society.

The main formal organization through which their interests are mediated is the government party, the Revolutionary Institutional Party or, as someone has said, 'the Revolution as an institution'. This party contains not only groups formally defined as political, but also occupational and other special-interest groups. It is a political holding company representing different group interests. Its major function is to establish channels of communication and mobility from the local community to the central power group at the helm of the government.

Individuals who can gain control of the local termini of these channels can now rise to positions of power in the national economy or political machine.

Some of the prerequisites for this new mobility are purely economic. The possession of some wealth, or access to sources of wealth, is important; more important, however, is the ability to adopt the proper patterns of public behaviour. These are the patterns of behaviour developed by the 'marginal' groups of colonial times which have now become the ideal behaviour patterns of the nation-oriented person. An individual who seeks power and recognition outside his local community must shape his behaviour to fit these new expectations. He must learn to operate in an arena of continuously changing friendships and alliances, which form and dissolve with the appearance or disappearance of new economic or political opportunities. In other words, he must learn to function in terms which characterize any complex stratified society in which individuals can improve their status through the judicious manipulation of social ties. However, this manipulative behaviour is always patterned culturally – and patterned differently in Mexico than in the United States or India. He must therefore learn also the cultural forms in which this manipulative behaviour is couched. Individuals who are able to operate in terms of both community-oriented and nation-oriented expectations then tend to be selected out for mobility. They become the economic and political 'brokers' of nation–community relations, a function which carries its own rewards.

The rise of such politician-entrepreneurs, however, has of necessity produced new problems for the central power. The Spanish Crown had to cope with the ever-growing autonomy of the colonists; the central government of the Republic must similarly check the propensity of political power-seekers to free themselves of government control by cornering economic advantages. Once wealthy in their own right, these nation–community 'brokers' would soon be independent of government favours and rewards. The Crown placed a check on the colonists by balancing their localized power over bailiwicks with the concentrated power of a corps of royal officials in charge of the corporate Indian communities. Similarly, the government of the Republic must seek to balance the community-derived power of its political 'brokers' with the power of other power-holders. In modern Mexico, these competing power-holders are the leaders of the labour unions – especially of the labour unions in the nationalized industries – and of the *ejidos*, the groups in local communities who have received land grants in accordance with the agrarian laws growing out of the 1910 Revolution.

Leaving aside a discussion of the labour unions (for limitations of time and personal knowledge), I should like to underline the importance of the *ejido* grants as a nationwide institution. They now include more than 30 per cent of the people in Mexican localities with a population below 10,000 (Whetten, 1948, p. 186). A few of these, located in well-irrigated and highly capitalized areas, have proved an economic as well as a political success (Whetten, 1948,

p. 215). The remainder, however, must be regarded as political instruments rather than as economic ones. They are political assets because they have brought under government control large numbers of people who depend ultimately on the government for their livelihood. Agrarian reform has, however, produced social and political changes without concomitant changes in the technological order; the redistribution of land alone can neither change the technology nor supply needed credit (Aguirre and Pozas, 1954, pp. 207–8).

At the same time, the Revolution has intensified the tendencies toward further internal differentiation of statuses and interests in the communities, and thus served to reduce their capacity to resist outside impact and pressure. It has mobilized the potentially nation-oriented members of the community, the men with enough land or capital to raise cash crops and operate stores, the men whose position and personality allows them to accept the new patterns of nation-oriented behaviour. Yet often enough the attendant show of business and busy-ness tends to obscure the fact that most of the inhabitants of such communities either lack access to new opportunities or are unable to take advantage of such opportunities when offered. Lacking adequate resources in land, water, technical knowledge and contacts in the market, the majority also lack the instruments which can transform use values into marketable commodities. At the same time, their inability to speak Spanish and their failure to understand the cues for the new patterns of nation-oriented behaviour isolate them from the channels of communication between community and nation. In these circumstances they must cling to the traditional 'rejection pattern' of their ancestors, because their narrow economic base sets limits to the introduction of new cultural alternatives. These are all too often non-functional for them. The production of sufficient maize for subsistence purposes remains their major goal in life. In their case, the granting of *ejidos* tended to lend support to their accustomed way of life and reinforced their attachment to their traditional heritage.

Confronted by these contrasts between the mobile and the traditional, the nation-oriented and the community-oriented, village life is riven by contradictions and conflicts, conflicts not only between class groups but also between individuals, families or entire neighbourhoods. Such a community will inevitably differentiate into a number of unstable groups with different orientations and interests.

This paper has dealt with the principal ways in which social groups arranged and rearranged themselves in conflict and accommodation along the major economic and political axes of Mexican society. Each rearrangement produced a changed configuration in the relationship of community-oriented and nation-oriented groups. During the first period of post-Columbian Mexican history, political power was concentrated on the national level in the hands of royal officials. Royal officials and colonist entrepreneurs struggled with each other for control of the labour supply located in the Indian communities. In this struggle, the royal officials helped to organize the Indian peasantry into corporate communities which proved strongly resilient to outside change. During the second period, the colonist entrepreneurs – and especially the owners of *haciendas* – threw off royal control and established autonomous local enclaves, centred on their enterprises. With the fusion of political and economic power in the hands of these intermediate power-holders, the national government was rendered impotent and the Indian peasant groups became satellites of the entrepreneurial complex. At the same time, their corporate communal organization was increasingly weakened by internal differentiation and the inroads of outsiders. During the third period, the entrepreneurial complexes standing between community and nation were swept away by the agrarian revolution and power again returned to a central government. Political means are once more applied to check the transformation of power-seekers from the local communities into independent entrepreneurs. Among the groups used in exercising such restraint are the agriculturists, organized in *ejidos* which allow the government direct access to the people of the local communities.

Throughout this analysis, we have been concerned with the bonds which unite different groups on different levels of the larger society, rather than with the internal organization of communities and national-level institutions. Such a shift in emphasis seems increasingly necessary as our traditional models of communities and national institutions become obsolete. Barring such a shift, anthropologists will have to abdicate their new-found interest in complex societies. The social psychological aspects of life in local groups, as opposed to the cultural aspects, have long been explored by sociologists. The study of formal law, politics or economics is better carried out by specialists in these fields than by anthropologists doubling as part-time experts. Yet the hallmark of anthropology has always been its holistic approach, an approach which is increasingly needed in an age of ever-increasing specialization. This paper constitutes an argument that we can achieve greater synthesis in the study of complex societies by focusing our attention on the relationships between different groups operating on different levels of the society, rather than on any one of its isolated segments.

Such an approach will necessarily lead us to ask some new questions and to reconsider some answers to old questions. We may raise two such questions regarding the material presented in the present paper. First, can we make any generalizations about the ways in which groups in Mexico interrelate with each other over time, as compared to those which unite groups in another society, such as Italy or Japan, for example? We hardly possess the necessary information to answer such a question at this point, but one can indicate the direction which a possible answer might take. Let me point to one salient characteristic of Mexican group relationships which appears from the foregoing analysis: the tendency of new group relationships to contribute to the preservation of traditional cultural forms. The Crown reorganized the Indian communities;

they became strongholds of the traditional way of life. The *haciendas* transformed the Indian peasants into part-time labourers; their wages stabilized their traditional prestige economy. The Revolution of 1910 opened the channels of opportunity to the nation-oriented; it reinforced the community-orientation of the immobile. It would indeed seem that in Mexico 'the old periods never disappear completely and all wounds, even the oldest, continue to bleed to this day'. This 'contemporaneity of the noncontemporaneous' is responsible for the 'common-sense' view of many superficial observers that in Mexico 'no problems are ever solved', and 'reforms always produce results opposite to those intended'. It has undoubtedly affected Mexican political development (Wolf, 1953, pp. 160–65). It may be responsible for the violence which has often accompanied even minor ruptures in these symbiotic patterns. And one may well ask the question whether bold processes of accommodation or conflict in Mexico have not acquired certain patterned forms as a result of repeated cyclical returns to hostile symbiosis in group relationships.

Such considerations once again raise the thorny problems presented by the national character approach. Much discussion of this concept has turned on the question of whether all nationals conform to a common pattern of behaviour and ideals. This view has been subjected to much justified criticism. We should remember, however, that most national character studies have emphasized the study of ideal norms, constructed on the basis of verbal statements by informants, rather than the study of real behaviour through participant observation. The result has been, I think, to confuse cultural form and function. It seems possible to define 'national character' operationally as those cultural forms or mechanisms which groups involved in the same overall web of relationships can use in their formal and informal dealings with each other. Such a view need not imply that all nationals think or behave alike, nor that the forms used may not serve different functions in different social contexts. Such common forms must exist if communication between the different constituent groups of a complex society are to be established and maintained. I have pointed out that in modern Mexico the behaviour patterns of certain groups in the past have become the expected forms of behaviour of nation-oriented individuals. These cultural forms of communication as found in Mexico are manifestly different from those found in other societies. Their study by linguists and students of kinesics would do much to establish their direct relevance to the study of complex societies.

A second consideration which derives from the analysis presented in this paper concerns the groups of people who mediate between community-oriented groups in communities and nation-oriented groups which operate primarily through national institutions. We have encountered several such groups in this paper. In post-Columbian Mexico, these mediating functions were first carried out by the leaders of Indian corporate communities and royal officials. Later, these tasks fell into the hands of the local entrepreneurs, such as the owners of *haciendas*. After the Revolution of 1910, they passed into the hands of nation-oriented individuals from the local communities who have established ties with the national level, and who serve as 'brokers' between community-oriented and nation-oriented groups.

The study of these 'brokers' will prove increasingly rewarding, as anthropologists shift their attention from the internal organization of communities to the manner of their integration into larger systems. For they stand guard over the crucial junctures or synapses of relationships which connect the local system to the larger whole. Their basic function is to relate community-oriented individuals who want to stabilize or improve their life chances, but who lack economic security and political connections, with nation-oriented individuals who operate primarily in terms of the complex cultural forms standardized as national institutions, but whose success in these operations depends on the size and strength of their personal following. These functions are of course expressed through cultural forms or mechanisms which will differ from culture to culture. Examples of these are Chinese *kan-ch'ing* (Fried, 1953), Japanese *oyabun-kobun* (Ishino, 1953) and Latin American *compadrazgo* (Mintz and Wolf, 1950).

Special studies of such 'broker' groups can also provide unusual insight into the functions of a complex system through a study of its dysfunctions. The position of these 'brokers' is an 'exposed' one, since, Janus-like, they face in two directions at once. They must serve some of the interests of groups operating on both the community and the national level, and they must cope with the conflicts raised by the collision of these interests. They cannot settle them, since by doing so they would abolish their own usefulness to others. Thus they often act as buffers between groups, maintaining the tensions which provide the dynamic of their actions. The relation of the *hacienda* owner to his satellite Indians, the role of the modern politician-broker to his community-oriented followers, may properly be viewed in this light. These would have no *raison d'être* but for the tensions between community-oriented groups and nation-oriented groups. Yet they must also maintain a grip on these tensions, lest conflict get out of hand and better mediators take their place. Fallers (1955) has demonstrated how much can be learned about the workings of complex systems by studying the 'predicament' of one of its 'brokers', the Soga chief. We shall learn much from similar studies elsewhere.

References

Aguirre Beltrán, G. and Pozas Arciniegas, R. (1954) 'Instituciones indigenas en el México actual', in A. Caso et al., *Métodos y resultados de la política indigenista en México*, Memorias del Instituto Nacional Indigenista, no. 6, Mexico.

Carrasco, P. (1952) 'Tarascan folk religion: an analysis of economic, social and religious interactions', *Middle American Research Institute Publications*, vol. 17, pp. 1–64.

Chávez Orozco, L. (1943) *Las instituciones democraticas de los indígenas mexicanos en la época colonial*, Ediciones del Instituto Indigenista Interamericano, Mexico.

Chávez Orozco, L. (1950) 'La irrigación en México: ensayo histórico', *Problemas Agricolas e Industriales de México*, vol. 2, pp. 11–31.

Chevalier, F. (1952) 'La formation des grands domaines au Mexique: terre et société aux XVIe–XVIIe siècles', *Travaux et Mémoires de l'Institut d'Ethnologie*, no. 56.

Fallers, L. (1955), 'The predicament of the modern African chief: an instance from Uganda', *American Anthropologist*, vol. 57, pp. 290–305.

Fried, M. H. (1953) *Fabric of Chinese Society*, Praeger.

Ishino, I. (1953) 'The *oyabun-kobun*: a Japanese ritual kinship institution', *American Anthropologist*, vol. 55, pp. 685–707.

Iturriaga, J. E. (1951). *La estructura social y cultural de México*, Fondo de Cultura Económica, Mexico.

Mangin, W. (1955) '*Haciendas*, *comunidades* and strategic acculturation in the Peruvian sierra', paper read before the American Anthropological Association, Boston, 18 November.

Mintz, S. W. and Wolf, E. R. (1950) 'An analysis of ritual co-parenthood (*compadrazgo*)', *Southwestern Journal of Anthropology*, vol. 6, pp. 341–68.

Redfield, R. and Tax, S. (1952) 'General characteristics of present-day Mesoamerican Indian society', in S. Tax (ed.), *Heritage of Conquest*, Free Press, pp. 31–9.

Tannenbaum, F. (1929) *The Mexican Agrarian Revolution*, Brookings Institution, Washington, DC.

Whetten, N. L. (1948) *Rural Mexico*, University of Chicago Press.

Wolf, E. R. (1953) 'La formación de la nación, un ensayo de formulación', *Ciencias Sociales*, vol. 4, pp. 50–62, 98–111, 146–71.

Wolf, E. R. (1955a) 'Types of Latin American peasantry: a preliminary discussion', *American Anthropologist*, vol. 57, pp. 452–71.

Wolf, E. R. (1955b) 'The Mexican *Bajío* in the eighteenth century: an analysis of cultural integration', *Middle American Research Institute Publication*, vol. 17, pp. 177–200.

Zavala, S. and Miranda, J. (1954) 'Instituciones indigenas en la colonia', in A. Caso et al. (1954), *Métodos y resultados de la política indigenista en México*, Memorias del Instituto Nacional Indigenista, no. 6, Mexico, pp. 29–112.

Related Items

3, 8, 10, 12, 27, 28, 30, 35, 37, 43, 49, 61, 62.

7

Peasantry as a Way of Living

Fei Hsiao Tung

Peasantry, the key toward understanding China, is a way of living, a complex of formal organization, individual behaviour, and social attitudes, closely knit together for the purpose of husbanding land with simple tools and human labour. Peasants are settled and sedentary. Growth of population on limited resources puts the law of diminishing returns in effective operation. Cultivation of land tends to be intensified. Minute care of the soil and delicate application of human labour hinder the utilization of improved tools. Standard of living lowers as population increases. Animal labour becomes uneconomical. Highly developed application of human skill in handling soil and crops yields a return only sufficient for a bare existence. When work is mainly done by hands and feet, the advantage of division of work is reduced. Extensive organization in such enterprises gives no appreciable profit but rather complicates human relations. This accounts for the fact that among the peasant society the basic group is usually small.

The smallness of the cooperative group is characteristic of peasantry. Peasants, unlike nomads, live in settled communities. They are non-aggressive because, on the one hand, extension of land beyond the ability of cultivation means little to them, and, on the other, living in a rural environment, they face no immediate threat of innovation or invasion. Security is a matter of course. There seems to be no necessity for any militant organization on a large scale.

This is perhaps one reason why the family is so predominant in the structure of social organization in a peasant community. The family in a peasant community is a sufficient unit to provide the necessary and minimum social cooperation in everyday economic pursuits. Such cooperation is maintained by, or rather an extension of, another main task of the human race, that of reproduction. The mutual reinforcement of the related functions of life achieves a strong solidarity. . . .

Excerpt from Fei Hsiao Tung, 'Peasantry and gentry', *American Journal of Sociology*, vol. 52, 1946, no. 1.

Among Chinese peasants, the basic social unit is numerically small and is mainly composed of parents and children. Evidence from various studies in rural China shows no exception. The average varies from four to six persons. However, from the point of view of structure, the basic group among the Chinese peasants is more than a family, as defined by anthropologists. It sometimes includes children who have grown up and married. I have called it the 'expanded family'.[1] If the principle of expansion carries far, the result will be a clanlike big house, as seen among the gentry; but among peasants such expansion is limited. As a rule, lateral expansion – brothers continuing to live together after marriage – is rare and unstable. The usual practice is that the aged parents stay with one of the married sons. Without any social provision for the old, it seems very natural that the parents should be taken care of by their son.

In a mobile community, nomadic or industrial, an individual has his own locus. He moves about by himself and acquires his social status on his own behalf. But for a settled peasant, it seems that all his activities are bound to the group. The family is a self-sufficient and self-supporting group, in which he maintains his existence and perpetuates his kind. It is the centre from which his relations and kinship, local, and professional, ramify. The singularism in extension of social relations differs in principle from the pluralism in modern society. Individuals in such a structure are counted only as members of a certain family.

The traditional ideology in China suppresses individualism in favour of familism. The meaning, or value, of the individual's existence is defined by its being a link in the chain of social continuity which is concretely conceived in terms of descent. The most important task of a man is to continue the family line. Of the three traditional charges against an undutiful son, failure in giving offspring comes first.

Farm work under primitive techniques is drudgery. It is quite conceivable that those who can afford to live without being engaged in hard work will do so even at the expense of their standard of living. It seems that there are two ways of reducing the painful experience in productive pursuits: either to improve tools and utilize animal and natural power or to shift the burden to others. The first is exploitation of nature and the second is exploitation of man.

Note

1 Fei Hsiao Tung (1939) *Peasant Life in China: A Field Study of Country Life in the Yangtze Valley*, New York, Dutton.

Related Items

1, 2, 4, 5, 9, 18, 21, 33, 37.

8

The Part-Societies with Part-Cultures

Robert Redfield

Until recently the peasantry of the Old World were the business, not of anthropology, but of other disciplines. European and Asiatic peasantry interested economists, sociologists and historians concerned with the origins of particular peasant institutions, especially agrarian institutions. To these students the relations of peasantry to forms of land-holding and to feudalism were topics of central interest. Folklore and the study of folk life (peasant life) were distinguished from the anthropologist's or ethnologist's study of primitive life (*Volkskunde* versus *Völkerkunde*). The student of peasant life characteristically did not make holistic community studies. . . .

Peasant society and culture has something generic about it. It is a kind of arrangement of humanity with some similarities all over the world. . . . In making these last assertions I am implying a definition of peasant society as a type. . . . It will be a type or class loosely defined, a focus of attention rather than a box with a lid. I do not think that any one definition of peasant society arises inevitably from the facts. The difficulties of a definition are admitted. Peasantry as a type are not as distinct as birds are from mammals or colloids from crystals. Many a definition is defensible; each is a fixing of attention on some characteristics chosen by the definer as important.

I shall follow Wolf's conception of peasantry as agricultural producers following a way of life on land the peasant controls. I shall add to this conception that emphasis on the relationship of peasant to an elite of the manor, town, or city. I want to think about peasants as the rural dimension of old civilizations. Kroeber puts it simply: 'Peasants are definitely rural – yet live in relation to market towns; they form a class segment of a larger population which usually contains urban centres, sometimes metropolitan capitals. They constitute part-societies with part-cultures.' But I am not inclined to limit the group of real peasant societies, within our view here, to those that form parts of admitted feudal societies.

Excerpts from R. Redfield, *Peasant Society and Culture*, Chicago University Press, 1956.

Related Items

33, 35, 36, 37.

9

Peasant Economy as a Category in History

Daniel Thorner

Peasant economies, we suggest, have been and still are a widespread form of organization of human society.[1] Because of their historical persistence, peasant economies would appear to be well worthy of study in their own right and in their own terms. When we search the literature of agrarian history for discussions of peasant economies we find them scattered among such diverse categories as 'subsistence', 'feudal' or 'oriental'. In discussions of the so-called 'under-developed' areas, peasant economies are frequently dealt with as conglomerations of 'small-scale' units or 'minifundia'. Or they may be relegated to an intermediate or transition stage between 'primitive' and 'modern' (or 'developed') economies. By contrast, we believe that there is hope of rich analytical yield if we can find a way of treating 'peasant economies' as a distinctive group.

For this purpose, it is essential to define peasant economy as a system of production and to distinguish it from other historical systems such as slavery, capitalism and socialism. We shall accordingly set out a tentative definition of peasant economy, and then illustrate it by several examples. These will show some of the varied forms which peasant economies have assumed in different continents in modern times. Beneath the apparent variety we shall find in each case a common core.

Before we specify the determining characteristics of peasant economy, we should make our level of analysis absolutely plain. We are dealing here with the features of the whole economy of sizeable countries. Our units will be at the scale of kingdoms or empires (Japan, Tsarist Russia, China), nations (Mexico) and grand imperial possessions (India, Indonesia).

We exclude from our coverage little possessions, tiny states, and sub-regions of larger states. Nor do we deal with peasant sectors of economies which, taken

Excerpts from Daniel Thorner, 'Peasant economy as a category in economic history', Deuxième Conférence Internationale d'Histoire Economique, Aix-en-Provence, vol. 2, Mouton, 1962, pp. 287–300.

as a whole, are not peasant economies. We do *not* exclude small nations. Quite a number of them, e.g. Ceylon, Paraguay, Syria, Sardinia, Ireland and Scotland before the Union, have had peasant economies, and a few still do today. But in the present paper we have thought it would be clearer if we presented as our examples only countries of a substantial size.

We use five criteria for determining whether the total economy of a given country, nation or large colonial area is to be taken as a peasant economy. All five of these must be satisfied before an entire economy of a given country can be termed peasant. Our first two criteria relate to production and working population. They are intended to help distinguish peasant economies from industrialized economies, whether capitalist or socialist. In a peasant economy, roughly half of the total population must be agricultural; and more than half of the working population must be engaged in agriculture. In a word, we are saying that, to be termed 'peasant', an economy must be primarily agricultural. In a capitalist or a socialist state which has been industrialized, there may remain thousands or even millions of peasants, but we would no longer apply the term 'peasant' to such an economy, *taken as a whole*. The question would rather become one of the 'peasant' sector in a non-peasant economy; the setting would then be different, and a different level of analysis would be required.

Our third criterion requires the existence of a state power and a ruling hierarchy of a particular kind: one in which the 'kinship' or 'clan' order has weakened sufficiently to give way to a 'territorial state'.[2] I am not saying that kinship or kin ties have disappeared, for that would be absurd. Rather I require the passage, in the sense of Moret on Egypt (1926), or, in the sense of ancient Greece, the formation of the territorial state.[3] The question of peasant economies in 'feudal' regimes is delicate. So are practically all questions involving that ticklish word 'feudalism'! If I were to be forced to specify now what I have in mind, I would say that I am concerned with the economies of the feudal monarchical states of Western Europe in the late twelfth and thirteenth centuries, rather than with those of the disintegrated and practically non-urban regimes in the ninth and tenth centuries. Here, however, our fourth criterion also comes into play, the rural–urban separation.

We presuppose, for peasant economies, the presence of towns, and a division or break between these towns and the countryside that is simultane-ously political, economic, social and cultural. In practice or belief, or both, the peasants are held to be a lesser or 'subject' order, existing to be exploited by all concerned. In social terms, this is considered to be the 'natural order'. We do not consider an economy to be 'peasant' unless it contains a significant number of towns with a definite pattern of urban life, quite different from that of the countryside.[4] Simply as a rough quantitative indication, we can say that the total urban population should amount to at least half a million persons; or, alternatively, that at least 5 per cent of the entire population of a given country should be resident in towns. By insisting that a peasant economy must have towns, we wish to do more than establish the mere fact that the economy is not purely agricultural. We posit a fairly marked degree of division of labour in society, and a distinct urban concentration of artisans, or other industrial and intellectual workers of various skills. By the same token we presume that agriculture is sufficiently developed to feed not only the peasants and the governing hierarchies, but also the townspeople.

Our fifth and final criterion, the most fundamental, is that of the unit of production. In our concept of peasant economy the typical and most representative units of production are the peasant family households. We define a peasant family household as a socio-economic unit which grows crops primarily by the physical efforts of the members of the family. The principal activity of the peasant households is the cultivation of their own lands, strips or allotments. The households may also engage in other activities: for example, in handicrafts, processing, or even petty trade. Some members of the family may work, perhaps be forced to work, outside the household from time to time. The household may include one or more slaves, domestic servants or hired hands. But the total contribution of these non-family members to actual crop production will be much less than that of the family members.

In a peasant economy half or more of all crops grown will be produced by such peasant households, relying mainly on their own family labour. Alongside of the peasant producers there may exist larger units: the landlord's demesne or home farm tilled by labour exacted from the peasants, the *hacienda* or estate on which the peasants may be employed for part of the year, the capitalist farm in which the bulk of the work is done by free hired labourers. But if any of these is the characteristic economic unit dominating the countryside, and accounting for the greater share of the crop output, then we are not dealing with a peasant economy. We also exclude specifically all economies in which the most representative agricultural unit is the Roman-style slave estate or the sugar- or cotton-growing slave plantation of modern times.

We may state categorically that in a peasant economy the peasant family members are not slaves. But we shall not try to specify whether the peasants are serfs, semi-free or free. There are, it hardly needs saying, other contexts in which this question is of the highest importance. For the definition of peasant economy, however, the distinction is unnecessary, and the effort to make it likely to prove analytically sterile. We have already indicated that in peasant economies the peasantry as a group is subject to and exists to be exploited by others. The peasant may very well have to work one or more days of the week for the baron or the lord of the manor. He may also be obliged to make payments or presents to landlords, functionaries, aristocrats or other important persons. At the same time, from the point of view of production, the peasant households constitute definite – one is almost tempted to say 'independent' – entities. Because of this duality in their position, these peasantries inevitably straddle the line between free and unfree. In a sense the peasant in such economies is simultaneously subject and master.

Within a particular country at a particular time, many varieties or blends of freedom and unfreedom may co-exist. It is usually difficult to say with any precision what proportion of the peasantry are serfs and what proportion are not serfs. With the passage of time, the proportions may change. In some areas, the working populations have oscillated over the centuries through most of the range from freedom to serfdom and back again.

In a peasant economy the first concern of the productive units is to grow food crops to feed themselves. But this cannot be their sole concern. By definition, they live in a state and are linked with urban areas. They must willy-nilly sustain the state, the towns, the local lords. Hence, in one way or another, they must hand over, surrender or sell to others part of their food crops. Although the conditions of exchange are such that the peasants usually give more than they get, they may obtain in return a bit of iron, some salt, spices, perhaps fancy cloth for a marriage.

We should be careful not to slip into the trap of imagining a 'pure' type of peasant household which consumes practically everything it produces and practically nothing else, as distinct from an 'impure' type which produces for a market as well as for its own immediate needs. The latter is historically more common and more characteristic. In point of fact, the household units in peasant economies frequently dramatize their dual focus by growing two crops. The first is the cereal essential to their own sustenance and that of society as a whole; the second is much more likely to be a non-food grain (perhaps a fruit, fibre or oilseed) produced precisely with an eye to barter, sale or exchange of some sort. It is as habitual with peasants in many areas to grow two crops as to walk on two feet.

We are sure to go astray if we try to conceive of peasant economies as exclusively 'subsistence' oriented and to suspect capitalism wherever the peasants show evidence of being 'market' oriented. It is much sounder to take it for granted, as a starting point, that for ages peasant economies have had a double orientation towards both. In this way, much fruitless discussion about the nature of so-called 'subsistence' economies can be avoided.

We might say that in a peasant economy roughly half or more of all agricultural production is consumed by the peasant households themselves, rather than being 'marketed'. We do not, however, include as 'marketed' produce those food grains handed over around harvest time by indebted or dependent peasant families to the local landlords, merchants, or money-lenders, and subsequently doled back before the next harvest, generally on unfavourable terms, to the same peasant families. Such food grains, in our view, have not passed through an organized market process. They have not moved on, via genuine commerce, for consumption by parties other than the original producers. Instead, they have remained in the village where they were grown and have returned to source, to the original producers. In effect, the productive unit is the household, and the consumption unit is the same peasant family household. This is certainly not the indirect process, mediated by a market, which is characteristic of capitalist agriculture. Instead, in a peasant economy, the movement of food grains inside the village away from the producing family and back again to that same family is tied in with long-established modes of economic domination and exploitation. When such relationships are typical at the village level, we have an almost sure sign, in an agricultural economy, that we are dealing with a peasant rather than capitalistic structure.

To summarize, we have defined peasant economies in terms of the predominance of agriculture, both in total product and in the working population. We have required the existence of a territorial state, and a separation between town and country. We have indicated that the characteristic unit of production must be the peasant family household with a double orientation, that is, both to its own sustenance and to the greater world beyond the village. We must emphasize that no single one of these elements will suffice to determine whether or not a given economy is indeed a peasant economy. All these features must be found together and must relate to the economy of a whole country.... My examples are Tsarist Russia, Indonesia, Mexico, India, Japan and China [within the two hundred years since 1750]. We [deal] only with peasant economies in their 'high' or 'late' phase. None the less, we have seen that conditions differed in several important respects, which may be worth listing:

1 Indigenous or colonial rule.
2 Small-scale cultivation only; or small-scale juxtaposed with large-scale cultivation and, if the latter, the arrangements for labour supply on the large-scale units.
3 Individual family holdings of land only; or individual family holdings in the context of larger group holdings or village community rights in land.
4 Hierarchy of peasantry at the village level; existence and social role of a class of agricultural labourers.
5 Urbanization and industrialization as factors in reducing the relative importance of the peasantry in the economy taken as a whole, and in leading to the transformation of peasant production.

We might say we have sketched in a preliminary way cases of countries at the exit, or seeking the exit, from peasant economy. It would, of course, be possible and desirable to take up cases of entrance into peasant economy. In the largest sense, the study of peasant economies should encompass the whole process of their appearance, the changes they undergo through time, and the ways in which they become – or fail to become! – transformed into modern industrial economies.

It may be of interest to situate peasant economy, as we have defined it, in relation to Karl Marx's well-known modes of production. Our peasant economies include societies falling under both Marx's feudal mode of production and his 'Asiatic Societies'. In addition, they take in those periods of history which he characterized as marked by small peasant agriculture and which he treated as transitions from one main mode of production to another.

We believe that our broader grouping, peasant economy, is justified analytically in terms of the common characteristics which we have just discussed and illustrated. It would, of course, be possible to extend the term 'feudal' (with or without the prefixes 'semi-', 'proto-' and 'pseudo-') to cover this whole range, but that would be unfortunate. The term feudalism originated in Western Europe and carries with it a set of specific connotations. We cannot help but be reminded of the feudal lord, the vassal, the fief, the feudal contract, the manor and the serf. This full complex of phenomena, however, occurs only in a small number of centuries in quite confined areas of extreme Western Europe and Japan. Peasant economies, by contrast, existed long before feudalism, alongside of feudalism, and long after it. They persist in our contemporary world. No matter how the content of the term is thinned out, feudalism cannot serve to cover a historical canvas stretching eastward from the Caribbean to the China Seas.

From our perspective, European feudalism of the high Middle Ages may be seen as embodying a particular form of peasant economy. Nothing is gained by trying to view *all* peasant economies as variations of that one rather special form. The time has arrived to treat European experience in categories derived from world history, rather than to squeeze world history into Western European categories.

Notes

1 Many writers have utilized the term peasant economy to describe the functioning of *individual* household units. We prefer to reserve the term for entire economies having certain characteristics which we shall specify in the course of this paper.

2 Re. criterion of existence of a state: the administrative structure of the state must comprise a total of at least five thousand officers, minor officials, flunkeys and underlings.

3 The area of the ancient Greek states, however, was so small that most of them would have to be excluded from our consideration because of failure to meet our initial precondition of sufficient size.

4 There is much literature on the separation between city and country. For the eighteenth century see Sir James Steuart (1767). Marx considered that the entire economic history of human society could be summed up in the movement of the antithesis between town and country (see Marx, 1867, p. 345). Robert Redfield was one of the twentieth-century writers much interested in this theme, particularly in cultural terms, see his study (1956). In an interesting article Lloyd A. Fallers (1961) has carried forward Redfield's line of work.

References

Fallers, L. A. (1961) 'Are African cultivators to be considered "peasants"?', *Current Anthropology*, vol. 2, pp. 108–10.

Marx, K. (1867) *Capital*, ed. D. Torr, London, 1939.

Moret, A. (1926) *From Tribe to Empire*, London.

Redfield, R. (1956) *Peasant Society and Culture*, Chicago University Press.

Steuart, J. (1767) *An Inquiry in the Principles of Political Economy*, vol. 1; reprinted by Oliver & Boyd, 1967.

Related Items

2, 13, 16, 17, 21, 25, 26, 31, 32, 49, 53, 56, 59, 62.

10

Metropolis and Peasant: The Expansion of the Urban-Industrial Complex

Andrew Pearse

This paper is concerned with the problem of the smallholding peasant rather than the estate tenant or worker, that is to say, the peasants belonging to communities the majority of whose member-families live by agricultural production on lands to which they have access rights. This sector, though it probably constitutes more than half of the agricultural population of the mainland countries, must be considered, in many ways, as marginal in Latin America. The reason for this is that, within the agrarian structure itself, the estate was the prevalent form of the economic organization, and the occurrence of large zones occupied by smallholders usually signified the non-existence or the decay of conditions as regards land and markets in which the great estate could prosper. Thus the quality and location of the smallholders' lands are both marginal, and offer an indifferent basis for a competitive market agriculture, either because they are poor, unwatered and hilly, or because they are too small to allow much beyond family subsistence, or because they are too distant from a suitable market for their products. They are marginal in the sense that the juridical institutions, elaborated for the regulation of the great property, offer instruments which are much too unwieldy or otherwise unsuited to the regulation of small properties, and consequently give place to custom and illegality. The smallholder may be said to be marginal in the sense that his participation in the general social system has been that of a dependent powerless element, disposed of by decisions of others, isolated by illiteracy from the circuit of ideas current in the society, rudimentary transport systems and cultural difference, and contractually inferior in his market relations. And

An original paper, which arose in the course of preparing a field study of ten peasant neighbourhoods in Chile when the author was working for the Food and Agricultural Organization of the United Nations, and attached to the Institute for Training and Research for Land Reform in Santiago. He is indebted to his colleagues Andrés Pascal, Christopher Scott and David Benavente, for their parts in the development of the ideas.

whatever his local situation may be, one of his obvious economic functions in the national system has been that of providing a labour reserve for the occasional and seasonal needs of estate and plantation agriculture.

As a contribution to the study of the changes taking place in rural Latin America and in problems of development, this paper draws attention to the expansion of the core of the great industrial (developed) societies, as the most important single factor in the alterations of rural life and social structure, laying down new conditions in which peasants make their decisions. It refers to a supra-political force of intervention which goes beyond and embraces those actions carried out by states and interest groups with specific intentions, such as the banning of the pill or a counter-revolutionary *golpe*; it is a 'vegetable' force with patches of intentionality. It is not aimed at peasants as such or underdevelopment as such, but at this stage of history it is reaching out into the rural areas of the underdeveloped world just as at an earlier period, and in a different manner, it set off transformations in the fabric of rural life in the now developed countries.

I arrived at a conviction of the importance of this approach from the rural pole of the axis rather than the metropolitan one, simply by seeing the acceleration and intensification of the impulses arriving at the periphery from the centre, and by being conscious that I was carried on one of these impulses myself, that in addition to trying to see the problem objectively I was a precise part of it as well as a UN expert in various technical assistance programmes.

We shall, then, take as our starting point the existence of an accelerating movement, emanating from the industrial urban centres of our society and making for the incorporation within its systems of the hitherto unincorporated, wherever it can gain access. In reaching the peasantry in Latin America, it is mediated by the national and regional capitals, which are in part local transmission stations and in part boosters of these impulses, adding their own force to the process. The most important driving force is the market complex, seeking out even marginal sellers of raw materials and cheap labour, as well as buyers for factory-made goods and for services. The stream is augmented by the natural expansiveness of bureaucracies, whether these be the national civil service, churches, health and education programmes, political parties, bilateral and multilateral aid agencies, missions and pilot schemes, or charity handouts, all competing hotly for clients, converts, 'natural' leaders, branch secretaries, and likely human types as material for training courses.

The great alterations taking place in agrarian structure, and in the values and behaviour of country people, must be seen as elements in a complicated process whereby the rural, social and economic systems respond to these exogenous impulses.

The 'incorporative drive', as we might call it, requires as a precondition the intensification of interaction between the local neighbourhood and the urban centres of the great society, made possible by improved transport, and the circulation between country and town of people, ideas and manufactured goods. It implies direct attachment of local production, exchange and consumption to the national market system (market incorporation), and the establishment, by the side of local customary institutions and traditional means, of standard national institutions (institutional incorporation). It results in modifications and transformations of values and the cultural goals which are in harmony with them, and in modifications and transformations of the social structure of neighbourhoods and rural localities, and of the structural relations between those and the larger society.

We shall now discuss the penetration of zones in which production for family use is the mainspring of the peasant economy, that is to say, where the subsistence system prevails. The elaboration of this process of commercial penetration must not, of course, be taken to imply a simple continuum from isolated economic autarky moving chronologically ever closer to complete integration in a market economy. During the historic period in Latin America there have always been communities of families each with functioning productive organizations linked directly to consumers by market relations and making use of money as a means of exchange. Coexisting with those, there have been isolated groups maintaining themselves with a minimum of exchange relations with local and national markets. But for historical reasons, the market linkage of communities of small producers working in relative independence (as also of estates in which small producers were organized under compulsion) has been intermittent rather than continuous. The rise and decline of heavily populated mining centres, the development of a new form of transport or periods of excessive demand in the metropolises for a particular natural product, such as gold, silver, sugar, hides, indigo, cotton, rubber, quinine, wheat, cacao, bananas, etc., have been typical inductors of market relations.

The present period is characterized by rapid growth of cities, and with them a growing internal market, rising population and the general extension of transport, bringing cheap manufactured consumer goods and agricultural elements of production to the rural zones, in exchange for money, and a much greater and more consistent demand for agricultural products, rather than random invasions, answering the rationality of mercantile or industrial capitalism, but not that of the dependent colonial or national economy, and still less of the producing regions. Thus it is now possible to speak about a persistent process of penetration and incorporation of the rural areas in the system of market relations. But incorporation in the larger market system is partial and does not lead to an evenly distributed economic development, involving increased productivity, income and capital formation.

The response to the incorporative drive is of course varied. In certain communities where a solidary system of collective defence against the larger society has been institutionalized, the response may be near zero, but there is usually a clearly identifiable reaction which may be radical in the alterations it produces, and depends on internal factors connected with the configuration and dynamics of the community as well as the intensity of the incorporative drive.

Local semi-autarkic economic systems, in which direct exchange of a variety of goods and of labour keep the circulation of specie to a minimum, are upset by the coming of cheap manufactured goods and the diffusion of certain kinds of machines. Manufacture for home consumption and arrangements for the exchange of labour fall into disuse. Money increases in importance, for the purchase of manufactured and processed necessities. As a consequence, there is an increase in the relative importance of commerce, transport and credit, and of those who manage or control them. Production does not advance generally, since both additional labour and technical inputs require cash or credit, which is not economically viable to the majority. There is less acceptance on the part of the younger men of the obligation to work for their fathers in exchange for subsistence, and more temporary migration for wage work, as well as permanent migration towards centres of urban or industrial employment. Thus the labour available at busy times is less than previously. Failing a really lucrative cash crop, the more accessible markets do not offer a secure and substantial return which could make possible a radical change of system, and most families are obliged to cling to subsistence agriculture for security.[1] The labour force available is devoted to securing a harvest of cereal or potatoes which will provide for the basic food requirements of the family, plus other items whose sale will provide the cash necessary for subsistence purchases the year round. A further obstacle to the commercial development of the small-holders' economy is the marketing mechanism. On account of the contractual inferiority of the peasant, and the usual concentration of three commercial functions in the hands of single individuals (purchaser of produce, supplier of credit and vendor of consumption goods), any surpluses developed by the little economy tend to be transferred to the middleman rather than remain available for reinvestment.

Full incorporation in the market would imply the establishment of competitive commercial farms. This requires certain additions to the peasants' assets of land, labour and traditional techniques, such as access to credit, knowledge of improved methods of production and the addition of some powered machines. It also would seem to imply a very difficult social transformation, namely the abandonment of a life guided by a network of community rights and obligations and its replacement by economically motivated activities in which neighbours and kin are manipulated like any other input. The traditional gearing of productive roles to family relationships must be modified by the submission of the latter to commercial exigencies.

Under these conditions, the commercial agriculturalist does not necessarily emerge directly from the peasantry, since the accumulation of the qualifications for success, namely technical know-how, credit and commercial ability, can only be acquired during a period following escape from an occupational status which carries with it continual dedication to manual labour, and from a social status which carries with it a network of particularistic obligations within the community and contractual inferiority in relations with the market. The commercial farmer may be the peasant migrant who returns from an industrial or commercial occupation to lands already in the possession of his family or which he acquires. He may be an outsider attracted by the productive and commercial opportunities of a community which are not perceived or not realizable by its members. Or he may be a member of the peasant community who has been able to establish himself in commerce or transport, and who has been exposed to urban socialization without necessarily living in the town. The outsider already lives within a circuit of ideas in which market intelligence and improved methods have currency, and he remains in contact with this circuit even if he now lives in the rural community, though his rural neighbours are not necessarily able to 'plug in' to it. And his economic behaviour suffers little restraint or control by this community, since he retains his urban reference-group. The other two types of modernizers will adopt free competitive economic behaviour in proportion to the decline of their community obligations and the growth of their identification with town reference-groups and other modernizers.

An alternative mode of change may be seen in which no commercial farmers emerge within the peasants' holdings, but in which entrepreneurs in modern inputs associate with the peasant, raising his productivity but securing his dependence and the lion's share of his surpluses. A current example of this mode of change can be given from a rather remote Bolivian estate which was appropriated by the Land Reform. Prior to the reform, its income was derived from the production for the market of high-quality potatoes, requiring chemical manures. After expropriation, the peasants became owners of the land, but within a comparatively short time came to rely on a group of commercially minded people (peasants, traders and lorry-owners) from a more prosperous zone, who brought them the manure necessary for planting and received payment of half the crop at harvest time. In effect, the lot of the traditional peasant is tied to the decline in the relative importance of the factors land and (unpowered) labour in the productive process, and the relative devaluation of recompense in respect of them.

The drive towards incorporation brings to neighbourhoods and rural localities a set of formally organized institutions (some a part of the state apparatus and some not) which are characterized by national standardization, conformity to urban cultural norms and developmental aims, such as schooling, public health, agricultural development, provision of credit, education of adults, mobilization of peasants in community organizations, or as voters, or in political associations, in football and sports clubs, as converts and as the recipients of charity. While market incorporation is a blind process in which individual agents and groups pursuing economic ends provide the motor, institutional incorporation contains a coherent aim-content, and is to some extent an instrument deliberately used by the state to fit out the 'lagging' peripheral subcultures for their prescribed roles in the national economy and society, though the degree of intentionality should not be exaggerated, however prominent the explicit aims are. Institutional incorporation offers partial alternatives and palliatives to the dilemmas of commercialization.

Education can be expected to diversify skills and prepare country people for easier acceptance of innovation. It undoubtedly facilitates the integration of migrants to the cities. The process of acculturation which accompanies institutional incorporation and the intensification of interaction with the larger society, diminishing the cultural differences between town and country people, also removes one of the props on which the contractual inferiority of the peasant is based. The implantation of the national institutions, organized at least formally on the basis of secondary relationship and standard norms, provides experience in leadership and membership through which local pressures may be exercised and local demands represented. Development agencies offering credit and technical services can be expected to provide some alternatives to local monopolies. Cooperatives may lead to the strengthening of bargaining positions, and political participation may give some consideration to peasant interests.

The incorporative drive, accompanied as it is by an intensification of communication and exchange of goods, persons and ideas between the rural neighbourhoods and the urban centres, puts on display, as it were, a series of alternative behaviours and orientations which may be adopted by the peasants. If they are adopted, then they replace elements of the traditional, local and particular subculture by elements of a national standard, contemporary (though not necessarily 'modern') urban culture. Penetration of the rural neighbourhoods by the incorporative movement brings 'facilities' in the most ample sense.

But at the same time it establishes a new kind of dependence of rural social organization on the urban centres. The obsolescence of the local economic institutions which grow up around subsistence is accompanied by the decline of other social institutions belonging exclusively to the neighbourhood, a loss of self-containment and valorative self-sufficiency. Exogamy becomes more general, local leadership diminishes in prestige and effectiveness. The new institutions offer apparently more efficient means to the fulfilment of social goals. But the status of the peasant in these new institutions is inevitably a dependent one, since their management requires urban skills (just as entrepreneurship does), and the greater the scope of the decision to be made, the more remote and metropolitan is the locus of decision making.

The forces operating to incorporate the smallholder sector in the national economy are differential in their effects, and lead to the counterposing of two groups. The entrepreneurs and the other groups in the rural neighbourhood who have experience of the urban world, and also are not dependent on their own manual labour applied to the land, seek to differentiate themselves socially from the remaining traditional peasantry. This is made possible by the increase in intensity of communications with the urban centres.

A new rural middle stratum begins to acquire identity, associating with the middle strata of the pueblo, and adopting behaviour and symbols taken from urban life. The values of the new rural middle strata are urban-oriented and they are sustained by urban reference-groups. Agricultural productive effort and investment are justified by urban rewards. 'Objective' justification must be found for the rejection of many traditional norms and disrespect for the traditional peasantry.

The expansion of the middle strata and the induction of the new institutions occur at the same time. It follows that the middle strata welcome the opportunity of validating their status by moving into the leading roles of the new institutions. This may mean that the use of the institution to demonstrate prestige or to exercise power may predominate over its dedication to its formal purposes. It almost certainly means the appropriation of the institution to the ends of this sector. Thus the replacement of the traditional, peculiar and local institution-set by the modern, standardized and national institution-set is accompanied by the taking over of the new authority-roles by the emergent middle strata.

With the growing importance of the national institutions and the decline of the local ones, the local solidarity based on a tightly knit network of loyalties and obligations gives way to emancipation from local control, to the increasing isolation of the nuclear family within the neighbourhood and, at the same time, an increase in controls exercised directly over the community from the urban centres. The importance of the neighbourhood as a community declines. The characteristic unique status of the traditional rural person is replaced by the enjoyment of different levels of status in different sub-systems. There is a tendency towards differentiation and multiplication of social as well as of economic roles. Action sequences which have been valued because they fulfilled the tradition are now valued as means to economic ends.

The other group consists of the peasants who, as it were, are left behind. They may own the land and dispose of their own labour and traditional skills. Their change of status is subtle and gradual. It is likely to be initiated when pressure of the market economy renders inadequate instrumental, techno-logical, economic and institutional means belonging to the subsistence system. Substitutes are sought for and in the new phase attempts are made to reach goals and enjoy the gratification thereof by the use of new techniques, changed productive and market relations, and the adoption of roles in the new national institutions.

The adoption of new techniques can take place without important social consequences, provided it is instrumental in reaching the desired goals. But the abandonment of the subsistence elements of the economy and of the local institutions, and full delivery to the commercial system and the national institutions, is fraught with far-reaching consequences since both exact stern conditions. To play the role of agricultural entrepreneur in the new system requires technical skill and 'bureaucrability', and access to credit on a considerable scale, assets which very few of the traditional peasantry are likely to possess individually or to dispose of jointly by collective action. The majority must be expected to suffer progressive decapitalization and to rely more and more on the sale of wage-labour, either locally or in other fields or cities. As regards the substitution of new institutional roles for old, the traditional local institutions allocated roles according to local criteria and a status system with a local apex based on local realities, such as kinship situation, control of resources essential to functioning of subsistence economy, special knowledge of lore and custom, etc. The new national institutions are profoundly and systematically hierarchical, having their apex situated in the national capital and beyond it, in Rome, Washington, Moscow, or wherever, and each one is a status sub-system in which the individual rank is derived from the measure of bureaucratic and schooled skills (which have not hitherto been available to rural peoples) and the measure of power enjoyed in the general social system, in regard to which the peasant is inevitably placed at the lowest point in the scale. Thus the new institutions, though they may aspire formally to equity in the distribution of rights in the new society, nevertheless offer to the peasant essentially dependent roles, whose norms have not been adapted to local conditions. Their performance, therefore, is regarded as 'inadequate'.

The new dependence of the traditional peasantry on the bureaucracies of the new institutions and controllers of transport and market takes the place of the former patterns of dominance exercised by local bosses such as *caciques*, priests and big land-owners of neighbouring estates. The personal ascendance of the latter is replaced by the attachment of the peasants as clients of specific organizations.

Thus the penetration of the rural areas by commercial relations and new institutions may be seen as a flow of action from the centre to the periphery of the society making for incorporation, but the reactions to it are varied, and result in contrasting forms of incorporation, as well as in differential speeds. It can be conceived of as the catalyst of a whole set of forces latent within the local rural structure. However, in the light of the variety of qualities of incorporation, three general dimensions of change can be conceptualized, as seen from the point of view of the destiny of the peasant and his communities:

In the economic dimension. Movement from family-bound production towards productive enterprises largely dependent on industrial inputs.

In the structural dimension. Movement from membership of a neighbourhood community marked by 'structural peninsularity' towards membership of a national class-society.

In the cultural dimension. Movement from territorially defined cultural variety towards national cultural homogeneity modified by sub-cultural class-differentiation.

For traditional country or market-town people, change in each of these dimensions implies decisions leading to the free or forced alteration of behaviour, usages, forms of economic activity, techniques, acceptance of rules about rights and duties pertaining to new relationships and participation or deliberate abstention from participation in some of the new institutions. What generally operative principles can be adduced to explain why the traditional peasant decides to change his way of life? The answer seems to be that the alternative to changing his behaviour is a deterioration of his condition, as a result of the obsolescence of traditional technical and institutional means. At the same time, new means become available to replace them; and new goals come within the range first of his aspirations, and then of his expectations. This phase marks the passage from a static to a dynamic situation, since the new 'facilities' offering an infinitely wider range of goals than hitherto available must be competed for. Competition for the appropriation of new facilities now takes place, but their distribution is differential because the competitors are unequally equipped for the struggle: not all facilities are scarce. Primary schooling is not a scarce facility, secondary schooling is. Land, labour and traditional agricultural skills are widely held by the peasantry, while the 'industrial inputs', credit and bargaining power, are scarce facilities. Economic differentiation is amplified in accordance with each family's potential for appropriating facilities. Those with least tend towards the provision of labour, those with most towards entrepreneurial performance. What begins as a quantitative difference becomes a qualitative one.

A third stage can be discerned in which the two differentiated groups, at odds over the price of labour, access to land and the monopolization of scarce facilities, take on the conformation of social classes, each embracing common symbols, seeking organized strength and making common cause on a national scale. The new dynamic consists of the competition and conflict between classes, and the struggle for social ascension from one class to another.

Note

1 The schematic answer to queries about why the subsistence orientation of family productive units should survive is simple enough: the peasant does not perceive the existence of a secure system of distribution of goods and facilities necessary for family livelihood based on money-exchange, and his perception generally corresponds to the real situation. The crisis is not in the long life of the subsistence systems, but in the dysfunctional straddle between these and a reliable money-market system.

Andrew Pearse

Related Items

13, 15, 16, 17, 21, 28, 31, 41, 49, 53, 54, 55, 56, 57, 59, 61.

Part IB

Diversity and the Analytical Margins

11

African Peasantries

J. S. Saul and R. Woods

The terms 'peasant' and 'peasantry', in addition to their popular and political usages, have been used in the social sciences for the description and analysis of types of rural society with reference to a wide range of geographical settings and historical periods. Despite considerable usage, there has been no consistent definition of the term. This conceptual inconsistency has had the consequence that analyses of 'peasant society' are by no means readily comparable in either their scope or their theoretical underpinnings. There have been, it is true, attempts at a more systematic categorization in which peasants have been differentiated from 'primitive agriculturalists' on the one hand and from 'farmers' or 'agricultural entrepreneurs' on the other (Wolf, 1966, p. 2). Yet what appears to be a successful way of specifically differentiating 'peasants' from other agriculturalists and non-agriculturalists in any particular area often presents difficulties when applied to another. Thus the variety of peasant types and the variety of approaches by social scientists to them promises to provide sufficient fuel for a virtually endless debate on the appropriate dimensions of the concept. There is a danger, however, that the definitional exercise will obscure the real point at issue. For the value of any concept lies in its ability to illuminate and explain empirical data when used in a theoretical argument. Thus the proper questions to ask before trying to define the 'peasant' in an African context are: what are we trying to explain, and will a concept defined in a particular way do justice to the empirical data and be logically appropriate to the argument?

Our interest lies in identifying and explaining the patterns of change and development in contemporary Africa, and we are therefore concerned to use terms such as 'peasantry' and 'peasant' as effective concepts within an analytical framework which does usefully structure such an explanation. A precise identification of the phases of social evolution and world economic

An original paper.

history during which the peasant may become an important actor on the African stage and his role a crucial one in the understanding of the process of historical change thus becomes of central importance in pinpointing this category. Moreover, as we shall in fact see, the changing African social structure has thrown up, during certain periods, strata which may be usefully so identified in structural terms.

It should also be stressed, however, that any definition must not aggregate together uncritically all peasants under a monolithic category, for the peasantry may also be differentiated internally in terms of certain structurally significant variables. This becomes all the more important an emphasis in light of our focus upon the changing context within which the peasantry operates, for the category will of necessity remain fluid at the margins as various segments of society pass in and out of the relevant range of social involvements which it epitomizes and at different rates. Not surprisingly, in certain circumstances different segments of the peasantry can come to play diverse historical roles with important consequences for the pattern of historical development. In brief, there can be among the peasants *different peasantries* – differentiated according to their structural position at a specified moment of time.

This much having been said, we must still specify some criteria for differentiating peasants from other rural people. Our emphasis here is twofold and highlights economic characteristics. Firstly, our concern with the structural position of the peasantry suggests that it must be seen as being a certain stratum within some wider political and economic system. A second dimension centres on the importance to the peasantry of the family economy.[1] Thus peasants are *those whose ultimate security and subsistence lies in their having certain rights in land and in the labour of family members on the land, but who are involved, through rights and obligations, in a wider economic system which includes the participation of non-peasants.*[2] The fact that for peasants ultimate security and subsistence rests upon maintaining rights in land and rights in family labour will be seen to be an important determinant shaping and restricting their social action. It is also the characteristic which peasants share with 'primitive agriculturalists', though not with capitalist farmers. For while the capitalist farmer may *appear* to depend upon his land and even upon family labour in some cases, he is not *forced* to rely solely upon these in the last instance; he has alternative potential sources of security and investment. What the peasant does share, in general terms, with the capitalist farmer (though not with the primitive agriculturalist) is his integration into a complex social structure characterized by stratification and economic differentiation. In fact, it is precisely the characterization of the peasantry in terms of its position relative to other groups in the wider social system which has particularly important explanatory value in the analysis of development.

The work of elaborating upon such criteria can only be begun here, but it is certainly possible to carry the discussion beyond the point reached by Fallers, for example, in his article entitled 'Are African Cultivators to Be Called

"Peasants"?' (Fallers, 1961). Confining himself to the discussion of 'traditional' social systems rather abstractly conceived and working partly in the anthropological tradition of Kroeber and Redfield, he defined peasant society as being a society 'whose primary constituent units are semi-autonomous local communities with semi-autonomous cultures'. This semi-autonomy he broke down further into economic, political and 'cultural' dimensions. He demonstrated the involvement of many Africans in the trade and exchange of agricultural produce and even the existence, albeit more limited in scope, of political states which in some areas allowed for the emergence of many political attributes of a peasantry. But crucial to his argument was the non-existence, as he saw it, of any juxtaposition between high- and low-cultures even in those African societies which had, in effect, economic and political proto-peasantries. Fallers concludes, in fact, with the suggestion 'that one of the reasons why Christianity, Islam and their accompanying high cultures have been so readily accepted in many parts of Africa is that many African societies were structurally "ready" to receive peasant cultures'!

Yet such a conclusion graphically demonstrates the dangers of looking for cultural aspects of peasant societies within the framework of an abstract and a historical approach.[3] For the history of colonial Africa shows, on the contrary, not any structural readiness to accept, and consequent acceptance of, a 'high culture', but rather a clash between different types of social systems in which the resulting system, independent of its cultural content, was the product of the interaction of the two systems. Moreover, despite the existence of some prefigurings of a peasant class in earlier periods, it is more fruitful to view both the creation of an African peasantry, as well as the creation of the present differentiation among African peasantries, as being primarily the result of the interaction between an international capitalist economic system and traditional socio-economic systems, within the context of territorially defined colonial political systems.

Sub-Saharan Africa viewed in continental perspective is still predominantly rural in its population, but the ubiquitous reach of colonialism has ensured that no significant numbers of the primitive agriculturalists who previously comprised the vast majority of the population have remained outside the framework of a wider economic system. Under our usage most of this rural population has thus been transformed into a peasantry. Of course, in certain areas, not only have non-African immigrants established themselves as capitalist farmers but a significant number of African cultivators have moved out of the peasant category and must also be called capitalist farmers. In addition, as the logic of capitalist development has worked itself out in Africa, other peasants have lost their land rights and have been *proletarianized* in either the rural or industrial sectors of the economy. In other words the further development of capitalism has begun to phase out the very peasantry at first defined and created. Moreover in most of the continent it is a capitalist route to development that is favoured and in so far as capitalism does have the inherent strength to transform African societies fully the existence of a peasantry could be viewed all the more as a transitional phenomenon. The possibility of a realization of this kind of transformation is of course most problematic and, in any event, remains a very long-term proposition.[4] The identification of a continental bias towards the further encouragement of this possibility may therefore help to explain the fluidity at the margins of the peasant category referred to earlier; it does not relieve one of the necessity of analysing the contemporary characteristics of that peasantry itself or of suggesting its likely response to the social structures which are emerging and serving to reshape it.

The colonial situation was everywhere one in which the local populations were both exposed to new goods and services and, in many cases, subjected to specific government-enforced economic or labour demands, with the result that new needs were generated which could only be met by participation in the cash-based market economy. Two ways of participating were open to them: sale of their labour or sale of their agricultural produce. Within this broad process four variables have been of particular importance in defining the nature of the 'participation' in the overall system by primitive agriculturalists through which they acquired, in effect, their peasant characteristics.[5] These variables are:

1 The presence, or otherwise, of centres of labour demand, such as mines, plantations, industries and the like.
2 The presence, or otherwise, of a suitable local environment for the production of agricultural crops for sale, combined with the degree of availability of marketing opportunities for these crops.
3 The presence, or otherwise, of an immigrant settler group of capitalist farmers who would be competitors with African producers.
4 And, at a later stage, the presence, or otherwise, of an indigenous elite (basing themselves upon educational attainment and, in some cases, upon political skills) which in certain circumstances (notably the absence of an immigrant settler group) could take over formal political power from the colonial regime. This new stratum might be complemented and reinforced in its exercise of authority by a newly emergent, indigenous 'national bourgeoisie', to be found in trade and in agriculture itself.

Equally important, it must be remembered that these variables have operated upon a pre-colonial Africa that was itself characterized by a large number of ethnic and political groups at different levels of political and economic organization. Taking full cognizance of such a wide variety of factors it may make it easier to get a clear idea of the full range of permutations and actual consequences possible within the overall process of 'peasantization'.

It is perhaps worth extending briefly the discussion as to the importance of environmental potential, a factor which helps to define both the character of the traditional agro-economic systems as well as their subsequent responses.

For the extent to which labour-exporting peasantries developed was not only a function of the labour demand/economic need dimension introduced by an absence of readily available cash-crops. It also reflected in some instances the degree to which adult men were underemployed in the traditional agricultural system and hence the extent to which they could be absent without threatening the security of minimal subsistence production. Similarly the extent to which a peasantry could respond to cash-cropping also depended on the adaptability of the traditional agricultural system to the incorporation of new crops or the expanded production of established crops *without threatening the security of minimal subsistence production*. Of course, these complexities further contribute to the process whereby a number of 'African peasantries' are tending to be created rather than a single monolithic stratum. But the reiteration of the italicized phrase is equally significant, for we are reminded of the second of the general characteristics of the peasantry mentioned earlier. In so far as particular African cultivators can continue to be identified as peasants, one will observe such a calculation to be central to the defining of their existence and to the grounding of their activities.

A distinctive African peasantry exists, therefore, though it may find itself involved in broader national systems which can have a range of possible characteristics – societies in which the dominant elements will be a variable combination of international corporations, immigrant settlers and immigrant trading groups, indigenous elites and indigenous national bourgeoisies. Secondly, in each territory we can distinguish a number of peasantries who are differentiated according to locality – some localities being labour exporting, some food-crop exporting, some cash-crop exporting and some with varying proportions of each. In addition, these differentiations will often coincide with, and be reinforced by, localized cultural identifications, often of an ethnic or tribal nature. Of course the pattern will not be a static one, but rather one changing over time as the system develops. Thirdly, the dynamic of capitalist development tends to introduce a further element which cuts across the differentiation of peasants by locality with a differentiation based on the degree of involvement in the cash economy. This involves, as we have seen, the possible movements towards proletarianization of migrant labourers on the one hand and toward capitalist agriculture on the other, and these too can chip away at the peasantry, pulling it in different directions.

It will be apparent that these complexities make any attempt to identify the historical role which the African peasantry is likely to define for itself a most treacherous one. For even were 'peasants', under certain circumstances, to become conscious of their common interests and act politically on the basis of that awareness, the likely results are not readily predictable. Upon occasion, for example, one might find that the bulk of the peasantry in a given territory was available for an attempt to press its demands upon the other classes and interests in the society – where abuses by an alien authority or a highly compromised indigenous urban elite become so unbearable as to override consciousness of other fissures. More often, perhaps, localisms of various sorts (e.g. tribal consciousness) will prevail, to the point where even those aspects of the peasantry's economic and social grievances which might be generalized on to a territorial scale become obscured.[6] Similarly, where it is nascent horizontal dimensions which define a variety of peasantries these may become the overriding determinant of peasant intervention in the historical process. Thus wealthy peasantries may move merely to open their own paths to capitalist farming (thereby altering the options for other peasants, some of whose passage to the agrarian proletariat may be correspondingly accelerated).[7] Or the 'lower' peasantries may awaken to the burden of their condition and the quality of their likely fate before the latter is in fact sealed, and act on that awareness. For the latter the means of their gaining consciousness, much less power, are particularly circumscribed, and as yet this is perhaps the most speculative of the alternatives which we have thrown up.

But in any case such a discussion cannot be taken far in the abstract. Continental trends may be fruitfully discussed, of course, but cumulative insight into the peasant's role is more likely to be gained by bringing together an analysis of the nature of a particular national social system (situated within the context of the world economy) with a characterization of the internal dynamics of its peasantry. And this can be done satisfactorily only through case-studies of actual historical experiences. We will therefore conclude with some brief reference to three such experiences, not under any pretence of exhausting their complexity but merely in order to *begin* the task of exemplifying the various criteria which we have presented and of underscoring the range of historical possibilities which we have hinted at.

In the context of Southern Rhodesia, where the capitalist framework of colonialism was characterized by the existence of a significant settler farming community able to establish political dominance over the various forces contending for control, the ability of the local African population to develop cash-crop agriculture on a scale that would have allowed the growth of a class of non-peasant capitalist farmers was checked (Arrighi, 1966; 1967). In this specific situation only the development of tightly controlled small-scale cash farming has been permitted. The involvement of the peasantry has been forced into a pattern of subsistence agriculture with only small cash sales of agricultural produce on the one hand and periods of paid employment for most males of working age as a means of meeting cash needs on the other. An attempt to stratify the peasantry by allowing the acquisition of smallholdings with individual tenure through what was termed 'native purchase' has been on too small a scale to have significant structural effects. As population pressure on impoverished land increases and circular patterns of labour migration become more difficult to sustain, almost all African agriculturalists within Rhodesia have therefore to accept the fate of increased proletarianization for at least some among their number, as well as a declining standard of living.[8] The alternative to this situation is a growth in consciousness about their class position and a revolutionary response to it.

In Ghana where, by contrast, there was no large-scale European farming community and hence a very different economic and political cast to the colonial situation, other patterns among the peasantry emerged. Thus in certain regions the cultivation of cocoa allowed the growth of large-scale cocoa farming by Ghanaian farmers. The peasants who developed these cocoa plantations were largely migrant farmers who quickly became capitalist farmers – to them we can hardly apply the term peasant (Hill, 1963). But their emergence profoundly affected the position of other peasants in the Ghanaian political economy. Certain areas not well endowed with agricultural resources now developed labour-exporting peasantries, these travelling not only to some mines and to the cities, but also to the cocoa farming areas. A group of tenant farmers or debt farmers also emerged and these can properly be seen as a peasantry, with a distinct class position.

Historically the capitalist cocoa farmer and wealthier peasants have been a politically conservative force, underpinning right-wing political parties as well as the post-Nkrumah military regime. In contrast, however, the lower peasantry was never fully and effectively enlisted into Nkrumah's movement, for the latter retained too many of the characteristics of a parasitic urban group to effectively mobilize their support. Market forces have therefore continued to chip away at the peasantry, albeit indecisively, for a deteriorating international market situation has sapped the power of cocoa to transform the rural economy and neither the Nkrumah regime nor its successor have developed strategies for industrialization which would provide an effective substitute. The peasantry's place has not therefore been eliminated by capitalist development, but neither have the abuses of incumbent elites proven a sufficient prod to generate its active intervention in the political arena (cf. Fitch and Oppenheimer, 1966).

By contrast, Tanzania has not seen the development of one sizeable and homogeneous group of cash-crop farmers from her peasant ranks. In many different areas (in accordance with the environmental potential that existed) annual or perennial crops have been developed as marketable cash crops, and in each such area some degree of differentiation has emerged among farmers. This differentiation is expressed not simply in terms of economic status, but by differential involvement in cooperative organizations and other modern institutions and privileged access to the advantages which they make available (Saul, 1971). Increasingly there have been for the early movers paths leading out of the peasantry into the farmer class. But once again the economic mobility of some agriculturalists changes the nature of the system in which others begin to move. Thus the unhindered play of this process promises to result in a complex pattern of stratification, one marked by a number of strata of agriculturalists stretching all the way from capitalist farmer to landless labourer. In addition regional differences which spring in part from the realities of different agro-ecological environments and marketing opportunities may give rise, as has happened elsewhere, to 'local' peasantries (sometimes wearing the cloak of tribalism) which have different structural positions, and conflicting interests, in the total system.

The Tanzanian government has been aware of the first stirrings of these possibilities and – almost alone among governments in sub-Saharan Africa – has chosen to confront the tasks of *pre-empting* them. So far this has involved only the tentative beginnings of that radicalization of the political structure which might enlist the support and involvement of the mass of the rural population. But the leadership does argue for the possibility of a *socialist transformation* of the peasantries and has embarked upon a search for the modern collective forms appropriate to that end (Nyerere, 1967). There has been some parallel attempt to redefine the nature of the country's relations with the international capitalist system and by so doing effect a basic change in the peasants' structural position. Whether this attempt will withstand the opposition of those non-peasants (and advanced peasants) whose positions are threatened by such a strategy remains to be seen.

It is hoped that such 'case-studies', though derisory in their brevity, will at least have indicated the importance of continuing the study of the African peasantry along some of the lines which we have indicated. It scarcely requires stating that a great deal of additional work in the spheres of conceptualization and historico-sociological investigation remains to be done.

Notes

1 Chayanov's theory of the peasant economy (see Chayanov, 1925) with its emphasis on the dual role of the peasant *household* as both a productive and a consumptive group is a valuable conceptual tool in any study of peasants. In much of Africa the concept needs to be extended to that of a *homestead* economy as a basic unit of analysis. The homestead, which is based on the joint property rights of an extended family, frequently has rights to farm land rather than rights to a particular farm.

2 Pastoralists are an important category of the rural population in a number of African countries. Since these predominantly pastoral people are subject to the same kinds of political and economic forces as their predominantly agricultural brethren and since their productive economy (in as much as it involves rights to, and control over, the family herds) is based on a similar kind of 'homestead' principle, they would fulfil our own limited criteria for peasants. We would thus include them in any study of African peasantries, however much this might offend 'peasant purists'.

3 See Frank, 1967, and Harris, 1964 for two very different but illuminating studies which situate Latin American peasantries in historical and structural terms.

4 See the article by Arrighi and Saul (1968, pp. 141–69) which assesses the socio-economic patterns to be found in the 'modern sector' of African countries in terms of their ability to transform the rural economy.

5 Our attention was drawn to the importance of seeing peasant aggregates in certain of these terms by an unpublished paper of D. L. Barnett, n.d.

6 On this point as well as for further discussion of the likely range of political roles for the peasantry in contemporary Africa see Arrighi and Saul, 1969.
7 An important variable which we have not been able to explore here is the pressure of population upon the land. Taken as a whole African land resources are considerable but areas of 'population pressure' do exist and in these areas the options open to individual peasants are much more limited. There the growth of a farmer class tends to mean the proletarianization of others.
8 A forthcoming study by Roger Woods on the 'Native purchase area of Rhodesia' will elaborate upon these and related points.

References

Arrighi, G. (1966) 'The political economy of Rhodesia', *New Left Review*, no. 39, pp. 35–65.
Arrighi, G. (1967) *The Political Economy of Rhodesia*, The Hague.
Arrighi, G. and Saul, J. S. (1968) 'Socialism and economic development in tropical Africa', *Journal of Modern African Studies*, vol. 6, no. 2, pp. 141–69.
Arrighi, G. and Saul, J. S. (1969) 'Nationalism and revolution in sub-Saharan Africa', in R. Miliband and J. Savile (eds), *The Socialist Register 1969*, London.
Barnett, D. L. (n.d.) 'Three types of African peasantry', Dar es Salaam, mim.
Chayanov, A. V. (1925) *Organizatsiya krest'yanskogo khozyaistva*. Translated as *The Theory of Peasant Economy*, D. Thorner, R. E. F. Smith and B. Kerblay (eds), Irwin, 1966.
Fallers, L. A. (1961) 'Are African cultivators to be called "peasants"?', *Current Anthropology*, vol. 2, no. 2, pp. 108–10.
Fitch, B. and Oppenheimer, M. (1966) *Ghana: End of an Illusion*, Monthly Review Press.
Frank, A. G. (1967) *Capitalism and Underdevelopment in Latin America*, Monthly Review Press.
Harris, M. (1964) *Patterns of Race in the Americas*, Walker.
Hill, P. (1963) *Migrant Cocoa Farmers of Southern Ghana*, Cambridge University Press.
Mitchell, J. C. (1959) 'The causes of labour migration', *Bulletin of the Inter-African Labour Institute*, vol. 6, pp. 12–47.
Nyerere, J. K. (1967) *Socialism and Rural Development*, Dar es Salaam; reprinted in J. K. Nyerere, *Freedom and Socialism: Uhuru na Ujamaa*, Oxford University Press, 1968.
Saul, J. S. (1971) 'Marketing co-operatives in a developing country', in P. Worsley (ed.), *Two Blades of Grass*, Manchester University Press.
Wolf, E. R. (1966) *Peasants*, Prentice-Hall.

Related Items

1, 2, 7, 8, 9, 19, 21, 25, 26, 27, 29, 35, 36, 38, 53, 55, 56, 57, 62.

12

Latifundios and Agricultural Labour in Latin America

Ernest Feder

Land tenure is sometimes defined in a relatively narrow sense as concerned principally with rights to land and their distribution. In reality much more is involved. In the first place, there are many farm people – the rural 'wage' workers – who have no rights to land whatever. These farm families are tied to the land because they have to make a living from working for others who *have* rights to land. In some countries, they may be the majority. In Latin America as a whole, landless families form 40 per cent of all farm families, no doubt a conservative estimate based on censuses which habitually under-report the lowest strata of the farm population.

In the second place, in predominantly agricultural societies the ownership of land is the main source of economic, political and social power. As a simple rule, it can be affirmed that the greater the amount of land owned, the greater the power of its owner. Farm people who have no land whatever have therefore no direct economic, political and social power. They could obtain higher incomes, political influence and greater social prestige if they were allowed to organize into cooperatives, peasant leagues or workers' syndicates, although even then our simple rule would probably hold. But in an agriculture where land is highly unevenly distributed, as in Latin America, where 1 per cent of all farm families control, conservatively speaking, one-half of all farm land (and probably as much as 60 per cent), the power of the landed elite is used precisely to keep the peasantry disorganized, poor and dependent. The curious thing is that economic wealth derived from agriculture is today no longer crucial to the total power of the landed elite. As will be pointed out, Latin American economies are characterized by a high degree of integration of the various sectors. However, political power has had, and continues to have, its base in the ownership of land, and now, with their continued political influence, the

Ernest Feder, 'Tenencia de la tierra y desarrollo socio-económico del secto agricola: América Latina', unpublished Regional Report for the Comité Interamericano de Desarrolla Agricola, March 1968. Abridged by the author.

landed elite has priority access to the newly developing resources of their countries. This political influence seems to be challenged in countries with a higher rate of economic development by the newly formed small groups of industrial, commercial and financial magnates. But on closer analysis, this challenge may prove to be more apparent than real, whenever the functions of land ownership, banking or marketing, for example, are fused in the same individuals, as is usually the case. In any event, even if this were to be true only partially, the interests of the Latin American financiers, industrialists or merchants are much closer to the interest of the nation's landed elite than to those of the peasantry, and the same holds true for foreign holders of investments.[1] For these reasons there are now few expectations that in the foreseeable future the status of the peasantry of Latin America can be improved.

Perhaps the most significant conclusion of this brief comment on the political and social implications of Latin America's land tenure system is the evident existence of an enormous and growing *class conflict* between the landless peasants and the producers on inadequate plots of land (smallholders), on one side, and the landed elite and their allies, on the other. In Latin America as a whole the landless and the smallholders now form 72 per cent of all farm families. Their number is growing in absolute and in relative terms. Access to land becomes every day more difficult, real incomes decline and unemployment is rising.

Latifundismo, Rural Autocracy and Absenteeism

How power relations find their expression in Latin American agriculture is best described through a brief characterization of the *latifundio* system. Autocracy is a fundamental aspect of Latin America's *latifundismo* and it affects all phases of the relations between employers and workers. *Latifundismo* is a system of power. An estate is normally an autocratic enterprise, regardless of the number of people working on it or whether the owner lives on it, nearby or far away. The owner may not be directly responsible for the day-to-day operation of the farm, which may be left to a tenant or an administrator (farm manager); but the final decisions on important issues such as what and how much to plant or what, when and where to sell, or even on any 'minor' issues if necessary, rest with him. Minor matters may be those regarding the life and welfare of his workers which in advanced societies have been taken over by public authorities or are resolved through cooperative and collective action. The power of the landlord extends therefore over the farming activities properly speaking as well as over the individuals who participate in these activities, including their 'private lives' and very often over people who are only indirectly involved with his farm operation.

What makes this power distinctive is the lack of check on its exercise. The organization of a *latifundio* is not unlike that of a military organization in which the top command retains the exclusive privilege of making decisions on all matters concerning the soldiers' activities and where delegation of power exists only within certain narrow limits – qualified always by the right to intervene, even arbitrarily. Decisions on minor issues made by subordinates to whom some power of decision making is granted are always subject to explicit or implicit sanctions by the top command. It is in this sense that a Brazilian sociologist could speak of estate owners as having the power of life and death over the men working for them.

It is also characteristic of estates that the *patrón* is non-resident and that he 'supervises' the management of his estate only on the occasion of visits of greater or less frequency, leaving the day-to-day management in the hands of his administrator (farm manager). Absentee management actually reinforces the autocratic nature of *latifundismo* because it increases the distance between the *patrón* and the workers.

The Economic and Social Function of Administrators (Farm Managers) and Other Agents of Authority

Absentee landlordism is too narrowly defined from a sociological viewpoint if only residence is used as a criterion. Even if an owner or producer resides on the farm, his administrator (farm manager) provides for a certain degree of absentee or indirect management because of the role played by the administrator and his functions. In fact, for the rural worker almost every estate owner is an absenteeist, as the bulk of the large estates is managed by administrators. In *Brazil*, for example, nearly 50 per cent of the *latifundios* had administrators (C I D A, Brazil, p. 132), and in *Colombia* 53 per cent of the land in the *latifundios* is managed through administrators (C I D A, Colombia, p. 168). These statistics may be conservative.[2]

With some exceptions an administrator is not a skilled and experienced person with the latest knowledge in good farming methods. In general, he is merely a worker who has been on the landlord's payroll for some years and distinguished himself by his thorough knowledge of local customs, which he respects, and his loyalty to his employer. He supervises the farm operation under orders of the landlord within a strictly limited sphere of action. He makes no major decisions with respect to the use of the land, the number and kind of livestock to be raised or fed, or what to buy or sell. His powers over operational expenditures are normally limited to small cash transactions or charge-accounts with merchants. From the point of view of the landlord, the administrator is merely another worker although he receives higher wages – usually not much higher – and certain minor privileges not accorded other workers. But the administrator is the boss's 'man of trust'.

From the point of view of the worker, the administrator represents in nearly all respects the nearest authority, because his most decisive function lies in the day-to-day handling of the farm workers. He assigns the daily work, pays wages, punishes, fires a farm worker and hires a replacement – within the framework set by the landlord. This implies that decisions regarding the number or type of workers to be hired and their remuneration are exclusively with the owner. The latter may receive a request for more workers from his administrator and dispose of it as he sees fit, and he may as likely as not consult his fellow-landlords in setting the terms of their employment without resorting to his administrator's advice.

Farm workers rarely enter into direct contact with the employer and any complaints or sentiments the workers may harbour with respect to the treatment received or the 'system' as such are first directed against the administrator.[3] The administrator is then their first object of respect or (more frequently) of resentment. He also represents the worker's main contact with the outside world. He is the delegated judge and jury in most routine matters regarding the work and the life of the worker and his family. In practical terms this implies that from the viewpoint of the productive work force there is no fair mechanism which can ensure that justified claims of the workers can be vented. The chances that any claims heard will be solved in favour of the workers are always slim, but the chances that they are heard at all slimmer still. Workers simply have nowhere to turn to, unless it be to a worker's syndicate or a labour court. But the latter are extremely scarce throughout Latin America.

Given his power, and although the general employment policy is laid down by the landlord, the administrator's treatment of the men can be severe and arbitrary without disapproval because the landlord needs his administrator more than he does the workers. Since he is by far the workers' most powerful superior, he usually is distinguished, like an officer in the army, by some symbol of authority, such as a horse on which he rides around the estate to supervise, a pick-up truck, and almost always a whip or a stick, and very often a gun. One Brazilian sociologist remarked that: 'The administrator, overseers, foreman are characteristic figures in the human landscape of Sape. Always robust, young, with clean, starched jackets, a long cape, elegantly mounted on their fiery horses, they are indispensable for two types of owners: the absentee owner and the physically weak who take recourse to these agents to impose their authority' (C I D A, Brazil, p. 150).

The interposition of administrators as a 'sponge' absorbing the immediate reactions of farm people fulfils an important function, namely that of contributing to the stabilization and fortification of the existing power structure. The ruling class's aloofness allows its members to appear *vis-à-vis* the workers and small producers as the innocent element, in the constant role of moderators, even benefactors, as actual or potential conciliators when conflicts come to their personal attention directly or via their administrator who, in turn, absorbs the blame for any harsh treatment. Thus absentee management in the wider sense, i.e. management through administrators, is both a convenience for the landlord whose main interests normally lie outside agriculture and whose incomes from non-farm sources often exceed his farm income, and a method to maintain the existing power structure.

Administrators are also an important element in maintaining the existing production pattern, its level of efficiency or inefficiency and of technology. Absentee landlordism is a guarantee that customary methods of farming are strictly observed though they may be antiquated. Most administrators are not allowed to introduce changes in the farming pattern, and landlords hesitate to introduce them because this may require changes in the tenure status of the workers. Therefore the high rate of absenteeism is an obstacle to technological progress and improved farming. Management practices cannot improve beyond that permitted by the sparse interest and knowledge of farming of most absentee landlords, and the limited abilities and responsibilities of their administrators.

The administrators' functions to preserve the *status quo* are reinforced by the fact that on many large estates and plantations, the authority of the landlords and their agents, the administrators, is reinforced by strong-arm men, a private police force. A typical example are the *capangas* of the sugar plantations in north-eastern Brazil who make the workers 'toe the line', who intimidate or terrorize them, or give them corporal punishment. At times they kill. These 'policemen' prevent workers from joining syndicates by threatening the workers and keeping union organizers off the farms, or dismissing workers who become active union leaders. They contribute a great deal to the violent conflicts between workers and administration, and cases of great brutality arise frequently.[4]

The Impact of the Divided Interests of Landowners on Labour Relations

The traditional rural elites of Latin America commonly show indifference to, if not ignorance of, the world of the peasants. The estate owner, whether he is an absentee landlord or not, seldom participates in the rural community in which he owns property. He does not share its institutions, nor its moods and ambitions. The schools are not for his children, the homes not for his entertainment, the hospital not for his care and the roads not for his travel unless they lead to his urban residence or are useful for his pleasure. His and his children's religious, social, political and other affiliations are in the capitals of the region, the state or the nation. Not using the facilities of the countryside, he has little interest in improving them, except for his convenience.

Lack of interest in the affairs of the rural communities can be explained by the owners' involvements in other activities – professional, financial, industrial or business. They endow landlord-absenteeism with its third dimension. By and large estate owners have little economic incentive to improve farm management or their relations with the rural community when they derive substantial incomes from many estates or from non-agricultural sources. Even at a low level of farm management their total earnings are sufficient for more than adequate levels of living and large savings. The sociologist Semenzato noted of the cacao area in Brazil:

It is invariably the same men who are in the cacao production, who are in the directorates of the banks, in the top organs of the co-operatives . . . and at times in the export houses. On the other side these very firms are also owners of the cacao plantations. There are banker-cacao farmers and livestock farmers. There are members of the directorate of the co-operatives who are influential politicians, large cacao growers, livestock men and great merchants. . . . Besides, these are the same men who are tied, directly or indirectly, by reason of their prestige and social position, to the industry of cacao by-products. And so forth. The greatest portion of the economic sector is in the hands of the large producers. (C I D A, Brazil, p. 171)

This description closely fits other Latin American countries. Relations between community and landlord are weakest when the landlord considers his properties only as a 'distraction' for spending weekends hunting or entertaining friends (p. 175).

The implication of these facets of *latifundismo* is that estate owners cannot help solve the problems of the *campesinato*, of rural labour. If this conclusion is correct, then a policy aimed at enlisting the aid of the landlords to solve these problems lacks realism.

Besides being complex, the social structure of the estate tends to be rigid from the point of view of economic development. For farm people dependent upon estate owners this has serious consequences. An autocratic organization is well adapted to having orders from above carried out efficiently: it is efficient with respect to the use and distribution of power. However, this efficiency is highest when matters go their usual way, in a routine manner. It can be quickly diluted, in terms of the management of the farm and of its people, when emergency situations or major changes arise. But while the landed elite has no interest in the peasants' aspirations and keeps aloof from their world, it is still keenly aware of its obligations to keep the peasants in check and subservient. It can achieve this simply through inaction – as the social structure automatically ensures obedience up to a point – or actively, through coercion, sanctions and total hostility to any peasant organization.

Estate owners at times mete out physical or other punishments either directly or through their representatives or by calling on police or military forces. This makes the estate owner at times accuser, judge, jury and enforcement agent, all in one. As a result, fear and sometimes even terror have become a component of the lives of many *campesinos*. Punishments of individual workers are given for real or alleged misdeeds or for carelessness, partly to terrorize the men and 'set examples', partly to deprive them of their belongings.

The severest sanctions are saved for efforts to unionize farm workers. Acts of terrorism also occur to deprive peasants of their land, both in established farming communities, as was mentioned earlier, and in the frontier areas.

The opposition of the estate owners to collective action is systematic and accompanied by drastic counter-measures which seem warranted only as an expression of the principle that to admit rightful claims in an individual case is tantamount to the landlord's surrender of the authority to determine unilaterally the working and living conditions of farm people. The *ligas camponesas* rose out of the workers' determination to fight feudal work obligations. Many of the members were small-farm owners. The history of the *ligas* is one of violence and persecution and assassination of labour leaders. In 1963, a member of one of the local organizations in the north-east said: 'The political situation here is very tense. Whoever speaks in favour of the *liga* can expect to be shot at any moment. None of us who are here in this shed are safe. A shot can come out of the dark from one of the *capangas* who must be watching us now.'

Rural Wage Levels and Labour Supply

Rural workers, including smallholders and working members of their families, receive lower average wages than any other significant sector in the society.[5] Indeed, a low-cost and obedient labour force is the cornerstone of the region's *latifundio* agriculture. To the extent that estate owners who control the bulk of the physical resources in agriculture have a vested interest in preserving such an economically and politically advantageous system, their opposition to proposed changes in land tenure institutions can be expected to continue. It is in the continuing interest of the large estate owner to have a large supply of labour on call. The existence of this pool of workers, both unemployed and partly occupied, means that wages continue low. The existing political structure in most countries offers the estate operators various means to ensure that there will be no change in this situation.

In the seven countries studied by C I D A, wages remain 'naturally' at a low level because there are many more applicants for rural jobs than available work opportunities. This condition prevails because employment opportunities have not opened up in line with the natural increase in the labour force as a result of a traditional under-utilization of the land. In some cases the opportunities have been reduced by the introduction of labour-saving machinery, and secondly because the access to farm land is practically closed to farm people. Therefore there is an absolute excess of rural labour because of the growing farm population and a relative excess in comparison to the existing jobs on the land. Excess supplies of labour exert a sharply depressing influence on the wage level, and by systematically limiting employment opportunities estate owners keep this influence alive.[6]

The Trend towards Hired Cash-Wage Workers and Conflicts Associated with It

In addition to these general structural elements of a *latifundio* agriculture which affect the level of wages and employment, one must keep in mind the nature of the work contracts under which rural workers are employed by the owners of land. Payment or part-payment of remuneration in terms of some right to the use of land still has considerable advantages for rural employers in most areas of Latin America. It attaches the workers to the land and guarantees the employers an adequate – even a more than adequate – supply of labour. It reduces the employers' need for cash and allows control over their workers' activities.

In recent years the proportion of hired landless workers who work only for cash wages has increased. This has resulted both from the 'pull' of the workers who abandon rural communities to escape onerous working conditions there and seek the greater freedoms of the villages and towns, and from the 'push' of the employers who replace their workers by motorized equipment or shift to pure wage employment, both of which simplify their labour problem.[7] But the shift to cash-wage workers is in most instances only partial. In São Paulo, for example, the share-croppers and *colonos* in coffee plantations increased, although at a slower rate than daily workers and piece-workers. The former therefore still outnumbered the latter by almost two to one in 1960 although São Paulo is considered to have one of the more dynamic agricultures of Brazil (C I D A, Brazil, p. 182).

The long-run decline of traditional resident rural workers is due to a number of economic and socio-political factors. The right to the use of land is becoming for the workers an increasingly unsatisfactory type of income. Cash is needed by the workers and their family to acquire necessities of life, even in the most remote rural communities of the hemisphere. On the other hand the traditional terms under which workers are hired and work their plots allow them every day less opportunity to grow enough food or provide for their own clothes and other items to satisfy their needs. As a result, many workers now seem to be paid both in kind, i.e. through the proceeds of their produce which may also bring in some cash from the sale of the produce, and in cash, usually as wage workers.

Demands for cash have accompanied many conflicts between estate owners and workers when the latter requested from the former better terms of employment and more ample access to the land resource. These demands are one of the ways in which these conflicts come out into the open. In other words, since the access to more land is practically closed, demands for better terms of employment normally imply more cash earnings and these are often opposed by the rural employers.

In Brazil, the slow shift from one type of labour use to another has been and still is exceptionally violent. In the north-east's marginal sugar-cane areas, for example, absentee landlords had rented their land to small tenants during the period of low sugar prices. They planted fruits and vegetables with which they supplied Recife and other cities and paid annual rentals, besides providing some free labour for the landlord under feudal arrangements. When prices of sugar rose after the Second World War, the owners evicted workers or forced them to destroy their permanent crops. Sometimes the owners paid compensation, but more often they did not. The conflicts which arose out of the tenants' treatment gave rise to the *ligas camponesas*. The conflicts continue as large landowners seek to reduce the number of their resident workers who live on the estates and usually are allotted a tiny garden plot. The normal method is to refuse to build new houses for the workers when the old ones become uninhabitable, or not to allow new workers to enter the houses when they become vacant, or to tear them down. All this has given rise to violent, even armed, clashes between rural workers and organized 'vigilantes' in this region.[8] The expulsion of workers is practised, however, in many parts of Brazil. It does not always have the dramatic consequences described above, since open clashes occur only when workers are organized and can resist the landlords.

In Ecuador's *sierra*, numerous conflicts have arisen out of the *hacienda*-owners' attempts to reduce the number of tenancy units (*huasipungos*) and to restrict the workers' or small owners' access to the land, and the subsequent extreme subdivisions of the *minifundios*. Demands for better wages and farm workers' aspirations toward better conditions of life are looked upon by *haciendados* as subversive (C I D A, Ecuador, p. 97). Being accustomed to request and receive free or nearly free labour services from their workers and to allow changes only when they originate under their own initiative, they see in these wage demands an attack on their status and prerogatives.

On one large typical *hacienda* of 12,000 hectares, for example, the landlord had adopted a strict policy of limiting and even decreasing the area of the *huasipungos* which caused increased deterioration and erosion of the land assigned to them. Yields became progressively smaller since the workers could not shift their cultivation to other parts of their farm, as the owner could. Furthermore, the landlord recuperated the *huasipungo* land for his own use when the head of the family of *huasipungo* died. This represented a certain break with tradition, and obliged the remaining family members to live on other *huasipungos* without obtaining new living quarters. The result was great overcrowding on the remaining *huasipungos*. Although the majority of *huasipungos* had existed on the farm for a long time, new land had been allotted to only a few and there were more families of non-*huasipungueros* (*allegados*) than there were *huasipungueros*. The conflict was of such magnitude that a solution through mutual concessions appeared to be impossible (C I D A, Ecuador, pp. 280 ff.). To this – says the C I D A observer – one must add the results of another process which occurs all over the area, namely that landlords are increasingly less in a position to meet the workers' growing refusal to work without remuneration and the pressure to pay cash wages in view of the low productivity of their own estates. The Indian population which for centuries was glued to particular plots of land has lost this security and is migrating in search of some means of livelihood. Human settlements are being destroyed; everywhere are abandoned huts, stables without animals, and *huasipungos* cultivated by the landlords (p. 295). The prevailing conditions oblige the workers to seek work elsewhere in order to subsist.

By and large, the shift towards cash wages is not likely to alleviate the financial hardships facing most of the workers. It does not solve the basic problem of unemployment in agriculture. This means that workers are mistaken in their expectation that remuneration through cash wages necessarily implies an improvement in their economic status.

Potential Employment Opportunities in Latin American Agricultures

It has been argued that in order to improve the level of living of farm people it is necessary to shift the excess rural population into urban-industrial jobs and to speed up the colonization of unopened frontier areas. This theory has merit if one assumes that at present rural employment cannot be expanded in existing farming areas.[9] Except for regions such as the excessively densely populated *minifundio* area bordering Lake Puno in Peru,[10] by and large the land now controlled by multi-family farms appears capable of absorbing many more farm workers if it were utilized more intensively (even at prevailing levels of technology) and under improved land tenure conditions. An examination of the possibilities of providing additional employment for farm people on existing farms leads to the conclusion that there is no immediate need for a massive shift of farm families to the frontier or to the cities. In the seven countries examined by C I D A it would appear that about fifty million more workers could find rural employment on existing multi-family farms and potential new job opportunities appear to be considerably in excess of the estimated underemployment or unemployment in agriculture.

The persistent pattern of rural unemployment in Latin America is an indication that under prevailing conditions the 'expansion' of agriculture – through modest intensification of land uses and through the widening of the frontier – translated into increased rural employment takes place at best at the same, but more likely at a slower rate than the growth of the active rural labour force. In other words the creation of new rural jobs is at present inadequate to relieve unemployment. What is more, the large estates probably contribute proportionally less to new employment than the smaller units.

Notes

1 It might be expected that the new magnates should be more interested in developing broader markets for their products or services and welcome an improvement in the status of the peasantry. But this may only be the theorists' viewpoint, for two major reasons. A developed peasantry threatens to upset the existing social structure and the power of the landed elite and the magnates alike; for example, an organized peasantry might take over the marketing of an important export product. Equally important, however, is the fact that urban business now thrives on cheap labour, constantly replenished from rural–urban migration as the peasants seek work in urban areas.

2 Owners of several estates with one administrator each may also employ a general or business manager (*gerente*) who accounts periodically to the owner.

3 See for example C I D A, Brazil Report (p. 155). But there are exceptions. In one instance, a rich landlord listened at regular intervals to 'complaints' of his workers, seated at a large table and accompanied by his administrative assistants (staff), with the workers standing twenty feet apart so that they could not converse. The circumstances were rather intimidating for the workers (p. 153).

4 A number of examples of violence can be found in C I D A, Brazil Report, chapter 4, or Ecuador Report, part 2, chapter 4.

5 The term 'wages' in this context includes returns in cash or kind to sharecroppers, tenants or other workers with plots.

6 Whether the large landowners limit employment opportunities as a deliberate policy is a debatable question. It is one of the characteristics of Latin American *latifundismo* that physical resources are under-employed. For example, only 4 per cent of all the land in large estates is actually in crops and there is more land held idle (fallow) than there is land in crops. It is estimated that if only the land held idle were used more intensively (without reference to any pasture land, for example, which could be cropped), the labour force on the *latifundios* could be doubled, at existing levels of farm management and technology. In recent years, some large estates have intensified their use of the land. But the use of machinery has sharply reduced the possibility of employing more labour. At best, seasonal labour is being employed on those estates.

7 The type of employment – traditional or pure wage employment – is not necessarily a function of the type of land use. Livestock enterprises may employ salaried workers or sharecroppers; plantations sharecroppers, tenants or workers with or without plots of land. Employment is influenced by tradition, the owners' participation in the management of the farm, and institutional arrangements, such as labour laws, credit and banking facilities.

8 One grave clash occurred when the C I D A team was making its field studies in Paraiba. See C I D A, Brazil Report (pp. 230–3). In the same community, another fight occurred exactly a year later in which at least nineteen people were killed. This incident was reported in the Rio de Janeiro press.

9 The immediate possibilities of absorbing rural labour in urban industries are limited because of urban unemployment and the anticipated slow increase in industrial employment even with a massive industrialization programme.

10 Another example is described in C I D A, Brazil Report (pp. 377 ff.). C I D A

estimated in 1966 that in the Peruvian sierra there is sufficient land available for a massive land reform and hence for a sharp increase in rural employment. If one takes into account the fact that there is considerably more land in multi-family farms than is now reported by the Census, the large-scale settlement of unopened frontier areas does not have to be considered seriously for a couple of decades.

References

The sources of the references are the seven C I D A reports on Land Tenure Conditions and Socio-Economic Development of the Agricultural Sectors of Argentina, Brazil, Chile, Colombia, Ecuador, Guatemala, Peru or the appendix tables 1A–12A of the Regional Reports.

Related Items

9, 13, 15, 17, 23, 29, 42, 52, 61.

13

Rural Social Change: General Typology, Family Farms, Collectivization

Boguslaw Galeski

The Structural Transformations of Agricultural Production

As in the past, there are two main types of agricultural production in the contemporary epoch – two institutions or chief forms of organization of production. One is the family farm, and the other is the large-scale farm in which work is performed not by family members but by serfs and peasants – in the past, or by hired workers – today.

The various kinds of farm organization existing today arose on the basis of analogical types of the past, which persist in some countries. These past types are the *latifundium*, or plantation, and the *peasant family farm*. If we ignore some reliquary and marginal forms, e.g. the Israeli *kibbutz*, the following processes of social transformation of agricultural production may be accordingly distinguished:

1 The dissolution of former *latifundia* as well as plantations or manorial estates as the result of an agrarian reform. The land from *latifundia* is distributed to landless peasant families or to peasant families owning farms of inadequate size.
2 The transformation of former *latifundia* into collective farms, their membership composed of former serfs, hired workers or landless peasant families.
3 The transformation of former *latifundia* into large-scale commercial farms, owned by private capital or by the state and based on hired labour.
4 The transformation of traditional peasant farms into modern family farms, fully commercialized and specialized but based on family labour and management.

An original paper based on Boguslaw Galeski, 'Social organisation and rural social change', *Sociologia Ruralis*, vol. 8, 1968, nos 3–4, pp. 258–81.

5 The transformation of peasant family farms into collective farms.
6 The transformation of poorer peasant family farms into part-time family
   farms with the head of the family employed off agriculture.
7 The enlargement of the family farm and its transformation into large-scale
   commercial farm based on hired labour.
8 The change of collective farms into state farms based on hired labour.
9 The dissolution of collective farms and their transformation back into
   separate family farms.

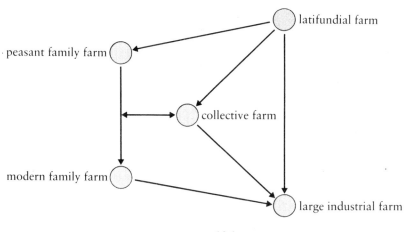

FIGURE 13.1

The above nine types seem to exhaust the basic patterns of evolution in
organization of agriculture. These types of transformation cannot be regarded,
however, as different evolutionary continua, isolated or independent of each
other. A somewhat closer characterization of each of them justifies the
assumption that they differ from each other with regard to their potential for
further transformation. Also, they can form links in continua or even different
stages of the same general evolutionary process. (The only exception is part-
time farming which is located 'in between' agriculture and other sectors of the
economy and requires separate analysis.) Thus the former *latifundia* may in
some socio-economic situations be transformed into a large industrial-type
enterprise as well as undergo parcellation into small peasant farms based on
family labour. The new peasant farms emerging from agrarian reform can be
united into multi-family collective farms or be modernized and change into
contemporary small agricultural enterprises based on family labour. Some of
them may be further transformed into industrial-type farms. This continuum
shows a very high potential for transformation. Other types do not possess such
marked tendencies. On the other hand nowhere were the industrial-type farms

converted into *latifundia*, nor did modern family farms change into the traditional peasant units. The collective farm is marked by a certain elasticity. It may serve as a transitional form for family farms as a result of agrarian reform. Or it may develop into a large agricultural enterprise. It is therefore a reversible form, i.e. family farms may be converted into a collective farm, while the collective farm may be transformed into family farms.

The Family Farms

The traditional peasant farm and the *latifundium* stand at either end of a continuum of intermediate forms which can be defined according to the degree and proportions of economic and non-economic dependency of the peasant families on the owner (or manager) of a large farm. The *latifundial* and industrial farms occupy extreme places on a scale constructed according to the degree of economic and socio-political dependence of the producers on the enterprise, and the use of manpower, i.e. family labour versus the wage workers of specialized occupations. The traditional peasant farm and the modern family farm occupy positions on the scale according to the degree of separation of the domestic family economy from the agricultural enterprise, as well as to the character and intensity of the family productive functions. The modern family farm and the industrial farm are placed on the scale according to the size of the enterprise and the professional or family character of the labour.

The conversion of the traditional family farm into a family-conducted enterprise takes place under the conditions of a market economy which impels specialization, increased marketable production and the lowering of costs. By undermining the autarky of the traditional family farm, the market makes it dependent on contractors, primarily in the field of outlets for produce and of credit. In terms of the penetration of agriculture by capital seeking effective investment areas (which leads to the growth of the division of labour) the previous activity of the peasant family becomes the foundation of specialized enterprises.

The family-conducted enterprise limits itself to a phase of production: raising raw materials (fodder, for example) or to the processing of a given raw material (converting fodder into meat, for instance). Other phases of the productive cycle are undertaken by specialized enterprises. The enterprise is also an intermediary in the transfer, most often accompanied by conversion, of raw material from one family farm to another. This process has been called the vertical integration of agriculture or, more precisely, vertical integration is one of the chief elements of the process. It embraces both family farms and industrial farms, but the degree of limitation of the producer-enterpriser's area of decision is less in the second case.

With reference to the family farm this process may be defined as the emergence of 'a manufacture in agriculture', if that term is understood as the organization of production based on domestic family labour on behalf of an enterprise engaged in marketing products, and at times also in the finishing phases of production and the preparation of articles for sale. Agricultural 'manufacture' also involves a certain number of producers, the producing families, linked with a large organizational unit by means of contracting with a processing and marketing enterprise (or enterprises). The difference consists in: (a) the fact that the family farm produces articles of basic consumption and hence has the possibility of supplying its own family; (b) the tools and often also the basic means of production, the land, are the property of the producers; and (c) the farming family conducts highly diversified activity and is connected with contractors not only of one but generally of many enterprises which specialize in processing and marketing given products and of providing certain services to the producers. These differences make doubtful the rapid conversion of the agricultural manufacturing organization into an organization analogous to industry. All the more so since, as indicated, the industrial farm too is most often linked with the above characterized organization.

The Collective Farms

A separate place is occupied by collective-type farming, which constitutes an intermediate phase between industrial farming and traditional, or modern, family farming.

The particular features of the collective farm require some elucidation. Collective farms differ not only according to size and level of commercialization and specialization of production (like industrial farms or modern family farms) but also according to the level of socialization of property, labour and outcome of production. From this point of view collective farms may be placed on the continuum ranging from aggregates of family farms linked by certain forms of cooperation to the fully integrated collective operation. Forms like 'Associations for Joint Cultivation' (*TOZ*) in the Soviet Union in the 1920s, the 'compact farms' in the Philippines, *moshavim* in Israel, joint farms in Japan, etc. are examples of collective farms being aggregates of individual family operations. In these forms some property might be owned and/or used jointly (installations, heavy agricultural equipment, buildings, etc.); some productive practices might be performed jointly (cultivation of the whole or part of land, harvesting etc.); some collectives might also purchase agricultural inputs and market their products through trade cooperatives, founded and run by the collective. In all those forms, however, the basic unit is the family farm (modern or traditional) cooperating more or less extensively with other family farms constituting the membership of the collective.

At the other pole the fully integrated collective farms might include consumption in their collectivized economy or act like an extended family.

Soviet communes in the 1920s, Israeli *kibbutzim*, and some religious groups in the US could exemplify this form. Requiring exceptionally strong ideological commitment, communes did not appeal to the majority of agricultural producers and failed when imposed by authorities. In the USSR communes together with the family farms aggregated into cooperative arrangements (*TOZ*) were forcibly transformed into the one form of a part-integral collective farm (*Kolkhoz*). In this model, adopted subsequently as a standard in Eastern Europe and a number of other areas, land property and other means of agricultural production are socialized but members of collective farms are also entitled to keep a small plot of land for family use, raise and sell privately limited numbers of poultry and livestock, grow and sell vegetables, fruit, eggs, etc. Such a collective farm is in fact composed of two different parts – one is an integral operation, the other an aggregate of very small family operations. The first part is usually subordinated to national plans, run by nominated managers and specialized personnel and delivers all products (as contract production or as obligatory deliveries) to trading and processing enterprises owned and administered by the state. The only difference between this form and state farms – like industrial plants fully owned and operated by state administration and based on hired personnel – is the distribution of bonuses in the form of dividends paid to the members according to results of production and their contribution to labour. There are also the mostly ritual meetings, with voting, discussion, etc. but usually without much impact on the actual decision making. The second category of collective farm activity is composed of the 'family plots', that is family mini-farms, self-managed and producing food for the family and for the market.

Between these two categories some forms of interdependence might develop – the family may raise animals (poultry, calves, etc.) for the fulfilment of the plan of deliveries imposed on the collective farms. This may be paid for by money or by some produce-input (fodder, fertilizers, etc.). Opposition of interests persists, however, and expresses itself in contrasting tendencies. For example, in Soviet agriculture managers representing both the interests of the state and their own interest as administrators tend to eliminate the 'relics of family farming', to reduce the size of family operations which are competing with integral farms particularly for family labour. On the other hand member families often attempt to extend their family operation and subordinate the profile of collective farm to the needs of their operations. One tendency is leading then to the transformation of integral collective farm to forms very similar to the state farm. The other is to transform integral collective farms into aggregates of family farms with some form of joint operation. The *agro-gorod* ideas of Khrushchev and recent process of integration of agriculture in the USSR – amalgamation of state and collective farms, creation of new, strongly specialized, super-units, etc. offer examples of the first tendency, the collective *ejidos*, or collective farms in India, Burma, Sri Lanka, Tunisia and Yugoslavia, of the second.

In countries where the first tendency is stronger, the transformation of the whole agriculture into one organizational form – state farms – might be expected in the future. (In the Soviet Union more than 70 per cent of land is so organized already.) Yet, at least for a time, family-controlled mini-farms have been tolerated and even encouraged because of the notorious inefficiency and low productivity of 'command' agriculture. This indicates that in favourable conditions an alternative tendency might become dominant, leading to the return to extensive family farming, though strongly cooperativized.

State farms are large-scale, industry-like operations based on hired labour. In their organization they differ little from plantations or large estates run by private owners and corporations in the United States and other non-socialist countries. There is one substantial difference, however. State farms are usually subordinated to central planning and management and have no opportunity for independent decision making. General limitations of command economy – bureaucratization, waste of resources, inadequate supply, bad planning, disregard for local natural requirements, etc. – reduce the ability of this form to reach levels of efficiency and productivity comparable to the large industrial farm in market economy. In particular cases, however, like that of the state farms in Hungary, this type of organization may be even more efficient and productive than large farms owned by corporations in the US.

The collective farm, having arisen on the grounds of the former village community, generally constitutes its continuation. The traits of such a community are even reinforced by the fact that the families living there are workers and co-owners of a common enterprise. Moreover the stratification system in these villages, primarily according to economic power and prestige, still affects the formal structure of the working force in the enterprise, or, on the other hand, the stratification system, functional and occupational, and creates conflicts within it.

The Interactive and the Directive Economic Systems in Rural Social Organization

Interactive and directive systems can be distinguished by the manner of linking consumption with productive activity. In the system denoted as *directive* (or 'command economy') the producers are assigned tasks by central planning bodies. The tasks are evaluated and their performance is punished or rewarded. Distribution of the goods produced is directed by a corresponding economic apparatus on the basis of the same principles. The consumers may of course purchase one or other article within the choice offered by the distribution channels, although examples of obligatory purchasing are also known. This behaviour has no direct influence on producers' or distributors' activity. The planning body is always a mediating factor here. It is not obliged to reckon with consumers' reaction in its decisions, especially since the consumer cannot refrain from buying articles which are basic necessities.

The extent of central body efficiency and rationality differs. Assuring proper incentives to economic institutions and correct criteria for evaluating their functioning is difficult, while the inflexibility of the co-ordinating apparatus is a constant source of social tension. However, this is not the main trait of the system. It is rather the indirect character of the links between production, distribution and consumption, which are realized in relations between each of these spheres and the central planning and co-ordinating bodies.

In the system denoted as *interactive*, productive activity and demand come into direct contact on the market. Consumers' behaviour is the direct source of reward or punishment for the producers. Satisfaction of demand is the condition for realizing the production process and determines producers' opportunities. Naturally, the latter try to shape demand by introducing new goods, by advertising and price manipulation, thus modifying or creating new patterns of consumption. But the spontaneous adaptation of production to demand threatens cyclical recession, the squandering of labour and periodic economic chaos, side by side with the highly advanced specialization and rationalization of production on the enterprise level.

The above economic systems are ideal models which do not exist in pure form. The directive system is usually now being modified by the introduction of elements of interaction to a greater or lesser extent. The interactive type, universal in the capitalist countries, has also been modified by state intervention in the form of investment, regulating enterprise capacity, as well as the level of prices, wages, etc. But there are still important differences between the two systems, which cannot be defined simply as differences between the socialist and capitalist economic systems. Undoubtedly, the principle of private ownership of the means of production makes it difficult to introduce a directive system, while the socialization of the means of production not only makes easier but directly induces the introduction of such a system. However, the two systems may appear under the conditions of both, the private and state ownership of the means of production (though with certain modifications). Economic control may be exercised not only by direct orders but also through 'steered' processes of interaction.

The nature of the economic system bears many-sided social implications in the spheres of structure, patterns of social mobility, types of interpersonal relations (of the superior–subordinate and seller–client types), and for the sources and direction of social conflict.

The following question arises. What is the relation of the two systems to the appearance of collective farming, industrial farming and of continua of change, such as the transformation of the traditional peasant farm into the modern family farm?

Starting from the observation of collective forms of production in different parts of the globe and in disparate social systems, we may distinguish four situations in which these forms appear. The first is where the principle of collective farming rests on the desire to realize given ideals (religious, political, patriotic) or, to put it differently, on motivations of a religious, social, political kind (for example, egalitarian ideology or serving the national aim to settle given territories). Some religious agrarian communities of the USA, as well as some of the first communes established in the Soviet Union immediately after the revolution, have been of this nature. The collective farm based on these principles may be dismissed from further consideration since it is strictly speaking not a movement of farmers who desire to transform their farms and live in that manner. Even if small groups of farmers' families engage in this kind of initiative, these are marginal groups and the possibility of their attracting other farmers by example is insignificant, as is the possibility of this structure maintaining itself for an extended period in either the directive or interacting system.

The second situation is the emergence of collective farms as a result of agrarian reform, i.e. when families of producers take over the lands of former *latifundia* or when landless peasant families settle on hitherto unused fallow lands. In both cases, families who thus obtain land are experienced at productive labour in agriculture, but they lack experience of independent farm operation. These families are as a rule inclined to maintain the former farm *in toto*, or to take over land in larger compact groups and to farm together. But agrarian reform is not limited to distributing land. As a rule, investment is also necessary so that the land may be properly husbanded and the producers ensured of a rapid improvement in living conditions. The needs are still greater in the case of new settlements on hitherto fallow land. Investment and credit, various kinds of state material aid, as well as agricultural instruction are necessary here. Under the conditions of an interactive system the situation may be regarded as transitional. As the farm becomes economically stronger, and in measure with the acquisition of experience, independent operation of a private farm becomes more attractive than collective farming with its internal conflicts and the need to adjust oneself to others. In consequence, the more efficient producers soon leave the farm. Under the directive system, the incentives to independent farming may be so weak, and the possibility of separating oneself from large-scale common farming may be so difficult to realize, that the collective farms hold on for a long time while the families involved adapt themselves to the situation.

The third situation prevails when the state carries out a universal collectivization of peasant farms. In doctrinal and political terms the most frequent motive for adopting such a decision is the industrialization of the country which requires internal accumulation by means of tight control of the peasant population's consumption level or shifting of considerable manpower from agriculture to industry. Such collectivization can be accomplished only under the conditions of a directive economic system where the idea of agricultural consolidation is in accord with the characteristics of that system.

It is possible to conceive a resulting consolidation on the industrial-type farm but its realization may effect sharp social conflicts and burden the state with heavy investments. It would also require directing a corps of specialists to agriculture, which is not suitable in conditions where a country's agriculture has to bear the burden of industrialization and there are no specialists available. Collective farming, in these circumstances, represents a compromise. The producers may make use of this by intensifying production on the plots of which they have usufruct, with the desire to rebuild individual peasant farms and to convert the collective farms into auxiliary enterprises.

The fourth situation appears in the system of extended interaction. Here the large farm may show superiority over the small ones because of the lower costs of production. Under a market economy this leads to the possibility of the emergence of collective farms in economically developed countries with the interactive system. But there is every indication that such organizations with collective traits will be very unstable for two reasons. First, it is so because of the action of centrifugal forces, i.e. the unavoidable difficulties of adaptation of the collective's members and the constant need to decide anew whether to retain collective farming, particularly with changing generations. Secondly, it is so because of the interplay of external forces, i.e. the many alternatives open in the conditions of an interactive system. Such an organization may therefore partly or entirely lose its collective character: partly, when the task of directing the enterprise is left to one member while the role of the others is limited to co-ownership (of land, or capital); entirely, when they are eliminated as co-owners from the enterprise. Be that as it may, collective farms established by family farmers in the interactive system would turn into industrial farms operated by a company or a single entrepreneur (or owner).

Examination of various situations in which collective farming arises inclines one to the view that this organizational form serves, in an interactive system, as a temporary method to husband land acquired from agrarian reform, or, on newly settled land, preceding the formation of modern family farming; or it is one of the roads (thus far a subordinated one) to the transformation of modern family farming into industrial farming. In the directive economic system this organizational form serves as an instrument of control over the agricultural producers in the interests of the economy as a whole. It is transitional also in this system, regarded as a compromise by the directing centres whose objective is to transform it into industrial farming. Among the collective farm producers there is on the other hand a tendency to take advantage of the compromise by subordinating this organizational form to the family farm in the shape of the private allotment which is limited in area but is productively developing.

Collective farming is a transitional form which appears particularly as a consequence of agrarian reform, or when there is an attempt to subordinate the agricultural producers to the needs of industrialization. It leads to modern family farming, to industrial farming or to intermediate organizational forms. Because of the social difficulties and conflicts connected with collective farming, it is difficult to foresee its future. Perhaps new, autonomous forms of producers' organization will arise on its foundations connected with industrial-type farming, which will make collective farming more attractive. On the other hand this form will appear no doubt also in the future where it is a matter of husbanding new lands or where centralized investment in agriculture become important.

The directions of change indicated do not provide an image of a uniform, world-wide social organization of agriculture. Future social organization in agriculture must be seen as at least as polymorphous as it is today. Nor can we exclude the possibility that future technical development in agriculture would basically confound our prognosis. But such a change would project new fundamental problems for the organization of society as a whole, of which rural change would constitute only a part.

Related Items

14

Hungary: Collective Farms which Work

Nigel Swain

The reasons underlying Soviet collectivization's relative failure can be summarized as follows. Initially, because resources were directed towards industry, funds were insufficient to establish successful large-scale production; in later years, when aid was provided, the government failed to develop an effective structural model for collective farms and failed to solve incentive problems within them. Farm managers' autonomy is restricted by party interference and by a system of quota planning which is overly centralized and unresponsive to local conditions. Collective farm members receive low wages and poor pensions from the communal farm, and produce from their family plots is used predominantly for home consumption because family production is not actively encouraged and no adequate network exists to market the produce. Marketing of goods produced on the communal farm suffers from the normal bottlenecks of the Soviet economy. Low incomes in the agricultural sector have had the further knock-on effect of negative selectivity. Only those who cannot get out of agriculture stay there, so the quality of leadership and the workforce tends to be poor. More generally, to borrow Chayanov's terminology, Soviet collectivization has focused on 'horizontal cooperation' (that is increasing the size of the production unit) at the expense of developing forms of 'vertical cooperation'. The latter accepts the need for specialization, a division of labour and production organized so as to ensure optimal conditions in each sector given the prevailing level of technology.

But collectivization can be very different. Under Hungary's brand of decentralized 'market socialism' collective farms and buying enterprises do not receive administrative quotas. They respond rather to market forces, albeit tempered by official guidelines. Farms enjoy genuine autonomy, not even being restricted to agricultural products; taxation and pricing structures ensure that they retain control over a significant proportion of additional income

An original paper based on research published in *Collective Farms which Work?*, Cambridge University Press, 1985.

created; and local party officials take minimal interest in day-to-day production. They have also been allowed to develop a mix of 'horizontal' and 'vertical' cooperation appropriate to their changing technological base. Specialization and diversification is permitted in products, processing, sales and the dissemination of technical know-how; and farms have benefited from innovative policies in such problem areas as capital-intensive versus labour-intensive development, team-based versus family-based work organization, and communal versus private production.

Capitalizing on their freedom to experiment, agricultural specialists in Hungary quickly learned two lessons about collectivization independently of Chayanov's writings. First it was discovered that, accepting the impossibility of the immediate mechanization of all branches of production, the decision to allow a significant amount of labour-intensive production to take place on members' private family plots need not pose a threat to the socialist sector. Precisely because of the technology gap, the relationship can be complementary rather than competitive. A socialist small-scale solution could therefore be developed. Family plot farming was positively encouraged by tax concessions and grants, collectives were exhorted to co-ordinate such activity, and a network of consumer cooperatives was established to furnish its supplies and channel its produce into the national economy.

Second, within the communal farm it was recognized that the Soviet solution of an annual share-out based on individuals' 'labour day' units within their work teams was inappropriate for both labour-intensive and capital-intensive sectors. In the latter the introduction of the wage form proved more appropriate. In the former more archaic forms of remuneration, variations on the theme of family-based sharecropping, were introduced which established a more direct relationship between effort and reward. Wages and pensions were also quickly brought into line with those of industry, made possible in part by government aid, a factor which also allowed the acquisition of Western machinery and the improvement of the rural infrastructure, but also by higher producer prices which furnished farms with relatively large disposable incomes. These higher agricultural sector incomes first stemmed and then reversed the flow of the young and the skilled out of agriculture.

Hungarian collective farms have created forms of socialist integration and associated systems of reward appropriate to the level of technical development present in each branch of production. Their economic efficiency as farms might be questioned; but yields and members' incomes are high, there are no food shortages to pose political threats to the regime, and agricultural exports constitute a vital component of hard-currency trade with the West. Collectivization Hungarian-style has shown that collective farms can work. The viability of the general should not be dismissed because of the failings of the Soviet particular.

Related Items

9, 13, 15, 18, 21, 25, 35, 51, 61.

15

Worker-Peasants in the
Three Worlds

Chris Hann

Worker-peasants have maintained a shadowy presence in the literature for a long time: it is high time we stopped treating them as marginal or transitional and placed them where they belong, at the centre of the stage.

I became aware of the phenomenon in a fuzzy way during fieldwork in a Hungarian village in the mid-1970s (Hann, 1980). The room I was renting overlooked the main road at the only bus-stop. Six days a week I would be woken long before dawn as an ancient engine spluttered to life. In the winter months, the driver used to arrive early and rev more noisily, presumably to generate some warmth for his passengers, some of whom had had a long walk from outlying farms. Eventually the bus would pull off, and the worker-peasants receded from my consciousness. During winter, it was dark when they returned in the afternoon. As the evenings grew lighter, I saw that some of them went along to the *bisztró* at the end of their shift, and settled down at the bar for the evening; but others hurried back to their farms to start another shift.

In so far as its worker-peasants were concerned, this village was quite typical of the Hungarian countryside in recent decades. Of course not all worker-peasants are daily commuters; many rural inhabitants can find wage-labour jobs in their own communities, e.g. in cooperatives, or in administration; others have members who return to the village only weekly, monthly, or at irregular intervals. Migration frequency depends largely upon the location of the village, and it has important consequences for the future of farming. In more isolated regions, when the farmwork devolves more completely on to the women because the men are long-distance migrants, production is more likely to be for self-provisioning only. In the longer term such households may become more recognizably proletarian, regardless of whether they retain their rural base or whether they eventually move to the city. But small-scale farming is encouraged by the state in Hungary, and most rural households maintain significant commodity production as a supplement to wage income. They

An original paper.

specialize in small-scale, labour-intensive activities, which are difficult (or very expensive) to mechanize, but important to the national economy both domestically and for foreign trade. A fruitful division of labour between the collectivized and the small-scale sectors has been one of the keys to the relative success of Hungarian agriculture in the socialist period (Swain, 1985).

At the same time, like the rest of Eastern Europe, Hungary has undergone rapid development in other fields. The completion of collectivization followed immediately the period of most intensive industrialization. The new industries needed labour, and the satisfying of this demand was facilitated in the short term by the substantial dislocation occasioned by collectivization. However, the sheer speed with which the country industrialized made it impossible to accommodate the new workers in the cities; no resources were available for housing and urban infrastructure. In such a context the advantages of re-cruiting a workforce from the countryside were obvious: it was cheaper to keep an old bus on the road than to build new housing estates, and doubly profitable if the rural workers were not merely producing a large part of their own food supply but also helping to provision the towns and to earn foreign exchange. Hence within a few years about one-half of all industrial workers in Hungary were domiciled in villages, and this proportion has been fairly stable in recent years. If one uses a broader definition of the worker-peasant household, to include all households combining independent small-scale farming with wage-labour, then one should add not only those families who find their wage-labour jobs in the countryside, but also many urban families who make similar use of 'auxiliary' plots allocated to them.

The phenomenon is also conspicuous in other state-socialist countries, including those which have not collectivized agriculture (Poland and Yugoslavia) and also those which do not encourage small-scale market production as explicitly as Hungary. It is present also in the developing countries of the Third World, but one need look no further for appropriate examples than to other parts of the European periphery. Thus the moderniza-tion of the agrarian structures of southern Europe has been proceeding more gradually, without the abrupt shock of collectivization; but aspects of the interrelations with the expanding industrial sector correspond to processes at work in the Second World. Worker-peasants are prominent in both, but there are also major contrasts. One difference between Turkey and Hungary lies in the relative role of trans-national migration: the Hungarian peasants are contributing to their own country's industrialization, but Anatolian peasants have also been drawn in large numbers to occupy particular niches in the economies of Germany and Scandinavia (Castles and Kosack, 1973; Shanin, 1976). When the capitalist economy is depressed such peasant migrants may find themselves in an intolerable position in their 'host country'. It is not clear what long-term economic benefits have been obtained by 'sending' countries such as Turkey. Yet the sums earned abroad stabilized quite a number of family farms 'back home', provided opportunities for new peasant farms to be established, and enabled some peasants to modernize their farms and/or to diversify into non-agricultural activities (Kudat, 1975). Further contrasts between Hungary and most Third World countries can be found in rates of population growth and employment opportunities which are constraining peasants to leave the villages of the Third World, and entailing the general tolerance there of 'shanty-towns'. Thus instead of commuting one may find more permanent forms of urban settlement, often substandard. The families of the urban 'informal sector' often maintain their rural links, and 'repeasantization' of some members is not unusual when households fission.

The ubiquity of the worker-peasant becomes more puzzling when one scrutinizes the allegedly most developed regions. The type may be rare in Britain, for reasons peculiar to the history of English industrialization (it survives in parts of the Celtic periphery, such as the crofting communities of the outer islands of Scotland – see Ennew, 1980), but in West Germany one finds that even today some two-fifths of all farms are in fact 'part-time', i.e. the families which run them have significant supplementary sources of income. To the extent that this means, as it usually does, a way of living that combines farming with wage-labour employment, the similarities with the worker-peasants of the Third and Second Worlds are striking. Among the differences, one should note that the element of 'self-provisioning' is likely to fall, though it seldom falls to zero. Furthermore, most of these farms are likely to be highly mechanized, at least by the standards of worker-peasants in the Second and Third Worlds, if not by those of the agribusiness sector in the First. But only those part-time farmers whose supplementary income is derived from some non-agricultural activity which they control, and run perhaps as a capitalistic business, transgress our conceptualization of worker-peasants. Of course this kind of diversification too represents an adaptation of traditional peasant economy, and we should not forget that peasants have very often engaged in a variety of sideline, artisan activities. Nevertheless, although this variant falls within a wider framework of 'multiple job holding' (or what the French call *pluriactivité*), it falls outside the notion of worker-peasant household as used here which requires that some member or members work for wages or salary outside the household.

Thus defined, worker-peasant households could be classified along a continuum, ranging from a near-proletarian pole, at which the farm is perhaps more like a 'hobby garden', making a very limited contribution to self-provisioning, to an entrepreneurial pole, at which the farm is the main focus of household activity and the off-farm work is relatively minor. Such a continuum could then be applied in each of the countries mentioned above. For example, in Hungary the sheer numbers of the worker-peasants have led some analysts to view them as a surrogate proletariat or 'new working class'. More specifically, some of those of poor peasant origin who were first to become migrant workers in the 1950s have by now become proletarians in the cities, or if they have kept their rural base, it is unlikely to be finely tuned to the market. At the other pole, it has recently been pointed out that some worker-peasant households are running highly profitable enterprises, and these often seem to be the descendants of the more prosperous peasants of the pre-socialist period, now resuming a process of 'interrupted embourgeoisement' (Szelényi and Manchin, 1986). In identifying these poles as 'proletarian' and 'bourgeois' one should still be very cautious in trying to fit the worker-peasants into conventional categories; in particular, few rural families have the accumulation dynamic of the classical bourgeoisie, and a household's position along this continuum may vary greatly from one year to the next, and is certain to change over its developmental cycle. However, the evidence from a country in which, following collectivization, inherited property differentials are no longer so significant, is instructive in showing that even here the most profitable combinations of agriculture with the new industrial opportunities are likely to be managed by those who were already more successful in the previous agrarian society.

There is therefore a need for complex analysis of the impact over time of this 'class', part owner of its means of production and controller of its own labour process, and part proletarian, upon the wider social structure of each of the Three Worlds. We should not assume that worker-peasants constitute a homogeneous group, or one that has made other lines of cleavage irrelevant. Indeed, there is much to be said for a sharper terminology, which would distinguish the local commuter from the trans-national migrant, and both of these from the part-time farmer in a developed Western agrarian structure. But there are also common features which may continue to justify applying the term worker-peasant to all three.

The most important such feature is that the rural family remains the base of the farming operation. Even the mechanized family farm in the West is not 'capitalist' in its deployment of its labour resources. Such households do not pay their members wages, nor do they depend significantly on hiring the labour power of others. In this respect the expectations of the classical economists of the nineteenth century have been disappointed, for the parallelism that they assumed between industry and agriculture is not valid. Kautsky's book of 1896 (1987) has more insight into the peculiarities of the countryside and the ways in which small-scale producers can co-exist with and perhaps underpin capitalist agriculture; but he did not succeed in reconciling his empirical observations of German peasants in an early phase of transformation with orthodox Marxist theory, which continued to stress the greater efficiency of large-scale, factory-type organization in agriculture. The awkward reality, as documented for Europe, is that family farming has survived and flourished, and worker-peasants have remained a prominent feature, in both East and West Germany and elsewhere. Two decades ago Franklin argued that, as some worker-peasants became capitalists and others proletarians, the stratum was ultimately sure to disappear (1969, pp. 61–2). However, more recent work in Germany has shown that, though not a static stratum, part-time farmers are maintaining, as in Hungary, a relatively stable presence in the occupational structure, with newcomers moving in as fast as others move out. Many were predicting the demise of the small-scale farms and the proletarianization of their owners already at the end of the nineteenth century. Now, as the twentieth century draws to a close, it would be wiser to refrain altogether from such prediction, and to ask instead *why* the family-labour farm has been so resilient, and what consequences this has had, not only at the level of social structure, but upon the household itself.

To take the latter question first, there have of course been radical changes in the internal structuring of the household, above all the feminization of agricultural work that has been reported wherever men have taken up wage-labour employment. The exact implications for the position of women in society will vary between cultures (in some it may impose an added burden on women without any gain in status, but this is perhaps unusual), but there can be little doubt that the worker-peasants have everywhere shattered the old stereotyped sexual division of labour. Almost as important has been the questioning of the traditional authority structure of the household by its younger members, as they take up off-farm jobs and register demands for greater independence.

To justify viewing various types of worker-peasant as adaptations of peasantry, rather than as entirely novel elements in the social structure, we can point not merely to economic structures, as in most of the preceding discussion, but to the life-histories and motives of the worker-peasants themselves. In each of the Three Worlds the key to the persistence of the worker-peasants may be argued to lie in the advantages to households of a combination of regular and secure income from a routine, unpleasurable job off the farm with both the material and non-material rewards of a non-alienating labour process on the farm. Freed from their 'closed', patriarchal communities of old, the worker-peasant households of today are *choosing*, wherever possible, to combine improved access to modern, consumerist society with what they value most from their traditional culture. The latter generally includes a strong attachment to the land, and also to the family group, despite the changes in its internal organization. There may also be an abiding preoccupation with risk-aversion, which the worker-peasant solution enables to be reconciled with a flexible maximization strategy. It is a precious combination, which may give the rural household some bargaining power for the first time. Thus a worker may refuse to put in overtime in the factory unless the rate is brought clearly above the rate that can be earned through working extra hours on the farm; or the household may decline to produce agricultural commodities for the market when the price offered is too low, a step that few peasants could afford to take in the past.

Conclusion

Worker-peasant households have been discussed here at two levels, a macro-level, at which there are some major differences between the kinds of worker-peasants one finds in different frameworks of political economy, and a micro-level, at which the similarities in motivations and household structure may be more striking than these differences. At the micro-level, the Chayanovian theory of the family-labour farm remains illuminating long after the element of 'self-reproduction' has gone into decline. At the macro-level we have noted that some theoretical formulations have been unsatisfactory. It may be true that already, in all Three Worlds, the small-scale farms are 'dominated' by an antagonistic mode of production, whether capitalist or state-socialist. Yet, with part-time farming proving so resilient and perhaps about to expand significantly as European farm policies are subjected to fundamental economic and ecological questioning, it would still be premature to claim that worker-peasants have disappeared even from the First World. It would be equally rash to assume that developments elsewhere will take similar courses to those followed so far in Europe. In some countries the worker-peasants have been a large and stable stratum for many decades. The combination of wage-work (usually in industry) with family work on a small farm may be economically attractive to industrializing states, but it can also be attractive to households themselves. Worker-peasants may provide a basis for long-term development that could be compared favourably with the path followed by countries which either eliminated their peasants rapidly, or never had any to begin with, and are now suffering acute social problems in their cities.

References

Castles, S. and Kosack, G. (1973) *Immigrant Workers and Clan Structure in Western Europe*, London.
Ennew, Judith (1980) *The Western Isles Today*, Cambridge.
Franklin, S. F. (1969) *The European Peasantry: The Final Phase*, London.
Hann, C. M. (1980) *Tazlar: A Village in Hungary*, Cambridge.
Kautsky, Karl (1987) *The Agrarian Question*, London.
Kudat, Ayse (1975) *Stability and Change in the Turkish Family at Home and Abroad*, Berlin.
Shanin, T. (1978) 'The peasants are coming: migrants who labour, peasants who travel and Marxists who write', *Race and Class*, vol. 19, no. 3.
Swain, Nigel (1985) *Collective Farms which Work?* Cambridge.
Szelényi, Iván and Manchin, Robert (1986) 'Peasants, proletarians, entrepreneurs: transformations of rural social structure under state socialism', *Sociologia Ruralis*, vol. 25.

Related Items

2, 3, 5, 10, 13, 17, 22, 23, 25, 26, 49, 57.

16

V. P. Danilov on the Analytical Distinction between Peasants and Farmers

Orlando Figes

In order to define 'peasantry' as a social and economic factor, we need to make some analytical distinctions between 'peasants' and 'farmers'. Such distinctions have been recently questioned by some writers who rejected 'peasant' as an economic category and advocated its replacement by a concept of 'simple commodity producer' (Ennew, Hirst and Tribe, 1977; with an opposite view in Shanin, 1983). Others agreed that distinguishing peasants from simple commodity producers and from farmers may be useful in tracing the emergence of rural capitalism in, say, early modern Europe or modern Asia. But the methods of making these distinctions have been called into doubt by the failure to define peasant economy through analysis of the household unit of production (Harrison, 1975; 1977). An article by Harriet Friedmann has tried bridge this gap by rejecting inductive definitions of the peasantry, with their assumption of a 'peasant mode of production', in favour of 'analytical specification of forms of production based on internal characteristics of the unit and external characteristics of the social formation' (Friedmann, 1980, pp. 160–1).

Definitions of the peasantry, in contradistinction to farmers, have usually focused on the ratio of commodity to subsistence production (the integration into market); the degree of peasant mobility of labour, land and credit; the peasants' 'subsistence' motivation for production (in contrast to 'agricultural entrepreneurs'); the individualization of productive enterprises and law of property; the replacement of family labour by hired labour, etc. (Shanin, 1973/4, pp. 70–5, 188–9; Wolf, 1955, p. 454; 1966, pp. 37–40; Bernstein, 1979, p. 7). For example Friedmann's distinction between peasants and farmers centres on *commoditization*, or the penetration into the social reproduction of commodity relations, by which the peasant household abandons

An original paper.

personal, reciprocal ties for renewal of means of production in favour of market relations. 'Peasant' production is thus 'defined negatively . . . by the resistance of their reproduction to commoditization, which in turn rests on immobility of labour, land and credit within the larger economy' (Friedmann, 1980, p. 170).

In an article co-written with L. V. Danilova and V. G. Rastiannikov in 1977, the Soviet agrarian historian Viktor Petrovich Danilov added a further analytical dimension to the definition of peasant production, related to Marx's distinction between living and objectified labour (Marx, 1977, pp. 364f., 374f., 384–5, etc.). In doing so he offered a way which can help substantively to sub-categorize the family-based units of agricultural production:

In Marxist political economy a natural economy is understood as that which is based upon a natural system of productive forces; that is, a system in which means of production arising from nature dominate over those attained through history. . . . The chief means of production in this system is land, with all the natural factors and processes belonging to it. As a part of production, these appear as productive forces. Despite the application of objectified labour, these means of production remain natural both in origin and character. Man as a labourer and also represented in the natural system of productive forces primarily in his natural, physical aspect – as muscular power, though the very existence of agriculture . . . is unthinkable without the specific productive experience of man, his skill and knowledge. Man-made means of production (agricultural implements, irrigation structures, domesticated animals, handicraft tools, buildings, roads, etc.) serve, along with production experience, as a means by which to include natural factors in the work process. . . .

The predominance of naturally arising productive forces over historical ones and, accordingly, living labour over objectified labour, which characterizes the natural system of productive forces, predetermined the internal order of peasant production, its aims and tendencies, the character of labour cooperation and its realization and potentialities, the limits of its development and, as a result, its place in the social system. (Danilov et al., 1977, p. 11)

Danilov applied this generalization to his study of the Russian peasantry under NEP. From the budget studies of family farms done in 1925, Danilov showed that manual labour represented from 56 per cent of the total cost of production in oats, to 75 per cent of the total cost of production in flax. He also showed that, excluding land and human labour, seed and cattle accounted for 75–80 per cent of the total costs of production, while machines and tools accounted for less than 5 per cent of costs. In areas of extensive grain farming the predominance of living labour over machine power was even greater (Danilov, 1977, pp. 266–7). Moreover, in a productive system dominated by manual labour, intensified cultivation, such as in flax, sunflower and sugar beet, meant the more intensified application of physical labour: 'The increased costs of specialized cultivation were met by the peasant simply working harder with his hands and not by the use of more productive machines and tools. This was at the root of the inertia in peasant economy and the slowness with which it intensified production' (Danilov, 1977, p. 266).

The conclusions Danilov draws from his study are clear enough to be cited without further comment:

> The correlation between manual labour and machine power is the most important index of the development of productive forces in a given society. It defines the limits of production and the productivity of labour. . . . The low productivity and small degree of commoditization of agricultural production [at the end of the 1921–1925 period] were inevitable under a system of production based upon manual labour. It was precisely this factor which hindered development in agricultural production. . . .
>
> Social forms of production and relations of production correspond with the structure of productive forces in agriculture. The overriding significance of individual manual labour, with its horse and hand tools, objectively determined the development of agriculture in the form of petty, private production, scattered over millions of small and tiny individual units. Petty individual production is inextricably connected with the dominance of manual labour, animal draught power and their corresponding technology. . . .
>
> The character of productive forces in peasant economy and the correlation of their structural elements show the productive forces to be essentially natural (land, cattle, seed, manure, etc.). These natural productive forces include the labour power of the peasant himself, for human labour in peasant economy is represented as simple, muscular power. The ease with which basic productive forces can be reproduced in peasant economy maintains its natural-consumption character, its traditionalism, its autarky. Consequently, peasant economy is able to survive with minimal dependence on the market.
>
> In the mass of peasant households the dominance of natural productive forces prevailed. Along with family cooperative labour, . . . this factor determined both the relative stability of peasant economy – its ability to survive and revive itself in the most unfavourable circumstances – and its relative stagnation, its low level of labour productivity and its inability to broaden production. Under these conditions, market integration could only take place at the level of surplus production. (Danilov, 1977, pp. 268–9)

Danilov gives primacy to the system of production forces in determining social formation. This, of course, does not rule out social and market relations as objective indicators of development in social forms of production. In *Sovetskaia dokolkhoznaia derevnia*, vol. 2, Danilov presents us with figures on the social differentiation of proletarians, petty commodity and capitalist producers as an objective index of the distintegrating peasant social form (Danilov, 1979, pp. 296–321). He also analyses market relations to document Lenin's thesis about peasant Russia at the stage of 'primitive capitalism', in which commercial and natural exchange were mixed, along with market and patriarchal exploitation, so that the 'kulak was still in large measure the old Russian *mir*-eater . . . and a long way from being a farmer' (Danilov, 1979, pp. 347, 159–77). Danilov looks at the development of market relations in three chronological stages: the marketing of the surplus product; the commoditization of the reproduction of labour; and the commoditization of the means of production. It is central to his view that the last of these stages not only marks the final

124   *Orlando Figes*

destruction of natural economy, but also involves a fundamental change in the *nature* of means of production: from the mostly natural means of production (which do not essentially serve as capital) to what Marxists define as the material side of capital, i.e. the man-made means of production. In this way Danilov moves away from assuming the exclusivity of market relations and/or relations of production in determining the rural social form and emphasizes instead the changing nature of production forces as an objective system distinguishing peasants from farmers.

References

Bernstein, H. (1979) 'Concepts for the analysis of contemporary peasantries', *Journal of Peasant Studies*, vol. 6, no. 4, pp. 421–44.

Danilov, V. P. et al. (1977) 'Osnovnye etapy razvitiia krestianskogo khoziaistva', in *Agrarnye stuktury stran vostoka: genezis, evoliutsiia, sotsialnye preobrazovaniia*, Moscow, pp. 6–48.

Danilov, V. P. (1977) *Sovetskaia dokolkhoznaia derevnia: naselenie, zemlepolzovanie, khoziaistvo*, Moscow. (Published in English by Verso, London.)

Danilov, V. P. (1979) *Sovetskaia dokolkhoznaia derevnia: sotsialnaia struktura, sotsialnie otnosheniia*, Moscow.

Ennew, J., Hirst, P. and Tribe, K. (1977) '"Peasantry" as an economic category', *Journal of Peasant Studies*, vol. 4, no. 4, pp. 295–332.

Friedmann, H. (1980) 'Household production and the national economy: concepts for the analysis of agrarian formations', *Journal of Peasant Studies*, vol. 7, no. 2, pp. 158–84.

Harrison M. (1975) 'Chayanov and the economics of the Russian peasantry', *Journal of Peasant Studies*, vol. 2, no. 2, pp. 389-417.

Harrison M. (1977) 'Resource allocation and agrarian class formation: the problem of social mobility among Russian peasant households', *Journal of Peasant Studies*, vol. 4, no. 4, pp. 127-61.

Marx, K. (1977) *Selected Writings* (ed. D. McLellan), Oxford.

Shanin, T. (1973/4) 'The nature and logic of the peasant economy', *Journal of Peasant Studies*, vol. 1, no. 1, pp. 63–80; vol. 1, no. 2 (1983), pp. 186–206.

Shanin, T. (1983) 'Defining peasants: conceptualizations and deconceptualizations', *Sociological Review*, vol. 30, no. 3.

Wolf, E. (1955) 'Types of Latin American peasantry: a preliminary discussion', *American Anthropologist*, vol. 57, no. 3, pp. 452–71.

Wolf, E. (1966) *Peasants*, Englewood Cliffs, NJ.

Related Items

2, 5, 6, 9, 12, 15, 18, 21, 22, 25, 26, 52.

17

Family Farmers and Classical Conception versus the Experience of Monopoly Capitalism

Göran Djurfeldt

The classical conception of the development of capitalism in agriculture is that, as in industry, the agrarian class structure will tend to polarize; the petty commodity producer will tend to disappear: a capitalist relation of production will develop, involving agrarian bourgeoisie and rural proletariat. According to this classical notion, the agrarian future would be one of big estates, managed by capitalist farmers, run with machinery and other capital intensive methods of production, and employing landless labourers. In other words wage-labourers in bread-and-meat factories would be the effect of capitalism in agriculture.

Close to a hundred years later, history has falsified this notion: in Europe the big estates have decreased in importance. The typical unit today is the family farm. The rural proletariat has decreased, not only in absolute size, but as part of the rural labour force. In the six original countries of the EEC in 1966/67, for example, 14 per cent of the rural labour force was 'non-family', i.e. mainly hired (OECD 1974, table 36). In the United States the percentage of hired labour in total farm employment has fluctuated around 25 per cent since 1910, with no discernible trend to increase (US Bureau of the Census, 1975, p. 467). Both these figures are expressed in man-year units and thus mask the fact that the modern rural proletariat is part-time: students, housewives, etc. drawn into agriculture during certain peak periods, as for example during the harvest of vegetables and fruit. Full-time agricultural labourers form a surprisingly small group; in the US, for example, an estimated 670,000 persons in 1972 (McElroy, 1973).

The petty-commodity producing farmer has thus not only survived, but has become typical of Western agriculture. At the same time, agriculture has gone

Excerpts from 'Hvad skete der med det agrarr borgeskap', *Den Ny Verden*, vol. 12, 1978, no. 3.

through a revolution in the forces of production which can be symbolized by the tractorization carried through in 30 years. The increase in productivity has at times even surpassed that in industry, as in the example given in table 17.1.

TABLE 17.1 *Increase in output per worker in agriculture and the rest of the economy, annual rates 1953–1967*

Country	Agriculture (% increase)	Rest of the economy (% increase)
Austria	5.0	3.8
Belgium	5.2	3.0
Denmark	3.9	2.7
Finland	4.4	2.9
France	4.0	2.9
Germany, Federal Republic of	6.0	3.7
Ireland	3.8	2.4
Netherlands	5.6	3.3
Norway	1.7	3.4
Sweden	4.7	3.0
United Kingdom	5.4	2.1
Italy	5.8	4.9
Portugal	2.9	4.7
Spain	4.8	4.2

Currently there are many indications of an increasing exploitation of farmers' labour. While their productivity increases faster than the rest of the economy, their living standard increases slower, i.e. in Marxist terms *they are producers of relative surplus value*. One indication of this is the terms of trade between agriculture and industry which seem to have a steady tendency to disfavour agriculture. Unfortunately, I have data for only three countries on this point: in the United States 1946–70 prices paid by farmers have increased much faster than the prices received (US Bureau of the Census, p. 488); the same is true for France 1946–62 (Amin and Vergopoulos, p. 193); while in Denmark 1963–74 the consumer price index has increased much faster than the farm-producer price index.

Conclusions after Rereading the Classics

Why did capitalism not develop in agriculture according to the classical conception?

1 The mechanism of price-determination of grain was subverted
2 when international competition got free rein

3 due to the dominant influence of the industrial bourgeoisie (in alliance with the working class?) on the state and its trade policies,
4 which eliminated rent and landlordism and hampered the reproduction of capitalist farmers, but permitted the middle farmers to reproduce themselves and even strengthen their position.
5 Proletarianization only befell the poor peasants; this proletariat, however, emigrated to the towns and to industry.
6 Capital fled agriculture, but flowed into agro-industry
7 in which capitalism developed, by moving production process from the farms and into the agro-industrial sector.
8 The development of monopoly capitalism, with the consequent intertwining of industrial and bank capital, paved the way for the development of *capital foncier* (fixed capital on the farms)
9 via mortgage credit.
10 Sometimes this process took on a cooperative form, which changed little in essence.
11 The farmers became producers of relative surplus value
12 and owners of their means of production only in a formal, juridical sense.

The above twelve points form a series of hypotheses which can be derived from the classics; they remain to be tested, of course, by a rigorous study of the history of agriculture and agro-industry in the Western countries and the United States.

Since for my own part this was a detour from the study of peripheral agriculture in the so-called 'developing societies', I want to return to that subject. What are the conditions for a development along classical lines in agriculture? From the above we can see that capitalist agriculture requires profit, which can derive from three sources:

a *more productive land* (this is why we tend to find capitalist farmers in the West in the most fertile areas, often on old feudal estates converted into capitalist farms);
b *a protected market* where prices are kept above cost price. (Many countries in the periphery have a protected grain market; it may even be possible to find a correlation between the level of protection and landlord dominance in these countries.)

It is implied in (b) that capitalist farmers often cannot compete in a free market. Since in the international market, countries with different agrarian structures tend to compete between themselves, capitalist agriculture can endure in this competition only in special circumstances, the most important of which seems to be:

c *depressed wage-level* which may originate either from a big reserve army of labour, or from a sizeable poor peasantry.[1]

Since (b) and (c) tend to characterize the countries in question, i.e. those of the capitalist periphery, we might conclude that a development along classical lines is not impossible in the periphery. A sizeable shifting out of agricultural production from centre to periphery has occurred in recent years. But we must hasten to add that for capitalist farmers to prevail over the middle peasantry requires also economies of scale which, as we have seen, cannot always be taken for granted.

Further complications have to be kept in mind: both (b) the prices of grain in the domestic market and, to a certain extent, (c) agrarian ownership structure, are possible to manipulate politically. The possibility to reproduce these conditions for a capitalist development depends, then, also on the political representation of the agrarian bourgeoisie, and its alliance with other classes. Here the relationship between profit and rent becomes important: in many circumstances, as we have seen, the mass of rent tends to increase at the expense of profit; moreover, it can be argued that agrarian capitalism is not as expansive in terms of productivity as usually imagined. Therefore it cannot be taken for granted that the agrarian bourgeoisie and the landlords will be able to secure an alliance with the other ruling classes, notably with the national and international bourgeoisie. They may be pushed out of the ruling-class alliance, as they have been in the West.[2] Some have taken the World Bank's newly awakened interest in small farmers as a sign of this.

This, of course, is speculative; but one conclusion seems firmly grounded: those who take over the original predictions of the classics and attempt to apply them wholesale to contemporary agriculture are engaged in a futile and dogmatic exercise.

Notes

1 Both (b) and (c) are present in the South African case of 'pure' agrarian capitalism of the Prussian variety. In the United States capitalist agriculture similarly seems to presuppose the low wages of Afro-American, Mexican, etc. labour.
2 It has been noted that 'bought out' might be more appropriate than 'pushed out' as a description of the elimination of landlordism in Europe. The landlord estates were gradually sold out to peasants, financed by state credit. Thus landed capital was transformed into capital, often invested, as noted above, in agro-industry.

References

Economic Commission for Europe (1973) *Present and Forseeable Trends in Mechanization and Their Impact on European Agriculture*, Agri/mech. report no. 51, United Nations, New York.
McElroy, R. C. (1973) *The Hired Farm Working Force 1972: A Statistical Report*, Washington, DC.

OECD (1974) *Agricultural Policy of the European Economic Community*, Agricultural Policy Reports, Paris, table 3b.

Samir, Amin and Vergalopoulos, Kostas (1974) *La question paysanne et le capitalisme*, Éditions Anthropos-idep, Paris.

US Bureau of the Census (1975) *Historical Statistics of the United States, Part 1*, Washington, DC.

Related Items

1, 2, 3, 9, 10, 13, 16, 18, 21, 23, 25, 26, 27, 31, 32, 41, 49, 52, 55, 61, 62.

Part II

Peasantry as an Economy

Part II traces the processes of production, exchange and consumption typical of those social structures where the family farm and the peasant village are the major units of social interaction. The fundamental social significance of 'making a living' and some collective particularities related to it make the delimitation of peasant economy central for the definition of peasantry as such. At the core of these particularities stand the operational logic and the patterns of social reproduction of the family farm. These imply the prevalent use of unwaged labour, land- and animal-husbandry as main occupation (usually supplemented by out-of-farm wage labour and/or crafts and trades) and the self-consumption of part of the produce. The diversity of actual farmers is considerable and can be represented on a number of quantitative scales, e.g. of the extent of commercialization, the extent of involvement in or usage of wage labour, etc., and of their correlants, like for example the size of the farm or of the investments in it. Ecological particularities and the actual production packages offer some further variations. Also, the broader societal contexts powerfully influence peasant economies, their dynamics and transformations. None the less, the resulting heterogeneity does not preclude some similarities of the content and logic of peasant economies. These find their expression in the characteristic strategies of the peasant family farms as well as in the broader context of regional, national and international economies.

Section A of part II begins with Galeski's discussion of the characteristics of peasant family farming as an occupation. The contributions of Dumont, Omvedt and Malita develop this issue further by looking at different aspects of agriculture as the human use of and interdependence with nature. Robinson offers a pointer to the particular issue of peasant income supplements and a survival strategy based on the underselling of their labour power. It is followed by Taylor's discussion of the differential impact of peasant family labour as against rural wage labour (see also the contributions by Feder, J. Harriss and Hann, items 12, 31 and 15). A 'snippet' by Susan George points to credit and investment as another side of the rural smallholders' equations of production.

Part IIA ends with Kerblay's discussion of Chayanov's theory of peasantry as a specific type of economy, and Alavi's discussion of peasantry in the capitalist mode of production: two major theoretical traditions concerning family farming. Kerblay looks at peasantry in terms of the survival strategies of family farmers, Alavi in the light of the developing new Marxist analysis of capitalism in its differing forms (see also Galeski, Thorner, Figes and de Janvry, items 13, 9, 16 and 49).

In section B of part II our attention is directed farther still towards the extra-village context of the economy discussed. This section also advances farther the issue of political economy. Any division into 'internal' and 'external' is evidently relative; we are speaking of different sides of a similar coin. The contributions of Nash concerning peasant producer markets in Latin America is followed by Barbara Harriss's considerations of rural markets controlled directly by the merchants (see also Wolf, item 6). Capital accumulation here offers an important analytical problem. While in item 28 Barbara Harriss looks at it *vis-à-vis* trade credit and control (see also de Janvry, item 49) Nash in item 27 pays particular attention to the socially determined de-capitalization trends within the peasant society (see also Stirling, item 5). Sen and Rahman then consider markets and exchange. Sen introduces the issue of political economy, that is of the domination of humans by other humans through the control of means of production and distribution. It is approached at its most direct level *vis-à-vis* the issues of famine and starvation (see also Scott, item 37). Rahman brings once more to the forefront the interdependence of power and economy whenever peasant land control is concerned. Next comes John Harriss's discussion of the capitalist characteristics and the diverse results of the so-called green revolution and of related analytical problems of socio-economic differentiation, polarization and possible de-peasantization. (See also Figes, Ortiz and de Janvry, items 16, 36 and 49). The contribution of Friedmann in item 32 brings part II to a close by considering its topic at its broadest. She looks at the present and the future of the family farms (i.e. a category inclusive of, but broader than, that of the peasant economies) and considers this issue within the changing context of international food regimes since the 1870s (see also Pearse, Figes and de Janvry, items 10, 16 and 49).

In part II as elsewhere preference has been given to the treatment of economy not in its narrow sense but within the context of societal structure treated within a historical process. In this spirit Galeski's contribution is not only about the farmer's occupation but also about the broader social context of professionalization, and the way it influences and transforms peasant economies; Malita suggests not only a taxonomy but a direction in which in his view food production is moving, etc. A final point is that political economy forms a major aspect of peasant social life and its transformations. It also offers one of the major connecting links between the subject matter of part II and that of the other parts of this volume. We have not singled it out, therefore, as a specific section but introduced its aspects in part II as well as elsewhere in the book.

Part IIA

Farming and the Farm

18

Farming as an Occupation

Boguslaw Galeski

When can a person be said to follow the vocation of farming? The answer seems obvious in the case of an agronomist, zoo-technician, agricultural worker on a state farm, a cow barn overseer, a production worker or engineer in an industrial fats factory, etc. But those engaged in big agricultural enterprises constitute such a large and differentiated community that the term 'agriculturist' is perhaps hardly suitable. As is the case with industry, it may be more suitable to speak of agriculture as an occupational division. The distinction between occupation, trade or vocation, speciality or job may present certain difficulties, but this applies to all branches of employment. And if it is accepted that agriculture presents greater difficulties, then it is only a matter of difference in degree.

Agriculture, however, presents a particular difficulty. For involved here is a category in relation to which the term 'agriculturist' cannot be simply rejected as too general. This may aptly apply to employees of agricultural institutions and enterprises. But this category involves the family cultivating an individual peasant farm. Of course, it is possible in this case too to distinguish between fruit growers, pig breeders, apiarists, tobacco growers, etc. Yet, the majority of peasant families engage in such differentiated production that the general term agriculturist may be misleading here and rather apply to employees of agricultural enterprises. The proposition that a family operating its own farm follows the farming vocation raises many doubts, and not only because of the general character of the term farmer. It is the fact that the family is involved, and not a person, that raises an immediate doubt. If the term vocation is nevertheless used in reference to families operating their own farms, then this vocation must be distinguished as a particular one, essentially different from others, in relation to the traits which determine that a given kind of work is considered following a vocation. But the term vocation is then not used in relation to other traits.

Boguslaw Galeski, 'Sociological problems of the occupation of farmers', *Annals of Rural Sociology*, Special Issue, 1968, pp. 9–26. Translated by Jerzy Syskind.

Definition of the Term Vocation

The term vocation (or profession) is generally used to designate a complex of activities which:

are distinct from other activities and are continuously performed;

are rendered on behalf of, or serve other people (society);

constitute a steady source of maintenance;

require certain preparation entitling one to follow a vocation, i.e., to work at it steadily on behalf of others, in exchange for means of subsistence.

None of these characteristics (which flow from each other) in itself suffices to define some given complex of activities as a vocation. It is possible to point to many distinct complexes of internally connected activities which – as J. Szczepanski (1963a) writes – nobody calls practising a trade or vocation (a housewife preparing meals for the family, for instance). Nevertheless under different conditions these same activities can unhesitatingly be defined as following a vocation (cooking in a restaurant, for example). So it is possible to indicate many individuals with steady sources of maintenance who pursue no vocation whatever (persons maintained by their families or those with bank accounts). Or there may be activity one is entitled to pursue after special preparation which is not a vocation. Such is the case, for instance, with driving an automobile – unless it is done for pay and serves other people (taxi driving). Many occupations, such as street cleaning, for instance, require no preparation or qualifications. Then there are people who pursue some activity without any gain in mind, which indicates that working on behalf of others is not always a sufficient vocation-distinguishing criterion, although it is undoubtedly the most important one. Hence the co-appearance of a complex of characteristics constitutes the basis for distinguishing a vocation, which may be defined as a complex of activities constantly performed on behalf of other people in exchange for means of subsistence; or more briefly – a complex of continuously performed activity which consists of exchanging individual for social labour. The term vocation is thus understood in the present paper.

It should be noted parenthetically that the term is often used to designate occupational or professional communities. One thus speaks, for example, of the doctor's vocation having in mind the totality of physicians. The term 'vocational category' will be used here in that sense, meaning a community of people pursuing the same vocation.

According to the above definition, many occupations listed in censuses cannot be regarded as vocational categories. It is difficult, for instance, to accept ownership (of land, buildings or capital, etc.) as a vocational category, if the activity is limited to profit making and does not involve management of an enterprise; whereas the majority of political leaders today should be reckoned in the vocational category since their activity is the basis of their maintenance. As we saw above in reference to the housewife and automobile driver, in certain cases, given complexes of activities sometimes bear the character of vocations and the people performing them may be defined as belonging to given vocational categories, and sometimes do not. Essential here is whether or not the activity becomes a vocation, and under what conditions. It may be said in relation to some types of activity that they are undergoing a social process of professionalization. The above traits determining vocation may serve not only as criteria for regarding some complex of activity as a vocation, but also as determinants of the process of professionalization transpiring in a given field. With the above enumerated traits as a criterion, it may be accepted that the process of professionalization of some work is the more advanced and that the activity may be more basically defined as practising a vocation:

the more clearly the considered complex of activity is distinguished from others – in contradistinction to household activity;

the more interlinked is the system of the social division of labour – in contradistinction to creative (or family) work for oneself;

the more it serves as a durable basis of maintenance – in contradistinction to casual occupations;

the more clearly defined are the necessary qualifications for practising it and the more specialized the institutions where the qualifications entitling one to pursue the given activity may be acquired – in contradistinction to work which anyone can do.

Because of the tendency of the family's economic function to disappear in the present epoch, it may, of course, be maintained that the work of the housewife is undergoing a process of professionalization, which as measured by the above determinants is already evident in some countries. The same may perhaps be said about the work of a political leader (the process of professionalization is highly advanced here). This process is most evident in relation to the social changes in the characteristics of the labour of families operating individual farms.

Peculiarities of the Farmer's Vocation

As applied to the labour of a family on an individual farm the term vocation implies social characteristics which clearly distinguish it from other occupations. The following are among its most important characteristics (Galeski, 1963a):

1   The work is done by the family. What is more, the generally accepted pattern of the organization of labour on an individual farm assumes family participation.[1] Otherwise, it is either not fully accomplished, not done properly or it meets with considerable difficulties. Contrary to the case of domestic production, which often involves the family but where it can be easily substituted by some other group, on the individual farm the range and system of activity are harmoniously linked with the family as the production crew, according to the physical capacities of the family members and their places in it.

2   The farmer's (family's) place in the vocational category is designated by his class position. His vocational advance is connected with the degree of possession of means of production. This characteristic is not peculiar to the farming vocation, for class position is in general closely correlated (sometimes very closely, as in the handicrafts, for instance) with the vocational position. The director of a capitalist factory is often a co-owner, an office worker is generally a wage worker. But with the farmer there is an identification of the class and vocational position. The farmer's role as owner and as producer are inseparable. Here the class position of the owner is defined as that of producer. The richer the farmer, the more he is also an organizer and manager, while the small farmer works also as an executive not only for himself but also among his neighbours.

3   The farmer's labour is to a great degree autonomic. He produces objects which satisfy his own basic needs. Every other vocation may be pursued only in connection with the practice of other vocations. Otherwise the individual producer could not work or even exist. True, the modern farmer too could not exist without the labour of people in other occupations. But it was not so long ago when the peasant family produced almost everything necessary for its existence. The relation between the farmer's vocation and other occupations is hence not of equal weight on both sides. Society could not exist without the farmer, while the life of the farmer would be immeasurably more difficult if he were not linked with a system of the social division of labour, but he would be able to keep alive.

4   The activity composing the farmer's labour covers not only a wide scope but is also the basis for separate occupations. It is not just a matter of the farmer having to know many things. There are many occupations where knowledge in many fields is useful or even necessary. Though a certain knowledge in the field of building, for example, is useful for the director of a larger enterprise so as to be able to orientate on the enterprise's building investment, he doesn't work as a carpenter or mason. The farmer, however, must often engage in labour which constitutes the basis of other occupations. He first of all carries on the farming occupation proper (breeding, gardening, production organizer, etc.), then the other trades connected with agriculture (food processing, for

example), or even non-agricultural occupations (tool and implement repair, transport, minor building activity, etc.). The farmer cannot have the necessary preparation for all the jobs he does, but the most important thing is that he does them in the same manner as repairing an electric light in one's home, i.e., not professionally. It is precisely all these tasks which compose the farmer's vocation.

Hence consideration of the peculiarity of the farmer's vocation suggests the following conclusion. The work of a family running its own farm may be defined as practising a vocation only on the grounds that, as productive labour raising means of subsistence, it occupies a definite place in the modern organization of production based on the social division of labour. In essence, however, this labour does not bear the characteristics of a vocation, and constitutes a relic of a different mode of social organization of production, one not based on the division of occupations. The range of activity composing the labour of a family farm is, however, already considerably limited and is in the process of being further restricted by the development of the social division of labour outside the farm. There is hence in effect a process of adaptation of this type of labour to the occupational pattern of the organization of production in society.

The Process of Professionalization of the Farmer's Labour

The process of professionalization of the farmer's labour may be analysed on a broad range. For it is expressed in many directions due to the character of the individual farm: the changes in the farm and the family, the farmer's manner of working, the fields of activity composing it, the farmer's mode of thinking about the farm and his attitude to his work. This process may also be conceived on the background of the general social transformations expressed in changes of the socio-occupational or class-vocational social structure.

The formulation class-vocational structure is used because of the fact that under conditions of the private ownership of the means of production there is a clear connection between the place of the individual in the class and the vocational structure; in reference to farmers this relation has been defined as identification. The farmer (family operating an individual farm) is most often at the same time an owner of land, an entrepreneur, a producer and seller of his products. If 'owner' signifies an exclusively class, and 'producer', an occupational position – though connected with one or another class status – then the positions of entrepreneur and seller may also be of a class (if connected with ownership of means of production) as of a vocational character (production or sales manager, a worker employed at storing, shipping or processing and serving clients). Under capitalist conditions it is proper to speak of concentration of the land, primarily in the form of the mortgage debt holders. There is also the concentration and centralization of other means of production as a result of indebtedness and the activity of enterprises renting out farm equipment or providing farm services (for instance, firms conducting a number of operations for farmers with their own crews and machinery). Also in effect is the concentration of the production and marketing of agricultural produce through the operations of special food industry corporations, by contract production for private firms, complete control of the market, etc. This leads, in the words of Marx, to a situation where under capitalism 'The small holding of the peasant is now only the pretext that allows the capitalist to draw profit, interest and rent from the soil, while leaving it to the tiller of the soil himself to see how he can extract his wages' (Marx, 1852, p. 178). The farmer is reduced by the development of capitalism to the class position of a worker (and not as definite as that of an industrial worker), and to the occupational role of a producer. This process of class polarization is hence simultaneously one of the professionalization of the farmer's labour. However, the basis has not been removed for the appearance of both class and occupational elements in the farmer's situation, as long as this process has not eliminated the peasant farm. One expression of this process, however, is the fact that these elements differ in individual types of farms and appear in different proportions. Although this process has thus far not abolished the individual peasant farm, its direction is clear and definite.

Under socialist conditions, both in the sphere of existence of individual farms (or in the socialist model which assumes its persistence) as with the prevalence only of multi-family farms (producers' cooperative farms) the process of professionalization, consisting of the separation of the functions of production organizer, producer and salesman, is not connected with class polarization. And though this process is far advanced in some countries, it has not been fully realized.

The process of the division of the farmer's labour into the tasks of organizer and director of production, of producer and distributor, is connected under both capitalism and socialism with the emergence of large agricultural enterprises integrated vertically or horizontally. It is certain that in large agricultural enterprises there is not only a separation of the functions in question here (first of all of the organizational–managerial and productive functions). There is also a division of activities composing the farmer's labour into different occupational specialities: for instance, agricultural accounting, stock breeding, gardening, field cultivation. There emerges besides a hierarchy of occupational or professional posts: enterprise director, agrotechnician, team foreman, agricultural worker. The same applies to an enterprise based on vertical integration, except that the functions of salesman, processor and producer are clearly separated here. But there is also a differentiation of the organizational–managerial functions which are removed from the farm and concentrated in the enterprise. This is accompanied by a narrowing of the field of productive activity of the peasant family because of the production-service agencies, such as the machine station, for instance.

The emergence of large agricultural enterprises is connected with the acquisition by the individual farm of elements of an enterprise and the separation of the household economy from the production establishment. The characteristics distinguishing the farmer's vocation from other occupations hence tend to weaken. The result of the emergence of agricultural enterprises and the growth in the peasant farm of elements of an enterprise is a rise in the agricultural division of labour and the formation of differentiated vocational structures in this division of the national economy. With the formation of these structures the term farmer becomes less and less suitable, and it becomes more proper to speak of various vocational categories in agriculture in an ever broader sphere. And with the progress of the process of professionalization the term peasant class or stratum also becomes less and less applicable. These questions, however, require separate treatment.

It must be borne in mind though that the individual farm is not only an enterprise but also a household economy. The process of professionalization of the farmer's labour is effected not only by the narrowing of the scope of the family's productive activity, but also by the reduction of its tasks in the household economy. With the expansion of the general social division of labour, a number of traditional activities of the farm family (for instance, sewing clothes) are definitely transferred to industrial establishments. Other economic and upbringing tasks of the farm family are also reduced (by the school, clubroom, crèche, kindergarten) although this process is slower than in the urban areas. For it is confronted with a number of difficulties connected with the existence of the farm and the existence of family patterns subordinated to the functioning of the farm.

Finally, connected with the professionalization process is a rise in the number of small farm owners who are steadily gainfully employed in non-agricultural occupations. Here the professionalization process takes place not in connection with the formation of agricultural labour occupational structures and the growth of the network of productive and non-productive social services for the benefit of rural families; the process is rather effected by the changes in the very character of rural settlements which are to a great extent becoming residential centres of populations occupationally connected with the city and industry. Consideration of the family pattern of production which constitutes the foundation of the individual peasant farm and of the farmer's vocation requires noting also the above trend, for it is the cause of the family production pattern being limited, in this case by the owner going to work in non-agricultural occupations, and of the individual farm losing the characteristics of an enterprise and assuming the traits of a household economy.

It is impossible for any discussion of the professionalization process not to note that its source lies outside the farm. For it is the market and industry which create the main impulses for change. State intervention plays an important role here. Prohibition of land fragmentation, the introduction of social security and retirement pensions, the requirement of agricultural education for heirs, the dissemination of agricultural services, etc. – such are some expressions of this intervention.

On a macro-sociological scale, an analysis of the professionalization of labour, of its tempo, the difficulties it confronts and which it creates, requires investigation of the variables of the agricultural population's socio-occupational structure as well as of that of the rural inhabitants generally. This has been treated elsewhere (Galeski, 1963b) and there is no need to develop the question here. But the process of professionalization of the farmer's labour can be analysed from another angle – that of the farmer's attitude to his labour and occupation.

The Farmer's Occupational Activity and Attitude to his Labour and the Farm

We continue to use the term 'farmer' in the sense of a family operating an individual farm or a multi-family farm. As pointed out above, this term is too general and hardly suitable in relation to other individuals employed in agriculture: on large agricultural enterprises, processing plants and establishments serving the peasant farm (and the agricultural economy in general), the agricultural administration, agricultural stations and scientific institutions as well as in the system of diffusion of agricultural knowledge. In reference to this agricultural personnel the sociological subject matter does not differ basically from the general theme of the sociology of labour, although there appear here certain variations connected with the small number of work establishments, the comparatively undeveloped division of labour, the relation between the place of work and residence (moreover, living in the country) as well as variations connected with the technical characteristics of agricultural production. The question of the occupational attitudes of the agricultural personnel employed off the farm is touched here only peripherally, for it is a matter of outlining primarily questions beyond the range of other branches of sociology, which are subjects of rural sociology. Only one problem of agricultural workers requires at least a few sentences here.

The conviction has been expressed in recent years in sociological literature, and first of all in journalism, that the main motive of the flight of the young people from the village is the way of life based on the individual farm, and not the conditions of life in agriculture. In other words, that it is not a flight from agriculture, but from the peasant way of life. On the whole correct, this conclusion seems to be oversimplified. The rural youth undoubtedly reject this way of life which denies them the values they aspire to (first of all, a vocation or profession) which are connected with the town and industry. However, the phenomenon applies to an even greater extent to large farms, where the farming methods do not necessarily generate the characteristics of the peasant way of life, while these characteristics certainly do not appear on a larger scale than on the peasant family farm. It therefore seems that the decisive role here is played by the difficult conditions of labour in agriculture. But then there are other factors inclining young people to leave the village which are connected with the way of life based on the individual peasant farm as well as factors which check this phenomenon. It must be said without elaborating that this question too indicates the need of a separate study of the situation of young people on individual farms. This situation is not comprehensible without considering the particular traits of the peasant family, for when they leave the farm the rural youth leave not only their place of work but also their family homes. The aversion of young people to work in agriculture in general should be regarded as a separate problem, since the matter of the peasant way of life seems to play no important role here.

We now turn to the first sociological problem in connection with the question of the incentive to occupational activity or with the attitude on which it is based. When determining the factors which influence the level of occupational activity in some sphere, economists are usually inclined to regard as decisive the income attained as a result of the activity. This is undoubtedly an oversimplification. Work may be undertaken not only in order to obtain means of subsistence and without regard to the magnitude of the earnings it assures. Ideological incentives: the spirit of emulation, the satisfaction of a job well done, etc., may operate – besides economic incentives. Motivations for labour transcending the economic one are firmly related with certain situations (war, revolution) or with given environments (inventors, artists, scientists, writers, civic leaders), but their impact on occupational activity is undoubted. There is nevertheless a basis for the economist's simplification. Thus in both the capitalist and the socialist systems income determines an individual's access to very many generally desired values. Under conditions of socialism, the influence of the material incentive is undoubtedly limited on account of the considerably reduced spread between incomes and the more limited stock of values money can acquire. Then there is the limited significance of money with respect to the values it can acquire. For instance, the acquisition of rare goods is determined under socialism not only by the amount of money one possesses (the short supply of articles does not always affect their price fixed by the state), but also by other factors, such as the system of distribution, for instance. Nevertheless, the principle 'to each according to his performance', adopted by socialism, finds its expression also in income differentiation, hence of access to generally desired values. This principle is the basis for the proposition that income magnitude under socialism expresses the degree of social recognition of the individual's work. It is hence obvious that the desire to obtain means of subsistence and to raise one's income is the most potent and, on a mass scale, the decisive factor of occupational activity – except for unusual situations or for particular social circles. Thus where economic policy has a decisive influence on the behaviour of incentives it to a great extent affects not only the level of occupational activity and its direction but, because of the weight of economic life, also the totality of interpersonal relations.

While recognizing the basic role of economic incentives, it would be incorrect to reduce them, in reference to the peasant family, exclusively to market incentives. For that is not their only source of income, while for some it mainly lies elsewhere.[2] What is most important, it would be erroneous to think that the peasant family regards the farm only as a means of income. This is perhaps so in relation to some farms of a clearly enterprise character: capitalist farms, for instance, or some 'specialized' commercial farms in Western Europe and the USA. Firstly, the peasant farm is directly geared to the satisfaction of the needs of the family, hence some changes effected by the family are not connected with the market situation. Secondly, the farm is also where the peasant family lives, therefore any improvements or major investment aim directly to improve the family's living conditions. Family income may in great measure be directed to improvements (new buildings, for instance) not so much with a view to produce more, or to lower costs, but simply so the family may live more comfortably. In many cases the production and consumption aspects of investment cannot be separated. In building a new dwelling house, which is as a rule first in the order of priority of the family's investment intentions (Galeski, 1962), the family improves the farm and raises its level of living at the same time.

Thus the basis of the occupational activity of the farm family is the farm – but the farm regarded as both a source of acquiring and raising income and a goal of spending income on it as a residence and living quarters. The problem of the functioning of the incentives to occupational activity, and of economic incentives in particular, is therefore a sociological question of a specific content in relation to the farmer's vocation (to the peasant farm). It is similar with the question of the direction of this activity.

As noted above, the situation of the farm family is based on the identification of the class and vocational position. Occupational activity may perhaps therefore be examined in either aspect. The traditional desire to enlarge the farm (rarely manifested today under Polish conditions) is a type of activity which definitely leads to changes in the class as in the occupational situation. The enlargement of his holding eliminates the need (or even the possibility) of the farmer working in other occupations or for his neighbours. It often requires the employment of agricultural workers and always changes the farmer's position in his occupation, since there is a change in the proportion of his managing and executive activity with the growth of his role as entrepreneur and seller of commodities.

But remaining on the grounds of occupational activity – the established fact that the mechanism proper to capitalism of rural stratification does not function in Poland and other socialist countries (or has only a marginal scope) justifies the proposition that the very combination of the functions of producer, entrepreneur and seller in the farmer's vocational activity projects the necessity of regarding this activity as a factor of formation of various agricultural occupations and of the farmer's self-determination in the framework of the emerging agriculturists' occupational structure. But as long as the individual peasant farm continues to exist, that long will the farmer's vocation be an amalgam of various occupations. Consequently, when dealing with the farmer's occupational activity it is necessary to state the direction of that activity. For activity here may be measured by labour input, the result of production, the rational organization of the labour process, market orientation, introduction of technical improvements, etc. Furthermore, since the time and interest the farmer devotes to the farm cannot be separated into interest in a production establishment and in a domestic economy, all general and quantitative comparisons of the vocational activity of the farmer and non-farmer seem highly problematical. It is consequently necessary to clearly define the activity under consideration: whether it is a matter of comparing different groups of the rural population, or of the connection between individual and group activity (Galaj, 1961). But in any of its conceptions, the question of the farmer's occupational activity cannot be examined without taking into account the fact that involved here is a vocation which combines the activity of various occupations and which is the basis for their formation as separate occupations. Activity in the farmer's vocation is therefore always one leading to some other occupation.

The above proposition also applies to the question of the so-called good farmer. This conception, so often used in public addresses and in journalism, is by no means a uniform one in the countryside. First of all, in some regions of a traditional peasant culture a 'good farmer' is as a rule one who has much land.[3] Secondly, even where occupational traits possess an independent value, this conception contains different contents – a 'good farmer' is a good organizer of the labour processes, a diligent person, one who knows what is profitable to produce, an innovator in some agricultural speciality, a person of much experience, the director of an agricultural school or a popularizer of agrarian science. The accepted 'good farmer' stereotype may differ in individual communities and be the basis for the characterization of the more general changes they are undergoing as well as for grasping the difficulties confronted by activity which aims to convince the farmers of one or another measure advantageous to them. For example, the activity of an agronomist in convincing farmers that it is irrational to own horses may be in vain if in the given community a farmer's prestige is based on possession and not on the economic effects of his labour (Mendras, 1958). This is why it is necessary to recognize distinctions between different types of 'good farmers' in practical determinations and in research; while in propagating the ideal 'good farmer' image one must be clear which 'good farmer' he has in mind.

This leads to the problem of the paths to advancement in the farmer's vocation. It follows from the character of the peasant farm that the hierarchy of positions in the vocation is connected with that held in the family. Becoming head of the family is synonymous with attaining vocational independence. Advancement in the vocation is consequently connected with changes in the family and not with qualification. Reaching maturity means acquisition of experience. The farmer's vocation begins with apprenticeship and proceeds from tending geese, pasturing the cows and serving as farm hand to the status of farmer.

As shown above, advancement in the farmer's vocation takes place also on the class plane by passage from the position of owner of small means of production to that of operator of a larger farm. The place of the individual in the family and the position of the family in the class hierarchy thus determine the main paths of advancement in this vocation. Undoubtedly, here too acquiring a speciality in some of the above mentioned fields of activity is essential for attaining generally desired values, and recognition by the community of neighbours, in particular. Research on the farmer's occupational ambitions would enable one to establish the exact importance of this factor. So far, though, this factor has not designated the main paths of advancement in the vocation. The relatively lesser significance of preparatory schooling, of acquiring qualifications (here primarily the qualification of landownership) to vocational advancement is the consequence of particular variables of this occupation which alienate many young people from tying their future to the farm.

The process of professionalization of farm labour and the emergence of large agricultural enterprises with a differentiated occupational structure open new paths of advancement in the vocation. But as long as the individual peasant farm persists, a considerable part of the population will continue to be excluded from that mechanism.

A young adult generally acquires enough experience on a peasant farm to be able to manage it. Activities which the boy or girl perform on the family farm are connected with their age and prepare them for the role of farmer (Chalasinski, 1937, vol. 1). The transmission of knowledge consists in the gradual initiation of the apprentices in all the rites of the occupation (Dobrowolski, 1937), which goes hand in hand with the inculcation of given standards and moral values, beliefs and customs. But the nature of the knowledge which consists of the accumulated experience of their forefathers and the mechanism of its transmission bear the heavy weight of tradition and constitute the foundation of conservatism in the farmer's mode of labour. The school in this system of knowledge transmission is a foreign element, coming from the outside. It limits the family's rearing influence, tears the child from the harmonious system of work and life and introduces into its consciousness patterns which are dissonant with, and values foreign to or impossible of realization within that system (Chalasinski, 1937, vol. 4): hence the resistance confronted by the school in rural areas. But the constantly growing orbit of conflicts between the farmer and society outside the village impels recognition of the need for this institution and is the basis for its acceptance. Still, while the general academic school has been fully accepted in many countries, the agricultural vocational school still meets with considerable reluctance to recognize its value in preparing a young person to run a farm,[4] and even more to accept its actual utilization for that purpose (Galeski and Wyderko, 1959). As in the case of the general school, the agricultural school becomes an indispensable element of vocational preparation mainly as a result of government regulations, hence of pressure from the outside. Nevertheless most countries have taken steps to diffuse agricultural services.

In the majority of countries the press, radio and television conduct chats with farmers, along the same lines as the practical advice programmes for women. This is due to the specific characteristics of farm labour which is only formally and not actually regarded – and cannot be regarded – as a vocation. No other vocation is surrounded with such all-sided activity calculated to diffuse scientific knowledge. Sociological themes in relation to this activity are most often of a practical character and the aim of research in this field is usually to work out effective principles guiding the activity. Thus sociologists investigate how agricultural knowledge reaches the farmer, the effectiveness of the advice by agronomists or suppliers of agricultural means of production (feed, machinery, fertilizers). They also investigate the penetration mechanisms of new technological information originating with agronomists or farmer-innovators and disseminated by leading farmers to the rest, as well as the mechanisms of the anchoring of some technology as an obligatory standard in a given community (Rogers, 1960, p. 149), etc. But the process of diffusion of agrotechnical knowledge has a broader sociological scope. We have in mind first of all the nature of resistance to technical innovations in the countryside. Often this resistance has an economic content. It is not easy for a small farmer to purchase the necessary equipment, the risk of introducing some branch of production is great and the labour input is high. Most often though the economic motive is not the only one for the farmer's reluctance to introduce improvements. As indicated earlier, economic arguments may not convince the farmer if he is activated by other considerations, such as prestige based on ownership and not on productivity, for instance.

Technical improvement changes the manner of working fixed as the standard by family upbringing and, as already pointed out, meets with opposition from rural conservatism. Changes in the mode of labour also alter the division of obligations in the family or cause their unequal distribution. They furthermore alter the prevailing family way of life, its customs and order of tasks fixed for generations. Questions connected with improvement are therefore inseparable from the whole system of rural life on which the farm is based.

Moreover, the penetration of technical innovations originates first of all in the system of neighbourly contacts, which are elements of the rural social structure. Outside influences which ignore this structure may effect some change or another but will be of little effect. The initiation of any measure by a family low in the rural prestige hierarchy, for instance, is rarely successful. The opinion of neighbours and self-evaluated social position may consequently exert an essential influence on whether the farmer undertakes some initiative or not. Also of importance in this respect is the kind of contact with the farmers by those who conduct vocational educational work among them, i.e., whether the positions of imparters and receivers of information are those of equals or not, and what their personal relations are. An agronomist enlightening a farmer head of the family in the presence of his wife and children how he is to manage his farm is an example of an ineffective way of diffusing agricultural science. Hence this question cannot be treated in separation from the rural family and the village community.

The diffusion of agrotechnical knowledge is carried on by the state and farmers' professional organizations. This question, like the problem of the farmer's place in the occupational structure as well as the related question of the position occupied by prestige in the farmer's vocation, require separate treatment. But it is worth noting here that farmers' professional organizations generally bear particular traits in comparison with other professional organizations. These are traits connected with the peculiarities characterizing the farmer's vocation. They are generally of a more or less clear class character, though that is not their specific trait. They are organizations of representatives of small enterprises and household economies. Their function is therefore to organize the combined activity of producers and consumers, who are at the same time sellers and entrepreneurs in fields profitable to them. Hence the priority of economic questions. Simultaneously the farmers' professional organizations must deal with matters concerning the families living in given territorial communities. They must hence acquire a communal character. This type of professional organization thus combines the characteristics of a political party, a cooperative (producers, consumers), and of a territorial self-government. Under socialist conditions, with the lack of a foundation for rural stratification (as a result of the socialization of the means of production) or of conditions for its deepening, the class role of the farmers' professional organizations either vanishes or is limited. There may thus ensue an identification of professional, cooperative and farmers' self-government organizations. However, the formation of the vocational structure of agricultural labour prepares the ground for vocational organizations in other occupations too. Organizations of this type do not embrace the peasant farm even where they are of a multi-family character, i.e., producers' cooperatives.

The questions connected with the farmer's vocation treated above constitute at least a preliminary basis for explaining the farmer's place in the occupational structure of society. Omitting the connection between occupational and class structure, which appears with special sharpness here, it must be asserted that because of the objective characteristics of the farmer's vocation it is necessary rather to separate it from the system of occupations, as that part of the social division of labour which has so far not been fully mastered by the occupational model, but which is subjected to and adopted by that model. This accounts for the fact that the relatively high social evaluation of the farmer's occupation (Wesolowski and Sarapata, 1961) does not correspond to its objective attractiveness, i.e. attractiveness measured by the influx of people into agriculture. In considerations of the decline of the farmer's vocation there is usually a lack of perception of the contradictions between the declared recognition and that expressed in behaviour. Nor is it adequately perceived that this situation cannot be basically altered as long as agriculture remains the domain of the family production model.

The sociological problems of the farmer's vocation outlined here pertain, as indicated, to the peasant family farm. The question of agricultural workers may be successfully treated (despite its undoubtedly distinct features) by the sociology of labour (of occupations). For rural sociology is interested specifically in the occupations pursued by the peasant family, so basically different from others and so inseparably connected with reliquary elements of rural life: the peasant farm, the family, rural society.

The thematology of this vocation embraces:

the determination of its general uniqueness;

disclosure of the paths followed by the process of professionalization of the farmer's vocation.

Expressions of the professionalization process and the distinctness of the farmer's vocation may be observed in sociological problems involved in the investigation of occupation, consequently in the problems of:

the foundation for occupational activity and its incentives;

the direction of that activity;

authority and roads to occupational advancement;

manner of acquiring knowledge and the necessary qualification to pursue that vocation;

the paths to the penetration and diffusion of occupational know-how.

The subject of the farmer's vocation is related to the specific character of farmers' professional organizations and the place of the vocation in the social occupational structure. But this question is more closely connected with the sociological problems of rural society and peasant strata and requires separate treatment.

Notes

1 Farms operated by single males or females are not considered to have full value. See, for instance, Wierzbicki, 1963.
2 For example the families of so-called part-time farmers.
3 Research conducted in 1960 by the Workshop of Rural Sociology at the Institute of Agricultural Economy shows that 70 per cent of respondents consider that one with little land cannot be a good farmer.
4 In a poll conducted by the Public Opinion Poll Centre 20 per cent of farmers considered the agricultural school unnecessary for the farmer.

References

Chalasinski, J. (1937) *Mlode pokolenie chlopow* [*The Young Generation of Farmers*], Warsaw.
Galaj, D. (1961) *Aktywnosc spoleczno-gospodarcza chlopow* [*Socio-Economic Activity of Farmers*], Warsaw.
Galeski, B. (1962) 'Badania nad aktywnoscia zawodowa rolnikow' ['Research on farmers' occupational activity'], *Studia Socjologiczne*, no. 1.
Galeski, B. (1963a) *Chlopi i zawod rolnika* [*Peasants and the Farmers' Occupation*], Warsaw.
Galeski, B. (1963b) 'Zawod jako kategoria socjologiczna: Formowanie sie zawodu rolnika' ['Occupation as sociological category: Formation of the farmers' vocation'], *Studia Socjologiczne*, no. 3 (10).
Galeski, B. and Wyderko, A. (1959) 'Poglady chlopow na przyszlosc wsi' ['Peasants views on the future of the village'], *Wies Wspolczesna*, no. 4.
Marx, K. (1852) 'The Eighteenth Brumaire of Louis Bonaparte', in Karl Marx and Frederick Engels, *Selected Works*, vol. 1, Lawrence & Wishart, 1950.
Mendras, H. (1958) *Les paysans et la modernisation de l'agriculture*, Paris.
Szczepanski, J. (1963a) 'Czynniki ksztaltujace zawod i strukture zawodowa' ['Factors shaping occupation and the occupational structure'], *Studia Socjologiczne*, no. 3 · (10).
Wesolowski, W. and Sarapata, A. (1961) 'Hierarchia zawodow i stanowisk' ['The hierarchy of occupations and positions'], *Studia Socjologiczne*, no. 2.
Wierzbicki, Z. T. (1963) *Zmiaca w pol wieku pozniej* [*Zmiaca after Fifty Years*], Warsaw.

Related Items

2, 3, 6, 11, 13, 15, 16, 17, 19, 21, 22, 25, 26, 27, 28, 32, 33, 35, 37, 60, 61.

19

Agriculture as Use and Transformation of Nature

René Dumont

The principal aim of agriculture may be defined as follows: to supply mankind with food and with those raw materials which are of animal or vegetable origin (Dumont, 1949). Evidently some of these requirements can be provided in other ways and the earliest mode of subsistence was simply by gathering products of untended nature. Today, fishing is still an invaluable resource, and together with hunting it still forms the mainstay of certain primitive economies. As late as 1936 there was an old peasant woman at Murols, in the Auvergne, who gathered wild hazelnuts from the hedgerows, shelled them on the hearth and, after two months of spare-time work, produced three or four litres of 'wild' oil. Her only concession to progress was the use of an old mechanical press. There are few of us who have never gathered wild berries, picked dandelions from the meadows in the spring or mushrooms from the woods in autumn. We have often, without realizing it – like Monsieur Jourdain – imitated the example of the old peasant woman.

The difference between mere collecting and agriculture is that the latter endeavours to modify the natural environment so as to secure the most favourable possible conditions for various useful species of plants and animals whose utility is further enhanced by a conscious process of selection. Agriculture tempers the extremes of the climate; with irrigation the farmer fights aridity; he houses his animals and protects his market gardens with frames and glass against wind and cold. Above all, agriculture modifies the soil. Unlike climate, this should not be regarded as part of the natural endowment of a region, the only exception being the case of certain virgin soils which have retained their original vegetation of grass or forest and which have provided the basis for pedological classification. Our own soils are highly artificial. In many

Excerpts from René Dumont, *Types of Rural Economy: Studies in World Agriculture*, Methuen, 1957, pp. 1–9. Translated by D. Magnin.

cases they have been worked with plough and harrow for thousands of years, corrected for deficiencies and enriched with manure and every kind of fertilizer, natural or artificial.

Agricultural science is the practical farmer's consultant. Its domain is the whole range of organic life utilized by man. It raises the productivity of useful species by methods of selection which were once empirical but now rely increasingly on the science of genetics. It transforms the living conditions and, more particularly, the feeding of animals. Thus the stage of development of any rural economy can be estimated by noting the degree to which the natural environment has been changed and the techniques employed to this end.

In a region developed on an extensive basis, the original features are only slightly modified and are still very apparent. In the case of a pastoral economy, where the grazing animal forages – and concentrates – the natural produce of the grassland, there is no modification whatsoever and there is very little even in the permanent grasslands of Western Europe, to which the term 'natural' is often applied with good cause;[1] indeed, as is still all too often the case in Normandy, rational methods of management, with fertilizing and other forms of improvement, are on the whole unfortunately absent. So long as the soil is not actually worked, permanent grassland remains, in effect, natural grassland; in the strict sense of the term therefore it is not a form of agriculture, the symbols of which are the plough and 'ager', the ploughed field.

We must now examine the distinctions which are usually made between the two main methods of raising the level of agricultural productivity. Intensification aims primarily at high yields even if they are costly in terms of labour and the maintenance of soil capital (by means of improved seeds, fertilizers, etc., whereby biological processes are modified). This is the method which must be urgently applied in overpopulated areas where the overriding consideration is that the productivity of the scarce factor – that is, of the land – should be increased. The soil is cultivated repeatedly and with such minute attention that the commonest implements are often the rake and the spade; the land is heavily manured and the water resources are carefully husbanded. The net result is a greatly modified landscape, and a good example of an intensive system of this type, with high yields per unit of area, is found in a typical market garden, where the climate is completely artificial and the soil is transformed by massive additions of fertilizing substances. The same practices, though to a lesser degree, can be recognized in the Spanish *huertas*; here, however, the climate is extremely favourable.

At the other end of the scale, mechanization aims at cutting down labour and increasing its productivity. In every type of operation, cultivating and harvesting included, human energy is replaced as far as possible by the work of animals and the power of machines. The hand tool is replaced by the motorized implement. The combine-harvester does all the work which previously was performed by scythe and sickle, flail and winnowing basket. It is in sparsely populated regions such as the 'new countries' that this type of mechanization is most needed, for, contrary to the general situation elsewhere, these are sometimes afflicted by a dearth of men on the land, and the special attribute of the machine is that it increases the farmworker's daily output. . . .

Whether it be farm, estate or collective, it is the individual undertaking which, by its work on the land – present and past – turns the forces of nature to advantage. For the most part, however, agriculture is still the domain of the family enterprise and is therefore carried on by a great multitude of highly dispersed units of production, some of them quite small and many of them very small indeed. The provision of machinery is thus inherently more difficult and costly than in manufacturing industry, where the trend is for ever-increasing concentration, while the discontinuous use of farm equipment heightens the contrast still further.

In some advanced types of economy, both capitalist and collectivist, the scale of agricultural enterprise is being increased, though more rapidly in some areas than in others. This is a significant trend; it is generally accompanied by the introduction of an appreciable volume of machinery and agriculture is therefore brought into line, in certain important respects, with manufacturing industry. In dealing with a particular type of farming, we shall therefore give some indication of the average size of the undertakings concerned. For instance, in the capitalist world, the family enterprise is the rule, and it gives ample proof of vitality when there is no shortage of space or of capital, as in the United States.

The farm unit operates in the context of a legal system which regulates the appropriation and disposal of the various factors of production, including the land. It also determines the farmer's relationship with the moneylender, banker or financier and, if he does not own the land himself, with his landlord. The law may either help or hinder the modernization and equipping of the countryside, but is notoriously slow in adjusting itself to technical developments and is, in consequence, rarely of much assistance. We shall indicate in outline some of the legal conditions which favour progressive farming.

Each individual farm is conditioned by its economic and social setting. Fertilizers, tractors and machines are the products of highly organized industries characterized by the efficient use of manpower and mass production methods, and commanding all the resources of modern technology. Apart from the natural environment of a region, therefore, its degree of industrialization stands out as the most important criterion in any evaluation of its agricultural future. Quite apart from the fact that it manufactures equipment for sale to the farmer, industry breaks down the barriers of self-sufficiency and precipitates the transition to a commercial economy by creating in its labour force a market for farm produce which, saving periods of depression, is well endowed with purchasing power.

Having already amassed a great fund of capital, an industrial region can the more easily continue to accrue its wealth. Moreover, increments generally accumulate more quickly in manufacturing industry and commerce than in agriculture, where the returns march in slow rhythm with the seasons. Thus, whereas the methods of former times demanded hard manual work most of all, today the farmer needs the modern tools of his craft, but almost inevitably lacks the means to buy them, and this is the most formidable obstacle which bars the way to rapid progress. The land is rarely short of hands, but very often it has neither capital nor machines.

The density of population is another important element in our analysis. When the density is high, the law of diminishing returns hinders the necessary intensification of production unless better techniques are constantly evolved and applied, but this is rarely the case in underdeveloped countries where research and education are both limited in their scope. In areas such as Spain and the Far East, where industrialization is still in a very early stage, there is the problem of finding useful outlets for the superabundant labour of the countryside where low productivity is all too often the rule.

Where the density of population is very low, the problem of rapid development is one of finding enormous quantities of equipment as quickly as possible. But this is not always practicable, and there is always the risk that the materials will be misapplied or used inefficiently, as may so easily happen, for example, in the administration of transport services.

A large part is also played by the educational system, and in this connection standards of professional training are of particular significance, for successful intensive agriculture demands a very high level of competence. Whereas a large undertaking needs to fill only a small number of key posts, the proportion of highly qualified men needs to be very much greater when every farmer is the manager of his own small family enterprise.

When all these factors have been considered in turn, a clear picture will emerge of the conditions under which the farmer has to operate, and at this juncture it will be appropriate to study the broad features of his techniques of production; in a general survey such as this we cannot concern ourselves with the minutiae of his methods. We shall, however, attempt to classify various systems according to their degree of intensiveness, with particular emphasis on permanent improvements, such as schemes of drainage or irrigation, on the frequency of soil workings and above all on methods of fertilization.

In some cases, no attempt whatsoever is made to fertilize the soil, and instances of this neglect are to be found in many primitive societies and even sometimes in those generally considered to be 'civilized', although here this adjective hardly seems appropriate. The next stage is when fertilization is practised sporadically; its value is hardly understood, and it exists mainly as a convenient method of waste disposal. In the final stage, soil enrichment, in one form or another, is practised consciously and for its own sake. So long as transport remains difficult and expensive, however, only the ground in the immediate vicinity of the home is affected. The first kind of fertilizer to be used is generally the residue of ashes from the hearth, and only later is the value of night soil, animal droppings, and plant remains, which are all available on the farm itself, fully appreciated. The most advanced stage of all is reached when fertilizers are brought in from outside the farm, especially when, like chemical fertilizers, they are the product of a factory process.

The degree of mechanization in an economy is indicated by the relative proportion of work done by hand, by animals, and by machines, respectively. A small proportion of manual labour obviously points to an advanced stage of development. In a primitive system, man is the beast of burden, but later he becomes a director of operations, driving the tractor which pulls or drives the machinery; furthermore, the efficiency of the latter in the performance of its highly specialized functions is constantly being improved. At the same time the need for equipment increases and fresh improvements are continually added to the work of the past.

The more he improves the physical environment, the greater is man's freedom in choosing the plants he wishes to cultivate. Having increased the volume and reliability of crop yields, he can also afford to add to his list of domestic animals. Thus, technically, he may select the precise combination he wishes to pursue from a very large number of possible enterprises.[2] In other words, he chooses a 'type' of agriculture or animal husbandry,[3] and the description of these types, together with the varying rates at which they have been developed, is an integral part of the study of the different forms of rural economy with which they are associated.

In subsistence farming, where nothing is brought in from outside, there is generally an even greater variety of produce than in the primitive type of economy, where a wide range of necessities is supplied by collecting rather than by agriculture. Similarly, subsistence farming is more varied than modern commercial agriculture, which has grown up thanks to improvements in communications and methods of distribution – although the efficiency of the latter is more open to doubt. Commercial agriculture is free to specialize in one or several of the products best suited to the overall conditions.

Once certain crops have been selected, they will often be cultivated on the same land year after year, and the form of the rotation will be designed to make tillage and fertilizing as convenient and economical as possible. The sequence sugar-beet, wheat and barley, for instance, represented the basic rotation practised in northern France during the latter part of the nineteenth and the early part of the twentieth centuries. Land utilization, on the other hand, is the proportion of a given area devoted to each crop: twenty-five acres of sugar-beet, twenty-five of wheat and twenty-five of barley in 1953–4, for example.

Type of farming, crop-rotation system and land utilization are the appropriate criteria for the classification of modern rural economies. When properly balanced, they facilitate soil conservation and avoid extremes of seasonal labour demands. At one time, however, the same land was not cropped continuously, and even today in some backward areas periods of cultivation are separated by long intervals of fallow. Thus cultivation may be either continuous or intermittent, and the former is characteristic of all the more advanced kinds of farming, except in semi-arid regions.

In Africa and Asia especially the rearing of animals is still carried on by nomadic herdsmen who practise no form of agriculture whatsoever. They rely solely on the unimproved pastures and undertake seasonal migrations in areas where the climatic regime restricts plant growth at certain times of the year. Such an economy becomes more intensive as its interest in crop production increases; its animals then provide power for tilling the land and manure for fertilizing it.

Such a system is more productive and certain commodities plentiful at one time of the year can be stored for use when needed: hay, for example, bundles of leafy twigs and various other items culled from forest, steppe, scrub or low-lying marshland. Next, certain fields may be set aside for cattle and converted into permanent grassland. This, however, may be a retrograde step for it is often associated with a fall in productivity.

The introduction of rotation grasses, roots, kale and other fodder crops, however, always represents a very real advance, although even here, as in the case of direct food production, the intensiveness of the system will depend on how much the land is cultivated and fertilized. Later, the fodder crops may be supplemented by the purchase of feeding-stuffs – mostly industrial by-products and often rich in proteins – like cattle-cake, bran and offal. Finally comes the use of various substances, such as mineral salts and vitamins, advocated by modern science. Once this stage is reached, selective breeding can safely begin for, although pedigree animals are more delicate, the farmer is now in a position to give them the care and attention they need. It was during the eighteenth century that these techniques of selective breeding and large-scale fodder-crop cultivation began to be applied, first in England and later in the rest of Western Europe (Veyret, 1951).

Except in its very highly specialized forms – like pig-rearing and poultry-keeping, which rely almost wholly on purchases of feeding-stuffs – animal husbandry is generally an integral part of the modern type of farming system. The size of the animal population will, of course, determine the volume of fodder crops to be grown and the size of reserves needed to tide over the season of restricted plant growth. Apart from the Equatorial zone, a modern system of intensive farming should provide for a high density of animals in order to satisfy the growing demand for meat and milk derivatives from the more advanced and highly industrialized countries. The extent to which an agricultural system meets this need will enable us to evaluate its stage of development. On a number of occasions we have already pronounced most unfavourably on the position in regions which do not conform in this respect (density of cattle too low in the Paris Basin, for example).

The various ways in which different types of farming are carried on and the proportion in which the various factors of production are employed result in different levels of productivity. The effectiveness of a given type cannot be measured exactly, but estimates can be made in terms of yield per unit area or of yield per working day (productivity of labour). The number of working days required to produce a certain quantity of a specified crop can be used as a basis of comparison between the various kinds of rural economy, and the most representative unit is the hundredweight of grain.[4] But only large differences between the indices thus obtained are of any significance.

In a modern economy, agriculture can feed a large number of people while employing a relatively small labour force,[5] but although this feature is characteristic of the advanced countries the reverse is true of primitive economies. Except in countries like England which import large quantities of food, the efficiency of a nation's farming bears an inverse relationship to the proportion of the working population employed on the land. This, however, is only true if the soil is not being exploited wastefully. A further characteristic of modern farming, and of specialized farming in particular, is that the greater part of the produce is marketed. In a primitive economy, on the other hand, almost everything is consumed by the producer himself.

Notes

1 In Norway 'cultivated', i.e. fertilized, grasslands are classified separately.
2 But he is increasingly forced to produce at the lowest possible costs by economic factors.
3 Bergmann defines them in terms of: type of product (crop and animal) and factors of production employed (land, labour, capital).
4 This is not to imply, as some have suggested without proof, that technical progress is limited to this type of product.
5 Food products make up about four-fifths of the world's agricultural output, by value. But industrial raw materials, and, foremost among them, textiles, must also be taken into account if a true picture of overall agricultural productivity is to emerge.

References

Dumont, R. (1949) 'Observations monographiques sur quelques fermes et communes de France', *Bulletin de la Société française d'Économie Rurale*.
Veyret, P. (1951) *La géographie de l'élevage*, Paris.

Related Items

2, 3, 6, 11, 13, 20, 21, 27, 28, 34, 35, 37, 56, 57, 60.

20

Nature, Ecology Movements and Peasant Communities

Gail Omvedt

Ecology – the interlinkages between human society and nature – has been of concern to peasant communities ever since the adoption of agriculture began a process of 'artificialization' of nature.

There is evidence that some of the earliest civilizations, such as the Mayan and Harappan, collapsed because the agricultural systems they were based on ravaged the resources of their environment. Later feudal societies could survive such 'natural disasters' as floods, famines and plagues only at the cost of uncounted lives lost among their peasant producers.

Capitalist development, particularly in the last half of the twentieth century, has impinged on the lives of the world's remaining peasant communities not least through its environmental effects. Huge dams have been built, often at the neglect of village irrigation systems that formerly provided some water to all – displacing hundreds of thousands, leaving reservoirs that silted up, and creating over-irrigated fields liable to salinization, waterlogging and accompanying diseases. Chemical fertilizers and high-yielding varieties of seeds have pushed a 'green revolution' heralded for increasing agricultural productivity – but often at the cost of seeping the spill of its natural nutrients and destroying thousands of indigenous varieties. Peasants and agricultural labourers have provided numerous victims to pesticide and fertilizer poisoning, along with the thousands killed in such disasters as at Bhopal.

Finally, deforestation, which is proceeding at a rapid pace in the Third World, affects both forest-dwelling and plains peasant communities. The plains peasants of northern India lost their village forests long ago to the plunder of colonialism – which is why they burn cow-dung for fuel, thereby depriving their fields of one of its best natural fertilizers. Now they are victims of droughts and flash floods, increasing in recent years owing to the ongoing

An original paper.

deforestation of the hilly regions. As for forest-dwelling communities, whether they were foragers, shifting, or settled cultivators, their traditional way of life is now receiving its final blows from the massive road-building, mining, dam-building, industrial construction and deforestation brought by post-independence capitalist development. 'Social forestry' programmes have actually worsened the situation, for they normally mean imposition of monocultural commercial plantations at the expense of indigenous mixed forests.

It is not surprising, then, that mass 'ecology movements' developed in many Third World countries. In India movements had their beginning with the 'tree-hugging' or *Chipko* movement of Himalayan peasants who threw their bodies in front of trees in 1973 to save them from logging contractors. The movement has expanded to include village-level tree-planting, and fights against alcoholism and for employment. It has formulated the principles that reforestation should be under local control and be based on trees adapted not for commercial purposes but for providing the 'five Fs' – fodder, fuel, fertilizer, fibre and food. In 1978, tribal peasants in south Bihar state initiated a movement to *cut down* trees planted by the government under World Bank programmes – because the teak monocultural plantations were replacing indigenous forests and in particular their multi-purpose and religiously sanctified sal tree. 'Sal is ours, teak is the exploiters,' was the slogan – and it led to confrontations with the police and dozens killed in one case of vicious firing. The Bihar tribals have also opposed the building of dams, as have indigenous people in many parts of the world.

Forest-dwelling communities have often been the first to act on such 'ecological' themes because the links of exploitation are very direct and visible. Peasant communities in plains areas have not found it so easy to trace the social causes behind the floods and droughts they suffer from. In addition, the class divisions created or intensified by capitalist development have hampered their resistance. The rich farmers who benefit from irrigation and cash-crop agriculture, the merchants who profit from distress sales by poor peasants, the technicians and bureaucrats who manage large-scale projects – all find it convenient to hide behind an ideology of 'development'. In India, while movements around issues of drought and dams have very often been led by left political parties, their demands are usually distributional: for jobs, water, relief work, alternative land, etc. They have rarely questioned the direction and nature of the development or focused on the basic causes of droughts, floods or other 'natural disasters'. However, with the increased environmental problems of the 1980s new trends can be seen – alliances of villages opposing the building of a river-polluting factory, mass demands for distributing irrigation water on a widespread basis for food crops rather than let it be monopolized by cash-crops such as sugar-cane. With the growing consciousness among the rural political activists of environmental issues and those concerning new agricultural and community experiments, the future may see a qualitative change in peasant and agricultural labourer movements. One thing is clear: 'ecology' is no longer a middle-class or European–North American pre-occupation.

> **Related Items**

18, 19, 21, 30, 31, 33, 34, 37, 41, 42, 59, 60, 61, 62.

21

Agriculture as a Productive Activity

Mircea Malita

There are four distinct stages in man's productive activities: gatherer, grower, manufacturer, and creator. These coexist today. Man is still a gatherer when he fishes the oceans, a grower in agriculture, a manufacturer in industry, and a creator in scientific research. This scale represents steps of increasing independence of man in relation to nature. Each period has its own specific rules and features. The great revolution in food took place with the passage of mankind from the gathering to the growing stage.

We are now witnessing a vast and significant transition. Fishing, the gatherer's last stronghold, is about to provide the location for systematic cultivation activities, over definite areas and by particular methods of husbandry. The fisherman is becoming a farmer. The technical and scientific revolution is, ultimately, but a massive penetration into industry of the features of scientific discovery. Automation, quick and imaginative adjustment, and a high degree of training are helping to convert the factory into a science laboratory.

The transformation which we are interested in is, however, that of agriculture into industry, which corresponds to the passage from cultivation to manufacturing. All modern changes in agriculture eventually amount to so many reductions of its specific features, which are being replaced by features peculiar to industry. Mechanization is the aspect easiest to grasp. Large-scale introduction of fertilizers, irrigation and high-productivity seeds imply a radical change of attitude rather than a mere attempt to improve the crops. Food production is no longer a natural process occurring in the immense oven of the sun, with man's corrections and amendments, but the result of a typically industrial calculation for turning certain prime factors into a finished product. Man apportions these factors so as to obtain an optimal result. Under such

Excerpts from Mircea Malita, 'Agriculture in the year 2000', *Sociologia Ruralis*, vol. 11, 1971, pp. 301–4.

conditions the producer's intervention is stronger than the facts of nature: any land will become productive, as a possible location for the chemical elements capable of sustaining plants.

The climatic factors seem to remain beyond human control, but they are not so impregnable in the long run. A wide range of plants and vegetables have already been wrenched away from the seasonal cycle. Hothouses are becoming ever more numerous, fields are covered with plastic sheets, meteorology is advancing significantly, heralding the era of climate determination. This escape from the sway of nature, which is specific to industrial production, has begun to characterize the new agriculture. It is not accidental, therefore, that in studies of the year 2000 agriculture is not a subject one often meets. This may be seen as a perception of its forthcoming industrialization and gradual transformation into a different activity, which is, perhaps, entitled to a new name.

Three conclusions emerge from the above remarks:

1   The cycles described are different not only in their features, but also in their types of management. The introduction of the scientific management of enterprises, of computers and programming into industrial production is one symptom of its passage into a scientific phase. One cannot say, however, that agriculture is, to the same degree, undergoing a process of transition towards the methods of classic industrial administration: efficiency, production line methods, concentration or association of capacities, etc. The conservatism inherent in traditional agriculture hinders the introduction of this new administration. Hence the need for a thorough study of the impact of industrial methods on agricultural production.

2   The four cycles are characterized by different rates of expansion. For the gatherer, there can be no expansion. The crop is destroyed cyclically, which leads to nomadism. Cultures mark the first steady, but arithmetical growth. One of Malthus' premises was correct. Industry brings with it geometric expansion. Science, in its turn, is characterized by the highest exponentials. Placing agriculture in a new stage of geometric growth will settle an age-old controversy. The possibility of catering for the needs of an expanding humanity thus finds a new theoretical basis.

3   Finally, if we accept the change of agriculture into an activity with industrial features, we implicitly recognize the importance of labour sociology applied to this passage. The conversion of country people into townspeople is not an isolated phenomenon, but one aspect of the global transfer of man's activities. There is an industrial outlook which the grower must wear as a new garment. Comparative studies on the (rural) grower and the (industrial) manufacturer are not merely exercises whose practical use is restricted to the comprehension and control of certain social phenomena. They could throw light upon the acquisition of a new field of activity, supplying answers of a

practical and economic interest to the question concerning the goals of this activity.

The year 2000 will find the farmer to be an industrialist, and the industrial producer as a scientific research worker.

We shall finally outline the answers to two questions that may legitimately arise. What will become of science? Possibly, mathematical epistemology. And as to agriculture, can it not leap together with industry directly into the realm of science? No, not by the year 2000, no matter how much it may benefit from the results of the latter. One stage which farming must necessarily go through, and which cannot be skipped, is that of industry at the turn of the twentieth century. Yet this is sufficient to help solve the problem of food and make the earth appear as a geometric and artificial structure freed from the terrors and vagaries of nature.

Related Items

1, 2, 3, 7, 9, 13, 16, 17, 18, 19, 20, 22, 27, 37, 53, 55, 59, 60, 61, 62.

22

Crafts and Trades among the Russian Peasantry

Geroid T. Robinson

Whether by choice or by necessity, the peasants were often something more than farmers – sometimes not farmers at all, for millions of them were engaged, at home or in the cities, for a part or all of their time, in self-directed non-agricultural work of some sort, or in agricultural or industrial wage-labour. Among all these activities, the handicrafts of the forest *guberniias* have held a very special interest for students of peasant life, for the reason that these craft-industries belonged in a peculiar sense to the peasantry themselves. The crafts were not free from external influence, and yet in their methods and their products they were still a rich repository of peasant science and peasant art. The workers produced an endless variety of work in wood, bark, cloth, leather, felt, clay and metal, varying in quality from the crudest articles of mass-consumption (wooden snow-shovels, brooms made of twigs, unglazed milk-pots, thick felt boots, heaped up by hundreds in the village markets), to silver ornaments and religious pictures which sometimes fully merited the name of works of art. Production was carried on sometimes quite independently in the peasant's home; sometimes at the order of an entrepreneur who distributed the raw materials to many home-workers, paid for the labour at a piece-rate, and collected and disposed of the product; sometimes, too, in a small shop set up cooperatively by an artel of workers, or maintained by a master who hired other craftsmen to work under his direction. The entire household, men, women, and children, often worked through the short winter day and well into the night, for a beggarly return; but when the brief agricultural season did not yield a living for the peasant family, then to work for less than a subsistence through the long winter months was better than to be altogether idle – and perhaps to be buried in the spring. Strong traditions of the village, close legal restrictions upon the mobility of the peasant, favoured an attempt on his part to find a source of side-earnings in the handicrafts rather than in some distant factory.

Excerpts from Geroid T. Robinson, *Rural Russia under the Old Regime*, Macmillan, 1949, pp. 104–5. First published in 1932.

The craft-industries might still live, even though they did not produce a living; they were generally supplementary to agriculture and, in effect, subsidized by agriculture, and it was this, above all, that enabled them to maintain a footing in a country where the Industrial Revolution was now well under way. Some of the craft-industries had not yet been subjected to factory competition, some survived in spite of competition, some collapsed and disappeared. Exactly what was happening will never be known, in terms of statistical accuracy; the number of persons engaged in handicraft production, though perhaps diminishing toward the turn of the century, still very much exceeded the number employed in the factories; and yet the crafts could not be called prosperous, nor did they offer opportunities of increasing promise to a peasantry hard pressed to find help in one direction or another.

Wage work in agriculture and other rural non-industrial occupations was also an important source of peasant income. . . . It is in the very nature of the highly specialized grain production of Russia that for brief periods it demanded whole armies of extra ploughmen and especially of harvesters, but of these short-term workers the census took no account, nor does there exist a dependable estimate of their number. If there were more than a million and a half of long-term labourers, those hired for the harvest alone probably counted several millions more.

Related Items

2, 10, 18, 27.

23

Labour Shortage in Egyptian Agriculture: A Crisis for Whom?

Elizabeth Taylor-Awny

The migration of Egyptian male labour to Arab states following the oil boom of the early 1970s has given rise to pockets of labour shortages within the domestic labour market. One of the major sectors to have evidenced shortages has been agriculture, which has seen a steep rise in male real wages since the mid-1970s, producing in the terms of the Ministry of Agriculture, 'one of the major crises facing Egyptian agriculture today'. On the basis of eighteen months' fieldwork carried out in one village in 1981/2, the following notes examine the nature of this 'crisis' as it affects agricultural labour markets and production relations in the village.

The village of Dahshur lies on the fringe of the Western Desert, 45 km south of Cairo in the governorate of Giza. The migration of village labour to Arab states began as a trickle at the end of the 1960s. The direction of this early migration flow was to Libya where, in increasing numbers as the 1970s wore on, village labour was incorporated into Libya's expanding agricultural and construction sectors. Until the borders between Libya and Egypt were closed in 1976 most migration was clandestine. Migrants travelled overland, without travel documents or labour contracts. Migration was thus cheap and free from bureaucratic procedures; it was therefore accessible even to the poorest strata of the village – landless agricultural labourers and small peasants, who indeed formed the majority of migrants out of Dahshur until the mid-1970s. After relations between Egypt and Libya further deteriorated following the Camp David agreement between Egypt and Israel, the main direction of migration changed to Saudi Arabia and by the early 1980s had diversified still more to include Jordan and Iraq. From the mid-1970s, the composition of village migrants also increasingly diversified to include labour drawn from most sectors of the village economy. In 1981, about 10 per cent of village households had members working abroad, and about 50 per cent of all migrants were drawn from the agricultural sector.

An original paper.

Of Dahshur's 800 or so households, almost 60 per cent are engaged in agriculture. The main cash-crops cultivated are vegetables, produced primarily for the Cairo market, and clover as fodder, for the local village market. In addition, peasants grow subsistence crops, such as maize and clover, for their own and their animals' consumption. Vegetable production is highly labour-intensive and cultivation is continuous throughout the year, with four or more crops being grown on any one small plot of land. Farming methods are mainly traditional, with only threshing and irrigation being to any significant degree mechanized. In general, then, both the cropping patterns and techniques of farming go to make the demand for agricultural labour in Dahshur amongst the highest in any region in Egypt.

Landholding in Dahshur like that throughout rural Egypt is highly fragmented; 50 per cent of village landholders (compared with 49 per cent on the national level) work less than one feddan (1.038 acres) of land; and 90 per cent work less than three feddans (cf. 82 per cent nationally). The tip of the national land distribution pyramid, the 2 per cent of landholders who farm between 10 and 50 feddans, is not represented in Dahshur, where the largest landholders work just under six feddans. Agricultural production in Dahshur, and across Egypt's agricultural sector, is carried out by two distinct types of farming unit: peasant farms, which are worked primarily by household labour and which produce both for their own consumption and for the market; and capitalist enterprises on which land is farmed solely by hired wage labour and production is for the market. Peasant producers comprise 90 per cent of Dahshur's landholders, the remaining ten per cent farming their land as small-scale capitalist enterprises. Within Egypt's agricultural sector as a whole, peasant producers account for approximately 95 per cent of landholders and farm about two-thirds of Egypt's land. Peasant production thus forms not only the basis of Dahshur's agriculture, but also, in terms of these criteria, is the most important sector of agriculture at the national level.

In spite of the fragmentation of landholdings and the fact that the majority of producers are peasants, hired agricultural labour is an essential component of village agricultural production. For only 12 per cent of Dahshur's peasant producers work their land *solely* by household labour. Although the rest rely primarily on household labour, all use additional labour at peak seasons (which are numerous in this type of vegetable production), and most use some additional labour weekly. The employment of non-household labour is thus not marginal to peasant production in the village, but rather an integral part of the production process.

In the 1950s and 1960s, landless wage labour was by all accounts readily available in the village. Hired for the most part on a casual basis, labourers worked both on capitalist farms and peasant holdings. Today, however, both capitalist and peasant farmers alike are reporting a shortage of agricultural labour. This is confirmed by trends in agricultural wages in the village which have followed the pattern documented at the national level, showing a steep rise in male real wages since the mid-1970s. It is the migration of village labour abroad that is held by Dahshur farmers to be the prime cause of the labour shortage, which some maintain has reached crisis proportions in recent years. However, although all farmers are united in reporting a shortage of agricultural labour, it is clear that the implications of the shortage for the two types of production unit vary considerably.

Capitalist farmers maintain that the labour shortage has meant not only an increase in agricultural wages but also that labour is unavailable in the required quantities for much of the agricultural year. Peasant producers, however, report that although hired male labour is less readily available than in the past, none the less it can always be found. The labour shortage has affected peasants primarily through increased labour costs.

What then needs to be explained is how it is that within the same village, one sector of agriculture, the capitalist, is complaining of an acute tightening of labour supply, while the peasant sector finds little difficulty in meeting its labour needs. The obvious fact that there is a greater dependency on hired labour on capitalist enterprises is not an adequate explanation, for as we have seen hired labour is an integral part of peasant production as well. Fieldwork observations suggest that three factors, all of which impinge differently on the capitalist and peasant sectors, are of significance here: first, the mechanisms available to farmers for regulating the flow of labour out of agriculture; second, the composition and functioning of village agricultural labour markets; and third, the ability of the two sectors to employ substitute labour to compensate for the male wage labour shortage.

Control over Labour Supply

Between 1972 and 1979, Egypt's agricultural labour force declined by 14 per cent, representing a loss of over half a million male workers.[1] Most of this labour has been incorporated either into the labour markets of other Arab states or into the domestic construction industry.[2] The only means available to the capitalist farmer to constrain the flow of wage labour out of agriculture is to raise wages to a competitive level. Real agricultural wages have indeed risen, but still lag behind those of the construction sector and far behind those offered abroad. Meanwhile capitalist farmers are complaining of an un-supportable profit squeeze.

The shift of peasant labour out of agriculture is, however, significantly regulated by the production and reproduction needs of the peasant household. This is clearly apparent in the migration patterns of peasants observed in Dahshur. The departure abroad of one male household member is typically delayed until the return of another, and the role of migrant within the house-hold is assumed in stages according to an evident pattern of priorities. Thus, for example, household heads generally only migrate if their sons are immature; sons take over the migrant role after reaching maturity; and sons nearing the age of marriage assume priority in the 'migrant queue' over those who are younger or already married. Here both the labour requirements of peasant production and the reproduction needs of the household (migration being a common means of accruing the necessary savings for marriage) provide the underlying 'logic' of migration patterns and act as one set of constraints over the flow of labour abroad. This is not to suggest that these constraints are all-powerful. Conflicts between household heads and would-be migrant sons are numerous. However, what is evident is that whereas there has been a wholesale flow of landless wage labour out of agriculture, the requirements of peasant reproduction have significantly impeded the unregulated flow of labour out of the peasant sector.

The Composition and Functioning of the Village Agricultural Labour Market

In the 1950s and 1960s the male agricultural wage labour market, in Dahshur and nationally, comprised primarily the landless or near-landless.[3] Today, landless male labour has virtually disappeared out of agriculture,[4] having been absorbed as previously indicated into the labour markets abroad or into the local construction sector. The male agricultural wage labour market now comprises primarily small peasants. This change in composition of the market has also involved a change in its functioning. For unlike the landless, the small peasant typically enters the wage labour market only *irregularly* and at times dictated by the labour requirements of his own land and his cash needs. These needs may, and often do, clash with those of capitalist production. The peasant, for example, is least available for wage work at peak seasons, when market demands and wages are at their highest. In other words the market no longer functions according to the logic of capitalist production but according to the needs of the peasant household.

These observations based on fieldwork in Dahshur would seem to explain the results of village surveys conducted elsewhere in Egypt. In a study, for example, of five villages in the Delta governorate of Sharqiyya, carried out in 1978/9, Richards et al. found the supply of male agricultural wage labour to be inelastic and non-responsive to wage levels.[5] These survey results would then seem to confirm my own observations and imply that a wage labour market composed primarily of small peasants is not an equivalent substitute to the capitalist farmer for that comprising 'doubly free' landless labour which responds to the demands of capitalist production.

Alternative Labour Supplies

In the 1950s and 1960s both peasants and capitalist farmers were assured an abundant supply of male labour in the wage labour market, a market which I have suggested has now not only 'tightened' but changed in its functioning. Female wage labour is however still readily available since village women have neither migrated nor shifted in significant numbers out of agriculture into other sectors of the economy. The female wage labour market in Dahshur comprises primarily widows, divorcees and female household members of unsuccessful peasant and landless migrants. These women maintain that employment opportunities fall short of their availability for work. Elsewhere in Egypt a surplus of female wage labour, at least seasonally, has likewise been reported.[6] However, in Dahshur, as in other regions recently surveyed, a rigid division of labour still pertains in the wage labour market.[7] In spite of the shortfall in supply of male labour, and in spite of the surplus of female and child labour, women and children are not performing tasks traditionally defined as male. Farmers are therefore not able to substitute non-male for male *wage* labour.

Within the peasant household, however, no such rigid division of labour pertains. In situations of labour crisis women and children frequently perform tasks normally undertaken by men. On their own land, for example, it is not uncommon to find women employed in one of the most strenuous of 'male' agricultural tasks – operating the *tanbour* (Archimedes' screw) used to raise irrigation water, although as wage labour this would only be performed by men. Peasants are therefore able to compensate for the lack of a cheap and readily available supply of male wage labour, not only by intensifying the labour input of their own household males, but also by deploying female and child family members in 'male' tasks. Dependent solely on the wage labour market, capitalist farmers are unable to employ women and children as substitute labour.

Studies of Egyptian agricultural labour in the 1960s concluded that surplus male labour was 'locked into' peasant households.[8] In spite of the tightening of agricultural labour markets this would still seem to pertain in Dahshur today. Much of this surplus labour does not enter the wage labour market and therefore cannot be tapped by capitalist farmers. Peasants are, however, able to make use of this surplus by entering into *exchange labour relations* with other specific, and often related, peasant households. Such exchange relations now normally involve the payment of a 'wage' in cash and/or in kind, but the obligation to return labour remains the basis of the arrangement. Having no household labour of their own to exchange, capitalist farmers are unable to enter into such relations. Peasants are thus able to draw on surplus labour outside their own households and outside the wage labour market by means inaccessible to capitalist farmers.

In response to the labour shortage peasants are employing strategies which although not those of capitalist economics none the less make good economic sense. Indeed, in both their ability to regulate the flow of labour out of agricultural production and in their ability to deploy remaining labour supplies, peasant producers in Dahshur stand in an advantageous position compared to that of capitalist farmers. The labour 'shortage' has thus unevenly impinged on the two sectors of agriculture within the village – a point further confirmed by the different responses of the two types of production unit to the shortage.

In response to the tightening of wage labour supply and to increased labour costs peasants in Dahshur may, in some seasons, grow less labour-intensive crops. From peasant accounts, for example, the extension of land given over to clover in the village in recent years is not only a response to higher market prices but also to the fact that clover requires a lower labour input than most vegetables. In addition, due to the less readily abundant supply of non-household labour, some agricultural tasks may be delayed beyond their optimum timing. The yields of most crops have, however, continued to rise for the period 1975–80, and at the same, or somewhat higher rate than for the preceding five years.[9] Peasant production shows no sign of having been 'critically' affected by the labour shortage.

Capitalist production in the village has, however, been threatened as a *form*. For in response to the labour shortage, capitalist farmers are increasingly renting out all or part of their land to peasants. The type of tenancy arrangement takes one of two forms: various types of share-cropping agreement, or the leasing out of land for one crop against a cash rent in advance determined by the value of the crop to be cultivated. In both cases the renting out is on a seasonal basis to avoid the relatively low annual rents fixed by land reform law and also to avoid the possibility of a sitting tenant. By these means, land worked by capitalist farmers is increasingly being brought under peasant production and peasants in recent years have gained increased access to village land. As a result of the labour shortage, then, a 'peasantization' of agriculture has occurred in the village.

At the national level, the share of land worked by peasants in recent years has also increased, along with a concomitant decline in the share worked by capitalist farmers (cf. table 23.1). From holding just over half of the total agricultural land in 1965, in 1977/8 peasants worked 67 per cent. Over the same period the share of land *owned* by peasants has declined from 57 per cent in 1965, to 52 per cent in 1977/8. Peasants' increased access to land has thus been achieved by the renting in of land from capitalist farmers.

The net renting in of land by the peasant sector evident since 1965 runs contrary to the trend of previous years. For between 1952 and 1965, the overall trend was that of a net leasing out of peasant land to the capitalist sector, i.e. for small plots of peasant land to be consolidated into landholdings of larger capitalist enterprises. The increased 'peasantization' of Egypt's agriculture

TABLE 23.1 *Share of total agricultural land owned and worked by peasants 1952–1977*

	1952 (prior to land reform)	1961 (after land reform law)	1965	1977/8
% land owned by peasants[a]	35	52	57	52
% land farmed by peasants	23[b]	38	52	67

[a] Peasants are here equated with owners or holders of less than five feddans of land. This crude identification of production relations based on farm size is conventionally made, and is based on the 1961 Agricultural Census which shows that farms under five feddans are predominantly worked by household labour.

[b] As no data on landholdings in 1952 are available, the figure used here is for 1950.

Sources: Data on land ownership: 1952-65 *Statistical Yearbook, 1978*, CAMPAS, Cairo; 1977/8 B. Hansen and S. Radwan (1982) *Employment Opportunities and Equity in Egypt*, ILO, Geneva, 1982, p. 107. Data on landholdings: 1950 and 1961 *Economic Bulletin*, National Bank of Egypt, vol. 31, no. 4 (1978); 1965 and 1977/8 Agricultural Census Section of the Ministry of Agriculture, Cairo.

since 1965, whereby land owned by capitalist farmers has been brought under peasant production, thus represents a reversal of previous trends.

These observations suggest that even in situations in which capitalist agriculture exists alongside a peasant sector incorporating surplus labour, capitalist farming is highly vulnerable if landless or near-landless labour is not readily abundant. For where peasant production is thriving, the wage labour of small peasants is not an equivalent substitute for landless wage labour.

Notes

1 Cf. B. Hansen and S. Radwan (1982) *Employment Opportunities and Equity in Egypt*, ILO, Geneva, pp. 59, 60.
2 G. Amin and E. Taylor-Awny (1985), *International Migration of Egyptian Labour*, IDRC, Ottawa.
3 *Agricultural Census, 1961*, Ministry of Agriculture, Cairo and A. Mohie-Eldin, 'The development of the share of agricultural wage labour in the national income of Egypt', in G. Abdel-Khalek and R. Tignor (eds) (1982) *The Political Economy of Income Distribution in Egypt*, New York and London.
4 G. Amin and E. Taylor-Awny, *International Migration*, pp. 252–3.
5 A. Richards, P. Martin and R. Nagaar (1983) 'Labour shortages in Egyptian agriculture', in A. Richards and P. Martin (eds) *Migration, Mechanisation and Agricultural Labour Markets in Egypt*, Colorado and Cairo.
6 Ibid.
7 Ibid.

8 E.g. A. Mohie-Eldin (1976) 'Underemployment in Egyptian agriculture', in *Manpower and Employment in Arab Countries*, ILO, Geneva.
9 Crop yield records, Agricultural Administration, Badrashin, Giza and Department of Agricultural Statistics, Ministry of Agriculture, Cairo.

Related Items

1, 2, 3, 4, 9, 13, 17, 18, 25, 26, 32, 36, 52, 53, 54, 55, 56, 57, 59, 60, 61, 62.

24

Rural Credit in Peasant Societies

Susan George

In the sphere of credit the small Third World farmer again gets the short end of the stick. In Latin America just the top 15 per cent of the farming community has access to state or private credit, while in Africa there is only 5 per cent. In most underdeveloped countries, very little credit is available to the agricultural sector *as a whole* – rich or poor. There is *no* credit available to some 100 million small farmers who are worst off because they are considered poor risks and because the lending institutions don't want to be bothered with the administrative expenses of setting up very small – to them – loans. 'In countries as disparate as Bangladesh and Iran, less than 10 per cent of institutional credit is available in rural areas; in Thailand, the Philippines and Mexico less than 15 per cent; in India less than 25 per cent. And only a fraction of this is available to the small farmer,' says Robert McNamara.

The result is that the average small farmer invests only about $6 per hectare – if he can afford that – when to get a halfway decent yield he should be spending anywhere from $20 to $80 on vital inputs. The smallholder is trapped coming and going, because he is financially strapped: he must sell his crop immediately after harvest when prices are at their lowest. He is indebted to the local usurer who 'tides him over' – for an exorbitant fee – between harvests. Even supposedly 'free' farmers who are neither share-croppers, squatters or landless can thus be reduced to peonage by the lack of a credit system worthy of the name. Agricultural extension services, sometimes managed or influenced by the international agribusinesses that sell inputs, also tend to benefit the larger landholders on a priority basis.

The smaller farmer in an underdeveloped country who cannot make ends meet usually has only one alternative to starvation – and that is the unsavoury 'private credit' network. . . . Smallholders are paying anywhere from three to twenty times as much for credit from the money-lender as they would have to pay a bank – if it would condescend to look at them. In a tiny minority of

Excerpt from Susan George, *How the Other Half Dies*, Penguin, 1976.

underdeveloped countries, a substantial number of small farmers can get normal bank credit: in Taiwan 95 per cent, in South Korea 40 per cent, in Colombia 30 per cent. But in Ethiopia, Nigeria and Malaysia only 1 or 2 per cent. Not surprisingly, the small farmers in these countries must then pay whopping rates for private credit: yearly interest rates in Ethiopia are (were?) 66 per cent, in Malaysia 58 per cent; while first prize for all countries goes to Nigeria, where usurers can get no less than 192 per cent interest per annum.

Related Items

6, 16, 17, 21, 28, 29, 31, 32, 39, 46, 50, 51, 53, 55, 56.

25

Chayanov and the Theory of Peasant Economies

Basile Kerblay

For some decades after its establishment in the 1870s the Russian provincial administration (the *zemstva*) conducted a series of detailed surveys of the peasantry, published in more than 4,000 volumes. On the basis of this extensive literature there emerged a flourishing school of agricultural economists who continued to play an influential role in Russia up to the end of the NEP in the 1920s. Their main aim was to help the peasant modernize his farming techniques. In contrast with Populists and Marxists, both of whom saw the agrarian problem in terms of property relations, they felt that land redistribution was an insufficient palliative (and implied a social upheaval whose consequences could not be predicted). They stressed the need to transform the entire organization of peasant agriculture by a series of essentially 'Western' innovations such as cooperatives, stock selection and the use of fertilizers, etc. This is the reason why they have been called 'the organization and production school'. Among them were A. Chelintsev, A. Chayanov, N. Makarov and many more.

Kossinsky (1906, p. 165)[1] and Brutskus (1913) of that group were the first to contrast the peasant and capitalist economies not so much on the political plane as on the plane of economic theory.

But, it was Chayanov's genius to formulate, from *zemstva* data, the theory of a specific peasant economy (i.e. peasant ownership but *without hired labour*) as an economic system *sui generis*. He tried to show that to the distinctive categories and modes of production Marx had recognized (slavery, feudalism, capitalism, socialism) there should be added another: the peasant economy.

Alexander Vasil´evich Chayanov was a man of wide interests. He wrote not only in the realm of economics and rural sociology but also in art, history and literature.[2] He became, after the Revolution, director of the Institute of Agricultural Economy. But as Soviet agricultural policy drew to an extensive collectivization he was increasingly attacked as a petit bourgeois idealizer of

An original paper.

peasant economy and a pro-*kulak* ideologist. In 1930 Chayanov was arrested and he died in 1939.

Chayanov's main contribution was firstly to provide a theory of peasant behaviour at the level of the individual family farm, and secondly to show that at the national level peasant economy ought to be treated as an economic system in its own right, and not, as the Marxists claimed, as a form of incipient capitalism, represented by petty commodity production. In Chayanov's view peasant motivations are different from those of the capitalist; they aim at securing the needs of the family rather than making a profit. That is why a central role is given in Chayanov's theory to the notion of balance between subsistence needs and a subjective distaste for manual labour (dis-utility) for this determines the intensity of cultivation and the size of the net product.

Chayanov proceeds to show that the prevailing concepts of classical economics as well as the marginalist theory explaining the behaviour of a capitalist entrepreneur do not apply in a peasant family which depends solely on the work of its own family members.[3] For in this type of farm the decreasing returns of the value of marginal labour do not hinder the peasant's activity so long as the needs of his family are not satisfied; that is, when an equilibrium has been achieved between needs and the drudgery of his effort.

All the principles of our theory, rent, capital, price and other categories have been formed in the framework of an economy based on wage labour and seeking to maximize profits. ... But we must by no means extend its application to all phenomena in our economic life. We know that most peasant farms in Russia, China, India and most non-European and even many European states are unacquainted with the categories of wage-labour and wages. The economic theory of modern capitalist society is a complicated system of economic categories inseparably connected with one another: price, capital, wages, interest, rent, which determine one another and are functionally interdependent. If one brick drops out of this system the whole building collapses.

In a natural economy human economic activity is dominated by the requirement of satisfying the needs of a single production unit, which is at the same time a consumer unit; therefore budgeting here is to a high degree *qualitative* ... quantity here can be calculated only by considering the extent of each single need. ... Therefore, the question of comparative profitability of various expenditures cannot arise – for example, whether growing hemp or grass would be more profitable or advantageous for these plant products are not interchangeable and cannot be substituted for each other.

On the family farm, the family equipped with means of production uses its labour power to cultivate the soil and receives, as a result of a year's work, a certain amount of goods. A single glance at the inner structure of the labour unit is enough to realize that it is impossible, without the category of wages, to impose on its structure net profit, rent and interest on capital as real economic categories in the capitalist meaning of the word. ... Thus it is impossible to apply the capitalist profit calculation. (Chayanov, 1925, pp. 1–5)

Chayanov saw no validity in circumventing the absence of wages by imputing values to unpaid family labour. The annual product minus outlays is indivisible and undifferentiated. It could not be broken down into wages and other factor payments.

The family labour product (the increase in value of material goods which the family has acquired by its work during the year, or, to put it differently, their labour product) is the only possible category of income for a peasant or artisan working family unit. . . . The amount of labour product is mainly determined by the size and the composition of the working family, the number of its members capable of work, then by the productivity of the labour unit and – this is especially important – by the degree of labour effort, the degree of self exploitation through which the working members effect a certain quantity of labour units in the course of the year. . . . Thorough empirical studies on peasant farms in Russia and other countries have enabled us to substantiate the following thesis: the degree of self exploitation is determined by a peculiar equilibrium between family demand satisfaction and the drudgery of labour itself. . . . It is obvious that with the increase in produce obtained by hard work the subjective valuation of each newly gained rouble's significance for consumption decreases, but the drudgery of working for it which will demand an ever greater amount of self exploitation will increase. . . . As soon as the equilibrium point is reached continuing to work becomes pointless. . . . Farm size and composition and the urgency of its demands determine the consumption evaluation. . . . The significance of each rouble gross income for consumption is increased in a household burdened with members incapable of work. This makes for increased self exploitation of family labour power. . . . Thus the objective arithmetical calculation of the highest possible net profit in the given market situation does not determine the whole activity of the family unit: this is done by the internal economic confrontation of *subjective evaluations*. (Chayanov, 1925, pp. 5–7)

The peasant producer would make an increased effort only if he had reason to believe it would yield a greater output which could be devoted to enlarged investment or consumption, but he does not push the drudgery beyond the point where the possible increase in output is outweighed by the irksomeness of the extra work. That is why this social mechanism has been called labour–consumer balance. Chayanov showed how, for different families, the balance between consumer satisfaction and the drudgery involved is affected by the size of the family and the ratio of working members to non-working members, and analysed effort curves and consumption–demand curves. He calculated also in what conditions the machine is preferable to manual labour for a peasant economy. He particularly emphasized the fact that calculations of the limits of possible land improvements for peasant economies must take into account the cost of the land and not the foreseeable increase in the rent, for in a peasant economy the prices agreed for the purchase of land or for land improvements are not set at the level represented by the capitalization of the rent as in a capitalist economy. That is why Chayanov concluded that the practical range of land improvements is larger for a peasant than for a capitalist economy.

In the capitalist economy land and labour are the variable factors which the entrepreneur tries to combine to obtain the maximum remuneration from his capital, considered as a fixed factor. In a typical peasant economy labour, proportionate to the size of the family, is the stable element which determines the change in the volume of capital and land.

For the capitalist entrepreneur the sum of values that serves to renew the work force is, from his private economic view-point, indistinguishable from other parts of the capital advanced to the undertaking, and is determined by the objective national economic category of wages and number of workers required for the particular volume of activity. This in its turn is determined by the total size of entrepreneur's capital. (Chayanov, 1925, p. 197)

It is obvious that the family labour unit considers capital investment advantageous only if it affords the possibility of a higher level of well-being; otherwise it re-establishes the equilibrium between drudgery of labour and demand satisfaction. (Chayanov, 1925, pp. 10–11)

Our analysis of the on-farm equilibrium's influence on capital circulation on the family farm enables us to formulate the following propositions:
   At any particular level of technology and in a particular market situation, any working family unit able to control the amount of land for use can increase its labour productivity by increasing to a certain level optimal for this family. Any forcing up of capital intensity beyond the optimum increases labour drudgery and even reduces its payment, since, on the one hand, increased expenditure to replace exhausted capital will counteract the useful effect of further capital intensification, while on the other, the economic realization of this capital requires the farm family to intensify its labour more than is permitted by the equilibrium of on-farm factors. (Chayanov, 1925, pp. 222–3)

From this thesis a distinct theory of social differentiation and mobility has been derived. Chayanov traced the natural history of the family (from the time of marriage of the young couple through the growth of the children to working age, etc.) and stressed demographic differentiation in contrast to the Marxist concept of class differentiation of·the peasantry.

Only by taking the family through the full extent of its development starting at birth and finishing at death, can we understand the basic laws of its composition. If we take it that a surviving child is born every third year in a young family . . . we should try to explain how the relationship of the family labour force to its consumer demands changes as the family develops. (See tables.)

We note a rapid increase in the proportion of consumers to workers. In the fourteenth year of the family's existence, this proportion reaches its highest point, 1.94. But in the fifteenth year the first child comes to the aid of the parents when he has reached semi-working age and the consumer–worker ratio immediately falls to 1.64. . . . In the twenty-sixth year of the family's existence, the ratio falls to 1.32. . . . Since the working family's basic stimulus to economic activity is the necessity to satisfy the demands of its consumers and its work hands are the chief means for this we ought first of all to expect the family's volume of economic activity quantitatively to correspond more or less to these basic elements in family composition. (Chayanov, 1925, p. 60)

TABLE 25.1 *Family members' ages in different years*

Years of family's existence	Husband	Wife	Age of children									Number of persons
			1st	2nd	3rd	4th	5th	6th	7th	8th	9th	
1	25	20										2
2	26	21	1									3
3	27	22	2									3
4	28	23	3									3
5	29	24	4	1								4
6	30	25	5	2								4
7	31	26	6	3								4
8	32	27	7	4	1							5
9	33	28	8	5	2							5
10	34	29	9	6	3							5
11	35	30	10	7	4	1						6
12	36	31	11	8	5	2						6
13	37	32	12	9	6	3						6
14	38	33	13	10	7	4	1					7
15	39	34	14	11	8	5	2					7
16	40	35	15	12	9	6	3					7
17	41	36	16	13	10	7	4	1				8
18	42	37	17	14	11	8	5	2				8
19	43	38	18	15	12	9	6	3				8
20	44	39	19	16	13	10	7	4	1			9
21	45	40	20	17	14	11	8	5	2			9
22	46	41	21	18	15	12	9	6	3			9
23	47	42	22	19	16	13	10	7	4	1		10
24	48	43	23	20	17	14	11	8	5	2		10
25	49	44	24	21	18	15	12	9	6	3		10
26	50	45	25	22	19	16	13	10	7	4	1	11

Source: Chayanov, 1925, p. 57.

Taking the sown area as a measure of peasant wealth and the volume of economic activity, Chayanov shows a clearly expressed dependence between development of a peasant family and the size of area sown by it. He supports his proof with regional statistics of the evolution of peasant holdings and families from 1882 to 1911.

When we study the dynamics of these farms with the view that family size is entirely determined by its economic situation we might expect that farms sowing small areas will in the course of fifteen years continue to sow the same small areas and that farms well endowed will as before sow large areas and retain a large family. The works of Chernenkov, Khryashcheva, Vikhlyaev, Kushchenko and others, however, tell us

TABLE 25.2 *Family members expressed in accounting consumer-work units*

Years of family's existence	Married couple	Children									Total in family		Consumers/ workers
		1	2	3	4	5	6	7	8	9	Consumers	Workers	
1	1.8										1.8	1.8	1.00
2	1.8	0.1									1.9	1.8	1.06
3	1.8	0.3									2.1	1.8	1.17
4	1.8	0.3									2.1	1.8	1.17
5	1.8	0.3	0.1								2.2	1.8	1.22
6	1.8	0.3	0.3								2.4	1.8	1.33
7	1.8	0.3	0.3								2.4	1.8	1.33
8	1.8	0.3	0.3	0.1							2.5	1.8	1.39
9	1.8	0.5	0.3	0.3							2.9	1.8	1.61
10	1.8	0.5	0.3	0.3							2.9	1.8	1.61
11	1.8	0.5	0.3	0.3	0.1						3.0	1.8	1.66
12	1.8	0.5	0.5	0.3	0.3						3.4	1.8	1.88
13	1.8	0.5	0.5	0.3	0.3						3.4	1.8	1.88
14	1.8	0.5	0.5	0.3	0.3	0.1					3.5	1.8	1.94
15	1.8	0.7	0.5	0.5	0.3	0.3					4.1	2.5	1.64
16	1.8	0.7	0.5	0.5	0.3	0.3					4.1	2.5	1.64
17	1.8	0.7	0.5	0.5	0.3	0.3	0.1				4.2	2.5	1.68
18	1.8	0.7	0.7	0.5	0.5	0.3	0.3				4.8	3.2	1.50
19	1.8	0.7	0.7	0.5	0.5	0.3	0.3				4.8	3.2	1.50
20	1.8	0.9	0.7	0.5	0.5	0.3	0.3	0.1			5.1	3.4	1.50
21	1.8	0.9	0.7	0.7	0.5	0.5	0.3	0.3			5.7	4.1	1.39
22	1.8	0.9	0.7	0.7	0.5	0.5	0.3	0.3			5.7	4.1	1.39
23	1.8	0.9	0.7	0.7	0.5	0.5	0.3	0.3	0.1		6.0	4.3	1.39
24	1.8	0.9	0.9	0.7	0.5	0.5	0.5	0.3	0.3		6.6	5.0	1.32
25	1.8	0.9	0.9	0.7	0.5	0.5	0.5	0.3	0.3		6.6	5.0	1.32
26	1.8	0.9	0.9	0.9	0.7	0.5	0.5	0.3	0.3	0.1	6.9	5.2	1.32

Source: Chayanov, 1925, p. 58.

Basile Kerblay

TABLE 25.3 *Areas sown in 1911 by 1882 area groups (%)*

Desyatinas sown in 1882	Desyatinas sown in 1911					
	0–3	3–6	6–9	9–12	12	Total
0–3	28.2	47.0	20.0	2.4	100	
3–6	21.8	47.5	24.4	8.2	2.4	100
6–9	16.2	37.0	26.8	11.3	2.4	100
9–12	9.6	35.8	26.1	12.4	16.1	100
12	3.5	30.5	28.5	15.6	21.9	100

Source: Chayanov, 1925, p. 67.

something completely different as may be seen from the table [25.3]3 comparing the 1882 and 1911 censuses for Surazh uezd, Chernigov guberniya.

We see that a considerable part of the farms that sowed small areas gradually acquired a labour force as family age and size increased and by expanding their sown area passed into the higher groups thus also expanding the volume of their activity. Conversely, former large farms passed into lower groups corresponding to small families created after division. This shows us that demographic process of growth and family distribution by size also determine to a considerable extent the distribution of farms by size of sown area and livestock numbers. . . .

In saying this of course we are not removing from our usage the concept of social differentiation; but this form of differentiation is not to be seen simply by grouping by sown areas; it has to be studied by . . . direct analysis of capitalist factors in the organization of production, i.e. hired labour on farms, not brought in to help their own, but as the basis on which to obtain unearned income and oppressive rents and usurer's credit. (Chayanov, 1925, pp. 67, 68)

Whereas the majority of Marxist economists believed in the advantages of concentration because such is the tendency of the capitalist mode of production, Chayanov maintained that horizontal concentration of production offered only limited advantages in agriculture. In an area of extensive cultivation where 2,000–8,000 hectares of grain land can be farmed with appropriate machinery, the optimal dimensions of productive units will not be the same as they are in a region of sugar-beet cultivation where the more intensive use of machines makes transport costs grow disproportionately beyond an optimum of 200–250 hectares. In other words, natural conditions themselves impose certain limits on the possibilities of a horizontal concentration. These difficulties disappear, however, for vertical integration: small farms can benefit from all the advantages of scale by using the formula of cooperatives. That is why the competitive power of peasant farms versus capitalist farms or collective farms was much greater.

The whole point of this vertical integration was to reconcile the maintenance of peasant farms in the biological processes of intensive cultivation and livestock breeding where they were more productive than capitalist units with the requirement of technical progress, where the large enterprise had an advantage in mechanization and marketing. Chayanov had doubts about collective agriculture because the incentive problem had been solved more flexibly by cooperatives based on small family farms with their individuality intact than by the artels. Socialist society according to him had not yet found the stimuli that would impel the production units to attain their optimal organization and the economy was destined to be the victim of a gigantic bureaucracy.

The dynamic processes of agricultural proletarization and concentration of production, leading to large-scale agricultural production units based on hired labour are developing through the world and in the USSR in particular, at a rate much slower than was expected at the end of the nineteenth century. . . .

The sole form of horizontal concentration that at the present time may, and actually does, take place is the concentration of peasant lands into large-scale production units . . . but it is not and cannot be of such massive size that we would be able to construct on it our whole policy of agricultural concentration. Therefore, the main form for the concentration of peasant farms can be only vertical concentration and, moreover, in its co-operative forms, since only in these forms will it be organically linked with agricultural production and be able to spread to its proper extent and depth. (Chayanov, 1925, pp. 257, 267)

Many of Chayanov's views were questioned by a variety of scholars. For example, he sometimes confuses the optimal dimension of an enterprise with the optimal dimension of cultivated areas or considers the peasant economy as a static entity independent of possible capitalistic environments, etc. He has also often shown more indulgence to the traditional peasant economy than to the future of industrial agriculture, yet one can hardly accuse him of simply turning his back on progress. In the chapter that Chayanov wrote in 1928 for the collection of essays on *Life and Technology in the Future*, he foresaw the prospect offered in a more or less distant future by soil-less agriculture, by factories for food products and synthetic textiles. He also predicted that man would be able to control the climate and forecast harvests.

Chayanov's theory was devised to take account of Russian conditions and, as Daniel Thorner has shown, works better for thinly populated countries than for densely populated ones where peasants could not readily buy or take in more land. Nevertheless the problem raised over forty years ago by the leader of the Russian organizational school, and the basic approach focusing analysis of peasant economies on the dynamics and structures of family farms, are just as pertinent today for developing countries where peasant economies still predominate.

Notes

1 'The peasant, by providing simultaneously land and labour, does not differentiate the value created in the process of production between costs of production and surplus value. All the value thus created returns to him to be used as a whole and is the equivalent of wages and the capitalist's surplus value. This is why the idea of surplus value and of interest on capital is foreign to him. He considers his net income as the product of his own labour.'
2 Several of Chayanov's studies have been published in German, in English (Chayanov, 1925) and Japanese. Eight volumes of selected studies by Chayanov are available in Russian: *Oeuvres choisies de A. V. Chayanov* (1967).
3 For the same reason, according to Chayanov, the accounting methods used in Western Europe at the time – see for example Laur, 1904 – do not apply in weakly monetized economies like those in Russia.

References

Brutskus, B. (1913) *Ocherki krest'yanskogo khozyaistva v zapadnoi evrope*.
Chayanov, A. V. (1925) *Organizatsiya krest'yanskogo khozyaistva*. Translated as *The Theory of Peasant Economy*, D. Thorner, R. E. F. Smith and B. Kerblay (eds), Irwin, 1966.
Chayanov, A. V. (1967) *Oeuvres choisies de A. V. Chayanov*, Johnson reprint, S.R. Publishers, Mouton.
Kossinsky, V. A. (1906) *K agrarnomu voprosu*, Odessa.
Laur, E. (1904) *Landwirtschäftliche Buchhaltung bäuerliche Verhältnisse*.

Related Items

1, 2, 3, 6, 9, 13, 14, 16, 17, 18, 21, 22, 23, 31, 32, 37, 49, 51, 53, 55, 60, 61, 62.

26

Peasantry and Capitalism: A Marxist Discourse

Hamza Alavi

In a commonsensical way people would have little difficulty in picturing what they mean by the word 'peasant', although academics have devoted much effort to figuring out a precise definition. Given differences in conditions in which particular peasant communities are located, whether in their ecology or in the economic and political regimes under which they function, they will differ. There may be differences also between categories of peasants within communities. Nevertheless, the word 'peasant' has a semantic core, a continuity of meaning, that locates it, as a category that embraces rural cultivators of different times and epochs. That essential component of its definition lies in the unity of the peasant family farm as a unit of production as well as that of consumption.

Much of the debate about the peasantry has been concerned with the question whether peasant production has a distinctive economic logic of its own that is different from that of non-peasant production. There are two features, in particular, that are central to this debate. Firstly, members of the peasant family participate in the division of labour on the family farm for which they are not paid either a time wage or individually on the basis of piecework. The benefits as well as the tasks of the peasant farm economy are shared by the whole family, on the basis of generalized reciprocity i.e. all produce goes into a common pool from which the needs of the family as a whole are met, under the authority of the family patriarch. Secondly, peasants produce a large part of their own subsistence requirements as well as some inputs, on the farm. To that extent they are independent of the market and have a capacity to survive, to a degree, in the face of adverse market conditions. This second feature distinguishes the peasant economy from that of urban petty commodity producers (craftsmen), who must buy their inputs from the market and sell their products likewise, before they can secure their subsistence. It is argued that peasant responses to changes in market conditions are different from those

An original paper.

that are expected by economic logic. The various propositions of that debate refer, by their nature, to an historically specific peasantry that is located within a well developed market economy, and, in particular, within capitalism (cf. A. V. Chayanov, Teodor Shanin and Mark Harrison in the Further Reading List). We do not propose to pursue this Chayanovian debate here. Our object rather is to examine the manner in which the impact of capital transforms the structures and operation of pre-capitalist peasant societies.

We may begin therefore by considering briefly different types of pre-capitalist societies of which the peasantry is a major component. Marxist theoretical discourse would distinguish between the different 'modes of production' within which particular peasant societies are located.[1] The concept 'mode of production' refers to social relations on which production and the mode of appropriation of the product are based. It denotes a particular set of social relations between the direct producers and a class of non-producers who appropriate the surplus product, and the basis on which the surplus is extracted. For example we have one set of relations between feudal lords and their unfree serfs and rather different ones between capitalists and the free labourers working for them. The concept of a particular mode of production entails its specific economic, political and ideological conditions on the basis of which its social relations are reproduced. In each case, these conditions constitute, together, a single articulated structure, an 'organic unity'. Peasants were found in a variety of pre-capitalist modes of production and now they operate also within the capitalist mode of production which has spread globally and dissolved pre-capitalist modes of production virtually everywhere in the world. In each case there are differences in the ways in which they function and relate to their own and the wider world.

For our present purposes we may take note of three *pre-capitalist modes of production* in which peasants were to be found. The pre-capitalist mode of production that existed before the impact of colonial capital which was most common in many parts of Africa, for example, was that of relatively unstratified, 'segmentary', communities of independent small peasants. Their economy centred primarily on the domestic household, but not exclusively so for the division of labour for certain purposes and, especially, their political system involved wider groupings, such as lineages and clans or the village community. Such small peasant societies tended to remain relatively egalitarian, for the peasant family farm, as an economic and social unit, was reproduced generationally, so long as land was available to settle each new family when young peasants married. The family farm was replicated generation by generation and produced primarily for self-consumption. Peasant communities produced not only agricultural commodities but also a varied assortment of articles that they needed, such as clothing and simple tools, making them virtually self-sufficient. Surplus goods were exchanged, by means of gifts as well as barter and sale in local markets; long distance trade, if any, was marginal to their economies. The peasant economy was essentially self-sufficient, a condition that has sometimes been referred to as a 'natural economy', which is geared to the production of 'use values', instead of commodities for exchange. These small and localized societies constituted the widest social units for their members, unlike those that we shall describe below. Sahlins designates their structure as the *Domestic mode of production*, although he inappropriately extends the concept to the contemporary peasantry also, which is incorporated into global capitalism (Sahlins, 1972). Samir Amin labels them *Primitive communal modes of production* (Amin, 1976). Such peasant communities were ordinarily self-governing and relatively undifferentiated and free from exploitation by other classes, although a degree of stratification and structures of domination were sometimes found amongst them (Fortes and Evans-Pritchard, 1941).

Another pre-capitalist mode is the *Asiatic mode of production*, although examples of such modes of production were not found in Asia alone. Samir Amin refers to them as *Tribute-paying modes of production* (Amin, 1976, chapter 1) which sounds more appropriate. Its principal feature was that a superior external force subordinated small peasant communities and extracted tribute from them through the exercise of state power. In this mode of production, at the local level, peasants remained organized in the form of internally self-governing and relatively self-sufficient corporate communities. The state which extracted a surplus from them, and the ruling class amongst whom it was distributed, were external to the peasant community.

Finally, a third pre-capitalist mode of production that is relevant to our present discussion is the *Feudal mode of production*, where peasants were enserfed by a lord, to whom they rendered tribute which took a variety of forms, its classic form being one where the serf possessed his own land which he cultivated for his subsistence but, at the same time, he was under obligation to render labour services for the cultivation of the lord's ('demesne') land. The key condition of the feudal mode of production was its requirement that the peasant was *unfree*, i.e. he was not free to leave his lord and seek his livelihood elsewhere. If he were to run away, the lord had the right to pursue the fugitive and reclaim him. The feudal mode of production tended to develop several strata of lords and overlords, the entire hierarchy crowned by a king, and supported in the ideological sphere by lords of religion. Despite such superstructures of feudal societies, the locus of power, economic, social and political, was essentially local. The basic condition of the feudal mode of production was the fusion of economic and political power at the point of production, of the lord over the peasant, with relatively little scope for outside mediation. It was the lords who inhabited wider domains of political and social life. English feudalism, for example, was based on the local manor, ruled over by the manorial lord through manorial courts. The manorial economy was largely self-sufficient, although a part of the surplus extracted by the lord found its way to urban markets to finance his purchases. The age of feudalism was also one that coincided with the rise of world commerce and early colonial conquests.

Capitalism began to develop in the womb of feudal society. As it developed there was a conflict between the dominant classes located in the respective modes of production culminating in bourgeois revolutions, violent or otherwise, when feudal structures were dissolved and replaced by structures of the capitalist mode of production. The central feature of that transformation was the separation of the producer from the means of production and the creation of 'free' labour; free in a double sense, namely free not only from feudal obligations but also 'free' from the possession of the means of production (land). Marx illustrated this process by referring to the enclosure movement in England when peasants were evicted from the land, thus creating a mass of dispossessed free labourers available for industrial employment (Marx, 1976, chapters 26 and 27, pp. 873 ff.). But this was by no means the only process that generated a supply of free labour for employment in industry. Not enough account is taken of the large mass of labour power that was extracted from the peasant societies all over Europe to fuel the industrial development of Western Europe and the USA, which drew on the peasantry from all over Europe for their supply of labour power. The labour of Irish peasants has catered to the needs of British capitalism to this day. The processes through which this was achieved has yet to be treated adequately in theoretical analyses.

In colonies with a 'feudal' structure, such as India, where indigenous industrial capitalism had yet to appear and the production base was essentially agricultural, the dissolution of feudal social relations of production proceeded along lines that were different and more subtle, so that scholars have often failed to perceive the change and have fallen into the error of regarding landownership in colonized and post-colonial India as 'feudal'. This is partly because in both cases the surplus was extracted through share-cropping; what was not perceived was that the structural basis of share-cropping was changed. After the colonial transformation the peasants were no longer unfree, under the direct power of the landlord as before. The locus of power was shifted from the landlord to the colonial state and its local agencies. However, at the same time the landlords were turned into *landowners*, for the peasants' land was given over to them by the colonial state as their property: the producer was separated from the means of production. Instead of sharecropping being a method of extracting a feudal surplus from an unfree peasantry, it was now surplus value extracted as rent from the share-cropping peasants. Whereas under feudalism the landlord pursued and held an unfree peasantry to exploit, now it was the peasants who pursued landowners for access to land to cultivate, as share-cropping tenants. It is hardly surprising that the major peasant movements in India, in the colonial period, were around demands for tenancy rights and security of tenancy (Alavi, 1980).

In the case of the colonial peasantry living under 'primitive communal modes of production' the penetration of metropolitan capital and the colonial state into the local peasant society was more complex, problematic and long-drawn-out. But in both cases (the transition from the feudal mode as well as that from the primitive communal mode), the impact of capital and that of the colonial state brought with it destruction of local self-sufficiency and the incorporation of peasant production into a (global) system of 'generalized commodity production'.[2] The concept must be qualified in this case, for the peasant was now a producer and consumer of commodities but his labour power itself was not yet a commodity, for he cultivated his own land. Peasant production was now much more susceptible to the vicissitudes of the market and, in cases of specialization in cultivation of commercial crops, the peasant produced less and less of his susbsistence needs from his own farm and he was increasingly dependent upon the market. There was therefore an internal disarticulation of the peasant economy by way of the destruction of some of its activities and its external integration into world capitalism. Changes in colonial land laws made land itself into a commodity.

Peasant societies began to get increasingly stratified, with 'rich peasants' at the upper end, who acquired large holdings and began to employ wage labour to supplement their family labour. At the other end 'poor peasants' with substandard holdings could not secure a livelihood without some members of the family taking to wage labour to supplement the family income. Some of them migrated, to work as labourers on capitalist enterprises and remitted savings home. The colonial state was a major instrument to force the pace of such change. Despite such a radical transformation of the 'primitive communal mode of production' under the impact of capital, there were also apparent continuities, such as kinship-based organization of local peasant communities. As a result some scholars suffer from an illusion that these societies are still pre-capitalist (or 'tribal'). Such a view obscures the far-reaching ways in which a long period of subordination to colonial and indigenous capital and the colonial and the post-colonial state have transformed them. They have long ceased to be 'pre-capitalist'.

In Marxist debates about the impact of capital on peasant production we encounter three main alternative propositions. The first of these is that the peasant family farm is just another instance of pre-capitalist petty commodity production, its conditions of reproduction being thought to be identical with those of small-scale production of manufactures, where the producer is the owner of the means of production. Just as capitalist development with the advance of large-scale industrial production destroys urban petty commodity production in manufacture, likewise, it is argued, peasants too are doomed to disappear, to be displaced by a rural society that is polarized between capitalist farmers and landless wage labourers.[3] This was the view held by Karl Kautsky towards the end of the nineteenth century, before he embarked on a systematic analysis in *The Agrarian Question* (Kautsky, 1966). The logic of treating the peasantry as another instance of petty commodity production was to relegate it to irrelevance, not least in the political domain, for it was doomed to disappear in the course of capitalist development. For Kautsky peasants were not only politically inconsequential but worse, they would dilute the revolutionary purity of the working-class movement. He therefore led the attack of proletarian exclusivists in the SPD in 1895 to defeat proposals for an agrarian programme. By contrast, Marx had earlier attacked just such an anti-peasant (Lassallean) tendency in the SPD in his 'Critique of the Gotha Programme' (Marx and Engels, 1968, pp. 325–6).

A second, different, line of argument about the effects of capital on the peasantry has emerged since the 1960s, originally amongst Africanist scholars but is now held more widely (e.g. Meillassoux, 1981, and for a good survey see Foster-Carter, 1978). They fail to recognize the far-reaching structural transformation of the peasant societies which they characterize still as pre-capitalist. Contrary to the Marxist view that when a new (capitalist) mode of production develops in a social formation, there is a contradiction between it and the preexisting (pre-capitalist) mode and through that confrontation the latter is dissolved, they take instead the view that this results only in the 'dissolution/ preservation' of the latter, a notion that in its uncertain formulation betrays a lack of theoretical clarity. They argue that the pre-capitalist peasant communal mode of production is 'articulated' into the developing capitalist mode, but in a subordinated relationship. Capitalism 'dominates' it and makes it subserve its needs and purposes, notably by making it generate (migrant) labour power, and also by providing a market for capitalist production. This argument posits a non-antagonistic and functional symbiosis between the pre-capitalist mode of production and the dominant capitalist mode of production. It sets aside the fundamental Marxist notion of *contradiction* and conflict between two modes of production in a 'social formation', through which structural changes are brought about in societies.

A third position, which will be maintained here, is that contemporary peasant societies everywhere have undergone a profound transformation under the impact of capital. Peasant production, although continuing to function on the basis of the family farm, is incorporated within the structural framework of the dominant capitalist mode of production and is transformed by it. The conditions of peasant production and reproduction are radically changed by the impact of capital. They now reproduce themselves as producers and consumers of commodities within a capitalist system of generalized commodity production and, not least, as producers of the commodity 'labour power', to provide migrant workers for capitalist enterprises. This view does not propose that peasant societies, so transformed and integrated into the global capitalist economy, co-existed with it in a non-contradictory and symbiotic equilibrium, free from the disintegrating and centralizing tendencies of capitalist development. But the contradiction between capital and the exploited and disintegrating peasantry is now internal to the capitalist mode of production of which the peasant economy is now a part. Capital dominates and exploits peasants as it does industrial workers. This common fate of the two subordinate classes within capitalism is the objective basis of their revolutionary alliance against capital, the alliance between the proletariat and the peasantry that was proclaimed equally by Lenin and Mao. That is in marked contradiction to the Kautskyian view that, as petty commodity producers, peasants have no place in a revolutionary movement.

The thesis that the peasantry was rapidly and inexorably being eliminated in the course of capitalist development was argued most strongly by young Lenin, who in 1899 had not yet emancipated himself from the intellectual legacy of his teacher Plekhanov (nor Kautsky), as he was soon to do. In 1899 he said: 'The old peasantry is not only differentiating; it is being completely dissolved, it is ceasing to exist, it is being ousted by absolutely new types of rural inhabitants – these types are the rural bourgeoisie (chiefly petty bourgeoisie) and the rural proletariat – a class of commodity producers and a class of agricultural wage workers' (Lenin, 1977, p. 177). In the light of the large mass of the Russian peasantry, whose weight and importance Lenin was later to recognize, this was something of an overstatement. Learning from the experience of the Russian revolution of 1905–7, Lenin soon changed his views radically and accorded a much greater importance to the peasantry in his revolutionary strategy. But by contrast with the Chinese revolution where the peasantry was fully mobilized, the Bolshevik failure to mobilize the peasantry was to bequeath to the Russian revolution a massive problem of a huge and intractable peasantry which had not been involved in the revolutionary process.

Kautsky began, as Lenin initially did also, with the prevailing view of peasants as petty commodity producers, whom capitalist development would eliminate. However, as he proceeded with his *Agrarian Question* the weight of evidence and logic forced him away from that simplistic view. His analysis began with the recognition that pre-capitalist peasants were not pure agriculturists, for they also engaged in a wide range of domestic crafts to provide for their varied needs. With the impact of capitalist development, there was an 'agriculturalization of the peasant', with the destruction of his domestic crafts. Parallel with the agriculturalization of the peasant was the process of commercialization of peasant production. The peasant was soon drawn into the orbit of capitalist generalized commodity production. The degree of specialization in agriculture had progressed so far that in some regions the peasant depended upon a single major crop, leaving him extremely vulnerable to the vagaries of the world commodity markets. The family farm, to that extent, was less and less able to meet the peasant family's subsistence needs.

Kautsky identified two aspects of capitalist development: 'accumulation', which is turning surplus value into capital, and 'concentration', the consolidation of small capitals into bigger units. He then differentiated between the impact of capital on urban petty commodity production and on peasant production. He pointed out that for the development of large-scale industry the prior destruction of small urban petty commodity producers was not a necessary precondition. On the contrary, it was the development of large-scale industry that took precedence in the process and its greater competitive power subsequently destroyed the economy of the small producers. That was not, however, the case in agriculture. 'The prime distinction is that in industry it is possible to multiply means of production at will; in agriculture the decisive means of production, land, constitutes a fixed magnitude under given circumstances and cannot be increased at will' (Kautsky, 1966, chapter 7, section c, p. 142). For the process of concentration to occur in agriculture there must be a prior dispossession of adjoining small farms to bring them together into a larger one. That was a difficult obstacle to overcome, which was not encountered in industry. Kautsky's argument so far only modified partially his earlier stance, for he now presented the process of centralization in agriculture as only a very slow one.

Kautsky then turned to the function of peasant societies in relation to capitalism. The fundamental problem of capitalist development was that of maintaining an adequate supply of workers. The role of peasant societies as reproducers of labour power had a special advantage for capital, for in this case the main cost of reproduction of labour power is borne by the peasant societies, and wages can be lower than those needed to maintain a permanently urbanized working-class family. This recognition by Kautsky was a major advance over earlier conceptions of the production and reproduction of free labour for capitalist exploitation. He concluded: 'The best conditions for bringing up a plentiful supply of able-bodied labour are found amongst the owners (or tenants) of small farms on which an independent household is linked with independent farming' (Kautsky, 1966, chapter 7, section f, pp. 159–60). He described peasant farms as 'production sites for new labour'. Thus Kautsky finally arrived at a conclusion that reversed his original position: 'Despite its technical superiority the large farm can never completely prevail in any given country. ... As long as the capitalist mode of production continues, there is no reason to expect the end either of the large scale enterprises or the small.' He then elaborated a number of both economic and political tendencies that would ensure 'the re-multiplication of the small farm' (ibid.). In Kautsky's eyes, that did not make peasants a feudal survival but a particular component of the capitalist mode of production. Nevertheless, Kautsky's political prejudice against the peasantry was to remain impervious to his most perceptive economic analysis and he was soon to revert to an anti-peasant position.

Kautsky's theoretical work provides us with a valuable basis from which to carry our analysis forward in order to identify the specific forms that capital takes when subsuming peasant production. According to the labour theory of value, taken very strictly, surplus value is extracted only from free labour purchased by the capitalist who appropriates the whole of the product of labour, but pays the labourer only his price, determined by the socially necessary labour time required to produce commodities of the value needed for his subsistence and reproduction. But Marx himself did not adhere too rigidly to this formula, for he records exceptions to the general rule. In the course of his discussion, 'Results of the Immediate Process of Production', where he expounds his well-known distinction between 'formal' and 'real' subsumption of labour under capital, he writes:

In India, for example, the capital of the usurer advances raw materials or tools or even both to the immediate producer in the form of money. The exorbitant interest which it attracts, the interest which, irrespective of its magnitude, it extorts from the primary producer, *is just another name for surplus value*. It transforms its money into capital by extorting unpaid labour, surplus labour from the immediate producer. *But it does not intervene in the process of production itself* which proceeds in its traditional fashion. (Marx, 1976, p. 1023, emphasis added)

Marx discusses here 'transitional subforms (which survive and reproduce themselves) within the framework of capitalism', even though the stage of 'formal subsumption of labour under capital', i.e. the separation of the producer from the means of production, has not yet been reached (ibid.). Marx's category of 'formal subsumption of labour under capital' entails that while social relations of production have changed, with the separation of the producer from the means of production, the labour process remains what it was before. With the further stage in the development of capitalism and capital accumulation, there is a movement towards 'real subsumption of labour under capital' when the labour process itself is revolutionized, so that there is a movement from 'absolute surplus value' to 'relative surplus value'. In the case of peasant production subsumed under capital, it is clear that we have not even reached the stage of 'formal subsumption of labour under capital'. But, nevertheless, the case is comparable to instances that Marx provides where surplus value is extracted by capital from the direct producer without the separation of the producer from the means of production. It is clear that Marx does not posit this separation as the absolute and indispensable condition of extraction of surplus value.

We must, however, consider how surplus value is generated and extracted where the peasant producer is not separated from the means of production (land). To understand the method by which 'surplus value' is extracted from peasant production we must begin by recognizing that the peasant's labour is objectified in the commodities that he produces for the market, for which he receives less than full 'value' by virtue of the operation of 'unequal exchange' (Emmanuel, 1972); what he receives is the 'value' of only a portion of his labour power that is objectified in the commodity, namely that which is equivalent to 'necessary labour time', the cost of reproduction of his labour power and not the full value of the labour incorporated in the product. The difference, the 'surplus value' that is appropriated by capital, enters into extended reproduction of capital by virtue of its acquisition and accumulation by the capitalist. Emmanuel, and others following him, in using the concept of 'unequal exchange', have been criticized on the ground that 'the characterization of capital–peasant relations *at the level of exchange* is inadequate' (Bernstein, 1979, p. 426, emphasis added). Bernstein's reservation is correct, for it is a misconception that it is merchants' capital alone and by itself that exploits the peasant. The mediation of merchant capital, which directly confronts the peasant, is only one moment in the operation of capital as a whole, which exploits the peasant as a totality. Fractions of capital do not exist in and by themselves; they are facets of a unified whole. Through the mediation of commercial capital, capital as a whole (that is financial and industrial capital as well as commercial) articulates with peasant production. Peasants of Pakistan or Uganda were made to produce cotton for the mills of Lancashire, not just for the benefit of the traders who encountered them directly. Capital as a whole appropriates 'surplus value' extracted from the peasant in the form of the unpaid part of his labour, as embodied in his commodity. The surplus value so extracted enters into extended reproduction of capital on a global scale contributing to capital accumulation mainly in the metropolis within the structure of peripheral capitalism or the colonial mode of production, the form in which capitalism extends itself globally (Alavi, 1982). Furthermore, in post-colonial states ruling bureaucracies have emerged as locally powerful and rapacious social groups that add to the burdens laid on a starving peasantry, on an unparalleled scale.

Clearly therefore we can distinguish two forms of capitalism in agriculture, one which is based on the separation of the producer from the means of production (land) and the other without such separation, on the basis of the peasant farm. Given these two forms, a question arises whether we are to accord the two forms of capitalism the same level of significance. My answer would be in the negative for I would maintain that capitalism based on the separation of the producer from the means of production remains its primary and fundamental form, the basis of industrial capitalism as well as that of 'capitalist agriculture' where capitalist farmers operate with wage labour. However, the subsumption of peasant production under capital, without separation of the producer from the means of production, brings to our attention the fact that capitalism is not restricted to that single original form but that in the course of its development and extension it also takes on, as in this case, another, complementary, form in subsuming peasant agriculture. This second form satisfies every criterion of the capitalist mode of production except that of the separation of the producer from the means of production. One would add that the two forms are not of equal status. This second form of capitalism, without the separation of the producer from the means of production, cannot exist as such without the prior existence of capitalism in its fundamental and primary form which is its general form. The reverse is not possible. Finally one would add that all this theoretical argument does not have just formal significance. There is an important political corollary that follows from it. If peasant production were merely another instance of petty commodity production, the development of capitalism itself would be sufficient to dissolve it. That is how Kautsky and others, the proletarian exclusivists, saw it. For them the peasantry, as petty commodity producers, had little significance with regard to contradictions within the capitalist mode of production and the alignment of forces directed towards its transcendence. But if we recognize the peasantry to be an integral part of the capitalist mode of production from whom surplus value is extracted, we can see it taking its place beside the proletariat as a component of the revolutionary alignment of forces against capitalism, a force for the future rather than a relic of the past.

Notes

I am obliged to Tim Allen, Paul Kelemen, Phil Leeson and Teodor Shanin for helpful criticism. The usual disclaimer about responsibility for ideas expressed here applies, of course.

1 For an explanation of the concept of 'mode of production' see Alavi, 1982.
2 Those readers who are not familiar with the Marxist concepts used here may refer to Sweezy, 1942 and Marx, 1976.
3 This position has been restated recently by Peter Gibbon and Michael Neocosmos in 'Some problems in the political economy of African socialism', in Bernstein and Campbell (1985). In the Introduction to that volume Bernstein has repudiated his earlier influential thesis that depicted the peasant under the sway of capitalism as 'wage labour equivalent' (Bernstein, 1979, p. 436) and has affirmed the pre-1897 Kautskyian view of peasants as petty commodity producers, as reiterated by Gibbon and Neocosmos, 1985.

References

Alavi, Hamza (1980) 'India: transition from feudalism to colonial capitalism', *Journal of Contemporary Asia*, vol. 10, no. 4, reprinted in H. A. Alavi et al. (1982) *Capitalism and Colonial Production*, London.

Alavi, Hamza (1982) 'The structure of peripheral capitalism', in H. Alavi and T. Shanin (eds), *Introduction to the Sociology of 'Developing' Societies*, London.

Amin, Samir (1976) *Unequal Development*, Hassocks.

Bernstein, Henry (1979) 'African peasantries: a theoretical framework', *Journal of Peasant Studies*, vol. 6, no. 4.

Bernstein, Henry and Campbell, Bonnie (eds) (1985) *Contradictions of Accumulation in Africa*, London.

Emmanuel, Arghiri (1972) *Unequal Exchange: A Study of the Imperialism of Trade*, London.

Fortes, Meyer and Evans-Pritchard, E. (eds) (1941) *African Political Systems*, London.

Foster-Carter, Aidan (1978) 'Can we articulate articulation?', in John Clammer (ed.), *The New Economic Anthropology*, London.

Gibbon, Peter and Neocosmos, Michael (1985) 'Some problems in the political economy of African socialism', in Bernstein and Campbell (eds), *Contradictions*.

Kautsky, Karl (1966) *Die Agrarfrage*, Hanover. English translation, *The Agrarian Question*, Manchester University Press, forthcoming.

Lenin, V. I. (1977) *Development of Capitalism in Russia*, Moscow.

Marx, Karl (1976) *Capital*, vol. I, Pelican Marx Library.

Marx, Karl 'Critique of the Gotha Programme' section I(4) in Marx and Engels (1968) *Selected Works*, London, pp. 325–6.

Meillassoux, Claude (1981) *Maidens, Meals and Money*, part II, Cambridge.

Sahlins, Marshall (1972) *Stone Age Economics*, London.

Sweezy, Paul (1942) *The Theory of Capitalist Development*, New York and London.

Related Items

13, 16, 17, 25, 28, 29, 31, 32, 36, 44, 46, 47, 49, 50, 51, 59, 61, 62.

Part IIB

The Extra-Village Context

27

Peasant Markets and Indian Peasant Economies

Manning Nash

The economic organization of the Indians of Middle America ranges over a wide gamut. It runs from the virtual isolation, little trade and almost no money of the tribal remnants of the Lacandon in the Peten to complete market interdependence of specialized communities producing for cash returns in an impersonal and competitive economic organization. There are all kinds of subtle gradations and variations between these extremes, but without doing violence to the ethnographic reality, it is feasible to sort the economic complexity of the region into three major types, each tending to be structurally, and frequently regionally, distinct. Each type carries with it some differences in the social structure and cultural pattern of which the economy is but a sub-system. The social and cultural correlates, concomitants and prerequisites of the varying economic organizations may form the basis for providing important indices to the dynamics of social change and stability among the Indians of Middle America.

The three kinds of economic organizations in Middle America are:

The regional marketing system. Communities are linked into a system of rotating markets. In its most developed form the rotating markets look like a 'solar system'. A major market centre is in daily operation. To it flow commodities produced throughout the region, goods from all over the nation and even items from international trade. Around the major market are a series of market places which have their special days. Each of these market places tends to specialize in a given produce or commodity and to carry a reduced selection of the goods available in the central market. Goods, buyers and sellers move around the solar system in terms of the days of the week when market activity centres in a particular market place. Such solar systems of regional interdependence are characteristic of the western highlands of Guatemala (where they are most

Excerpts from Manning Nash, 'Indian economies', in the Handbook of Middle American Indians series, University of Texas Press, 1967, pp. 87–101.

highly developed), the valley of Oaxaca, central Mexico, Michoacan, and eastern Guatemala among the Chorti and Pokomam. Without the marked solar qualities, regional market interdependence is found in the highlands of Chiapas among the Tzeltal and Tzotzil and in parts of the Alta Verapaz in Guatemala and a pattern of intense daily markets in the Isthmus of Tehuantepec. The regional marketing system is 'money economy organized in single households as both consumption and production units with a strongly developed market which tends to be perfectly competitive' (Tax, 1953, p. 13).

The adjunct export economy. Communities produce chiefly for home and local consumption, but tend to have one or a few commodities produced for cash and market exchange. Specialization is rare; from community to community the products, skills and economic organization are homogeneous. The economy is pecuniary, but there is much exchange of items for other items, albeit in terms of price-money equivalents. The market and the market place tend to be in the hands of non-Indians, and the Indian is more seen as seller than buyer. This sort of economy varies from the coffee growers of Sayula (Guiteras Holmes, 1952) who are mainly concerned with the export of a cash-crop, or the vanilla growers of the Totonac region around the major market of Papantla (Kelly and Palerm, 1952) to the coffee, melon and citrus growers of the Sierra Popoluca (Foster, 1942). Another axis of variation is toward the paid labour role of Indians on plantations where the export economy is organized in the hands of non-Indian entrepreneurs. The paid labour, or Indian rural proletariat (Mintz, 1953), often coexists with communities growing the basic subsistence crops. In the Yucatan peninsula (Redfield, 1941) the henequen plantations approach this; in parts of the Verapaz in Guatemala, and in the coastal regions where Indians are workers on coffee, sugar, rice or banana plantations, there occurs the extreme form of the adjunct export system.

The quasi-tribal system. Economies are concerned chiefly with meeting locally defined demands. Economic effort is directed toward subsistence needs with handicrafts for home use, and attention to the crops of the milpa. Money is part of the daily life but tends to be scant, and transactions are not a daily occurrence. The Indians with this kind of economic system tend to be in remote or not very accessible upland regions, or to be remnants of former unintensive village agriculturalists. The economic type is found among the Cora and Huichol, the Tarahumara, the Tepehuan, the Maya, and other groups of north-west Mexico, and, except for the Lacandon of the Mexico–Guatemala border, does not exist south of Mexico City, and is absent from Guatemala (except possibly for the Kekchi around Lake Izabal, Dr Nancy Solien de Gonzales reports).

The three types of economies are different in scale, in the number of Indians they include, and in the areas where they are able to function. All the economies are tied, more or less tightly, to the national and international economies; none is free from the effects of national and world fluctuations. Everywhere the Indian and his communities are enmeshed in a network of economic relationships well beyond the local ethnic unit. Even the very isolated groups like the Lacandon or the Tarahumara, or the Xcacal of Quintana Roo get involved with the passing agents of the larger economy. . . .

The facts of ecological variation, the proximity of highland and lowland, are the physical basis for the cultural and economic diversity of the region. It is the occurrence of distinct local societies, however, with strong endogamous tendencies, which inclines to restrict handicrafts, trades and industries to a single community. The present distribution of agricultural patterns, handicrafts and special skills is the result of the operation of comparative advantage over a long time, and shifts do take place. Apparently shifts in kind of crop (other things being equal, like land availability) take place more easily and rapidly than the cultural incorporation of a new handicraft or industry. This, of course, is tied to the facts of enculturation, since a handicraft or industry passes from father to son, or mother to daughter, whereas an agricultural speciality will pass from adult to adult. In addition, Indians work for each other as agricultural labourers across community lines (as they work for Ladinos) and hence are able to learn agricultural techniques more readily. But even crop shifts in a community's inventory are not easily undertaken. Indians must compete with the already established way of making a living in their own community and with the reputation of the other producing communities in the market place. For example, potatoes of Todos Santos are less valued in the Quezaltenango region than potatoes of Nahuala, or the vegetables from Zunil are thought to be the best. Indians from these communities wear their distinctive costumes, which serve as 'brand' identifications; and the customers assume that a man in the Todos Santos striped pants is selling his own potatoes, or that the blue-skirted Almolongera is selling her own vegetables, though this is often not the case. So there is some stickiness even in the transfer or diffusion of agricultural techniques and products. Specialities, of course, are subject to competition from both Indian and non-Indian producers. Many handicrafts have been lost, like the hat making of Aguacatenango which could not compete with factory-made hats, or the reduction in palm-leaf rain capes with the spread of cheap plastic tablecloths used as ponchos. Conversely, new things are stimulated through competition and contact: tourists who visit Chichicastenango favour a sort of risqué pattern on napkins; the Ladinos of Chiapas are the consumers of large pottery flowerpots. Skills and agricultural patterns change over time and in response to changing market conditions, in the context of possibilities of technique transfer and development among communities. . . .

The market, as an institution, rests on the free interplay of buyers and sellers, with price established through the interaction of buyers who are not large enough to set price, and sellers who do not control enough of the supply to affect the price. There is also the feature of impersonality in an open market system. Entry (as buyer or seller) is not restricted. Anyone who pays the small tax can enter the local markets and set up a stall, though in the city markets there are some larger installations requiring more outlay than many of the vendors can muster. The interaction between buyer and seller shows indifference to person, with attention only to price. In these markets, haggling and bargaining are characteristic but they are the means of establishing the going price, and shopping is the way of getting price information where price is not posted or advertised. Vendors of similar products are usually grouped together, and from the bids of buyers and the asking of sellers a price is quickly reached. The price prevails until there is some change in the supply and demand factors. Bargaining in any single transaction reflects the state of the market place as a whole, and the market place as a whole reflects the operations of the entire regional and national markets.

Looked at closely, these markets are a series of buyer–seller transactions, an exchange of money for goods. Except for some of the food sellers, some of the medical suppliers and a few of the stores in the market or in the towns where markets are held (and to which people may be tied by credit), there does not exist a clientele for any seller, or a body of loyal customers for any purveyor of commodities. The market relationships are truly dyadic contract and fleeting (Foster, 1961). This characteristic of the market is a symptom of a prevailing fact of the economic organization of Indian communities, a fact with far-reaching structural and economic consequences. Indian buyers and sellers in the market place are members of households, and they act as members of households. These households are economic units in only one of their aspects, and they tend to see the economic sphere as only one of the areas in which maintenance needs may be met. Households are limited in the numbers and kinds of persons they can recruit, the capital and savings they can command, the sort of economic opportunity to which they can respond. Given the fact that households, not firms, are the economic organizations around which the market economy is built, the limits of planning, continuity, scale and technological complexity in economic life become readily apparent. What makes these economies different from a modern, dynamic economy with a built-in drive toward economic and technological development is thus clear. They do not lack economic rationality, the matching of means and ends for best outputs; they do not hedge economic activity with a host of traditional barriers; they do not despise wealth and hard work; and they exhibit the free market where each man follows his own economic interest. Thus they have the values, the markets, the pecuniary means of exchange, the ability to calculate, and the interest in economic activity. (In Mitla, Parsons (1936) complained that it was a 'ritual of price' that marked these Zapotec; Malinowski and de la Fuente (1957) have spoken of a 'commercial libido'; and others have reported the keen interest in price and economic activity.) What is lacking is the social organization of an entity like the firm, an autonomous, corporate group dedicated to and organized for economic activity.

That such social organizations have not grown up in Indian communities is tied to the larger social structure and cultural pattern. The specialized communities with their distinctive cultural and economic cast, maintained through endogamy and organized around a variant of the civil–religious hierarchy (Cámara, 1952; Wolf, 1955; Nash, 1958), are not conducive to a social entity based strictly on economic ends. The communities are organized to protect their corporate existence and as such have specialized controls over the free use of accumulation of resources and mechanisms to ensure a democracy of poverty. In the social structure of communities like Panajachel, Cantel, Santa Eulalia or Santiago (Wagley, 1941) in Guatemala, or Amatenango, Aguacatenango, Zinacantan in Chiapas, or Mitla, Yalalag and others in Oaxaca, there operates a levelling mechanism. The levelling mechanisms (Wolf, 1955; Nash, 1961) operate to drain the accumulated resources of the community for non-economic ends, and to keep the various households, over generations, fairly equal in wealth. They are mechanisms to keep economic homogeneity within the community, so that socially important heterogeneity – age, sex, previous service to the community, control of or access to the supernatural – remains the basis of role differentiation. They militate against the rise of social classes based on wealth and economic power distinctions. The levelling mechanism rests on the following interrelated aspects:

1 Low level of technology and limited land, so that absolute wealth and accumulation are small in virtue of poor resources in relation to population and a technology which is labour-intensive and not highly productive.
2 Fracture of estates by bilateral inheritance. Whatever is in fact accumulated in capital goods is scrambled among sons and daughters in nearly equal shares. Almost everywhere in the region bilateral inheritance prevails. The few places with patrilineal descent groups do not vest property rights in a corporation, but exhibit a pattern of division among the patrilineally related families.
3 Forced expenditure of time and resources in communal office. The posts in the civil and religious hierarchies require some loss of work time, and the higher the post the more time is lost and the more direct costs in taking on the post.
4 Forced expenditure by the wealthy in ritual. Those who have been skilled or lucky and have accumulated wealth must expend it for communal ends, chiefly in feasting and drinking, so that the wealth is consumed.

The levelling mechanism keeps the fortunes of the various households nearly equal and serves to ensure the shift of family fortunes from generation to generation. The sanctions behind the operation of the levelling mechanism are generally supernatural, with witchcraft as the means to keep the economic units oriented to the communal drains and claims on their wealth. These economies, then, are market – competitive, free, open – but set into a social structure without corporate units dedicated to and able to pursue economic ends. Working with a cultural pattern forcing the accumulation of wealth into non-economic channels, and buttressed by a system of supernatural sanctions against those who do not use their wealth, they show a lack of dynamism, a technological conservatism almost equivalent to that of the most isolated communities, and an inability to seize and exploit or create economic opportunity.

This combination of features presents a startling social fact: the presence of markets, economic rationality and money form a single complex, but in addition firms, credit mechanisms, deliberate technical and economic invest-ment are needed for economic dynamism. The latter features are part of a social structure not found in the corporate peasantry of Middle America, and their coexistence in a single society (like our own) appears a historical precipitate rather than a functionally linked set of social characteristics. Experience in other parts of the world where the market economy is set into a social structure that is not modern in the sense of organizations dedicated to purely economic ends (e.g. the bazaars of the Arab world, the regional markets of Africa or the peasant markets of Java and Haiti) leads to the expectation that such organizations do not develop from the dynamics of internal social and economic life but are a product of social change induced by pressures or privileges generated in the modern economy.

This survey of the broad type of economy in the regional marketing areas of Middle America has been taken from an aerial view, a height which may give rise to misunderstandings. The tendency toward economic homogeneity, for example, does not indicate that a given community or village is, at any one time, virtually without wealth differences. Lewis (1947) describes a three-class wealth division for Tepoztlan and relates it to the types of land and technology that different families own. Tax (1952) finds a wealth division into quarters convenient for Panajachel, and describes the functions of wealth in office-holding, marriage choice and prestige. Similarly, the emphasis on households as economic units appears to play down the role of the community as a property holder. Nowhere is land fully communal; nowhere is it fully in individual hands. Some lands (often the *monte*, scrub land, pasture land or firewood land) is owned by the community and open to use by all members. Frequently there are means to prevent the sale of land from Indians to Ladinos (as in many communities in Chiapas). But the communal control of productive resources in the form of ownership was everywhere eroded and destroyed by the middle of the 1800s, and one of the persisting problems of the corporate communities has been to hold on to their territorial base.

References

Cámara Barbachano, F. (1952) 'Religious and political organization', in S. Tax et al. (eds), *Heritage of Conquest: The Ethnology of Middle America*, Free Press.

Foster, G. M. (1942) 'A primitive Mexican economy', *Monograph, American Ethnology Society*, vol. 5, pp. 1–115.

Foster, G. M. (1961) 'The dyadic contract: a model for the social structure of a Mexican peasant village', *American Anthropology*, vol. 63, pp. 1173–92.

Guiteras Holmes, C. (1952) *Sayula*, Socieded Mexicana de Geografia y Estadistica.

Kelly, I. T. and Palerm, A. (1952) 'The Tajin Totonac', part 1, 'History, subsistence, shelter and technology', Smithsonian Institution, pub. 13.

Lewis, O. (1947) 'Wealth differences in a Mexican village', *Scientific Monthly*, vol. 65, pp. 127–32.

Malinowski, B. and de la Fuente, J. (1957) 'La economía de un sistema de mercados en México', *Acta Anthropologica*, ser. 2, vol. 1, no. 2, Mexico.

Mintz, S. W. (1953) 'The folk urban continuum and the rural proletarian community', *American Journal of Sociology*, vol. 59, pp. 136–45.

Nash, M. (1958) 'Political relations in Guatemala', *Social and Economic Studies*, vol. 7, pp. 65–75.

Nash, M. (1961) 'The social context of economic choice in a small community', *Man*, vol. 61, pp. 186–91.

Parsons, E. C. (1936) *Mitla: Town of the Souls*, University of Chicago Press.

Redfield, R. (1941) *The Folk Culture of Yucatan*, University of Chicago Press.

Tax, S. (1952) 'Economy and technology', in S. Tax et al. (eds), *Heritage of Conquest: The Ethnology of Middle America*, Free Press.

Tax, S. (1953) 'Penny capitalism: a Guatemalan Indian economy', Smithsonian Institution, pub. 16.

Wagley, C. (1941) 'Economics of a Guatemalan village', *American Anthropology Association Mem.*, no. 58.

Wolf, E. R. (1955) 'Types of Latin American peasantry: a preliminary discussion', *American Anthropologist*, vol. 57, pp. 452–71.

Related Items

5, 6, 9, 11, 16, 17, 18, 22, 24, 28, 30, 31, 33, 35, 37, 56, 57, 60, 62.

28

Merchants and Markets of Grain in South Asia

Barbara Harriss

Introduction

Scene: a market town in south India

It is early. Long fingers of shadow throw the image of the row of palmyra thatched awnings out over the newly swept dirt road, over the long, orderly procession of bullock carts and over the dust which their somnambulations have freed into the cool air. There are forty mandis, grain merchants' depots, in this market. They are as but one for Gopal, who sits rewinding his headcloth astride bags of paddy on one of the carts. He, like many others in the line of carters, has never known the privilege of choice. Gopal's father has asked him to sell all his family's grain not necessary for seed and stock in the place where the household has always sold it: to the merchant who gave them a loan in the difficult time before harvest so that they could pay the day labourers in food and also feed their own household.

Gopal's merchant's shop is just like the others: narrow and deep, fortified by bags of grain and patrolled by coolies dressed in loin-cloths with knives at their waists. Inside it is airless and dark. Here Gopal's pallid mercantile friend sits, in immaculate white, cross-legged by his rosewood writing table. His great bulk (more eloquent testimony to his diet and his material wealth than the musty surroundings of the shop where he spends almost all his waking hours) is supported by a bolster, his fat cream-coloured fingers supporting the weight of unobtrusive but, it has to be confessed, diamond rings.

Gopal feels like a fly in a spider's web. The spider is cheerful, offering the essential greeting: 'Have you eaten?' The fly is given a hot sweet tea to pour down his throat and refresh himself with. Having satisfied himself that his client has eaten, the spider moves into action. The great account book is opened (the one which is never shown to prying officials). The coolies, who

An original paper.

unload, weigh and rebag the grain, jump to attention and it is all over very quickly.

The price is not an issue. It is not a secret. It's a commonplace of every journey, hailed from every bus the length and breadth of the land. Gopal's merchant would not cheat him, as others are reputed to do: not on deductions for 'poor quality', nor in fraudulent weights and measures, nor because he has only brought one small cartload. Nor does he tarry long months over paying Gopal: the money is there for him if he wants it, there behind the doors of that large, impregnable safe. Admittedly Gopal does have to tip the man who weighs and sews his gunny bags, and the noseless cripple who sweeps the road outside the merchant's shop. No, what is important to both seller and buyer is that Gopal has to sell all his surplus (far more than what covers his debt) right now at the low prices after harvest. It was all arranged like this when he took out his loan; and the merchant's clerk came out on a motorbike to Gopal's father's plots to have a good look.

Gopal leaves some money in free deposit with the merchant, twists the change he needs into a knot in his cloth, slides a bundle of notes into his pocket and heads for the centre of town, leaving his animals in the care of the merchant's coolies.

It has been a good harvest, breaking the run of low and untimely rains and only too timely caterpillar infestations. During the two years of bad weather he had had to buy rice for the first time. The women of the house laboured in the fields of other farmers for the first time. Their jewellery went to sojourn at the pawnbroker's. Gopal had to scour the market for money with which to pay the labourers who broke the hard crust of earth on fields uncultivated for a year and who dealt with the weeds. His merchant was the only one to oblige. Now, after he has paid the harvesting gang in grain and given an annual token in kind to the village washerman, the potter, the priest and the barber, he has still got enough cash from the sale to attend to matters outstanding: to pay the rent on one well, to pay the businessman from whom he got fertilizer and pesticide at the government decreed fair price and on interest-free credit, to pay a provisions trader for a long list of odds and ends on the never-never and the medicine seller for the pills on credit which had cured his son of fever. Since the government amortized his (and thousands of others') outstanding electricity bill, there is one problem the less for his own well, where the water is getting lower by the year. Some other time, not today, not mixing business with pleasure, he will bring his sons' mother to the temple and to the cinema.

Today, Gopal buys a coconut, banana and a twist of jasmine petals and lays them with grateful piety before the golden deity in the splendid new market temple erected recently by the wealthiest merchant. Then he redeems jewels from his pawnbroker, tours the cloth shops for a headtowel, purchases without negotiation a pair of plastic shoes for his wife and rests in a tiffin hotel over coffee and a dosa.

On barren ground at the edge of town, as the heat and light intensify, noise is rising from a scene of chaotic colour. Laid out in neighbourhoods is the patchwork quilt of the weekly market: live cattle, goats and poultry, leaf vegetables, root vegetables, salt, fodder, spices, haberdashery, human hair and cosmetics, plastic buckets and utensils, leaf plates, fruit, chewing tobacco, dried salt fish, millet, rice, recycled tins, locally made implements, soothsayers, cobblers, cart repairers and carpenters, blacksmiths and sellers of factory-made cotton goods all have their pitches. Commerce here is, as in town, a confrontation but one of a different kind where Gopal feels superior: a confrontation of gender, of caste, status, and exchange. Male purchasers clad in white stand and buy from equally large numbers of low-caste women traders clad in bright saris and seated on the ground. The small size of the heaps of goods is a pretty eloquent indication of these traders' poverty. And the languid negotiations and haggling which precede a deal contrast with the fixed prices of trade in town and are also an eloquent indication of the different system of exchange in which the distribution of local goods takes place. Gopal parks his cart and circles the shandy on foot, gossiping with castefolk from neighbouring villages about the weather and an imminent pilgrimage, absorbing the implications of a new marriage alliance, speculating about the rising popularity of the opposition party in the towns and in the agricultural regions of the south, brooding with other men over whether the young leader of the farmers' agitations here will turn into a vote-winning non-party candidate in the next state elections (what havoc that would play!), discussing the exorbitant fee necessary to bribe a local government official to demonstrate his unofficial skills as the region's water diviner, seeking bargains, slowly filling his cloth shopping bag but avoiding the ritually polluted but actually rather cheerful area reserved for the butchering of cattle and goats. Well pleased with his day, Gopal hoists some children from his street in the village on to the bare planks of his cart and returns to his fields and his father.

What we may learn

In this scene a number of lessons about the market may be learned. First, marketing is one of a number of ways produce is exchanged. Reciprocal arrangements between castes is another. Government-administered distribution is one more. Second, just as there are status relations within the peasant household (here the grown son with children of his own deferring to his father who is still the head of the household, ultimate manager of decisions on the production and consumption of food) we can see that buying and selling express relations of power and status among the actors. Gopal as the producer is subordinated to the merchant via ties of credit which have eliminated his capacity to choose the time, place and intermediary for his marketing and which even encourage him to leave money in trust with the merchant. In turn Gopal has better negotiating power than the impoverished female petty traders who people the periodic market. He is also engaged in some non-exploitive marketing and credit relationships with interest-free credit on goods sold at prices fixed to be fair by the government.

A third lesson concerns the variety of intermediaries within a market place: they include specialized and wealthy merchants and their family members; their agents and employees who may have specialized jobs to do; petty commodity dealers of varying degrees of specialization; general traders dealing in consumer goods as well as food; artisans, providers of services and unspecialized producer–retailers. The Indian market place is the arena in which a process of economic specialization or a social division of labour works itself out, revenue from sales of produce generating custom for craftsmen and artisans (carpenters, cobblers, carters) all of whom are of different castes in rural India but whose activities are just as likely to be specialized by tribal group or by region elsewhere in the world (Nash, this volume, item 27; Smith, 1976).

But in the eighties, in India at least, revenue from the sales of produce by peasants is beginning to be generating demand for commodities from factory production in distant cities. Toothpaste and brushes and factory-made soap replace sugar-cane or neem twigs and soapnut. Non-biodegradable polythene bags and plastic twine are spurned by the pigs and goats who used to feed on wrapping leaves and who are reduced to eating cinema posters. Plastic, stainless steel and aluminium plates and pots, glasses, and kerosene wick stoves have robbed the potters of their clientele. Some of them in turn make tiles which replace the palm thatches and thus displace the thatchers. Viscose is playing havoc with cotton. Commercial paints are preferred over the shells hauled from the seashore to be crushed for limewash. Factory-made beer, whisky and cigarettes replace bidis and toddy and threaten the livelihoods of toddy tappers and bidi wrappers and those who trade these goods. The glass bangle dealers had a beautiful but breakable product. Plastic bangles, both cheaper and lasting longer, divert and soak up demand. And mats face competition from modern and specialized articles of furniture, previously thought to be the preserve of filmstars and the richest: beds, Formica-topped tables and chairs.

This has opened up opportunities for business livelihoods in an increasingly diversified rural economy. But for every traditional washerman who has modernized and opened a dry cleaning shop, for every cobbler becoming a 'Bata' agent, for every goldsmith becoming a moneylender and financier, for every blacksmith becoming an agro-engineer, for every carter becoming a lorry driver, many more can be in process of impoverishment (Harriss and Harriss, 1984).

For this is no land of arcadian serenity. It is thought that over two-thirds of the people live below what the technical men in Delhi have calculated is the poverty line, describing minimum conditions of nutrition, clothing and shelter. Risk aversion is a necessary survival strategy when harvests are uncertain, as we saw has been Gopal's experience in recent years. The threat of disaster hangs over the lives of most toiling people, especially the disaster of sickness – to animals, crops or to people, which is costly in terms of treatment (whichever of the four systems of medical therapy is approached) and in terms of time lost from work. So much so that certain family members (little girls in much of northern India, young children everywhere) may suffer a neglect which, combined with their burden of labour in fields and homes, makes their life expectancy unusually lower than that of men.

Last but not least we learn that the economic aspects of marketing are enhanced by and linked with religious, political and administrative aspects of life. Building a temple with the profits of trading is an act of generally appreciated piety by the merchant-philanthropist. Unpaid social brokerage in marriage negotiations is as proper a function of a periodic market as is brokerage in the resolution of disputes, and as is brokerage in vegetables. The market place is an institution for political transactions.

The Commercialization of Grain

Grain provides energy, protein, vitamins and minerals. Without grain, most societies would find it hard to maintain themselves either biologically or socially. Grain is also a medium for social messages and for religious actions. The production and distribution of grain provides employment, incomes and entitlement to agricultural inputs, industrial consumer goods, the products of artisanal workshops and food with which to diversify the diet. Understanding the commercialization of grain not only shows us how the market permits and facilitates a social division of labour and mingles the economic with the social but also how it acts as a means of exploiting peasant societies. For peasants can be defined not only in terms of their ownership of land and the use of household labour in production, not only in their practice of self-exploitation using uncosted labour, but also in terms of their subordination to other social classes and to the state. Our theme is how such subordination may come about through the medium of marketing and commercializing grain and yet how an unequal and subordinated peasantry may still retain a certain independence. Two contrasting examples from India will illustrate the general points which we turn to introduce.

We shall use the word marketing for the process of transacting: the buying and selling of grain. The word commercialization we take to mean the historical process of increasing the proportion of production that is destined for the market rather than for home consumption. Usually, but not always, that process involves increasing total production.

Both marketing and commercialization are components of the much wider process of circulation of goods, after they have been produced. In some peasant societies, and in certain peasant households in most peasant societies, goods may circulate hardly at all. The grain is brought from the fields to the homestead where it is stored and eventually consumed. But this is becoming increasingly less the rule. More frequently the process of circulation results in a transfer of control over goods out of the hands of those who produced them. You can see this most clearly when agricultural wage labourers produce goods for a landowner. But this may even be the case within households, for instance in societies like that of northern Ghana, where women are the most important producers of grain and are furthermore individually responsible for feeding their own children but where it is the male household head alone who takes charge of the grain store, who allocates grain each day to each adult woman to prepare and cook, and who, in certain circumstances, may actually purchase the cooked food from his wife (Whitehead, 1981).

Control over the fruits of a peasant household's labour can be transferred in the process of circulation in a number of ways: through kind rental payments, for instance. The peasant then exchanges grain for the temporary right to cultivate another's land. Or through usury: the payment in kind (or cash or labour) for money or goods loaned at interest rates which are so high that they are not the result of a competitive money market, are unjustifiable in terms of the costs and risks of lending but reflect instead the lender's power over the borrower. A third way of transferring control over goods is through taxation – on land, property, people, on goods sold and (rarely) on income. The state then receives grain or cash got from necessary sales of grain and the peasant household may or may not receive in return the services of law and order, infrastructure and welfare that modern states usually declare that they will provide. It is obvious that it is the terms and conditions on which these transfers take place, rather than the transfers themselves, which determine the degree of exploitation of producers via the sphere of circulation and thereby their subordination to classes controlling the market and to the state.

Marketing itself involves a transfer of control and an exchange of grain for cash. Grain is marketed for a variety of purposes in order to purchase goods not produced by the household. Grain may be sold for cattle, salt, mill cloth, kerosene and jewellery. Grain may be purchased when grain production has failed in order to buy goods produced but not owned by the households. Payments in grain to labouring peasants may be sold by them in order for them to purchase goods (cloth, vegetables, cheaper types of grain) – which they may also have laboured to help to produce in order to obtain cash, in turn to pay taxes, rents for land or for the house, debts, the costs of marriage, the costs of production and so on.

Peasant households can be exploited by these transactions under several conditions:

where the market for their produce is reasonably competitive and efficient but where the production and marketing of the goods they need to buy are concentrated and controlled in such a way that peasants have to market more and more of their goods over the years to obtain the same type of consumer good (such as a saree) or input to agriculture (such as a ploughshare);

where one or a few merchants are so much more powerful than peasant sellers that they have no choice but to sell at prices which are below what they would be if formed in an open auction attracting many traders;

where the government or where independent state marketing boards or corporations endowed with monopoly powers practise prices below those of private markets and compel peasants to sell to them alone.

So the circulation of grain can be a means of extracting invisible resources from producers as well as a means of distributing physical resources to consumers. Profits in the hands of private merchants, or state marketing boards, grain repayments to merchants and money-lenders, taxes in the hands of the government are all resources which are then put to use directly or via channels of savings and investment. Houses, stores or temples may be built, land and lorries purchased, children educated, political parties funded or marriage alliances negotiated with the proceeds. The government may use its revenue for the salaries of its own officials, for its army and police, its education and medical system, its roads, electricity-generating stations or sports stadia. It may plough some of it back into grain production through subsidies or fertilizer, or investment in agricultural research, or irrigation. Though the process is 'bafflingly diverse', it is the agricultural sales of peasant producers which are now at the heart of it. We shall contrast two instances.

South-east India

Stretching from the foot of the battered and dissected Javadi Hills in Tamil Nadu state lies the Coromandel Plain, a mosaic of gullied and mostly dry watercourses, irrigation reservoirs called tanks, livid green rice fields, barren red watersheds, clumps of trees round villages of mud and thatch, brick and tile and people – 4 million of them in one district alone. About 35 per cent of the population is rural landless labour. Those who are landed farm on average only 3 acres. Eastern North Arcot District lies on this plain. Its simple agricultural economy is dominated by paddy (the name for rice before its husk is removed by milling) and groundnuts (peanuts), the former grown mostly on land irrigated by tank and well water and the latter on land fed by rain. The region is surplus in the two major grains. Here, as John Harriss shows in chapter 31 of this volume, despite a structure of landholdings which is by Indian standards relatively egalitarian, a class of capitalist farmers is emerging. The productivity of these farmers is greater than those of small peasants. But the expansion of this class is constrained by a relative shortage of land in which they can invest.

Little land is sold, for two types of reason, one being social. The kinship system (involving norms of marriage to cross-cousins) serves to maintain land within a tight circle of kin. The second reason concerns the economics of marketing. Local grain merchants see it in their interests not to foreclose on paddy-producing debtors, even instead to persist in lending money to them on reasonably competitive, not excessively exploitive terms. In turn there are two reasons for this. One is that merchants and peasants belong to the same castes, in contrast to scenarios for elsewhere in (north) India. Naturally transactions with relatives constrain the ability of a merchant to exploit them. The other reason is that the objective of a merchant who supplies loans in this way is to guarantee supplies of paddy with which he may subsequently make speculative profits on a market which is nevertheless characterized by crowding of intermediaries. This paradox needs further explanation.

Merchants' capital in North Arcot

Grain is commercialized in eastern North Arcot by over 2,000 trading firms supplying over a thousand rice mills. These trading firms are polarized. On the one hand there is a small elite of large businesses which dominates the trade through its command of information, contacts, credit and commodities. Less than 10 per cent of firms control as much of the grain trade as do the remaining 90 per cent. These large firms tend to be old, often having started in village locations with the centre of gravity of their operations switching to town in recent years. These firms began big and tend to remain so. Large-scale wholesale merchants are closely linked to each other by marriage alliances. Sons of one big house will marry daughters of another. They will also commonly serve apprenticeships, acquiring skills and contacts in the shops of a member of their kin group, perhaps someone better able than father to provide the right mix of stick and carrot. Trading in grain is typically one of a number of business activities in the portfolios of such houses, where several generations and/or brothers and their wives all live as a joint family under one roof. Larger traders have the larger agricultural properties of the region and are part of the small landlord class. Generally unentrepreneurial in their business dealings, they expand into commerce in other agricultural products and build urban property. They tend to own the fabric of the local market towns. They own some of the small fleets of lorries and carts. Few are migrants. Most are well embedded in social terms: the dominant trading caste is the dominant agricultural caste with niches in the bureaucratic apparatus as well.

Within such firms there is a precise division of labour, but only to a limited extent is role differentiation related to caste or to traditional occupation (for example Brahmin accountants and bookkeepers, or at the other extreme Harijan sweepers). First there is the relatively well-paid salariat: clerks, machine fitters in mills, etc. Clearly it is in the interests of the merchant to prevent a high turnover of his permanent workforce, hence such people may benefit from patronage in the form of profit sharing, or gifts at the time of marriage, or for educating a relative, or at times of sickness: a rudimentary and arbitrary means of compensating for the lack of a proper welfare state. Such people may equally well be tied to the patron by debt relations. Second there is the daily wage labour force: of weighers, baggers, watchmen, whose kind and cash wages vary greatly according to the particular tie (of caste, debt, years worked) between employer and employee. Lastly there is casual labour (male loaders and humpers, female paddy driers). These people are not patronized by the trader. After all from his point of view there is a massive labour surplus among which to choose the daily unskilled workforce. In some places and for some jobs these casual coolies have been able to retaliate by creating gangs and a closed shop. Elsewhere many political parties have created as much chaos as they have resolved by trying to organize, each, their own unions. Women, anchor points for the milling process, have as yet proved impossible to organize.

The big firms dominate market-town society. They appear as notable philanthropists, office bearers of the Lions and Rotary Clubs whose humanitarian activities reinforce their prestige and serve to foster useful social connections with local bureaucrats and with the professional elite of small-town lawyers and medical doctors. These mercantile firms are local financial *eminences grises* behind many political parties. They offer a supply of competent candidates for office in local government and in the cooperative agricultural credit and marketing societies. They dominate the committees running the regulated grain markets originally designed to improve the conditions of marketing for small producers. Their own commodity associations oppose threats from government intervention into their trade and from the labour unions by back-room lobbying at high political levels, where connections of kin with state ministers come in handy.

By contrast there exist a large number of small family firms, nevertheless more wealthy and more landed than the average peasant producer from the ranks of whom some have recently sprung. The rate at which the smaller merchants can accumulate profits is constrained by a number of factors to do with their smaller size and their dependence on the mercantile elite. The costs of renting shops, warehouses and mills, the fees for negotiating transport will be higher when the trader does not own these items of technology necessary for his business. The consumption expenses of the merchant's family, a return for their unwaged work, reduce pure profits. The third constraining factor is their need for private sector 'informal' credit, obtainable from large merchants, private registered 'finance corporations', 'private parties' (monied and propertied individuals living off money-lending) and, if all else fails, pawn-brokers. The further down the hierarchy of trading credit, the more urgent the need, the more risky the purpose, the more exploitive the terms and conditions in these compartmentalized money markets.

Competition in lending money to paddy-producing peasants is necessary to cement the particularistic social regulations guaranteeing supplies for speculative activity. The social obligations of traders to 'their' peasants then extend to exercise books for the education of a peasant boy, a few rupees free for urgent

Barbara Harriss

medicines, help with a pilgrimage. Money is lent to producers relatively cheaply not only because of kinship ties and competition from subsidized credit through the government's cooperative associations but also from credit supplied officially to fertilizer dealers in order to encourage them to expand their firms, and from modestly expanding but subsidized production credit for agriculture distributed by nationalized commercial banks. Lastly the 1970s saw the development of further competing suppliers of production credit from pawnbrokers, finance companies and even minor government officials.

While money-lending has not grown more remunerative, the rate of profit to be had from trading grain has increased, despite the increase in the number of merchants. The key to this paradox lies in the way merchants can manipulate government policies designed to curb mercantile power in such a way as to secure greater distortions in the prices which give merchants their profits. It operates like this. The government buys for its fair price shop system a fixed proportion of what merchants in turn buy from peasants. The state purchases at prices which are always below that of the market. Traders lose out but they more than compensate for their losses by hoisting the prices of all the paddy and rice that they have not sold to the government. Government regulation of the grain trade also means that the regional transport of grain is strictly controlled by permit only – a recipe for black market profits from smuggling and evasion. A moment's thought will show that there is no conflict of interests between the merchants and the government, for local officials benefit enormously from bribery and corruption and therefore are also in favour of this state of affairs. Merchants live in a state of apparent symbiosis with peasants and with the state but actually they dominate the rural economy.

Despite close social ties between peasants and merchants, the mercantile sector is slowly unhitching itself from agriculture proper. Private grain-trading capital is coming increasingly not from the investment of profits of agriculture but from the profits of trade as firms split up, branches are created, as urban employees serve their apprenticeships, save their initial capital and/or attract a large dowry from a rural bride and start out on their own. The rate of return from grain trading exceeds respectively those of private money-lending, grain milling, official money-lending and agricultural production. Fewer and fewer mercantile profits are being reinvested directly in land or in agriculture.

The rural economy is ever more rapidly integrated into national life and the big-city economy to which the savings of merchants and peasants alike flow via the investment activities of the mushrooming commercial banks. Over the last fifteen years, market towns have grown in importance as wholesaling centres not only of local agricultural produce but of agricultural goods exotic and unfamiliar a decade back (eggs, 'European' vegetables, Himalayan fruits, processed breads, for example) all produced hundreds of miles away. Also wholesaled are the industrial consumer goods (cosmetics, ready-made clothes, plastics, steel furniture) produced in metropolitan factories and increasingly retailed not only from the stalls of traditional periodic markets but also in small, young, but permanent village shops to followers of the urban fashions disseminated through the village TV and the cinema (Harriss and Harriss, 1984).

North-east India

There are many elements of comparison between North Arcot's granary and that of Birbhum District in West Bengal. Their physical environments and the total rainfall they receive are similar. They share a relatively simple rice-based cropping system. They have a net surplus of rice. They are both regions of smallholder agriculture with the same average holding size.

But there the comparison ends. The reason for the small size of holdings in Birbhum is not a long history of independent and relatively egalitarian landownership. Quite the reverse. The region has been dominated by a numerically very small class of controllers of land, money and commodity markets. Share-cropping, the production relation of landless cultivators, was commonplace and still is much more common and more exploitive than is tenancy in North Arcot. Nevertheless a relatively successful land reform has given many Bengali peasants rights over what they cultivate. There was no property reform to complement land reform so that the marketing structures of the pre-reform economy have been left, as we shall see, not quite intact. There is a marked contrast to North Arcot in the technology of rice production. Irrigation is unusual. Rice is rainfed. The new high-yielding technology is not as diffused as in the south. The labouring peasantry is poorer. The average income from rice cultivation in Birbhum is equivalent to that of a landless labourer in North Arcot. Despite (or because of) the local government's being a 'left front', a coalition of socialist parties, the vast mass of peasants have less power than in North Arcot, possibly because the forces which oppress them in Birbhum are more powerful. We shall look again at the role of grain merchants in this contrasting agrarian economy.

Merchants' capital in Birbhum

The commercialization of rice is more complex than in North Arcot. More people gain a livelihood from trade and more of it is openly illegal, by which we mean that it breaks one or more of the dense tracery of laws regarding licensing, storage, transactions, movement of goods, interest rates on credit and the taxation of trade which have been legislated by this, and every other, Indian state. There is a greater diversity of private intermediaries. The system is more highly stratified with the most powerful intermediaries contracting in number and the least powerful expanding.

Among the intermediaries which are expanding are village grocers who not only sell essentials (salt, rice, chillies, dhal, betel nut, spices and soap) on credit to paddy producers but also extend consumption loans in grain to be repaid after harvest at very high disguised interest. There are also rural 'husking' mills which dehusk paddy for villagers' own consumption in return for a fee. There are purchasing agents for the major rice mills and illegal petty traders rising from the ranks of the rich peasantry. In the latter two categories are estimated to be about 3,500 livelihoods, comparable with North Arcot to the south. Increasingly these intermediaries are unlicensed and therefore illegal and more of their mercantile activity is illegal.

Contrast this with the large-scale licensed intermediaries of whom there are a hundred in the district. The decline in their numbers does not spell decay but instead masks an economic concentration in activity. The 'satanic mills'[1] in Birbhum, whose long chimneys tower over the palm trees and bamboo thickets, not only are powerful relics of an earlier pre-land reform era and witness to the profits of the landlord class but also point to the needs for rice of the contemporary state (which we explain below) and both provoke and challenge the mushrooming illegal market. Since 1965, many of the erstwhile landlords' mills have been bought up by Marwaris, a specialized and successful migrant trading caste from north-west India, perhaps the only social group in India with the cash to surmount the formidable barriers to entry into large-scale, modern rice milling. The average rice milling firm in Birbhum is 22 times more wealthy than its counterpart in North Arcot and its official net income from milling is 90 times that of the average paddy producer, compared to a factor of only 7 in North Arcot.

Exchange relations in Birbhum are more exploitive than in North Arcot. Cheating by merchants on quality and on weights and measures is routine and hard for the peasant to circumvent. But disguised interest on pre-harvest loans in cash or in food can be up to ten times higher, because of the concentration of control over money in the hands of the great rice milling families. Grain prices veer more widely from season to season in Birbhum district than in North Arcot. Daily prices in villages vary more greatly according to the debt relationship of the seller and his status in local society. These social relations reduce the returns to paddy cultivation for many poor peasants and they also reduce the attractiveness of investing in risky new technology.

The state government gains from this process of subordination through the market. Since 1967 it has conferred upon the powerful milling oligopoly legal rights to control the wholesale trade in grain. It has also discriminated towards this class by subsidizing the costs of modernizing the technology for milling and the costs of operating new machines. Why does a left front government which has pressed through a land reform maintain and support such reactionary marketing institutions? Because it needs to supply Calcutta with rice and it can obtain that rice most easily using a levy system like that of North Arcot but with two crucial differences. Firstly the proportion that must be sold to the state is much higher in Birbhum (and thus the corresponding price distortions that give merchants their profits are much greater). Second, the fewer the mills, the more easy they are to police.

While the state finds no option but to persist in perpetuating this mutually reinforcing relationship with the merchant-millers, it finds itself in two debilitating contradictions. The first is this. The management of Calcutta's food supplies, and those to plantations and mining settlements, requires the greatest degree of centralization and concentration. The market distortions which arise from this concentration attract massive numbers of new entrants to the petty grain trade. To a popular socialist government these livelihoods are desirable; but they are also illegal. The second contradiction is as follows. The more livelihoods profiting from the price margins, the more rice is diverted away from the official system, the more difficult it is to provide Calcutta legally with food, the greater the incentive to increase the levy on rice mills even further, the even greater the compensating distortions to rice prices and the larger the flood of petty traders. This particular instance of subordination of peasants to legal and illegal, small and large merchants, millers and the state may be the most important explanation for the slow pace of technological change in paddy production. In this case the marketing system is indeed devouring its own 'nutrient base' in a way which makes its resolution difficult to predict.

Summing Up

Circulation or exchange is no new thing and it has not always needed the market to be its facilitating mechanism. Witness, for example, the hierarchical flows of goods and services mediated through the caste system, or the presents of the potlatch. These are socially stabilizing 'reciprocative' forms of exchange. Or witness the centralization of surplus by an authority, be it via flows of tax to a state fisc or via feudal dues. Such redistributive systems usually match the right to extract surplus with an unsymmetrical obligation to maintain the providers of surplus in some way, an obligation which needs institutions of distribution. These other forms of exchange may coexist with market exchange in combination and permutation (Polanyi et al., 1957, pp. vii–ix).

But markets are an increasingly pervasive means of circulation. The market has been characterized sociologically as a price-making institution which acts fluidly and randomly with respect to individuals (Polanyi, 1957, pp. 255–67). Nash's quasi-tribal and regional marketing systems (this volume, item 27) are of this sort and they integrate the economy alongside more or less reciprocal activity. Similar exchange systems have been identified in South Asia for regions dominated by small-scale producers (Blaikie, Cameron and Seddon, 1980). Trade, whether periodic or fixed in space and time, is impersonal, competitive and little specialized. Here the market integrates different ecological and cultural regions and/or castes or tribal groups exchanging crops and produce in the production of which they have specialized. This sort of market is also said to act as a leveller. Nash shows how technological, cultural and ritual factors exert control over accumulation.

But our two case-studies of more deeply commercialized localities in contemporary India show markets which do not resemble competitive archetypes, which also coexist with the degraded remnants of a reciprocal exchange system and with redistribution by the state. Here the levelling mechanisms have grown weaker and market activity is associated with a dissolution of older social structures.

North Arcot's grain-marketing system is imperfectly competitive. Mercantile intermediaries are numerous and polarized, with varying degrees of specialization. Relations of marketing tend to be particularistic and not impersonal. Trade and money comprise different institutions but in this case tend to be linked in order to secure a quantity and timing of grain transactions wherein producers receive the lowest possible open market prices. The conditions of concentrated production and oligopoly trade of industrial consumer goods comprise another manifestation of the subordination of peasants to the market. Through the operation of this market a new, specialized mercantile class emerges. This class is increasingly urban and allies itself with the local professional and bureaucratic bourgeoisie. Although not entrepreneurial, this mercantile class uses new technology. There are no technological controls over accumulation. Big mercantile houses appear with varied investment portfolios, increasingly divorcing land-based activity from trade, processing and money-lending. Equally, we can observe the consolidation of a large class of small producers 'compulsively involved in interlinked markets' (Bharadwaj, 1985). They are deprived of choice in grain and money markets, often selling grain at low harvest prices only to buy it back again for household consumption at high pre-harvest prices, deprived even of the ability to sell their land, thus preventing for the time being the full development of the land and labour markets. In such a system of exchange a peasant's independence is conditioned by his unindebtedness.

Here, it is the network of periodic markets which most closely approximates Nash's systems. But this similarity is deceptive. Actually North Arcot's periodic markets are used by poorest and lowest-caste people and form a spatially and socially distinct system from the marketing system focused on towns. Certainly levelling mechanisms operate. We saw that caste still acts as a constraint on accumulation even though other institutions (for example, competitive state credit) also have the same effect and even though non-market factors such as the scattered geographical distribution of plots belonging to chronically indebted producers prevent merchants from accumulating land and proletarianizing marginal peasants.

In Birbhum the manner in which peasants are subordinated to merchants and to the state is easy to see. Producers support a baroque edifice of intermediaries, some of whom are a hundred times more wealthy than they, and some of whom are significantly assisted by government subsidies. Mercantile wealth derives from their ability to exact resources from producers in the form of high interest on loans, depressed prices, arbitrary deductions for quality, cheating on weights and measures, and in certain cases illegally high share-cropping rents. Merchants are able to exploit in this way partly because of their historical concentration of power and partly because there are no compromising ties of kinship as there are in the south. As a result peasants get lower prices for their grain than they do in North Arcot. They also get a lower share of what local consumers pay for their rice (85 per cent in Birbhum), than they do in the south (93 per cent). In this region the dissolving effects of the market are tantamount to a de-peasantization. The indirect control by merchant-millers over the production process is so thorough that the share-cropper or the marginal peasant is a thinly disguised labourer. Their households depend substantially upon retail markets for grain.

The independence of such a peasantry resides in its ability to make more or less unfettered decisions about crop choice and technology, and about which party shall represent it in government; and in its ability to use uncosted family labour for productive work. Even this oligopolistic marketing system has its levellers: if there are few constraints to accumulation, then there are also few constraints (other than the merely juridical) to entry. Peasants can thus enter illegal petty trading, which, if they do so in sufficient numbers, actually threatens both the baroque mercantile edifice and the local state government. The evolution of a more competitive petty trading sub-system can also be seen as the gradual emergence of a marketing system appropriate to conditions of production after a land reform, even if this was not quite what the reformist state had intended.

Note

1 For William Blake these were the universities, whereas here the mills are more literal!

References

Bharadwaj, K. (1985) 'A view on commercialisation in Indian agriculture and the development of capitalism', *Journal of Peasant Studies*, vol. 12, no. 1, pp. 7–25.

Blaikie, P., Cameron, J. and Seddon, D. (1981) *Nepal in Crisis: Growth and Stagnation at the Periphery*, Clarendon: Oxford.

Harriss, B. and Harriss, J. (1984) '"Generative" or "parasitic" urbanism? Some observations from the recent history of a south Indian market town', in J. Harriss and M. Moore (eds) *Development and the Rural—Urban Divide*, Cass: London, pp. 82–101.

Polanyi, K. (1957) 'The economy as instituted process', in Polanyi et al. (eds), pp. 243-69.

Polanyi, K., Arensberg, C. M. and Pearson, H. W. (eds) (1957) *Trade and Market in the Early Empires*, Free Press: New York.
Smith, C. E. (ed.) (1976) *Regional Analysis: I Economic Systems*, Academic Press: New York.
Whitehead, A. (1981), 'I'm hungry Mum: the politics of domestic budgeting', in K. Young, C. Wolkowitz and R. McCullagh (eds) *Of Marriage and the Market: Womens' Subordination in International Perspective*, CSE Books: London, pp. 86-111.

Related Items

2, 4, 6, 9, 10, 16, 17, 18, 19, 22, 24, 25, 26, 27, 31, 32, 35, 36, 37, 43, 53, 55, 59, 60, 62.

29

Political Economy of Starvation

Amartya Sen

Starvation is the characteristic of some people not having enough food to eat. It is not the characteristic of their *being* not enough food to eat. While the latter can be a cause of the former, it is but one of many *possible* causes.

... If one person in eight starves regularly in the world, this is seen as the result of his inability to establish entitlement to enough food; the question of the physical availability of the food is not directly involved.

The approach of entitlements is quite inescapable in analysing starvation and poverty. If, nevertheless, it appears odd and unusual, this can be because of the hold of the tradition of thinking in terms of what *exists* rather than in terms of who can *command* what. The mesmerizing simplicity of focusing on the ratio of food to population has persistently played an obscuring role over centuries, and continues to plague policy discussions today much as it has deranged anti-famine policies in the past.

... A food-centred view tells us rather little about starvation. It does not tell us how starvation can develop even without a decline in food availability. Nor does it tell us – even when starvation is accompanied by a fall in food supply – why some groups had to starve while others could feed themselves. The over-all food picture is too remote an economic variable to tell us much about starvation. On the other hand, if we look at the food going to *particular* groups, then of course we can say a good deal about starvation. But, then, one is not far from just describing the starvation itself, rather than explaining what happened. If some people had to starve, then clearly, they didn't have enough food, but the question is: *why* didn't they have food? What allows one group rather than another to get hold of the food that is there?

... A person's ability to command food – indeed, to command any commodity he wishes to acquire or retain – depends on the entitlement relations that govern possession and use in that society. It depends on what he

Excerpts from Amartya Sen, *Poverty and Famines*, Clarendon Press, 1982, pp. 7–8, 154–6, 161–6.

owns, what exchange possibilities are offered to him, what is given to him free, and what is taken away from him.

... It is sometimes said that starvation may be caused not by food shortage but by the shortage of income and purchasing power. This can be seen as a rudimentary way of trying to catch the essence of the entitlement approach, since income does give one entitlement to food in a market economy. ... But the inadequacy of the income-centred view arises from the fact that, even in those circumstances in which income does provide command, it offers only a partial picture of the entitlement pattern, and starting the story with the shortage of income is to leave the tale half-told. People died because they didn't have the income to buy food, but how come they didn't have the income?

... The entitlement approach requires the use of categories based on certain types of discrimination. A small peasant and a landless labourer may both be poor, but their fortunes are not tied together. In understanding the proneness to starvation of either we have to view them not as members of the huge army of 'the poor', but as members of particular classes, belonging to particular occupational groups, having different ownership endowments, and being governed by rather different entitlement relations. Classifying the population into the rich and the poor may serve some purpose in some contexts, but it is far too undiscriminating to be helpful in analysing starvation, famines, or even poverty.

... Viewed from the entitlement angle, there is nothing extraordinary in the market mechanism taking food away from famine-stricken areas to elsewhere. Market demands are not reflections of biological needs or psychological desires, but choices based on exchange entitlement relations. If one doesn't have much to exchange, one can't demand very much, and may thus lose out in competition with others whose needs may be a good deal less acute, but whose entitlements are stronger. In fact, in a slump famine such a tendency will be quite common, unless other regions have a more severe depression. Thus, food being *exported* from famine-stricken areas may be a 'natural' characteristic of the market which respects entitlement rather than needs.

... In a peasant economy a crop failure would reduce both availability and the direct entitlement to food of the peasants. But in so far as the peasant typically lives on his own-grown food and has little ability to sell and buy additional food from the market anyway, the immediate reason for his starvation would be his direct entitlement failure rather than a decline in food availability in the market. Indeed, if his own crop fails while those of others do not, the total supply may be large while he starves. Similarly, if his crop is large while that of others goes down, he may still be able to do quite well despite the fall in total supply. The analytical contrast is important even though the two phenomena may happen simultaneously in a general crop failure. While such a crop failure may superficially look like just a crisis of food availability, something more than availability is involved. This is important to recognize also from the policy point of view, since just moving food into such an area will not help the affected population when what is required is the generation of food entitlement.

The focus on entitlement has the effect of emphasizing legal rights. Other relevant factors, for example market forces, can be seen as operating *through* a system of legal relations (ownership rights, contractual obligations, legal exchanges, etc.). The law stands between food availability and food entitlement. Starvation deaths can reflect legality with a vengeance.

Related Items

9, 10, 13, 22, 24, 28, 30, 31, 32, 42, 45, 59, 62.

30

Landed Property in Bengal: Power and Faction as an Economic Factor

Hussain Zillur Rahman

With the imposition of British colonial rule in Bengal towards the close of the eighteenth century, property rights in land became subject to two fundamental but contradictory influences. On one hand, colonial rule gradually led to the supersession of the localized, customary contexts in which land rights had hitherto been manifest. This was partly a matter of legislation whereby a legal framework of property was established and, more concretely, the creation of a network of rural police stations (*thana*) and a network of law courts which over time supplanted the two customary adjudicating roles by which rights in land had up till then been held. These adjudicating roles had been those of the zamindar or the local lord and of the customary leadership of village communities. One consequence of colonial rule, thus, was that property rights in land lost their localized, customary basis in the power of the landlord and the institutional cohesion of village society. Instead, their proof and their guarantee became vested in colonial state-power.

Contradictorily, however, on these very questions of proof and guarantee, a fundamental ambivalence marked the actual functioning of colonial state-power. First of all, a definitive record of rights never came to be established for Bengal, a factor which greatly impaired the ability of the courts to provide conclusive adjudication. Secondly, the growth of law was oriented not towards securing the social consolidation of legal property but towards strengthening the hegemony of the colonialist state authority over civil life. Among other features, this was evident in the marked underdevelopment of laws of trespass by which the injured party could secure compensation in favour of a strengthening of the criminal judicial power of the Executive authority, a feature which sharply distinguished British colonial rule in Bengal from the

An original paper.

corresponding experience of Britain itself. Lastly, the judicial procedure which came to be introduced militated against the 'ascertaining of truth' of cases in dispute. The combined effect of these key features of colonial rule was that instead of functioning as the definitive arbiter enforcing the structure of legal property in land, the judicial and police institutions of the colonial state only imposed themselves on agrarian society as necessary arenas for manœuvring by parties in dispute. In effect, therefore, the legal title by itself did not guarantee the right of property but neither could it be disregarded, any more than could the institutions of law and police themselves by which it was circumscribed.

By divesting land rights of their customary basis but failing to act as a definitive 'universal arbiter', British colonial rule 'politicized' land-property and functionalized village life. The stability of the individual right became crucially dependent on the holder's political capacity to manœuvre both within the local arena and within the institutions of the state. This political capacity, however, was not institutionalized, for that would have meant supplanting the functions of the law courts and the rural police stations or the creation of a duality of state and local power, neither of which occurred. The ambivalent adjudication by colonial state-power and the individualized political manœuvring by which the stability and the effectiveness of the right of property was secured were two sides of a single structural process, the former being the precondition for the latter.

Inasmuch as land-property rights came to be underpinned by individualized political manœuvring, they were continually vulnerable at the individual level. This was a further twist to the 'politicization' of land-property. Power and participation in processes of power in the village became a sine qua non for effective and stable property rights, but such power was necessarily informal and individualized and hence continually open to challenges. Power, in this sense, became a directly economic concern for members of the agrarian society. Land use and control relate directly to rural faction.

Within the substantive evolution of agrarian society shaped by broader economic and demographic factors, a structural instability was thus brought into operation by the British colonial rule, a dynamic which permeated alike the political and economic life of village society. Its twin manifestations were the dynamism of the land structure (property, control or use) and the political dynamic of unstable factionalism. Both of these entered village life in colonial Bengal, and indeed this very much remains so in contemporary Bangladesh in so far as the specific system of law courts and police which engendered the particular property–power nexus has not been superseded by the ending of British colonial rule.

Related Items

5, 6, 18, 21, 25, 26, 29, 35, 37, 39, 43, 44, 46, 52, 58, 61.

31

Capitalism and Peasant Production: The Green Revolution in India

John Harriss

Introduction

Theories about peasants and capitalism

It is generally held that the process of economic development connotes increasing diversification and specialization of productive activity, probably increasing scale of units of production, and that these tendencies in turn imply concentration in urban centres. Another way of regarding the process is to see it as involving a 'structural transformation' in which there is a progressive shift of the labour force out of agriculture and into secondary and tertiary activity. The agricultural sector must supply not only labour for other activities, but also raw materials, food and resources for investment in the course of this transformation. The conception of 'structural transformation' on these lines implies that there should be a progressive dissolution of peasant production. The contradictory character of peasants as both owners of means of production and direct producers (workers on the land) is seen as retarding diversification and specialization. Their ownership of resources, too, is thought to make it possible for them to retreat from involvement in the market into subsistence production, so making it difficult for state organizations to acquire the necessary resources for investment in other sectors. This is Hyden's argument with regard to the Tanzanian peasantry, which he considers to have been 'uncaptured' by the market (Hyden, 1980). In the context of dominant ideas about the process of development, therefore, the continued existence of peasants may be seen as a problem. It should be noted that these ideas are held in common both by many liberal thinkers and by Marxists and socialists.

An original paper.

But it has been argued with force and tenacity, especially since Lenin's work *The Development of Capitalism in Russia*, published in 1899, that increasing commercialization of rural economies encourages more and more social and economic differentiation amongst producers (essentially as a result of the forces of competition). Over time, therefore, it is to be expected that a class of relatively large-scale, capitalist agricultural producers is formed, while the mass of the peasants is transformed into a proletariat. The same process expands the home market for the goods and services of more specialized agricultural and non-agricultural production (the mechanisms involved are considered in more detail below). Thus, according to this model of the relations between capitalist development and the peasantry, Hyden's problem is solved by commercialization and the development of capitalist relations in agriculture.

Against this line of thought, however, there is set another tradition which holds both that the peasant economy is a very distinctive form of production and that it is relatively efficient in various ways, so that there is no necessary process whereby the peasantry will be dissolved. Some thinkers in this tradition are critical of the conceptions of development to which we have referred; and most if not all of them reject the assumption of the backwardness of peasant production which is associated with these ideas. Peasant production is efficient for a variety of reasons – because of the peasants' knowledge about the agro-climatic environment in which they work; because of those special features of agricultural production processes, including their pronounced seasonality and the difficulties of the supervision of labour, which make agriculture relatively unpromising from the point of view of capitalist investment; because of the flexibility of family labour; and because peasant producers economize in the use of scarce resources. Both as a result of their efficiency, and because the peasant form of production can survive without 'profits' so long as the costs of peasant labour (subsistence) are met, it is held that the development of capitalism does not necessarily lead to the dissolution of the peasantry.

An extension of this reasoning shows that the development of capitalism may involve the subordination of peasant producers to industrial or to commercial capital, in such a way that the household form of production is continuously reproduced though under conditions in which its autonomy is undermined. A particularly clear form of this relationship is that in which agribusiness firms intervene in the organization of production on apparently independent peasant farms, by offering credit and inputs, laying down technical conditions, and providing a market.[1] As peasant producers come to depend on the agribusiness concern for inputs, they may effectively be converted '. . . into a labour force working with other people's means of production' (Thorner et al., 1966, p. 262). Capitalist development in agriculture may take place in this way, therefore – by means of vertical concentration rather than horizontal concentration involving the creation of spatially larger and larger units of production.

Vertical concentration based on agro-processing (dairying, sugar refining, freezing or canning of vegetables and fruit, and even rice milling) means that capitalists can benefit from the relative efficiency of peasant production, because (for example) the costs of supervision of labour are reduced or eliminated, being borne by the peasants themselves. Other variants of this relationship between capital and peasant production are possible, notably that in which peasant producers are dependent for inputs or for part of the costs of their subsistence, on merchant capitalists whose interests are in gaining control of the peasants' output at the lowest possible price. But whatever the specific form of the relationship (which must be investigated empirically), it involves the continued reproduction of the peasant form of production under conditions partly determined by the interests of capital. This is no more of a 'necessary' development than is the differentiation and dissolution of the peasantry. It is historically contingent and will be affected by factors like those of population pressure and environmental degradation which may undermine the viability of peasant production.[2]

The purpose of this essay is to amplify these arguments concerning the relations between capital and peasantry by reference to a specific case. The 'green revolution' in South Asia was widely understood, in the late 1960s and early 1970s, to be having the effect of encouraging the differentiation of peasant producers along the lines of Lenin's analysis. We examine the reasoning behind this judgement and the evidence for it, and explain by reference to material from regions of north India and from a micro-level study of trends of agrarian change in a region of south India, how and why actual changes have been much more complicated and contradictory than either the Leninist 'differentiation' model or a model, on Chayanovian lines, of independent peasant economy would suggest. The essay shows the analytical usefulness of both models in comprehending historical process, whilst also demonstrating that neither is satisfactory and sufficient in itself.

The 'green revolution'

The term 'green revolution' came into use in the late 1960s to refer to the effects of the introduction of higher-yielding varieties (HYVs) of wheat and rice in 'developing' countries. The expression was deliberately coined to contrast with the phrase 'red revolution', and the notion that 'developing' countries were to undergo far-reaching changes as a result of an agricultural revolution, rather than because of radical political transformation, gives a clue to the political interests involved in the generation of the new agricultural technology. Research foundations established by the American capitalists Ford and Rockefeller played a very important role in organizing and funding the agricultural research which produced the HYVs. And the strategic, geopolitical interests of the United States in changing rural social and economic conditions in Asia and Latin America, with a view to the containment of communist expansion, were clear. The papers of the American agricultural expert Wolf Ladejinsky, for example, show how strong were the interests of the United States government in the 1940s and 1950s in encouraging distributivist land reforms in Asia, aimed at both increasing agricultural output and improving social distribution. As hopes of achieving effective land reforms receded, so attention came to be focused on bringing about increased production by means of the intensification of agriculture, involving the application of fertilizers and agro-chemicals, irrigation, and the search for improved varieties. This was the message of an influential report for the Government of India prepared by Ford Foundation staff in 1959, following which India embarked upon a strategy aimed at intensification, initially in specially selected, supposedly favoured areas. It was in this context that research was carried out on which the 'green revolution' was based.

Plant breeding research directed at improving the productivity of crops was not new, certainly in the South Asian context but scientists working first of all on wheat in Mexico in the 1940s and 1950s, and later on rice at the International Rice Research Institute (IRRI) in the Philippines, achieved a breakthrough with the breeding of varieties that were particularly responsive to inputs of chemical fertilizers, which were shorter-strawed than existing varieties and thus, being more resistant to lodging, adapted to carrying bigger ears, and which were also sometimes of relatively short duration. These are important botanical characteristics of varieties with the potential of doubling or more than doubling average yields and of permitting more intensive cultivation by making it possible to increase the frequency of cropping of the land. But to achieve these results the first generation of HYVs required high fertility conditions. The new varieties usually required high levels of application of fertility-enhancing inputs (principally chemical fertilizers) in circumstances of adequate and controlled water supply (often requiring irrigation). Further, the conditions of their cultivation encouraged infestation by insects and disease, so that they also needed application of plant-protection chemicals. The successful use of the HYVs thus required the adoption of what came to be called a 'package' of inputs (new seeds, fertilizers and agro-chemicals) and cultivation practices (controlled irrigation and more systematic planting). And the package required cultivators to dispose of cash for the purchase of most of its components. Whereas before they had been able to use their own seed, they now had to purchase it, if not every season, certainly quite frequently. Before, when they fertilized their fields it was mostly with manure obtained from their animals or from the commons. But now these sources of fertility were inadequate and fertilizers had to be purchased, as did plant-protection chemicals, which had not been much needed before. The use of the HYV package brought with it an enhanced demand for cash, and involvement in the markets for both inputs and output.

The 'Green Revolution' and the Peasantry

It has often been pointed out that the HYV package, of seed, fertilizer and chemicals, is highly divisible and that it is therefore 'scale neutral' – that there are no particular economies of scale associated with it. So, it is argued, it may be used with as much benefit by very small as by very large producers. It should be possible to assist small producers, if necessary, to meet the cash requirements of the package, by extending credit to them on normal banking terms. In principle all this may be perfectly correct, but the principle does not amount to much in the circumstances of Third World rural economies, characterized by wide disparities in economic and political power and the existence of very large numbers of impoverished producers. The new technology may theoretically be 'scale neutral' but it is certainly not 'resource neutral'.[3] Perhaps the crucial point here is that those disposing of more resources are in a much better position to cope with the risks associated with this more cash-intensive technology. A small producer who has to borrow extensively in order to meet the cash costs of HYV cultivation runs the risk, in the event of failure because of miscalculation or unfavourable agro-climatic conditions, of becoming deeply indebted and thereby of placing the household in more precarious circumstances than before. Failure is a serious matter for producers with more resources, too, but they at least have a buffer which is not there for the poor small producer. It has been found very commonly, and for reasons which are clear, that those with more resources, whether economic or political, have better access to the controlled irrigation necessary for HYV cultivation, perhaps because they have been better able to invest in groundwater irrigation or because they are able to influence the distribution of water in a bureaucratically controlled canal irrigation system. Those with more resources in the first place are more likely to be able to obtain credit for the purchase of inputs at low rates of interest; if inputs like fertilizer are in short supply then they are more likely to be able to obtain them, or they may be able to obtain them at a lower price; and those with more resources are more likely to enjoy easy access to extension and other services supplied by the state. Those well endowed with resources are also more likely to be able to command sufficient labour at the most appropriate times for successful cultivation; and where the hiring of labour is necessary (as it is for almost all producers at some stages in the cultivation of wet rice), the big people may well be able to pay lower wages because some labourers are indebted to them over long periods.[4] These are some of the more important reasons why the HYV package is not 'resource neutral', and they often mean not simply that those with more resources are able to make better use of the package than the small producers but also that conditions are thereby created which are even more unfavourable to small producers (because the success of the relatively well-off makes it more difficult for poorer cultivators to obtain labour, or credit, or fertilizers). Further, the success of the few better-endowed producers, and the advantages to them in the mechanization of operations, especially when the increased labour demands of the HYVs have tightened labour markets, pushed up wage rates and encouraged the political mobilization of labour, can encourage displacement of labour, eviction of tenants and the physical expansion of already large farms at the expense of the smaller.

In spite of the difficulties which they have encountered in securing access to the HYV package, very many small producers have taken up the new varieties. Their mode of economic calculation may be different from that of large producers, for they are perhaps concerned above all with the total quantity of grain coming from their fields rather than with a profitability calculation. If HYVs make it possible for them to double the yield, then they may have a powerful incentive to adopt them even in the face of high cash costs which mean that when standard farm management accounting is done it appears that their 'profits' are no more, and may even be less than with the older varieties. They may attempt to meet cash costs from work off their own holdings. But the cultivation of HYVs by such producers has often meant that they have had to start taking or to take larger advances of credit in order to meet cultivation costs; and that they have then had to sell all or a large part of their product immediately after harvest, when prices are low, because of their debts. It may be said that they have become 'compulsively involved' in markets – selling grain even when they have no real surplus at all.

All the conditions described have been observed in different parts of the Third World where the HYV package has been taken up. And the operation of the processes referred to has led to the expectation that the 'green revolution' will lead to the differentiation of peasant producers, where this term is used not simply in the descriptive sense of 'greater socio-economic differentiation between people' but rather to refer to the process of formation of classes. Thus Andrew Pearse, who directed a major international research project on the impact of the introduction of HYVs in the early 1970s, wrote:

The discriminatory nature of (the) package strategy . . . and of the obligatory leap into capital intensive commercial farming . . . (results in) . . . a self-fuelling pressure towards polarisation magnified by a variety of political, economic and social factors pushing larger cultivators towards a qualitatively more profitable agriculture and greater competitive strength in the market, accompanied by increased political power. . . . The problem is not that which is generally posed, . . . the intractability of 'subsistence agriculture', but its decline to the point where it does not even provide subsistence. The movement out of agriculture implied in this process is a long term trend that can be expected to take place, and which is a positive feature of development so long as alternative earning opportunities exist, but in most of the countries studied the alternative opportunities for productive occupation were so few that they were frequently insufficient to absorb the natural increase in urban population. . . . (Pearse, 1980, pp. 169, 181)

This statement reflects an understanding of the effects of the introduction of the new varieties as stimulating the development of capitalism in agrarian society, where such development is conceived of in terms like those of Lenin in his work *The Development of Capitalism in Russia* (1899). On the basis of an exhaustive analysis of the evidence available for Russia in the late nineteenth century Lenin concluded then:

> The system of socio-economic relations existing among the peasantry . . . shows us the presence of all those contradictions which are inherent in every commodity economy and every order of capitalism: competition, the struggle for economic independence, the grabbing of land (purchasable and rentable), the concentration of production in the hands of a minority, the forcing of the majority into the ranks of the proletariat, their exploitation by a minority through the medium of merchants' capital and the hiring of farm labourers. . . . The sum total of all the economic contradictions amongst the peasantry constitutes what we call the differentiation of the peasantry. The peasants themselves very aptly and strikingly characterise this process with the term 'depeasantising'. (Lenin, 1899, p. 172)

This conception of capitalist development as entailing the differentiation of rural producers and 'de-peasantization' has been enormously influential despite contemporary and subsequent criticism. A number of writers, like Pearse, have seen in the 'green revolution' the working out in practice of Lenin's model. In the next section of this essay we will review some of the evidence on the introduction of HYVs and peasant differentiation in India.

The New Technology and Peasant Differentiation in India

It is, of course, extremely difficult to make sensible generalizations about India as a whole. But one generalization which is undisputed is that the impact of the 'green revolution' has differed widely between regions. It has increased regional disparities and had considerable impact upon the agrarian structures of some regions and almost none at all elsewhere. It has had particularly profound effects in the predominantly wheat-growing region of north-west India (the states of Punjab and Haryana, and the western part of Uttar Pradesh); a very moderate impact on the rice-growing areas of eastern India and rather more effect on those of the south: and it has had very little impact at all over much of the central plateau. There is, however, widespread and abundant evidence that the new technology is not 'resource neutral' for the reasons we have outlined; and an authoritative survey of quantitative evidence has concluded that

> labourers and landowners both benefited [though] landowners cornered most of the benefits which resulted in increased disparity between them and the labourers . . . [while] . . . the relative disadvantage of the small owners vis-a-vis the new technology

[has meant that] income disparity among different classes of landowners measured also by concentration ratio has increased. (ICSSR, 1980, p. 15)

The same survey points out, however, that there has been some *reduction* in the concentration of landownership and that

... [the] shift in land distribution in favour of the medium and small cultivators not only seems to have restrained the adverse income distribution effects of technological change but also reduced marginally the rural disparity of incomes [consumption] at the aggregate level. (ICSSR, 1980, p. 16)

The quantitative evidence both from large-scale surveys and from micro-level research showing that landlessness and the concentration of land ownership have tended to decline, not increase, over the period in which the new technology has been introduced certainly seems to contradict the thesis of 'de-peasantization'. But the analysis of differentiation as a social process calls for more than simple inspection of indices of concentration.

There is a good deal of evidence showing that the new technology has increased differentiation amongst rural producers in the wheat-growing belt of the north-west, though it also shows that this process is more complicated than in the classical model (based on Lenin's 1899 study). In the north-west intensive utilization of the new technology has greatly increased the demand for agricultural labour, and wage rates have been pushed up. These circumstances have also encouraged cultivators to mechanize operations (and by the early 1970s, indeed, the states of Punjab, Haryana and western UP had more than 50 per cent of all India's tractors on less than one-fifth of the net sown area). Evidence on the dispossession of poor peasants is not unambiguous, for in Punjab as elsewhere the proportion of rural households not owning land has tended to decline. But it appears that there has been a shift in the distribution of the *operated area* in favour of rich peasants and that this has not come about through the complete dispossession of poor peasants, but rather as a result of the reversion of land formerly tenanted by poor peasants and of 'reverse tenancy' under which small landholders rent out land to bigger owners. Byres concludes his review of the evidence by suggesting that a process of *partial proletarianization* has been in effect, and that this process, though not initiated by it, has certainly been hastened by the operation of the new technology:

That process has added to the already large number of landless labourers ... it has not done this on a large scale, however. Rather its most significant contribution has been to throw into increased wage employment large numbers of poor peasants who continue to own some land, and to bring some share-croppers near to the state of pure wage labour. (Byres, 1981, p. 432)

At the same time the rich peasants of north-west India have become effectively organized as a class, reflected in their capacity to avoid taxation and to maintain high agricultural prices, and in their forceful political presence.

Bhaduri, Rahman and Arn have developed a similar but more general argument about the partial nature of the process of proletarianization. They found in an intensive survey of four villages in Bangladesh that land ownership was relatively stable over time and that small ownership households in agriculture persisted on more or less the same footing as the larger-sized landowning households. They show that the process of polarization of rural producers may actually generate a contradictory process of stabilization of the poor peasantry through the creation of supplementary income opportunities. Thus many small landholders retain their holdings by engaging extensively in wage employment, or because of the availability of other income obtained from activities outside the cultivation of their own land (Bhaduri et al., 1986).

The effects of the introduction of the new technology are diverse and complicated, and may be contradictory. In order to tease out some of the relations of capitalist development and the peasantry, therefore, we turn to a specific, detailed case-study.

The 'Green Revolution' and the Development of Agrarian Capitalism in Northern Tamil Nadu, South India

The region in question is the eastern part of North Arcot District, situated on the broad coastal plain of south-eastern India, and with a rural population of 1.85m. in 1971 (average density of 0.4 ha per person).[5] The climate is monsoonal, with most rain falling in October–November, and a long dry period. There is a water deficit through the year except in the months from August to November and cultivation is heavily dependent upon irrigation. An extensive system of 'tank' irrigation (based on reservoirs formed by the construction of earth bunds across the lines of intermittent water courses) has been in existence for many centuries, supplemented by the use of groundwater lifted from big open wells. Latterly, in the 1960s and 1970s, groundwater irrigation has greatly expanded as a result of rural electrification and the widespread introduction of small (3 and 5 hp) electric pumping sets. The cropping systems of the area are quite simple. Irrigated rice (or 'paddy') is cultivated wherever possible, and in tracts with good groundwater resources three crops may be fitted in on the same land in one year. Then non-irrigated 'dryland' between the irrigated areas usually carries one crop per annum, overwhelmingly of groundnuts, of which the district as a whole was an important exporter earlier in this century and of which it remains a major producer. There is usually only a short lean season with little agricultural activity (in mid- to late November). In the early 1970s paddy covered about 50 per cent of the gross cropped area and groundnuts (then giving an income to the cultivator on average 65 per cent of that from an acre of paddy) occupied another 40 per cent.

Eastern North Arcot has never been a region of large estates or of extensive tenancy, but rather has been characterized by the prevalence of smallholding peasantry. In a random sample survey conducted in 1973–4 only 5 per cent of cultivators were found to be tenants, accounting for 6 per cent of production and 6 per cent of cultivated land. But the same survey showed that 36 per cent of households were landless; that only 49 per cent of households derived the major part of their incomes from cultivation, 35 per cent from agricultural labour and 16 per cent from non-agricultural activity. It has been quite reliably estimated by Washbrook that in such predominantly 'dry' districts of southeast India already by the end of the nineteenth century about 80 per cent of households were 'marginal' in the sense that they did not own sufficient productive resources of their own to be able to satisfy their own livelihood requirements, except by working for others. Commodity relations were extensive by 1900 and a class of agricultural wage workers (sometimes understood to be the condition of the development of agrarian capitalism) was in existence. In these circumstances a small class of rich peasants, through their control over land, also exercised extensive power over labour, credit in cash and kind, and in the product markets: and they came to enjoy considerable political power as well (Washbrook, 1976, chapter 1). Their dominance has continued to the present.

The introduction of the new HYVs of rice was preceded in North Arcot by rural electrification and widespread adoption of electric pumpsets. Investment in these was partly financed by formal, state credit agencies (set up to encourage agricultural development) but the bulk of it (70 per cent according to surveys in 1973–4) came from producers' own funds and from private loans. The new rice varieties began to be introduced in the late 1960s but they occupied less than 20 per cent of gross paddy acreage until after 1975. By the early 1980s they occupied more than 90 per cent of the gross paddy area in many villages; consumption of chemical fertilizers and agro-chemicals had increased correspondingly; and even between 1976–7 and 1980–1 the number of electric pumpsets in use increased by 26 per cent (from an already high base). It is an area where it makes sense to talk of a 'green revolution' as having taken place, for it has been estimated that the output of paddy increased by more than 50 per cent over the 1970s, with average yields having doubled since the introduction of HYVs.

The process of adoption of the modern technology, and the distribution of benefits accruing from it, have been no less subject to the 'talents effect' (Andrew Pearse's evocative phrase, referring to the biblical parable), relating to basic differences between people and households in terms of their control over resources, than they have elsewhere. Research in the early 1970s showed that the extent and the success of adoption were crucially related to access to groundwater irrigation and that to the amount of land or other resources or sources of incomes owned by different households. When farm operations were accounted for using a standard frame appropriate to capitalist units of production, it was found that while HYVs were very much more profitable than the older varieties for rich peasants, they were not necessarily so for middle and poor peasants. This was because of higher unit costs paid out by these smaller producers, for cash inputs like draught power, fertilizers, and water, and also for labour (for in the cultivation of irrigated rice even very small producers cannot substitute household for hired labour in operations like transplanting; and in circumstances in which there is sometimes a shortage of labour so that wage rates are bid upwards, it is often necessary for smaller farmers to pay higher rates than rich peasants who have a retinue of more or less permanently indebted client labourers). In spite of the difficulties which they faced poor peasants were often keen to adopt the new technology, for the reasons relating to their mode of economic calculation which we discussed above. While it was possible for poor peasants to derive benefit from the cultivation of the modern varieties, it seemed highly likely also to reinforce the extent of their compulsive involvement in the market.

'Compulsive involvement' in markets and the persistent indebtedness associated with it are circumstances which have been thought likely, in principle, to lead eventually to loss of land and thus to 'de-peasantization'. The research showed, however, that a majority of peasants (rich and poor) relied extensively upon advances of cash from paddy traders. But traders did not commonly foreclose on debts because their interests were primarily in securing and controlling supplies of grain at the lowest possible price, which could be achieved by establishing the dependence of cultivators upon them so that the cultivators were forced to sell their grain immediately after harvest when prices are lowest, and in circumstances in which they could not afford to protest too forcibly over rates and the precision of weights. Rates of profit were considerably higher in paddy trading and agro-processing than in agricultural production itself, and there seemed to be no reason why traders should want directly to take over land so long as this was the case.

In summary, therefore, research in the early 1970s suggested that the introduction of the new technology was responsible for a deepening of commodity relations in this rural economy, as cultivation became more extensively monetized because of producers' needs for more and more costly cash inputs. At the same time the potential profitability of HYV cultivation had given a filip to the expansion of capitalist production in agriculture. Yet it seemed that this expansion was already being constrained because of a set of interlinking factors. Capitalist farmers could not easily expand their activities because of the land constraint and the difficulty of expanding the size of their farms. Some had already invested as much as it was safe to do in groundwater irrigation and in circulating capital, and could only expand further by taking over more land. But this they could not easily do because of the continuing reproduction of smallholding property. And the needs of smallholding producers for advances of cash meant that the uses of money capital in money-lending, as well as in trading, were more profitable than in agricultural production itself. The system of partible inheritance, by breaking up larger units of production, also contributed to the reproduction of small property;

and the survival of small peasants was assisted by the operations of the kinship
system which worked to keep property in a small circle of kin. In addition state
interventions, in the interest of 'rural development' (desirable for the expansion
of agricultural output and perhaps even more to satisfy political aims,
including the maintenance of support for the regime), such as those supplying
cheap credit through 'cooperative' institutions, played a part in the continuing
reproduction of small property.

It makes little sense to regard the wider economy of which the rural economy
of eastern North Arcot is a part as anything other than fundamentally
structured by capitalism. The majority of rural producers, however, are not
capitalists but combine in themselves the contradictory characteristics of being
both owners of some means of production *and* direct producers. The introduction of new technology created conditions for some expansion of capitalism in
agriculture, but it did not appear likely in the early 1970s that it would lead to
widespread 'de-peasantization' on the lines of the classical model.[6]

Further research, in 1983–4, in which the histories of the same households
studied a decade earlier were analysed in detail, confirmed and amplified these

TABLE 31.1 *Landholding class mobility matrices, Randam village, 1984*

Landholding: position at inheritance	LL	1	2	3	4	Total	
LL	112	4	5	4	5	130	
1 (*lowest quartile*)	4	29	5	3	1	42	
2	7	2	20	4	8	41	*upward* 15.5%
3	5	7	3	19	7	41	
4 (*upper quartile*)	1	1	1	3	35	41	
Total	129	43	34	33	56		*no change* 73%
			downward 11.5%				

The matrix describes what has happened to households' landholdings since the time at
which each household head inherited land, up to 1984. The categories distinguished are
those of the landless, and the quartile groups of the distribution of landholders. Thus the
first, or lowest quartile, is made up by those household heads in the bottom 25 per cent of
the distribution. Of the households which were in the lowest 25 per cent at the time of
inheritance, 29 were still in the lowest quartile of the distribution in 1984, four had become
landless, five had acquired so much more land as to have moved up into the second
quartile, three had moved up into the third quartile, and one household had moved into the
top quartile. The figures on the upward side of the diagonal lines refer to households which
have been upwardly mobile, i.e. have acquired more land so as to have moved into higher
quartiles of the landholding distribution; the figures on the downward side refer to those
households which have been downwardly mobile in terms of landholding.

conclusions. Little or no change was found in the incidence of landlessness or in the distribution of land ownership, and indeed there had been more upward than downward mobility in terms of landholding (see table 31.1 for data for one village). At the same time there had been a decline in the numbers of house-holds depending primarily upon agricultural wage labour for their livelihoods; the numbers of male agricultural labourers had remained roughly constant, though the numbers of female labourers had increased; and the numbers in the labour force of those who were primarily cultivators had also tended to decline. There had been a marked shift into other activities outside agriculture, especially into handloom weaving, where incomes were higher than for agricultural labouring; into trading; and into a variety of 'service' occupations including casual labour jobs in local towns and minor public sector jobs in the villages; as well as into livestock husbandry (dairy cattle and sheep). There had also been an increase in the numbers of people who had migrated to major cities for work, especially to Madras and Bangalore, though some as far afield as Bombay. In most of these cases entire households had not moved out, but only individuals who continued to be considered as members of the village based family (in the context of what has been aptly described as 'share family' arrangements). This general shift into these other activities had the effect of tightening the agricultural labour market in many if not in all villages, and real wage rates had risen in consequence.

The net effect of these changes is summed up in the (household) class mobility matrix for one village between 1973 and 1984 (table 31.2) when it is considered together with the landholding data (table 31.1). There may have been some *levelling down* (mainly as a result of substantive changes – principally the partitioning of households, which accounts for most of the downward movement shown in the matrix), but it has not been on a large scale. Rather there has been a shift into increased dependence on non-agricultural activities, including some in distant cities, so that there has been a proletarianizing tendency in operation. But there is no evidence at all of a process of dispossession or for 'de-peasantization' in that sense. As Bhaduri and his fellow-authors point out, the tendencies which may exert a push towards polarization also give rise to increased income-earning activities, which have the effect of stabilizing small property holding.

There is evidence on changes in incomes and their distribution which shows that there have been real gains accruing to most rural people from the expansion of agricultural output. But there are also indications from this region as from elsewhere in Tamil Nadu that returns from the cultivation of HYVs have been squeezed by increased costs of inputs, not reliably compensated for by increases in paddy prices (which, anyway, continue to exhibit wide intra- and inter-seasonal variance). It is unlikely that poor peasants are any less 'compulsively involved' in markets than they were before, except where they have been able to find good income-earning opportunities outside agriculture. The role of paddy merchants as suppliers of credit remains significant, as the

John Harriss

TABLE 31.2 *Class mobility in Randam village, 1973–1984*

		A Capitalist farmer	B Rich peasants	C Middle peasants	D Poor peasants	AL	Other	Migrated out	Extinct
A	(9)	7	5	—	—	—	—	—	—
B	(22)	3	25	10	—	—	4	1	—
C	(32)	—	2	22	4	—	5	2	1
1973 D	(39)	—	—	—	21	12	12	5	—
AL	(93)	—	—	—	6	62	15	13	5
Other	(80)	—	—	1	4	6	50	12	8
Migrated in		—	—	3	6	4	12	—	—
Total 1973:		275							
Total 1984:		10	32	35	42	84	98	(33)	(14) = 300

AL = agricultural labourers

This matrix is to be read in a similar way to table 31.1. It shows, for example, that there were 22 rich peasant households in the village in 1973 and that as a result of partitioning and other substantive changes as well as of the changing relations of production, by 1984 three had become 'capitalist farmer' households: there were still 25 households of rich peasants, formed from amongst the original 22; while 10 middle peasant households had been formed and four households were no longer primarily involved in agriculture. One household had emigrated from the village.

great majority of all cultivators of paddy have regular relations with a particular merchant. But this mercantile credit is less important quantitatively than it was before, because of the expanded supply of formal, public sector credit and of credit from the nationalized banks (under the 'needs-based approach' to banking which has been officially encouraged in India over the last decade). There has been a high rate of default on the repayments of such loans, and the question of overdues has been an important political issue in Tamil Nadu. But state intervention under 'Integrated Rural Development Programmes' has come to play an increasingly important role in the continuing reproduction of smallholding peasant production.

Perhaps the particular significance of the expansion of formal credit has been that it has further intensified the direct relationships between a broad spectrum of rural people and the state. A many-stranded relationship has developed; it involves electricity supplies and tariffs – so vital for the success of cultivation; state interventions in paddy and groundnut markets – another major political issue has been that of the level of product prices; the supply of basic consumer goods at regulated prices through so-called 'cooperative' shops; latterly a scheme for supplying 'nutritious noon meals' to all children of school-going age; and credit supplied through rural development programmes. These different interventions have had the effect of encouraging the formation of overlapping alliances of rural people, in a sense 'against' the state though in a context in which the state is regarded as, and does indeed partially conform to, the role of 'patron'. It is certainly not the case that rural people are seeking to overthrow the state. Rural politics in Tamil Nadu as a whole, including eastern North Arcot, in the late 1970s and early 1980s were dominated by Farmers' Movements which won support from a range of agrarian social groups. Though led principally by the dominant peasants, they also mobilized middle and poor peasants and at least sought to win support amongst agricultural wage workers by making demands upon the state on their behalf. Intra-rural class antagonisms have not generally been intensified. Even though the benefits of increased production have not been distributed equally, there is evidence that most rural people have derived some benefit, and any potential antagonism between rich and poor peasants has been dampened because of the participation of the poor peasants, too, in the 'green revolution', and shared experience of problems over the supply of power to pumpsets, supply of credit, and product prices. There has not been a swelling of the male agricultural labour force; and thus far, at least, political activity by landless, poor people, has been caste- rather than class-based.

Relations of Capital and Peasantry: General Observations

It would be misleading to attempt to derive any general statements about the relations of the development of capitalism and the peasantry from this particular case-study. It does show, however, that even in circumstances where the introduction of the new varieties has been relatively successful and has had the effect of deepening commodity relations and of encouraging agricultural capitalism, the dissolution of small peasant production with a process of 'de-peasantization', does not necessarily occur.

It will be helpful before we consider further the implications of this case-study to refer to another classical account of the impact of the development of capitalism upon peasant production – that of Karl Kautsky, who wrote an analysis of the agrarian situation in Germany which was published shortly before Lenin's *Development of Capitalism*.[7] There is an ambiguity in Kautsky's work, for he was concerned to demonstrate the reality of capitalist development involving centralization and concentration, in agriculture as in industry, but at the same time his empirical work showed quite clearly that Western agriculture of the late nineteenth century was not developing in this way. Djurfeldt (1982) has recently elaborated upon Kautsky's discussion and developed some key arguments from it. The statistical data that Kautsky cited showed that big estates had lost and middle peasants gained land in late nineteenth-century Germany, while smallholdings had been fragmented. Kautsky refers to the land constraint on the development of capitalism in agriculture but he also points out that the intensification of capital in agriculture does not necessarily require a larger area and may be associated with a smaller size of farm, especially in the context of technical innovation and the development of specialized dairy farming and market gardening to supply rapidly growing urban markets, characteristic of the period. Further, the proliferation of smallholdings in late nineteenth-century Europe seems partly to be explained as the result of the giving out of small allotments of land to agricultural workers by estate owners. This had the effect of binding labourers to the estates and of keeping down labour costs, because agricultural labourers with such small allotments effectively subsidized the costs of reproduction of their own labour power by producing some of their food requirements on their own land. Djurfeldt points out that keeping down labour costs in this way may have been vitally important to the survival of capitalist enterprises in European agriculture at that time. This was a long period of agricultural depression as Europe faced the effects of the competition of cheap imports from the colonies, the USA, Argentina and Russia, and it seems that farmers could not afford to pay the wages necessary to keep labourers from migrating to industrial centres or to the USA: 'In other words the farmers were forced to circumvent the "freedom" of the labourers by settling them on the land' (Djurfeldt, 1982, p. 142). Kautsky in fact pointed to the role that peasant production may play in reproducing labour power for capital. It seems that the agricultural labourers' domestic production was effective for capital accumulation, in just the same way that food production by migrant workers' households is effective for capital accumulation in southern Africa now, or the reproduction of small peasant producers is effective in relation to capitalist agriculture in the Cauca valley of Colombia (see Taussig, 1978), because it 'subsidizes' the costs of reproduction of labour power in all these cases.

The context of crisis, due to international competition, also explains the gains made by middle peasants in late nineteenth-century Europe because '. . . those farms which are least dependent upon the exploitation of hired labour, the middle peasants, according to the Marxist definition, are least affected by the crisis, and are best able to reproduce themselves when prices are lowered by foreign competition' (Djurfeldt, 1982, p. 156). Others have argued that, by the same token, such peasant production may be efficient from the point of view of urban capital because it does not need to produce profits but only the socially determined livelihood requirements of the household in order to survive, and can therefore deliver supplies of agricultural products at relatively low cost. This argument is broadly borne out by Kautsky's discussion of the role of agro-industrial capital in late nineteenth-century Europe. He saw this as bringing about concentration and centralization without the formation of physically larger farms, because of the way in which it could integrate together large numbers of small units of production, though 'vertically' rather than 'horizontally'. He gave the example of the Nestlé company. Nestlé's malted milk factory at Vevey in Switzerland '. . . processes 10,000 litres daily, produced by 12,000 cows and coming from 180 villages. The 180 villages have lost their economic autonomy. . . . Their inhabitants still appear to be proprietors (owners of the means of production) but they are no longer free peasants.' (Djurfeldt, 1982, p. 156). Kautsky here described a mode of development of capitalism in agriculture which, far from requiring the dispossession of smallholding peasants, is based upon them and seeks to take advantage of their relatively lower costs whilst also being able to derive economies of scale in such activities as processing and marketing. It is a mode of development in which peasant production is subsumed under capitalism without being destroyed by it; and it is found widely in contemporary agriculture both in the advanced capitalist countries and in the Third World (for example in out-grower schemes of sugar production or in the smallholder production of tea). A comparable pattern is found in some socialist economies, and notably in Hungary where there has been a deliberate effort to foster the interrelationships of large-scale collectivized agricultural production and that on small private plots.

Kautsky's analysis suggests that the development of capitalism in an economy does not necessarily require 'de-peasantization', and why this is so (though there are also other factors which mitigate class differentiation among the peasantry and to which we have referred in passing, such as the demographic and social factors that determine household size, and the mode of inheritance). But the significance of the analysis goes far beyond this, partly because it shows substantively different possible relations of capital and rural producers. There are peasant producers whose relations with capital are like those of the allotment-holding wage labourers (we gave some examples);[8] there are others who are like the middle peasants of Kautsky's discussion. Neither argument quite applies, as we will go on to explain, to the small peasantry of eastern North Arcot.

Our case-study shows that the dissolution of small peasant production, with a process of 'de-peasantization', does not necessarily occur. But it also exposes the absurdity of the quite common assumption that the reproduction of smallholding peasant production comes about because it serves the interests of capital, even though it may do in some cases, as Kautsky argued. Such a conception of the 'articulation' of the peasant 'mode' or 'form' of production with capital relies on functionalist logic (reasoning of an inherently tautological kind). In eastern North Arcot the increasing incidence of 'share family' arrangements might be taken to indicate that urban wages are being subsidized by rural household production; but the way in which those wages, when remitted back to the villages, help to stabilize small property is almost certainly a more important effect. Urban wages subsidize rural production rather than the reverse. The small peasantry continuously reproduces itself partly because of the 'efficiency' of peasant production to which we have referred, and which relies in part on the peasants' capacity for what some describe as 'self-exploitation'. But the circuit of reproduction of the North Arcot peasantry involves relations with merchant capital rather than with agro-industry, and, increasingly, relations with the state. Marx argued in *Capital* that the development of capitalism is in inverse proportion to that of merchant capital. In this region of south India the profitability of usury and speculative trading locks up a large amount of money and diverts it from productive uses. So from this point of view it is hard to see how the reproduction of smallholding peasant production is 'functional' for capital accumulation. Similarly the use of public resources by the state for various rural development and other activities which contribute to the persistence of the smallholding peasantry seems to inhibit accumulation. In the state of Tamil Nadu industrial development has latterly been retarded for reasons which include serious problems over the supply of power. Part of the 'opportunity cost' of rural subsidies is lack of investment in the infrastructure necessary for industry. There are circumstances in which the reproduction of small peasant production is effective in relation to capital accumulation, but it is not the case in the region of our study.

The last point to be made, therefore, is to emphasize the diversity of what can be described as 'peasant production', and of its relations with capital. There are substantial differences between, for example, poor rural producers reproducing themselves through their relations with landlords, or with merchants' and usurers' capital, and who are thus the base of a backward form of development, characterized by low levels of productivity, on the one hand; and on the other, those peasant producers who, though they may be subject to domination by agro-industrial capital, are part of an expanding economy. There are important differences between largely pauperized peasantries like those of much of South Asia, and 'substantial' peasantries still endowed with adequate means of production. An essentialist conception of 'peasantry', involving the assumption that 'peasants' are in some way everywhere and at all times 'the same', is quite as misleading as the teleology of the differentiation perspective.

Notes

1 See Thorner et al., 1966, p. 262; and for an historical example, the activities of the Nestlé company in Switzerland.

2 See de Janvry, 1981, pp. 85 ff.
3 For an elaboration of this point see Byres, 1981.
4 All these arguments are attested in Pearse, 1980.
5 Evidence and detailed argument in support of the analysis presented in this section will be found in Farmer, 1977; B. Harriss, 1981; and J. Harriss, 1982, 1985.
6 Several authors have suggested that in circumstances like those described here, where apparently independent peasant producers in fact depend upon advances from monied capitalists in order to initiate the production cycle, then their real status is comparable with that of workers in the putting out system of manufacture. It is argued that they should be considered to be workers 'formally' subsumed under capital, like for example weavers in the early stages of capitalist industrialization, according to Marx's analysis in volume 1 of *Capital*. Following this line of argument, it is suggested that many peasants, like the weavers, while appearing to be independent producers, are in fact 'disguised wage workers', and that after they have repaid advances to the capitalists who control their production, they are left with only the equivalent of a wage.

There are a number of reasons why this argument doesn't hold up, elaborated by Adnan, 1985. He points out that a producer who continues to own some means of production cannot be indifferent to the outcome of production, nor to the efficiency of the labour process because his/her share of the product depends upon it: 'This, then ... distinguishes him from the wage worker. For the latter labour power is alienated and hence unburdened by operational accountability – it is this which impels the capitalist to supervise the labour process. It follows that the indebted peasant cannot be reduced to a wage worker. Equally the merchant-usurer cannot be analytically equated to the capitalist' (1985, PE-59).
7 Kautsky's *Die Agrarfrage* was published in 1899. Some extracts were published in English in Banaji, 1976.
8 See also de Janvry, 1981, for a major argument about Latin American agriculture constructed around this point.

References

Adnan, S. (1985) 'Classical and contemporary approaches to agrarian capitalism', *Economic and Political Weekly*, vol. 22, no. 20. Review of Political Economy, pp. PE-53–64.
Banaji, J. (1976) 'A summary of Kautsky's *The Agrarian Question*', *Economy and Society*, vol. 5, no. 1, pp. 2–49.
Bhaduri, A., Rahman, H. Z. and Arn, A. L. (n.d. *c*. 1984) 'Persistence and polarisation: a study in the dynamics of agrarian contradiction', mimeo. (subsequently published in *Journal of Peasant Studies*, vol. 13, no. 3, pp. 82–9).
Byres, T. (1981) 'The new technology, class formation and class action in the Indian countryside', *Journal of Peasant Studies*, vol. 8, no. 4, pp. 405–54.
Djurfeldt, G. (1982) 'Classical discussions of capital and peasantry: a critique', in J. Harriss (ed.), *Rural Development: Theories of Peasant Economy and Agrarian Change*, Hutchinson Education.
Farmer, B. H. (ed.) (1977) *Green Revolution?: Technology and Change in Rice-growing Areas of Tamil Nadu and Sri Lanka*, Macmillan.

Harriss, B. (1981) *Transitional Trade and Rural Development*, Vikas.

Harriss, J. (1982) *Capitalism and Peasant Farming: Agrarian Structure and Ideology in Northern Tamil Nadu*, Oxford University Press.

Harriss, J. (1985) 'What happened to the green revolution in south India? Economic trends, household mobility and the politics of an "awkward class"', University of East Anglia, School of Development Studies, Discussion Paper No. 175.

Hyden, G. (1980) *Beyond Ujamaa in Tanzania: Underdevelopment and an Uncaptured Peasantry*, Heinemann.

Indian Council of Social Science Research (1980) *Alternatives in Agricultural Development*, Allied Publishers.

Janvry, A. de (1981) *The Agrarian Question and Reformism in Latin America*, Johns Hopkins University Press.

Lenin, V. I. (1899) *The Development of Capitalism in Russia* (Collected Works, vol. 3), Progress Publishers.

Pearse, A. (1980) *Seeds of Plenty, Seeds of Want*, Oxford University Press.

Taussig, M. (1978) 'Peasant economics and the development of capitalist agriculture in the Cauca Valley, Colombia', *Latin American Perspectives*, vol. 18, no. 53, pp. 62–90.

Thorner, D. et al. (eds) (1966) *A. V. Chayanov: The Theory of Peasant Agriculture*, Irwin.

Washbrook, D. A. (1976) *The Emergence of Provincial Politics: The Madras Presidency 1870–1920*, Cambridge University Press.

Related Items

9, 13, 16, 17, 18, 21, 24, 25, 26, 28, 29, 30, 32, 43, 49, 50, 51, 52, 53, 55, 56, 59, 60, 61, 62.

32

The Family Farm and the International Food Regimes

Harriet Friedmann

Food production has long been remarkable at both extremes of scale: in the organization of the enterprise and in the international division of labour. Commercial family farming arose in conjunction with the consolidation of capitalism in the areas of European settlement in the last quarter of the nineteenth century. It displaced not only self-supplying peasants in Western and Eastern Europe, but also farms depending exclusively on hired labour. It persists to the present day in the advanced capitalist countries. Internationally, many of the formerly self-sufficient agrarian societies of the 'Third World' have become dependent on food imports. Through the widening and deepening of international markets over the past century,[1] the world's basic food has come increasingly to centre on family farms in the advanced capitalist countries, especially the United States.

Of the whole array of issues related to food and agriculture – from the world's food supply to the ecological effects of prevailing agricultural practices – one key is to understand the family farm. In the first part below, I situate family farming in relation to *concepts* of value theory and family labour enterprises. These concepts contribute in the second part to the *historical analysis* of international food regimes.

Simple Commodity Production and Family Labour Enterprises

Two dimensions distinguish family farms in capitalist societies: the combination of property and labour, or *simple commodity production*, and the *unity of the domestic group and the productive group* in the labour process. A theoretical tradition exists for each, with parallel strengths and faults. The strength of each is at the enterprise level. Criticisms of invalid generalizations to the larger

An original paper.

economy lose sight of this particular strength. By relating each to the other and both to capitalism, the two approaches can usefully be retheorized.

We need a concept to analyse the unexpected situation in which worker-owners have for a century predominated in so major a branch of capitalist production as basic foodstuffs. Commercial family farms lack two of the distinguishing features of capitalist enterprises: their labour is not social, in the sense that it is not monetized through markets in labour power; and profit is subjective, in that it cannot be structurally distinguished from other components of the total return to the enterprise, which prevents any tendency towards equalization of rates of profit. Weeks (1981, pp. 27–40) argues, in the most rigorous tradition of value theory, that these are precisely the reasons why a simple commodity 'mode of production' cannot exist. However, family farms exist not as a mode of production but as enterprises within branches of capitalist economies. In this perspective, it is practically possible to use the concept simple commodity production to refer to the unit of production, the farm, and the sector in which these units predominate. Simple commodity production is a *form* of production (Friedmann, 1980), that is, it must be specified simultaneously through the external relations to the larger capitalist society, and through the internal labour process.

As I define it, simple commodity production refers to the unity of property and labour in an economy characterized by the general circulation of commodities and therefore by the separation of capital and labour; it does not apply to family labour farms in formations without developed markets in labour power, land rights and money, as well as in products. The positive features of simple commodity production in agriculture are typically a high level of technology and investment and a great deal of competition, in combination with a family-based division of labour. For all except the last aspect, the concept of simple commodity production is useful. Weeks's objections are not decisive. First, as investment in purchased inputs overshadows returns to labour, private labour causes a less significant deviation from value. Second, subjective profit does not prevent expansion and contraction of the family farm sector, since competition forces many enterprises to fold, though without transforming the simple commodity character of the remaining, larger enterprises.

Family enterprises are unique within capitalism in the division of labour based on kinship, notably on gender and age. Although it is not included in the concept of simple commodity production, it is crucial for historical analysis. The tradition that explains the internal labour process of family enterprises derives from Chayanov (1966). His attempt to construct a 'peasant economy' is just as flawed as the notion of a simple commodity 'mode of production'. Yet his focus on the intersection of economics and demography in household enterprises, both within and across generations, is indispensable (Friedmann, 1978a, pp. 560–63). The Chayanovian argument is consistent with simple commodity production in defining the internal dimension of the unit of production as absence of a profit category and flexibility of labour costs. The latter points usefully to norms of consumption and relations between sexes and generations. To use these ideas critically, we must go beyond Chayanov to understand the family as a site of inequality and domination and an arena of struggle. Both the 'opportunity cost' of alternative employment for family members, and the degree of deference or independence of wives and children, determine just how flexible the composite consumption fund can be.

Once capitalism subordinates family enterprises,[2] they take on for the first time the specific features of simple commodity production: only within capitalism is the combination of property and labour *contradictory*. What distinguishes simple commodity production from other productive domestic groups (whose lineage is ancient) is its external relations, which tie it completely into the general circulation of commodities, including markets in labour power, rights over land, and money capital. Since capitalism is based on the separation of labour and property, and their combination through the wage contract, the specific and opposing interests of capital and labour are joined in simple commodity production. This accounts for the notable volatility and unpredictability of politics and ideologies which characterize simple commodity producers, especially farmers (Wilson, 1978). Much depends on which aspect of the unity is drawn upon in relation to larger politics; given the complexity of human experience even within simpler social relations, it is not surprising that farm politics often draw on both elements of the contradiction in different weights and configurations. Although property eventually triumphs (Davis, 1985; Conway, 1981), the cooperative and anti-capitalist politics of family farms have been surprisingly vital and influential at crucial moments, such as the American New Deal (Finegold, 1982) and the formation of social democratic parties in Denmark (Christiansen, 1984) and Canada (Lipset, 1968; Whittaker, 1976).

Simple commodity production, though historically contingent,[3] bears logical relations to other forms. It shares with capitalist enterprises certain general conditions of reproduction deriving from the context of generalized circulation: competition and pressure to increase the productivity of labour, concentration and centralization leading to increased scale and decreased numbers of enterprises, and for agriculture increasing dependence on credit as land becomes subordinated to capital. These features contrast sharply with the status relations governing ties within households and communities in what is often called 'peasant' production.[4] Simple commodity production also shares with the capitalist form a particular dependence on markets in labour power. For simple commodity production, the labour market provides a way to coordinate the definite labour requirements of the enterprise, which are fixed by competition, with the demographic cycle of the family. It provides additional labour to compensate for seasonal shortages and in periods when children are too young or have left. The labour market is also a source of wages earned outside by family members to supplement the enterprise income when necessary and to save for generational reproduction in the shape of 'fission' (Bogue, 1968; Friedmann, 1978b). Though paid labour is intertwined with simple commodity production, it functions in ways distinct from capitalist enterprises.

The enterprise and family coincide within household production, and all three entities emerge in response to the deepening of capitalist relations. Their flexible labour costs and ability to forgo profit give family farms definite advantages over competing capitalist enterprises. Of course, the latter have the advantage of flexibility in the number of labourers, if not the cost per labourer. Consequently, the advantages of simple commodity production depend on the appropriate technical conditions, which keep labour requirements within the range of the residential family. While agricultural technologies are largely supplied by public research and subsidies and generally favour increased scale and accumulation (Kloppenburg, forthcoming; Hightower, 1978), they also to some extent respond to the demand created by existing simple commodity producers – this at least was the case for the diminished scale of the mechanical harvester after its initial introduction in the late nineteenth century, and could again be the case for technologies appropriate to family farms in the Third World if they had the cash to pay for what they wanted. At the same time, family property depends on the persistence or adaptation of the patriarchal family. Struggles for independence and equality by women and potential heirs and successors often conflict with the maintenance and transmission of family property. Family law, which serves as a sort of substitute for labour law in family enterprises, is evolving in a context where most families live on wages and salaries, while the transfer of productive property at divorce or death is uneasily managed through inheritance laws appropriate to corporate forms (Bennett, 1982).

The family farm is doubly marginal to capitalism. As simple commodity production, it is marginal in that its existence is not theoretically (i.e., definitionally) necessary (Banaji, 1977). As a family labour unit, it is similarly marginal to capitalism. Just as capitalism 'domesticates the family' (Briskin, 1985), it domesticates family enterprises. Like the family, simple commodity production is vital to the people involved, whether they seek to enforce, change, or escape the bonds of patriarchal property. From this clash between what is socially marginal and what is individually central spring deeply felt ideas and actions. Depending on the numbers, social location and tenacity of family farmers, people in these theoretically marginal categories can have dramatic and profound effects on the histories of capitalist societies.

This conceptual discussion has two implications pointing to historical analysis. First, family farms must be examined concretely in relation to capitalism and family structures in specific nations. Second, politics are crucial. Because their existence is contingent, family farmers even more than other classes and groups, secure lasting conditions for their reproduction through politics. Typical policies in this regard are price supports and related marketing procedures, which tie farmers and the state together in complex but remarkably stable ways. Yet such policies vary in their origins and effects, which take shape through international food regimes. I shall leave behind all the determinants of family farms at the enterprise level – including their interaction with national agricultural policies – and turn now to the interactions between national policies and international regimes.

The International Political Economy of Food

The changing relations of family farms to states, capital, and the international division of labour, is a story that requires three further concepts.[5] First the *agro-food complex* allows us to trace the changing products, as well as the activities and industries associated with them, which together have defined diets and food production over the past century. Second, the history of food and agriculture consists of two periods, defined by *regimes of accumulation*. Following Aglietta (1979), an extensive regime in which capital organizes production but not the mode of life existed from the last decades of the nineteenth century until the First World War; an intensive regime, in which capital organizes the mode of consumption, that is, in which commodity relations prevail over traditional ones in daily life, developed after the Second World War. Third is the *international food regime* which unifies the first two and has specific origins and effects in the First, Second, and Third Worlds. Extensive accumulation was occurring in the state socialist and under-developed worlds simultaneously with intensive accumulation in advanced capitalism, and must be understood both comparatively (in relation to the history of extensive accumulation in Europe) and relationally, within the post-war context of intensive accumulation in the developed world.

The *extensive* international food regime of 1870–1914 supplied the needs of the expanding working classes of Europe and countries of European settlement. The commodification of food occurred within the framework of diets characteristic of the various parts of Europe, and carried by European colonists to the Americas and the Antipodes. Under this regime, basic food available on the market expanded to an unprecedented scale. Qualitatively, it represented the historic European cultural desire for a diet containing wheat (in contrast to coarser grains and potatoes) and meat. The vast supplies of wheat and meat in this period came from simple commodity producers recruited to the areas of new European settlement through state-sponsored colonization projects. The advantages of simple commodity production, once established, led to the displacement of both capitalist and peasant agriculture in Europe. The result was a spiralling number of displaced Europeans available for recruitment as settlers in the New World. The constellation of state projects, simple commodity producers, and international free trade led to a new international division of labour, with exports of grain coming from the now dominant export areas, notably the United States.

This regime went into crisis after the First World War and despite brief booms never recovered. Its legacy was the concentration of grain production in settler regions of the United States, Canada, Australia, and parts of Argentina, and agricultural transformations in many countries of Europe. Like their beleaguered competitors in the Old World, the export-dependent and regionally based classes of farmers in the New World became highly organized during the turbulent 1930s, and pressed claims for state assistance. New Deal price support programmes were to have enormous effects internationally with the rise of American power after the Second World War. They created state-owned surplus stocks which presented a problem of disposal, but which could be mobilized for various projects abroad. These would be the key to the new international food regime.

The second international food regime of 1945–73 was at once *intensive* in the advanced capitalist world and *extensive* in the underdeveloped regions. For the advanced capitalist diet, intensification meant more highly processed, standardized food. The norms of consumption in the intensive or 'Fordist' regime called for mass-produced, durable (packaged and especially frozen) foods appropriate for private 'family' consumption making use of a wide range of appliances, from the car to the freezer and ultimately the microwave oven. In the Third World, as earlier for Europe, extensive accumulation involved a quantitative extension in the commodification of food. But it occurred in conjunction with an intensive development of the agro-food complex already existing in the advanced capitalist world and already based on European dietary staples. Part of the story is the pathos of cola drinks, white bread, and infant formula in conjunction with widespread malnutrition. But the more devastating impact was the displacement rather than the commodification of traditional foods, through the substitution of foods already produced on a massive scale for European diets. This shows up in aggregate statistics on per capita consumption between the early 1950s and the late 1970s: while total per capita grain consumption in the underdeveloped world increased only 12 per cent per capita, consumption of *wheat* increased 60 per cent (for the world as a whole, the increase was 21 per cent for all grains and 32 per cent for wheat). As a rough indicator of the displacement of traditional diets, per capita consumption of all other grains and root crops in the non-socialist Third World *decreased* by 15 and 31 per cent respectively.

The agro-food complex changed in conjunction with consumption in the advanced capitalist countries. The rise of a complex food processing sector, plus increased investment in mechanical and chemical means of production in agriculture, created a new set of relations for simple commodity producers of grain and livestock. The constellation of simple commodity production/ merchant capital/direct consumption of flour and meat, which had character-ized the extensive regime, gave way to a greater density of relations between farmers and large capital, both in buying means of production and in selling to processors. That simple commodity production remained viable, despite a radical decline in numbers, was due to agricultural policies reflecting national alliances between farmers and states. Particularly important for the international regime were the European Common Agricultural Policy, which reconstructed self-sufficiency in wheat and meat (but not in animal feeds), and the US system of price supports and export subsidies (Bertrand et al., 1983; Johnson, 1975; Fennell, 1979; Pearce, 1981).

The second international food regime involved a new shape and density of international relations of food (Friedmann, 1982). Within the framework of the mutually exclusive trading blocs of the Cold War, American exports replaced European imports at the centre of the regime: the US supplied Europe with feedstuffs for intensive commodification of food and the former European colonies and dependencies with wheat for extensive commodification.[6] The key to this recomposition was international food aid, primarily American bilateral aid. The *aid-centred* food regime began with Marshall aid to Europe, which developed mechanisms for overcoming foreign exchange barriers to imports of surplus grain generated by domestic American farm programmes. Except for the soya and maize 'hole' in European agricultural protection, this aid helped the transition to self-sufficiency and ultimately export competition with the US – also using aid. For the Third World, however, the result was Public Law 480, through which imports of American wheat increased so much that international trade was completely reorganized along an American/Third World axis. At its peak, US aid accounted for 80 per cent of American wheat exports and more than 35 per cent of *world* wheat trade, and Third World countries accordingly bought more than three-quarters of American wheat exports (Friedmann, 1982, S264–5). The governments of the Third World generally welcomed the aid, since cheap food for rapidly expanding urban populations was part of a larger attempt to promote rapid industrialization. Of course, all this took its toll on Third World agriculture, undercutting local farmers who might provide food to national markets.

The second regime went into crisis in 1973. The US–Soviet grain deals of 1972–3, which are outlasting the general detente they initiated, virtually ended the American wheat surpluses whose continual reproduction underlay the regime. The conditions of the aid-centred regime were in any case disappearing through both export competition (including various export credit arrangements) and a shift to commercial sales to the Third World. Its most dramatic legacy in much of the underdeveloped world is the destruction of the peasantry as a viable social and economic structure and the accompanying growth of impoverished rural and urban populations. In national accounting terms this has meant import dependence endangered by balance of payments crises and indebtedness in the 1970s and 1980s. As a result, governments and international agencies have adopted a new focus on agriculture, all too often accompanied by a criticism of state intervention that ignores the history of international regimes (e.g. Bates, 1981).

Another legacy of the post-war regime is serious disarray in international trade. The fierce export competition between the United States and the European Community periodically erupts into trade wars. Renewed over-production in the advanced capitalist countries faces stagnant demand by the underdeveloped world, which despite increasing need is short of foreign exchange. Between East and West agricultural trade has become implicated with Great Power politics, whose complexities are revealed by the ill-fated embargo of US grain shipments to the Soviet Union after the invasion of Afghanistan: it helped defeat the president in the next election; the reinstate-ment of trade by the Reagan administration was a counterpoint to its general Cold War policies and rhetoric, an inconsistency often noted by European governments asked to embargo one or another aspect of Soviet trade.

Finally, the last years of the aid-centred food regime saw a burst of speculative investment that now threatens agricultural and ecological crisis in the advanced capitalist world. American farmers, like others, incurred enormous debts in response to the land boom that accompanied spiralling food prices in the early 1970s. Banks encouraged them to expand production on credit just as they encouraged Third World governments to expand purchases of American food on credit. When prices fell and interest rates rose, farm trouble was back with a vengeance, and those farmers who did not go bankrupt had little choice but to abandon ecological practices designed to avoid the massive erosion of the 1930s. Falling prices were not enough to revive export demand, which now depends on the state socialist and underdeveloped countries, and there is little prospect of diminishing export competition in agriculture. New biotechnologies, which have the potential to restructure agriculture completely, are on the horizon of a world in disarray.

What Now?

Both simple commodity production and international food relations are in flux. Superficially similar ideologies favour 'the free market' in advanced capitalist, underdeveloped and state socialist societies. Beneath the surface, however, the problems are more complex in each and certainly not like one another. At home in advanced capitalism, simple commodity production is in trouble. With farmers reduced in numbers by their very success, and more directly integrated with large capital in the agro-food complex, price support policies have become less appropriate and less politically viable.

Yet along with American diets, policies in the Second and Third Worlds look to shifting images of American agriculture. For both this means pursuing productivity at the expense of equality and the environment. In centrally planned economies, 'second economy' agriculture based on private, often family, labour complements a general attempt to restructure agriculture. It is not simple commodity production according to my definition, since the context is not generalized circulation as in capitalism (celebrations or denunciations of capitalist restoration are certainly premature). In Hungary where it has proceeded furthest and achieved greatest success, private agriculture is intimately bound up with restructured and technically dynamic cooperatives, suggesting that the dynamism of each depends on the other (see Swain, 1981; Juhasz, 1984).

For the underdeveloped world, establishing simple commodity production would mean greater agricultural unemployment and commodification of food, both in a context of increasing international integration through agro-food capitals. The political instability associated with food shortages lends urgency to agricultural restructuring. In the wake of failed transformations of large-scale agriculture in many Third World countries, emphasis by many governments and international agencies has shifted towards the transformation of Third World peasants into simple commodity producers. They envision an era of productivity like that of the recent American past, ignoring the present acute crisis of simple commodity production in the United States, as well as the particular conditions of the two international regimes which allowed it to emerge and thrive for a century.

Whatever their success in improving productivity in various social contexts, these projects are based on technologies associated with high-yielding agriculture, which tend to import the energy- and chemical-intensive monocropping practices of advanced capitalism. Even success in production means probable ecological damage (perhaps more serious in tropical and subtropical areas), increased foreign exchange requirements for inputs, and reduced employment in agriculture. Hope for changing techniques, orientated to ecologically sound farming and consumer demands for healthier foods, may also be the hope for simple commodity producers. Experiments in 'sustainable' agriculture suggest smaller scale and greater labour intensity, for a change. These will involve, for each social and ecological region, a conscious restructuring of agro-food complexes and politics around socially defined needs and resources.

A new international regime will have to avoid the extremes of autarchy and the sacrifice of natural environments and human diets on the altar of 'free trade'. It must be based on self-conscious politics in *all* countries to augment local agriculture and renew its connection to local consumption. One step is to understand the power of choice and action. A corrective to any sense of historical inevitability is the recovery and criticism of a lost alternative to the second international food regime: the proposals (defeated in 1947) for a World Food Board working within an international economy subordinated to national development projects (Peterson, 1979, pp. 173–84). It was fatally flawed – it assumed continued European colonialism – yet it was part of a general attempt by the various parties and movements who had fought valiantly against fascism to construct a world of self-governing peoples. Present proposals, such as buffer stocks to stabilize international markets, hark back to that time, but have lost some of the spirit. The technical proposals for agriculture, as for international money, increasingly presuppose that governments co-ordinate decisions, leaving less and less scope for democracy. The challenge is to create forms of international co-ordination consistent with control by all people over their environments, nations, and communities.

Notes

1 With the crucial exception of mutually exclusive trading blocs during the Cold War. This exception reinforces the point about family farming in the US.
2 This is a complex process involving the interaction between commodification and gender/age relations. Commodification bounds households, and increasingly narrows membership to first the ideal nuclear family and then fewer people still. It defines a separate and devalued sphere of domestic life, a process central to the subordination of women in capitalism (Harris, 1981; Whitehead, 1981; Maher, 1981). This process, which generally accompanies the separation of work from family ties and place of residence, occurs *within* the family farm. Sachs (1983) has an excellent account of the process. For discussions of the changing division of labour within Canadian and American family farms, see also Bennett (1982), Kohl (1976) and Wilkening (1981); within English farms, see Gasson (1984) and Bouquet (1982).
3 It can be demonstrated (e.g. Friedmann, 1978b) that it is historically contingent in a double sense: like capitalist enterprises, it is specific to the modern epoch; unlike capitalist enterprises, simple commodity production need not exist at all.
4 The contrast is overdrawn for expositional purposes. For a critique of the strong distinction between commodified external relations and non-commodified internal relations, plus a nicely argued alternative perspective on the interpenetration of all the categories, see Lem (forthcoming).
5 The following summarizes Part I of my forthcoming book *The Political Economy of Food* (London: Verso).
6 It also increased the US export share relative to Canada, Australia, and Argentina.

References

Aglietta, Michel (1979) *A Theory of Capitalist Regulation: The American Experience*, London: New Left Books.
Banaji, Jairus (1977) 'Modes of production in a materialist conception of history', *Capital and Class*, no. 3.
Bates, Robert H. (1981) *Markets and States in Tropical Africa*, Berkeley and Los Angeles: University of California.
Bennett, John W. (1982) *Of Time and Enterprise: North American Family Farm Management in a Context of Resource Marginality*, Minneapolis: University of Minnesota Press.
Bertrand, Jean-Pierre, Catherine Laurent, and Vincent Leclerq (1983) *Le monde du soja*, Paris: Maspero.

Bogue, A. G. (1968) *From Prairie to Cornbelt*, Chicago: Quadrangle Books.

Bouquet, Mary (1982) 'Production and Reproduction of Family Farms in South-west England', *Sociologia Ruralis*, vol. XXII, no. 3/4, pp. 227–44.

Briskin, Linda (1985) 'Theorizing the Capitalist Family/Household System: A Marxist Feminist Contribution'. PhD Thesis, York University, Toronto.

Christiansen, Niels Finn (1984) 'Denmark: end of the idyll', *New Left Review*, no. 144.

Conway, J. F. (1981) 'Agrarian petit-bourgeois responses to capitalist industrialisation: the case of Canada', in Frank Bechhofer and Brian Elliott (eds), *The Petite Bourgeoisie*, London: Macmillan.

Davis, Mike (1985) *Prisoners of the American Dream*, London: Verso.

Fennell, Rosemary (1979) *The Common Agricultural Policy of the European Community*, London: Granada.

Finegold, Kenneth (1982) 'From agrarianism to adjustment: the political origins of New Deal agricultural policy', *Politics and Society*, vol. 11, no. 1, pp. 1–27.

Friedmann, Harriet (1978a) 'World market, state and family farm: social bases of household production in the era of wage labour', *Comparative Studies in Society and History*, vol. 20, no. 4, pp. 545–86.

Friedmann, Harriet (1978b) 'Simple commodity production and wage labour in the American Plains', *Journal of Peasant Studies*, vol. 6, no. 1, pp. 71–100.

Friedmann, Harriet (1980) 'Household production and the national economy: concepts for the analysis of agrarian formations', *Journal of Peasant Studies*, vol. 7, no. 2, pp. 158–84.

Friedmann, Harriet (1982) 'The political economy of food: the rise and fall of the international food order of the postwar era', in Michael Burawoy and Theda Skocpol (eds) *Marxist Inquiries*, special supplement to the *American Journal of Sociology*, vol. 88: S248–86.

Friedmann, Harriet (forthcoming) *The Political Economy of Food*, London: Verso/New Left Books.

Gasson, Ruth (1984) 'Farm women in Europe: their need for off-farm employment', *Sociologia Ruralis*, vol. 24, no. 3/4, pp. 216–28.

Harris, Olivia (1981) 'Households as natural units', in Kate Young, Carol Wolkowitz and Roslyn McCullagh (eds), *Of Marriage and the Market*, London: CSE Books.

Hightower, Jim (1978) *Hard Tomatoes, Hard Times*, Cambridge, Ma.: Schenkman.

Johnson, David Gale (1975) *World Food Problems and Prospects*, Washington: American Enterprise Institute.

Juhasz, Pal (1984) 'The Transformation of Management, Work Organization and Worker Endeavors in Hungarian Cooperative Farms', MS, Budapest, Cooperative Research Institute.

Kloppenburg, Jack (forthcoming) *First the Seed*, Cambridge University Press.

Kohl, Seena B. (1976) *Working Together: Women and Family in Southwestern Saskatchewan*, Toronto and Montreal: Holt, Rinehart, and Winston of Canada.

Lem, Winnie (forthcoming) 'Les rapports interpersonnels en production marchandise simple: l'exploitation familiale à Murviel-les-Beziers (l'Herault)', in Louis Assier-Andrieu (ed.) *Les Transmissions Ideologiques et Symboliques de la Parente en Occitanie*, Paris.

Lipset, S. M. (1968) *Agrarian Socialism: The Cooperative Commonwealth Federation in Saskatchewan*, New York: Doubleday.

Maher, Vanessa (1981) 'Work, consumption, and authority within the household: a

Moroccan case', in Kate Young, Carol Wolkowitz and Roslyn McCullagh (eds) *Of Marriage and the Market*, London: CSE Books.

Pearce, Joan (1981) *The Common Agricultural Policy Royal Institute of International Affairs*, Chatham House Papers, 13, London: Routledge & Kegan Paul.

Peterson, Martin (1979) *International Interest Organizations and the Transmutation of Postwar Society*, Stockholm: Almqvist & Wiksell International.

Sachs, Carolyn (1983) *The Invisible Farmers: Women in Agricultural Production* Totowa, NJ: Rowman & Allenheld.

Swain, Nigel (1985) *Collective Farms Which Work?*, Cambridge: Cambridge University Press.

Weeks, John (1981) *Capital and Exploitation*, Princeton University Press.

Whitehead, Ann (1981) ' "I'm hungry, Mum": the politics of domestic budgeting', in Kate Young, Carol Wolkowitz and Roslyn McCullagh (eds) *Of Marriage and the Market*, London: CSE Books.

Whittaker, Reginald (1976) 'Introduction' to William Irvine's *The Farmer in Politics* [1920], Toronto: McClelland and Stewart.

Wilkening, Eugene A. 'Farm families and family farming', in Raymond T. Coward and William M. Smith, Jr (eds) *The Family in Rural Society*, Boulder, Colorado: Westview Press.

Wilson, Graham (1978) 'Farmers' organizations in advanced societies', in Howard Newby (ed.), *International Perspectives in Rural Sociology*, London: Wiley.

Related Items

2, 3, 13, 16, 17, 18, 21, 25, 26, 28, 29, 31, 49, 50, 51, 53, 54, 60, 61, 62.

Part III

Peasantry as a Culture

Part III focuses on peasant culture. The term 'culture' is used here not in its broadest anthropological sense (i.e. as substantively everything created by humans), but to designate typical collective cognitions and values. We are talking of the, often implicit, models as well as ideals of social reality with the help of which social experience is perceived, felt, understood and judged. These 'lenses through which men see', to use C. Wright Mills's metaphor, are loaded with emotional charge and result in patterns of plausibility and marked predispositions for some types of cognition, expressed in collective behaviour of which political action offers a prime example. Life experience, social organizations and collective cognition are linked by mutual dependency.

Peasant culture is intertwined with and in reality inseparable from the life of small rural communities and the particularities of family farming. Lack of anonymity, powerful normative controls and conformism treated as a virtue, relative egalitarianism and mutual dependence in the face of powerful 'external forces' (of nature as much as of markets or of state policies) and collective identities are expressed in what James Scott described as 'subsistence ethics' – the mutual links of peasant consciousness and community are powerful and clear.

Part III begins with Dobrowolski's description and analysis of peasant customs, values and views which pays particular attention to oral cultural transmission within small 'traditional' localities and to its particularities. (See also Thomas and Znaniecki, and Womack, items 1 and 47.) Next comes an original contribution by John Berger devoted to peasant aesthetic sense, where perceptions and emotions meet, as expressed in a life work and the imagination of a peasant son from a French province. This is followed by Bailey's discussion of peasant cognitive maps *vis-à-vis* those of India's contemporary modernizers (see also part V). Oritz's comment challenges definitions of peasant economic behaviour as rooted in tradition or peasant particularity and points to the general economic rationale behind it – a contribution to a controversy which proceeds to divide the social scientists in the field. The extract from Scott's book devoted to 'moral economy' and a 'subsistence ethic' explores the social parameters of peasant cognitive response to the economy of permanent risk to survival (see also Sen and Wolf's items, 29 and 46). Ranger's paper devoted to the transformation of peasant consciousness in Zimbabwe closes part III. It traces the history of ideological hegemony of a colonial regime over a peasantry it subjugated, of this hegemony's erosion and eventual collapse in the struggle against its white settlers' regime. It offers a direct bridge to part IV (see also Omvedt and Esteva, items 20 and 59).

33

Peasant Traditional Culture
Kazimierz Dobrowolski

Introduction

The present essay is an attempt at a theory of traditional peasant culture as it existed in the area of southern Poland (Southern Malopolska) in the nineteenth and twentieth centuries. It is based in the first place on field material which was collected by the author in the inter-war period and partly after the Second World War. It is not an exhaustive view of the subject; merely an attempt to extract from a great many individual facts a pattern of typical, recurring processes which reflect the cultural dynamics of definite phases of historical development. These generalizations aim at grasping: (a) the main forces shaping and maintaining traditional culture, (b) the basic characteristic features of that culture and (c) the dynamics of its disintegration. Together these may reveal the real mechanism behind the functioning of a given traditional culture. The present essay does not give all the generalizations which could be extracted from the source of material, nor does it claim to offer wider generalizations reaching beyond the said territory of southern Poland

The Concept of Traditional Culture

Generally speaking, 'tradition' covers the total cultural heritage handed down from one generation to the next. Two basic media of transmitting social heritage are known. The first comprises transmission by means of speech and other sound stimuli (e.g. musical sounds), which are received by the sense of hearing, as well as demonstration of actions and objects which are perceived by visual organs. This mode of transmission always involves direct human contact. Secondly, there exist transmission media which possess a mechanical

Kazimierz Dobrowolski, 'Peasant traditional culture', *Ethnografia Polska*, vol. 1, 1958, pp. 19–56. Abridged by the author and translated by A. Waligorski.

character. These include print, musical scores, various iconographic techniques and phonographic apparatus. Such media relieve the producers and receivers of the cultural content from direct human contact, and they establish indirect, impersonal human relationships.

It has become customary for ethnographers and culture historians to speak about 'traditional culture', meaning all those cultural contents and values *which are transmitted orally*. We have accepted this linguistic convention, and in that sense the term 'peasant traditional culture' has been used in this paper.

In all domains of social life, in all efforts of human cooperation, in the production and accumulation of cultural gains and achievements, we can always observe two fundamental, though contrasting, tendencies which manifest themselves with varying intensity in different phases of historical development. Firstly, there is a tendency which is essentially conservative and stabilizing, which is expressed in a propensity for the preservation and maintenance of the existing social order. It is always based on the acknowledgement of previous experience and is essentially focused on the past. The past, here, supplies a pattern of living and provides a model for human action. Conversely, there exists a tendency which has grown out of doubt and dissatisfaction and which is invariably conducive to social change. This tendency is often destructive and revolutionary *vis-à-vis* the existing social order, and has often been expressed in terms of a more or less violent opposition to, and negation of, the surrounding reality. This tendency is usually born out of the deep human craving for new and better forms of social life, new moral truths and more adequate technical innovations. Such a vision of new life, forward looking, yet generated by concrete conditions of human existence, can become a powerful, driving force for human action.

These tendencies reflect two fundamental needs of human existence: (a) that of the regulation and ordering of human relationships founded on a set of established values, skills and capabilities, truths and experiences; and (b) that of the improvement of human existence by the securing of greater mastery over the natural environment, by extending knowledge of the surrounding reality, by obtaining a greater security and protection against hostile forces, by the reduction of human effort and by making human cooperation rest on a more balanced foundation.

Now, the first tendency is known to manifest itself with greatest strength in all those cultures which rely exclusively on oral transmission and direct demonstration in handing down their cultural contents and experience. The second, on the other hand, is apt to come to the fore in the crucial periods of social upheaval and revolution which are known to have opened up new eras in human history.

The glorification of the past, which finds its expression in so-called traditionalism, occurs also in literate civilizations, i.e. in those cultures which, for some length of time, have employed writing as a principal means of social transmission. What is more, cases are on record where writing itself has become a factor strengthening the importance of tradition. This has been often the case with sacred texts which for many centuries acted as canons regulating and controlling human behaviour. In the majority of cases, however, the written word has been a positive, if not altogether decisive factor of change. For literacy invariably carries with it unlimited possibilities for the quantitative transmission of cultural contents, between generations. By its very nature, writing implies the possibility of a more intensive cultural accumulation in all spheres of human activity. Writing makes possible a more adequate and precise transmission of those contents, values and achievements which form the essence of a given culture. In literate societies the process of transmission and diffusion of cultural contents are always much more widespread, rapid and effective than in oral cultures. Finally, writing, by the very fact of accumulation of texts, implies an infinitely greater scope for comparison and for critical examination, including a critical appraisal of the achievements of past generations and of their handed-down knowledge – technical, natural, historical, etc. – than was ever possible with an orally transmitted heritage.

Hence when discussing the dynamics of a conservative, traditionalist culture, we inevitably turn our attention to such communities as hand down their cultural contents by oral transmission. Here it will be seen that the process is both diachronic and synchronic. It is diachronic in the sense that the passing generation hands over its cultural experiences to its successors. But it is also synchronic, in so far as the achievements of individuals or groups of individuals are directly spread by actual human contacts.

The basic transmission process in traditional culture consists of education, which introduces the novice into a definite world of both material and immaterial values. This takes place by means of intentional teaching and demonstration as well as by a corresponding reception of the above instruction through auditory and visual perception. These processes may have a conscious character which is the case when the transmission takes place in a deliberate, purposeful and institutionalized manner; but they must also be natural or spontaneous when they result from mere contact and imitation.

The classical domains of traditional cultures are, of course, the so-called primitive, preliterate communities which can still be found in more remote parts of the globe. But their numbers are rapidly dwindling, and only a few such pure, uncontaminated communities exist, unaffected by the impact of higher civilizations and relying essentially on mechanical means of transmission.

Of a different character are peasant traditional cultures which originated out of class divisions prevailing in feudal Europe. They developed under the influence of the ruling class and the educated minority, though that influence took quite a different form in various phases of historical development. In the early medieval period, for instance, the cultural distance between the peasants and the feudal knights resolved itself chiefly into the differences in wealth and material endowment, but there were no marked differences in education and mentality. The situation changed during the Renaissance when education became increasingly based upon institutionalized schooling, embracing much wider groups of lay classes, who succeeded in partially emancipating themselves from the influence of the Church and who in the course of time obtained a dominant cultural role within society. Ruling class influence was and is different again in particular phases of the capitalist and socialist systems.

The Basic Conditions of the Existence of Traditional Culture

Traditional culture is a reality *sui generis* with its own specific dynamics. A low level of agricultural technology and stability of peasant settlement represents, perhaps, its most important foundations. In the Beskid villages, studied by the writer, agricultural tools and implements were simple, made chiefly of wood, and as late as the 1880s iron was only used on a small scale. Equally simple was the organization of work which, combined with a tendency towards economic self-sufficiency and with mystical and magical patterns of thought, reflected a rather simple state of economic and social development. When to the above is added a more or less permanent peasant occupation of the land, inherited together with the farmstead from fathers and involving very little spacial mobility, we shall have in a nutshell a picture of peasant traditional culture as well as the condition in which such cultures are apt to thrive.

Another important factor of peasant conservatism was the patriarchal family and kinship system which was expressed in the father's authority and power over children, in the children's economic and intellectual dependence upon parents, and the young people's submissive attitude. In a peasant family close cooperation between the generations (usually three and sometimes even four) was a rule, extending over family affairs, work and recreation in the household and on land attached to it. This too was conducive to the maintenance of traditional culture.

In this connection, the social situation of the peasantry has to be briefly reviewed. Legal and economic oppression of peasants in the feudal system greatly hampered their economic development and debarred them from a wider participation in national culture. Legal barriers, too, blocked any possible social advancement. In these circumstances, a strong feeling of social degradation and inferiority often arose in peasant minds, animated by the deprivating experience of many centuries of oppression. This did not preclude a simultaneous attitude of hatred, and more active opposition raged from time to time against the dominant class. Thus the steadily deepening social distance between the upper classes and the peasantry up to the abolition of serfdom produced a stagnant peasant living standard reflected in their material culture, in their dress, and in their food and household equipment, and which by association came to typify, in all outward aspects, a distinct peasant social class. Despite the breakdown of the feudal system in Galicia in 1848, this state of affairs survived tenaciously for a long time afterwards.

Oral Transmission and its Social Functions

Relying mainly on the field data, the consequences of transmission of culture orally are now examined.

We have already seen that one of the most important effects of this was the limited possibility of cultural transfer from generation to generation. This limitation affected not only the number of elements transferred, but also their quality, i.e. their exactness and lasting character. Thus quantitative limitations were particularly pronounced in cases where new technological inventions and new literary and philosophical contributions were concerned. This type of intellectual achievement, coming mainly from anonymous members of the highland community, never had an enduring character. Usually expressed in agricultural practice, in natural science and medical observations, in literary and musical production or ideological conceptions, it was never written down, and in the great majority of cases it perished with the death of the original creator.

Thus an important consequence of the oral transmission of culture was a gradual decline in the public memory for older usages and artefacts. Now technological advances, new terms, customs and songs began to oust the old ones, and ultimately, despite long coexistence, in some cases completely replaced them. This usually happened when the old form did not find a material embodiment or iconographic representation or was not preserved in a written shape. Then it fell into the limbo of social oblivion and was irrevocably lost.

Selection in Cultural Transmission

The process of selection in cultural transmission acquired a characteristic pattern. When analysing what was likely to become preserved in a given society, and what was likely to perish, the writer was able to establish a set of rules and general principles, which were valid for the type of culture under investigation, but which even there could show deviations and modifications according to phase of historical development.

In the first place it would appear that all that had an individual character, all that resulted from the capability and skills of individuals, that did not become objectified during the lifetime of its originators, at least in a small community, tended to disappear. In other words, all that failed to enter into a concrete scheme of action, that did not become a pattern for behaviour, or a set of mental attitudes, or a stereotype of a given culture, can safely be regarded as potentially lost. Many examples are on record; they include such non-material products as songs, tunes, folk-tales, popular artistic productions, ideas and concepts connected with a *Weltanschauung* of the members of a given community. This type of cultural production met with a much better chance of survival when it encountered men with similar interests, capabilities and dispositions to the original creator. In material production and technology the position was similar; when a new technological invention or improvement in production became a part of the routine of a working team connected with the original creator, there was a much greater chance of its being permanently established.

Passing to the factors which helped to maintain a product, its practical utility must be stressed above all else. As long as it was important in the life of the community, and satisfied, effectively, the needs of its members – economic, technological, social and emotional – and did not compete with new, but related, or rival products, it had a chance of long survival. In this connection prominence must be given to various objects of material culture which would have been particularly difficult to change, as this would have required an enormous output of labour. A classic example is the field system, which in certain villages of Podhale has retained its original medieval arrangement of fields and strips. If certain products well tested during several centuries' experience, despite their outward simplicity, met productive needs, e.g. certain items of farming equipment, they also had a chance of survival. The same is true of numerous techniques of work connected with soil cultivation, harvesting, flax processing, wood working and pottery.

Specific Instruments of Social Transmission in Traditional Culture

Apart from direct oral transmission and practical demonstration, the peasant community developed other means which allowed knowledge to be transmitted with greater precision. These included, above all, the compact and highly expressive linguistic formulae, often put into rhyme, which contained meteorological statements, facts about climate, information relating to agriculture and animal farming, religious and moral instruction, as well as a whole realm of experiences, forming what is popularly known as 'wise sayings'. Many of these formulae belonged to the category of proverbs. They are common in current speech, adding much to its vigour and expressiveness.

The verse form was also used to an extent in magical formulae, which improved the chances of faithful repetition of the formula during the magical performance. Some versification was also applied with gusto, in various folk-tales with a dramatic plot. These stirred popular imagination and were for the most part sung, by wandering musicians and beggars. Such a form was more suitable for chanting reproduction by the audience.

Connected with this was the application of traditional schemes and models which served as guiding principles in practical action. For example, the old village carpenters in Podhale did not make use of any drawn plans of blueprints, or resort to written-down calculations. Their entire technological knowledge was based exclusively on memory and was reduced to the repetition, in practical action, of a few basic models. Thus there existed a model of a larger, two-roomed house and a smaller one having one room only, with certain variants which consisted of adding summer-rooms and stores (*komora*). Similar basic schemes existed in the work of rural tailors and other craftsmen.

Sociability in Traditional Life

Institutionalized social gatherings were very important media for the preservation of traditional culture. They consisted of meetings at home, in the inn, in the summer often outside the building in the open, or else contacts made during the journey to church, to the market, or to the annual church fête on patron saint day. With each type of social intercourse were connected certain definite groupings of people, as well as traditionally prescribed subjects of conversation. Thus men walked separately to the local parish church, while women formed another group, young and old people still another. Groups based on neighbourhood walked together to the local fair. The church fête was mainly attended by the young, the journey providing many opportunities for making new acquaintances.

Of special importance, however, were the neighbours' meetings, which gathered for certain ceremonial occasions like spinning or tearing feather, as well as for more informal events like regular evening gatherings, especially in the winter months. These gatherings, common in southern Poland by the end of the nineteenth century and early twentieth century were the forerunners of the modern book or newspaper.

The subject matter of these evening talks embraced gossip about local events and household and community affairs, as well as 'news from the wide world'. There were also numerous tales, often legendary, mystical and magico-religious in character. The tales carried a great power of attraction, and the narrator became the centre of popular interest and general social recognition. Their subjects centred on various figures belonging to the world of popular demonology – spirits of the dead, ghosts and devils, but also various types of fairies and gnomes, on the whole rather malignant, but some of them at least propitious. To this, various saints must be added, as well as the figure of Jesus wandering over the earth.

Passing to the social function of these tales, it should first be observed that they probably grew out of age-old human ideas and discoveries, by means of which early mankind sought to explain the forces which govern the world of nature and human destiny. Their contents acted, both for the narrator and the recipients, as a living truth, a concrete reality. In these circumstances these tales constituted an important instrument of the strengthening of the old, mystico-magical outlook. They contained many practical hints on how to protect oneself from evil forces, or how to placate them. Often the tales, especially those which contained religious motifs, had additional ethical and moral objectives, stressing the reward for good deeds, and punishment for wrongdoers. In this way various moral precepts were enhanced, which from Church lore made their way into traditional culture, usually with characteristic local adaptations. A special category of tales referred to hidden treasures and benevolent robbers, who aided the poor in acts of revenge over the cruel nobles. The unusual popularity of these legends probably reflected the deep peasant desire to improve their lot, to compensate for their grief and humiliations suffered in real life.

Anonymity of Products

One of the most characteristic features of traditional culture is the anonymous character of its original producers and contributors. The introduction of new and better tools and techniques, the invention of new ornamental patterns, new tunes or harmonic discoveries were often connected with the process of objectivization which meant that a given community adopted and incorporated an individual product. At first, the identity of the original contributor or innovator was common knowledge. In the course of time, however, this person was forgotten, the product became separated from its original creator, lost its individual character and became indistinguishable from other techniques. It is but seldom that the name of the original creator penetrated and survived in the collective consciousness of the community, although such cases are on record.

The Power of the Village Authorities

A very slow rhythm and tempo of development is a characteristic feature of every traditional culture. Many technological arrangements and economic habits have shown unusual tenacity throughout centuries of feudalism, and even after the nineteenth-century emancipation the position was not radically altered. As late as the inter-war period one could find in the remote villages of the Beskid mountains as well as in the older forest settlements in the central Polish plain an astonishing number of traditional relics of material culture (farm tools and implements, agricultural techniques, land tenure systems, interiors of peasant cottages), to a lesser extent, of social organization (e.g. certain forms of patriarchal family and even some relics of the old clan system), as well as of certain interesting manifestations of the traditional peasant mentality. As a result, the permanent unchanging character of social institutions developed, implying belief in their intrinsic value. 'Thus our fathers and grandfathers have always done, thus we shall do', is a statement which can be accepted as typical and which is often heard from peasants from the old traditional culture. In these circumstances any conscious rational motivation for economic activity or manner of conduct was of little relevance. Similarly of little importance was the rationalization of the character and peculiarities of any social institution, or economic and legal norm, or rule of conduct. What was of great importance was any action undertaken without a deeper intellectual reflection; one which consisted of a passive reception of the existing cultural system on the one hand, and a strong emotional attachment to it on the other. In this way, cultural contents and institutions acquired an unusual importance, becoming a working authority which exerted a binding influence upon human beings. The essence of this authority consisted in the acknowledgement of a definite cultural product, which as a rule was devoid of any cultural judgement, but which was further enhanced by a strong belief in its intrinsic value, and sometimes even developing into certain manifestations of religious reverence or a cult. Closely connected with this attitude was the consequent high authority vested in the main carriers and transmitters of traditional culture. Clearly, the most influential were the old people, whose long life and numerous contacts with people permitted them not only to accumulate the greatest amount of traditional knowledge but also to gain the richest experiences through economic and social practice. Owing to the lack of written knowledge, they inevitably constituted the main source of information on work and production, on the world and on life from which younger generations could amply draw.

In order to understand properly how this authority worked, it is necessary to stress another important aspect of traditional knowledge. It is explained by the fact that many of its elements were esoteric and jealously guarded from general circulation. These secret contents could only be passed to a small number of chosen people. Even in agricultural pursuits, before the introduction of official farming knowledge and agricultural instructors, not every son had the fortune to be entrusted by the father with full knowledge of traditional farming methods. This idea of the secrecy in production can also be found in various economic pursuits other than agriculture as well as in the craftsmen guilds. It was naturally most pronounced in folk-medicine and veterinary knowledge as well as in various magical practices. In these circumstances the intellectual as well as the economic superiority of the elderly was enhanced. The economic dominance resulted in the children's submission to parents and found expression in the division and the allotment of work. Food and living quarters were provided in return but no cash. Paternal authority also controlled endowment at marriage, the disposal of property at death, and generally made the leaving of the parental home and migration in search of alternative work extremely difficult.

The Role of Magic and Religion in Traditional Culture

One of the salient features of traditional culture was the unusually great role allotted to magical beliefs and practices compared with activities based on empirical and rational foundations. Among Polish highlanders, dairy farming was most permeated with magical beliefs and practices. Nearly every activity connected with sheep rearing, grazing, milking as well as the milk processing was associated with certain practices which aimed either at securing success or averting pending danger or misfortune. They formed a body of secret lore which was passed on by the senior shepherd (*baca*), often after reaching an advanced age or even sometimes at his deathbed, to his successors. The latter, before they could be entrusted with the magical power they entailed, had to undergo a kind of initiation ceremony.

A strict observance of the traditionally prescribed order and sequence of rites and formulae played a very important part in highlanders' magical practices, as, in fact, in any magic. To reverse the order, to change a formula could be very dangerous, for it might turn success into misfortune, and even bring about magical retaliation, of which the frail and dependent human being has always been afraid. It is interesting to note that this important magical attitude in traditional highland culture was often extended to the domain of rational and empirical action. Thus any rejection of the usual and traditionally sanctioned technological activity, any change of the old tools and techniques, any abandonment or breaking of traditional custom would be commonly dreaded and regarded as a dangerous act, which might invite misfortune, or produce disaster. For that reason matches were never used for making fire in the old mountain dairy huts, but the traditional method of flint and steel was employed. This was also the reason why the introduction of new equipment in the mountain chalets, like tin vessels in the inter-war period, met with resistance, for this, it was feared, might reduce the proceeds from sheep. When by the end of the nineteenth century iron ploughs became common in the Galician villages, the peasants, especially the older generation, often expressed fear that the soil cut with iron might retaliate and refuse to yield crops. Similar forebodings were expressed with regard to farm machinery, like chaff-cutters or threshing-machines, which, it was feared, might adversely affect the crops.

Such a magic-ridden frame of mind was therefore a serious obstacle to progress in all branches of culture, and at the same time became an important factor in the preservation of the old regime. In this mental climate, permeated with belief in ancestral authority and deeply saturated in the magical *Weltanschauung*, any attempt at change, in material culture as well as in customs and social relations, met with apprehension and fear of retaliation by the mystical powers who acted as guardians of the old established order. It should be added that magical thinking confirmed the authority and social position of a certain category of people, like the *bacas* (sheepmasters), medicine-men and blacksmiths. The village commoners believed in their secret lore and their ability to control hidden forces which could bring about success or misfortune. For that reason they often acted as intermediaries between the world of the supernatural and peasant rank and file, who, feeling helpless, looked for support to these highly influential people.

A few words must now be said about those religious beliefs which played an important part in the preservation of traditional values. Underlying them was a deep-rooted belief in 'divine omnipotence' which created and controls everything, in the 'will of God' regulating equally the social order and the destiny of individuals as well as controlling the laws of nature. Against this there developed a system of transcendental sanctions, including religious commands and prohibitions, exerted over the peasantry by the clergy and the ruling class. These acted as powerful safeguards of the feudal system, and afterward of capitalism. Such commands and prohibitions extended to the sphere of family life, and also to the wider network of human relations. Those who broke them would meet with 'God's punishments', those who accepted them and acted in accordance with the 'will of God', could reckon on His support, since the ultimate mastery of things and people lay with Him.

Tendency towards Cultural Uniformity

We have already said that in every human community, irrespective of time and space, we can find a collective tendency towards the maintenance and conservation of the existing state, and, conversely, an individualistic, emancipating tendency towards the introduction of new elements into culture.

The old peasant culture in southern Poland at the close of the feudal era and also to a certain extent under capitalism, had a predominantly traditional character. But it is important to realize that it never constituted a uniform egalitarian cultural monolith with regard to the consumption and share in the production of cultural goods. It was a highly differentiated culture, both socially and economically; its social contrasts were often considerable, especially those which existed between rich peasants and the village poor. Thus there were great differences in the sizes of farms and the number of cattle, in the interior of peasant cottages, furniture, implements, food, dress, etc. In social and ceremonial life, there was much splendour and pomp among rich peasants, best seen at such occasions as weddings, christening feasts and funerals. This sometimes developed into a consciousness that certain material objects accompany a certain social status, such as the gate in front of the house, one or even two chimneys on the roof of the cottage, chests for personal belongings, certain types of furniture and dress. The consumption of certain types of food was regarded as a duty associated with social rank. On the other hand, the scale of consumption of social goods by the village proletariat was much smaller. In addition, there was a strong pressure exerted by the rich peasants on the poorer section of the community (the landless and village labourers) which aimed at debarring them from using such elements of culture which the rich claimed as their sole prerogative. Yet it was the poor who played a very conspicuous part in the creation of cultural values. They were the main carriers of technological knowledge in various branches of production, like wood- and metal-working, pottery, weaving, tailoring, and so on. They possessed wide knowledge of wild fruit, roots, herbs and the like collected in forests and fields to supplement their diet. It was they who provided the great majority of craftsmen-carpenters, coopers, wheelwrights, weavers, blacksmiths, potters. The village proletariat produced a large number of folk-artists, sculptors, painters, ornament makers, tailors, singers and players, saga-tellers and folk-writers.

Despite this differentiation, traditional culture manifested a tendency towards uniformity. It was expressed in the social pressure towards a common, unchanging pattern of social institutions and ideological contents within particular classes or village groups. The individuals who deviated from the commonly accepted pattern of behaviour obtaining within their respective classes or groups met with such repressive measures as ridicule, reproach, moral censure, ostracism or even the application of official legal sanctions.

It is a significant feature of the type of peasant culture we are analysing that there is a relative paucity of material examples in contrast to the highly developed system of behavioural patterns. Thus, on the one hand, we have a limited number of such material arrangements as types of houses, plans of the interior, furniture, dress, ornaments, etc., and on the other, a great number of highly differentiated social situations, each demanding a special, customarily prescribed form of conduct. These extended both over the sphere of family life, as well as over neighbourly relations, village affairs and inter-village relationships. Connected with these regulated forms of conduct were numerous attitudes, evaluations, moral and legal norms. However, despite these strong tendencies towards uniformity, the village community was never a levelled, well-adjusted social reality. Different starts in life, personal abilities and unequal opportunities played a very important role in a peasant community. An inquiring individual often led to the discarding of mechanical lines of thought. In my many years of field study I came across several village philosophers whose thoughts upon life were independent and bold. Thus among a variety of peasant thinkers I found sceptics who doubted the reality of heaven and hell, and even the existence of the human soul.

The Poverty of Historical Perspective

The peasant population which in the feudal period was divided up into small and isolated village and parish communities and into somewhat larger sections within the so-called patrimonial estates (*latifundia*) lived under conditions which did not favour the development of a broader historical perspective.

It is clear that in a community which relied mainly on oral tradition, the memory of the past must have had a limited, local character. Apart from topographical facts (village and field boundaries), it was mainly concerned with the events which, owing to their unusual character and their far-reaching effects, left deep traces in the mind of the people. Thus events associated with vital aspects of human existence, such as famines, epidemics, wars, class struggles with landlords, were remembered above all. These form the destructive nature of peasant history. In a later period, they consisted of memories of the conditions of living under serfdom, of constant and sometimes angry disputes with the squire, of his economic oppression of the villagers, of his robbing of their land to enlarge his own estates; they also included tales of great highland robbers, some of them becoming figures of legendary fame. It should be stressed that such traditions of serfdom retained their strength even in modern times, becoming one of the factors mobilizing the peasant masses in their struggle for social and political emancipation. Here, however, they concern us above all as an important factor in the awakening of peasant interest in their past and of the deepening of their general historical perspective.

The poverty of historical perspective was also the result of a short collective memory, caused simply by the continual process of death of one generation and succession by a new one. This may seem obvious enough, yet the stressing of this simple process leads to the discovery of another interesting aspect of the peasant historical sense, namely that historical events were assigned no clear-cut chronology. Often events remote from each other merged, in the peasant memory, into one picture without a definite sequence, sometimes even passing into synchronic vision.

The Village Community in Traditional Culture

A very significant feature of the peasant traditional culture was a strong bond of social cohesion which, despite the existing class differentiation, joined the population of individual settlements into well-defined territorial groupings, the village communities. The Beskid villagers of that time had relatively little contact, economic, administrative, religious and educational, with the town and other villages. This, combined with the almost complete absence of a wider peasant organization, resulted in a situation where village communities of that time lived their own lives, being practically self-sufficient. Somewhat closer relations existed only between those villages which formed a common parish. The village bond was above all manifested in a strong community of interest, which operated within the village.

Although sharp social contrast existed among the village population, which was divided into several landowning classes as well as into different types of landless peasantry, there existed a well-developed sense of internal solidarity.

Outwardly it was expressed in a common name, like 'we the Porebianie', 'we the Bubkowinianie', etc., i.e. we, the people of Poreba, Bukowina, etc. The common ownership of pasture-land, bogs and forest, in which even the smallest owners of land had their share, provided an additional link. The institution of mutual neighbourly assistance, as well as an elaborate system of exchange of gifts, was practised on a large scale. Another manifestation of the solidarity was the practice of common migration in groups for seasonal work and the formation of work parties on the basis of a common village or parish origin. The same principle of grouping obtained in common pilgrimages to the acknowledged shrines or places of religious worship. There was also a tendency towards settling down together in towns and industrial settlements, as well as towards seeking employment in the same factories. This principle was maintained in the Polish emigration settlements abroad, in the United States, for example.

A village community with a strong sense of internal solidarity had also a well-defined sense of distinctness in relation to the outside world. Thus the inhabitants of neighbouring villages were always treated as strangers. They were treated differently, though with varying degrees of antipathy. The following statement by one of my informants will best illustrate this ethical relativism: 'It is not permissible to beat the people from our own village [*swojacy*, dialect] but the people from other villages can (and should) be beaten.'

Such an attitude often led to conflicts with the inhabitants of other communities, which sometimes developed into prolonged and acute antagonism. These often passed into open brawls, in which groups mainly of youngsters took part. There were many locations in which such a fight could take place, the usual ones being the boundary between the two villages, the inn, or fêtes and parties, mainly in connection with the courting of local girls by the *niepilce* (dialect for strangers).

Attitudes towards strangers were thus, on the whole, antagonistic. They found expression in depreciatory and sometimes even abusive nicknames for people of other villages. Their evaluations, descriptions and stories of them were usually totally distorted. Numerous examples are on record, though it would be difficult, if at all possible, to reproduce in English the atmosphere and the expressiveness of the local dialect.

It should also be added that an important function of the above-mentioned village antagonism was to provide a barrier to the access of strangers into the village. For they, by marriage or by other means, it was thought, would get hold of the land, of which there was always a great shortage in southern Poland.

The Dynamics of Disintegration of Traditional Cultures

Before we branch into a discussion of the process of disintegration of traditional peasant culture under the impact of capitalism, a few words must be said about its historical antecedents. We have already seen that any traditional culture, based exclusively on oral transmission, could maintain its pure form only in those situations where the community that carried it was not subject to the influence of more advanced, literate civilizations. But such a situation never existed in Europe, where the peasant cultures since the earliest times had developed as dependent products, in a state of symbiosis with the cultures of the ruling classes. The latter, since feudal times and then throughout the period of capitalism, have always applied writing and later on printing as a means of accumulation and perfecting of cultural achievements. The position was similar in Poland, where the development of peasant culture was not independent, but contained within a framework of a political and social system imposed by the ruling classes. In the feudal system there were two principal ways of transferring the elements of ruling-class culture to that of the peasantry: (a) by a conscious pressure and coercion on the part of the ruling class, or (b) by imitation on the part of the peasantry.

The peasantry in the feudal system constituted – as is generally known – the most numerous, and at the same time the most exploited and oppressed class, on whose labour the well-being of the nobles, gentry and clergy depended. Hence the tendency for the ruling class to control the social and economic life of the peasants, as well as other aspects of their culture. The result was that various cultural elements of the upper classes were inevitably introduced in the life of the villagers. To illustrate this process, which was, of course, gradual and extended over a long time, it is enough to mention the role of the ruling class in the regulation of the land system and rural housing, and in numerous rules and instructions issued (most of them in writing and some even in a printed form) to the peasantry regulating various aspects of their material well-being (e.g. peasant dress and costumes). Or one may mention the role of the clergy and the products of Church culture, for centuries transmitted by written and printed media, which extended over vital systems of peasant life and mentality such as religious concepts and practices, family life, views on life and the world, and literary motifs which from the sermons passed to folk-tales. It should be added that the institution of parish schools, although in feudal times they trained a relatively small number of children, had existed for several centuries and its teachers, the rectors, were often of peasant stock.

Of considerable importance was the fact that in numerous villages the actual organizers of settlements, the so-called 'locators', were often townsmen, while the legal foundations of these settlements consisted of written civil and penal codes brought from Western Europe. Shortly afterwards, during the fifteenth century, a large number of the village scribes were of village origin. For that period saw a powerful drive for social advancement among the villagers, who on an increasing scale began to send their sons to schools. The latter afterwards took up lower administrative posts in the Church and municipalities. It is therefore no accident that already at that time the countryside was producing a number of eminent men, scholars, writers and poets. However, the great majority of peasants who became literate took minor posts in the villages as the rectors of parish schools, vicars, church organists, scribes in village courts and accountants in large estates. It was from this group that the leaders of peasant movements and jacqueries were recruited as well as the originators of a rebel peasant ideology, searching in the gospels for a justification for peasant rights. In this respect, attention should be drawn to a very real connection which existed between peasant culture and the peasants' prolonged struggle for emancipation, which often led to violence. For it was in that struggle that many peasant songs originated with a strong anti-nobility bias, condemning the manor and life in it.

Apart from the social coercion exerted by the ruling class, another process was simultaneously in operation, that of imitating certain cultural forms and practices belonging to the privileged classes. Although this process was much more voluntary in character, it was not quite spontaneous. For it should not be forgotten that for the exasperated peasantry various culture elements pertaining to the dominant classes must have looked attractive, be it custom, etiquette, music or literary production.

In this way non-peasant cultural elements penetrated – by enforcement or imitation – into folk-culture. At the same time they often perished in the culture of the ruling classes, e.g. in literature, official science or other branches of artistic production. Having been retained in the peasant culture, they often underwent changes, both in quality and in quantity, acquiring after some time a folk-character. This important process, which had already taken place with varying intensity in the feudal period, remained, so far as the mechanism of development was concerned, little altered in the nineteenth and twentieth centuries.

Generally it may be said that the peasant culture of southern Poland showed a preponderance of the traditional elements until the emancipation of the peasants in 1848, and even beyond that to about 1870. The disintegration of traditional peasant culture was a long process. The dissolution of traditional elements after 1848 was due to a strengthened forward-looking perspective among the peasantry. Among the factors which heralded this tendency were:

1 the growing infiltration into the villages of products demanding higher technical skill and knowledge about how to use them, improved agricultural tools and machinery, for example;
2 a more intensive exchange of goods between town and country and the breaking up of the spatial isolation of the countryside;
3 the development of rural education;
4 the wider connection of village populations with social, political and cultural movements on a national scale.

The tide of displacement of elements of traditional culture among the villages was not an even one; slow at the end of the feudal epoch, it speeded up at the turn of the nineteenth and early twentieth century, and became rapid in the new Poland.

Note

1 Thus among the landed peasantry there were owners of full fields (*kmiecie*), half-fields (*pokmiecie*), half a *rola* (another type of field) (*oorolnicy*), quarter-rola (*ewiererol-nicy*), owners of forest-recovered fields (*zarebnicy*) and finally the owners of quite small plots (*zagrodnicy*, *hortulani*). The landless population were differentiated into craftsmen (*rzemieslnicy*), village labourers (*wyronicy*) who either had a household of their own, or a room (*komora*) and food provided by a rich peasant for whom they had to work (*komornicy*).

Related Items

1, 3, 4, 5, 6, 7, 8, 27, 30, 34, 35, 36, 37, 38, 42, 44, 59, 60.

34

The Vision of a Peasant
John Berger

Very few peasants become artists – occasionally perhaps the son or daughter of peasants has done so. This is not a question of talent, but of opportunity and free time. There are some songs and, recently, a few autobiographies about peasant experience. There is the marvellous philosophical work of Gaston Bachelard. Otherwise there is very little. This lack means that the peasant's soul is as unfamiliar or unknown to most urban people as is his physical endurance and the material conditions of his labour.

It is true that in medieval Europe peasants sometimes became artisans, masons, even sculptors. But they were then employed to express the ideology of the Church, not, directly, their own view of the world.

There is, however, one colossal work, which resembles no other and which is a direct expression of peasant experience. It is about this work – which includes poetry, sculpture, architecture – that I want now to talk.

A country postman, as my 27,000 comrades, I walked each day from Hauterives to Tersanne – in the region where there are still traces of the time when the sea was here – sometimes going through snow and ice, sometimes through flowers. What can a man do when walking everlastingly through the same setting, except to dream? I built in my dreams a palace passing all imagination, everything that the genius of a simple man can conceive – with gardens, grottoes, towers, castles, museums and statues: all so beautiful and graphic that the picture of it was to live in my mind for at least ten years. . . .

When I had almost forgotten my dream, and it was the last thing I was thinking about, it was my foot which brought it all back to me. My foot caught on something which almost made me fall: I wanted to know what it was: it was a stone of such strange shape that I put it in my pocket to admire at leisure. The next day, passing through the same place, I found some more, which were even more beautiful. I arranged them together there and then on the spot and was amazed. . . . I searched the ravines, the hillside, the most barren and desolate places. . . . I found tufa which had been petrified by water and which is also wonderful. . . .

An original paper.

This is where my trials and tribulations began. I then brought along some baskets. Apart from the 30 km a day as postman, I covered dozens with my basket on my back, full of stones. Each commune has its own particular type of very hard stone. As I crossed the countryside I used to make small piles of these stones: in the evenings, I returned with my wheelbarrow to fetch them. The nearest were four to five km away, sometimes ten. I sometimes set out at two or three in the morning.

The writer is Ferdinand Cheval, who was born in 1836 and died in 1924, and who spent 33 years building his 'palace passing all imagination'. It is still to be found in Hauterives, the village where he was born, in the Department of the Drome, France.

> In the evening when night has fallen,
>   And other men are resting.
> I work at my palace.
> No one will know my suffering.
> In the minutes of leisure
> Which my duty allows me
> I have built this palace of a thousand and one nights –
> I have carved my own monument

Today the Palace is crumbling, its sculptures disintegrating, and its texts, inscribed on or cut into the walls, are being slowly effaced. It is less than 80 years old. Most buildings and sculptures fare better, because they belong to a mainstream tradition which lays down principles for whom they should be made, and, afterwards, for how they should be preserved. This work is naked and without tradition because it is the work of a single 'mad' peasant.

There are now a number of books of photographs about the Palace but the trouble with photographs – and even in film – is that the viewer stays in his chair. And the Palace is about the experience of being inside itself. You do not *look* at it any more than you look at a forest. You either enter it or you pass it by.

As Cheval has explained, the origin of its imagery was stones: stones which, shaped during geological times, appeared to him as caricatures. 'Strange sculptures of all kinds of animals and caricatures. Impossible for man to imitate. I said to myself: since nature wants to make sculpture, I will make the masonry and architecture for it.' As you look *into* these stones they become creatures, mostly birds or animals. Some look at you. Some you only glimpse as they disappear back into the stones from which they emerged briefly as profiles. The palace is full of a life that is never entirely visible.

Except for a few exceptions which I will discuss later, there are no definitively exterior surfaces. Every surface refers, for its reality, inwards. The animals return to within the stones; when you are not looking they re-emerge. Every appearance changes. Yet it would be wrong to think of the Palace as dream-like. This was the mistake of the Surrealists, who were the first to 'discover' it in the thirties. To psychologize it, to question Cheval's unconscious is to think in terms which never explain its uniqueness.

Despite its title, its model is not a palace but a forest. Within it are contained many smaller palaces, chateaux, temples, houses, lairs, earths, nests, holes, etc. The full content or population of the Palace is impossible to establish. Each time you enter it, you see something more or different. Cheval ended up by doing far more than just making the masonry and architecture for the sculptures of nature. He began to make his own. But nature remained his model: not as a depository of fixed appearances, not as the source of all taxonomy, but as an example of continual metamorphosis. If I look immediately in front of me now, I see:

a pine tree
a calf, large enough for the pine tree to be its horn
a snake
a Roman vase
two washer-women, the size of moles
an otter
a lighthouse
a snail
three friends nestling in coral
a leopard, larger than the lighthouse
a crow

Such a list would have to be multiplied several thousand times in order to make even a first approximate census. And as soon as you realize that, you realize how foreign to the spirit of the work such an exercise would be. Its function is not to present but to surround.

Whether you climb up its towers, walk through its crypts or look up at a façade from the ground, you are aware of having *entered* something. You find yourself in a system which includes the space you occupy. The system may change its own image, suggesting different metaphors at different times. I have already compared it with a forest. In parts it is like a stomach. In other parts it is like a brain – the physical organ in the skull, not the abstract *mind*.

What surrounds you has a physical reality. It is constructed of sandstone, tufa, quicklime, sand, shells and fossils. At the same time all this diverse material is unified and made mysteriously figurative. I do not now speak of the population of its images. I speak of the mineral material as a whole being arranged to represent a living organic system.

A kind of tissue connects everything. You can think of it as consisting of leaves, folds, follicles, or cells. All Cheval's sustained energy, all his faith, went into creating this. It is in this tissue that you feel the actual rhythm of his movements as he moulded the cement or placed his stones. It was in seeing this tissue grow beneath his hands that he was confirmed. It is this tissue which surrounds you like a womb.

I said the basic unit of this tissue suggested a kind of leaf or fold. Perhaps the closest I can get to defining it, or fully imagining it – inside the Palace or far away – is to think of the ideal leaf which Goethe writes about in his essay 'On the Metamorphosis of Plants'. From this archetypal leaf all plant forms derived.

In the Palace this basic unit implies a process of reproduction: not the reproduction of appearances: the reproduction of itself in growth.

Cheval left the Drome once in his life: as a young man to work for a few months in Algeria. He gained his knowledge of the world via the new popular encyclopaedic magazines which came on the market during the second quarter of the nineteenth century. This knowledge enabled him to aspire to a world, as distinct from local and partial, view. (Today modern means of communication are having, in different parts of the world, a comparable political effect. Peasants will eventually visualize themselves in global terms.)

Without a global aspiration, Cheval could never have sustained the necessary confidence to work alone for thirty-three years. In the Middle Ages the Church had offered a universal view, but its craftsmen mostly worked within the constraint of a prescribed iconography in which the peasant view had a place but was not formative. Cheval emerged, alone, to confront the modern world with his peasant vision intact. And according to this vision he built his Palace.

It was an incredibly improbable event, depending on so many contingencies. Of temperament. Of geography. Of social circumstance. The fact, for instance, that he was a postman and so had a small pension. If he had been a peasant working his own land, he could never have afforded the 93,000 hours spent on the Palace. Yet he remained organically and consciously a member of the class into which he was born. 'Son of a peasant, it is as a peasant that I wish to live and die in order to prove that in my class too there are men of energy and genius.'

The character of the Palace is determined by two essential qualities: physicality (it contains no abstract sentimental appeals, and Cheval's state-ments all emphasize the enormous physical labour of its construction) and innerness (its total emphasis on what is within and being within). Such a combination does not exist in modern urban experience but is profoundly typical of peasant experience.

The notion of the *visceral* may perhaps be used here as an example. A word of warning, however, is necessary. To think of peasant attitudes as being more 'gutsy' than urban ones is to miss the point and to resort to an ignorant cliché.

A stable door. Hanging from a nail, a young goat being skinned and eviscerated by a grandfather deploying the point of his pocket-knife with the greatest delicacy, as if it were a needle. Beside him the grandmother holding the intestines in her arms to make it easier for her husband to detach the stomach without perforating it. One yard in front, sitting on the ground, oblivious for a moment of his grandparents, a four-year-old grandson, playing with a cat and rubbing its nose against his own. The visceral is an everyday, familiar category from an early age to peasants.

By contrast, the urban horror of the visceral is encouraged by unfamiliarity, and is linked with urban attitudes to death and birth. Both have become secret, removed moments. In both it is impossible to deny the primacy of inner, invisible processes.

The ideal urban surface is a brilliant one (e.g. chrome) which reflects what is in front of it, and seems to deny that there is anything visible behind it. Its antithesis is the flank of a body rising and falling as it breathes. Urban experience concentrates on recognizing what is outside for what it is, measuring it, testing it and treating it. When what is inside has to be explained (I am not talking now in terms of molecular biology but in terms of everyday life), it is explained as a mechanism, yet the measures of the mechanics used always belong to the outside. The outside, the exterior, is celebrated by continuous visual reproduction (duplication) and justified by empiricism.

To the peasant the empirical is naive. He works with the never entirely predictable, the emergent. What is visible is usually a sign for him of the state of the invisible. He touches surfaces to form in his mind a better picture of what lies behind them. Above all he is aware of following and modifying processes which are beyond him, or anybody, to start or stop: he is always aware of being within a process himself.

A factory line produces a series of identical products. But no two fields, no two sheep, no two trees are alike. (The catastrophes of the green revolution, when agricultural production is planned from above by city experts, are usually the result of ignoring specific local conditions, of defying the laws of natural heterogeneity.) The computer has become the storehouse, the 'memory' of modern urban information: in peasant cultures the equivalent storehouse is an oral tradition handed down through generations; yet the real difference between them is this: the computer supplies, very swiftly, the exact answer to a complex question; the oral tradition supplies an ambiguous answer – sometimes even in the form of a riddle – to a common practical question. Truth as a certainty. Truth as an uncertainty.

Peasants are thought of as being traditionalists when placed in historical time; but they are far more accustomed to living with change in cyclical time.

A closeness to what is unpredictable, invisible, uncontrollable and cyclic predisposes the mind to a religious interpretation of the world. The peasant does not believe that Progress is pushing back the frontiers of the unknown, because he does not accept the strategic diagram implied by such a statement. In his experience the unknown is constant and central: knowledge surrounds it but will never eliminate it. It is not possible to generalize about the role of religion among peasants but one can say that it articulates another profound experience: their experience of production through work.

I have said that a few surfaces in Cheval's Palace do not refer inwards for their reality. These include the surfaces of some of the buildings he reproduces, like the White House in Washington, DC, the Maison-Carrée in Algiers. The others are the surfaces of human faces. All of them are enigmatic. The human faces hide their secrets, and it is possible, as with nothing else in the Palace, that their secrets are unnatural. He has sculpted them with respect and suspicion.

Cheval himself called his Palace a temple to nature. Not a temple to the nature of travellers, landscapists, or even Jean-Jacques Rousseau, but to nature as dreamt by a genius expressing the vision of a class of cunning, hardened survivors.

In the centre of the Palace is a crypt, surrounded by sculpted animals – only towards his animals did Cheval show his capacity for tenderness. Between the animals are shells, stones with eyes hidden in them, and, linking everything, the tissue of the first leaf. On the ceiling of this crypt, in the form of a circle, Cheval wrote: 'Here I wanted to sleep.'

Related Items

1, 3, 4, 5, 7, 19, 21, 33, 35, 37, 42, 47, 61, 62.

35

The Peasant View of the Bad Life

F. G. Bailey

For a number of reasons, tracing the cognitive map of a culture not one's own is difficult.[1] In recent years linguistic anthropologists have developed a technique which may provide the scientific exactness so far lacking, but as yet these tools have been used to elicit the categories through which people perceive their kinsmen, or the types of food they eat or the way they think about the consumption of alcohol, or about disease, or about the land on which they grow their food. The more general moral categories which which I am here concerned – good and bad, success and failure, and the difficult idea of the moral community – remain beyond the reach of these techniques. My account, therefore, will be impressionistic and difficult to verify.[2]

Anthropologists begin by selecting native concepts and teasing out their meanings. A one-word translation is always inadequate. Often the concepts are presented in the native language: *mana*, *taboo*, *totem* are well-known examples, and they can be described only by specifying the contexts in which they may be correctly used. Sometimes the people themselves have no general term. For example the concept of an 'outsider' is my summary of a range of terms which peasants have for particular outsiders: *sircar* (government); *marwari* (a trader); *gujerati* (another kind of trader); *kataki* (a man from the coastal plain); and so forth. In short, there are quite considerable problems of translation.

Thirdly, it is not easy to decide at what level of generality to make the translation. Perceptions of the world vary according to sex, to age, to caste status, and so forth. In the context of modernization in peasant India it is usually appropriate to look at the cognitive maps of adult males, but this does not get round variations in caste and ethnic allegiances. I shall be talking of the hill peasants of Orissa who, in the area in which I lived, are either Oriyas or Konds.[3] The cognitive maps of both these peoples contain the same element of xenophobia, but they differ radically in their perceptions of human inequality.

A shortened version of F. G. Bailey, 'The peasant view of the bad life', *Advancement of Science*, December 1966, pp. 399–409.

To average out these differences makes nonsense; there is nothing to do but make two cognitive maps, for ideas of rank are clearly relevant in the modernization process. In what follows I shall be talking mainly about the Oriyas, who, being a caste society, see the social world in categories of rank. The other themes which I shall discuss are found to a greater or lesser degree in many peasant societies; but I could not claim that they are universal.

Every society discriminates between different categories of persons, giving to the highest full status as members of the community, able to bear social responsibilities and commanding the corresponding social rights, and relegating the lowest into a category which is scarcely human at all. Those who are so marginal as to be considered outsiders can be used as if they were objects or instruments, providing the user has the power to do so; this is not regarded as a moral relationship, but as one of exploitation. Standards of honesty, respect and consideration in so far as they are moral imperatives are diminished as the status of the person at the other end of the relationship becomes more marginal. Moreover, one expects him to reciprocate. One justifies cheating government agencies by saying that the officials concerned are cheating you. This perception is often so firm that even behaviour which is patently not exploitative, but benevolent, is interpreted as a hypocritical cover for some as yet undisclosed interest: by definition all horses are Trojan.

The steps by which categories of people are charted as marginal are not evenly spaced. For the villagers whom I knew the moral community comprises their own family, the members of their own caste in the same village, their fellow villagers (markedly graded according to their distance from ego in the caste system), their kinsmen in other villages and their caste fellows in other villages, and getting near to the limit, people of other castes in those same villages.[4] Then, after a gap, come people who are villagers like oneself, with the same style of life and speaking the same dialect, but with whom, as yet, no connection can be traced: if they desire to be admitted to the moral community, the villagers use elaborate and rigorous techniques to test their cultural credentials.

Beyond this category are people whose culture – the way they speak, the way they dress, their deportment, the things they speak about as valuable and important – places them unambiguously beyond the moral community of the peasant: revenue inspectors, policemen, development officers, health inspectors, veterinary officials, and so on; men in bush shirts and trousers, men who are either arrogant and distant or who exhibit a camaraderie which, if the villager reciprocates, is immediately switched off; men who come on bicycles and in jeeps, but never on their feet. These are the people to be outwitted; these are the people whose apparent gifts are by definition the bait for some hidden trap.

The significance of this for political modernization and for development is obvious. Suggestions or commands to assume modern political or economic roles come from outside the moral community; they are therefore automatically categorized as dangerous and sinful, and those villagers who adopt the new roles run the risk of being marked as deviants and punished. Equally if any innovation does in fact turn out to be harmful (for example, the improved seed that fails) the villager does not feel obliged to search for what he would regard as a rational scientific cause; he finds a perfectly satisfactory explanation in the fact that it came from outside; and he also finds confirmation of his perception that external things are evil and dangerous (cf. Bailey, 1959, pp. 252–4).

It is, therefore, something of a paradox that the way a peasant tries to exploit a politician or an official, or to avoid being exploited by him, is by transforming the modern specialized relationship which he has with that man into a multiplex relationship, a type which is characteristic of his own peasant world. The peasant dealing with a clerk finds a broker to help him establish a personal relationship which will soften the rigorous unpleasantness of the official relationship. The politician seeking votes or the development official seeking peasant cooperation will call them 'brothers and sisters'. When the peasants want something out of the official they will address him as if he were a king and therefore has the obligation to be generous, or perhaps by that opening to many Indian petitions 'You are my mother and my father. . . .' The implication in all these cases is that the official relationship, which is single-interest and specialized, is not enough: it must be reinforced with other relationships.

Relationships within a peasant or tribal community are for the most part multiplex: that is to say, they are not specialized to deal with a single activity. There is, of course, some division of labour, as, for example, between the landowners and the landless: but even then this relationship, which I have described through its economic strand, will also carry political and ritual and possibly familial strands. This, indeed, is the characteristic pattern of the caste system as it works inside an Indian village.

It is to be noticed that whether the initiative comes from the official and politician or from the peasant, it is the supplicant who seeks to make the relationship diffuse: to make it a moral relationship. The dominant partner will usually play hard-to-get; if the official or politician is dominant he will try to retain the transactional character of the relationship and not have the sharp edge of the bargain blunted by moral considerations; if the peasant is dominant, he is likely to reject the proferred relationship, because it comes from an outsider, or to accept it simply as a transaction and get what he can out of it. I have ample evidence that this was overwhelmingly the attitude of villagers towards campaigning politicians in India.

When, as a supplicant, the peasant tries to bribe a clerk, or to establish a dependent relationship with an official in the idiom of family relationship or of a courtier at the king's palace, he is in fact trying to coerce the clerk or the official by including him within his own moral community. He is trying to transform the transaction, which he knows is one of exploitation, into a moral relationship, *because it is in his interest to do so*. In just the same way, when the campaigning politician addresses him as 'brother', the peasant sees this as an act of hypocrisy, and looks behind the façade of symbolic friendliness for the hidden interest.

The watershed between traditional and modern society is exactly this distinction between single-interest and multiplex relationships. The hallmark of a modern society is the specialized role and the whole apparatus of its productive prosperity rests upon the division of labour between specialized roles. Of course we have diffuse institutions like the family, but the public official who finds jobs for his relatives, or the fact that a large part of Macmillan's cabinets could be shown on a chart of kinship and affinity, is something which our modern culture condemns: or at least we feel uncomfortable about it.

This feeling of ethical disquiet may be the reason why planners in India resolutely close their eyes to the fact that the society they are attempting to modernize is founded upon multiplex relationships. No doubt there is bribery and nepotism; but it is loudly condemned. Even in situations which could be met without bruising the modernist conscience, the official gaze is resolutely averted: for example, when the zemindari holdings in Orissa were abolished, the zemindar's place was taken by an official specializing in the collection of revenue; but the zemindar's other functions – money-lending, dispute settling, and so forth – were not systematically provided for.

The attitude of the peasant towards single-interest relationships is not, I think, marked by ethical displeasure. Such relationships, being with outsiders, are not *im*moral so much as *a*moral: when one is dealing with an instrument, standards of what is just and unjust do not apply: one wants only to use the instrument most effectively.

A second important theme in the peasants' cognitive map is what we would call leadership. Villagers recognize two kinds of big men: a secular leader whom we will call 'chief' and a man of religious eminence whom the villagers call a 'yogi' or a 'guru' (teacher) but whom we will call a 'saint'. I will argue that the idea of disinterested service to the community is only a minor element in one of these categories and is absent altogether from the other.

A chief is a man who is able to take care of his honour (*mohoto*), and who regards honour as the supreme value in social life. Honour entails the notion of competition and conflict, for a man gets honour by demonstrating, in various stylized ways, that his rivals have less honour: that is to say, by shaming them. Heads of families, especially wealthy men of high caste, are all chiefs, and they treat one another, when not in combat, with a dignified formality and restraint.

In so far as a man is a chief he is expected to protect the interests *not* of the community at large, but the interests of his own followers against rival chiefs and their followers. Moreover, even within this relationship between chief and follower the notion of disinterested service is weakly developed: loyalty, except for the innermost circle of followers, is bought by the protection which the chief gives and by the largesse which he hands out to his own followers. If the chief cannot provide these things, then the follower is not expected to go through an agony of heart searching but to use his head and find a stronger and richer chief. There is an element here of the amorality found in the 'outsider' relationship. Notice also that although the chief is expected to provide a service for others, the notion of this service is the very antithesis of what we mean by '*public* service': as their equivalent in our civilization might say, 'chiefs are not in business just for their health'. Notice also that the idea of service from a posture of humility is entirely absent.

Some of these chiefs, when they become old men, turn into 'philanthropoids'. They build temples, or rest-houses for pilgrims, or plant trees to give shade, or excavate bathing pools where the devout may take purifying baths. Peasants certainly mark with approval wells and bathing ghats and shade trees: but the act of giving is considered cynically as a kind of conscience money. A man in a village close to where I lived had cheated and bullied his way to great eminence, but in middle age was still without a son. He then invested in a number of spectacular public works and in a new young wife; in due time she presented him with a son. This son lived to manhood, but, as the man who told me noted with satisfaction, the old man outlived him and there were no grandchildren.

Villagers look more kindly on a man of religious eminence than upon a chief. But, like the chief, the saint too is looking after himself and his own soul, as we would say: his life is not spent in the service of others. Even if he is a guru (a teacher), he is a consultant helping individuals with their particular difficulties, rather than a man active in the public service. The saint is respected – even loved in a special numinous sense of that word – not for what he does for the community, but simply for what he is – a holy man.

Some traditional ideas about secular leadership are relevant to political modernization and economic development. Notice that the appropriate relationship between a leader and a follower is not inconsistent with the attitude which one has towards an outsider. Leader–follower relationships within a moral community have a degree of hardness and calculation of self-interest: when the relationship crosses the boundary of the moral community, wariness hardens into suspicion and double-dealing. Within the moral community the peasant understands the range of possible action; within limits, he knows what his opponent will do, because he and his opponent (whether leader or follower) share certain basic values; furthermore the relationship is seen to be regulated by councils or *panchayats* or superior leaders. But outside the moral community none of these controls apply: official action is unpredictable; values are not shared; and adjudicative institutions like courts of law are not part of the peasant moral community but are regarded as instruments or weapons to be used in the contest. Within the moral community, one looks carefully to see if the leader is fulfilling his side of the bargain; outside the moral community, one knows that a bargain will not be fulfilled, and one must therefore insure oneself by anticipatory cheating.

Secondly, the language of cooperation is almost completely absent from the traditional leader–follower relationship. The language of cooperation is, of course, found in the village but it is a language used between equals and within the moral community. It is found in the formalized equality symbolized in the procedures of the village council or in the ceremonial meeting of the senior kin of a bride and groom; it is also found, with less formality, in cooperative work parties or in hunting when the men, after a rest, urge one another to resume the chase with those strange staccato cries of mutual encouragement that one hears coming out of a pack of rugby forwards. Everyone gives the orders to no one in particular. But leaders do not appeal to their followers to pull together as a matter of moral obligation: rather they offer them inducements (rewards or punishments) to do so.

Traditional leaders do not ask for cooperation. Outsiders *cannot* effectively ask for cooperation from the peasants. But they do so continually, and to the villagers this seems either a joke or something to be very worried about, as a football player would be if he heard himself being urged on and urged to cooperate by the captain of the opposing team.

The peasant looks upon outsiders (including officials) as his enemies. But there are also, within his conceptual world, a number of persons whom we might see as peacemaking or mediating. How does the peasant see these persons? The men could be traitors; they could be enemy agents; or they could be accepted and given moral status as true mediators, thus widening the boundaries of the peasant moral community.

At first sight some chiefly roles – in India rajas or non-absentee zemindars – could span the gap between officials and the peasant world. These statuses combine in the one-person general administrator, tax collector, justice of the peace, welfare officer and money-lender, custodian of sacred symbols and organizer of collective rituals at harvest or sowing time or on other religious occasions. All these people have now been legally – but not always effectively – dethroned in India. They were to some extent a part of the moral community of their peasants. We anthropologists have made much of a relationship of this kind: emphasizing that the king, as the custodian of sacred objects and the performer of sacred rituals, symbolized the unity of his people and their values. I am sure we were right to do so, and not a few difficulties in enforced modernization arise from ignoring non-political components of traditional leadership roles and neglecting to make provision in modern institutions for these components.

But, for several reasons, it is hard to see rajas or landlords as mediators in the modernizing situation. Firstly, they were not allowed to do so because the cognitive map of the modernizing elite marked them as enemies identifying them correctly as an important part of the political system created by the British authoritarian administration. Secondly, since they are the very apogee of the chiefly role, their status as members of the peasant moral community was somewhat precarious. One Orissa ex-raja, who had been elected – almost unanimously – to the Legislative Assembly, told me that he did not bother to campaign and that if he had chosen to nominate his elephant the people would have returned it to the Assembly. But, in the next election, he was defeated. His state had been abolished for ten years and the many roles that he had combined in his person were either not being performed or were being done by a scatter of administrators. I think he underestimated the transactional nature of his tie with his former subjects. The love, of which he boasted, turned out to be cupboard love (the contents of the cupboard being, of course, culturally defined). Thirdly – and the fate of the raja will serve to illustrate this too – once such men begin to behave like outsiders, then inevitably they take on the role of outsiders and lose their place in the moral community of the peasants. A few exceptional men – there were two striking examples in Orissa – built up a transactional following in the modern role of politician: no doubt they were helped by their royal status to make a start, but this status alone would not carry them for very long. Incidentally, the modernizing elite was very reluctant to admit that these two men were in fact playing modern roles.

The second kind of potential mediator is the man who has recently made the jump into the elite, and who still has close kinsmen who have remained peasants. In most parts of tropical Africa the indigenous elite are new boys: so too, in India, are many politicians at the state and even at the national level; but this is less true of the civil services. This happens because the children of the elite acquire education and the children of the poor do not. This has been the case for many generations in India. I suppose it will also become true of Africa, and one already hears reports from West Africa that the elite is hardening into a class (see Lloyd, 1966, introduction).

How do peasants regard a kinsman who has become part of the elite? He is still part of their moral community and is expected to take the responsibilities and obligations of a kinsman. That these obligations may conflict with his modern roles is not countenanced. Such a man must take care what role-signs he displays: when he goes on leave, he discards the bush shirt and trousers for a *dhoti* before he enters his village. Indeed those actions which the modern world stigmatizes as nepotism and corruption are in fact often the fulfilling of a man's obligations in the traditional world. The conclusion must be – and it is something of a paradox – that the newly joined member of the elite can act neither as a mediator between the two worlds nor as a modernizing agent among his own people: he can in fact only retain the tie with his own people so long as he acts in accordance with their values.

The third category of brokers are those who use religious symbols which are valued by the peasants, in order to seek membership of the peasant moral community: or (which perhaps more accurately describes the motives of the most famous of them), in order to disclaim membership of the modernizing elite. How do the villagers look upon such men and women?

The saintly figure is part of their known world. He stands for something – however vague – which they value; one might call it personal salvation. They do not bargain with or try to exploit a saint. For most people the relationship is distant and impersonal, one of respect and reverence symbolized by giving alms and receiving what we call blessing. Those who form a closer relationship as pupils or disciples choose to do so for ideological or moral reasons; the saint does not drum up a following in the way that a chief does.

But the politician who presents himself in the saintly style, clad in a *dhoti* and sandals and arriving on his feet, does not always behave in the manner which the villagers associate with his appearance. The visitor does not sit silently under the tree or give his advice only to those who ask for it; he makes speeches. Moreover, what he advocates must seem to the villagers very surprising, like sacred music sung to rock-and-roll. He talks about hygiene, or basic education, or why the poor should be given land – all topics which suggest to the villagers *sircar*, the government. Vinoba Bhave's men came to the village where I lived and were rejected as completely as if they had been government agents – indeed, more completely, for it was known that they had no force to back up their requests. We talk easily of charismatic leaders since Weber gave us the word, but I think we are often taken in by the propaganda of those who have ambitions to be charismatic leaders.

The remaining mediating role has probably been the most effective in spanning the gap between peasants and elite. This is the village broker: the man who makes a profession of helping officials or politicians and peasants to communicate with one another, and is paid either directly or indirectly for doing so. He knows how to get licences and remission of tax, he knows where to place bribes, he can get real medicine from the hospital dispensary. For the other side he recruits voters or agents or people to make a good showing when some superior visitor is coming down; he can do privately and discreetly all those jobs which the rulers of modern institutions forbid, but which modern people find must be done (see Bailey, 1963, pp. 55–67).

Although his stock in trade is the favours he has done for people, such a man is not honoured or even trusted by the villagers. He is a renegade, a half-outsider, albeit necessary to temper the cold winds of bureaucracy. But no such man could possibly achieve moral status as a mediator between traditionalists and modernizers. Both sides place him in the category of outsider. In fact he does positive harm: his makeshift activities perpetuate the gap in communication between peasants and elite.

From the point of view of those who wish to modernize, the picture which I draw is not encouraging. There are a few exceptional people who can become, so to speak, honorary members of the peasants' moral community and yet urge peasants to take on new and modern roles. But they can do this only to a very limited extent, for the peasants have a very low threshold of tolerance for those of their own members who connect too closely with the outside world.

The root of my argument is that building a modern society is not a routine process in which all the steps are known and all contingencies anticipated. On the contrary: it is a world of mistakes, frustrations, disappointments, anxiety and conflict. On the quite rare occasions when peasants enter this world voluntarily, they do so because they think they are going to get something out of it: they are out to exploit. If their expectations are disappointed, they withdraw, as they would withdraw their allegiance from an unsuccessful leader. Only people who have a moral commitment to a modern society will persist in the face of disappointment and failure. I have been discussing a number of roles which, at first sight, might seem to provide this moral commitment by holding the trust of the peasants. But in virtually all cases this trust is withdrawn if the broker is seen to be a missionary for modernization.[5]

I have talked about the peasants' categories of outsiders, leaders and brokers: that is, about persons. Now, at a more abstract level I shall ask what peasants think, not about politicians, but about policies. Much has been written about what particular peasants or tribesmen think about particular policies; but not so much about the idea of policy making.

In this idea, there are two main components, neither of which forms part of peasant culture. The first is that man has a good chance of controlling his own destiny and his environment: no one would continue to formulate policies if he thought that he could never implement them. Indeed the essence of policy making is that it is a plan for manipulating variables which we know we can control, in order to adapt ourselves to those variables which we know we cannot control, and so, in a paradoxical way, to achieve some kind of control over the uncontrollable.

One of the components of our romantic view of rural life is its certainty and dependability. The four seasons follow one another: year after year life renews itself in the same way. This cycle of eternity, recorded and edited and abridged for us in poetry or at the cinema, gives us a sense of security. We do not doubt, when we go to sleep, but that the same world will be there when we wake up in the morning.

I do not know whether the peasants with whom I lived have this mystical sense of life's continuance; I doubt it, since, unlike us, they know rural life in the raw, unexpurgated, unabridged and uncleaned for dramatic presentation. Certainly, whatever the stability of nature's grand design, they see little security in their own life. No one can be sure whether the harvest will be good or bad: no one can be sure who will be alive this time next year, or even next week. In two or three years a rich man can become poor or a poor man rich. Women die in childbirth: there were women in Bisipara (a village where I lived) who had had five or eight or, in one case, ten children and raised not one beyond its second year. In circumstances like this, no one can feel that man is the master of his environment: nature may have had a grand continuing design, but a man's life is filled with discontinuities. No peasant thinks in terms of five-year plans, and I would argue that the idea of planning can exist only in those cognitive maps which include the idea of man in control of predictable and controllable *impersonal* forces.

Even in our cognitive maps, persons seem less predictable and controllable than things. Sometimes we attribute our failures to other people's malevolent actions; we do this particularly when the undertaking is difficult and a gamble – if the five-year plan fails, that is because of the wicked internal opposition, the stupid peasants and the intrigues of the neo-colonialists: witch-hunting is found in everyone's culture. But we also stress and widely employ the idea that failures can be the result of our miscalculation of variables which are purely impersonal, which have no will of their own, and which cannot be held to be morally responsible. In such cases the idea of punishment or revenge or deterrence makes nonsense: it is the mistake that must be corrected, not the person. To the extent that a cognitive map does not include the idea of impersonal non-moral forces, it also cannot include the idea of planning. To a much greater extent than we do, peasants blame failure upon the malevolence of human agents.[6] It is true that in India and in some other cultures, fate is used as an explanation; but fate, although predictable, cannot be controlled. Success, too – spectacular success – is attributed to human wickedness. The man who, as we say, makes a killing, is not reaping the rewards of hard work and correct calculation, but made his way through sorcery or magic or at least in some way which was harmful to his fellows. Judging from the stories I was told of how men in Bisipara first became wealthy the peasant mythology contains no category of honest riches. Notice the significance of this for innovation and modernization: any peasant who adopts new ways, and becomes rich, must have cheated, must have exploited his fellows, and to that extent should be punished or put outside the moral community.

In brief, both the uncertainty of peasant life and the fact that peasants explain failure by blaming people rather than by supporting a miscalculation or impersonal forces means that policy making and planning are not part of their cognitive map of the world and human society. They do not reject the idea of planning as wicked: they simply do not have the category.

At first sight such a statement seems wrong, for no peasant could survive unless he planned the use of his resources. Peasants breed cattle; they save for marriages; nowadays they make wills; they plan with Machiavellian subtlety ways of doing one another down; and, to name the simplest and most fundamental act of planning, they keep seed for next year's sowing. But, I would argue, such activities are not to be considered planning in the way in which that word is used in, for example, the phrase 'five-year plan'. This brings me to the second component in the idea of policy making.

The second component in policy making is innovation. The policy maker sees a future which is different from the present not just because it is separated from the present by a week or a year, but because life then will be of a different kind from what it is now. Let us separate these two kinds of thought about the future by calling the first 'the round of time' and the second 'time's arrow' (Bourdieu, 1963).

The peasant plans for the round of time. He allocates resources as if he held the assumptions that with minor variations and barring accidents next year will be this year over again. Each resource is seen against a round of time: so many years before the ox must be replaced; so many years before the son replaces the father; thatching every third or second year. In this world, too, people are not so ready to look for the witch behind every failure. A man whose crop is poor when all around have good crops cannot blame witches if he is known to be a slovenly cultivator: it is recognized that with luck (i.e. the absence of human malevolence and adverse fate) good crops are the result of hard work and skilled cultivation. But, as is perhaps true also in our society, few people think hard work and skill a means of changing a poor man into a rich man in twenty years' time: if changes like that happen, they come overnight by mystical means, by magic, or fate or luck; by finding a crock of gold; in our culture by devious and anti-social property deals or by winning on the football pools.

Those who make five-year plans are thinking of time as an arrow. The work has a beginning and an end; there is a target to be reached. The end is a state of affairs quite different from the beginning, and itself is a starting point for further ventures. We have no difficulties with this notion. To plan a future state of affairs which is radically different from the present is to us quite rational. But those who think in terms of the round of time see such changes as coming from mystical forces like fate, or luck, or witchcraft or acts of God, and to plan for such events makes nonsense. The politician who promises a good life in store for everyone, if they help to implement the plan, is heard by the peasants as we would hear a man promising everyone a first dividend on the pools every week.[7]

These are cultural categories and, as with statistical norms, they allow that individuals can be found holding different ideas. Some peasants have learned to see time as an arrow; and most peasants, at least in countries like India, are from time to time compelled to behave as if they saw time that way. But when there is a failure, where accidents occur and the arrow misses the target, then they look for explanations and they take initiatives in the idiom of the round of time – in terms of human wickedness rather than of scientific error. Even those who make the plans, in whom the idea of time as an arrow is internalized, may react to failure by looking for the scapegoat rather than the cause.

This concludes my examination of a few basic cultural themes in the cognitive map of the Indian peasant. These themes hang together: the relationship with a leader is instrumental and exploitative; still more so is that with an outsider. Spectacular success is evil because your success means my failure; my failure is caused by your malevolence. Outsiders talk about spectacular change and spectacular success, but we peasants can only be instruments in their schemes; in any case, if their fantasies were realized, this could only be by anti-social means.

How shall I conclude this discourse, which for a modernizer is certainly a jeremiad? I would insist that to look upon the bright side, and simply deny what I have said, is to pretend that the enemy's bullets will turn to water and his tanks are made of cardboard.

Furthermore, it makes little sense to ask why people hold these values, in the hope that, discovering the causes, we can bring about change. At this level values and categories of thought are ultimate and given; they have no causes and they cannot be further reduced. Indeed it is as pointless as to ask *why* peasants think in the round of time as it is to ask why the Oriya numeral for unity is 'eko' while we say 'one'. We can explain values by relating them to one another, as one analyses the structure of a painting or a poem; but we cannot ask what is the cause of a set of values.

What we can do, however, is to show how a particular set of ideas, such as those I have been discussing, and the experience of the people validate one another. The connection is a functional one and the line of causation between ideas and experience points in both directions. Belief and action are connected with one another. My argument is that fundamental categories of thought (like those of time) and fundamental values (like those attached to leadership and authority) are impervious to direct ideological attack – at least in the short run and given the resources at the disposal of modernizing elites in most of the new nations. The sensible tactic, therefore, is to change the 'action' element (which is another word for 'experience'), in those sectors of action that are at least connected with ideological convictions.[8]

The operational prospects are not in fact so bad. I have been talking about collective representations – about thought; and thought is not the same as action. People can be pressured by carrots or sticks into doing things which they consider are evil or foolish; and a long enough experience may convince them that in fact these things are neither evil nor foolish. Vaccination and DDT spraying and some agricultural innovations (especially some cash-crops) have this kind of success. But parliamentary democracy or other kinds of political modernization and many economic innovations and social reforms do not and could not show such immediate and tangible returns; they may in fact seem to produce immediate and tangible disasters. The conclusion must be that, given peasant resistance, a radical policy of political and economic modernization can only be achieved by pressure and by continued success in material terms.

Short of this – but consistently – those resources which are available for modernization are wasted if they are used directly for propaganda about duty, service, self-sacrifice, and so forth. Modernization is an end too vague and too complex to be readily symbolized and understood: even 'swaraj' (independence) was a non-message so far as Indian peasants were concerned: they listened when Congress began to exploit agrarian discontents. 'Democratic centralization' is a non-message; remission of rent or the removal of a greedy landlord will be understood and accepted (with due suspicion). Any plan for modernization which is based on the assumption that peasants will feel an immediate moral commitment to modernity as such, and will persist voluntarily in the face of failure and frustrations because they are so committed, must be ineffective.

Let me repeat that my discourse is about collective representations – about the way peasants think. This is but one – indeed, the last – of the variables with which the modernizer must operate. If his plans fail, clearly his first question should be about physical and technical matters. Leaving aside human wishes, is it possible for anyone to carry out that particular plan? Perhaps there is something special about the soil of the demonstration farm, absent from most peasant farms? Perhaps the price of fertilizer is too high, so that even if the peasants want it, they cannot buy it? There are many factors of this kind, and their control is usually far easier than attempts to influence and control peasant values and categories of thought.

Secondly, there is a set of variables which belong to peasant social structure rather than to peasant values. The line between social structure and values is a difficult one to draw, but I have in mind a great variety of particular role constraints which affect the peasant's life. For a simple example, given a certain level of poverty, the contribution which children make to transplanting paddy can be crucial: where I lived in India the village schools were closed at planting time and this seemed to me a sensible recognition of the productive role of children in the peasant family. Again – an all too familiar example in many Indian villages – to give the vote to untouchables in elections for village *panchayats*, without the additional protection of a secret ballot, is to invite failure. In other words, innovations may have social costs, which are unknown to or have been ignored by the modernizer.

Both the technical and the structural factors can only be discussed against the background of particular cases. What prospect there is of successful modernization in India, and other developing nations, rests upon the willingness of the planning elite to improve continuously their manipulation of technical and structural variables – to make sure that the price of water from the canal is reasonable and is seen by the peasants to be reasonable, that improved seed developed on the demonstration farm will in fact grow on peasant plots, and to remember that the headman will come under great pressure from his kinsmen, and so forth. I suspect that there is a temptation to evade the drudgery of seeking technical – and I suppose we might say 'structural' – efficacy by saying that the peasants need a change of heart and rushing out to make a speech. If all the technical and structural variables have been correctly handled and the project still fails, one might argue that there is no recourse but to bring about a voluntary change of heart in the peasants. To argue this is to argue that the task is impossible.

From this there emerges one broad strategic directive. Resources for modernization, if they are limited, are most effectively spent if they bring about a change in the physical environment, which the peasant must accept willy-nilly and which force him to adapt himself to the new conditions. When change has come about, at least in village India, it is generally because new methods of irrigation have been introduced, or a road has been built to the market, and so forth. Such measures, of course, do not always succeed; but I suspect that they succeed more often than does a direct onset upon peasant social structure, and still more often than an attack upon those generalized and internalized values and perceptions about which I have been talking here.

Cognitive maps do change; but for the most part they do so slowly as the result of experience. As the flow of water can change the course of a river, so experience can erode received ideas and allow others to settle in their place. With this most modernizers must be content. Occasionally force of circumstances or a massive expenditure of resources can produce a flood of new experiences that change the map overnight; but this is rare. For the most part modernizers must think small; and the least effective use of their resources is to plan directly that the peasants shall have a change of heart. The cultural themes which I have been discussing here are like swamps and rocky mountains; the modernizers should plan to make a detour.

Beyond that, one can make few recommendations. The gnarled oak of peasant alienation (as the modernizers would see it) is only one tree in the forest. It is a tree which takes many different forms, even in India, even within the one village from which I have drawn my material. One needs a much wider sample. One should also look at some of the other trees, at the many divisions within the elite. What view do they have of themselves, of each other, and of the peasants? Armed with all these maps and with a systematic knowledge of technical factors and of social structure, one might begin to understand some of the diverse changes which have occurred – or failed to occur – in the new nations.

Notes

1 There are many near synonyms for 'cognitive map', some more and some less inclusive: ethos, world view, collective representations, beliefs and values, ideology and – most inclusive – culture. The metaphor of a map is appropriate because it suggests a guide for action. Cognitive maps consist of a set of value directives and existential propositions which together help to guide social interaction.

2 I am not competent to discuss psychological techniques for ascertaining peasant attitudes.

3 For a detailed account of Konds and Oriyas see Bailey (1960, pp. 121–93).

4 The concept of a moral community is complex and difficult. In everyday language this is the distinction between 'we' (the moral community) and 'they' (the outsiders). For those who follow Durkheim the adjective 'moral' is perhaps redundant, since the

society (or community) is co-extensive with moral action. Nevertheless, I retain the adjective to emphasize the continuous judgement of right and wrong which characterizes interactions within the community. Beyond the community such judgements do not apply: to cheat an outsider is neither right nor wrong: it is merely expedient or inexpedient.

It is also difficult to draw a boundary around a particular moral community, for each one varies according to the ego who is chosen as the point of reference. The Brahmin and the Sweeper do not have the same moral community even within the one village. Nevertheless, for both of them, there are some common – and large – discontinuities, so that *vis-à-vis* for instance outsiders, it is possible to regard both Brahmin and Sweeper as members of the one moral community.

5 There is an extensive literature on 'hinge men': those who mediate between different cultures or between different levels in the same culture. A good example is Wolf (1956). The range of such roles extends from simple transactions (for example, the petition-writer at an Indian administrative headquarters) to highly developed patron roles which come near to attaining moral status, see Boissevain (1961). The roles considered in this essay are not those of '*cultural* brokers' in the sense of providing a communication of ideas and a meeting of minds: on the contrary the village broker at least is a device which enables the peasants and the elite to avoid a meeting of minds. By providing pragmatic contracts they render unnecessary normative communion.

6 The best-known exposition of this outlook on life is in Evans-Pritchard (1937).

7 For peasants social life is a zero-sum game. One man's gain is, of necessity, another's loss. See Foster (1965).

8 Peasants are generally distinguished from tribesmen by their contact with towns, markets and high cultures. Routine experiences in traditional towns are unlikely to modify the broad features of the map of peasant cognition sketched here, since these experiences are part of this same map. But the traumatic experience of migrant labour and factory work in 'modern' towns is likely to bring change in peasant values and beliefs: so also is production largely for a market, which turns the peasant into a farmer. I cannot here discuss urban contacts, except to say that my argument applies to peasants and not to farmers or to industrial workers.

References

Bailey, F. G. (1959) *Caste and Economic Frontier: Village in Highland Orissa*, Manchester University Press.

Bailey, F. G. (1960) *Tribe, Caste and Nation*, Manchester University Press.

Bailey, F. G. (1963) *Politics and Social Change*, Oxford University Press.

Boissevain, J. (1961) 'Patronage in Sicily', *Man*, n.s., vol. 1, pp. 18–33.

Bourdieu, P. (1963) 'The attitude of the Algerian peasant towards time', in J. Pitt-Rivers (ed.), *Mediterranean Countrymen*, Mouton.

Evans-Pritchard, E. E. (1937) *Witchcraft, Oracles and Magic among the Azande*, Clarendon Press.

Foster, G. (1965) 'Peasant society and the image of limited good', *American Anthropologist*, vol. 67, no. 2, pp. 293–315.

Lloyd, P. C. (ed.) (1966) *The New Elite of Tropical Africa*, Oxford University Press.

Wolf, E. R. (1956) 'Aspects of group relations in a complex society', *American Anthropologist*, vol. 58, no. 6, pp. 1065–78.

Related Items

1, 2, 4, 5, 7, 8, 18, 22, 24, 28, 29, 30, 33, 37, 38, 40, 41, 42, 45, 47, 58, 59, 61, 62.

36

Peasant Culture, Peasant Economy
Sutti Ortiz

Peasants are described as traditionally oriented and slow to change their patterns of behaviour. This behaviour may not be the result of tradition but a withdrawal or coalition in response to unrewarding competitive relations. The pattern of behaviour, language, etc. are used as symbols of distance. The degree to which Indians, peasants or minority groups make use of such a device depends on their evaluation of their success in the competitive game. This success in turn depends on opportunities available to the Indians, to the non-Indians, the political power of each group, knowledge and ability to manipulate circumstances. Not all communities face the same situations and hence not all are 'traditionally oriented'.

Peasants are described as individuals resigned to their fate (Banfield, 1958) and passive when faced with prospects. A good harvest is said to be the result of supernatural intervention and misfortunes are blamed on fate. Such an attitude of mind, according to some writers, discourages efforts of self-help, a point I discuss later. First let us examine why peasants are ready to explain events as the result of fate. Oscar Lewis (1960, p. 77) feels that fatalism is due to upbringing in an authoritarian family structure. A more direct explanation is possible if we examine the degree of uncertainty which pervades the agricultural activities of peasants. Crops suffer from drastic climatic changes, attacks by pests, rodents, damage by animals, etc. Variability of yields to an individual farmer may be 400 per cent. A farmer can formulate an expectation about his harvest only if he can have a mental picture of the outcome and if he has any confidence about the likelihood of his prognosis. With such a high degree of uncertainty few individuals could formulate an expectation; it should not surprise us that as uncertainty decreases farmers are less likely to express prospects in terms of fate or supernatural events. Farmers with non-irrigated land answered questions about future plans with 'what God wishes'. Neigh-

Excerpt from an original paper, 'Reflections on the concept of "peasant culture" and "peasant cognitive systems"'.

bouring farmers who had access to irrigated land where yields are less variable answered the same question with concrete plans; they could think ahead because they could estimate future outcomes.

Peasants are believed to be fearful of the world at large, hostile in interpersonal relations and resigned to the will of God. Holmberg (1967) indicates that these attitudes are objective evaluations of their own experiences and not distorted by cultural preconceptions. Accidents and illness took their toll amongst the serfs in *haciendas* of highland Peru, others died executed by the police at the instigation of *hacienda* owners. Throughout his life the Indian serf has also become accustomed to endure corporal punishment. Every highland *hacienda* used to jail Indians without trial, either in punishment for insubordination to the *hacendero*, or for transgression of his property, or unwillingness to cooperate in regional projects. Serfs have limited opportunities to better their levels of living and almost no political protection against the excesses of administrators and *hacenderos*. It is not surprising that they are fearful of authority, fearful of losing their animals or land and fearful of hunger. In order to minimize conflict with authority they behave meekly and are always ready to comply verbally, furthermore they teach their children to avoid contact with strangers. In order to alleviate hunger they steal from the *hacendero* and from each other. Holmberg suggests that behavioural patterns similar to the ones he describes are exhibited by any population suffering the same degree of deprivation and domination. The 'culture of repression', as he describes such a behaviour, discourages social change. Poverty is accepted as inevitable and innovation is regarded as pathological behaviour. Thus Holmberg argues very much like Foster. The 'culture of repression', like the 'image of the limited good', are objective perceptions of the peasant world. Their perceptions become internalized and institutionalized and constitute the lens through which they view the real world, even when that real world changes and offers them more rewarding opportunities. Both writers suggest that peasant communities will not develop unless their 'culture' or 'cognitive systems' are first changed.

The sequel to the argument that peasants share a culture, regardless of whether it is considered distinct or not, is that their economic behaviour can be explained in terms of their attitudes, values and cognitive systems. Some scholars like Foster are careful to indicate that peasant-like attitudes are also shared by other agriculturalists (Foster, 1965). But more often than not it is assumed that Western farmers allocate resources rationally in such a way as to maximize profit. I have indicated that this is not exactly correct; Western farmers are just as much influenced by values, social rewards and desire for satisfaction of their own personal needs and family needs as a peasant farmer. Social factors are always relevant and their understanding helps to elucidate the outcome of decisions made by producers. But although sociological analysis helps elucidate economic behaviour, it does not fully explain it. Peasants after all produce for a market and buy in a market; some of their decisions or inactions may just as easily be explained in terms of the state of the market. Furthermore, in order to attain a goal – regardless whether the goal is profit or satisfaction of social obligations – all producers have to develop economic strategies. When a peasant decides how much maize to plant – the amount varies from year to year – he has to consider the cash to buy seeds, the labour he will need, his ability to attract labourers, as well as the implication of this choice on all other economic activities. He will very likely evaluate chances of a yield and the certainty of the same. There is thus an economic context to productive actions; the outcome of these actions has also to be explained in terms of limitation of resources as well as in terms of goal gratification, cultural values and culturally determined perceptions.

. . . Many so-called traditional techniques are no more than well-tested ways of minimizing the chance of total loss and starvation. Without government price supports, peasants have to devise other means of insuring themselves. I mentioned earlier that the Páez condemn as morally wrong the sale of large quantities of food by other Indians in the market place. It was not a rigid rule imposed on anyone who sold food. In fact few Indians produced food for sale to traders and they remained as good members of the community. Their behaviour was not judged simply in terms of the rule but was evaluated in terms of the economic significance of the rule, that is, whether or not it threatened the security of those who did depend on them.

New agricultural techniques imply usually a cash cost which may be out of proportion with the increase in yield promised by experts. They often also entail long-range cost, e.g. in upkeep of equipment, and hidden indirect costs often perceived only by the peasant farmer. For example a new seed may require a higher labour input which may affect the time the farmer has for other *safer* farming activities. Social consequences have also to be considered. Furthermore new techniques suggested by extension workers are not properly tested and adjusted to the highly variable local conditions. Rogers (1962), while holding to the idea that peasants' attitudes explain reluctance to accept changes, remarks that the higher the income of the farmer the more likely he is to accept new techniques. It has been estimated that the cost of fertilizer can absorb most of the benefits that a low-income farmer can gain from the innovation, hence commercial farms are more likely to try new techniques. Only a high degree of confidence in a new method can induce a poorer farmer to accept it. Farmers accept a new technique only as long as the annual risk does not endanger the subsistence level.

When making a decision an individual selects, from innumerable opportunities offered by the environment, a set small enough to be able to evaluate the probable outcomes of each and to compare them against each other. The opportunities included are those which are obvious to him. Cultural condition does indeed affect perception but does not define it. Past experiences by the individual have a bearing, too. The opportunity also has to have immediate relevance to the individual in question. Furthermore the individual has to be able to estimate the chances of an outcome with sufficient conviction to allow him to choose. If he is terribly uncertain about all outcomes and if all the opportunities are equally desirable, the farmer delays actions and searches for more opportunities (see Edwards, 1967; Johnson, 1961; Shackle, 1952). If a search does not lead to the discovery of a more suitable set of opportunities from which selection can be made, then either aspirations are lowered (see Simon, 1959) or passivity ensues until the event forces the farmer to act. The passivity and distrust of the Indians described by Holmberg (1967) can be understood in the context of the uncertainty of their social and economic environment and not simply as determined by the culture of oppression.

References

Banfield, E. C. (1958) *The Moral Basis of a Backward Society*, Free Press.

Edwards, W. (1967) 'The theory of decision making', in W. Edwards and A. Tversky (eds), *Decision Making*, Penguin.

Foster, G. M. (1965) 'Peasant society and the image of limited good', *American Anthropologist*, vol. 2, pp. 293–315.

Holmberg, A. R. (1967) 'Algunas relaciones entre la privación psicobiológica y el cambio cultural en los Andes', *Amer. Indigena*, vol. 27.

Johnson, G. L. (ed.) (1961) *Study of Managerial Processes of Midwestern Farmers*, Iowa State University Press.

Lewis, O. (1960) *Life in a Mexican Village; Tepotzlán Re-studied*, University of Illinois Press.

Rogers, E. (1962) *Diffusion of Innovations*, Free Press.

Shackle, G. L. S. (1952) *Expectations in Economics*, Cambridge University Press.

Simon, H. A. (1959) 'Theories of decision-making in economics', *American Economic Review*, vol. 49, pp. 253–83.

| Related Items |

9, 13, 18, 19, 21, 23, 25, 26, 31, 32, 33, 35, 37, 38, 41, 53, 54, 62.

37

Peasant Moral Economy as a Subsistence Ethic

James C. Scott

There are districts in which the position of the rural population is that of a man standing permanently up to the neck in water, so that even a ripple is sufficient to drown him.[1]

Tawney was writing about China in 1931 but it would not stretch his graphic description much to apply it to the peasantry of Upper Burma, Tonkin and Annam in Indochina, or East and Central Java in the early twentieth century. Here too, lilliputian plots, traditional techniques, the vagaries of weather and the tribute in cash, labour, and kind exacted by the state brought the spectre of hunger and dearth, and occasionally famine, to the gates of every village.

The particular ecological niche occupied by some sectors of the peasantry in South-East Asia exposed them, more than most, to subsistence risks. Upper Burma's Dry Zone, always at the mercy of a capricious rainfall, suffered a catastrophic famine in 1856–7, shortly after Britain's conquest of Lower Burma. 'The rains failed and the rice withered in the fields . . . and the people died. They died in the fields gnawing the bark of trees; they died on the highways while wandering in search of food; they died in their homes.'[2] In Annam, in north-east Thailand, and elsewhere where nature is unkind, most adults must have experienced, within living memory, one or more times of great scarcity when the weak and very young died and when others were reduced to eating their livestock and seed paddy, to subsisting on millet, root crops, bran – on what they might normally feed their animals.

The great famine of 1944–5 experienced by the peasantry of North Vietnam, however, was of such magnitude as to dwarf other twentieth-century subsistence crises in the region.

If the Great Depression left an indelible mark on the fears, values, and habits of a whole generation of Americans, can we imagine the impact of periodic food crises on the fears, values and habits of rice farmers in monsoon Asia?

Excerpts from James C. Scott, *The Moral Economy of the Peasant*, Yale University Press, 1976, pp. 1–11.

The fear of food shortages has, in most pre-capitalist peasant societies, given rise to what might appropriately be termed a 'subsistence ethic'. This ethic, which South-East Asian peasants shared with their counterparts in nineteenth-century France, Russia and Italy, was a consequence of living so close to the margin. A bad crop would not only mean short rations; the price of eating might be the humiliation of an onerous dependence or the sale of some land or livestock which reduced the odds of achieving an adequate subsistence the following year. The peasant family's problem, put starkly, was to produce enough rice to feed the household, buy a few necessities such as salt and cloth, and meet the irreducible claims of outsiders. The amount of rice a family could produce was partly in the hands of fate, but the local tradition of seed varieties, planting techniques and timing was designed over centuries of trial and error to produce the most stable and reliable yield possible under the circumstances. These were the *technical arrangements* evolved by the peasantry to iron out the 'ripples that might drown a man'. Many *social arrangements* served the same purpose. Patterns of reciprocity, forced generosity, communal land and work-sharing helped to even out the inevitable troughs in a family's resources which might otherwise have thrown them below subsistence. The proven value of these techniques and social patterns is perhaps what has given peasants a Brechtian tenacity in the face of agronomists and social workers who come from the capital to improve them.

The purpose of the argument which follows is to place the subsistence ethic at the centre of the analysis of peasant politics. The argument itself grows out of a prolonged effort on my part to understand some of the major peasant rebellions which swept much of South-East Asia during the Great Depression of the 1930s. Two of those insurrections, the Saya San Rebellion in Burma and what has been called the Nghe-Tinh Soviets in central Vietnam, are analysed in some detail.

In a broad view of colonial history in South-East Asia, these rebellions and others like them might be considered epiphenomena, though they were hardly trivial for the men and women who fought and died in them. Both uprisings were ultimately crushed; both failed to achieve any of the peasants' goals; both are considered minor subplots in a political drama that was to be increasingly dominated by the struggle between nationalists and colonizers. In still another and more profound historical sense, these movements were marginal. They looked to a closed and autonomous peasant utopia in a world in which centralization and commercialization were irresistible. They were more or less spontaneous uprisings displaying all the trademarks of peasant localism in a world in which the big battalions of secular nationalism were the only effective opposition to the colonial state. Along with other backward-looking movements of peasants or artisans, they were, in Hobsbawm's phrase, 'inevitable victims' inasmuch as they ran 'dead against the current of history'.[3]

Viewing from another perspective, however, we can learn a great deal from rebels who were defeated nearly a half-century ago. If we understand the indignation and rage which prompted them to risk everything, we can grasp what I have chosen to call their moral economy: their notion of economic justice and their working definition of exploitation – their view of which claims on their product were tolerable and which intolerable. In so far as their moral economy is representative of peasants elsewhere, and I believe I can show that it is, we may move toward a fuller appreciation of the normative roots of peasant politics. If we understand, further, how the central economic and political transformations of the colonial era served to violate systematically the peasantry's vision of social equity, we may realize how a class 'of low classness' came to provide, far more often than the proletariat, the shock troops of rebellion and revolution.

It is this 'safety-first' principle which lies behind a great many of the technical, social and moral arrangements of a pre-capitalist agrarian order. The use of more than one seed variety, the European traditional farming on scattered strips, to mention only two, are classical techniques for avoiding undue risks often at the cost of a reduction in average return. Within the village context, a wide array of social arrangements typically operated to assure a minimum income to inhabitants. The existence of communal land that was periodically redistributed, in part on the basis of need, or the commons in European villages functioned in this way. In addition, social pressures within the pre-capitalist village had a certain redistributive effect: rich peasants were expected to be charitable, to sponsor more lavish celebrations, to help out temporarily indigent kin and neighbours, to give generously to local shrines and temples. As Michael Lipton has noted, 'many superficially odd village practices make sense as disguised forms of insurance'.[4]

It is all too easy, and a serious mistake, to romanticize these social arrangements that distinguish much of peasant society. They are not radically egalitarian. Rather, they imply only that all are entitled to a *living* out of the resources within the village, and that living is attained often at the cost of a loss of status and autonomy. They work, moreover, in large measure through the abrasive force of gossip and envy and the knowledge that the abandoned poor are likely to be a real and present danger to better-off villagers. These modest but critical redistributive mechanisms none the less do provide a minimal subsistence insurance for villagers. Polanyi claims on the basis of historical and anthropological evidence that such practices were nearly universal in traditional society and served to mark it off from the modern market economy. He concludes: 'It is the absence of the threat of *individual* starvation which makes primitive society, in a sense, more human than market economy, and at the same time less economic.'[5]

The provision of subsistence insurance was not confined to the village sphere; it also structured the moral economy of relations to outside elites. As Eric Wolf observed,

It is significant, however, that before the advent of capitalism . . . social equilibrium depended in both the long and short run on a balance of transfers of peasant surpluses to the rulers and the provision of minimal security for the cultivator. Sharing resources within communal organizations and reliance on ties with powerful patrons were recurrent ways in which peasants strove to reduce risks and to improve their stability, and both were condoned and frequently supported by the state.[6]

Again, we must guard against the impulse to idealize these arrangements. Where they worked, and they did not always work, they were not so much a product of altruism as of necessity. Where land was abundant and labour scarce, subsistence insurance was virtually the only way to attach a labour force; where the means of coercion at the disposal of elites and the state was sharply limited, it was prudent to show some respect for the needs of the subordinate population.

Although the desire for subsistence security grew out of the needs of cutivators – out of peasant economics – it was socially experienced as a pattern of moral rights or expectations. Barrington Moore has captured the normative tone of these expectations:

This experience [of sharing risks within the community] provides the soil out of which grow peasant mores and the moral standards by which they judge their own behaviour and that of others. The essence of these standards is a crude notion of equality, stressing the justice and necessity of a minimum of land [resources] for the performance of essential social tasks. These standards usually have some sort of religious sanction, and it is likely to be in their stress on these points that the religion of peasants differs from that of other social classes.[7]

The violation of these standards could be expected to provoke resentment and resistance – not only because needs were unmet, but because rights were violated.

Despite striking parallels, a good case can be made that the process of transformation was, if anything, more traumatic for colonial peoples. For one thing, it telescoped a process which had taken as much as three centuries in England or France into a forced march of mere decades. In Europe, moreover, as Polanyi eloquently shows, the indigenous forces which had much to lose from a full market economy (including, at times, the Crown, portions of the aristocracy, artisans, peasants and workers) were occasionally able to impede or at least restrict the play of market forces by invoking the older moral economy. In Germany and Japan the creation of strong conservative states allowed what Moore has called 'a revolution from above' which kept as much of the original social structure intact as possible while still modernizing the economy. The results, while laying the ground for fascism and militarism at a later date, were somewhat less traumatic in the short run for the peasantry. But in the colonial world the political forces which would have opposed or moderated the full impact of the market economy had little or no capacity to make themselves felt except at the level of insurrection.

The problem for the peasantry during the capitalist transformation of the Third World, viewed from this perspective, is that of providing for a *minimum income*. While a minimum income has solid physiological dimensions, we must not overlook its social and cultural implications. In order to be a fully functioning member of village society, a household needs a certain level of resources to discharge its necessary ceremonial and social obligations as well as to feed itself adequately and continue to cultivate. To fall below this level is not only to risk starvation, it is to suffer a profound loss of standing within the community and perhaps to fall into a permanent situation of dependence.

The pre-capitalist community was, in a sense, organized around this problem of the minimum income – organized to minimize the risk to which its members were exposed by virtue of its limited techniques and the caprice of nature. Traditional forms of patron–client relationships, reciprocity, and redistributive mechanisms may be seen from this perspective. While pre-capitalist society was singularly ill-equipped to provide for its members in the event of collective disaster, it did provide household social insurance against the 'normal' risks of agriculture through an elaborate system of social exchange.

In more recent times, of course, the state itself has assumed the role of providing for a minimum income with such devices as countercyclical fiscal policy, unemployment compensation, welfare programmes, social medicine, and the negative income tax. One effect of these guarantees, incidentally, has been to make it more rational for individuals to engage in profit-maximizing behaviour.

The colonial period in South-East Asia, and elsewhere for that matter, was marked by an almost total absence of any provision for the maintenance of a minimal income while, at the same time, the commercialization of the agrarian economy was steadily stripping away most of the traditional forms of social insurance.[8] Far from shielding the peasantry against the fluctuations of the market, colonial regimes were likely to press even harder in a slump so as to maintain their own revenue. The result was something of a paradox. In the midst of a booming export economy, new fortunes for indigenous landowners, officeholders, and money-lenders and, occasionally, rising average per capita income, there was also growing concern with rural indebtedness and poverty and an increasing tempo of peasant unrest. It was not unlike the discovery of pauperism in the midst of England's industrial revolution.[9] The explanation for this paradox is to be sought in the new insecurities of subsistence income to which the poorer sector of the population was exposed. Although the average wage rate might be adequate, employment was highly uncertain; although the average prices for peasant produce might be buoyant, they fluctuated dramatically; although taxes might be modest, they were a steady charge against a highly variable peasant income; although the export economy created new opportunities, it also concentrated the ownership of productive resources and eroded the levelling mechanisms of the older village economy.

The moral economy of the subsistence ethic can be clearly seen in the themes of peasant protest throughout this period. Two themes prevailed: first, claims on peasant incomes by landlords, money-lenders, or the state were never legitimate when they infringed on what was judged to be the minimal culturally defined subsistence level; and second, the *product* of the land should be distributed in such a way that all were guaranteed a subsistence niche. The appeal was in almost every case to the past – to traditional practices – and the revolts I discuss are best seen as defensive reactions. Such backward-looking intentions are by now a commonplace in the analysis of peasant movements. As Moore, citing Tawney, puts it, 'the peasant radical would be astonished to hear that he is undermining the foundations of society; he is merely trying to get back what has long been rightfully his'.[10] The revolts were, by the same token, essentially the revolts of consumers rather than producers. Except where communal land had been appropriated by local notables, the demand for the redistribution of land itself was strikingly absent. Protests against taxes and rents were couched in terms of their effect on consumption; what was an admissible tax or rent in a good year was inadmissible in a bad year. It was the smallness of what was left rather than the amount taken (the two are obviously related, but by no means are they identical) that moved peasants to rebel.

Notes

1 R. H. Tawney (1966) *Land and Labor in China*, Boston: Beacon Press, p. 77.

2 From the *Government of Burma Report on the Famine in Burma 1896—97*, quoted by Michael Adas (1974) in *Agrarian Development and the Plural Society in Lower Burma*, Madison: University of Wisconsin Press, p. 45.

3 E. J. Hobsbawm, 'Class consciousness in history', in Istvan Mezaros (ed.) (1971) *Aspects of History and Class Consciousness*, London, pp. 11–12.

4 Michael Lipton (1969) 'The theory of the optimizing peasant', *Journal of Development Studies*, vol. 4, p. 341, cited in E. R. Wolf (1969) *Peasant Wars of the Twentieth Century*, New York: Harper & Row, p. 279.

5 Karl Polanyi (1957) *The Great Transformation*, Boston: Beacon Press, pp. 163–4. Even the term seminal, applied as it is without discretion, is too weak a tribute for this book. His analysis of pre-market and market economies has been formative for my own work. The emphasis in this quote has been added.

6 Wolf, *Peasant Wars* p. 279.

7 Barrington Moore, Jr (1966) *Social Origins of Dictatorship and Democracy*, Boston: Beacon Press, pp. 497–8. I believe the emphasis in most peasant societies is not so much on land *per se* as on the right to a share of the product of the land; hence I have added 'resources' in brackets.

8 A possible exception to this rule was the Dutch East Indies where, at least on Java, colonial policy was bent to extracting a marketable surplus while at the same time preserving – not to say fossilizing – as much of rural society as possible.

9 See Wolfram Fischer (1966–7) 'Social tensions at the early stages of industrialization', *Comparative Studies in Society and History*, vol. 9, pp. 64–83.

10 Moore, *Social Origins*, p. 498.

Related Items

1, 2, 3, 4, 5, 6, 7, 18, 19, 20, 21, 27, 33, 35, 36, 38, 39, 41, 42, 44, 46, 56, 59, 61, 62.

38

Peasant Consciousness: Culture and Conflict in Zimbabwe

Terence Ranger

Introduction

For many years and by many people peasants were seen mostly as victims or objects. Scholars focused on what was done *to* peasants by landlords, or the state, or international capitalism, or on what might be done *for* peasants by movements of liberation or revolution. If peasant beliefs or perceptions were regarded as at all worthy of study they were seen as negative in significance, a consequence of hegemonic manipulation and a barrier to modern political activity. In the early 1980s, however, students of peasant societies throughout the world began to proclaim the crucial importance of establishing peasant agency and of understanding peasant consciousness.

Thus the introduction to a special issue of the *Radical History Review* on 'Colonialism and Resistance' in Latin America, published in 1983, spelt out a general departure from underdevelopment perspectives and dependency theory:

Agrarian social structures are not thought to derive from the logic of early capitalism; nor are peasants . . . considered to be merely its victims. Peasants . . . were both the products and sources of historical change. Through their action and struggle, they often impinged on the intent of colonizers and even altered the terms of their own exploitation. Imbued with these perspectives, social historians have reintroduced culture, consciousness, and ideology into the research agenda. (Larson, 1983, pp. 11–12)

In the same way the preface to a formidable collection of studies of *History and Peasant Consciousness in South East Asia*, published in 1984, tells us that:

this symposium treats the peasantry . . . as the subjects of history, as conscious actors in the troubled histories of these countries, and as contributors to traditions and forms of

An original paper.

culture which are often muted or absent in official historiography. This marks a significant break with approaches which view the peasantry as only subject or subjected peoples. The importance of this newer approach can hardly be over-estimated in a region with a population of nearly 400 million, the majority of whom are peasants. (Ishii, 1984)

One of India's leading rural historians, in an article published in 1986, asserts that hitherto changes in Indian rural societies have been explained as processes imposed upon the peasantry. It is important now to attempt 'to restore subjectivity to the peasantry, to look at its political actions not as "primordial", "pre-political", "irrational", and hence inherently inexplicable, "spontaneous" acts, but as actions informed by its own consciousness' (Chatterjee, 1986, p. 202). Even social historians of rural Western Europe, where there are not millions of contemporary peasants, are developing the same research agenda. Thus David Sabean, in a study of early modern Württemberg, published in 1984, seeks to explain rural social change in terms of 'popular culture and village discourse' rather than of the 'constant reception of elements of high culture' (Sabean, 1984, pp. 3–4).

Plainly a general movement of historiographical reinterpretation has been taking place. Moreover, there are many more detailed agreements among the historians of these vast and varied regions of the world both as to subject matter and as to method.

One such agreement is on the importance of 'peasant consciousness not as an abstract realm of thought but as concrete social force' (Turton and Tanabe, 1984, p. 1). Peasant consciousness, we are told by the contributors to the South East Asian volume, expresses itself in practice or discourse. Sabean lays a similar stress on discourse for the study of peasant consciousness in early modern Germany:

One of the problems with the present investigation of popular culture is that it seeks to get at culture as if it were a set of ideas, different from but analagous to that of 'high culture'. On the one hand, action and practice are not studied as part of culture. On the other, the ideas and values are not grasped as part of practice but remain reified.

His own work is an exercise 'in the study of culture and practice, belief and action' (Sabean, 1984, p. 221).

Another agreement is on the centrality of 'community' in peasant consciousness. Almost everywhere the notion of the primordial legitimacy of the community provides 'both reasons and forms of organization for resistance, and also contributes to the idea of a transformed society.' But it is also widely agreed that in very many cases 'the village entity is the ... product of new forces' (Turton and Tanabe, 1984, p. 3). For West German peasants, 'community was not something "pre-modern", unchanging, structural, but was constructed, changed with time, and can only be grasped as historical process.'

Indeed, for Sabean, 'what is common in community is not shared values or common understanding so much as the fact that members of a community are engaged in the same argument . . . the same discourse, in which alternative strategies, misunderstandings, conflicting goals and values are thrashed out' (Sabean, 1984, p. 29). For Indian peasants, belief in an ancient community is a mobilizing myth rather than a historical statement, since 'the bonds which are believed to define the community are not immutable. . . . They are historically evolved solidarities and are subject to change, sometimes extremely sudden change' (Chatterjee, 1986, p. 201). It is the many different ways in which communities may be imaginatively constructed and the rapidity with which solidarities can change which make peasant political action so unpredictable.

Finally, there has been agreement in this recent work on the importance of situating peasant consciousness within the context of 'traditional' or 'inherited' culture and ideology. Such traditions are not regarded, however, as circumscribing peasant creativity. Traditions are a resource. Practice or discourse which can claim to be rooted in tradition, no matter how much it has changed shape, acquires legitimacy, furthers mobilization, puts moral pressure on landlords and officials. So these students of peasant consciousness have studied both the 'great' religious and cultural traditions of governing elites and the 'little' traditions of peasant orality, and studied the ways in which they have been used to construct ruling-class hegemonies but also peasant counter-hegemonies.

Social historians of rural Africa have been caught up in this re-evaluation of peasant consciousness. There are, after all, millions of peasants in contemporary Africa. It makes as much sense in Africa as it does in South-East Asia or Latin America to claim that peasants and their perceptions are crucial to the prospects of reform, or revolutionary change, or modernization or escape from famine. Moreover, many social historians of Africa have come to share the organizing assumptions of recent rural historians elsewhere. Africanists, too, have focused on peasant discourse; on the construction of community; on the uses of tradition (for example, Beinart and Bundy, 1987; Fields, 1985; Vail and White, 1980). But what strikes me about the growing literature on African peasant consciousness is not the similarity with the findings of the historiography of peasants in other parts of the world so much as the difference.

This is not surprising. The shared propositions of the new historiography of peasant consciousness necessarily lead towards difference. There are so many styles of discourse; so many different ways of constructing community; so many distinct 'great' and 'little' traditions; so many different political potentialities. Inevitably, few generalizations can be borrowed from the study of one peasantry in order to apply them to another. It is particularly necessary to stress this in relation to Africa, however. Until the 1960s African cultivators had been discussed as 'tribesmen' rather than as 'peasants'. It was a breakthrough towards a more effective agrarian historiography when the term 'peasant' began to be almost universally applied. Thereafter African cultivators ceased to be treated primarily as members of immemorial tribal societies, locked in traditional cultures, and came to be discussed and defined in terms of their situation within modern colonial/capitalist social formations. But this gain has had to be paid for. Making up for lost time, historians and sociologists of African rural societies borrowed all sorts of ideas about the peasantry of other continents and applied them to Africa, and to make matters worse they usually borrowed from the older school of peasant studies rather than from the new and more flexible historiography.

So we began to hear a good deal about 'typical' peasant conservatism, irrationality and pre-political ideology. In this way, African peasants came to be regarded as 'archaic', even though in most parts of Africa peasantries were the creation of colonialism itself. African peasants were almost by definition held to be incapable of acting effectively against colonial capitalism. In many parts of Africa cultivators had been turned into peasants – 'peasantized' in the ugly jargon – in order that colonial capitalism could enjoy its own period of primitive accumulation. Nevertheless, peasants were not thought to be a class essential to the colonial capitalist mode of production and hence were not thought to be a class capable of taking effective revolutionary action against it. Peasants were pre-eminently thought of as the victims of colonial capitalism – captured by the colonial state, super-exploited and eventually proletarianized as the needs of colonial capitalism changed. In this way the particular features of African peasantries – their Africanness on the one hand and their modernity on the other – were more or less lost sight of.

In such an intellectual context the new emphasis on peasant consciousness has been very salutary. A focus on peasant discourse, on the construction of peasant communities and on the balance of custom and innovation in peasant ideology allows us to escape from inapplicable and over-generalized models and to begin to establish the particularities of African peasantries. The lesson is that nothing can be taken for granted. We think of peasants as living in villages but in much of Africa villages are recent creations rather than long-established micro-societies. Ethnic consciousness in Africa is often a twentieth-century ideological innovation rather than the lingering effect of a long-established 'great' tradition. Rural religion in Africa is often a response to and reflection of colonial realities rather than a surviving and irrational archaism. At the same time, while all these innovations have been taking place, African peasants have often sought to enmesh their rulers by appealing to a common respect for 'tradition'. (Simultaneously, of course, their rulers were often seeking to enmesh them through the codification of custom.)

So far from being perpetual victims, many African peasantries have come to be described as 'uncaptured', retaining too great an autonomy for the good of either the colonial or the post-colonial state. Becoming a peasant is coming to be seen as a process in which African cultivators themselves often participated by making choices and taking initiatives. 'Self-peasantization' has joined 'peasantization' in the jargon of African agrarian historiography. In the African context, as well as the Latin American one, peasants have 'through their struggle . . . altered the terms of their own exploitation'; in Africa, as well as in South-East Asia, peasants have been 'conscious actors in the troubled histories of these countries'.

But of course African peasantries *have* been much exploited and their histories have certainly been troubled. To say that African peasants have been conscious actors is not to deny that they were participants in a most uneven contest with the colonial state or with settler agriculture. African peasants experienced eviction from their land, discriminatory pricing systems, de-stocking of their cattle, coercive extraction of labour from peasant farming for the benefit of capitalist plantations, state interference in peasant agricultural techniques and tenurial systems. Hence students of African peasant conscious-ness have paid much attention to peasant political and revolutionary potential, a question of as much significance to activists as to academics. Here, too, nothing can be taken for granted. African peasants are not French or Russian or Chinese peasants. Their political potential can be assessed only by means of a thorough examination of the protest implications of African peasant discourse, construction of community and flexibility of tradition.

The Making of Peasant Consciousness in Zimbabwe

All this can best be illustrated by taking one particular case. Zimbabwe serves this purpose well. It presents a stimulating combination of a colony in which settler power was strong; in which African peasant production was persistently raided and undercut for the benefit of capitalist farming; in which peasants were evicted from millions of acres of land – but in which a successful guerrilla war was fought on the basis of peasant support and inspired by peasant religion and consciousness. Post-independent Zimbabwe presents an equally provoca-tive combination of a country in which a dominant party and state bureaucracy simultaneously fosters capitalist farming, expresses its aspirations towards a Marxist–Leninist reconstruction of the countryside, and gives vent to periodic technocratic criticisms of the backwardness of peasant farming – and yet also a country in which peasant production is rapidly expanding and peasant consciousness, without any formal organization, appears to be powerful enough to inhibit the state from enforcing either collectivization or destocking. Zimbabwe has generated, moreover, recent historical, anthropological, sociological and political studies of peasant experience, perceptions and aspirations (Callear, 1982; Dillon-Malone, 1979; Fry, 1976; Lan, 1985; Ranger, 1985). Drawing on these, and work as yet unpublished, it is possible to present a brief outline of the history of peasant consciousness in Zimbabwe.

Cultivators became peasants in Zimbabwe in a way that struck a complex balance between tradition and innovation. Some cultivators in Zimbabwe had embarked upon regular production of a surplus to satisfy market or tribute demand long before colonial occupation (Bhila, 1982). But in general cultivators turned themselves into peasants only after the imposition of British South Africa Company rule in the 1890s. Where they could Africans chose to relate to the colonial state and the colonial economy by meeting demands for produce rather than for labour. This process of self-peasantization was crucial but it was also undramatic. It did not involve to begin with any radical change in methods or technology.

The Rhodesian colonial economy needed foodstuffs rather than cash-crops. In particular it needed cereals to feed its African labour forces in the towns and on the mines, most of whom were drawn from other colonial territories. There was no need for colonial administrators to monitor early colonial African pro- duction or to enforce new methods. African cultivators, of course, had always grown cereals and now they went on growing them in much the same way, so that to European observers the only perceptible change was that increasing amounts of African produce reached the market. Although whites depended in the first twenty years of colonial rule on African production of food they resented this dependence and hoped that it would soon be replaced by the output of settler capitalist farming. So there were no attempts to reorganize African production or to introduce new technologies or tenures. There *were* attempts, on the other hand, to extract labour from African rural societies. The future of African men, in the eyes of administrators, lay in industrial labour rather than in petty commodity production.

All this meant that African foodstuffs seemed to come on to the market from a fully 'traditional' African rural society. African cultivators still operated within systems of communal tenure, within which there was no permanent ownership of land, which was distributed to family groups according to their capacity to use it. They still recognized the authority of chiefs, however diminished by colonial 'direct rule'. Most still made offerings to spirits of the land in elaborate territorial cults. They used hoes, not ploughs. They continued with a traditional gender division of labour. However much they were now devoted to annual production of a marketable surplus, African cultivators did not look like peasants to white administrators, who continued to regard them as tribesmen.

And yet, under this surface, African cultivators were turning themselves into peasants by a series of innovations. Here indeed is a good example of the importance of a focus on practice rather than on articulated bodies of ideas, since it is only by studying practice during this early colonial period that one can observe the emergence of a day-by-day, common-sense peasant conscious- ness. African cultivators took a series of steps to ensure that their chosen peasant option was successful. Groups of families migrated so that they would be close to roads or railways or stores and often such migrations were effected without the consent of chiefs or headmen, who found themselves with greatly reduced followings. Large settlements around the residence of a chief or headman broke up and there developed a much more scattered pattern of homesteads. Much more male labour was invested during the early colonial period in agricultural production and much less in hunting or craft production or 'tribal' politics and adjudication. New crops were introduced and there was a new emphasis upon maize, which was the cereal most in demand by traders and employers of African labour. Gradually maize replaced millet as the staple. African cereal producers showed an awareness of the market which led them to boycott traders who offered low prices for grain or asked high prices for goods, and sometimes, when traders combined to fix prices, African producers collectively withdrew grain from the market. When there were droughts African cultivators refused to accept famine relief from the administration in order to avoid having to repay by sending out labour, and concentrated instead on opening up more ground in hopes of a large marketable surplus the following year. Plainly a great deal of thought was going into the business of being a peasant.

African cultivators still had access to tradition but these changes and initiatives had transformed their relationship to traditional authorities. In the past chiefs had extracted tribute in the form of grain and cattle. Now, gradually but inexorably, cultivators withheld such tribute since they needed everything they produced to make the peasant option a reality. Chiefs came to rely on their official salaries. In the past chiefs had controlled the agricultural year in the name of the ancestors. Spirit mediums who were believed to incarnate dead chiefs had determined when planting could begin, controlled the use of fire, enforced frequent rest-days in honour of the ancestral spirits. Now peasants increasingly planted as soon as it was advantageous to do so, used fire to clear hitherto protected areas, and worked through many of the proclaimed rest-days.

In so far as they had become peasants, then, African cultivators were not burdened by inheriting centuries of conservatism. Instead, becoming a peasant meant breaking from tradition and opening oneself up to new ideas. In so far as they remained tribesmen, African cultivators were in a position to select and adapt tradition. In fact, Zimbabwean peasants were able to draw upon both African and European 'great traditions' for their own purposes.

In the first two decades of the twentieth century many Zimbabwean peasants began to draw on the European 'great tradition' in the form of mission Christianity. If the colonial government and administration did not, in this period, seek to transform African rural society so as to bring about a prosperous peasantry, most missionaries took a very different attitude. By the early twentieth century almost all missionaries were hostile to godless and exploitative urban and industrial society and wished to protect Africans against its effects. Nearly all of them worked for a stable Christian peasantry. Some of them – like the American Methodists – preached the 'Gospel of the Plough' and sought to produce black rural entrepreneurs. Others – like most Roman Catholic missionaries – aspired to realize a more egalitarian society of devout peasant villages. The Catholics imported into Zimbabwe the peasant cults of nineteenth- and early twentieth-century European Catholicism. The Anglicans

aimed at a characteristic middle way, encouraging a decently restrained entrepreneurial enthusiasm but also insisting upon the unity of the Christian village.
All of them set up schools, reduced the vernacular to writing, taught literacy and
published material in the vernacular.

Historical discussion of missionary Christianity has tended to see it as
cultural imperialism. It is certainly true that just as Africans 'chose' the peasant
option only in the context of the constraints on choice imposed by the colonial
economy, so Africans in Zimbabwe only 'chose' Christianity after colonial
conquest. Nevertheless, the element of choice ought not to be overlooked.
There *were* many aspects of mission Christianity which could be useful to
cultivators trying to become peasants. In the district I know best, indeed, a
rough fit came about, partly by means of African choice, between types of
peasant aspiration and the types of Christian mission ideology most appropriate to them.

In the area of Makoni district closest to urban markets and with flat land to
plough there grew up an American Methodist ploughman elite. In other areas,
less favourably situated but still able to get smaller quantities of grain to market
by head-carriage, there grew up a network of Anglican villages, under the
leadership of an African teacher/evangelist, where functional literacy helped
peasants to deal with traders. On the huge farm granted to the Roman
Catholics, locked up behind the mountains, where production for the market
was impossible, there grew up a subsistence peasant society, in which a devout
female peasantry laboured and to which male labour migrants regularly
returned on pilgrimage. In each area Methodism, Catholicism or Anglicanism
became a folk religion, their symbols, rituals and assumptions mingling with
African needs and ideas.

In this way African peasants obtained a purchase on the European Christian
'great tradition', making use of it as well as being used by it. The same duality
existed with peasants who did not choose Christianity but who continued to
participate in territorial cults of eco-religion. It is important to understand here
that in Zimbabwe such cults had constituted a pre-colonial 'great tradition'
rather than a localized set of village practices. The oracular cave-shrines of the
High God Mwari in the south-west of the country and the networks of spirit
mediums representing dead ancestors or heroes in the centre and east had
legitimated secular power and controlled exploitation of the land. The
relationship of the chief to the Mwari shrine or the senior spirit medium had
legitimated his demand for tribute. It was the founding ancestors who 'owned'
the land that was distributed by the chief within the system of communal
tenure. It might have been thought, therefore, that African cultivators who
continued to participate in these territorial cults would have been locked in
pre-peasant tradition, bound still to pay tribute to the chief, and hostile to
Christian production for the market.

In fact, the circumstances of early colonial Zimbabwe meant that an African
peasant could make use of this indigenous 'great tradition' as well as being

used by it. As chiefs became more and more the salaried agents of the colonial state, there developed a separation between chiefs and Mwari priests and mediums. In any case, the territorial cults had abundantly proved their adaptability to new political and economic patterns in the past. Now they adapted to peasant production. Mwari priests and spirit mediums often condemned innovations in African agriculture, but it turned out that they were condemning entrepreneurial innovations, which separated the achiever from his collective obligations. Cult spokesmen often prohibited the sale of produce to whites, but it turned out that they did this when it was necessary to put pressure on traders. In short, small-scale peasants, who were growing food crops by established methods, and whose marketing did not disrupt communality, could derive much from the 'great tradition' of the territorial cults – a promise of fertility and rain, occasional co-ordination of defensive or protest measures, an assurance that in justice the land was theirs.

It can be seen then that rural religion in early colonial Zimbabwe was *not* a mere continuance of archaic forms of belief. It was rather an engagement with those aspects of both European and African great traditions which were most relevant to the new business of being a peasant. Throughout the colonial period in Zimbabwe Europeans described African peasants as stuck in pre-colonial modes of agricultural production, and radicals described them as imprisoned in immemorial superstition. Both ideas were very far from the truth even of early colonial peasantization.

A focus on peasant practice and an exploration of peasant use of the 'great tradition' is, therefore, as pertinent to peasant consciousness in Zimbabwe as in Latin America, or India or early modern Germany. So too is an examination of the fluidity of the idea of community. At various times European administrators found it advantageous to define 'traditional communities'. At first they tried to hold together the large villages around the homesteads of chiefs or headmen. Later they accepted the more dispersed patterns of settlement which had developed under colonialism and defined the basic rural community as the 'ward', a segment of the chiefdom presided over by a headman, to whom all its residents took their cases for settlement. Such local courts were, indeed, places where members of the community were engaged in argument and thrashing out conflicting goals. But administrative definitions were attempts to characterize rural Africans as tribesmen rather than as peasants and to impose a single rather than a multiple potentiality of community.

The developments I have been describing had given rise to a whole series of possible identities, which could be combined into a whole series of possible communities. A rural Zimbabwean in the 1920s could think of himself as the follower of a particular chief or headman. But he could equally think of himself as a member of a particular Christian community.

The closest things to villages in colonial Makoni district, in fact, were Christian settlements clustered around the church and school. Their inhabitants were encouraged to think of themselves as related to each other, and to other Christian villages, through shared faith rather than through kinship. During the First World War the Makoni Native Commissioner reported that neither the chiefs nor the administration commanded any loyalty and that the real units of belonging in the district were the folk churches. Everyone expected that war would soon break out between the 'English' folk Anglicans and the 'German' folk Catholics, with the 'American' Methodists standing by in armed neutrality!

Sometimes rural Zimbabweans could even think of themselves as primarily peasants – as when meetings of Native Boards, chaired by Native Commissioners, gave opportunity for vociferous complaint about prices for grain. Incipient class differences between large-scale entrepreneurs and smaller peasants rarely found expression, however, but were subsumed either into distinctions between religions or into the solidarities of general peasant grievance.

Community did not express itself, therefore, purely in traditional 'tribal' forms. An equally important point, though, is that when tribal identities *were* expressed they were often newly forged. Educated and literate Christians made use of the new written forms of the vernaculars to write and publish local histories which gave an authoritative modern expression of tribal traditions. The black teacher or cleric, author of the printed school history, now rivalled the spirit medium or the tribal elders, with their oral traditions, as owners of the past. And while in this way local identities were brushed up and streamlined and modernized, there also began to grow up a wider sense of ethnic identity. Mission language work had resulted in the emergence of a number of alleged dialects of the Shona language and these came to be associated with particular churches as well as particular regions. These dialects – Chikaranga, Chizezuru, Chimanyika and the rest – served first to invent and then to actualize regional cultural identities and solidarities, so that in both town and country Africans began to speak of themselves as Karanga or Zezuru or Manyika. As in so many other cases, what soon came to be accepted as long-standing traditional identities were in fact cultural innovations.

These multiple identities have made Zimbabwean peasant society hard to understand and hard to predict for either administrator or historian. Everything in the Zimbabwean rural areas was referred back by peasants either to 'tradition' or to the rapidly established canons of a moral economy which supposedly guided relations between traders and peasants or landlords and tenants. Peasant rights were thus anchored in an imagined past. But it was a past in constant reformulation. It was hard to tell at any one moment whether a group of rural Africans would react as defenders of the rights of a chiefdom, or as exponents of a larger Manyika culture, or as men outraged by a breach of the peasant moral economy or as men outraged by an offence against the tenets and practices of popular Christianity. These ambiguities, and the rarity of instances of unambiguous class solidarities, have persuaded political radicals in Zimbabwe, as of course elsewhere, to write off the peasantry as an effective political agent and still more as a potential revolutionary force. And it is indeed true that the complex of ideas and identities I have been describing arose as part of a process of accommodation to rather than rejection of the colonial economy. Becoming a peasant was plainly a matter of entering into that economy rather than of seeking to repudiate it.

Nevertheless, it would be a mistake to write off peasant consciousness in Zimbabwe as merely passive, divided and accommodationist. The varying identities were not imprisoning and divisive shackles of false consciousness; rather they were a series of resources, each to be deployed at the appropriate moment. Moreover, if these resources were usually drawn upon in order to enter the colonial economy on the best available terms, they could be deployed very differently once the whole peasant option was under threat. There is no space here to continue a chronological narrative of the Zimbabwean peasantry. But it is instructive to explore how the resources of peasant consciousness were used and enlarged during the three great crises for the peasant option, crises in which it seemed quite possible that it would be destroyed altogether. These were the crisis of the Great Depression of the late 1920s and early 1930s; the crisis of the Great Eviction of the late 1940s and early 1950s; and the crisis of the Great Destruction of the 1970s during the guerrilla war and government counter-action. I shall take each briefly in turn.

Peasant Consciousness and Protest in Zimbabwe

The Depression meant a collapse of prices for peasant grain and cattle; it also meant a collapse of industrial employment and the return of labour migrants to the countryside; finally, it meant discrimination by the settler state in favour of white farming and at the expense of peasant production. The Zimbabwean peasantry was not destroyed during the Depression and by the late 1930s the colonial economy had recovered, so that the peasant option once again became viable. Nevertheless, the Depression represented a watershed for peasant consciousness, as peasants had to contemplate the possibility that all the accommodations they had made and all the initiatives they had taken had been in vain, and as they came to realize both the power and the partiality of the colonial state. There was little formal political protest in the early 1930s, even though returned labour migrants preached the radical ideologies they had learned in the towns of South Africa. But there was intense ideological conflict.

On one side there was a drawing together of the missionaries and the administrators, both of whom were now anxious to ensure rural stability and to avert a breakdown of authority. For their part missionaries ceased to push for modernizing change and the emergence of peasant entrepreneurs; they began to feel that commoners had become too disrespectful of chiefs, wives of husbands and youths of elders. Missionaries became more sympathetic to those traditional ideologies that had sustained political order. The administrators, for their part, became yet more anxious to sustain rural patriarchy but at the same time began to intervene in peasant production so as to avert total economic collapse. A conservative alliance of state and church, chiefs and elders was struck. The creative tensions between mission church and state and traditional religion which had allowed room for peasant choice and manœuvre were coming to an end. In their place there was emerging a composite authoritarian ideology in which missionaries, chiefs, native commissioners and spirit mediums seemed to combine to enforce a single identity – that of local tribesman. Within the churches there was in any case less freedom of belief and practice as professionally trained black teachers and clergy began to replace the old locally based teacher/evangelists. Within traditional religion there was also less freedom for popular innovation as the old close alliance of chiefs and mediums was for a time restored.

Against this foreclosing consensus there beat various youth ideological challenges. Returned labour migrants tried to set up associations which would link rural protest with that of the towns and in one or two places, as in the rural districts around Bulawayo, they were briefly successful. More influential than this political protest, however, was religious innovation. This was no matter of peasants relapsing into irrationality. The authoritarian colonial order was sustained specifically by religious ideology and in the 1930s had managed to combine mission Christianity and traditional religion. Discontented peasants, exploited women and excluded youth needed a means of repudiating both – and a more convincing one than the importation of secular urban ideas. Thus there arose in most areas of Zimbabwe African prophetic and Holy Spirit churches. These denounced the missions, attacking their emphasis on schools whose teachings had done no good to African peasants when the crunch of the Depression came. Turning the tables on the missionaries, African prophets attacked their materialism and lack of spirituality. In particular they attacked the demand for church dues and fees. At the same time the prophets denounced spirit mediums and priests of Mwari, who were seen as equally corrupt and useless proponents of established religion. The spirit churches called on youth to abandon the churches and the cults; to withdraw from both the colonial and the traditional economic order; to cease to produce for the market, cease to sell labour, cease to pay dues to churches or to make offerings to spirits of the land. Instead the prophetic churches offered new communities – Zion Cities in the Reserves – where there would be collective agricultural production for the church itself and the development of artisanal skills.

These prophetic churches, with their huge followings of youths and women, have often been seen as merely escapist irrelevancies, as inward-turning retreats from reality. Yet, so far from being inward-turning and small-scale, they were linked to and inspired by the global counter-establishment movements of Zionism and Pentecostalism, which from white America to Scandinavia and white South Africa had provided a new sense of identity to people who had found themselves marginalized by industrial capitalism. Some of these Zimbabwean churches have become international. Above all, in the 1930s, they kept open the range of possibilities, the multiplicity of possible identities, at a time when there was a danger of closure and stasis.

By the end of the 1930s the crisis of the Depression had passed. As markets began to recover it began to make sense once again to make use of mission education and literacy; entrepreneurial self-confidence was regained and the conservative alliance repudiated; within the mission churches folk Christianity was given a new vitality by Revival movements led by African Anglicans, Catholics and Methodists. The old multiplicity of identities and strategies seemed to have been restored. But things had changed. The prophetic churches survived and grew and continued to represent an alternative to collaboration with the colonial economic system. Meanwhile, the intervention of the state, begun during the Depression, intensified after it. The state was viewed with general distrust; its aid had not been needed in the formative period of peasantization; it had blatantly aided whites against blacks and continued to do so; its advocacy and increasing enforcement of intensive small-scale cultivation was seen merely as a justification for large-scale evictions of black cultivators from land which would then be given to whites. There could never again be a positive emphasis upon entering the colonial economy as peasants on the best terms. After the 1930s peasant consciousness was always defensive and watchful.

All these suspicions and fears were abundantly justified in the late 1940s. The state intervened to evict hundreds of thousands of peasants from land on which many families had been farming since the 1890s. In order to make room for the expansion of white capitalist agriculture, which was at long last booming, they were moved to arid land, remote from roads and railways. In the Reserves the state intervened to destock cattle, to limit arable holdings and to enforce rules of conservation and of intensive farming. The population of the Reserves greatly increased and there was acute land shortage. The peasant option was once again gravely threatened and this time not by general economic collapse but because of state policy.

In this crisis every peasant resource and identity was made use of, though mostly without avail. The prophetic churches, which had from the beginning preached withdrawal from the peasant option and the state economy, gained more converts. But those who wanted to defend the peasant option adopted a wide range of strategies. Some turned to chiefs for leadership in protest, especially in Matabeleland, where urban politicians joined traditional *indunas* and black clergy to oppose eviction. Some tried to make the best of intensive farming methods, drawing on the resources of the mission churches. Some consciously acted and spoke as tribesmen – promises of security of tenure made to the Ndebele by Cecil Rhodes, it was claimed, were now being broken. Others acted and spoke as mission Christians – the progressive ideology of self-help was being betrayed. Others turned increasingly to the spirit mediums or to the Mwari cult – the territorial cults literally embodied the claim of Africans to be the real owners of the land.

Meanwhile, as peasants everywhere became aware of the role of the state and realized that peasants in other districts were as much affected as themselves, there developed another enlargement of identity. People had come to think of themselves as Manyika or Zezuru or Karanga. Now they came to think of themselves as Shona, or even as Africans. This developing identity did not imply a departure from concepts of tradition but an enlargement of them. Educated Africans, who had once written local tribal histories or helped create mission vernaculars, now wrote histories of past Shona empires. Such expansions of tradition now prepared many peasants for interaction with nationalist movements. In the mid 1950s when such movements were founded in the towns they at first assumed that they must focus on mobilizing urban discontent. By the end of the 1950s, however, nationalist leaders had discovered the protest potential of the complex consciousness of the country-side. Peasants from arid zones where the peasant option had become impossible sent their own emissaries to the towns to seek legal and political help. Soon rural nationalism threatened to undermine the carefully maintained stability of the Reserves.

In shorthand we can thus write of rural nationalism. But things were much more complicated than that. Peasant consciousness was very far from identical with that of the urban leaders. Peasants were at once more cautious and more radical than the nationalist leaders of the early 1960s. They were more cautious because they had a better sense of rural power realities and were more exposed to official retaliation; they were more radical because by now the erosion of the peasant option had brought them to desire a sweeping transformation. Peasants wished, if it were remotely possible, to drive whites out of the alienated lands; to chase authoritarian government experts out of the peasant areas. These were not objectives which the nationalists were yet ready to proclaim. Moreover, while peasants joined nationalist parties and appealed for legal aid, they did not by any means automatically accept nationalist politicians as more legitimate than the various spokesmen of their own range of communities and identities. The nationalists found that generalized attacks on chiefs or on mission Christians misfired in areas where a powerful chief opposed the state in his own way or in areas where folk Christianity retained its utility and vitality. When young nationalist labour migrants, returned from the towns, proclaimed a return also to pre-colonial culture, and declared themselves as mediums, they alienated the real spirit mediums, who resented and despised these interlopers.

Nationalist leaders in this period often used to debate whether they could most trust the urban or the rural 'masses', often finding themselves dis-illusioned with both. Such leaders attacked the 'conservatism' and 'irration-ality' of the peasantry. But the truth was that they had not bothered to discover that the peasant 'mass' had to be analysed in all its complexity or that peasant 'tradition' had to be understood as a series of enabling inventions. Peasants often wondered in turn how far they could trust leaders whose vocabulary was so different from their own and who seemed more concerned to capture intrusive state machinery than to destroy it.

By the 1970s much had changed. The crisis of peasant agriculture was now acute. Confronted with international sanctions, the Smith regime had responded by throwing state support once again behind white farming. It aided white farmers to move out of export cash-crops and back into maize and cattle, thereby competing directly and on favoured terms with black peasants. Moreover, as the guerrilla war spread and intensified, so peasant production came under attack. Peasants in many areas were moved to 'protected' villages and subjected to curfews which made tending their fields almost impossibly difficult. Towards the end of the war the 'Security Forces' launched 'Operation Turkey', designed to destroy crops so as to deny food to guerrillas. Thousands of peasant cattle were seized or killed as punishment for aiding guerrillas. By the end of the 1970s the peasant share of the internal food market had virtually disappeared. On the other hand, the old urban-based nationalist movements had given way to younger guerrillas whose relationship with the peasants was quite different.

It was crucial to the success or failure of these guerrillas to understand the complexities and potentials of peasant consciousness. It was no longer a question of intellectual theory whether or not the peasantry were a revolutionary class. It was a matter of daily practice. This daily practice was very different from the dominant model of how a people's war *should* work and to understand it we need to bring to bear our developing comprehension of the course of Zimbabwean peasant consciousness since 1890. Peasant hostility to the state had intensified greatly since the 1950s but otherwise the ingredients of peasant consciousness remained the same in the 1970s as they had been twenty years earlier. The difference lay in their interaction with armed guerrillas.

We have seen that throughout the twentieth century, and despite the adherence of many peasants to mission Christianity, to independent churches and to nationalist parties, the pre-colonial 'great tradition' of the territorial cults had never lost its relevance. Many different groupings had tried to draw upon it as a resource. Small peasants had sought fertility, rain and ecological advice from spirit mediums; administrators in the 1930s had shown respect for African religion in the hope of shoring up chiefly authority; nationalists in the early 1960s had called for a return to ancestral veneration as a mark of authenticity. Now in the 1970s there was a contestation for control of this resource. The Rhodesia Front administration belatedly tried to achieve genuine tribal political institutions as a bulwark against the guerrillas and so they sought to persuade spirit mediums to endorse 'legitimate' chiefs; district commissioners made charts of all the spirit mediums in their area and toured round making appropriate gifts to their spirits. Some ambitious mediums, who claimed wide regional influence, did ally themselves with the authorities and condemned the pollution of the land by guerrilla shedding of blood. But many more mediums were open to use as a resource by the guerrillas and their peasant supporters.

The mediums represented in the most effective symbolic way the peasant claim to the lost lands. They were savage critics – in the name of traditional management of the land – of the enforced agricultural rules. Hence they represented the political programme of most of the peasantry, which demanded restoration of alienated lands and the cessation of state inter-ference in farming. At the same time, through their dominance of the creation and enunciation of oral tradition and myth, the mediums could 'make history' not only by working with guerrillas in the present but also by operating on the shape of the perceived past. Mediums produced new or modified oral traditions which integrated the strange young guerrillas into the inheritance and territory of the ancestors, legitimating them by use of the most funda-mental metaphors of the pre-colonial great tradition. They imposed prohibitions and constraints on the guerrillas which allowed the peasantry some degree of control over the armed men. Hence the role of the mediums in the 1970s was neither atavistic nor dysfunctional. Rather it was another stage in the fusion of innovation and tradition; another stage in the redefini-tion of communities. By some past definitions the guerrillas were strangers to existing rural communities. The mediums redefined and reordered those communities.

But other peasant resources and identities were not rendered redundant. In zones of intense folk Christianity the guerrillas worked with priests or African catechists rather than with mediums. If spirit mediums could turn command of oral historiography to the service of guerrilla war, African Catholic intel-lectuals could turn their skills of literacy and their access to the presses to effective use as well. Now it was not a matter of writing local tribal history or nationalist tracts, but a matter of recording and publishing the brutalities of the government forces. Just as some mediums collaborated with the authorities, however, so some traditions of rural folk Christianity stood opposed to the guerrillas, the most notable being the Methodist church under Bishop Abel Muzorewa. Similarly, past nationalist identities were sometimes an advantage in bringing about easy collaboration between peasant elders and guerrillas and sometimes a disadvantage. In some places elders who had dominated rural nationalism resented the new authority of intrusive armed young men; in others a long record of radical opposition to the state singled out an elder as the natural intermediary between guerrillas and people. One or two peasant resources and identities *were* irrelevant to the war. Thus the communities of the prophetic churches, with their principled abstention from politics, neither collaborated with nor opposed the guerrillas but did their best to live apart in the middle of a war. The regional identities – being Manyika, or Zezuru or Karanga – do not seem to have been mobilized as constituencies during the war, since peasants might be of one such perceived identity and guerrillas of another.

In general, however, what took place was certainly neither the total mobilization of all types of peasant consciousness in support of the guerrillas, nor was it a total transformation of peasant consciousness through guerrilla political education and the teaching of radical secular self-help. What took place was the mobilization of most adherents of most peasant identities and communities, and the introduction of some new ideas and identities. Guerrillas and peasants came to share in a fused and composite ideology, the most fascinating examples of which are the *chimurenga* (liberation war) songs of the 1970s.

Conclusion

This brief account of Zimbabwean peasant consciousness has shown that it is profitable to ask in the Zimbabwean case the questions which have been articulated by the new peasant historiography. It has also shown how different can be the answers. In its origins, its relation to the great traditions, its potentials for political action and for rebellion, Zimbabwean peasant consciousness was and is quite different from Asian, or Latin American or indeed from peasant consciousness in much of the rest of Africa. This lesson of particularity is one that needs to be constantly learned and relearned.

It needs to be relearned even by political leaders in independent Zimbabwe, who know how important peasant participation and ideology was in the guerrilla war, but who are tempted nevertheless to apply to the peasantry in peace-time all the old lumping generalizations. Even as the Zimbabwean peasant option has been resumed with greater success than ever before, so that peasants now produce well over half of the country's maize and a third of its cotton, official reports describe peasant farming as 'tradition-bound', 'backward' and 'subsistence oriented' (Chavunduka, 1982; Ministry of Lands, 1985). Even while scholarly publications record the radical role of peasant consciousness during the guerrilla war, party ideologues in Zimbabwe speak of the inevitable leading role of the urban proletariat and the need to break down rural conservatism. Maybe such lumping generalizations are never seriously intended to describe any particular peasantry but merely to legitimate the programme of planners and politicians. If so, Zimbabwean peasant consciousness no doubt has still some surprises in store.

References

Beinart, W. and Bundy, C. (1987) *Hidden Struggles: Rural Politics and Popular Consciousness in South Africa*, London.

Bhila, H. K. (1982) *Trade and Politics in a Shona Kingdom: The Manyika and their Portuguese and African Neighbours, 1575–1902*, London.

Callear, D. (1982) *The Social and Cultural Factors Involved in Production by Small Farmers in Wedza Communal Area, Zimbabwe*, Unesco, Paris.

Chatterjee, P. (1986) 'The colonial state and peasant resistance in Bengal, 1920–1947', *Past and Present*, vol. 110, February.

Chavunduka, G. J. (1982) *Report of the Commission of Inquiry into the Agricultural Industry*, Harare.

Dillon-Malone, C. M. (1979) *The Korsten Basket-Makers: A Study of the Masowe Apostles*, Manchester.

Fields, K. (1985) *Revival and Rebellion in Colonial Central Africa*, Chicago.

Fry, P. (1976) *Spirits of Protest*, Cambridge.

Ishii, Y. (1984) 'Preface' in Andrew Turton and Shigeharu Tanabe (eds) *History and Peasant Consciousness in South East Asia*, Senri Ethnological Studies no. 13, Osaka.

Lan, D. (1985) *Guns and Rain. Guerrillas and Spirit Mediums in Zimbabwe*, London.

Larson, D. (1983) 'Shifting views of colonialism and resistance', *Radical History Review*, vol. 27, May.

Ministry of Lands, Resettlement and Rural Development (1985) 'Communal Lands Development Plan. A 15 year development study', Harare.

Ranger, T. O. (1985) *Peasant Consciousness and Guerrilla War in Zimbabwe*, London.

Sabean, D. W. (1984) *Power in the Blood: Culture and Village Discourse in Early Modern Germany*, Cambridge.

Turton, A. and Tanabe, S. (1984) 'Introduction' in Turton and Tanabe (eds) *History and Peasant Consciousness in South East Asia*, Senri Ethnological Studies, no. 13, Osaka.

Vail, I. and White, L. (1980) *Capitalism and Colonialism in Mozambique*, London.

Related Items

7, 9, 10, 11, 13, 19, 20, 21, 25, 26, 29, 33, 35, 37, 39, 40, 41, 42, 43, 44, 45, 46, 47, 53, 54, 55, 56, 58, 59, 61, 62.

Part IV

Peasantry as a Class

Part IV focuses on political processes, that is, on issues of power, authority and conflict. It treats peasants as a class, that is as a social entity with a community of economic interests, its identity shaped by conflict with other classes and expressed in typical patterns of cognition and political consciousness, however rudimentary, which makes it capable of collective action reflecting its interests. Part IV looks also at the content and forms of peasant village politics, considering the intra-peasant divisions involved. Particular attention is paid to the social roots of peasant resistance to oppression, the forms it takes and to peasants combining with other social forces in attempts to influence state policies or to establish in a revolutionary way an alternative society.

Views concerning peasants' potential for effective political action range widely from assumptions of its total nullity to the celebration of contemporary peasantry as the most decisive factor of the global political scene (see 'Peasantry in the Eyes of Others' in Part V, item 48). To a considerable degree peasant political action has been subject to broader societal context and particular historical conjunctures. Yet it was not simply a matter of extra-peasant multiple determinations. Both peasant action and peasant response to the extra-peasant political impact show particularities rooted in the social, economic and cultural patterns characteristic of them.

Part IV opens with a Marx contribution concerning the political characteristics of peasants as a class. It remains highly illuminating and there are, in fact, some lessons to be learned from our ability to use meaningfully these analytical findings of a century and a half ago. Hobsbawm and Tilly present and discuss next forms of peasant resistance in different periods and in the face of different challenges. (See also Alavi, Sen, Omvedt and Ranger, items 26, 29, 20 and 38.) Alavi's contribution considers peasant factionality in the village as well as a form of organization of the peasants in their confrontation with the big landlords (see also Rahman, item 30). A 'snippet' by Scott focuses attention on the indirect yet often very effective ways peasants face powers superior to their own. This is followed by Shanin's short excerpt concerning peasantry as a class and of the forms and categories of political and armed action typical of it (see also Ranger and Womack, items 38 and 47). The last three contributions in part IV deal with revolutionary struggles in the twentieth century. They begin with Moore's comment concerning the contemporary revolutions of the oppressed. It is followed by Wolf's discussion of peasant rebellions and of their place within revolutionary events and transformations (see also Ranger, item 38). A major exemplification of it as well as of revolutionized peasantry's political aims and forms of organization, as expressed in Mexico's state of Morelos under the rule of Zapata's peasant rebels, brings the part to completion (see also Sen, Bailey, Scott, Ranger, items 29, 35, 37 and 38, and the items in part V).

39

Peasantry as a Class
Karl Marx

10 December 1848, was the day of the *peasant insurrection*. Only from this day does the February of the French peasants date. The symbol that expressed their entry into the revolutionary movement, clumsily cunning, knavishly naïve, doltishly sublime, a calculated superstition, a pathetic burlesque, a cleverly stupid anachronism, a world-historic piece of buffoonery and an undecipherable hieroglyphic for the understanding of the civilized – this symbol bore the unmistakable physiognomy of the class that represents barbarism within civilization. The republic had announced itself to this class with the *tax collector*; it announced itself to the republic with the *emperor*. Napoleon was the only man who had exhaustively represented the interests and the imagination of the peasant class, newly created in 1789. By writing his name on the frontispiece of the republic, it declared war abroad and the enforcing of its class interests at home. Napoleon was to the peasants not a person but a programme. With banners, with beat of drums, and blare of trumpets, they marched to the polling booths shouting: *plus d'impôts, à bas les riches, à bas la république, vive l'Empereur!* No more taxes, down with the rich, down with the republic, long live the emperor! Behind the emperor was hidden the peasant war. The republic that they voted down was the *republic of the rich*.

10 December was the *coup d'état* of the peasants, which overthrew the existing government. . . .

Bonaparte represents a class, and the most numerous class of French society at that, the *smallholding [Parzellen] peasants*.

Just as the Bourbons were the dynasty of big landed property and just as the

Excerpts from Karl Marx, 'The class struggles in France 1848–1850' and 'The eighteenth Brumaire of Louis Bonaparte', in Karl Marx and Frederick Engels, *Selected Works*, vol. 1, Foreign Languages Publishing House, 1950; Lawrence & Wishart, 1950, pp. 159, 302–8. First published in 1850–2.

Orleans were the dynasty of money, so the Bonapartes are the dynasty of the peasants, that is, the mass of the French people. Not the Bonaparte who submitted to the bourgeois parliament, but the Bonaparte who dispersed the bourgeois parliament is the chosen of the peasantry. For three years the towns had succeeded in falsifying the meaning of the election of 10 December and in cheating the peasants out of the restoration of the empire. The election of 10 December 1848 has been consummated only by the *coup d'état* of 2 December 1851.

The smallholding peasants form a vast mass, the members of which live in similar conditions but without entering into manifold relations with one another. Their mode of production isolates them from one another instead of bringing them into mutual intercourse. The isolation is increased by France's bad means of communication and by the poverty of the peasants. Their field of production, the smallholding, admits of no division of labour in its cultivation, no application of science and, therefore, no diversity of development, no variety of talent, no wealth of social relationships. Each individual peasant family is almost self-sufficient; it itself directly produces the major part of its consumption and thus acquires its means of life more through exchange with nature than in intercourse with society. A smallholding, a peasant and his family; alongside them another smallholding, another peasant and another family. A few score of these make up a village, and a few score of villages makes up a Department. In this way, the great mass of the French nation is formed by simple addition of homologous magnitudes, much as potatoes in a sack form a sack of potatoes. In so far as millions of families live under economic conditions of existence that separate their mode of life, their interests and their culture from those of the other classes, and put them in hostile opposition to the latter, they form a class. In so far as there is merely a local interconnection among these smallholding peasants, and the identity of their interests begets no community, no national bond and no political organization among them, they do not form a class. They are consequently incapable of enforcing their class interest in their own name, whether through a parliament or through a convention. They cannot represent themselves, they must be represented. Their representative must at the same time appear as their master, as an authority over them, as an unlimited governmental power that protects them against the other classes and sends them rain and sunshine from above. The political influence of the smallholding peasants, therefore, finds its final expression in the executive power subordinating society to itself.

Historical tradition gave rise to the belief of the French peasants in the miracle that a man named Napoleon would bring all the glory back to them. And an individual turned up who gives himself out as the man because he bears the name of Napoleon, in consequence of the *Code Napoléon*, which lay down that *la recherche de la paternité est interdit*.[1] After a vagabondage of twenty years and after a series of gross adventures, the legend finds fulfilment and the man becomes Emperor of the French. The fixed idea of the Nephew was realized, because it coincided with the fixed idea of the most numerous class of the French people.

But, it may be objected, what about the peasant rising in half of France, the raids on the peasants by the army, the mass incarceration and transportation of peasants?

Since Louis XIV, France had experienced no similar persecution of the peasants 'on account of demagogic practices'.

But let there be no misunderstanding. The Bonaparte dynasty represents not the revolutionary, but the conservative peasant; not the peasant that strikes out beyond the condition of his social existence, the smallholding, but rather the peasant who wants to consolidate his holding, not the country folk who, linked up with the towns, wants to overthrow the old order through their own energies, but on the contrary those who, in stupefied seclusion within this old order, want to see themselves and their smallholdings saved and favoured by the ghost of the empire. It represents not the enlightenment, but the superstition of the peasant; not his judgement, but his prejudice; not his future, but his past; not his modern Cévennes, but his modern Vendée.[2]

The three years' rigorous rule of the parliamentary republic had freed a part of the French peasants from the Napoleonic illusion and had revolutionized them, even if only superficially; but the bourgeoisie violently repressed them, as often as they set themselves in motion. Under the parliamentary republic the modern and the traditional consciousness of the French peasant contended for mastery. This progress took the form of an incessant struggle between the schoolmasters and the priests. The bourgeoisie struck down the schoolmasters. For the first time the peasants made efforts to behave independently in the face of the activity of the government. This was shown in the continual conflict between the *maires* and the prefects. The bourgeoisie deposed the *maires*. Finally, during the period of the parliamentary republic, the peasants of different localities rose against their own offspring, the army. The bourgeoisie punished them with states of siege and punitive expeditions. And this same bourgeoisie now cries out about the stupidity of the masses, the vile multitude, that has betrayed it to Bonaparte. It has itself forcibly strengthened the empire sentiments [*Imperialismus*] of the peasant class, it conserved the conditions that form the birthplace of this peasant religion. The bourgeoisie, to be sure, is bound to fear the stupidity of the masses as long as they remain conservative, and the insight of the masses as soon as they become revolutionary.

In the risings after the *coup d'état*, a part of the French peasants protested, arms in hand, against their own vote of 10 December 1848. The school they had gone through since 1848 had sharpened their wits. But they had made themselves over to the underworld of history; history held them to their word, and the majority was still so prejudiced that in precisely the reddest Departments the peasant population voted openly for Bonaparte. In its view, the National Assembly had hindered his progress. He had now merely broken the fetters that the towns had imposed on the will of the countryside. In some parts the peasants even entertained the grotesque notion of the Convention side by side with Napoleon.

After the first revolution had transformed the peasants from semi-villeins into freeholders, Napoleon confirmed and regulated the conditions on which they could exploit undisturbed the soil of France which had only just fallen to their lot, and slake their youthful passion for property. But what is now causing the ruin of the French peasant is his smallholding itself, the division of the land, the form of property which Napoleon consolidated in France. It is precisely the material conditions which made the feudal peasant into a small-holding peasant and Napoleon into an emperor. Two generations have sufficed to produce the inevitable result: progressive deterioration of agriculture, progressive indebtedness of the agriculturalist. The 'Napoleonic' form of property, which at the beginning of the nineteenth century was the condition for the liberation and enrichment of the French country folk, has developed in the course of this century into the law of their enslavement and pauperization. And precisely this law is the first of the '*idées napoléoniennes*' which the second Bonaparte has to uphold. If he still shares with the peasants the illusion that the cause of their ruin is to be sought, not in this smallholding property itself, but outside it, in the influence of secondary circumstances, his experiments will burst like soap bubbles when they come in contact with the relations of production.

The economic development of smallholding property has radically changed the relation of the peasants to the other classes of society. Under Napoleon, the fragmentation of the land in the countryside supplemented free competition and the beginning of big industry in the towns. The peasant class was the ubiquitous protest against the landed aristocracy which had just been overthrown. The roots that smallholding property struck in French soil deprived feudalism of all nutriment. Its landmarks formed the natural fortifica-tions of the bourgeoisie against any surprise attack on the part of its old overlords. But in the course of the nineteenth century the feudal lords were replaced by urban usurers; the feudal obligation that went with the land was replaced by the mortgage; aristocratic landed property was replaced by bourgeois capital. The smallholding of the peasant is now only the pretext that allows the capitalist to draw profits, interest and rent from the soil, while leaving it to the tiller of the soil himself to see how he can extract his wages. The mortgage debt burdening the soil of France imposes on the French peasantry payment of an amount of interest equal to the annual interest on the entire British national debt. Smallholding property, in this enslavement by capital to which its development inevitably pushes forward, has transformed the mass of the French nation into troglodytes. Sixteen million peasants (including women and children) dwell in hovels, a large number of which have but one opening, others only two and the most favoured only three. And windows are to a house what the five senses are to the head. The bourgeois order, which at the beginning of the century set the state to stand guard over the newly arisen smallholding and manured it with laurels, has become a vampire that sucks out its blood and marrow and throws them to the alchemist cauldron of capital. The *Code Napoléon* is now nothing but a *codex* of distraints, forced sales and compulsory auctions. To the four million (including children, etc.) officially recognized paupers, vagabonds, criminals and prostitutes in France must be added five million who hover on the margin of existence and either have their haunts in the countryside itself or, with their rags and their children, continually desert the countryside for the towns and the towns for the country-side. The interests of the peasants, therefore, are no longer, as under Napoleon, in accord with, but in opposition to the interests of the bourgeoisie, to capital. Hence the peasants find their natural ally and leader in the *urban proletariat*, whose task is the overthrow of the bourgeois order. But *strong and ulimited government* – and this is the second '*idée napoléonienne*', which the second Napoleon has to carry out – is called upon to defend this 'material' order by force. This '*ordre matériel*' also serves as the catchword in all of Bonaparte's proclamations against the rebellious peasants.

Besides the mortgage which capital imposes on it, the smallholding is burdened by *taxes*. Taxes are the source of life for the bureaucracy, the army, the priests and the court, in short, for the whole apparatus of the executive power. Strong government and heavy taxes are identical. By its very nature, smallholding property forms a suitable basis for an all-powerful and innumer-able bureaucracy. It creates a uniform level of relationships and persons over the whole surface of the land. Hence it also permits of uniform action from a supreme centre on all points of this uniform mass. It annihilates the aristocratic intermediate grades between the mass of the people and the state power. On all sides, therefore, it calls forth the direct interference of this state power and the interposition of its immediate organs. Finally, it produces an unemployment surplus population for which there is no place either on the land or in the towns, and which accordingly reaches out for state offices as a sort of respect-able alms, and provokes the creation of state posts. By the new market which he opened at the point of the bayonet, by the plundering of the continent, Napoleon repaid the compulsory taxes with interest. These taxes were a spur to the industry of the peasant, whereas now they rob his industry of its last resources and complete his inability to resist pauperism. And an enormous bureaucracy, well-gallooned and well-fed, is the '*idée napoléonienne*' which is most congenial of all to the second Bonaparte. How could it be otherwise, seeing that alongside the actual classes of society he is forced to create an artificial caste, for which the maintenance of his regime becomes a bread-and-butter question? Accordingly, one of his first financial operations was the raising of officials' salaries to their old level and the creation of new sinecures.

Another '*idée napoléonienne*' is the domination of the *priests* as an instrumen-tality of government. But while in its accord with society, in its dependence on natural forces and its submission to the authority which protected it from above, the smallholding that had newly come into being was naturally religious, the smallholding that is ruined by debts, at odds with society and authority, and driven beyond its own limitations naturally becomes irreligious. Heaven was quite a pleasing accession to the narrow strip of land just won, more particularly as it makes the weather; it becomes an insult as soon as it is thrust forward as substitute for the smallholding. The priest then appears as only the anointed bloodhound of the earthly police – another *'idée napoléonienne'*. On the next occasion, the expedition against Rome will take place in France itself, but in a sense opposite to that of M. de Montalembert.

Lastly, the culminating point of the *'idées napoléoniennes'* is the preponderance of the *army*. The army was the *point d'honneur* of the smallholding peasants, it was they themselves transformed into heroes, defending their new possessions against the outer world, glorifying their recently won nationality, plundering and revolutionizing the world. The uniform was their own state dress; war was their poetry; the smallholding, extended and rounded off in imagination, was their fatherland, and patriotism the ideal form of the sense of property. But the enemies against whom the French peasant has now to defend his property are not the Cossacks; they are the bailiffs and the tax collectors. The smallholding lies no longer in the so-called fatherland, but in the register of mortgages. The army itself is no longer the flower of the peasant youth; it is the swamp-flower of the peasant *lumpenproletariat*. It consists in large measure of *remplaçants*, of substitutes, just as the second Bonaparte is himself only a *remplaçant*, the substitute for Napoleon. It now performs its deeds of valour by hounding the peasants in passes like chamois, by doing *gendarme* duty, and if the internal contradictions of his system chase the chief of the Society of 10 December over the French border, his army, after some acts of brigandage, will reap, not laurels, but thrashings.

One sees: *all 'idees napoléoniennes' are ideas of the undeveloped smallholdings in the freshness of its youth*; for the smallholding that has outlived its day they are an absurdity. They are only the hallucinations of its death struggle, words that are transformed into phrases, spirits transformed into ghosts. But the parody of the empire [*des Imperialismus*] was necessary to free the mass of the French nation from the weight of tradition and to work out in pure form the opposition between the state power and society. With the progressive undermining of smallholding property, the state structure erected upon it collapses. The centralization of the state that modern society requires arises only on the ruins of the military-bureaucratic governmental machinery which was forged in opposition to feudalism.[3]

Notes

1 Inquiry into paternity is forbidden.
2 In *Cévennes*, a mountainous region of France, a large uprising of Protestant peasants (the so-called Camisards) took place in the beginning of the eighteenth century.

Their watchwords were, 'No Taxes!', 'Freedom of Conscience!' The insurgents seized feudal castles, hid in mountains, engaged in guerrilla warfare. The struggle lasted almost three years.

Vendée: The region in France where massive peasant revolt took place against the government of the French Revolution of the end of the eighteenth century.

3 In the 1852 edition this paragraph ended with the following lines, which Marx omitted in the 1869 edition: 'The demolition of the state machine will not endanger centralization. Bureaucracy is only the low and brutal form of a centralization that is still afflicted with its opposite, with feudalism. When he is disappointed in the Napoleonic Restoration, the French peasant will part with his belief in his small-holding, the entire state edifice erected on this smallholding will fall to the ground and *the proletarian revolution* will obtain *that chorus without which its solo song becomes a swan song in all peasant countries*'.

| Related Items |

9, 13, 16, 26, 29, 30, 37, 38, 40, 41, 42, 43, 44, 45, 46, 47, 51, 55, 56, 58, 59, 61, 62.

40

Social Bandit as a Pre-Capitalist Phenomenon

Eric Hobsbawm

The characteristic victims of the bandit are the quintessential enemies of the poor. As recorded in tradition, they are always those groups which are particularly hated by them: lawyers (Robin Hood and Dick Turpin), prelates and idle monks (Robin Hood and Angiolillo), money-lenders and dealers (Angiolillo and Schinderhannes), foreigners and others who upset the traditional life of the peasant. In pre-industrial and pre-political societies they rarely if ever include the sovereign, who is remote and stands for justice. Indeed, the legend frequently shows the sovereign pursuing the bandit, failing to suppress him, and then asking him to court and making his peace with him, thus recognizing that in a profound sense his and the sovereign's interest, justice, is the same. Thus with Robin Hood and Oleksa Dovbush.

... The fundamental pattern of banditry, as I have tried to sketch it here, is almost universally found in certain conditions. It is rural, not urban. The peasant societies in which it occurs know rich and poor, powerful and weak, rulers and ruled, but remain profoundly and tenaciously traditional, and pre-capitalist in structure. An agricultural society such as that of nineteenth-century East Anglia or Normandy or Denmark is not the place to look for social banditry.... The bandit is a pre-political phenomenon, and his strength is in inverse proportion to that of organized agrarian revolutionism and socialism or communism. Brigandage in the Calabrian Sila went out before the First World War, when socialism and peasant leagues came in. It survived in the Aspromonte, the home of the great Musolino and numerous other popular heroes for whom the women prayed movingly. But there the peasant organization is less developed.

... In such societies banditry is endemic. But it seems that Robin-Hoodism is most likely to become a major phenomenon when their traditional equilibrium is upset: during and after periods of abnormal hardship, such as famines

Excerpts from E. J. Hobsbawm, *Primitive Rebels*, Manchester University Press, 1959.

and wars, or at the moments when the jaws of the dynamic modern world seize the static communities in order to destroy and transform them. Since these moments occurred, in the history of most peasant societies, in the nineteenth or twentieth centuries, our age is in some respects the classical age of the social bandit. We observe his upsurge – at least in the minds of the people – in southern Italy and the Rhineland during the revolutionary transformations and wars at the end of the eighteenth century; in southern Italy after Unification, fanned by the introduction of capitalist law and economic policy. In Calabria and Sardinia the major epoch of brigandage began in the 1890s, when the modern economy (and agricultural depression and emigration) made their impact. In the remote Carpathian mountains banditry flared up in the aftermath of the First World War, for social reasons which Olbracht has, as usual, described both accurately and sensibly.

But this very fact expressed the tragedy of the social bandit. The peasant society creates him and calls upon him, when it feels the need for a champion and protector – but precisely then he is incapable of helping it. For social banditry, though a protest, is a modest and unrevolutionary protest. It protests not against the fact that peasants are poor and oppressed, but against the fact that they are sometimes excessively poor and oppressed. Bandit-heroes are not expected to make a world of equality. They can only right wrongs and prove that sometimes oppression can be turned upside down. Still less can they understand what is happening to Sardinian villages that makes some men have plenty of cattle and others, who used to have a few, have none at all; that drives Calabrian villagers into American coal-mines, or fills the Carpathian mountains with armies, guns and debt.

Related Items

33, 35, 37, 38, 39, 42, 43, 45, 46, 58.

41

Conflict, Resistance and Collective Action versus Capitalization and Statemaking

Charles Tilly

Many fought the effects of capitalism and statemaking. In looking at how and when they fought, we do not observe all the varieties of rural conflict and collective action. Much of the time, European peasants found themselves dealing with marauding wolves, with floods, with thieves, with rapists, with abandoned children, with unholy priests, with neighbours who encroached on their fields; those unwanted conditions and persons provoked peasants to action against them. On the whole, such plagues had no strong connections with capitalization and statemaking. At the risk of taking the exceptional for the essential, then, let us concentrate on the occasions and forms of conflict, resistance and collective action which *did* wax and wane as a function of the development of capitalism and the growth of strong national states.

In what ways did capitalization and statemaking affect the interests of rural people? In simplest terms, the development of capitalism altered the viability of peasant life by making land, labour and commodities increasingly available and responsive to monetized markets in which holders of substantial capital predominated. That set of alterations increased the power of those peasants who managed to accumulate capital; weakened the effectiveness of multiple and collective claims on land, labour, or commodities; decreased the feasibility (and often the attractiveness) of supplying household goods and services from the household's own land and labour; set wage-labour in competition with unpaid household labour; reduced the chances for a household to maintain itself from one generation to the next; and favoured the concentration of land in the hands of people who maximized its monetary return. Although these changes offered splendid opportunities to some peasants, over the long run

Excerpts from Charles Tilly, 'Proletarianization and rural collective action in East Anglia and elsewhere, 1500–1900', *Peasant Studies*, vol. 10, 1982, no. 1.

they doomed the peasantry as a whole to disappear. And they provided spurs to resistance.

As for statemaking, the largest effects on European rural life were probably not the celebrated ones: the creation of national citizenship, the construction of standardized law, the eclipse of local and household authority, even the adoption of national policies governing the profitability of alternative crops. State reinforcement of the position of capital and capitalists probably had more impact on everyday rural life than any of these political changes. But the largest influence of statemaking most likely operated through the state's own demand for resources, especially the resources required for making war: men, food, lodging, clothing, arms, and the money to buy all of them. Certainly the most visible forms of direct rural resistance to statemaking in Europe involved those demands. Evasion of conscription, taxation, billeting, corvee, and requisition of goods for the military built the reputation of European peasants and other cultivators for dissimulation, stealth and stubbornness.

A tried-and-true taxonomy will help us do a first rough sorting of rural people's varied reactions to capitalization and statemaking. Thinking of the claims people make on others when they act, we can distinguish defensive, offensive and competitive forms of action. Defensive actions claim threatened rights which people have already exercised routinely, offensive actions claim rights due in principle but not yet established in practice, while competitive actions pit participants against each other within arenas in which their right to involvement is not at issue. Countrymen who fight off tax collectors' demands for their goods engage in defensive actions, countrymen who insist on their previously-denied right to buy noble land engage in offensive actions, and countrymen who join the inter-village fights engage in competitive actions. Within each of these categories, we may also define a range running from primary emphasis on the effects of capitalism to primary emphasis on the effects of statemaking.

Thus, in the simplest version of the scheme, we distinguish twelve types of reaction: an individual defensive reaction to capitalism (such as hunting on posted land), a collective offensive reaction to statemaking (such as creation of a movement for land reform), an individual competitive reaction to state-making (such as voting a personal interest), and so on through the permutations. Table 41.1 lays out the types, with examples of actions which occurred fairly often at one point or another in the European rural experience. The value, if any, of this sort of simplification eventually proves itself in the revelation of the relative frequency and infrequency of different reactions, and its identification of the characteristic conditions under which each reaction occurs. In the meantime, however, we can use it merely to get a sense of which forms of action belong together. If we don't let the taxonomy gain weight, and lumber off on its own to crush reality on its way, it will serve as a sturdy mount for a first tour of rural action, individual and collective.

On a first tour, let us make no effort to draft a complete map of the terrain. It will do to illustrate the variety of reactions to capitalism from English experience, before reflecting more generally on regularities and systematic variations.

TABLE 41.1 *A rough classification of rural reactions to capitalism and statemaking, with characteristic examples*

Reactions to	Claims made		
	Defensive	*Offensive*	*Competitive*
Capitalism			
Individual	hunting on posted land; arson	purchase of church property	bidding at servants' fair
Collective	invasion of newly enclosed fields; food riots	creation of marketing cooperatives	leaguing to buy land and keep it in local hands
Statemaking			
Individual	hiding taxable goods	suing local powerholders in royal courts	voting a personal interest
Collective	expulsion of military recruiters; tax rebellions	creating a social movement, e.g. for price supports, land reform	petitioning on bill before Parliament

Related Items

10, 13, 25, 26, 28, 29, 31, 35, 37, 38, 39, 40, 42, 46, 47, 49, 50, 51, 53, 54, 58, 59, 61, 62.

42

Weapons of the Weak: Everyday Struggle, Meaning and Deeds

James C. Scott

... revolutions are few and far between. The vast majority are crushed unceremoniously. When, more rarely, they do succeed, it is a melancholy fact that the consequences are seldom what the peasantry had in mind. Whatever else revolutions may achieve – and I have no desire to gainsay these achievements – they also typically bring into being a vaster and more dominant state apparatus that is capable of battening itself on its peasant subjects even more effectively than its predecessors.

For these reasons it seemed to me more important to understand what we might call *everyday* forms of peasant resistance – the prosaic but constant struggle between the peasantry and those who seek to extract labour, food, taxes, rents and interest from them. Most forms of this struggle stop well short of outright collective defiance. Here I have in mind the ordinary weapons of relatively powerless groups: foot dragging, dissimulation, desertion, false compliance, pilfering, feigned ignorance, slander, arson, sabotage, and so on. These Brechtian – or Schweikian – forms of class struggle have certain features in common. They require little or no co-ordination or planning; they make use of implicit understandings and informal networks; they often represent a form of individual self-help; they typically avoid any direct, symbolic confrontation with authority. To understand these commonplace forms of resistance is to understand much of what the peasantry has historically done to defend its interests against both conservative and progressive orders. It is my guess that just such kinds of resistance are often the most significant and the most effective over the long run. Thus, Marc Bloch, the historian of feudalism, has noted that the great millenial movements were 'flashes in the pan' compared to the 'patient, silent struggles stubbornly carried on by rural communities' to avoid claims on their surplus and to assert their rights to the

Excerpts from J. C. Scott, *Weapons of the Weak: Everyday Forms of Peasant Resistance*, Yale University Press, 1985.

means of production – for example, arable, woodland, pastures. Much the same view is surely appropriate to the study of slavery in the New World. The rare, heroic, and foredoomed gestures of a Nat Turner or a John Brown are simply not the places to look for the struggle between slaves and their owners. One must look rather at the constant, grinding conflict over work, food, autonomy, ritual – at everyday forms of resistance. In the Third World it is rare for peasants to risk an outright confrontation with the authorities over taxes, cropping patterns, development policies or onerous new laws; instead they are likely to nibble away at such policies by noncompliance, foot dragging, deception. In place of land division, they prefer piecemeal squatting; in place of open mutiny, they prefer desertion; in place of attacks on public or private grain stores, they prefer pilfering. When such stratagems are abandoned in favour of more quixotic action, it is usually a sign of great desperation.

Such low-profile techniques are admirably suited to the social structure of the peasantry – a class scattered across the countryside, lacking formal organization, and best equipped for extended, guerrilla-style, defensive campaigns of attrition. Their individual acts of foot dragging and evasion, reinforced by a venerable popular culture of resistance and multiplied many thousandfold, may, in the end, make an utter shambles of the policies dreamed up by their would-be superiors in the capital. Everyday forms of resistance make no headlines. But just as millions of anthozoan polyps create, willy-nilly, a coral reef, so do the multiple acts of peasant insubordination and evasion create political and economic barrier reefs of their own. It is largely in this fashion that the peasantry makes its political presence felt. And whenever, to pursue the simile, the ship of state runs aground on such reefs, attention is usually directed to the shipwreck itself and not the vast aggregation of petty acts that made it possible. For these reasons alone, it seems important to understand this quiet and anonymous welter of peasant action.

. . . The struggle between rich and poor in Sedaka is not merely a struggle over work, property rights, grain and cash. It is also a struggle over the appropriation of symbols, a struggle over how the past and present shall be understood and labelled, a struggle to identify causes and assess blame, a contentious effort to give partisan meaning to local history. The details of this struggle are not pretty, as they entail backbiting, gossip, character assassination, rude nicknames, gestures, and silences of contempt which, for the most part, are confined to the backstage of village life. In public life – that is to say, in power-laden settings – a carefully calculated conformity prevails for the most part. What is remarkable about this aspect of class conflict is the extent to which it requires a shared world-view. Neither gossip nor character assassination, for example, makes much sense unless there are shared standards of what is deviant, unworthy, impolite. In one sense, the ferociousness of the argument *depends* on the fact that it appeals to shared values that have been, it is claimed, betrayed.

Related Items

4, 5, 8, 20, 23, 30, 34, 35, 38, 44, 47, 58, 59, 62.

43

Village Factions

Hamza Alavi

'Faction' aptly describes the most pervasive form of peasant political interaction as it is observed in peasant societies; accounts of peasant societies are replete with examples of 'factionalism'. Beals and Siegel (1960) focus on faction as conflict, and speculate about types of conflict, the conditions in which it occurs, and 'strains' and 'stresses' which bring it about. A discussion of social conflict in such terms obscures rather than illuminates its causes and consequences and the social goals of the people who are involved in the conflict. Furthermore, as a description of factional conflict in peasant societies, that treatment of the subject misses the central fact about that mode of politics, namely that factional alignments cut across class alignments.

Factional conflict, therefore, has a significance which cannot be understood without an examination of the manner in which factions are recruited and led. Nicholas (1963, 1965, 1966, 1968) and Bailey (1969), rather more usefully, focus on factions as political groups and explore the resources of leaders who recruit them and the manner in which they organize political activity.

The analytical questions raised in the latter perspective express the fact that political cleavages in peasant societies are often vertical cleavages, which run across class lines, rather than horizontal cleavages of class conflict. Faction leaders are conceived either as local power-holders or as manipulating political entrepreneurs, who organize political groups with their retinues of labourers, share-croppers and other economic dependents – if they have them – and alliances with other influential individuals or groups. An important aspect of factional conflict is that rival factions are, in general, structurally similar, namely that they represent similar configurations of social groups, although that is by no means always the case. Where that is so, the faction model describes a segmental rather than class conflict. Such conflicts, therefore, do not have an ideological expression, because rival factions, or

Based in part on Hamza Alavi, 'Peasant classes and primordial loyalties', *Journal of Peasant Studies*, vol. 1, 1973, pp. 43–59.

faction leaders, fight for control over resources, power, and status as available within the existing framework of society rather than for changes in the social structure. Shanin describes the phenomenon, in rural Russia, as 'vertical segmentation [which] may be used to define social groupings, usually local, which cut across the major socio-economic stratification of modern society, indicating division into qualitatively similar, highly self-sufficient, hierarchical segments with relatively little interaction between them. . . . The segments show hierarchical structures of authority centred around a patriarchal leader or a traditional oligarchic leadership' (Shanin, 1972, p. 177). We may add that the concept of faction has also been applied to analysis of political activity at levels other than that of the local peasant community; but that will not concern us here.

Wolf (1966a, pp. 81ff.) uses the concept of peasant 'coalition' instead of faction, and suggests an ingenious classification of coalitions, based on three dichotomies: the number of persons involved, namely dyadic and polyadic; the number of ties that bind them in the coalition, namely 'single-stranded' and 'many-stranded'; and the relative statuses of parties to the coalition, namely 'horizontal' and 'vertical'. The system of classification is useful heuristically; but its limitations become apparent when it is applied to factions. For example, patron–client relationships, which Wolf classifies as 'many-stranded dyadic vertical' coalitions, are included in factional alignments but as only one of several modes of recruitment. Analyses of factions particularly emphasize 'transactional' relationships between leaders and followers, which Wolf classifies as 'single-stranded dyadic' coalitions, by which he refers, however, only to certain types of 'evanescent coalitions'. Factional recruitment makes use of single-stranded as well as many-stranded ties, 'vertical' as well as horizontal relationships. Furthermore, the term faction refers to the group as a whole and not to separate individual 'coalitions' between leaders and followers. The term 'dyadic' would therefore be inappropriate to describe the resultant set of relationships. Nor would it seem appropriate to describe them as 'polyadic' because the ties of followers all converge on the faction leader and do not imply direct ties amongst themselves, independent of their respective relationships to the leader. The concept of faction is therefore more complex than that of coalition; it leaves open the question of mode of recruitment and admits a multiplicity and complexity of ties. It seems to be a preferable concept. It is more flexible, analytically, than Wolf's classification of coalitions which imposes a set of rigid dichotomies on the analytical model.

Nicholas describes and defines the concept of faction by a set of five propositions, which he seeks to establish and illustrate. He states (1965, pp. 27–9) that:

1 factions are groups which emerge during conflict;
2 they are political groups engaged in organized conflict about the uses of public power;
3 they are not corporate groups: they are basically impermanent although they

may persist for long periods of time (unlike e.g., lineages, which exist by ascription and are permanent);

4 they are recruited by a leader; members can belong to a faction only through the activity of leader, since the unit has no corporate existence or clear single principle of recruitment. The leader, being responsible for organizing the personnel of a faction, is ordinarily a man with more political power than any of his followers;

5 'the faction members are recruited on diverse principles', or ties, with the faction leader.

Bailey offers one further distinction, that of 'core' and 'followers'. It is useful for analyses of recruitment of factions, although his own definition (or an elaboration) of the concept of faction would appear to exclude that application. Bailey uses the metaphor of 'team' (faction is a particular kind of team) in his own elaboration of a model for political analysis, and he distinguishes between a 'core' and a 'following' of a team. He writes: 'The core are those who are tied to the leader through multiplex relationships: the bond with a follower is transactional and single interest' (Bailey, 1969, p. 49). He conceives of the 'core' as 'an inner circle of retainers', whereas those whose ties with the leader are single interest and transactional constitute 'an outer circle of followers'. But with reference to factions Bailey emphasizes two characteristics: 'Firstly, the members (of a faction) do not co-operate because they have a common ideology which their cooperation will serve; secondly, they are recruited by a leader with whom they have a transactional relationship' (ibid., p. 52). The second condition, if accepted, would exclude 'core' from the definition of faction, whereas factions ordinarily are built around a core.

We might distinguish between the faction model as an organizing concept, enabling us to identify actual political alignments in peasant societies for analysis, and theoretical propositions and generalizations about the factional mode of politics in peasant societies. Our interest lies primarily in the former aspect. It allows us to identify actual alignments, whatever they may be, as a necessary preliminary step, so that we may then proceed to the next step of analysis by exploring reasons for observed alignments, identifying structural factors (in the Marxist sense of class alignments derived from the mode of production) which underly them and the immanence of change which inheres in structural contradictions. It provides us with a map of the pattern of social interaction and a statement of our initial problem. It takes us further than generalized statements about the power, say, of landowners as a class, by providing a framework in which we can identify the precise locus and operation of relationships of power and see how the power of individual landowners is articulated into the power of a class. It eschews *a priori* statements about class power or about horizontal solidarity of kinship, or caste or class, as alternative bases of political action. These are put before us in a problematic form, which then constitutes our project for analysis.

Two theoretical propositions which are made about factions call for some comment. One is a suggestion that the factional mode of politics, manifested in vertical cleavages, excludes class solidarity and class conflict, and that the factional mode is specific to certain societies, being inherent in their culture or social structure. One such widely debated view is put forward by Geertz, who uses the Indonesian word *aliran* (stream) to denote factions. He defines the term, however, as 'an ideologically defined political faction . . . a political party surrounded by a set of sodalites (i.e. a cluster of organisations through which factional conflict is manifested at certain levels)' (Geertz, 1965, p. 127). He adds 'An *aliran* is more than a mere political party, and it is more than a mere ideology: it is a set of interconnected social forms which act to group large masses of people into a generalised category' (ibid., p. 128). Geertz's perception of the phenomenon of faction which embraces ideology and political party affiliation is, it should be pointed out, derived from observation of factional politics at a variety of levels of political competition and is not confined to the village level. We have not discussed the manner in which factional cleavages at the village level are reproduced at higher levels, by alliances between rival faction leaders, and are institutionalized into political parties in electoral contest. The essential element in Geertz's exposition is his understanding of that mode of politics as a culturally determined one.

Nicholas emphasizes the constructive and necessary political functions of faction in societies which have been subject to 'disruption' by social change. He writes: 'A factional system is not the political "state of nature" of any of the societies which I have examined. The fact that factions are so often found *in rapidly changed or changing societies* and institutions has no doubt drawn the attention of Siegel and Beals as well as other observers to the disruptive features of factional politics. If we distinguish between the social disruption brought about by social change and *the social order brought about by almost any kind of political system*, our attention will be drawn to the functions' (Nicholas, 1965, p. 57, [italics added]). It is a common fallacy to suggest that a political system 'brings about' order in society. A political system is an aspect and expression of a given social order; the one cannot be conceived without the existence of the other. By the same token Siegel and Beals are no less in error in attributing a disruptive role to factional politics. In making the above statement Nicholas refers specifically to changes in the tribal political organization of some North American Indian communities, originally based on a segmentary lineage system, as a consequence of a breakdown of the lineage structure. But, typically, factional politics are found in peasant societies, such as those of South Asia, which have not been subject to rapid social change. On the other hand, rapid social change, associated with the 'green revolution' in those societies, has tended to replace the factional mode of politics by class conflict.

However, Nicholas takes up a position not very different from that of Geertz, but in rather more qualified terms, and argues: 'There are two factors, found repeatedly in Indian villages, which are conducive to the development of vertical political cleavages.' From an examination of a number of case-studies, he concludes: 'The dominant mode of conflict in Indian villages is between factions' (Nicholas, 1968, pp. 278–9).

A suggestion that a factional mode of politics is necessarily the only mode of politics that may occur in societies which have certain, given, characteristics would imply a static view of social process and social structure. Nicholas does not take quite such a deterministic view. The pivotal question on which the issue must turn is that of defining conditions which produce vertical cleavages and those in which such cleavages yield to new patterns of political conflict characterized by horizontal cleavages, and class solidarity of poor peasants. The Geertz thesis has been discussed by Wertheim (1973), who points out the crucial factor of patron–client relationships in bringing about vertical structuring of alignments, expressed in the form of *alirans*, at the village level. Wertheim's analysis focuses on a class domination of poor peasantry, and conditions in which such a domination is challenged. We find that, in the wake of the 'green revolution' in countries of Asia, such challenges have indeed been manifested in new forms of peasant militancy. The profound economic changes which are currently taking place have had the effect of disrupting patron–client relationships and the vertical alignments of factions dominated by wealthy landowners.

Writing about the effects of the 'green revolution' in India, Sharma points out:

What emerged in the later sixties was both qualitatively and quantitatively different. Unlike the traditional village-based conflicts between factions within the dominant land-owning groups, which involved localised symbols of power and prestige, the new conflicts emerged along class dimensions. . . . So pervasive has been the change in the political climate in India that only the most naive would ignore it. Violent confrontations have become so commonplace that daily newspapers now report them in a most matter-of-fact and perfunctory fashion, often as small items in obscure columns. Yet hardly a week goes by in which some such incident is not reported. (Sharma, 1973)

The issue therefore is not whether politics in peasant societies must run along factional lines of vertical cleavages or horizontal cleavages of class conflict. It is rather that of the conditions in which factional conflict gives way to cleavages of class.

The second theoretical proposition about the factional mode of politics which calls for consideration is the 'principle of diversity of factional recruitment'. That is an attribute of factions, by definition. It takes the form of a theoretical statement, however, when it is emphasized that the critical factor in factional recruitment is only that there should be a tie between leader and follower; but that the nature of the tie is, in itself, inconsequential. This emphasis in exposition derives from Nicholas's attempt to show that factions are not recruited on the basis of a single structural principle. But his proposition about diversity of factional recruitment obscures some of the most critical questions about structural factors underlying factional recruitment by suggesting that followers are recruited at random.

. . . Our framework of analysis, and the issues which it brings to the surface, can best be elaborated by a reference to a model based on politics in villages of the Punjab in Pakistan. The economic structure, and the pattern of alignments within it, are determined primarily by the distribution of ownership of land and the mode of its utilization. Land is a saleable commodity and its ownership is sanctioned by the laws of the state of Pakistan; its laws also affect relationships between landlords and share-croppers. The internal economic structure of the peasant society of the Punjab therefore depends upon its relationship to the larger entity of the state of Pakistan, which legitimizes and enforces the structure.

About 70 per cent of the land is owned by 5 per cent of the rural households owning more than 25 acres each. Much of it is cultivated by share-croppers; some of it is 'self-cultivated', by landlords who own tractors and employ wage labour. The two modes of production are sometimes distinguished as the 'feudal' (or 'semi-feudal, or 'feudalistic') mode of production – there is an evident semantic difficulty in the use of that concept – and the 'capitalist' mode of production. As I have shown elsewhere, in Pakistan such a dichotomy does not accord with the actual picture, because on about 90 per cent of the land affected by farm mechanization, the owners have also retained share-croppers, taking away only a part of their land for mechanized cultivation. They keep the share-croppers because they need them, as a source of seasonal labour. The two 'sectors' of the agrarian economy are not, therefore, separate and autonomous but are closely entwined; the one is not viable without the other. In this case we might speak of a 'multiplex' mode of production, which combines two types of relations of production, namely the 'feudal' and the 'capitalist'. What is common to both the share-croppers and labourers, however, is their exploitation by and economic dependence on the landlord for access to their means of livelihood, which is the aspect of the relations of production that is most relevant in the present context. There are also various categories of 'village servants' such as the barber, carpenter, blacksmith, potter, etc., whose domination by a single master arises only in the few cases where a single family owns a whole village or group of villages. In general, because the 'village servants' work for several employers at the same time, they enjoy a relative autonomy which share-croppers and labourers do not have. They are overshadowed by the power of big landlords of their village but are not in quite the same situation as the other two classes.

These relationships are characterized as 'patron–client' relationships, and it is often alleged that they signify a relationship of *reciprocity* from which each party gains some benefit. Powell, not untypically, describes it as 'a relationship involving an interchange of noncomparable goods and services between actors of unequal socio-economic rank' and he considers the exchange to be reciprocal (Powell, 1970, p. 412). In opposition to that paternalistic value judgement, another value judgement would consider the relationship to be based on the exploitation of the actual cultivator, the share-cropper and labourer, by a parasitical class. The implications of the opposition of the two views are too obvious to call for any elaboration. The issue, however, is not purely one of subjective value judgements. A whole corpus of Marxist literature is concerned with the mystification that underlies such a conception of 'reciprocity'.

Attention might, however, be drawn to the reinforcement of the master–subject relationship in South Asia by ritual ties and a set of 'rights' and 'obligations' known as the *'jajmani'* system. It confers 'rights' on the subject who has a privileged access to certain favours from his masters, and imposes 'obligations' on the latter (cf. Lewis, 1958; Beidelman, 1959). The *jajmani* system legitimates and reinforces the secular ties of the subject to his master by 'sacred', ideological, ties. These ties were of some importance when there was a relative shortage of share-croppers and labourers. But in recent years, they have been progressively eroded against the background of an acute shortage of land available for share-cropping. The ritual 'obligations' are disregarded by landlords and cannot be enforced by their weak clients. In the final analysis the relationship proves to be an unequal one. But the increasing shortage of land has made the dependence of the share-cropper on the landlord for access to land more acute. The ties of economic dependence and political domination are now stronger despite the erosion of the ritual relationships of the *jajmani* system.

In contrast to the domination and dependence which binds share-croppers and labourers to landowners, there are independent peasant proprietors, sometimes referred to as the 'middle peasants' who cultivate their own land. As an 'ideal type' they neither employ labour nor are they themselves employed as labourers or share-croppers by others. In practice, those who own much less than five acres must supplement their income by working for others and those who have much larger holdings tend to employ some labour, probably seasonal and casual labour, to assist with the harvest. We find that the relationships of dependence in the one case and those of autonomy in the other, as determined by relationships in the economic structure, have an important bearing on political alignments, and factors tending to bring about changes in the alignments.

The second differentiated, and institutionalized, structure is that of kinship. The kinship structure in Punjab is based on endogamous patrolineages, known as *biraderis*, which have a genealogical depth of about four or five generations. The kinship system of the Punjab has been analysed elsewhere (Alavi, 1972) and it is only necessary here to underline those aspects of it which reflect on the constitution of corporate groups and political alignments. What is of particular interest in this context are differences between different classes of the peasantry in the degree of kinship solidarity and organization of kin groups.

Biraderi solidarity is strongest in the case of independent peasant proprietors; in their case the rules of endogamy and the rituals of *biraderi* are practised most rigorously and the *biraderis* are constituted into corporate groups, with *biraderi panchayats* (councils) which govern internal affairs of the *biraderis* and represent the *biraderis* as a whole to the outside world, not least in the political arena. On the other hand, *biraderi* organization is the weakest in the case of *biraderis* of share-croppers and labourers; they are subject to the authority of the landlord, even in their private domestic affairs and disputes, and they are unable to establish an authority of their own in opposition to that of the landlord over them. *Biraderi* organization is also rather weak in the case of landlords, who are often in competition with each other for power and status in local political arenas. They do not always have duly constituted *panchayats* to give authoritative decisions binding on them; instead they meet in informal private gatherings to consult with each other either to act in concert or to part in disagreement.

The third structure through which ties are established between members of the peasant community is the 'political structure', primarily the administrative structure of government. Influential landlords set themselves up as political middlemen and mediate between members of the village, individually as well as collectively, and the government. They establish a wide network of links with government officials which enables them to extend their mediating roles. The government, on the other hand, has traditionally relied on influential landlords to establish links with the local-level power structure. Its interest in strengthening the links is no less than that of the landlords. That structure includes links with political parties and urban political movements. Factional alliances above the level of the village are institutionalized as political parties; or the latter induct faction leaders, the local power-holders, to establish their local bases. Revolutionary political parties, on the other hand, seek to change existing alignments and break the domination of the power-holders.

In Punjab villages there is also another element of the 'political structure'; although illegal, it is widely acknowledged as a local 'institution'. That is a kind of 'mafia', operated by rich and powerful landlords who have links, especially, with the police. They set themselves up in business as patrons (*rassagirs*) of local bandits (*goondas*), through whom they terrorize the peasants, particularly by stealing their cattle and abducting women. They offer 'protection' to small peasants in return for political support. For the independent peasant proprietors, the value of *biraderi* solidarity and tightly knit *biraderi* organization lies partly in the fact that such organization provides them a measure of security *vis-à-vis* the power of big landlords; by themselves they are too vulnerable. (That at least suggests that the 'function' of kinship cannot be sought purely in the sphere of 'kinship'.) A fuller account of these modes of 'political mobilization' is given in another article (Alavi, 1971). The inclusion of the system of robbery, terrorization and 'protection' by *rassagirs* and *goondas*, as part of the 'political structure', underscores the fallacy and invalidity of definition of structure by cultural norms and jural rules, for it violates both; it is recognized by the people only as an unpleasant 'fact of life'. It is lawlessness; but, by that token, it is not 'anomie' in the Durkheimian sense. What establishes it as structure is its regular, systematic and predictable mode of operation.

. . . *Biraderis* of independent peasant proprietors generally participate in the political arena as organized corporate groups. Their alliance with particular faction leaders may be based on a variety of factors. It may be a relationship of protector and protégé, the 'protector' being a *rassagir* who terrorizes them into submission. Or the faction leader may gain support by acting as an intermediary between the weak and uninfluential peasants and the bureaucracy. . . . Strong links with the bureaucracy are of great importance to a faction leader.

Biraderis of independent peasant proprietors sometimes unite against landowners. It is not always easy for a peasant, from amongst themselves, to present himself as a leader. *Biraderis* are often brought together by organizers of radical political parties or peasant unions: sometimes by one of their own class whose leadership role is legitimized by his position in a political party or a peasant union. Radical or 'revolutionary' political parties and peasant unions tend to become established with support derived primarily from this class of the peasantry, despite the commitment of the parties or unions, ideologically, to organize the 'poor peasants', namely the share-croppers and labourers. The example of bases of political alignment in Govindapur village, cited by Nicholas, appears to have been such a case. For this class of peasants, it might be said, their horizontal solidarity, as a kin group, is only a first stage in the manifestation of their class solidarity; the second stage is reached when they organize politically into peasant unions or in political parties.

In the case of landowners the problem of class solidarity does not arise in the village-level political arena in which members of their own class appear as rival faction leaders and the interests of their class are not threatened. For them horizontal solidarity of kinship is not an idiom for class solidarity but, rather, a resource to be exploited to consolidate political support. That is particularly evident in cases in which rich landowners have a large number of poor relations. To mobilize sufficient support, landowners enter into alliance with their peers; the alliances are based on 'transactional' ties which are weaker, of course, than the institutionalized ties of kinship. The *biraderi* of the faction leader and their economic dependants constitute the core of the faction – both horizontal as well as vertical ties constitute the core. They 'mobilize' the support of peasant proprietors with whom their ties, although nominally 'transactional', based on equality, are often unequal, based upon political dependence of the protégé on the 'protector' or upon patronage through mediation with government or otherwise.

This picture of the structural conditions which determine political alignments at the village level, dominated by the economic and political power of big landlords, reinforced by their links with the bureaucracy and dominant political parties, calls into question the usual assumptions about the working (and the significance of the results) of representative democracy and the electoral process, in predominantly peasant societies. It also reflects on the problems and the dilemmas of revolutionary political parties seeking mobilization of the poor peasantry through parliamentary political contests, having little to offer to break the power of the landlords over them other than their rhetoric and exhortations to arouse class consciousness. Recent events referred to above show that the class consciousness of the poor peasants, the sharecroppers and labourers, is aroused in certain circumstances and vertical alignments of the factional mode of politics have yielded to the pressures of class conflict. But the conditions in which that arises require consideration and analysis (Alavi, 1965).

Finally, we find that the factional model of politics in peasant societies is not a repudiation of the model of class conflict; the two depict different modes of political alignments, in different conditions. Furthermore, primordial loyalties, such as those of kinship, which precede manifestations of class solidarity, do not rule out the latter; rather they mediate complex political processes through which the latter are crystallized. Moreover, primordial loyalties and structures of kinship do not exist by themselves in 'functional' isolation. They are moulded by class relationships; as we have found, by identifying differences in the manifestation of kinship solidarity or the absence of it in the cases of different strata of the peasantry and among landlords. The complex mediations of the processes by which class solidarity is established and manifested escapes the attention of those Marxists who focus exclusively on dramatic demonstrations of class solidarity of peasants in revolutionary action. On the other hand, the idea of 'functional' separation of structures and analyses of primordial loyalties in themselves, outside the matrix of the class structure, vitiates the results of political sociology and social anthropology.

References

Alavi, Hamza (1965) 'Peasants and revolution', in R. Miliband and J. Saville (eds) *The Socialist Register 1965*, London: Merlin Press.
Alavi, Hamza (1971) 'Politics of dependence: a village in West Punjab', *South Asian Review*, vol. 4, p. 2.
Alavi, Hamza (1972) 'Kinship in West Punjab villages', *Contributions to Indian Sociology*, New Series, no. 6.
Bailey, F. G. (1969) *Stratagems and Spoils*, Oxford: Blackwell.
Beals, A. R. and Siegel, B. J. (1960) 'Pervasive functionalism', *American Anthropologist*, vol. 62.
Beidelman, T. O. (1959) *A Comparative Analysis of the Jajmani System*, Locust Valley, NY: Augustine.
Geertz, Clifford (1965) *The Social History of an Indonesian Town*, Cambridge, Ma.: Harvard University Press.
Lewis, Oscar (1958) *Village Life in Northern India*, Urbana: University of Illinois Press.

Nicholas, Ralph W. (1963) 'Village factions and political parties in rural West Bengal', *Journal of Commonwealth Political Studies*, vol. 2.

Nicholas, Ralph W. (1965) 'Factions – a comparative analysis' in M. Banton (ed.), *Political Systems and the Distribution of Power*, London: Tavistock.

Nicholas, Ralph W. (1966) 'Segmentary factional political systems' in Marc Swartz et al. (eds), *Political Anthropology*, Chicago: Chicago University Press.

Nicholas, Ralph W. (1968) 'Structure of politics in villages of southern Asia', in M. Singer and B. Cohn (eds), *Structure and Change in Indian Society*, New York, Chicago: Aldine Atherton.

Powell, J. D. (1970) 'Peasant society and clientelist politics', *American Political Science Review*, vol. 64, no. 2.

Shanin, Teodor (1972) *The Awkward Class*, London: Oxford University Press.

Wertheim, W. F. (1973) 'From *Aliran* towards class struggle in the country-side of Java', in W. F. Wertheim (ed.), *Dawning of an Asian Dream*, Anthropology–Sociology Centre, University of Amsterdam (mimeo.).

Related Items

5, 6, 8, 18, 19, 23, 24, 27, 28, 29, 30, 31, 35, 37, 38, 40, 41, 42, 61, 62.

44

Peasantry in Political Action

Teodor Shanin

The peasantry has acted politically often enough as a class-like social entity. Importantly, also in the world of industrial societies it has shown an ability for cohesive political action. These were not only belated battles of a pre-capitalist type, for their common interests have driven peasants into political conflicts also with capitalist landowners, various groups of capital-related townsmen and with the modern state.

The widely accepted picture of rapid de-peasantization proved oversimplified. The polarization of the countryside in an industrializing society – into capitalist owners and a rural proletariat – was checked or slowed down by the draining-off of capital and labour into the towns, as well as by the specific features of a peasant family-farm economy. Economic counter-trends have acted in the opposite direction and greatly influenced the final results. Furthermore the significance of specific culture and communities for the establishment of class position proved to be most important. All this made peasant cohesiveness as a potential basis for political class formation stronger than the predictions of the Russian Marxists or of the American strategists would have led us to believe.

On the other hand, inescapable fragmentation of a peasantry into small local segments and the diversity and vagueness of their political aims undermine their potential political impact. Hence, how far a peasantry may be regarded as a class should be seen rather as a question of degree and of the historical period and context. If we posit an imaginary scale or continuum, we could say that the peasantry would appear as a social entity of comparative low 'classness', which rises in crisis situations.

But the peasantry's specific features as a socio-political group are not just to be seen merely on a quantitative scale. Marx's description of the duality in the

Excerpt from Teodor Shanin, 'Peasantry as a political factor', *Sociological Review*, vol. 14, 1966, pp. 12–27.

social character of the peasantry (on the one hand, it is a class; on the other, it is not)[1] leaves the riddle unsolved. In so far as the peasantry is not a class, what is it – granting its qualitative existence?

A class position is basically a social conflict-relationship with other classes and groups. Outside this interrelation, a class ceases to exist. Yet it is indeed true that 'because the farmer's produce is essential and, at the lowest level, sufficient for human existence, the labour of the farmer is necessary for the existence of society; but the existence of society as a whole is not to the same extent necessary for the existence of the farmer' (Galeski, 1963, p. 49). Peasants prove this by withdrawing from the market in crisis situations and indeed, sometimes consciously use this ability as a means of exercising political pressure.

The fundamental duality of the peasants' position in society consists in their being, on the one hand, a social class (one of low 'classness' and, on the whole, dominated by other classes) and, on the other hand, 'a different world' – a highly self-sufficent society 'in itself', bearing the elements of a separate, distinctive and partly enclosed pattern of social relations. This is why peasantry is the social phenomenon in which the Marxist class analysis meets the main conceptual dichotomies of non-Marxist sociological thinking; Maine's brotherhood versus economic competition; de Coulange's familistic versus individualistic; Tönnies's *Gemeinschaft* versus *Gesellschaft* or Durkheim's mechanic (segmentary) versus organic societies. This unique duality (a 'class' and a 'society') leads to conceptual difficulties, yet may well serve as a definition of the peasantry particularity – especially when differentiating this entity from wider, more amorphous groupings such as 'middle groups', 'exploited masses', petty bourgeoisie or 'remnants of feudalism'.

As another way to extend dichotomies of classical sociology, A. L. Kroeber advanced a definition of peasants as those who 'constitute part-societies with part-cultures . . . definitely rural, yet live in relation to market towns . . . [They] lack the isolation, political autonomy and self-sufficiency of a tribal population, yet their local units maintain much of their old identity, integration and attachment to the soil' (Kroeber, 1923, p. 284). Redfield elaborated Kroeber's point and concluded accordingly that 'there is no peasantry before the first city' (Redfield, 1953, p. 31).

This approach, under which the extent of cultural self-sufficiency is used as an index of social development, is valid. However, Redfield's definition of the peasantry seems too narrow and his definition of pre-peasant society too absolute. Groups of settlers in many parts of the world, cut off from towns, far from noblemen and out of reach of the state and its tax collectors, can hardly *ipso facto* be labelled 'non-peasant'. They seem, indeed, to demonstrate peasantry's major characteristic, i.e. its self-sufficiency, its ability to exist outside the thrall of noblemen and town. It was the socio-political significance of these features which gave rise to the characteristic structure of power-relations found in pre-capitalist society – it was the potential for peasant self-sufficiency which made direct and harsh political control a necessity for the rulers.

The Peasantry in Political Action

The political impact of the peasantry has been marked on the whole by its socio-political weaknesses. The segmentation of peasants into families, local communities and clans and the differentiation of interest within the communities had made for difficulties in the crystallizing of nationwide aims and symbols and developing national leadership and organizations (this made in turn for what we have called low 'classness'). Technological backwardness, especially in the fields of communications, weaponry and tactical expertise, has brought to naught many attempts at political action. Peasantry has had its socio-political points of strength, however, especially its being the main food-producer, being dispersed in rural areas and being numerically preponderant. Monopoly of food production often proved of crucial importance in times of crises and provided for an extra measure of autonomy in confrontations. The vastness of the countryside served as a stronghold. Numerical strength could tip the balance. Yet in the long run it was rather the basic weaknesses of the peasantry which tended to stand out. The peasantry proved no match for smaller, closely knit, better organized and technically superior groups, and has, time and time again, been double-crossed or suppressed politically or by force of arms.

The spread of industrialization and mass culture gives peasantry some new possibilities of communication and cultural and political cohesion. Yet, at the same time, it lowers the importance of the countryside in terms of national production, curbs the impact of its 'food-monopoly' by developing international trade, stimulates village-level polarization and improves the government forces' relative advantage in terms of organization, mobility, weaponry and new forms of repressive power. Once again, the course of historical development seems to weaken the peasants' political power and potential. Granting this, peasantry cannot be ignored and its actions dismissed. For it is not only victors and rulers who determine political reality.

The peasants' chances of influencing the political sphere increase sharply in times of national crises. When non-peasant social forces clash, when rulers are divided or foreign powers attack, the peasantry's attitude and action may well prove decisive. Whether this potential is realized is mainly dependent upon the peasants' ability to act in unison, with or without formal organization. This, in turn, is dependent upon the cohesion of the peasantry, its economic, social and cultural homogeneity and the reflection of these in the ideological sphere.

A satisfactory broad comparison of peasantry's political and armed action in pre-industrial societies with that in contemporary ones is still to be made. In a modern society the particular patterns of peasant political action are determined by peasantry's character as a social entity. We may discern three main types:

1 *Autonomous class action*. In the sense suggested by Marxist theory as defined in Marx's own lifetime. In this type of action, a social class crystallizes in the course of conflict, creates its own nationwide organization, works out its ideology, aims and symbols, and produces leaders, mostly from within its own ranks. For today's peasantries, this pattern of political action is the least frequent. Some of the 'Green International' parties in Eastern Europe of 1920s, the peasant unions in Russia in 1905 and China of 1926, the Zapata movement in Mexico and their counterparts in the rest of the world need to be studied comparatively to understand the mechanics of this type of peasant action and its relatively limited occurrence.[2]

2 *Guided political action*, in which the social group concerned is moved by an external power-elite which unites it. This pattern of action is especially important when peasantry is concerned. The cyclical stability of the farm and the village and the political implications of this are generally overcome only by a severe crisis, met by an exogenous factor of sweeping political and emotional power. Such an external organizer of the peasantry may be found in millenial movements, secret societies, Russian cossacks, French Bonapartism or Mao's people's army, which provided the peasantry with the missing element of unity on a wider inter-village and inter-regional scale. The common element found in all these very different movements is the existence of a closely knit group of activists, with its own impetus, specific organizational structure, aims and leadership – a group for which the peasantry is an object of leadership or manipulation. The peasantry, in this case, may be 'used' (i.e. deliberately tricked into some action alien to its own interests) or 'led to achieve its own aims': but the very definition of 'aims' is in the hands of qualitatively distinct leaders. The peasants' interests and attitudes are only one of the factors taken into account. Marx expressed such a situation when referring to the French peasantry in the mid-nineteenth century to say 'they are ... incapable of enforcing their class interest in their own name, whether through a parliament or through a convention. They cannot represent themselves, they must be represented. Their representative must at the same time appear as their master ...' (cf. Marx and Engels, 1950, vol. 1, p. 303). The only thing to be objected to in this statement is its absoluteness, which was refuted by later events.

The low 'classness' of the peasantry makes the study of peasant movements especially illuminating for the sociological analysis of the external elites which lead them. The peasantry's limited influence on such leaders makes the elite group's dynamics appear in a 'purer' form. Moreover, it also helps us look at the problem of class-like masses (i.e. of social groups such as Russian soldiers in 1917–18 which act temporarily as class entities but do not bear all the features of a class) and at their place in political processes.

3 *Amorphous political action*. This pattern seems to be highly typical of peasants' impact on politics, and may take two forms:

(a) Local riots which 'suddenly' emerge as short outbursts of accumulated frustration and rebellious feeling. On the whole easily repressed by the central authorities, these riots may act as a check on the state policy and stimulate its change. When related to crisis in other spheres riots may develop into nationwide movements capable of a determining effect on major political development.

(b) Peasant passivity. The conceptual grasp of passivity as a factor of dynamics poses some complex questions. Yet the spontaneous restriction of production by the Russian peasantry in 1920 proved strong enough to frustrate the will of a government victorious in a war against numerous and powerful enemies. Government decrees and orders the world over have been voided of effect by their spontaneous, stubborn and silent non-fulfilment by peasantry. As suggested by R. E. F. Smith, passive resistance is actually a specifically peasant contribution to politics elaborated and sophisticated by Tolstoy and Gandhi. The relationship between basic social features of peasant society as discussed and passive resistance seems evident. It served dissent but, on the other hand, the influence of the conservative peasant 'apathy' has often proved decisive for the securing of the victory of the Establishment over the revolutionaries. Once again, this must be understood in relation to the peasant social structure, consciousness and experience.

The Peasantry in Armed Action

Armed action had a place of special importance in the political life of societies which include numerous peasants. Clausewitz's remark that 'war is an extension of politics by other means' holds true not only for the relations between states. As to this form of peasant political action, its particularities were expressed in army service, the guerrilla and in 'morale':

1 The modern conscript army is one of the few nationwide organizations in which the peasantry actively participates. The segmentation of the peasantry is thereby broken. The cultural intercourse involved, even when there is no indoctrination, teaches the peasant-soldier to think in national and not only village-limited terms. He is taught organization, complex cooperative action, co-ordination, modern techniques and military skills. The army provides him also with a hierarchial institution in which he may rise as a leader and receive the training necessary for it. This increase in the peasant's potential ability to act politically would, while in the army, be largely curbed by rigid discipline and by the controls exercised by the non-peasant officer corps. Yet, in a time of crisis, this power of authority and repression may decline and the actual

preferences and attitudes, reflected in the action or the refusal to act by a peasant army, may well become decisive. Moreover, the experience gained in army service acts as an important influence in the villages. The ex-serviceman may become a leader and a channel through which outside influences reach other villagers. In attempting to organize politically, peasants frequently refer back to their army experience. The Russian *Tamanskaya armiya* and 'Green Army of the Black Sea', the FLN, the Chinese 'People's Militia', the Zapata and Villa armies in Mexico served not only as the military organizations but also as the main political organizations – a political party in arms.[3]

The army may bear therefore the marks of both the first and second type of political action described, i.e. of peasantry as 'a class for itself' and as a 'guided' socio-political entity.

2   During the last decade, successful guerrilla warfare moved it into the centre of public attention. American strategists tend to approach guerrilla warfare as a military technique or tactic, to be taught by smart sergeants along with drill and target practice. Their failure in both guerrilla and anti-guerrilla warfare in Vietnam is the best comment on this view.

The social essence of guerrilla warfare is that it offers the most suitable form for armed peasant action. The record of it seems to be as old as the peasantry itself. Innumerable rebels, brigands and outlaws appear in the myth, the folk-memory of every people, as well as in its real history. The ability of the guerrilla 'army' to dissolve in times of need into the sympathetic peasant mass or to vanish into the expanses of the countryside, its ability to utilize various degrees of peasant militancy and friendly passivity, its capacity to survive without outside supplies and the adequacy for this type of warfare of relatively primitive weapons may make a guerrilla force unbeatable by modern military methods.

Yet the essentially peasant character of guerrilla warfare explains not only its strength but also its weaknesses – the segmentation, the lack of crystallized ideology and aims, the lack of stable membership. These essential weaknesses may be overcome by the injection of a hard core of professional rebels, turning the revolt into 'guided political action'. The professional rebels' nationwide ideological and organizational cohesion, their stability and zeal and their ability to work out a long-term strategy may transform peasant revolt into successful revolution. But the key to the understanding of successful guerrilla warfare has to be sought not in the marvels of the rebels' organization, but in their relationship with the peasantry; not in the military techniques of the few, but in the sociology of the masses.

3   Last, there are the subjective determinants of military action generally labelled 'morale' whose resistance to quantification does not negate their importance. Peasant revolts all over the world display common cultural features which seem to have been better caught in the synthetic expressions of the arts than when dissected by the analytical tools of the social sciences. The picturesque image of the young peasant rebel challenges the mundane nature

of everyday peasant life. The childish display of exhibitionism, described by Znaniecki, as typical of the peasant's attempts to establish his own personality when breaking out of rigid family ties (Thomas and Znaniecki, 1918, p. 103), explains much of the spirit of peasant fighters. The leader-hero, the legends which surround him, his 'personal charisma' – to a large extent may take the place of ideology and organization as unifying factors. All these features influence the general character of peasant units as a fighting force, especially so in conditions of a civil war.

The mainstream of contemporary sociology has by-passed peasantry.[4] Rural sociology has been localized in and financed by rich industrial societies and has consequently been centred upon the problem of how to promote members of farming minorities into fully productive and prosperous members of 'civilized society'. Few sociologists have so far elevated the peasantry from the footnote to the page. Yet, were historical and social significance the criteria for the choice of the objects of study, we should be flooded by publications on the peasantry. Innumerable problems of our world's political and economic development leads us to this subject and the understanding and misunderstanding of it by policy makers. To take but one example, the history of the Soviet Union has time and time again (in 1918, 1920, 1927–9, etc. – up to the 1960s) been largely shaped by unexpected rural responses to the ruling party's policies, based on such evaluation and prediction. Countless other examples could be cited from Africa, Asia, Latin America, etc.

Only a cross-disciplinary effort of both conceptual and factual studies may overcome the astonishing shortcomings in our knowledge of the peasantry. The methodological difficulties involved are grave but this is a reason to double the effort, not to retreat to a familiar path and to concepts of society which turn majorities of its population into a footnote.

Notes

1 Marx and Engels (1950, vol. 1, p. 303): 'In so far as millions of families live under economic conditions of existence that separate their mode of life, their interests and their culture from those of other classes, and put them in hostile opposition to the latter, they form a class. In so far as there is merely a local interconnexion among these small-holding peasants, and the identity of their interests begets no community, no national bond and no political organization among them, they do not form a class.'
2 For an important insight into the influence of the stratification of the peasantry on political action, see Alavi (1965) and Wolf (1969).
3 One such force is described by Marx in the *Communist Manifesto* when speaking of the early stage of bourgeois class organization as 'an armed and self-governing association in the medieval commune' (Marx and Engels, 1950, vol. 1, p. 34).
4 Written in 1965 at the very onset of the 1960s/70s wave of peasant studies (for discussion of which seem item 62).

References

Alavi, H. (1965) 'Peasantry and revolution', *The Socialist Register 1965*, Merlin Press.
Hobsbawm, E. (1965) 'Vietnam and the dynamics of guerrilla warfare', *New Left Review*, vol. 17.
Kroeber, A. (1923) *Anthropology*, Harrap.
Marx, K. and Engels, F. (1960), *Selected Works*, Lawrence & Wishart.
Redfield, R. (1953) *The Primitive World and its Transformation*, Cornell University Press.
Thomas, W. I. and Znaniecki, F. (1918) *The Polish Peasant in Europe and America*, Dover Publications, 1958.
Wolf, E. R. (1965) *Peasant Wars of the Twentieth Century*, Harper and Row.

Related Items

8, 9, 21, 25, 26, 28, 29, 30, 35, 37, 38, 39, 40, 41, 42, 43, 45, 46, 47, 61, 62.

45

Revolutions of the Oppressed: A Case Made

Barrington Moore, Jr

Because peasant discontent has frequently expressed itself in reactionary forms, Marxist thinkers often regard peasant radicalism with a mixture of contempt and suspicion or, at best, with patronizing condesension. To smile at this blindness, to point out that Marxist successes have come out of peasant revolutions, have almost become favourite anti-Marxist pastimes, so much so as to conceal more significant issues. As one reviews the spread of modern revolution from its starting points in the German *Bauernkrieg* and the Puritan Revolution in England, through its successful and abortive phases as it travels westward to the United States and eastward through France, Germany, Russia, and China, two points stand out. First, the utopian radical conceptions of one phase become the accepted institutions and philosophical platitudes of the next. Secondly, the chief social basis of radicalism has been the peasants and the smaller artisans in the towns. From these facts one may conclude that the wellsprings of human freedom lie not only where Marx saw them, in the aspirations of classes about to take power, but perhaps even more in the dying wail of a class over whom the wave of progress is about to roll. Industrialism, as it continues to spread, may in some distant future still these voices forever and make revolutionary radicalism as anachronistic as cuneiform writing.

For a Western scholar to say a good word on behalf of revolutionary radicalism is not easy because it runs counter to deeply grooved mental reflexes. The assumption that gradual and piecemeal reform has demonstrated its superiority over violent revolution as a way to advance human freedom is so pervasive that even to question such an assumption seems strange. . . . I should like to draw attention . . . to what the evidence from the comparative history of modernization may tell us about this issue. As I have reluctantly come to read this evidence, the costs of moderation have been at least as atrocious as those of revolution, perhaps a great deal more.

Excerpt from Barrington Moore, Jr, *Social Origins of Dictatorship and Democracy*, Penguin, 1967, pp. 504–6.

Fairness demands recognition of the fact that the way nearly all history has been written imposes an overwhelming bias against revolutionary violence. Indeed the bias becomes horrifying as one comes to realize its depth. To equate the violence of those who resist oppression with the violence of the oppressors would be misleading enough. But there is a great deal more. From the days of Spartacus through Robespierre down to the present day, the use of force by the oppressed against their former masters has been the object of nearly universal condemnation. Meanwhile the day-to-day repression of 'normal' society hovers dimly in the background of most history books. Even those radical historians who emphasize the injustices of pre-revolutionary epochs generally concentrate on a short time span preceding the immediate outbreak. In that way, too, they may unwittingly distort the record.

That is one argument against the comforting myth of gradualism. There is an even more important one, the costs of going without a revolution.

Related Items

35, 37, 38, 39, 40, 41, 42, 44, 46, 47, 61.

46

On Peasant Rebellions

Eric R. Wolf

Six major and social political upheavals, fought with peasant support, have shaken the world of the twentieth century: the Mexican revolution of 1910, the Russian revolutions of 1905 and 1917, the Chinese revolution which metamorphosed through various phases from 1921 on, the Vietnamese revolution which had its roots in the Second World War, the Algerian rebellion of 1954 and the Cuban revolution of 1958. All of these were to some extent based on the participation of rural populations. It is to the analysis of this participation that the present paper directs its attention.

Romantics to the contrary, it is not easy for a peasantry to engage in sustained rebellion. Peasants are especially handicapped in passing from passive recognition of wrongs to political participation as a means for setting them right. First, a peasant's work is more often done alone, on his own land, than in conjunction with his fellows. Moreover, all peasants are to some extent competitors, for available resources within the community and for sources of credit from without. Second, the tyranny of work weighs heavily upon peasants: their life is geared to an annual routine and to planning for the year to come. Momentary alterations of routine threaten their ability to take up the routine later. Third, control of land enables them, more often than not, to retreat into subsistence production should adverse conditions affect their market crop. Fourth, ties of extended kinship and mutual aid within the community may cushion the shocks of dislocation. Fifth, peasants' interests – especially among poor peasants – often cross-cut class alignments. Rich and poor peasant may be kinfolk, or a peasant may be at one and the same time owner, renter, sharecropper, labourer for his neighbours and seasonal hand on a nearby plantation. Each different involvement aligns him differently with his fellows and with the outside world. Finally, past exclusion of the peasant from participation in decision making beyond the bamboo hedge of his village deprives him all too

Eric R. Wolf, 'On peasant rebellions', *International Social Science Journal*, vol. 21, 1969.

often of the knowledge needed to articulate his interests with appropriate forms of action. Hence peasants are often merely passive spectators of political struggles or long for the sudden advent of a millennium, without specifying for themselves and their neighbours the many rungs on the staircase to heaven.

If it is true that peasants are slow to rise, then peasant participation in the great rebellions of the twentieth century must obey some special factors which exacerbated the peasant condition. We will not understand that condition unless we keep in mind constantly that it has suffered greatly under the impact of three crises: the demographic crisis, the ecological crisis and the crisis in power and authority. The demographic crisis is most easily depicted in bare figures, though its root causes remain ill-understood. It may well be that its ultimate cause lies less in the reduction of mortality through spreading medical care, than in the world-wide diffusion of American food crops throughout the world which provided an existential minimum for numerous agricultural populations. Yet the bare numbers suffice to indicate the seriousness of the demographic problem. Mexico had a population of 5.8 million at the beginning of the nineteenth century; in 1910 – at the outbreak of the revolution – it had 16.5 million. European Russia had a population of 20 million in 1725; at the turn of the twentieth century it had 87 million. China numbered 265 million in 1775, 430 million in 1850, and close to 600 million at the time of the revolution. Vietnam is estimated to have sustained a population between 6 and 14 million in 1820; it had 30.5 million inhabitants in 1962. Algeria had an indigenous population of 10.5 million in 1963, representing a fourfold increase since the beginning of French occupation in the first part of the nineteenth century. Cuba had 550,000 inhabitants in 1800; by 1953 she had 5.8 million. Population increases alone and by themselves would have placed a serious strain on inherited cultural arrangements.

The ecological crisis is in part related to the sheer increase in numbers; yet it is also in an important measure independent of it. Population increases of the magnitude just mentioned coincided with a period in history in which land and other resources were increasingly converted into commodities – in the capitalist sense of that word. As commodities they were subjected to the demands of a market which bore only a very indirect relation to the needs of the rural populations subjected to it. Where, in the past, market behaviour had been largely subsidiary to the existential problems of subsistence, now existence and its problems became subsidiary to the market. The alienation of peasant resources proceeded directly through outright seizure or through coercive purchase, as in Mexico, Algeria and Cuba; or it took the form – especially in China and Vietnam – of stepped-up capitalization of rent which resulted in the transfer of resources from those unable to keep up to those able to pay. In addition, capitalist mobilization of resources was reinforced through the pressure of taxation, of demands for redemption payments, and through the increased needs for industrially produced commodities on the part of the peasantry itself. All together, however, these various pressures disrupted the precarious ecological balance of peasant society. Where the peasant had required a certain combination of resources to effect an adequate living, the separate and differential mobilization of these resources broke that ecological nexus. This is perhaps best seen in Russia, where successive land reforms threatened continued peasant access to pasture, forest and ploughland. Yet it is equally evident in cases where commercialization threatened peasant access to communal lands (Mexico, Algeria, Vietnam), to unclaimed land (Mexico, Cuba), to public granaries (Algeria, China), or where it threatened the balance between pastoral and settled populations (Algeria). At the same time as commercialization disrupted rural life, moreover, it also created new and unsettled ecological niches in industry. Disruptive change in the rural area went hand in hand with the opening up of incipient but uncertain opportunities for numerous ex-industrial peasants. Many of these retained formal ties with their home villages (Russia, China, Algeria); others migrated between country and industry in continuous turnover (especially Vietnam). Increased instability in the rural area was thus accompanied by a still unstable commitment to industrial work.

Finally, both the demographic and the ecological crisis converged in the crisis of authority. The development of the market produced a rapid circulation of the elite, in which the manipulators of the new 'freefloating resources' – labour bosses, merchants, industrial entrepreneurs – challenged the inherited power of the controllers of fixed social resources, the tribal chief, the mandarin, the landed nobleman (see Eisenstadt, 1966). Undisputed and stable claims thus yielded to unstable and disputed claims. This rivalry between primarily political and primarily economic power-holders contained its own dialectic. The imposition of the market mechanism entailed a diminution of social responsibilities for the affected population: the economic entrepreneur did not concern himself with the social cost of his activities; the traditional power-holder was often too limited in his power to offer assistance or subject to cooptation by his successful rivals. The advent of the market thus not merely produced a crisis in peasant ecology; it deranged the numerous middle-level ties between centre and hinterland, between the urban and the rural sectors. Commercialization disrupted the hinterland; at the very same time it also lessened the ability of power-holders to perceive and predict changes in the rural area. The result was an ever-widening gap between the rulers and the ruled. That such a course is not inevitable is perhaps demonstrated by Barrington Moore (1966) who showed how traditional feudal forms were utilized in both Germany and Japan to prevent the formation of such a gap in power and communication during the crucial period of transition to a commercial and industrial order. Where this was not accomplished – precisely where an administrative militarized feudalism was absent – the continued widening of the power gap invited the formation of a counter-elite which could challenge both a disruptive leadership based on the operation of the market and the impotent heirs of traditional power, while forging a new consensus through communication with the peasantry. Such a counter-elite is most frequently made up of members of provincial elites, relegated to the margins of commercial mobilization and political office; of officials or professionals who stand mid-way between the rural area and the centre and are caught in the contradictions between the two; and of intellectuals who have access to a system of symbols which can guide the interaction between leadership and rural area.

Sustained mobilization of the peasantry is, however, no easy task. Such an effort will not find its allies in a rural mass which is completely subject to the imperious demands of necessity. Peasants cannot rebel successfully in a situation of complete impotence; the powerless are easy victims. Therefore only a peasantry in possession of some tactical control over its own resources can provide a secure basis for on-going political leverage. Power, as Richard Adams has said (1966, pp. 3–4), refers ultimately

to an actual physical control that one party may have with respect to another. The reason that most relationships are not reduced to physical struggles is that parties to them can make rational decisions based on their estimates of tactical power and other factors. Power is usually exercised, therefore, through the common recognition by two parties of the tactical control each has, and through rational decision by one to do what the other wants. Each estimates his own tactical control, compares it to the other, and decides he may or may not be superior.

The poor peasant or the landless labourer who depends on a landlord for the largest part of his livelihood, or the totality of it, has no tactical power: he is completely within the power domain of his employer, without sufficient resources of his own to serve him as resources in the power struggle. Poor peasants, and landless labourers, therefore, are unlikely to pursue the course of rebellion, *unless* they are able to rely on some external power to challenge the power which constrains them. Such external power is represented in the Mexican case by the action of the Constitutionalist army in Yucatan which liberated the peons from debt bondage 'from above'; by the collapse of the Russian army in 1917 and the reflux of the peasant soldiery, arms in hand, into the villages; by the creation of the Chinese Red Army as an instrument designed to break up landlord power in the villages. Where such external power is present the poor and landless labourer have latitude of movement; where it is absent, they are under near-complete constraint. The rich peasant, in turn, is unlikely to embark on the course of rebellion. As employer of the labour of others, as money-lender, as notable coopted by the state machine, he exercises local power in alliance with external power-holders. His power domain with the village is derivative; it depends on the maintenance of their domains outside the village. Only when an external force, such as the Chinese Red Army, proves capable of destroying these other superior power domains will the rich peasant lend his support to an uprising.

There are only two components of the peasantry which possess sufficient internal leverage to enter into sustained rebellion. These are (a) a land-owning 'middle peasantry' or (b) a peasantry located in a peripheral area outside the domains of landlord control. Middle peasantry refers to a peasant population which has secure access to land of its own and cultivates it with family labour. Where these middle peasants holdings lie within the power domain of a superior, possession of their own resources provides their holders with the minimal tactical freedom required to challenge their overlord. The same, however, holds for a peasantry, poor or 'middle', whose settlements are only under marginal control from the outside. Here land holdings may be insufficient for the support of the peasant household; but subsidiary activities such as casual labour, smuggling, livestock raising – not under the direct constraint of an external power domain – supplement land in sufficient quantity to grant the peasantry some latitude of movement. We mark the existence of such a tactically mobile peasantry in the villages of Morelos in Mexico; in the communes of the central agricultural regions of Russia; in the northern bastion established by the Chinese Communists after the Long March; as a basis for rebellion in Vietnam; among the *fellahin* of Algeria; and among the squatters of Oriente province in Cuba.

Yet this recruitment of a 'tactically mobile peasantry' among the middle peasants and the 'free' peasants of peripheral areas poses a curious paradox. This is also the peasantry in whom anthropologists and rural sociologists have tended to see the main bearers of peasant tradition. If our account is correct, then – strange to say – it is precisely this culturally conservative stratum which is the most instrumental in dynamiting the peasant social order. This paradox dissolves, however, when we consider that it is also the middle peasant who is relatively the most vulnerable to economic changes wrought by commercialism, while his social relations remain encased within the traditional design. His is a balancing act in which his balance is continuously threatened by population growth; by the encroachment of rival landlords; by the loss of rights to grazing, forest and water: by falling prices and unfavourable conditions of the market; by interest payments and foreclosures. Moreover, it is precisely this stratum which most depends on traditional social relations of kin and mutual aid between neighbours; middle peasants suffer most when these are abrogated, just as they are least able to withstand the depredations of tax collectors or landlords.

Finally – and this is again paradoxical – middle peasants are also the most exposed to influences from the developing proletariat. The poor peasant or landless labourer, in going to the city or the factory, also usually cuts his tie with the land. The middle peasant, however, stays on the land and sends his children to work in the town; he is caught in a situation in which one part of the family retains a footing in agriculture, while the other undergoes 'the training of the cities' (Tillion, 1961, pp. 120–1). This makes the middle peasant a transmitter also of urban unrest and political ideas. The point bears elaboration. It is probably not so much the growth of an industrial proletariat as such which produces revolutionary activity, as the development of an industrial workforce still closely geared to life in the villages.

Thus it is the very attempt of the middle and free peasant to remain traditional which makes him revolutionary.

If we now follow out the hypothesis that is middle peasants and poor but 'free' peasants, not constrained by any power domain, which constitute the pivotal groupings for peasant uprisings, then it follows that any factor which serves to increase the latitude granted by that tactical mobility reinforces their revolutionary potential. One of these factors is peripheral location with regard to the centre of state control. In fact, frontier areas quite often show a tendency to rebel against the central authorities, regardless of whether they are inhabited by peasants or not. South China has constituted a hearth of rebellion within the Chinese state, partly because it was first a frontier area in the southward march of the Han people, and later because it provided the main zone of contact between Western and Chinese civilization. The Mexican north has similarly been a zone of dissidence from the centre in Mexico City, partly because its economy was based on mining and cattle raising rather than maize agriculture, partly because it was open to influences from the United States to the north. In the Chinese south it was dissident gentry with a peasant following which frequently made trouble for the centre; in the Mexican north it was provincial businessmen, ranchers and cowboys. Yet where you have a poor peasantry located in such a peripheral area beyond the normal control of the central power, the tactical mobility of such a peasantry is 'doubled' by its location. This has been the case with Morelos, in Mexico; Nghe An province in Vietnam; Kabylia in Algeria; and Oriente in Cuba. The tactical effectiveness of such areas is 'tripled' if they contain also defensible mountainous redoubts: this has been true of Morelos, Kabylia and Oriente. The effect is 'quadrupled' where the population of these redoubts differs ethnically or linguistically from the surrounding population. Thus we find that the villagers of Morelos were Nahuatl-speakers, the inhabitants of Kabylia Berber-speakers. Oriente province showed no linguistic differences from the Spanish spoken in Cuba, but it did contain a significant Afro-Cuban element. Ethnic distinctions enhance the solidarity of the rebels; possession of a special linguistic code provides for an autonomous system of communication.

It is important, however, to recognize that separation from the state or the surrounding populace need not only be physical or cultural. The Russian and the Mexican cases both demonstrate that it is possible to develop a solid enclave population of peasantry through state reliance on a combination of communal autonomy with the provision of community services to the state. The organization of the peasantry into self-administering communes with stipulated responsibilities to state and landlords created in both cases veritable fortresses of peasant tradition within the body of the country itself. Held fast by the surrounding structure, they acted as sizzling pressure-cookers of unrest which, at the moment of explosion, vented their force outward to secure more living-space for their customary corporate way of life. Thus we can add a further multiplier effect to the others just cited. The presence of any one of these will raise the peasant potential for rebellion.

But what of the transition from peasant rebellion to revolution, from a movement aimed at the redress of wrongs to the attempted overthrow of society itself? Marxists in general have long argued that peasants without outside leadership cannot make a revolution; and our case material would bear them out. Where the peasantry had successfully rebelled against the established order – under its own banner and with its own leaders – it was sometimes able to reshape the social structure of the countryside closer to its heart's desires; but it did not lay hold of the state, of the cities which house the centres of control, of the strategic non-agricultural resources of society. Zapata stayed in his Morelos; the 'folk migration' of Pancho Villa simply receded after the defeat at Torreon; the Ukranian rebel Nestor Makhno stopped short of the cities; and the Russian peasants of the central agricultural region simply burrowed more deeply into their local communes. Thus a peasant rebellion which takes place in a complex society already caught up in commercialization and industrialization tends to be self-limiting and, hence, anachronistic.

The peasant Utopia is the free village, untrammelled by tax collectors, labour recruiters, large landowners, officials. Ruled over, but never ruling, they also lack any acquaintance with the operation of the state as a complex machinery, experiencing it only as a 'cold monster'. Against this hostile force, they had learned, even their traditional power-holders provided but a weak shield, even though they were on occasion willing to defend them if it proved to their own interest. Thus, for peasants, the state is a negative quantity, an evil, to be replaced in short shrift by their own 'home-made' social order. That order, they believe, can run without the state; hence peasants in rebellion are natural anarchists.

Often this political perspective is reinforced still further by a wider ideological vision. The peasants' experience tends to be dualistic, in that he is caught between his understanding of how the world ought to be properly ordered and the realities of a mundane existence, beset by disorder. Against this disorder, the peasant has always set his dreams of deliverance, the vision of a *mahdi* who would deliver the world from tyranny, of a Son of Heaven who would truly embody the mandate of Heaven, of a 'white' Tsar as against the 'black' Tsar of the disordered present (Sarkisyanz, 1955). Under conditions of modern dislocation, the disordered present is all too frequently experienced as world order reversed, and hence evil. The dualism of the past easily fuses with the dualism of the present. The true order is yet to come, whether through miraculous intervention, through rebellion, or both. Peasant anarchism and an apocalyptic vision of the world, together, provide the ideological fuel that drives the rebellious peasantry.

The peasant rebellions of the twentieth century are no longer simple responses to local problems, if indeed they ever were. They are but the parochial reactions to major social dislocations, set in motion by overwhelming societal change. The spread of the market has torn men up by their roots, and shaken them loose from the social relationships into which they were born. Industrialization and expanded communication have given rise to new social clusters, as yet unsure of their own social positions and interests, but forced by the very imbalance of their lives to seek a new adjustment. Traditional political authority has eroded or collapsed; new contenders for power are seeking new constituencies for entry into the vacant political arena. Thus when the peasant protagonist lights the torch of rebellion, the edifice of society is already smouldering and ready to take fire. When the battle is over, the structure will not be the same.

No cultural system – no complex of economy, society, polity and ideology – is ever static; all of its component parts are in constant change. Yet as long as these changes remain within tolerable limits, the overall system persists. If they begin to exceed these limits, however, or if other components are suddenly introduced from outside, the system will be thrown out of kilter. The parts of the system are rendered inconsistent with each other; the system grows incoherent. Men in such a situation are caught painfully between various old solutions to problems which have suddenly shifted shape and meaning and new solutions to problems they often cannot comprehend. Since incoherence rarely appears all at once, in all parts of the system, they may for some time follow now one alternative, now another and contradictory one; but in the end a breach, a major disjuncture will make its appearance somewhere in the system (Wilson and Wilson, 1945, pp. 125–9). A peasant uprising in such circumstances, for any of the reasons we have sketched, can – without conscious intent – bring the entire society to a state of collapse.

References

Adams, R. N. (1966) 'Power and power domains', *América Latina*, year 9, pp. 3–21.
Eisenstadt, S. N. (1966) *Modernization: Protest and Change*, Prentice Hall.
Moore, B., Jr (1966) *Social Origins of Dictatorship and Democracy*, Beacon Press; Penguin, 1969.
Sarkisyanz, E. (1955) *Russland und der Messianismus des Orients: Sendungsbewusstsein und politischer Chiliasmus des Ostens*, J. C. B. Mohr, Tübingen.
Tillion, G. (1961) *France and Algeria: Complementary Enemies*, Knopf.
Wilson, G. and Wilson, M. (1945) *The Analysis of Social Change*, Cambridge University Press.

Related Items

47

Zapata!

John Womack

. . . This was a feat neither political ambition nor military ferocity could accomplish. The machinery to dragoon local followers did not exist. If a village resented a self-appointed chief, it simply kept its men home. The contest for revolutionary command in Morelos was therefore not a fight. It was a process of recognition by various neighbourhood chiefs that there was only one man in the state they all respected enough to cooperate with, and that they had a duty to bring their followers under his authority. The one man turned out to be Zapata, who was a singularly qualified candidate – both a share-cropping dirt farmer whom villagers would trust and a mule-driving horsedealer whom cowboys, peons and bandits would look up to; both a responsible citizen and a determined warrior. But his elevation to leadership was not automatic, and never definitive. As he himself later wrote to Alfredo Robles Domínguez, he had to be very careful with his men: for they followed him, he said, not because they were ordered to but because they felt *cariño* for him – that is, they liked him, admired him, held him in high but tender regard, were devoted to him. It was because he was the kind of man who could arouse other eminently pragmatic men in this way that neither Tepepa, nor Merino, nor anyone else who cared about the movement ever tried to rival him. If he never bossed them, they never crossed him.

. . . Dispossessed and destitute families had indeed inhabited the place for centuries; now, psychologically, they arrived. What they conquered, cleared, levelled, and settled was not a territory, which they only recovered, but a society, which they thus recreated. Like other immigrants and pioneers, they proceeded fitfully – sometimes by the compulsion of immediate needs, sometimes by dreams they would not surrender. But in this social wilderness they moved in a remarkably constant direction toward the establishment of democratic municipalities, country neighbourhoods where every family had influence in the disposition of local resources.

Excerpts from John Womack, *Zapata and the Mexican Revolution*, Knopf, 1968, pp. 79, 224–8.

In central and southern Mexico the utopia of a free association of rural clans was very ancient. In various forms it had moved villagers long before the Spaniards came. Its latest vehicle was the Zapatista army: ironically, Morelo's country families had clarified their civilian notions in military service. The Liberating Army of the Centre and South was a 'people's army'. And to the men who fought in its ranks, and to the women who accompanied them as private quartermistresses, being 'people' counted more than being an 'army'. For leadership they still looked more readily to their village chiefs than to their revolutionary army officers. . . . Having supported and composed the revolutionary army, these country folk reasoned that they should be the beneficiaries of its success. More important, they had also learned in the war that military leaders ought to respect them, and that if they did not, others should appear who would. Village authorities all over the state espoused this new toughness, and it constituted the firmest inhibition against neighbourhood dictators.

Zapata and most of his chiefs shared these popular expectations about civilian rule. They also had not lost their sense of who they were – the sons of the pueblo, field hands, share-croppers, and rancheros. The original authority had been in local councils. And the pretentions they developed were honest, country pretensions. No native Morelos revolutionary dressed in khaki, the current national fashion for aspiring politicos. When a Morelos chief wanted to look elegant, as Zapata did at Xochimilco, he dressed as for a fair at the district market, in rings and gaudy colours and flashy silver buttons.

. . .The result was the real possibility of local democracies. Although the chiefs retained extraordinary power, passing it down to a trustee when they left on campaign, their control was never institutional nor so restrictive as the Porfirian bosses'. And although Zapata's personal provision of guarantees was irregular, because access to him was irregular, he was nevertheless a respected chief justice. The revolutionary society that actually developed in Morelos never outgrew contention between the new civil and military authorities, but at least the contest was genuine, and the location of legitimacy clear. From the beginning the movement had been a deliberate enterprise by country chiefs to restore the integrity of the state's villages, to gain local rights of participation in national progress. When Madero initiated the revolution in November 1910, Morelos rural leaders did not flock to his cause without weeks of hard reckoning and calculation. And when they did join him, it was for conscious, practical reasons – to recover village lands and establish village security. When later they reacted against Madero's refusal to keep his promises, they defined their opposition with a public plan. And despite Madero's great popularity, many villagers supported them, actively or passively. If, in the war against Huerta and afterward, their local concerns seemed a liability, the state chiefs remained uncomfortable with grander, vaguer projects: in the villages they were at home, and the rest they left to the secretaries. In this insistent provincialism was the movement's strength and its weaknesses.

Related Items

20, 33, 35, 37, 38, 39, 40, 41, 42, 44, 45, 46, 59, 61.

Part V

'Them' – Peasants as Objects of Policies and Studies

Part V focuses on the ways the non-peasants understand and shape the life of contemporary peasantry. Policies towards peasants have been determined to a considerable degree by exploitative interests of social classes and of organizations which treat them as an object – a resource necessary to pursue somebody else's goals and aims. Yet there is no simple correspondence between those interests, goals as declared or the actual aims of the policies followed and the results achieved. 'Objective circumstances', i.e. conditions which cannot be controlled by state and other organizations, such as the vagaries of nature, movements of the international market, flows of resources or changes of governments, are partly responsible for it. Peasant resistance, explicit as well as implicit, to being used contributed also to the unexpected results of rural planning (see also parts III and IV). One must consider as well the powerful impact of comprehension and miscomprehensions of the policy makers and their advisers who face peasants and try to use them or to help them.

Part V begins accordingly with a number of short pronouncements about peasants and rural life which reveal something of the outsider's approach to the issue. These views, their tremendous discrepancies and emotional charge, underlie the policies and ideologies directed towards the peasants of the contemporary world (see also Kerblay, Alavi and Ranger, items 25, 26 and 38).

The next item is a systematic discussion of state and state policies *vis-à-vis* the rural society put within the broader context of social and economic life of Latin America. It leaves behind the widespread tendency to see state impact on rural economy as restricted to land reform only and considers the extensive and changing range of state interventions in agriculture in what is formally categorized as the 'free market economies'.

Part V moves then to alternative analyses and strategies and to the assumptions which underlie them. These begin with Preobrazhensky's classic statement of the proposition concerning the necessity to have peasants pay for industrialization, a statement admirable in its clarity and refusal to hide behind a glib politician's phrase. It represents a tradition of analysis in the mainstream of the 'orthodox' Marxism of the Second International as well as of those in its Russian branch who debated later, in the 1920s, how to build socialism in the huge 'developing society' they came to rule. This mode of analysis is representative also of many non-Marxist and anti-Marxist 'development specialists' of today. Paradoxically an alternative to Preobrazhensky's view about capital formation came in Marx's own notes (which brings to mind their author's testy comment that 'he was never a Marxist').

Dore's discussion of the possible forms of land reform and their impact on agriculture leads us to a different approach and line of argument concerning transformation of peasant economy (see also Galeski, item 13). It is followed by McNamara's speech a decade later to the governors of the World Bank, which had become by then the major sponsor of 'rural development' *on par* with the governments of the 'developing societies'. The note of urgency and the 'interventionist' edge of McNamara's *Address* indicate how much and how fast the perception of rural conditions in the 'developing societies' changed with the more insightful Western politicians. Yet, the word 'peasant' is avoided with clear cognitive results (see page 439).

McNamara's speech is followed by items 54, 55 and 56 concerning the unfolding of actual policies of 'rural development', their criticism and some resulting issues that do not want to go away (see also Omvedt, John Harriss, Friedmann, items 20, 31 and 32). Kandyoti speaks next of rural women, while Bernstein's note sounds a warning to critics not to replace dogmatic disregard of peasants by as dogmatic philo-peasantism and state-phobia. Esteva offers an opposite warning and a different challenge. Speaking of rural Mexico – a 'more advanced' version of what clearly is a 'development society', he presents the most radical form of criticism of 'rural development', one which moves towards an alternative 'green' perspective, making the whole issue of 'development' stand out in particularly sharp relief. This perspective in the debate of ways and means to transform peasant societies is followed by Richards's call for ecological populism and by a description of an agrarian reform undertaken by revolutionary peasants themselves, when under Zapata they acquired power to do so. Esteva, Richards and Womack offer a counterpoint to the debate about 'What can we do for "them"?' by treating peasants as a subject rather than the object of history and social change (see Scott, Ranger, Tilly, Shanin, Wolf and Womack, items 37, 38, 41, 44, 46 and 47).

Part V and the book are brought to a close with a brief historiography of peasant studies which pays particular attention to their remarkable 1960s/70s ascent in Anglo-Saxon academic literature, and determinants, impact and directions of further development.

48

Peasantry in the Eyes of Others

The Barbarians	*Maxim Gorky*
The Revolutionary Proletariat of Our Times	*Frantz Fanon*
Those Who Pay the Bill	*Julius Nyerere*
Not Really True at All . . .	*Raymond Williams*

In the words of a great historian, 'The interrelations, confusions and infections of human consciousness are, for history, reality itself' (Bloch, 1954, p. 151). To history one can add here the science of the social scientists, the politics of the politicians and the plausibilities inbuilt into public opinion and the media. Or, as noted by an outstanding economist with a penchant for actual money and policy making, '. . . the ideas of economists and political philosophers, both when they are right and when they are wrong, are more powerful than is commonly understood. Indeed the world is ruled by little else. Practical men, who believe themselves to be quite exempt from any intellectual influence, are usually slaves to some defunct economist' (Keynes, 1946, p. 383). An overstatement surely, but also a well made point which is doubtlessly valid.

All this is the more true when peasants are concerned. Peasants do not write their own history nor is it written for them. It is written about and, often, without them. Their voice is barely ever heard at those places where decisions are made about policies and profits. It is the interests and images of non-peasants which define the ways the 'Peasant Question' is being put and resolved in economic and political planning by state and agrobusiness, impinging deeply on the peasants' existence in the modern world.

To social scientists and those who learned from them, peasants have often offered a major point of comparison as against contemporaneity, with a historiography to match based on the natural ascent from 'them' – backward, traditional, communalist and organic, to 'us' – progressive, scientific, individualist and alienated. Becoming civilized was associated with de-peasantization, the attitude to peasanthood or even to the existence of peasantry, often reflecting global schemes and hopes rather than rural actualities. Progress as the super-agenda as well as the actual social gulf between the peasant underdogs and those who rule and write (and, to some, the feelings of guilt associated with it) provided for powerful emotional undercurrents when peasantry was being discussed. So did the fact that in all revolutions of the twentieth century peasants played a role which was as large as it was unexpected. All these elements fed the dominant cognitions and policies in turn were reflected by them. That is why peasantry in the eyes of others, its perceptions and misperceptions alike, must be ever kept in mind when peasants, the studies of them and the policies toward them, are concerned.

References

Bloch, Mark (1954) *The Historian's Craft*, Manchester.
Keynes, John Maynard (1946) *The General Theory of Employment, Interest and Money*, London.

The Barbarians
Maxim Gorky

Western man from his very childhood, from the moment he stands up on his hind legs, sees all around him the monumental results of the work of his forefathers. From the canals of Holland to the tunnels of the Italian Riviera and the vineyards of Vesuvius, from the great workshops of England to the mighty Silesian factories, the whole of Europe is densely covered by grandiose embodiments of the organizational will of man – the will which puts forward as its proud aim to subject the elemental forces of nature to the intelligent interests of man. The land is in the hands of man and man is truly its sovereign. The child of the West soaks up these impressions; a consciousness of the value of man and a respect for his work, together with a feeling of his own significance, is raised in him, as heir to the marvel of the works and creations of his predecessors.

Such thoughts, such feelings and values cannot grow in the soul of the Russian peasant. The boundless plains on which the wooden, thatch-roofed villages crowd together have the poisonous peculiarity of emptying a man, of sucking dry his desires. The peasant has only to go out past the bounds of the village and look at the emptiness around him to feel in a short time that this emptiness is creeping into his very soul. Nowhere around can one see the results of creative labour. The estates of the land-owners? But they are few and inhabited by enemies. The towns? But they are far and not much more cultured than the village. Round about lie endless plains and in the centre of them, insignificant, tiny man abandoned on this dull earth for penal labour. And man

Excerpts from M. Gorky, *On the Russian Peasantry*, Ladyzhnikov, 1922, pp. 4–21. Translated by Paula V. Harry.

is filled with the feeling of indifference killing his ability to think, to remember his past, to work out his ideas from experience. A historian of Russian culture, characterizing the peasantry, said of it 'a host of superstitions, and no ideas whatsoever'. This judgement is backed up by all the Russian folklore. . . .

The technically primitive labour of the countryside is incredibly heavy; the peasantry call it *strada* from the Russian verb *stradat'* – to suffer. The burden of the work, linked to the insignificance of its results, deepens in the peasant the instinct of property, making him unresponsive to those views which place at the root of the sinfulness of man that very instinct. . . .

Even the memories of Pugachev [the leader of the major and most recent peasant–cossack rebellion] did not remain bright within the peasantry and memories of other less significant political achievements of the Russian people similarly faded.

It can be said about all this, in the words of a historian of the 'Time of Troubles' in Russian history, '. . . all these rebellions changed nothing, brought nothing new into the mechanism of the state, into the structure of understanding, into customs and inclinations . . .'.

To this judgement it is appropriate to add the conclusion of a foreigner who had closely observed the Russian people: 'This people has no historical memory. It does not know its past and even acts as if it does not want to know it.' . . .

But where is the good-natured, thoughtful Russian peasant, indefatigable searcher after truth and justice, who was so convincingly and beautifully depicted in the world of nineteenth-century Russian literature?

In my youth I searched for such a man across the Russian countryside and did not find him. I met there instead a tough, cunning realist who, when it was favourable to him, knew quite well how to make himself out as a simpleton. By nature the peasant is not stupid and knows it well. He has composed a multitude of wistful songs and rough, cruel stories, created thousands of proverbs embodying the experience of his difficult life.

He knows that 'the peasant is not stupid, it is the world which is the fool' and that 'the community [*mir*] is as powerful as water and as stupid as a pig'. He says: 'Do not fear devils, fear people', 'Beat your own kind and then strangers will fear you.' He holds no high opinion of truth: 'Truth will not feed you', 'What is wrong with a lie if it makes you live well?', 'A truthful man is like a fool, both are harmful.' . . .

Those who took on themselves the bitter, Herculean work of cleaning the Augean stables of Russian life I cannot consider 'tormentors of the people'; from my point of view they are rather victims.

I say this from a strong conviction, based on experience, that the whole of the Russian intelligentsia for almost an entire century courageously tried to lift on to its feet the heavy Russian people lazily, carelessly, incapable slumped on its land – the entire intelligentsia is the victim of the historical backwardness of the people, which managed to live unbelievably wretchedly on a land of fairytale richness. The Russian peasant, whose common sense has now been awakened by the revolution, could say of its intelligentsia: 'stupid like the sun, works just as selflessly'. . . .

[And in the future] the half-savage, stupid, heavy people of the Russian village, and all those almost frightening people spoken of earlier, will die out and will be replaced by a new breed, a literate, reasonable, cheerful people. To my mind this will not mean a very 'nice and likeable Russian people', but will be at last a businesslike people, mistrustful and indifferent towards everything that does not directly bear on its needs. . . .

The town, the unquenchable fire of all pioneering thoughts, spring of irritating, not always comprehensible, events, will not quickly gain its just appreciation on the part of this man. He will not quickly understand it as a workshop, constantly producing new ideas, machines, goods, the aim of which is to brighten and beautify the life of the people.

The Revolutionary Proletariat of Our Times
Frantz Fanon

The peasantry is systematically disregarded for the most part by the propaganda put out by the nationalist parties. And it is clear that in the colonial countries the peasants alone are revolutionary, for they have nothing to lose and everything to gain. The starving peasant, outside the class system, is the first among the exploited to discover that only violence pays. For him there is no compromise, no possible coming to terms; colonization and decolonization are simply a question of relative strength. . . .

The history of middle-class and working-class revolutions [in the West] has shown that the bulk of the peasants often constitutes a brake on the revolution. Generally in industrialized countries the peasantry as a whole are the least aware, the worst organized and at the same time the most anarchical element. They show a whole range of characteristics – individualism, lack of discipline, liking for money and propensities towards waves of uncontrollable rage and deep discouragement which define a line of behaviour that is objectively reactionary.

We have seen that the national parties copy their methods from those of the Western political parties; and also, for the most part, that they do not direct their propaganda towards the rural masses. In fact, if a reasoned analysis of colonized society had been made, it would have shown them that the native peasantry lives against a background of tradition, where the traditional

Excerpts from Frantz Fanon, *The Wretched of the Earth*, Penguin, 1967. Translated by Constance Farrington. First published in 1961.

structure of society has remained intact, whereas in the industrialized countries it is just this traditional setting which has been broken up by the progress of industrialization. In the colonies, it is at the very core of the embryonic working class that you find individual behaviour. The landless peasants, who make up the *lumpen-proletariat*, leave the country districts, where vital statistics are just so many insoluble problems, rush towards the towns, crowd into tin-shack settlements, and try to make their way into the ports and cities founded by colonial domination. The bulk of the country people for their part continue to live within a rigid framework, and the extra mouths to feed have no other alternative than to emigrate towards the centres of population. The peasant who stays put defends his traditions stubbornly, and in a colonized society stands for the disciplined element whose interests lie in maintaining the social structure. It is true that this unchanging way of life, which hangs on like grim death to rigid social structures, may occasionally give birth to movements which are based on religious fanaticism or tribal wars. But in their spontaneous movements the country people as a whole remain disciplined and altruistic. The individual stands aside in favour of the community.

The country people are suspicious of the townsman. The latter dresses like a European; he speaks the European's language, works with him, sometimes even lives in the same district; so he is considered by the peasants as a turncoat who has betrayed everything that goes to make up the national heritage. The townspeople are 'traitors and knaves' who seem to get on well with the occupying powers, and do their best to get on within the framework of the colonial system. This is why you often hear country people say of town-dwellers that they have no morals. Here, we are not dealing with the old antagonism between town and country; it is the antagonism which exists between the native who is excluded from the advantages of colonialism and his counterpart who manages to turn colonial exploitation to his account. . . .

The militants fall back towards the countryside and the mountains, towards the peasant people. From the beginning, the peasantry closes in around them, and protects them from being pursued by the police. The militant nationalist who decides to throw in his lot with the country people instead of playing at hide-and-seek with the police in urban centres will lose nothing. The peasant's cloak will wrap him around with a gentleness and firmness that he never suspected. These men, who are in fact exiled to the backwoods, who are cut off from the urban background against which they had defined their ideas of the nation and of the political fight, these men have in fact become 'Maquisards'. Since they are obliged to move about the whole time in order to escape from the police, often at night so as not to attract attention, they will have good reason to wander through their country and to get to know it. The cafés are forgotten; so are the arguments about the next election or the spitefulness of some policeman or other. Their ears hear the true voice of the country, and their eyes take in the great and infinite poverty of their people. They realize the precious time that has been wasted in useless commentaries upon the colonial regime. They finally come to understand that the change-over will not be a reform, nor a bettering of things. They come to understand, with a sort of bewilderment that will from henceforth never quite leave them, that political action in the towns will always be powerless to modify or overthrow the colonial regime.

These men get used to talking to the peasants. They discover that the mass of the country people have never ceased to think of the problem of their liberation except in terms of violence, in terms of taking back the land from the foreigners, in terms of national struggle, and of armed insurrection. It is all very simple. These men discover a coherent people who go on living, as it were, statically, but who keep their moral values and their devotion to the nation intact. They discover a people that is generous, ready to sacrifice themselves completely, an impatient people, with a stony pride. It is understandable that the meeting between these militants with the police on their track and these mettlesome masses of people, who are rebels by instinct, can produce an explosive mixture of unusual potentiality.

Those Who Pay the Bill
Julius Nyerere

Our emphasis on money and industries has made us concentrate on urban development. We recognize that we do not have enough money to bring the kind of development to each village which would benefit everybody. We also know that we cannot establish an industry in each village and through this means effect a rise in the real incomes of the people. For these reasons we spend most of our money in the urban areas and our industries are established in the towns.

Yet the greater part of this money that we spend in the towns comes from loans. Whether it is used to build schools, hospitals, houses or factories, etc., it still has to be repaid. But it is obvious that it cannot be repaid just out of money obtained from urban and industrial development. To repay the loans we have to use foreign currency which is obtained from the sale of our exports. But we do not now sell our industrial products in foreign markets, and indeed it is likely to be a long time before our industries produce for export. The main aim of our new industries is 'import substitution' – that is, to produce things which up to now we have had to import from foreign countries.

It is therefore obvious that the foreign currency we shall use to pay back the

Excerpt from Julius K. Nyerere, 'The Arusha Declaration', *Freedom and Socialism: Uhuru na Ujamaa*, Oxford University Press, 1968, pp. 242–3.

loans used in the development of the urban areas will not come from the towns or the industries. Where, then, shall we get it from? We shall get it from the villages and from agriculture. What does this mean? It means that the people who benefit directly from development which is brought about by borrowed money are not the ones who will repay the loans. The largest proportion of the loans will be spent in, or for, the urban areas, but the largest proportion of the repayment will be made through the efforts of the farmers.

This fact should always be borne in mind, for there are various forms of exploitation. We must not forget that people who live in towns can possibly become the exploiters of those who live in the rural areas. All our big hospitals are in towns and they benefit only a small section of the people of Tanzania. Yet if we have built them with loans from outside Tanzania, it is the overseas sale of the peasants' produce which provides the foreign exchange for repayment. Those who do not get the benefit of the hospitals thus carry the major responsibility for paying for them. Tarmac roads, too, are mostly found in towns and are of especial value to the motor-car owners. Yet if we have built those roads with loans, it is again the farmer who produces the goods which will pay for them. What is more, the foreign exchange with which the car was bought also came from the sale of the farmers' produce. Again, electric lights, water pipes, hotels and other aspects of modern development are mostly found in towns. Most of them have been built with loans and most of them do not benefit the farmer directly, although they will be paid for by the foreign exchange earned by the sale of his produce. We should always bear this in mind.

Although when we talk of exploitation we usually think of capitalists, we should not forget that there are many fish in the sea. They eat each other. The large ones eat the small ones, and the small ones eat those who are even smaller. There are two possible ways of dividing the people in our country. We can put the capitalists and feudalists on one side, and the farmers and workers on the other. But we can also divide the people into urban dwellers on one side and those who live in the rural areas on the other. If we are not careful we might get to the position where the real exploitation in Tanzania is that of the town dwellers exploiting the peasants.

Not Really True at All . . .
Raymond Williams

. . . I had been told that the rural experience, the working country, had gone; that in Britain it was only a marginal thing, and that as time went by this would

Excerpts from Raymond Williams, *The Country and the City*, Chatto & Windus, 1973, pp. 299–305.

be so everywhere. I accepted this, at one level, for much longer than now seems possible. It was one of the impulses, I can see now, that kept sending me back to old rural literature and history. And I cannot clearly remember when I suddenly realized that it was not really true at all. Even while I was showing in the novels a different and persistent experience, this idea had stuck. When at least I saw that it was false I knew that I had to look for its sources. There were not only, as might be supposed, the sentimental ruralists, though just because of my experience I had to face them. There were also, and more critically, the brisk metropolitan progressives, many of them supposedly internationalists and socialists, whose contempt for rural societies was matched only by their confidence in an urban industrial future which they were about in one way or another – modernization, the white heat of technology, revolution – to convert into socialism. There are so many writers and thinkers, still, of each of these kinds, that it takes a long time, a long effort, to look round and say that their common idea of a lost rural economy is false.

Is it then not false? Is it not obvious that in Britain a working agriculture is marginal? That was the first mode of error I learned to perceive: an unnoticed persistence, in the old imperialist countries, of a kind of abstract chauvinism: that what happened to them was what was happening or would happen to everyone. Still most countries in the world were predominantly rural, but within the imperialist division of the world they did not really count, were not in important ways there. Even those who saw that they were exploited, within the imperialist division of the world, did not necessarily go on to see that in and through this condition and its struggles a working agriculture, a rural economy in any of its possible forms, simply had to persist: in the exploited countries themselves and, if some elements of the exploitation were to be diminished, in what had been abstractly thought of as the developed metropolitan countries. Perhaps more of us now know this. The facts of the food and population crisis have been widely and properly publicized. If we are to survive at all, we shall have to develop and extend our working agricultures. The common idea of a lost rural world is then not only an abstraction of this or that stage in a continuing history (and many of the stages we can be glad have gone or are going). It is in direct contradiction to any effective shape of our future, in which work on the land will have to become more rather than less important and central. It is one of the most striking deformations of industrial capitalism that one of our most central and urgent and necessary activities should have been so displaced, in space or in time or in both, that it can be plausibly associated only with the past or with distant lands.

Some of this, now, is changing, even within old imperialist Europe. But it is still the case that the future of agriculture is seen, here and in the Third World, in mainly capitalist forms, and especially as involving massive social displacement. It could be done, and is elsewhere being done, in quite different ways. And the urgency of its doing, in ways that break with capitalism, is linked with that other complementary aspect of the crisis: the condition and the future of the cities and of industry. One of the real merits of some rural writers, often not seen because other elements are present, is an insistence on the complexity of the living natural environment. Now that the dangers to this environment have come more clearly into view, our ideas, once again, have to shift. Some of the darkest images of the city have to be faced as quite literal futures. An insane over-confidence in the specialized powers of metropolitan industrialism has brought us to the point where, however we precisely assess it, the risk to human survival is becoming evident, or if we survive, as I think we shall, there is the clear impossibility of continuing as we are.

. . . Look at socialism or communism: historically the enemies of capitalism, but in detail and often in principle, in matters of the country and the city, continuing and even intensifying some of the same fundamental processes.

This is a genuine historical and political difficulty. Trotsky said that the history of capitalism was the history of the victory of town over country. He then proceeded, in the critical first years of the Russian revolution, to outline a programme for just such a victory, on a massive scale, as a way of defeating capitalism and preserving socialism. Stalin carried through very much that programme, on a scale and with a brutality which made that 'victory' over the peasants one of the most terrible phases in the whole history of rural society. The local needs and priorities were desperate: a shattered economy and an appalling food shortage; rural capitalism, in new forms, undoubtedly spreading. But the way it was done, and the spirit in which it was done, were not only brutal; they drew on one element of an ambiguity in Marxism which in its turn had massive consequences on the character of the society as a whole.

. . . In the *Communist Manifesto* Marx and Engels argued that 'the bourgeoisie had subjected the country to the rule of the towns . . . has created enormous cities . . . has made barbarian and semi-barbarian countries dependent on the civilized ones': the familiar history of capitalism and imperialism. They argued that these relations of centralization and dependence had created the conditions for revolution, and in one sense they were right.

But there was an ambiguity at the core of the argument. They denounced what was being done in the tearing progress of capitalism and imperialism; they insisted that men must struggle to supersede it, and they showed us some ways. But implicit in the denunciation was another set of value-judgements: the bourgeoisie had 'rescued a considerable part of the population from the idiocy of rural life'; the subjected nations were 'barbarian and semi-barbarian', the dominating powers 'civilized'. It was then on this kind of confidence in the singular values of modernization and civilization that a major distortion in the history of communism was erected. The exposed urban proletariat would learn and create new and higher forms of society: if that was all that had been said it would have been very different. But if the forms of bourgeois development contained, with whatever contradiction, values higher than 'rural idiocy' or 'barbarism', then almost any programme, in the name of the urban proletariat, could be justified and imposed. The terrible irony has been that the real processes of absolute urban and industrial priority, and of the related priority of the advanced and civilized nations, worked through not only to damage the 'rural idiots' and the colonial 'barbarians and semi-barbarians', but to damage, at the heart, the urban proletarians themselves, and the advanced and civilized societies over which, in their turn, the priorities exercised their domination, in a strange dialectical twist. To see exposure creating revolution was one thing; to see more of the same producing more of something quite different was at best an apocalyptic hope.

This difficulty worked itself through, in a surprising way, in our own century. Revolutions came not in the 'developed' but in the 'undeveloped' countries. The Chinese revolution, defeated in the cities, went to the country and gained its ultimate strength. The Cuban revolution went from the city to the country, where its force was formed. In a whole epoch of national and social liberation struggles, the exploited rural and colonial populations became the main sources of continued revolt. In the famous Chinese phrase about world revolution, the 'countryside' was surrounding the 'cities'. This the 'rural idiots' and the 'barbarians and semi-barbarians' have been, for the last forty years, the main revolutionary force in the world.

. . . It can be restated theoretically. The division and opposition of city and country, industry and agriculture, in their modern forms, are the critical culmination of the division and specialization of labour which, though it did not begin with capitalism, was developed under it to an extraordinary and transforming degree. Other forms of the same fundamental division are the separation between mental and manual labour, between administration and operation, between politics and social life. The symptoms of this division can be found at every point in what is now our common life: in the idea and practice of social classes; in conventional definitions of work and of education; in the physical distribution of settlements; and in temporal organization of the day, the week, the year, the lifetime. Much of the creative thinking of our time is an attempt to re-examine each of these concepts and practices. It is based on the conviction that the system which generates and is composed by them is intolerable and will not survive. In many areas of this thinking there is not only analytic but programmatic response: on new forms of decision making, new kinds of education, new definitions and practices of work, new kinds of settlement and land-use.

| Related Items |

8, 18, 21, 25, 26, 29, 33, 34, 35, 36, 37, 41, 42, 46, 47, 53, 58, 61.

49

Peasants, Capitalism and the State in Latin American Culture

Alain de Janvry

The performance of agriculture and the position of peasants in the social division of labour cannot be analysed except in relation to the totality of the social formation of which they are part. This includes the structure of the economy and its insertion into the international market, the social class structure and the associated patterns of surplus control, and the set of institutions that constitute the state, including both the state apparatus and the government that has formal control over it. The study of peasants must, consequently, be specific to a particular historical, geographical, economic, social and institutional context. It is only by reference to this context that the production performance of peasant households; their levels of welfare; their differentiation into new social classes; and their permanence, elimination or transformation can be understood. The relationship between peasants, capitalism and the state is a dynamic, triangular relationship that is conditioned by this context.

Although the study of peasants is, thus, highly context-specific, there are a number of constants in peasant behaviour that are rediscovered among social formations and that unify the field of peasant studies. One is the family-based nature of production motivated by the rationality of insuring the reproduction of the producers and of the production unit itself. This gives peasant agriculture features that are markedly different from those of commercial farming, such as an absolute commitment to the productive use of family labour; indivisibility of factor incomes; partial market orientation of the product; incorporation in production of family members (such as children, elders, and women in the reproductive phases of their life cycles) with, eventually, zero-opportunity cost on the labour market; and behaviour toward risk dictated by safety-first objectives (Schejtman, 1984; Deere and de Janvry, 1979). Another constant is the socially dominated position of peasants that forces them to

An original paper.

surrender a surplus under a variety of forms such as rent in labour services, kind, or cash; unfavourable terms of trade and low wages; and usurious credit terms. Finally, the geographical dispersion of peasants and the personal nature of at least some of the relationships of domination to which they are subject make their forms of collective action discontinuous and often more defensive (evasive reaction, foot dragging, and other everyday forms of resistance) than expressive of clearly articulated and aggregate interests.

These peasant constants (family-based production, social domination and defensive strategies) occurring in the context of specific social formations lead to markedly different outcomes in terms of the production performance, welfare, social differentiation and permanence of peasants. We analyse in this item the position of peasants in present-day Latin America. Because of lack of space, we only provide a limited factual characterization of Latin American peasants today (for which see, e.g., Pearse, 1975; Goodman and Redclift, 1984; de Janvry, 1981) but develop a theoretical framework that permits an understanding of their continued permanence and continued poverty, stressing, in particular, the role that the state plays in these dynamic processes.

The approach we follow here is, in part, motivated by the need to dispel the myopia of many studies of rural development processes which do not attribute significance to the role of the state. This is the case for many orthodox Marxists, for whom there is capitalism with its laws of motion but no state, as well as for many liberal economists for whom there are market forces but no state either. As we shall see, not only does the state eventually engage in major reforms, such as redistribution of the land, but it also engages in widespread manipulation of prices, credit, wages, technological alternatives and educational opportunities, all of which have dramatic impacts on the welfare and permanence or disappearance of peasants. As we shall also see, the state cannot be reduced to a monopolistic instrument of rule for those in power; it is as well an object of struggle for the dominated groups, and it has limited effectiveness in implementing the reforms and policies it pursues.

Peripheral Capitalism or Cheap Labour as the Engine of Industrial Growth

We start by observing three well-known facts that have characterized the growth of Latin American nations during the last 20 years. The first is that many of these economies have been highly dynamic, displaying a high rate of industrial growth, but that the type of growth that occurred has been systematically inequalizing on the distribution of income and highly unstable over time. The best example is the case of Brazil, where the average annual rate of growth of the gross domestic product was 8.5 per cent between 1965 and 1980 but fell to -0.3 per cent between 1980 and 1982. The share of income of the richest 20 per cent in the population increased from 54 per cent in 1960 to 62 per cent in 1970 and 63 per cent in 1980. The second fact is that, in spite of considerable vertical mobility, the level of real wages of unskilled workers failed to rise significantly over the long term and growth failed to re-absorb surplus labour even during periods of economic booms. In Chile, for example, while the gross domestic product grew at an average annual rate of 8.5 per cent between 1977 and 1980, the official rate of unemployment was 18 per cent and real wages were 20 per cent below their 1970 level. A third fact is that the sectors of the economy with the most rapid rates of economic growth were not the wage-goods sectors but the sectors producing luxury consumption goods (cars and electrical appliances) and capital goods.

There are a number of theoretical explanations of why economic growth occurring in the particular economic and social structure of modern Latin American nations creates inequalizing spirals. They all have one element in common which is to make cheap labour the engine of growth for the modern sector. A highly unequal initial distribution of income, much more unequal than ever characterized the industrialized countries at levels of per capita income similar to those of Latin America today, is due to extreme inequality in the distribution of assets (land in particular); surplus labour and, consequently, low wages; use of skill-intensive technology in the modern sector which pushes upward the wages of skilled workers and employees; and terms of trade unfavourable to agriculture. These sources of inequality are reinforced by growth which valorizes the assets, by population growth as a rational response to poverty, and by biases toward adoption of labour-saving technology, thus perpetuating surplus labour. Increasing inequality in the distribution of income distorts the pattern of effective demand and, hence, the pattern of intersectoral allocation of investment toward luxury consumption goods.

An investment programme dominated by capital and luxury consumption goods tends to be self-reinforcing as the intersectoral allocation of investment is not only demand-led but, also, acquires a certain degree of autonomy from demand. This is due to the role of the state which favours public-sector investment in capital goods to accelerate future growth, to the influence of planning theory which recommends investment in capital and luxury-goods sectors for having high backward and forward linkages,[1] and to the role of foreign capital which invests in the production of commodities that are wage goods in the advanced economies but luxuries in the Third World due to large disparities in the levels of wages between more and less developed countries. With a bias toward investment in luxury goods and periodic emergence of excess capacity, the state is eventually pushed into creating effective demand to sustain growth. This takes the form of consumption credit and tax incentives on the purchase of luxury goods and real wage concessions for skilled workers and employees while minimum wages for unskilled workers are left to lag behind the rate of inflation.

The existing social class structure, the state, and the pattern of insertion of Latin America into the international division of labour all contribute to patterns of economic growth and result in inequalizing spirals for which cheap labour is the engine of growth. It is by reference to this general framework, with all the specificities and variations it assumes in particular countries and time periods, that the nature and future of Latin American peasants must be understood.

From Cheap Labour to Cheap Food

Starting again from facts, we make two additional observations. One is that there has been a systematic undervaluation of agricultural commodities in Latin American countries (of urban wage goods, in particular) by contrast to overvaluation in the more developed countries. Latin American cheap food policies have been principally implemented through overvalued exchange rates, trade restrictions and price fixing. Overvalued exchange rates lower the domestic price of both imported foods and exported agricultural products. Trade restrictions have taken the form of export taxes imposed by monopolistic marketing boards and export prohibitions. Price fixing leads to excess demand and requires imposition of rationing such as meatless days. The other is that we witness the permanence of large numbers of peasants in spite of extensive social differentiation in agriculture and decades, if not centuries, of development of capitalism. This is evidenced by the observation that the Latin American peasantry, as a share of the economically active population (EAP), increased from 60 per cent in 1950 to 65 per cent in 1980 (PREALC, 1982). The absolute number of peasant EAP increased by 31 per cent over the 30-year period, in spite of the fact that the share of agriculture in total EAP declined from 32 per cent in 1950 to 20 per cent in 1980. This indicates that, in spite of intense rural–urban migration and a significant displacement of the traditional sector toward the urban economy (the ratio of traditional urban EAP to peasant EAP increased from 41 per cent in 1950 to 98 per cent in 1980), the peasantry remains a large and growing social sector.[2]

The reasons that cheap food policies have been implemented are compelling. Holding down the price of food allows cheapening of labour for the modern sector to contain inflationary pressures and stimulate industrial investment, increasing of effective demand for modern-sector goods as a lower food bill frees purchasing power for other goods, and legitimizing governments in the eyes of politically important urban constituencies. The consequence of cheap food policies and of increasing inequality in the distribution of income has been a bias in agricultural production away from wage goods and toward export crops, inputs for industry and luxury goods. It has also been a generally poor performance of agricultural production with output barely following population growth and a rising share of imports in total consumption.

Capitalist farmers are generally partially or totally compensated for low product prices by socially discriminating 'institutional rents' handed out by the state. These include subsidized credit, public technology and extension services, infrastructure projects, and differential price treatments by crops according to who produces and who consumes them. The market thus takes away from producers through a distorted price system while the political economy selectively compensates to maintain the rate of profit in particular farms and activities. In Brazil, for example, large farms producing export crops have received the lion's share of subsidized credit. State intervention through price distortions and institutional rents thus creates serious biases in the allocation of resources which lead to inefficiencies and foregone production and accelerate social differentiation against the weaker groups, the peasants in particular, who are rarely benefited by institutional rents.

In this context of sharply uneven development by farms, activities, regions and time period, the peasantry (as well as the urban informal sector) finds itself functionalized in four different ways to the global pattern of accumulation. Peasants are here defined as those social groups with family-based agricultural production units that lie in a continuum of social differentiation between fully landless agricultural workers, at one extreme, and capitalized family farms able to insure a return to factors of production equal to their opportunity cost on factor markets at the other extreme.[3] Within the range of these limits, we find different types of peasants fulfilling four basic functions consistent with the logic of disarticulated growth.

Originating with upper-class peasants who have sufficient access to land to generate a marketed surplus, labour and capital market failures allow these peasants to deliver food in markets at a price eventually lower than that of capitalist farms. Their cost advantage is based on self-exploitation, i.e., on the use in production of labour categories recruited within kinship networks with zero-opportunity costs such as children, elderly, women in reproductive periods, and the seasonally unemployed. For the farm as a whole, the implicit total factor income is below opportunity cost on factor markets. If the capitalist sector cannot compensate for this cost advantage through either higher total factor productivity or discriminatory access to institutional rents, peasants can outcompete capitalists and deliver low-cost food on the market, for example, in situations where it is underpriced by cheap food policies. Functional dualism between peasants and capitalism where peasants are a source of cheap food for the rest of the economy has, thus, been used as an argument to explain the staunch permanence of peasantries under capitalist development. Peasants remain in existence both because they have the ability to resist elimination through efficient resource use (in spite of traditional technology) and through self-exploitation and because there is a structural logic to this exploitation as part of the cheap labour–cheap food requirements of disarticulated growth.

In situations where peasants are not freeholders, the surplus generated on the basis of their efficiency and self-exploitation can be captured in the form of rent. This is why we witness the perpetuation of share-cropping arrangements even under advanced capitalism. They allow mobilizing of labour within kinship networks when labour markets fail, bypassing labour legislation, avoiding the cost of supervisory labour, and passing to peasants part of the production and market risks.

Peasants with insufficient land resources to absorb family labour productively typically rely on survival strategies that lead them to engage in a variety of activities outside of the home plot – particularly wage labour. These semi-proletarian peasants are, thus, able to cover part of the cost of maintenance and reproduction of the household outside of the wage economy. Wages paid can fall below this cost, and employers benefit from a subsidy that originates in unpaid household labour applied to the peasant plot. Peasants become a source of cheap labour for the capitalist economy both directly, as workers in the modern sector, and indirectly as underpaid wage workers in food-producing capitalist farms that can transfer to cheap semi-proletarian labour the costs of cheap food policies.

The final function fulfilled by peasants is to provide household-financed social welfare, which allows both support and reproduction of surplus labour at no cost for the modern sector and political defusion of tensions created by rural dislocations and poverty. This is particularly important in periods of economic stagnation when unemployment increases, urban migration is sharply curtailed, and farm households have to absorb the brunt of lower food prices and increased unemployment. It is also important in the process of monetization and commodification of agriculture when traditional safety nets, such as patron–client relationships and guaranteed employment through belonging to social networks, are being dismantled. Finally, it is important when, as is typical of Third World development today and in sharp contrast to the history of industrialization in Western countries, the development of capitalism in agriculture displaces peasants from access to land while offering insufficient migration and employment opportunities in the rest of the economy. With limited mobility in the allocation of resources (by contrast to the typical assumption of orthodox economists), this process of rapid structural transformation creates large segments of population trapped in the peasant and urban informal sectors. With weak public protective institutions, kinship networks become the zero-cost alternative to social welfare. Peasants are then functional to the overall economy not as a source of cheap labour or cheap food, but as a source of financing systemic failures. In this case, their permanence does not provide evidence of superior efficiency relative to capitalist farms and of the success of peripheral capitalism in harnessing their capacity for self-exploitation of the product or labour market. It is, instead, a testimony to the social failure of peripheral capitalism.

Functional/Contradictory Dualism and the
Possibility of Cheap Labour

While peasants fulfil a number of functions that explain the systemic logic of their permanence, the key to this permanence is their capacity to resist, if not social differentiation, at least their complete removal from access to land. We start here from the observation that peasants display a wide variety of survival strategies through adaptations in the division of labour by sex and age at different stages of the life cycle. Off-farm sources of income are a large component of total household income for the medium and small-sized peasant households. Household surveys show that off-farm income accounts for 67 per cent of total income in Puebla, Mexico (farms of less than 4 hectares) with 71 per cent of the farm households in the region); 71 per cent in Cajamarca, Peru (farms of less than 11 hectares with 89 per cent of farm households); 61 per cent in Bolivia (farms of less than 5 hectares with 67 per cent of farm households); 58 per cent in Ecuador (farms of less than 5 hectares with 77 per cent of farm households); 76 per cent in Guatemala (farms of less than 1.4 hectares with 63 per cent of farm households); etc. (see de Janvry, 1981; Deere and Wasserstrom, 1981; Commander and Peek, 1983; and Hinter-meister, 1984). Among off-farm income sources, wages were in all cases by far the most important contributor. It is this wide variety of sources of income that allows the majority of Latin American peasants to remain in existence in spite of an insufficient land base to ensure household subsistence.

Another observation is that capitalist agricultural sector employment increased by only 7 per cent in 30 years, in spite of an increase in agricultural gross disposable product of 85 per cent during the same period (PREALC, 1982). At the same time, there was a widespread substitution of hired permanent workers by temporary workers. In Chile, for instance, the share of temporary workers in total paid employment in capitalist farms increased from 37 per cent to 56 per cent between 1965 and 1976 (GIA, 1983), while total paid employment increased by only 3 per cent. In some areas, labour market adjustment to this changing employment structure resulted in the rise of town-based farm workers (e.g. the *boias frias* in southern Brazil) with labour contractors mediating the meeting of supply and demand for labour. In most other areas, it is the peasantry which has delivered this seasonal labour force (e.g., the *enganche* system between the Altiplano and the coast in Peru). The dominant fact, however, is that there have been relatively few opportunities for full proletarianization created in Latin American agriculture in spite of sustained output growth.

Exploitation of peasants through cheap food (terms of trade), rent payment, cheap labour (low wages), and household-financed social welfare is, however, highly unstable; hence, it contradicts the reproduction of peasant exploitation over time. The combination of poverty and control of productive resources fuels demographic growth as it makes children instruments of production and protection for the household. The result is a declining land base per capita which reduces both the marketed surplus of food and the subsidy to wages. Agricultural census data thus show that the average farm size for peasant households decreased over the last 30 years in every single Latin American country, with the exception of Chile and Nicaragua (which had extensive land reforms), and of Venezuela. In Brazil, for instance, average farm size for farms less than 10 hectares, which represented 50 per cent of all farms in 1980, declined from 4.3 hectares in 1950 to 3.5 hectares in 1980.

Poverty also forces an extractivist use of natural resources and a short-run valuation of conservation. Like demographic growth, ecological degradation reduces effective resources per capita and lowers the food and wage subsidy contribution to peasants.

Migration is also enhanced by poverty. While it benefits the migrants and has many positive spillovers on the household and the community through remittances and consumption expenditures, it also seriously jeopardizes the reproduction of peasants. In many communities, absenteeism leads to abandonment of the land, inappropriate production practices and land speculation. Migration reproduces archaic social relationships and often deters productive investment because the returns from investing in migration are so much higher (Dominicans migrating to New York, Mexicans migrating to California, etc.). The result is the transformation of peasant communities into distant consumer suburbs of the destination of migration. This is, of course, not the case for all peasants and all communities. When local profitable investment opportunities exist, successful migrants can invest their labour earnings in acquiring the status of family farmers. In this case, wage labour is not a symptom of de-peasantization but a detour toward acquiring the status of upper-class peasant at a later stage in the life cycle.

Peasant exploitation and the contradictory demographic, ecological and migratory responses that it creates tend to transform the social relations of production that characterize peasants. While peasants increase in absolute numbers and some may acquire the status of capitalized family farmers, the majority sees its land base deteriorate, its marketed surplus decline, and its sources of income become increasingly dominated by wage earnings. Cornered between the successful expansion of capitalist farms and of capitalized family farms that concentrate the land, on one side, and lack of sufficient employment and migration opportunities on the other side, the peasantry has to cling tenaciously to land resources and becomes increasingly semi-proletarianized. The famous Latin American debate between *campesinistas* (advocates of the permanence of peasants) and *proletaristas* (advocates of the transformation of peasants into wage workers) was, thus, one in which both parties were partially right and partially wrong. Peasants do remain in numbers but not with unchanged social relations and, in particular, with increasing reliance on wage earnings; peasants are proletarianized but without, in the majority of cases, full loss of access to some productive land. Careful statistical observations indicate that the capitalization of family farms and full proletarianization are possible for a few but that the majority of Latin American peasants drifts to the status of semi-proletarianization. For those, the family unit is maintained and retains its agricultural residence while increasingly relying on wage income for its subsistence. During periods of economic crisis, as in the current debt squeeze on Latin American nations, migration opportunities are reduced and the role of peasants as providers of household-financed social welfare increases. As a refuge sector, the number of peasants thus changes anticyclically relative to economic growth.

The Policies of State–Peasant Relationships

The state is a complex and dynamic coalition of forces representing, in accordance with their relative political power, the interests of different segments of civil society and of the agents of the state (bureaucrats and politicians). Endowed with a certain degree of autonomy relative to civil society, the state can also transcend parochial interests to respond to systemic crises that compromise economic growth or the reproduction of the dominant social order. In peripheral capitalism, this relative autonomy will generally be used to subordinate peasants to the logic of disarticulated growth and to functionalize their survival strategies as purveyors of cheap food, rents, cheap labour, and household-financed social welfare. As we have seen, these interventions of the state tend to favour the dominant classes which have a greater rent-seeking capacity and are rewarded through the appropriation of institutional rents. State intervention thus tend to accelerate the development of capitalism in agriculture and to accelerate social differentiation among peasants. Because subordination is contradictory to the reproduction of peasants, however, the state may also periodically intervene through pro-peasant initiatives that protect peasants' access to land and increase the productivity of labour in their home plots.

The most important state interventions which have stimulated the development of capitalization in Latin American agriculture while institutionalizing functional dualism with the peasantry are the land reforms that started with Mexico in 1917 and terminated with Chile in the late 1970s. These reforms were basically anti-feudal in the sense of forcing elimination of different forms of labour bondage and rents in labour services and a shift to wage labour. In all cases, a dualistic agrarian structure was created. On the one hand, non-expropriated land was transformed under the threat of expropriation into either large-scale capitalist farms with the same boundaries as the former semi-feudal estates (Bolivia, Venezuela, Ecuador, Peru in 1964–9, and Colombia) or into medium-scale farms with ceilings on landownership (Mexico, Chile, and Peru after 1969). The reform sector was more extensive where revolutionary pressures existed (Mexico and Bolivia) or where democratic legitimization for the reform had to be obtained from the peasants (Chile) than where it served as a mere threat for the modernization of the reform sector (Colombia and Ecuador). In all cases, the reform sector had the principal purpose of achieving labour absorption and political stabilization, while the non-expropriated (but transformed) sector had the purpose of achieving productivity gains. Most of the peasantry remained unbenefited or was hurt by the reforms, e.g., the former share-croppers or workers with land rights who were expropriated in the process of transformation of the non-expropriated lands (Chile, Ecuador, and Colombia). The land reforms thus reinforced functional dualism between an expansive capitalist sector generously subsidized by institutional rents (including the technology of the green revolution) and a growing mass of semi-proletarians. The land-reform sector increased the number of both semi-proletarian peasants and family farms, the former delivering cheap labour to the capitalist farms, and the latter a marketed surplus of cheap food based on self-exploiting family labour in a context of cheap food policies without the compensating benefit of institutional rents.

With the successful end of anti-feudal land reforms in the early 1970s, the land-reform programmes, which were proving to be destabilizing of investment in capitalist agriculture as they legitimized land invasions and created further threats of expropriation, were replaced by programmes of agricultural development for capitalist farms and of integrated rural development for family farms. The purpose of these programmes was to enhance the productivity of family farms, to protect them from competition with capitalist farms, to increase their capacity to deliver a marketed surplus of food, and to create a politically stable buffer class between semi-proletarian peasants and capitalist farms. These programmes, which used credit and technology as their main instruments, had, of course, very little to offer to semi-proletarian peasants with insufficient land resources. Consequently, when successful, they helped to reinforce the economic and political viability of functional dualism. In recent years, the Mexican Food System (SAM) of the Lopez Portillo administration was the most ambitious state-initiated attempt at boosting the productivity of peasant farming to reduce national food dependency. For as long as bountiful oil and debt rents were available to Mexico, transferring resources to peasants was not opposed by the dominant political groups and the SAM project met with a fair degree of success. This was no longer the case when the economic crisis of 1982 suddenly created severe competition for public revenues. Lack of peasant political power to protect the budget of the project led to its elimination with a change in presidency.

While dominated by the logic of functional dualism, the relationship between state and peasants is highly dynamic. Peasants can employ a whole set of individual defensive strategies to protect themselves from aggression by the state. In other situations, defensive strategies give way to offensive strategies either in the form of participation in revolutionary movements or through grassroots initiatives that evolve into collective action with the aim of influencing policy in their favour.

Hirschman (1970) has usefully contrasted two types of patterns of civilian response to unacceptable behaviour of the state. One is 'exit', where the dissatisfaction is expressed individually by evasive actions, failure to obey, and shifts to alternative sources of services. These defensive actions are not intended to change what are regarded as unjust public policies or poor performance of the state but to escape bearing the burden of their consequences. If public institutions depend for their survival on support from their clientele, exit will induce reorganization and redrafting of policies; but, if the public sector has a large degree of autonomy relative to peasant support, the effectiveness of exit behaviour in inducing change will be very limited.

This behaviour is typical of the majority of Latin American peasants. Their defensive strategies in response to aggression by the state are principally individual and evasive. Examples are the emergence of black markets and of illegal private appropriation of collective lands in response to abusive price controls in Chile under Allende, smuggling across borders between Colombia and Ecuador in response to overvalued exchange rates, withdrawal from the market when credit or terms-of-trade conditions are excessively unfavourable, as during the oil and debt booms of the late 1970s with massively overvalued exchange rates and cheap food imports, and ignoring the authorities' prohibition of cutting trees in the watersheds of the Dominican Republic. These evasive actions induce state responses either toward laissez-faire or toward the use of force (Spittler, 1979). Force is, however, limited by the difficulty of controlling production (hence, the tendency to collectivize as a means of control), by lack of information on the objective conditions of peasants, and by bureaucratic inefficiencies. The result is limited effectiveness in the implementation of policies directed towards peasants and limited response to the evasive behaviour of peasants.

The other pattern of response which Hirschman (1970) identifies is 'voice', which implies collective action with interest articulation and aggregation. In exceptional situations, peasant rebellions and revolutions have played important roles in the course of Latin American history. Large-scale peasant participation was determinant in the Mexican, Bolivian and Nicaraguan revolutions (Huizer, 1972); but these movements are rarely initiated by peasants themselves, and the gains from these struggles are often captured by other groups. This was the case in Mexico, where the main beneficiary of the revolution has been the emerging bourgeoisie, and in Bolivia where peasants' gains in land were confined to infrasubsistence plots of land forcing them to offer their labour as semi-proletarians.

Peasant Consciousness and Collective Action

There has been considerable debate over the origins of collective action among peasants and over the types of political programmes in which they can be enlisted. In Mexico, for example, Bartra (1974) has argued that peasants assume petty bourgeois class positions and that a progressive alliance has to be sought between urban workers and the semi-proletarian peasants and landless agricultural workers. Esteva (1978), by contrast, argues that peasants (including those who are highly semi-proletarianized) are motivated by protection and modernization of their small plots of land and can organize into eventually large peasant movements to achieve these goals. Peasant political organizations can, in turn, achieve a logical alliance with urban workers as they have mutual interests deriving from an increased production of basic foods and reduced urban migration which alleviates a source of downward pressure on urban wages.

There cannot, of course, exist a single political line among peasants due to the extraordinary heterogeneity and instability of their objective and subjective conditions. Yet contradictory positions in this debate come from failure to acknowledge the fact that the class position of peasants, which is an inter-mediate location between the two essential classes of capitalism, is itself contradictory. Objectively, a majority of rural people in Latin America tend to be more dependent on wage income than on home production for their sub-sistence. Yet the seasonal and erratic conditions of their employment in a labour market marred by surplus labour and low wages force them to cling to plots of land for their survival, however small the contribution of land to total income. Rural wage earners are, thus, motivated to act collectively as small producers or in community struggles for public services, such as roads, potable water and schools, but rarely for better employment conditions and higher wages. As Paré (1977) clearly indicates, peasant demands for land and services should not be considered as reactionary nor should their heavy dependency on wage income be used to assume that they possess proletarian class conscious-ness. Collective action for greater access to land, to public assistance to the modernization of land use, and to improved community services has been at the base of grass-root initiatives in Latin America.

The conditions under which peasants' individual defensive strategies give way to collective action – not only to seek a collective solution to a common problem but also to act as a lobby and place claims on the state – are complex and varied. Huizer (1972), Castells (1983), and Hirschman (1984) have identified conditions such as

1 contacts with urban organizations and experiences derived from participa-tion in other struggles;
2 availability of strong and charismatic local leaders;

3 creation of awareness through cultural revival and information campaigns;
4 external aggression by nature, landlords, or the state; and
5 support from urban allies or foreign assistance groups.

Peasant political alliances have the distinctive characteristic of being generally aimed at the state rather than against other clearly defined class entities. In recent years, particularly under repressive forms of government that eliminate classical forms of organization as workers (unions) or producers (cooperatives), grass-roots initiatives have been an important alternative course of collective action even if dispersed and confined to specific groups. Rarely do these initiatives aggregate into large movements and become significant agents of social change. Yet the processes they set in motion can sometimes achieve substantial gains for participants and serve as springboards for more ambitious demands when the windows of opportunity suddenly open. They serve as nurseries for future leaders and breeding grounds for democratic values, and they are the most effective guardians against the potential barbarism of governments.

Notes

1 Backward and forward linkages are best understood in the context of input–output analysis. The backward linkages of a particular activity measure the demand for input-supplying industries that are necessary to sustain the activity. The forward linkages of an activity measure the use of the output of that activity as input by other industries. Investing in industries with strong linkages will thus induce large investments in input-supplying and output-using industries.
2 The traditional urban sector EAP is defined as being composed of workers on own-account, unpaid family members, and paid domestic services. Peasant EAP is defined as workers on own-account and unpaid family members.
3 The implicit wages to family labour are equal to market wages, and the implicit rate of return to capital is no less than the average rate of profit to which this capital would have access in the economy.

References

Bartra, R. (1974) *Estructura agraria y clases sociales en Mexico*, Mexico City: Era.
Castells, M. (1983) *Grassroots and the City*, Berkeley: University of California Press.
Commander, P. and Peek, P. (1983) *Oil Exports, Agrarian Change and the Rural Labour Process: The Ecuadorian Sierra in the 1970's*, World Employment Programme Research, Working Paper No. 63, Geneva: International Labour Office.
Janvry, A. de (1981) *The Agrarian Question and Reformism in Latin America*, Baltimore: Johns Hopkins University Press.
Deere, C. D. and Janvry, A. de (1979) 'A conceptual framework for the empirical analysis of peasants', *American Journal of Agricultural Economics*, vol. 61, no. 4, pp. 601–11.

404 *Alain de Janvry*

Deere, C. D. and Wasserstrom, R. (1981) 'Ingreso familiar y trabajo no agricola entre los pequeños productores de America Latina y el Caribe', in A. Novoa and J. Posner (eds), *Agricultura de ladera en America Tropical*, Turrialba, Costa Rica: Centro Agronomico Tropical de Investigación y Enseñanza.
Esteva, G. (1978) 'Y si los campesinos existen?', *Comercio Exterior*, vol. 28, June, pp. 699–732.
GIA (1983) *Capitalismo y campesinado en el agro chileno*, Santiago, Chile: Grupo de Investigaciónes Agrarias.
Goodman, D. and Redclift, M. (1984) *From Peasant to Proletarian: Capitalist Development and Agrarian Transitions*, New York: St Martin's Press.
Hintermeister, A. (1984) *Rural Poverty and Export Farming in Guatemala*, World Employment Programme Research, Working Paper No. 71, Geneva: International Labour Office.
Hirschman, A. (1970) *Exit, Voice and Loyalty*, Cambridge, Ma.: Harvard University Press.
Hirschman, A. (1984) *Getting Ahead Collectively: Grassroots Experience in Latin America*, New York: Pergamon Press.
Huizer, G. (1972) *The Revolutionary Potential of Peasants in Latin America*, Lexington, Ma.: Lexington Books.
Paré, L. (1977) *El Proletariado agricolo en Mexico*, Mexico City: Siglo XXI.
Pearse, A. (1975) *The Latin American Peasant*, London: Frank Cass.
PREALC (1982) *Mercado de trabajo en cifras: 1950–1980*, Chile: Regional Employment Program for Latin America and the Caribbean.
Schejtman, A. (1984) 'The peasant economy: internal logic, articulation, and persistence', in C. Wilber (ed.), *The Political Economy of Development and Under-Development*, New York: Random House.
Spittler, G. (1979) 'Peasants and the state in Niger (West Africa)', *Peasant Studies*, vol. 8, no. 1, Winter, pp. 30–47.

Related Items

12, 13, 21, 23, 25, 26, 29, 30, 31, 32, 39, 41, 42, 50, 51, 53, 54, 59, 61, 62.

50

Peasantry and the Political Economy of the Early Stages of Industrialization

Evgenii Preobrazhensky

For capitalist accumulation to begin, the following prerequisites were needed:

1 A preliminary accumulation of capital in particular hands to an extent sufficient for the application of a higher technique or of a higher degree of division of labour with the same technique.
2 The presence of a body of wage workers.
3 A sufficient development of the system of commodity economy in general to serve as the base for capitalist commodity production and accumulation. . . .

By *socialist* accumulation we mean the addition to the functioning by means of production of a surplus product which has been created with the constituted socialist economy and which does not find its way into supplementary distribution among the agents of socialist production and the socialist state, but serves for expanded reproduction. *Primitive socialist* accumulation, on the other hand, means accumulation in the hands of the state of material resources mainly or partly from sources lying outside the complex of state economy. This accumulation must play an extremely important part in a backward peasant country, hastening to a very great extent the arrival of the moment when the technical and scientific reconstruction of the state economy begins and when this economy at last achieves purely economic superiority over capitalism. It is true that in this period accumulation takes place also on the production base of state economy. In the first place, however, this accumulation also has the character of preliminary accumulation of the means for a really socialist economy and it is subordinated to this purpose. Secondly, accumulation of the former kind,

Excerpts from Evgenii Preobrazhensky, *The New Economics*, translated by B. Pearce, Clarendon Press, 1965, pp. 80–124. First published in 1924.

that is, at the expense of the non-state milieu, greatly predominates in this period. For this reason we should call this entire stage the period of primitive or preliminary socialist accumulation. This period has its special features and its special laws. . . .

Let us now examine systematically the main methods of primitive capitalist accumulation and compare them, so far as possible, with the analogous or closely related methods and processes of primitive socialist accumulation. We shall take for purposes of comparison not only the period preceding capitalist production but also the epoch of the first steps of capitalist production, because this primitive accumulation, as accumulation from outside the range of capitalist production, was also carried on under very varied forms, after the appearance of capitalist enterprises.

Let us begin with plundering of non-capitalist forms of economy. In essence the whole period of the existence of merchant capital, from the moment when the craftsman's work for the customer and the local market gave place to work for distant markets and when the buyer-up [putter-out] became a necessary agent of production, can be regarded as a period of primitive accumulation, as a period of systematic plundering of petty production.

Another form of plundering which was of very great importance was the colonial policy of the world-trading countries. We have in mind here not the plundering which is connected with the exchange of a small quantity of labour for a larger quantity on the base of 'normal' trade, but plundering in the form of taxes on the natives, seizure of their property, their cattle and land, their stores of precious metals, the conversion of conquered people into slaves, the infinitely varied system of crude cheating, and so on. To this category also belong all methods of compulsion and plundering in relation to the peasant population of the metropolitan countries. The robbery of small peasant production in the interests of primitive accumulation assumed many different forms. The celebrated 'enclosure movement', to which Marx devoted such brilliant pages of the first volume of *Capital*, was not the typical method of primitive accumulation for all countries. The most typical methods were, first, plundering of the serf peasants by their lords and sharing of the plunder with merchant capital, and, second, crushing taxation of the peasantry by the state and transformation of part of the means so obtained into capital.

When the landlord's estate began to be transformed from a purely natural economy into a money or semi-money economy, when the landlords thereby promoted trade on a large scale, and when the growth in their demands stimulated an increase in extortion from the peasantry, they entered into a certain kind of unconscious cooperation with merchant capital. Everything that was plundered in the countryside, except what was consumed on the spot, was sold to merchants. In return the merchants supplied the landlords with the products of urban or foreign industry which served to satisfy their growing and increasingly refined demands. Merchant capital sold these products at a profit of 100 per cent and more. Then it lent money to the ruined gentlefolk at usurious rates of interest. As a result, the feudal lords were in this period in a certain sense agents for merchant capital, transmission pumps for the plundering of small-scale rural production in the interests of primitive capitalist accumulation. Being 'higher class' in comparison with the third estate, legally speaking, they cooperated economically with the merchants, who took not the greater but the smaller share in the matter of extortion from the peasantry.

The other form in which petty production was plundered was state taxes. Out of their receipts from taxation the absolute states encouraged the development of manufacture, giving subsidies to merchants who had become industrialists to nobles who had transformed themselves into manufacturers. This support was rendered especially to manufactories which in one way or another served to supply the army: textile mills, arms works, metallurgical enterprises, and so on. This kind of transfer of resources from the channels of petty production through the state machine to large-scale production, especially to heavy industry, takes place also in a much later period.

On the role of the state, and in particular on the role of state pressure in the period of primitive accumulation, Marx wrote:

These methods depend in part on brute force, e.g., the colonial system. But they all employ the power of the state, the concentrated and organized force of society, to hasten, hothouse fashion, the process of transformation of the feudal mode of production into the capitalist mode, and to shorten the transition. Force is the midwife of every old society pregnant with a new one. It is itself an economic power. (1867, p. 776)

This force played a very big role also in the formation of national states as arenas for the activity of merchant capital. The profound class analysis, full of concrete historical truth, to which M. N. Pokrovsky subjected the policy of the Muscovite Tsars, evokes a clear picture of this aspect of the period under consideration. The conquest of the necessary territory, trade routes and so on, is also nothing else but a link in the chain of primitive capitalist accumulation, because without accumulation of the necessary territorial prerequisites the development of merchant capital and its transition to industrial capital could not be carried through successfully. From this standpoint the peasant paid tribute to the Moloch of primitive accumulation not only when part of the rent he paid passed through the hands of the lord into those of the merchant, not only when part of the taxes he paid passed via the state to the manufacturer, but also when he gave the blood of his sons for the winning of new trade routes and the conquest of new lands.

An important role in the process of primitive accumulation is played by the system of state loans, under which there takes place the transfer of part of the annual income of the small producers, in the form of interest payments, into the hands of the capitalist creditors of the state which has contracted the loan. In this connection Marx says:

> The public debt becomes one of the most powerful levers of primitive accumulation. As with the stroke of an enchanter's wand, it endows barren money with the power of breeding and thus turns it into capital, without the necessity of its exposing itself to the troubles and risks inseparable from its employment in industry or even in usury. The State creditors actually give nothing away, for the sum lent is transformed into public bonds, easily negotiable, which go on functioning in their hands just as so much hard cash would. But further, apart from the class of lazy annuitants thus created, and from the impoverished wealth of the financiers, middlemen between the government and the nation – as also apart from the tax-farmers, merchants and private manufacturers, to whom a good part of every national loan renders the service of a capital fallen from heaven – the national debt has given rise to joint-stock companies, to dealings in negotiable effects of all kinds, and to agiotage, in a word to stock-exchange gambling and the modern bankocracy. (1867, pp. 779–80)

Let us now dwell upon the method of primitive accumulation which we have enumerated, based mainly on plundering of small-scale production and non-economic pressure upon it, and let us see how matters stand in this connection in the period of primitive socialist accumulation.

As regards colonial plundering, a socialist state, carrying out a policy of equality between nationalities and voluntary entry by them into one kind or another of union of nations, repudiates on principle all the forcible methods of capital in this sphere. This source of primitive accumulation is closed to it from the very start and for ever.

It is quite different in the case of the alienation in favour of socialism of part of the surplus product of all the pre-socialist economic forms. Taxation of the non-socialist forms not only must inevitably take place in the period of primitive socialist accumulation, it must inevitably play a very great, a directly decisive role in peasant countries such as the Soviet Union. We must consider this point in some detail.

From the foregoing we have seen that capitalist production was able to begin to function and develop further only by relying on the resources obtained from petty production. The transition of society from the petty-bourgeois system of production to the capitalist could not have been accomplished without preliminary accumulation at the expense of petty production, and would thereafter have proceeded at a snail's pace if additional accumulation at the expense of petty production had not continued alongside capitalist accumulation at the expense of the exploited labour-power of the proletariat. The very transition presumes, as a system, an exchange of values between large-scale and petty production under which the latter gives more to the former than it receives. In the period of primitive socialist accumulation the state economy cannot get by without alienating part of the surplus product from the peasantry and the handicraftsmen, without making deductions from capitalist accumulation for the benefit of socialist accumulation. We do not know in how great a condition of ruin other countries in which the dictatorship of the proletariat is going to triumph will emerge from civil war. But a country like the USSR, with its ruined and in general rather backward economy, must pass through a period of primitive accumulation in which the sources provided by pre-socialist forms of economy are drawn upon very freely. It must not be forgotten that the period of primitive socialist accumulation is the most critical period in the life of the socialist state after the end of the civil war. In this period the socialist system is not yet in a condition to develop all its organic advantages, but it inevitably abolishes at the same time a number of the economic advantages characteristic of a developed capitalist system. How to pass as quickly as possible through this period, how to reach as quickly as possible the moment when the socialist system will develop all its natural advantages over capitalism, is a question of life and death for the socialist state. At any rate, that is the problem before the USSR today, and that will perhaps be the problem for a certain time for a number of European countries in which the proletariat will come to power. Under such conditions, to count only upon accumulation within the socialist field would mean jeopardizing the very existence of the socialist economy, or prolonging endlessly the period of preliminary accumulation, the length of which, however, does not depend on the free will of the proletariat. In the concrete part of this work, which will be devoted to the industry and agriculture of the USSR, we shall cite numerical calculations as to how long we should expect the restoration of our industry even to its pre-war levels to take if we were to rely only on the surplus product of industry itself. In any case the idea that socialist economy can develop on its own, without touching the resources of petit-bourgeois (including peasant) economy is undoubtedly a reactionary petit-bourgeois Utopia. The task of the socialist state consists here not in taking from the petit-bourgeois producers less than capitalism took, but in taking more *from the still larger* incomes which will be secured to the petty producer by the rationalization of the whole economy, including petty production, on the basis of industrializing the country and intensifying agriculture. . . .

We can formulate a law, or at least that part of it which relates to the redistribution of the material resources of production, in this way:

The more backward economically, petit-bourgeois, peasant, a particular country is which has gone over to the socialist organization of production, and the smaller the inheritance received by the socialist accumulation fund of the proletariat of this country when the social revolution takes place, by so much the more, in proportion, will socialist accumulation be obliged to rely on alienating part of the surplus product of pre-socialist forms of economy and the smaller will be the relative weight of accumulation on its own production basis, that is, the less will it be nourished by the surplus product of the workers in socialist industry. Conversely, the more developed economically and industrially a country in which the social revolution triumphs, and the greater the material inheritance, in the form of highly developed industry and capitalistically organized agriculture, which the proletariat of this country receives from the bourgeoisie on nationalization, by so much the smaller will be the relative weight of pre-capitalist forms in the particular country; and the greater the need for the proletariat of this country to reduce non-equivalent exchange of its products for the products of the former colonies, by so much the more will the centre of gravity of socialist accumulation shift to the production basis of the socialist forms, that is, the more will it rely on the surplus product of its own industry, and its own agriculture.[1]

Note

1 This law must of course, undergo certain modifications when there is a transfer of means of production from an advanced socialist country to a backward one.

Reference

Marx, K. (1867) *Capital*, ed. F. Engels, trans. S. Moore and E. Marx Aveling, Allen & Unwin, 1946.

Related Items

9, 13, 14, 15, 21, 25, 26, 35, 36, 37, 38, 39, 41, 42, 44, 51, 53, 58, 59, 60, 61, 62.

51

Primitive Accumulation Reversed: Society Owes Initial Expenses to the Peasant Communes

Karl Marx

As the latest phase in the [archaic] primitive formation of society, the agrarian commune is at the same time a phase in the transition to the secondary formation, and therefore in the transition from a society based on communal property to one based on private property. The second formation does, of course, include the series of societies which rest upon slavery and serfdom.

After the so-called emancipation of the peasantry, the state placed the Russian peasant commune in abnormal economic conditions; and since that time, it has never ceased to weigh it down with the social force concentrated in its hands. Exhausted by tax demands, the commune became a kind of inert matter easily exploited by traders, landowners and usurers. This oppression from without unleashed the conflict of interests already present at the heart of the commune, rapidly developing the seeds of its disintegration. But that is not all. At the peasant's expense, the state grew in hothouse conditions certain branches of the Western capitalist system which, in no way developing the productive premises of agriculture, are best suited to facilitate and precipitate the theft of its fruits by unproductive middlemen. In this way, it helped to enrich a new capitalist vermin which is sucking the already depleted blood of the 'rural commune'.

... In short, the state lent a hand in the precocious development of the technical and economic instruments best suited to facilitate and precipitate the exploitation of the farmer – Russia's greatest productive force – and to enrich the 'new pillars of society'.

Excerpts from T. Shanin, *Late Marx and the Russian Road*, Routledge & Kegal Paul, London, 1984.

Does this mean, however, that the historical career of the agrarian commune is fated to end in this way? Not at all. Its innate dualism admits of an alternative: either its property element will gain the upper hand over its collective element; or else the reverse will take place. Everything depends upon the historical context in which it is located.

Let us, for the moment, abstract from the evils bearing down upon the Russian commune and merely consider its evolutionary possibilities. It occupies a unique situation without any precedent in history. Alone in Europe, it is still the organic, predominant form of rural life in a vast empire. Communal land ownership offers it the natural basis for collective appropriation, and its historical context – the contemporaneity of capitalist production – provides it with the ready-made material conditions for large-scale cooperative labour organized on a large scale. It may therefore incorporate the positive achievements developed by the capitalist system, without having to pass under its harsh tribute. It may gradually replace small-plot agriculture with a combined, machine-assisted agriculture which the physical configuration of the Russian land invites. After normal conditions have been created for the commune in its present form, it may become the direct *starting point* of the economic system towards which modern society is tending; it may open a new chapter that does not begin with its own suicide.

... One debilitating feature of the 'agricultural commune' in Russia is inimical to it in every way. This is its isolation, the lack of connection between the lives of different communes. It is not an immanent or universal characteristic of this type that the commune should appear as a *localized microcosm*. But wherever it does so appear, it leads to the formation of a more or less central despotism above the communes. The federation of north Russian republics proves that such isolation, which seems to have been originally imposed by the huge size of the country, was largely consolidated by Russia's political changes of fortune after the Mongol invasion.[1] Today it is an obstacle that could be removed with the utmost ease. All that is necessary is to replace the *volost*,[2] a government institution, with a peasant assembly chosen by the communes themselves – an economic and administrative body serving their own interests.

It is understood that the commune would develop gradually, and that the first step would be to place it under normal conditions *on its present basis*.

... But where is the peasant to find the tools, the fertilizer, the agronomic methods, etc. – all the things required for collective labour? This is precisely where the Russian 'rural commune' is greatly superior to archaic communes of the same type. For, alone in Europe, it has maintained itself on a vast, nationwide basis. It is this place within a historical context in which the contemporaneity of capitalist production provides it with all the conditions for cooperative labour. It is in a position to incorporate the positive achievements of the capitalist system, without having to pass under its harsh tribute. The physical configuration of the Russian land is eminently suited to machine-assisted agriculture, organized on a large scale and performed by cooperative labour. As for the initial expenses, both intellectual and material, Russian society owes them to the 'rural commune' at whose expense it has lived for so long and in which it must seek its 'regenerative element'.

... Leaving aside all questions of a more or less theoretical nature, I do not have to tell you that the very existence of the Russian commune is now threatened by a conspiracy of powerful interests. A certain type of capitalism, fostered by the state at the peasants' expense, has risen up against the commune and found an interest in stifling it. The landowners, too, have an interest in forming the more or less well-off peasants into an agricultural middle class, and in converting the poor farmers – that is, the mass – into mere wage labourers – that is to say, cheap labour. How can a commune resist, pounded as it is by state exactions, plundered by trade, exploited by landowners, and undermined from within by usury!

What threatens the life of the Russian commune is neither a historical inevitability nor a theory; it is state oppression, and exploitation by capitalist intruders whom the state has made powerful at the peasants' expense.

... While the commune is being bled and tortured, its lands sterilized and impoverished, the literary flunkeys of the 'new pillars of society' ironically refer to the evils heaped on the commune as if they were symptoms of spontaneous, indisputable decay, arguing that it is dying a natural death and that it would be an act of kindness to shorten its agony. At this level, it is a question no longer of a problem to be solved, but simply of an enemy to be beaten. Thus, it is no longer a theoretical problem. To save the Russian commune, there must be a Russian revolution. For their part, the Russian government and the 'new pillars of society' are doing their best to prepare the masses for such a catastrophe. If the revolution takes place in time, if it concentrates all its forces to ensure the unfettered rise of the rural commune, the latter will soon develop as a regenerating element of Russian society and an element of superiority over the countries enslaved by the capitalist regime.

Notes

1 The text of Marx's 'drafts' which in 1881 advocated what would amount to the reversal of 'primitive accumulation' in a post-revolution society marked by a massive peasantry and the survival of its early forms of self-organization was probably unknown to Preobrazhensky when he presented his analysis (reproduced in our item 50) as universally Marxist.

2 *Volost'* was in the relevant period a self-governing peasant locality, usually consisting of several villages and communes and with its own elected leadership and magistrates' court but tightly controlled by the state authorities.

Related Items

2, 10, 13, 14, 25, 26, 28, 38, 39, 41, 45, 46, 47, 49, 50, 59, 61, 62.

52

Land Reform and Japan's Economic Development – A Reactionary Thesis

R. P. Dore

There is general agreement among the students of Japan's economic development that agriculture's contribution to the task of building a strong industrial base was a considerable one. It provided export earnings and import substitutes which helped in acquiring the machinery and raw materials which had to be bought abroad. It managed a steady expansion of the supply of staple foods which enabled a growing town population to be fed reasonably cheap food. It contributed through the land tax a substantial portion of the funds which provided the infrastructure of communications, government and education, and through the profits of the landlords some of the capital which developed especially the small industries. And it was in part a growth in productivity which made this 'squeeze' possible without such a drastic lowering of rural living standards as to cause uncontrollable political instability.

Was this in part because of, or in spite of, the nature of the land tenure system? It has by now become a truism that one important factor determining the productivity of agriculture is the system of property institutions under which land is owned and used. The question which naturally arises, therefore, is this: granted that agriculture made a substantial contribution to Japan's economic growth, was it the best that it could have made? Or is it possible that under a different land tenure system it could have done more?

This question, like all the other 'if' questions about human history, can only be answered by guesses derived from comparison with other countries. For such comparisons it is useful to have a typology. The one I suggest below has no particular merit except that it seems to be applicable to a variety of situations and is a handy basis for generalization.

R. P. Dore, 'Land reform and Japan's economic development', *Developing Economies*, Special Issue, vol. 3, 1965, no. 4, pp. 487–96.

The typology is little more than a distinction between two types of land reforms based on the kind of landlord whose power and property is affected. The key is therefore the definition of the two types of landlord. The first is typically one who acquires control of a territory by military conquest or by infeudation – being allocated a territory by a warrior chief who thereby secures his allegiance. At first he is lord and master in every sense; he draws produce from the cultivator by virtue of his monopoly of violence; political control and economic exploitation are one and indivisible and there is no conceptual distinction between rents and taxes.

At a later stage of development the autonomy and arbitrariness of his political power may become circumscribed by the development of a central state authority. The central government may claim the sole right to tax and the former feudal magnate now only draws a rent. He may still, however, exercise political power in his hereditary fief by ascriptive right, though he may exercise it through delegates, he himself living in the central capital and only occasionally visiting his estates for supervisory or ceremonial purposes.

The second type of landlord is characteristically one who achieves his position by *economic* means within the framework of a system of established political order; not by warfare or that milder type of warfare that is politics. Sometimes he is a merchant, sometimes a thrifty farmer who acquires land from the improvidence or misfortunes of others, sometimes a money-lender. He may also exercise some political power, but it is power exercised through the framework of a system of government in which he has no ascriptive right, only the power of manipulation gained by virtue of his superior wealth. Such landlords have smaller estates than the first kind, and they generally live near the land they own. They may, in Marxist terms, act as the rural wing of the bourgeoisie, a conservative political force which gains advantages for itself from contacts with the urban politicians, and provides the latter with a necessary basis of support in proto-democratic systems. They are not necessarily obstacles to all economic progress and can in some cases serve as the agents of economic development.

The next distinction follows logically from the first. What will be called a Stage I redistribution is one which expropriates, or in some way drastically reduces the power of, Type I landlords. A Stage II land redistribution is one which expropriates or weakens the second type of landlord.

For some countries the classification seems clearly apposite. One can pinpoint the two distinct historical events representing the two stages of land reform. In Czechoslovakia, Yugoslavia and other countries of the old Austro-Hungarian Empire the land reforms which took place after the First World War were Stage I reforms; those which came after the Second World War were Stage II reforms. In Russia one may take the land redistribution following the revolution as the first stage, and collectivization, destroying the power of the *kulaks*, as the second. There are other countries such as England where there has been no first-stage reform and where the Type I landlords have never disappeared. Their local political power has been whittled away to the point where only in the more remote areas of rural Scotland can the scions of noble families, such as Lord Home, claim a parliamentary seat almost as a hereditary right. Their economic hold over the land remains, however, though it is in no sense different from that of the Type II landlords – those who acquired their land by economic means, often by investing in small estates the profits derived from industry and commerce. (Already by the sixteenth century it is difficult to separate the two types of landlords, as witness the historians' disputes about the rise or fall of the 'gentry' or the 'aristocracy'.)

France, by contrast, quite clearly had a Stage I redistribution in the celebrated events which took place in 1789, but in neither France nor England has a Stage II redistribution taken place. Instead, in both countries, the Type II landlords who supported the bourgeois regimes of the nineteenth century were forced, as their political power waned, to accept tenancy reforms which redistributed income without redistributing the ownership of land. In these countries, and in England especially, industrialization *before* population growth created serious pressure on the land, and the ability of landlords to accept gradual reform (if only because they had already acquired substantial industrial interests too) has created a situation where the entrepreneurial tenant can be counted as a member of the prosperous middle class. In Ireland, on the other hand, greater population pressure, greater tenant distress and a more intransigent unwillingness of landlords to accept reform led, not to evolution, but to drastic changes which saw the virtual elimination of the Type I landlords in the space of a decade.

Again, there are countries where a first-stage land reform has only recently been carried out; India, for example, where the removal of the jagadirs and zemindars did not immediately affect the Type II landlords, and Iran where only the holders of whole villages were affected by the original land reform measure.

A new phenomenon in the modern world, however, is the accelerated spread of communications, education and political consciousness, one of the results of which is that the political demand for land reform can become irresistible in countries which are otherwise at a level of economic development at which, a century ago, effectively organized popular political demands of any kind would have been unthinkable. Hence the strong political pressure for a Stage II land reform in India, only a decade or so after the first. Hence the second wave of land reforms in Iran which is aimed, two years after the first, at the estates of the smaller landlords. Hence, too, countries where the land reform has taken place has been in effect a telescoped Stage I plus Stage II operation, jumping from a structure of large 'feudal' holdings to atomized peasant proprietorship. Bolivia is an oustanding recent example.

If the reader still thinks that the typology has any validity he will have no doubt where to fit Japan into the picture. The Meiji Restoration and the creation of a centralized system of government dispossessed (though with handsome compensation) Japan's Type I landlords, the *daimio*. They remained wealthy, but their wealth was no longer in landed property. They almost entirely lost local political influence and became a metropolitan aristocracy, and although they were granted, to be sure, a place in the political system in the House of Peers, at no time was the House of Peers at the centre of political power.

This fact in itself was of considerable importance for Japan's industrialization. Those who controlled policy after the Meiji Restoration were not landed gentlemen but members of a bureaucracy who depended for their income on the salaries, and on the less formal income channels provided by their more or less corrupt relations with the new industrial class. They had, therefore, no personal interest in protecting agricultural incomes at the cost of slowing the growth of industry. They could, and did, maintain a high level of taxation on agriculture. There is a marked contrast here with the situation in, say, England, where the landed aristocracy, with strong personal agricultural interests, maintained their political influence until a relatively advanced stage of industrial development. It was not until the middle of the nineteenth century that the repeal of the Corn Laws marked the final emergence of political supremacy of industrial interests. Similarly, in a good many Latin American countries today the continued political power of a traditional landlord class (fortified by those who have put urban wealth back into the purchase of landed estates and adopted traditional values) remains an obstacle to serious industrial development.

The removal of the *daimio* left a clear field for the Type II landlords, those smaller village landlords who had been acquiring control over land by economic means in the latter half of the Tokugawa period. The first decades of the new regime saw an extension of their power; various factors, but especially the operation of the new tax system, increased the amount of land which such landlords controlled, from about 30 to about 45 per cent of the total. They remained the dominant economic and political influence in the countryside until Japan's Stage II land reform put them out of business in 1947–9.

No one can seriously doubt that the Stage I land reform represented by the dispossession of the *daimio* was an essential precondition for Japan's development. The question whether or not the land tenure system after 1870 was the best one to promote that development resolves itself, therefore, into the question: could the Stage II land reform with advantage have come earlier? Supposing that the Meiji government had insisted that the land certificates issued in the 1870s should always be given to the actual cultivator and that all other claims and liens should be ignored or compensated for; and supposing that it had set rigid limits to the area of land which any family might subsequently acquire by purchase; supposing, in other words, that the Stage I and Stage II land reforms had been telescoped into one, thus establishing immediately a small peasant holding system; would the growth of agricultural productivity have been faster, or agriculture's contribution to economic development in general greater?

There are some good grounds for answering 'no'. One might list them as follows:

1   These landlords were village landlords, themselves often farmers, with an understanding of agriculture and personal motives for improving their tenants' standards of husbandry. (Though rents were generally fixed rents, in produce, the tradition of rent reduction in years of bad harvest preserved elements of a share system.) Many of them, through inexperience as village headmen and contact with the *samurai* class, had developed Confucian ideas of paternal responsibility which meant that their economic interests were sometimes reinforced by a sense of moral duty to improve their tenants' production methods for the latter's own good. As a consequence they had the *motive* to use their economically-based political control of village society to improve agriculture.[1]

2   Secondly, they also were in a better position than other villagers to have the *knowledge* to do so. Being richer they had more leisure and travelled more. They brought their brides from further afield and consequently had wider kinship connections. They could afford education and were sometimes the only literate members of their village. They were consequently in a better position to learn of superior methods practised elsewhere and to keep in touch with the national centres of technical innovation – as well as sometimes being inventors and experimenters themselves.

3   Many of the productive innovations in agriculture in this period required the creation of new formal organizations. Consolidated schemes for the reorganization of field sizes, irrigation and drainage systems certainly did. So did the creation of new marketing channels, of incentive-creating shows and competitions, of the primitive travelling-lecturer system of agricultural extension, and so on. Such organizations could be created much more easily in an authoritarian manner by use of the landlord's traditional power than they could have been if it had been necessary to persuade the majority of the villagers to come together to form such organizations on a footing of equality in a democratic manner.

4   The landlords' role as links in a communication system joining the villages to the centre of government was important for more than just the diffusion of agricultural improvements. They were interpreters of government policies without whom there might have been far more peasant uprisings and general political unrest than there in fact was. At the same time their own political ambitions forced the creation of local government systems which could be gradually expanded to meet increasing demands for political participation, whereas if there had been no landlord class to make demands

which were of a nature moderate enough to be acceptable with modifications to the ruling Tokyo oligarchy, concessions might have been delayed and really revolutionary forces built up which might have destroyed the whole structure of administration. The landlords were particularly important as interpreters of the government's educational policy and often played a leading part in the building and expansion of schools. As village landlords they sent their own children to the village schools, and hence had a direct interest in them. Even when they became absentees, for one or two generations they maintained close links with their village, and the desire to maintain the 'prestige of the house' in the village where the family land and graves were prompted many of them not to begrudge taxes and contributions for village schools and public works.

5   The landlords commanded the 'agricultural surplus'. In their hands it was more effectively taxable. Moreover, many of them used their wealth in productive ways – in the education of their children and in investment in food-processing and other local industries. If this wealth had not been squeezed out of their tenants it would have been used for direct consumption; the overall rate of savings would have been lower and economic development slower.

6   By analogy one might argue from situations such as Bolivia where a telescope Stage I/Stage II land reform left the villages without small landlords and without a structure of local leadership, and where there seems to have been not only no economic development but in fact a decline in production, and administrative anarchy.

As against these, one might set the following arguments for the contrary point of view:

1   The landlords may have brought new ideas and techniques to the villages, but this advantage was cancelled out by the well-known drawbacks of a tenancy system; the fact that tenants, with only insecure tenure, had no motive for carrying out improvements with long-term effects, and the fact that the burden of rents kept them so poor that they could not afford the kind of investment in, for instance, fertilizers, which was most capable of bringing big increases in production.

2   It is debatable whether the tradition-sanctioned authority of the landlords was a necessary condition for creating the organizational structure necessary to improve agricultural practices. The tradition of village coopera-tion between equals is an old one in Japanese rural areas. There were villages, particularly in the commercially more developed areas of central Japan from Gifu to Hiroshima, where landlord influence was less strong and a more egalitarian type of village structure prevailed. These areas were not notably slow in developing the cooperative organization required for agricultural development, and there is no reason to suppose that the more authoritarian

village could not have adapted to more egalitarian forms if the influence of the landlords was removed – as in fact they did after 1950.

3   The landlords may have invested some of the income they squeezed out of their tenants in productive ways, but they also consumed conspicuously, to some extent in luxury imported goods. If there had been a greater equality of village incomes there might not have been as much local investment in commerce and industry, but there would have been a quicker and wider diffusion of popular education. Many more villagers might have sent their children to school for, say, six years instead of four.

4   The pre-emption of local formal political authority by the landlords was a loss, not a gain, for agriculture. As soon as they were allowed representation in the national Diet their main interest was directed towards reducing their tax burden. This pressure on the national budget slowed the growth of agricultural research and extension services and of the development subsidy system. If the voice of the villages in the Diet had been the voice of practising farmers these things would not have been neglected.

5   The 'political stability' of the countryside ensured by the landlords' power was also a loss rather than a gain. If the demand for political participation had built up to revolutionary proportions before concessions were contemplated and a real revolution had taken place, there might earlier have emerged a democratic political system with a government really devoted to the cause of popular welfare.

It is impossible to reach any definite conclusions on this matter. On balance it seems difficult to believe, given the level of violence associated even with middle-class politics and even in the 1920s and 1930s, that a regime of any stability or any power to plan economic development could have emerged from a successful popular revolution at any time in the Meiji period. It equally seems difficult to believe that organizational and technical innovation in the villages could have proceeded as fast without the backing of traditional landlord authority. I am inclined to believe that economic development would have been slower if there had been a Stage II land reform at any time before, say, 1900.

But the situation was already different by 1920. By then most farmers were literate and more capable both of informing themselves individually about new agricultural methods and of forming the organizations necessary to put them into practice. (As Galbraith, 1963, has recently said, 'Nowhere in the world is there an illiterate peasantry that is progressive. Nowhere is there a literate peasantry that is not.') More important, if the landlords' traditional authority *was* put to productive purposes in the Meiji period, this was only because that authority was *accepted* by the tenants. By 1920 tenants were beginning to lose their differential submissiveness – as the growing number of disputes over rents and the formation of tenant unions testify. Hence, by this time, the advantages of landlord control had all but disappeared. Only the disadvantages of poor incentives and tenant poverty remained. A Stage II reform at any time after 1920 would probably have hastened economic development, as well as conducing to a more satisfactory internal political structure (more satisfactory by our present-day values) and possibly modifying Japanese external policies as well.

There are two further comments worth making on this issue. The first concerns the evaluative implications of the fact – if it is a fact – that the Meiji landlords contributed to the cause of Japanese economic development. Japanese historians are inclined to write off the landlord system in the Meiji period as a social evil. In part this is a back-projection into the past of judgements about recent situations, but in so far as this is not the case, what would they make of the assertion that on balance economic development took place more rapidly with landlords than it would have done without them? One answer, which would probably be favoured by the majority, is that the assertion is wrong and that my summary of the balance between the two sets of arguments is at fault. There is, however, another answer. One can accept the assumption and still argue that Stage II land reform was desirable at a very early stage. It may be granted that the landlords helped to hasten the pace of economic development, but this was done at the expense of miserable poverty on the part of the tenants, and at the cost of preserving a system of social relations in the villages which was an affront to human dignity. It would have been better, it can be argued, to have improved the lot of the Meiji tenant even if this meant a slower pace of economic growth; even if it meant postponing the arrival of television sets in the villages from 1960 to 1980, to the generation of those tenants' great-grandchildren rather than their grandchildren. This is a perfectly valid argument. Economic growth is not the only end in life. Just how much sacrifice of personal welfare by the present generation is justified by how much improved welfare for future generations is a difficult value question which every development planner must face.

The second comment is this: none should try, without very drastic modifications, to draw from the history of Meiji Japan the conclusion that a small village landlord system is a beneficial factor in the initial stages of economic growth and seek to apply this as a 'lesson' to the situation of the developing countries today. It is inappropriate as a lesson from many points of view. The population growth rate in most of the developing countries is much higher than it was in Meiji Japan, thus adding a new dimension to the problem of rural development. Communications techniques have improved considerably, making less necessary the informal intermediate policy-interpreting function of the Meiji landlord. Many countries have less need to squeeze industrial capital out of the traditional agricultural sector, because of mineral revenues, foreign aid or the taxation of agricultural exports produced by capitalist plantations. Above all, the political revolution of the twentieth century – the new assumption that all governments ought to derive their power from electoral consent – together with the development of mass media in even poor countries, has created a political demand for land reform even in economies which are characterized by an almost wholly subsistence agriculture. What this means is that the traditional *acceptance* of landlord authority – a necessary condition for landlords to play the kind of useful role they played in Meiji Japan – has already been destroyed. Social relations in the villages have often reached a level of conflict similar to that of Japan in the 1920s, even though agricultural development may remain at Japan's 1870 level.

The trouble with these 'if' questions about history is not only that one can rarely arrive at satisfying answers. Even if one gets an answer it is rare that one can draw any simple 'lessons' from it for the solution of contemporary problems. For if there are some senses in which the countries of the world are moving in different directions – the poor perhaps getting relatively poorer and the rich relatively richer – there are other ways – in the accumulating stock of scientific knowledge and political ideas – in which the world as a whole moves on.

Note

1 The literature available in English reflects only a fraction of the information available in the works of Japanese scholars, but a good general idea of the development of agriculture in Japan, and in particular the role of the landlords, may be gained from the following: Dore (1959), Dore (1960), Johnston (1962), Nakamura (1965), Ogura (1963), Ohkawa and Rosovsky (1960), Sawada (1965) and Smith (1956).

References

Dore, R. P. (1959) 'The Japanese landlord: good or bad?', *Journal of Asian Studies*, vol. 18, no. 2.

Dore, R. P. (1960) 'Agricultural improvement in Japan: 1870–1900', *Economic Development and Cultural Change*, October, part 2.

Galbraith, J. K. (1963) *Economic Development in Perspective*, Harvard University Press.

Johnston, B. F. (1962) 'Agricultural development and economic transformation: a comparative study of the Japanese experience', *Food Research Institute Studies*, vol. 3, no. 3.

Nakamura, J. I. (1965) 'The growth of Japanese agriculture: 1875–1920', in W. W. Lockwood (ed.), *The State and Economic Enterprise in Modern Japan*, Princeton University Press.

Ogura, T. (1963) *Agricultural Development in Modern Japan*, Japan FAO Association.

Ohkawa, M. and Rosovsky, H. (1960) 'The role of agriculture in modern Japanese economic development', *Economic Development and Cultural Change*, vol. 9, no. 1, pp. 43–67.

Sawada, S. (1965) 'Innovation in Japanese agriculture', in W. W. Lockwood (ed.), *The State and Economic Enterprise in Modern Japan*, Japan FAO Association.
Smith, T. C. (1956) 'Landlords and rural capitalists in the modernization of Japan', *Journal of Economic History*, June.

Related Items

13, 17, 18, 21, 23, 24, 25, 26, 28, 30, 31, 32, 35, 41, 49, 53, 55.

53

Paupers of the World and How to Develop Them

Robert S. McNamara

Poverty and Growth

The basic problem of poverty and growth in the developing world can be stated very simply. The growth is not equitably reaching the poor. And the poor are not significantly contributing to growth.

Despite a decade of unprecedented increase in the gross national product of the developing countries, the poorest segments of their population have received relatively little benefit. Nearly 800 million individuals – 40 per cent out of a total of two billion – survive on incomes estimated (in US purchasing power) at 30 cents per day in conditions of malnutrition, illiteracy and squalor. They are suffering poverty in the absolute sense.

... Among 40 developing countries for which data are available, the upper 20 per cent of the population receives 55 per cent of national income in the typical country, while the lowest 20 per cent of the population receives 5 per cent.

... policies aimed primarily at accelerating economic growth, in most developing countries, have benefited mainly the upper 40 per cent of the population and the allocation of public services and investment funds has tended to strengthen rather than to offset this trend.

... The Concentrations of Poverty

... Clearly, the bulk of the poor today are in the rural areas. All of our analysis indicates that this is likely to continue to be the case during the next two or three decades:

Extracts from the *Address to the Board of Governors, International Bank for Reconstruction and Development* (Nairobi, 1973) proclaiming a new strategy of the World Bank.

1 At present, 70 per cent of the population of our developing member countries and an equivalent percentage of the poor live in the countryside.
2 Although demographic projections indicate that 60 per cent of the population increase in these countries (an increase of two billion people by the end of the century) is expected to take place in the urban areas – largely through internal migration – in the year 2000 more than half of the people in the developing world will still reside in the countryside.
3 Rapid urbanization is already creating very serious problems. Under present policies, per capita public expenditures in urban areas are typically three to four times as great as they are in rural areas. Thus, efforts to relieve rural poverty by still greater migration to the cities will result in an even more inequitable division of public expenditures and only exacerbate the existing inequalities of income.
4 Within the rural areas the poverty problem revolves primarily around the low productivity of the millions of small subsistence farms. The truth is that despite all the growth of the GNP, the increase in the productivity of these small family farms in the past decade has been so small as to be virtually imperceptible.

But despite the magnitude of the problem in the countryside, focusing on rural poverty raises a very fundamental question: is it a really sound strategy to devote a significant part of the world's resources to increasing the productivity of small-scale subsistence agriculture? Would it not be wiser to concentrate on the modern sector in the hope that its high rate of growth would filter down to the rural poor?

The answer, I believe, is no.

Experience demonstrates that in the short run there is only a limited transfer of benefits from the modern to the traditional sector. Disparities in income will simply widen unless action is taken which will directly benefit the poorest. In my view, therefore, there is no viable alternative to increasing the productivity of small-scale agriculture if any significant advance is to be made in solving the problems of absolute poverty in the rural areas.

A Strategy for Rural Development

... The fact is that very little has been done over the past two decades specifically designed to increase the productivity of subsistence agriculture. Neither political programmes, nor economic plans, nor international assistance – bilateral or multilateral – have given the problem serious and sustained attention. The World Bank is no exception. In our more than a quarter of a century of operations, less than $1 billion out of our $25 billion of lending has been devoted directly to this problem.

It is time for all of us to confront this issue head-on.

1 There are well over 100 million families involved – more than 700 million individuals.
2 The size of the average holding is small and often fragmented: more than 100 million farms are less than 5 hectares; of these, more than 50 million are less than 1 hectare.
3 The possession of land, and hence of political and economic power in the rural areas, is concentrated in the hands of a small minority. According to a recent FAO survey, the wealthiest 20 per cent of the landowners in most developing countries own between 50 and 60 per cent of the cropland. In Venezuela they own 82 per cent; in Colombia 56 per cent; in Brazil 53 per cent; in the Philippines, India, and Pakistan about 50 per cent. Conversely, the 100 million holdings of less than 5 hectares are concentrated on only 20 per cent of the cropland.
4 Even the use of the land which the small farmer does have is uncertain. Tenancy arrangements are generally insecure and often extortionate. In many countries tenants have to hand over to the landlord 50–60 per cent of their crop as rent, and yet in spite of this are faced with the constant threat of eviction. The result is that their incentive to become more productive is severely eroded.

It has often been suggested that the productivity of small-scale holdings is inherently low. But that is simply not true. Not only do we have the over-whelming evidence of Japan to disprove that proposition, but a number of recent studies on developing countries also demonstrate that, given the proper conditions, small farms can be as productive as large farms. For example, output per hectare in Guatemala, the Republic of China, India, and Brazil was substantially greater on smaller farms than on larger ones. And it is, of course, output per hectare which is the relevant measure of agricultural productivity in land-scarce, labour-surplus economies; not output per worker.

There is ample evidence that modern agricultural technology is divisible, and that small-scale operations need be no barrier to raising agricultural yields.

. . . I suggest that the goal be to increase production on small farms so that by 1985 their output will be growing at the rate of 5 per cent per year. . . . the following are essential elements of any comprehensive programme:

1 Acceleration in the rate of land and tenancy reform.
2 Better access to credit.
3 Assured availability of water.
4 Expanded extension facilities backed by intensified agricultural research.
5 Greater access to public services.
6 And most critical of all: new forms of rural institutions and organizations that will give as much attention to promoting the inherent potential and productivity of the poor as is generally given to protecting the power of the privileged.

These elements are not new. The need for them has been recognized before. But they will continue to remain little more than pious hopes unless we develop a framework of implementation, and agree to a commitment of resources commensurate with their necessity.

| Related Items |

11, 18, 21, 22, 23, 24, 25, 26, 29, 31, 32, 35, 37, 38, 41, 42, 49, 52, 54, 55, 56, 57, 59, 60, 61, 62.

54

The World Bank's
Change of Heart

Susan George

There is no doubt that the World Bank has had a change of heart. For twenty-five years, it pushed development based on the trickle-down theory – from the top dogs to the underdogs – and these twenty-five years have proved that this conception has resulted in a monstrously expensive failure. The Bank is furthermore conscience-stricken that during so many years of heavy investment in roads and electricity, it gave only a tiny fraction, less than 5 per cent, to rural development; and thus to the places where most of the world's poor people live. The sheer weight of reality and of steadily deteriorating conditions in the Third World have forced the Bank's analysts – its far-flung teams of economists, financiers and sociologists – to arrive at conclusions that were news 120 years ago when an obscure scholar named Karl Marx announced them, but which are hardly original today. In the Bank's various papers, *Land Reform*, *Agricultural Credit* and *Rural Development* – and in McNamara's speeches – one can almost hear these anguished analysts crying out, 'Great Scott, there *is* a class struggle!' 'By George, poor people *are* exploited by rich ones!' In all these documents, the Bank is constantly sidling up to the only available verdict: that social upheaval is necessary if such exploitation and poverty – the real causes of hunger – are to be eliminated; then slinking away from it again.

QUESTION: What does the world's most formidable capitalist lending institution do when confronted with the inevitability of a quasi-Marxist analysis of present reality?

ANSWER: It abandons the hoary trickle-down credo of development in favour of what it calls 'new-style projects' with a 'comprehensive approach'. In no case does it call for social and political structural change, much less revolution. How could it do so when its major stockholders and lenders would not be exactly overjoyed at such a prospect? And it tries to find a middle

Excerpts from Susan George, *How the Other Half Dies*, Penguin, 1976, pp. 245–5, 251–2.

ground, because it 'measures the risks of reform against the risks of revolution'. This middle ground is constituted by a super-hyper-broad-scale technocratic approach with a scope far beyond that of the Bank's previous projects.

... McNamara's declarations and Bank documents are full of *implicit* criticism of the green revolution. The whole thrust of the green revolution has been to modernize the methods of the already better-off farmers to the detriment of the poor, who, unable to afford the costly inputs it requires, are being progressively pushed off their land. McNamara seems to realize this: 'There is only a limited transfer of benefits from the modern to the traditional [farming] sector. Disparities in income will simply widen unless action is taken which will directly benefit the poorest.' The zero-growth productivity of small scale agriculture must be improved. Elsewhere, speaking of the Bank's most-complex-ever programme in Mexico, he explains that it is necessary because 'although the nation has achieved over the last three decades the highest sustained growth in agricultural production in Latin America, *rural poverty appears to have worsened* in many regions throughout the country. ...' These three decades correspond exactly to the application of the green revolution in Mexico, which has created large, productive commercial farms of the agribusi-ness type side by side with the 'worsening rural poverty' for those left out. Or, again, we learn from McNamara that India had to add an extra $500 million in hard currency to its budget in 1974 in order to import fertilizer and 'India is the world's largest importer of this essential ingredient of increased agricultural production.' A few paragraphs later we learn that what the 'energy crisis' has added to India's outlays could have been avoided altogether! 'In many countries, for example ... [it will be possible] to generate power using alternative sources. Petroleum-based plants can be replaced with hydro-power, geo-thermal power or with coal, lignite or nuclear-fuel plants.' He does not add that the fertilizer base could also be changed – or could have been, before Westerners moved in. India's green revolution agricultural system has largely been based on oil. Now the Bank discovers that India could have been energy-independent (although this might have been less profitable for various US firms). An even more recent bank document tells us that 'poverty is found in the highly productive irrigated *areas* of Asia' (where the green revolution holds sway) and that 'the number of landless or near-landless workers is growing, especially in Asian countries' (for which we have given examples of land concentration in the hands of the largest farmers and of eviction suits).

McNamara and the Bank are equally hard – and much more explicitly so – on the glaring inequalities within the poor countries themselves. The President of the Bank speaks of the concentration of land in the hands of a privileged minority; he notes that 'the politically privileged among the landed élite are rarely enthusiastic over the steps necessary to advance rural development'; he knows full well that 'income distribution patterns are severely skewed within developing countries'; he castigates the many purely rhetorical land reforms that have been passed in underdeveloped countries and which have 'produced little redistribution of land, little improvement in the security of the tenant'. He even goes so far as to suggest that the answer for the small farmer lies in 'various types of communes' and says 'experience shows that there is a greater chance of success if institutions provide for popular participation, local leadership and decentralization of authority'.

Recognizing (at least implicitly) the pernicious effects of the green revolution and the obvious obstacles to a better life of an estimated 100 million poor rural families posed by present land tenure and power structures, what does McNamara propose in order to put his Bank's stated policy of 'reaching the absolute poor' into effect? Alas, more of the same.

Related Items

11, 13, 18, 22, 23, 24, 25, 26, 29, 31, 32, 35, 38, 41, 42, 49, 53, 54, 56, 57, 58, 59, 60, 61, 62.

55

Rural Development: A Change in Policy, Why and How?

Gavin Williams

The 'target' of rural development, in the military terminology of the World Bank, is the peasantry, that is, the class of independent smallholders. The existence of peasant producers appears to be an anomaly in a 'modern' capitalist world. Modernizers, of both liberal and Marxist varieties, have tended to assume the superiority of large-scale, capitalist production over peasant production, and thus the inevitability and desirability of replacing peasants by capitalist production. The problem is how to eliminate the peasantry as a class; an alternative solution is to subordinate peasants to the requirements of capitalism. Peasants have posed the same problem, even more sharply, for European socialist states, who have sought to replace them by collective and state farms, or have tried to make the peasantry finance industrial investment by the state. . . .

Rural development is an activity undertaken by governments and by international agencies, public and private. It takes a number of forms, many of which are combined with one another: credit programmes, irrigation schemes, farm settlements, extension services, marketing cooperatives, the provision of chemical fertilizers, herbicides and pesticides, and high-yielding varieties of seeds. Their purpose appears to be self-evident, namely, an increase in agricultural production and an improvement in living standards. However, at least in Africa, as several of the essays in this volume demonstrate, the historical record shows that rural development has often failed to achieve either of these ends, let alone both of them. By any criteria, successful projects have been the exception rather than the rule. There have been impressive examples of the expansion of agricultural production in Africa, during the colonial period in some countries and since then in others. This has been achieved by rural producers reorganizing production to take advantage of new or expanded

Excerpts from Gavin Williams, 'The World Bank and the peasant problem', in Judith Heyer, Pepe Roberts and Gavin Williams (eds), *Rural Development in Tropical Africa*, Macmillan, 1982. Abridged by the author.

markets for food and other crops. It required the provision of cheap transport by sea, rail and road; it owed little or nothing to the direct involvement of public agencies in agricultural production and marketing. With some significant exceptions, such involvement tended to hinder rather than to assist the development of agricultural production.

This bleak record has not discouraged the repetition of forms of rural development which have failed in the past. Old and discredited policies are offered as new recipes for rural development. International agencies have replaced colonial governments as the main promoters and financiers of rural development. This has increased the tendency to generalize formulas across ecological zones, national boundaries and colonial spheres of influence. Rural development is big business, offering contracts and employment to construction and consultancy firms, international experts and bankers, fertilizer, chemical and seed manufacturers and distributors, officials, extension workers and even, for short periods of time, labourers.

If rural development does not usually achieve its objectives, its increasing popularity needs to be explained in some other way. Clearly, a number of people benefit from it, even when farmers do not. The self-interest of the agents of rural development may not be sufficient to explain the activity, nor the particular forms it takes. A more adequate explanation needs to identify the purposes which the activity serves, both directly and indirectly, the justifications which are offered to legitimate the activity, and the assumptions, often implicit, by which its agents define their situation, objectives and actions.

. . . those rural development strategies which have succeeded in increasing agricultural production have been those which have solved the 'peasant problem' by increasing the dependence of producers on production for the market to provide both their means of subsistence and their means of production, and by subjecting them to private and state monopolies in the provision of inputs and the purchasing of commodities. . . . Peasants have benefited in some cases, at the cost of increasing dependence and even loss of control of the land. In others, they have been impoverished and dispossessed.

The apparent shift in World Bank agricultural policy in the 1970s arose out of the developments of the 1960s. Three major influences stand out. The first was the World Bank's intensified involvement in India. In 1965–7 India's foreign exchange crisis gave the World Bank the chance to direct India's economic policy towards devaluation, the elimination of import controls, and a shift in agricultural policy away from ineffective agrarian reforms and community development projects towards the promotion of technical improvement. The World Bank saw the biggest problem as a Malthusian increase in population, to be solved by birth control and the green revolution.

In India and Mexico, where the new technologies were first developed, dramatic improvements in yield were realized in the best irrigated and most suitable areas for wheat. It was more difficult to extend the new technology to dry areas, and to other crops. . . . What is more, the new strategy appeared to be increasing inequalities, marginalizing the rural poor, and developing capitalist farming. Hence the growing stress on employment and distribution. These problems would be solved by poor countries encouraging low-wage, labour-intensive export industries and small capitalist production, the latter being identified with assistance to the 'informal sector'. Integrated rural development projects would provide the infrastructure necessary to extend the new technologies to new areas, and international research institutes would develop technologies for new crops. . . .

The second major influence was the awesome example which Vietnamese peasants had provided to McNamara and his ilk of their capacity to resist the monstrous military machine he directed. McNamara argued simply that 'economic backwardness' breeds violence. Development would cure economic backwardness, and 'without development there can be no security'. To be successful 'development' would have to reach the poor, the World Bank's new 'target' group. Thus McNamara's translation from the Department of Defence to the Presidency of the World Bank was followed, successively, by the establishment of the Pearson Commission to plead for more 'aid', a concern with unemployment, underemployment, which means poverty – even among those who overwork and redistribution with growth and a shift in priorities towards rural development and the rural poor and redirected growth to meet 'basic needs'.

The third major influence was the shift in the strategy of multi-national corporations away from direct investment towards joint ventures, often with governments, and the international marketing of technology, services and physical commodities. Prominent agro-industrial corporations like Booker Bros and Brooke Bond had to sell their plantations in countries like Guyana and Sri Lanka, and opened up new sources of supply and profits in promoting outgrower schemes and managing irrigation projects. . . . Oil corporations and other suppliers have expanded their markets for fuel, fertilizer, pesticides and herbicides. Esso established 400 agro-service centres in the Philippines to distribute them to farmers, but closed the centres down because they did not make profits. The World Bank has established farm service centres, at public cost, on the Funtua scheme in Nigeria.

There is clearly an affinity between these developments and the establishment of a new economic orthodoxy in place of the previous assumption that development required a high rate of industrial investment, financed from agricultural production. It was argued that growth in output was not necessarily incompatible with more equitable asset income distribution or with strategies to expand 'employment' by encouraging labour-intensive production of crops and manufactured goods. Economists rediscovered old arguments for the efficiency of small farmers. Consequently, it would be possible to promote economic growth, more equal distribution of income assets, and political stability, all at the same time. . . .

The assumptions evident in the World Bank's new strategy for rural development are clear. The 'low productivity' of smallholders will be raised by providing them with 'new or improved service systems to support a modern system of agriculture' in the form of the 'new seed-fertilizer-water technology for wheat, rice and maize', and by integrating them into the market economy. Thus rural development 'is concerned with the modernization and monetization of rural society, and with its transition from traditional isolation to integration with the national economy'.

The small farmer is not considered a possible initiator of agricultural development, but as a 'beneficiary'. Rural development is not the business of farmers. It is accomplished by the state, by international agencies and their experts, and sometimes by international agro-capital. It is seen as an administrative process, through which planners design and execute their strategies. Consequently the local 'beneficiaries' of rural development must be organized to fit the administrators' convenience.

The World Bank's 'philosophy of agricultural development' is an ideology of benevolent technocracy. It treats the state as a machine, which serves the objectives of whichever group directs it, and not as a relation of production, which subjects the producers to the domination of their rulers. The technocrats, and the international experts who advise them, are the ghosts in the machine, costlessly and impersonally allocating resources in accordance with their criteria of economic rationality and social justice. The World Bank and its advisers recognize that state policies and resources may be diverted to serve the interests of privileged groups, and that it may prove difficult to identify appropriate policies and to execute them efficiently. They cannot ask whether these problems arise from the nature of the whole enterprise, and whether they should be involved in the business of rural development at all.

The efficiency of peasant producers in using resources contrasts sharply with the inefficiency of government institutions in providing those resources. Consequently there is an inherent contradiction in promoting the lower-cost expansion of production by small farmers through the provision of rural development schemes. The World Bank recognizes that it is much more expensive to provide benefits to large numbers of small farmers than to small numbers of large ones. Therefore a number of World Bank projects, like the Funtua scheme, focus their extension efforts on 'selected contact farmers', presumably on the assumption that the benefits will then trickle down to other farmers. Alternatively, settlement and outgrower schemes, cooperatives and crop authorities are used as instruments of administration, through which governments can provide services and reclaim debts. Settlement schemes benefit small numbers of farmers, if at all, at considerable cost. Cooperatives and 'progressive' ('contact') farmer policies tend to provide commercial opportunities to a small number of influential farmers and traders, and to consolidate their control of local patronage. It is of the nature of rural development itself, that is, of the intervention of public agencies in peasant production, that it should tend to distribute resources to the better-off and subject peasant producers to state control, and to agro-capital.

Related Items

11, 13, 18, 22, 23, 24, 25, 26, 29, 31, 32, 35, 38, 41, 42, 49, 53, 54, 56, 57, 58, 59, 60, 61, 62.

56

Updating 'Development Policies': The Berg Report as the Dust Settles

Tim Allen

In the 1970s, the World Bank was associated with the catch-phrases 'meeting basic needs' and 'redistribution with growth'. These terms encapsulated a strategy of development planning propagated by the institution's president, Robert McNamara. Recognizing the inadequacies of economic growth models fashionable in the 1960s, which had anticipated a 'trickle-down' effect to the very poor, McNamara called upon the Bank to concentrate its activities on directly assisting those most in need. By improving the redistributive capacities of Third World governments, it was hoped to 'solve' the problems of poverty and malnutrition through provision of essential public services like primary education and health care.

To what degree these schemes really assisted the world's poor is still a moot point.[1] Nevertheless, poverty-focused development projects moved the Bank away from the more neo-liberal, free-market position of the International Monetary Fund,[2] and provided the beleaguered aid industry with the sustaining ideal it needed to cope with structuralist and neo-Marxist critiques. How could it be wrong to try to help those incapable of helping themselves? Moreover, there is no doubt that during McNamara's long term of office between 1968 and 1981, the Bank itself was transformed. From being 'in many ways almost an appendage of the US Treasury Department' (Ayres, 1983, p. 7), it expanded into by far the largest international lender to Third World countries, and, in effect, the foremost 'think-tank' on development issues.

By the end of the decade, however, the much publicized failure of some Bank-funded schemes, and the continuing plight of the world's poor, had worn the 'basic needs' rhetoric very thin indeed. Always a target of attack from the Left, the Bank increasingly found itself under pressure from the Right.

An original paper.

Conservative opinion in the US was highly critical of 'soft' loans to countries like Tanzania, denouncing them as 'give-aways' which promoted socialism. Following Reagan's inauguration as US President at the beginning of 1981, it was made clear that the new administration would redirect funds away from multilateral organizations which it viewed as unresponsive to US foreign policy interests, and antipathetic to 'sound' economic principles. Such a threat was extremely serious, because, in spite of the growth of the Bank in the 1970s, the US remained its biggest single donor country. Thus, some compromise in the institution's poverty-oriented approach seemed inevitable, and the arrival of A. W. Clausen to take over from McNamara appeared to confirm this was imminent. Clausen, a well-known commercial banker, was seen by some as no more than the Reagan administration's tool for directing the Bank towards more overtly free-market/open-economy type strategies.

It is in this context that the heated debate which has surrounded the Bank's 'Accelerated Development in Sub-Saharan Africa' can best be understood. Published in October 1981, this report centred attention on that part of the Third World where past hopes had been most cruelly dashed. Written by a consultancy team under Professor Elliot Berg, a prominent supply-side economist, and with a foreword by Clausen himself, it was seized upon as the first statement of the Bank's new orthodoxy in the post-McNamara era.

What, then, was the revised agenda for action in the 1980s to consist of? The answer to this is by no means straightforward. The basic message of the Berg Report is clear enough: African states must cut back their public sectors, and private enterprise should be encouraged. But beyond this an adequate summary is virtually impossible, for it is not structured in the form of an integrated argument, and does not disguise its composite construction. Instead, it presents an attractively packaged hodgepodge of diagnosis, prescriptions, case-studies and statistics, which are not fully interrelated with each other, and not always consistent. The following points are those which tended to be emphasized by reviewers as being particularly significant.

First, although the Report continues to mention the importance of meeting basic needs, this is not perceived as the primary focus of development strategy, but rather as the likely consequence of higher productivity. Attempts to introduce universal free access to essential services is implicitly rejected as too costly and ineffective. Instead it is proposed that attention should be targeted at 'those areas where the physical infrastructure provides pre-conditions for rapid pay-off from additional investment'. It is accepted that some help should be given to arid and semi-arid regions, but it is also suggested that 'programs should be devised to facilitate the migration of people from the poorest regions to those better endowed' (World Bank, 1981, p. 52).

Second, it is maintained that the development record of sub-Saharan Africa in the 1970s has been disappointing, worse than any comparable part of the Third World, and that this is something that cannot be explained by 'external' factors alone. The Report contends that ultimately 'domestic policy issues are at the heart of the crisis' (World Bank, 1981, p. 121). Maladroit government action has led almost everywhere to a decline in export production, and seriously overextended state bureaucracies. There is consequently an urgent need for the retraction of public sectors, enabling private enterprise to flourish in the way that the lively 'black market' in many African countries indicates it would if given half a chance. Thus, while it is pointed out that the grim situation in sub-Saharan Africa necessitates a doubling of foreign aid, it is stressed that policy adjustments will be required from recipient governments.

Third, the Report emphasizes that the immediate solution to Africa's dilemma rests with agriculture. Its sluggish record in the 1970s is seen as 'the principal factor underlying ... poor economic performance' (World Bank, 1981, p. 45). The reasons for this stagnation are again linked to ill-advised state interference. It is argued that adoption of autarkic goals, urban bias, discouragement of export crop production, failure to promote adequate agricultural research, experiments at collectivization, and indirect taxation of farmers via low farm-gate prices have persistently stifled the enormous potential of Africa's smallholders. Such policies must be reversed. Highlighting the impressive productivity of smallholders in Kenya, and the apparent success of agricultural projects in northern Nigeria, the Report proposes that 'the smallholder sector should be the primary focus of a growth-orientated rural development strategy' (World Bank, 1981, p. 50). This will alleviate poverty, which is still predominantly a rural phenomenon in Africa, and will be far more effective than most other output-raising alternatives. Aid schemes should therefore concentrate on irrigation, feeder roads and relevant agricultural research. Above all, it must be recognized that 'smallholder energies and skills can only be mobilized voluntarily', and that therefore 'the incentive structure must be right' (World Bank, 1981, p. 54). This requires adequate prices and marketing arrangements, provisions of off-farm inputs and consumer goods, smallholder participation in decision making, and the adjustment of heavily over-valued exchange rates. It is appreciated that such policy changes will be 'technically difficult and politically thorny', but it is maintained that the rewards will be great. If implemented, the Report claims that there ought to be 'real gains in both development and income in the near future' (World Bank, 1981, p. 133).

Although controversial in both its diagnosis and prescriptions, here was not quite the neo-liberal tract that some World Bank watchers had been expecting. Nevertheless, it did appear to redraw the prospective relationship between the international agencies, national governments and the poor. Whereas the rhetoric of the 1970s was premised on the idea that the needy could be assisted via state structures, the rhetoric for the 1980s seemed to indicate that these could be by-passed. It is interesting in this respect that the Report avoided the term 'peasant', thereby implicitly rejecting class analysis and suggesting that rural Africa is inhabited by a mass of property-owning, profit-maximizing individuals. The impression was given that these inchoate capitalists would leap into action if only they could be protected (by international aid agencies?) from the machinations of parasitic bureaucrats. Questions were thereby raised concerning the independence of nation states, which were underlined by sections of the Report relating to exchange rates and conditionality of future funding. It seemed that the rhetoric of the Bank had moved back in line with that of the IMF.

The significance of this for hard-pressed African governments was swiftly appreciated, and ramifications for states in other parts of the Third World soon became apparent by the inclusion of similar arguments in the Bank's annual World Development Reports. Not surprisingly the Berg Report became the subject of a series of official discussions and reviews by African regional institutions, and, more generally, prompted a vigorous debate on rural development policies. In academic circles reactions to it were enormously varied. Commentators of neo-liberal persuasions, like Deepak Lal, emphasized the 'get the prices right' aspect of it, and agreed wholeheartedly. Others also accepted much of its diagnosis, but questioned its prescriptions on the grounds that doubling aid would only make matters worse (Eicher, 1984), or that it is unlikely that smallholders would respond to price hikes in the expected manner (Hyden, 1983). Many, however, found aspects of the diagnosis equally questionable. Jane Guyer, for example, pointed out that, partly because it overlooked the immense contribution of women to farm work, and relied too heavily on official statistics, the Report was far too pessimistic about the production of roots and tubers (ref. 4). Allison and Green (ref. 1), Colclough (ref. 1), Godfrey (ref. 1), and Loxley (ref. 4), were among those who argued that the external constraints on African states in the 1970s severely limited their room to manœuvre, and that generally they managed better than the Bank gives them credit for. Sender and Smith (1984), Loxley (ref. 4), Schultheis (ref. 3), and Williams (ref. 4) stressed the Report's misleadingly ahistorical perspective, which largely ignores such crucial matters as independence struggles, political forces, wars and class realities, giving the incorrect impression that African governments really are in a position to jettison 'bad' schemes and adopt 'good' ones.

Predictably, the most severe criticisms were put forward by neo-Marxist analysts. Much of what they said, therefore, was incompatible with the Bank's thinking which, like that of most development agencies, remains imbued with what is usually referred to as 'modernization theory'. Nevertheless, from any theoretical perspective, some of these arguments could not be ignored, and, no doubt partly as a consequence, the Bank has subsequently taken pains to 'clarify' its position in a series of updating publications (World Bank, 1983, 1984, 1986). It has been recognized that, at least since 1979, the external circumstances confronting African countries have seriously constrained government action, that promotion of primary agricultural exports will not be enough to facilitate recovery, and that food self-sufficiency is extremely important. The Bank has now stopped heaping opprobrium on recipient governments, and recently turned to muted censure of donors for not adequately supporting attempts at economic rationalization.

More generally it is possible to trace a relative shift away from the free market and anti-state arguments of parts of the Berg Report towards strategies which require bureaucratic or parastatal participation. Whereas in 1981 it was left vague how state contraction could be combined with the need for an extension of agricultural research and other essential services, the later studies have explicitly highlighted a need for increased expenditure in these areas, and have additionally called for the funding of programmes to curb population growth. In addition, eloquent apologists for the Bank have maintained that the Berg Report was misunderstood, that it never was meant to mark a dramatic change in policy, and it aimed only at initiating discussion about short-term responses to Africa's problems. In the longer term the Bank claims to be in full accord with the Lagos Plan of Action, adopted by the Organization of African Unity in 1980, which calls for regional cooperation and industrial growth. This is rather remarkable, since in 1981 the Bank had given some thoughtful commentators the impression of breaking with the Lagos Plan in crucial respects. Perhaps it is worth bearing in mind that, at the time Clausen took over, some kind of 'Reaganomic' rhetoric was essential to secure continued US funding. Yet it is unclear that this has actually affected what kind of project the Bank chooses to support. Just as the organization was not the dangerous champion of socialism which the Right imagined it was in the 1970s, it has not now become the mere instrument of international capitalist oppression which some on the Left would like to believe. In fact, all the turn-arounds and revisions in the Bank's views since 1981 have somewhat taken the wind out of its critics' sails. If nothing else, they highlight an important fact about the institution that is not always fully appreciated: it is above all else eclectic. Far from being a straw man that can be readily knocked down, it is like a sponge, which constantly seeks to render critiques partial by absorbing them and reforming them in its own image. Thus, just as some neo-Marxist scholars were disconcerted by the Berg Report's attack on state bureaucracies, which bore a marked resemblance to some of their own arguments, now populists calling for 'development from below' find that this is what the Bank wants too. Lately, it has even been suggested by former critics of the Berg Report that the debate it provoked has been beneficial in drawing attention to major development bottlenecks, and that a short-term semi-consensus has emerged between analysts of diverse political persuasions (Allison and Green, ref. 2; Colclough, ref. 2).

Ultimately, however, fundamental differences in approach remain. The World Bank, like other development agencies, largely ignores substantive processes of social transformation. It operates with the idea that enlightenment of one kind or another, combined with the transfer of some resources, leads to the solution of problems. Indeed, it is hard to see how most aid workers could do what they do without this assumption. In contrast, uncompromising observers whose perspective is more detached, or more broadly focused, historically and sociologically, continue to find such notions politically suspect, or, if sincere, naive. But, confronted with the worsening plight of so many of the world's poor, is it acceptable to do nothing to help? Criticizing the aid industry is not difficult, but the onus must be upon those who reject the possibility of the West implementing 'real' development to come up with an alternative more viable than socialist revolution, which, for much of Africa, is likely to remain a utopian dream for some time to come.

Notes

1 For an attack on the Bank's activities under McNamara, see Hayter and Watson, 1985. For a defence, see Ayres, 1983.
2 The International Monetary Fund and the World Bank were both formed at a conference of 44 nations held at Bretton Woods, New Hampshire in 1944. They are separate institutions, but relations between them are very close. Their operations are conceived as being complementary. Exchange rate issues and balance of payments equilibrium are the primary concern of the IMF, while development and investment programmes are the concern of the Bank.

References

There are four useful collections of short papers on the Berg Report and its follow-up publications.
1 'Accelerated development in sub-Saharan Africa: what agenda for action?', *IDS Bulletin*, vol. 14, no. 1, 1983; papers by: Allison, C. and Green, R., Daniel, P., Bienefeld, M., Colclough, C., Green, R., Godfrey, M., Harvey, C., Griffith-Jones, S.
2 'Sub-Saharan Africa: getting the facts straight', *IDS Bulletin*, vol. 16, no. 3, 1985; papers by Allison, C. and Green, R., Singer, H., Lipton, M., Allison, C., Godfrey, M., Colclough, C., Harvey, C., Daniel, P., Green, R., Bienefeld, M.
3 'The World Bank's accelerated development in sub-Saharan Africa: a symposium', *African Studies Review*, vol. 27, no. 4, 1984; papers by: Paul, J., Schultheis, M., Green, R., Selassie, B., Please, S. and Amoako, K.
4 'The World Bank's prescription for rural Africa', *Review of African Political Economy*, vol. 27/28, 1984; papers by: Guyer, J., Williams, G., Loxley, J.

Other references

Ayres, R. (1983) *Banking on the Poor; the World Bank and World Poverty*, MIT Press, London.
Eicher, C. (1984) 'Facing up to Africa's Food Crisis', in Eicher, C. and Staatz, J. eds *Agricultural Development in the Third World*, Johns Hopkins University Press, Baltimore.
Hayter, T. and Watson, C. (1985) *Aid: Rhetoric and Reality*, Pluto Press, London.
Hyden, G. (1983) *No Shortcuts to Progress*, Heinemann, London.

Lal, D. (1983) *The Poverty of Development Economics*, Hobart Publishing, London.

Sender, J. and Smith, S. (1985) 'What's right with the Berg Report and what's left of its critics?', *Capital and Class*, vol. 24.

World Bank (1983) *Sub-Saharan Africa: Progress Report on Development Prospects and Programs*, Washington, DC.

World Bank (1984) *Towards Sustained Development in Sub-Saharan Africa: A Joint Program of Action*, Washington, DC.

World Bank (1986) *Accelerated Development in Sub-Saharan Africa: An Agenda For Action*, Washington, DC.

World Bank (1986) *Financing Adjustment with Growth in Sub-Saharan Africa, 1986—90*, Washington, DC.

Related Items

11, 13, 18, 22, 23, 24, 26, 29, 32, 38, 41, 42, 49, 53, 54, 55, 57, 58, 59, 60, 61, 62.

57

Rural Women as Objects of Development Policies

Deniz Kandyoti

Policy interest in rural women started manifesting itself in the early 1970s at a time when widespread disenchantment with the effects of development policies on the agrarian sectors of the Third World countries was being felt. They had by and large resulted in stagnating levels of food production, nutritional decline and a destructuring of rural communities fuelling massive rural-to-urban migration. The problems of absolute poverty, and of rural and urban unemployment and underemployment started to occupy a very central place in policy concerns. As the emphasis shifted from modernization to the provision of the poorest people's basic needs (food, shelter, health, etc.), distributional issues increasingly appeared on the agenda but failed to recognize the effects of gender inequality above and beyond those of class membership. Meanwhile, a growing body of research documented the counter-productive effects of ignoring rural women's contributions and their special needs both from the point of view of agricultural productivity and of the overall welfare of rural families. Thus, policy proposals related to rural women became intimately linked to an ongoing assessment of strategies of agricultural development.

... Policy proposals relating to rural women have been fraught with an unusual amount of disagreement about policy objectives and fundamental divergences in the identification of priorities. The problem has been formulated by some as simply 'how best to tap the economic resources represented by Third World rural women', and rural women themselves have been defined as 'a semi-autonomous resource in the rural sector' (Michkelwait et al., 1976). The assumption here is that there are vast human resources lying idle and untapped, a view to which Presvelou (1975, p. 50) gives eloquent expression: 'Forsaken, these women cannot help perpetrating a corrosive social pattern of idleness and inefficiency: they are the *olvidadas*, the forgotten

Excerpts from Deniz Kandyoti, *Women in Rural Production Systems: Problems and Policies*, UNESCO, 1985.

human resources in rural development where they are forbidden to play any role at all.'

An equally prominent but somewhat contradictory view is that women are already overburdened with work and that the most pressing need is to alleviate the drudgery involved in providing the basic necessities of life (such as fetching water from long distances, time-consuming food processing, firewood collection, etc.). An ILO report proposes that 'especially in rural areas most women in developing countries are overworked rather than underemployed and a more appropriate technology for the tasks they perform implies labour saving in order to improve the *quality* of their employment, rather than employment *creation*.[1]

However, programmes primarily geared to assist and educate women in the Western 'home economics' vein have been strongly criticized for the limited awareness they show of women's roles as producers, and their exclusive emphasis on their tasks as reproducers whose labour could be rendered more efficient. Germain (1976/7) has provided a thorough criticism of the focus of typical programmes directed at rural women and involving welfare services (health and family planning), instruction in nutrition, child care and home economics. This approach not only assumes an exclusively domestic role for women but also imposes arbitrary and counter-productive ceilings on women's productivity and income-generating capacity by ignoring their current productive roles. Therefore, employment creation and increasing women's access to income sources are proposed as more appropriate policy objectives. The case for explicit support of rural women's productive activities is frequently presented as a human rights issue which also makes good economic 'development' sense. The extent to which the development or the human rights components of this equation are stressed can be very variable. Thus, we may be informed (Cain, 1981, p. 4) that 'the approach to the study of women's roles and status in a development context is not to be viewed as an end in itself but rather as a *means* to promoting more effective development overall [my italics]'.

. . . Tinker sees one of the solutions to world hunger in placing appropriate technology for subsistence agriculture where it properly belongs – in the hands of women. The three main strategies for meeting the world's food crisis – increased production, greater income-producing activities and a reduction in post-harvest food losses – in her opinion coincide with strategies for aiding poor rural women. She denounces the serious bias in the introduction of new technologies: they have often been geared to cash-crop production, drawing off land and labour from food crops; nutritional levels tended to fall even while cash incomes may have increased; and, in green revolutions which have affected only rice and wheat, the technology has been class- and sex-biased. Tinker (1981, p. 57) therefore concludes:

In order for the food crisis strategies to accomplish their goal of feeding the world, women must not only be included in planning, they must be central to it. Since development is essential to the introduction of new technologies, women must be consulted in the selection of new technologies, trained in their use, and given means to control those most related to their spheres of economic activity.

The assumptions in question may be roughly summarized as follows:

1 Women are *de facto* food producers in many parts of the Third World.
2 The main constraints on their productivity are related to the labour time involved in their daily household maintenance tasks.
3 A reduction or freeing of labour time from household tasks implies its possible diversion to income-generating activities.
4 Women's access to income is more likely to pay welfare dividends for the community at large (especially for children) than men's income.
5 Women's productivity and potential for income generation may be raised with minimal capital outlays.

These assumptions are so widespread in the women and development literature that they warrant further examination.

First, the involvement of women in food production is generally documented with extensive case material from Africa. Indeed, studies on Africa show that women are not only food producers and animal husbanders but that they are also involved in storage, processing and marketing of foodstuffs. However, their farming activities take place on an ever-shrinking resource base, with extremely primitive technology and with severely stretched time resources. The competition for their time comes from arduous and time-consuming household tasks on the one hand, and their need to accommodate additional activities which will provide them with cash earnings in an increasingly monetized rural economy on the other.

Clearly, though, the extent of women's involvement in subsistence farming is a function both of their access to resources and the degree of overall commoditization of the agrarian sector. In many parts of Asia and Latin America the women of landless or near-landless households can rely only on wage earnings from varied and intermittent sources. The agrarian sector of many Third World countries, and especially certain regions within them, have become commoditized to the extent that subsistence farming can account for an absolutely minimal fraction of a household's subsistence needs. It is no accident therefore that policies relating to rural women reflect these differences: those relating to Africa frequently stress the need to assist subsistence farming, whereas in Asia the accent is on employment creation programmes.[2] However, involvement in household tasks as a factor setting a limit to women's earning ability is uniformly stressed.

Second, a growing number of time–budget studies indicate that tasks such as water fetching, fuel collection, food processing and preparation can account for the better part of an adult woman's extremely long working day. Allocating resources to better sanitation, easy access to water points, cheap sources of fuel, improved means of porterage and transportation would have immediately beneficial consequences, as would the reduction in laborious food-processing operations through the introduction of labour- and time-saving appropriate technologies (Carr, 1978). However, the introduction of new technologies has different consequences for different classes of rural women. Improvements in overall sanitation have undeniably positive consequences on the quality of life of rural women, but they ultimately tend to be justified in terms of increments in productivity rather than welfare.

Third, a freeing of labour time from household tasks is explicitly related to its possible diversion to (a) agricultural production and animal husbandry, and (b) non-farm income-generating activities. Most proposals involve the upgrading of these areas of activity. Better access to productive resources, improved techniques and tools for cultivation, access to agricultural extension services and the provision of farm credit to women are some of the measures envisaged in the area of agricultural production. As far as non-farm income-generating activities are concerned, these may cover a myriad of rural-based cottage industries, from fruit canning and textiles to soap and brick making, depending on local skills and resources. Again, education and training, as well as the setting up of women's organizations, such as cooperatives, to facilitate obtaining credit and finding marketing outlets are advocated as desirable and realistic objectives.

A striking feature of many such proposals is that they seem quite oblivious of the insights gained from rural development projects geared to *male* peasants (such as credit schemes for smallholders, rural cooperatives, etc.) and of their possible shortcomings.

Fourth, another important assumption is that women's access to income is more likely to pay welfare dividends for the community, especially for children's health and nutrition, than that of men. According to Blumberg (1981, p. 43): 'Increasing the proportion of a class's resources in the hands of its females will have more rapid and more immediate consequences for the level of individual well-being than comparable increases in the hands of its males.'

... Finally, there is an implicit assumption that these goals can be achieved with relatively modest capital outlays, mainly through more rational use of local resources, the provision of some training and credit facilities, as well as reasonably priced, easy to maintain appropriate technologies. This is indicative of a tendency to emphasize strategies that optimize women's productivity without necessarily addressing broader distributional issues within the rural sectors of Third World countries. However, as should be clear from our review of regional case-studies, low productivity and poverty are not the result of inefficiency and poor use of resources. It should follow that increased efficiency and better use of resources are hardly remedies for it. It is hard not to concur with Burce (1981, p. 502) that 'new forms of discrimination against women are more symptoms than causes of larger problems facing Third World nations; it is unlikely that food shortages, exploitation of general under-development would be eradicated by changes in attitudes toward women'.

Notes

1 Director-General of ILO's report to the World Employment Conference, International Labour Organization, 1976 (my italics).
2 These are often official programmes of employment creation offering temporary work to the most disadvantaged and destitute of the rural population.

References

Blumberg, R. L. (1981) 'Females, farming and food: rural development and women's participation in agricultural production systems', in B. Lewis (ed.), *Invisible Farmers*, Washington, DC, AID.
Burce, A. (1981) Review of B. Rogers, *The Domestication of Women: Discrimination in Developing Societies*, *Signs*, vol. 7, no. 2.
Cain, M. L. (1981a) 'Java, Indonesia: the introduction of rice processing technology', in R. Dauber and M. L. Cain (eds), *Women and Technological Change in Developing Countries*, pp. 127–38, Boulder, Colo., Westview Press.
Cain, M. L. (1981b) 'Overview: Women and Technology – Resources for our Future', in: Dauber and Cain, *Women and Technological Change*.
Carr, M. (1978) *Appropriate Technology for African Women*, United Nations, African Training and Research Centre for Women of the Economic Commission for Africa.
Germain, A. (1976/7) 'Poor rural women: a policy perspective', *Journal of International Affairs*, vol. 30, no. 2, Fall/Winter.
Michkelwait, D. R., Riegalman, M. A., Sweet, C. F. (1976) *Women in Rural Development: A Survey of the Roles of Women in Ghana, Lesotho, Kenya, Nigeria, Bolivia, Paraguay and Peru*, Boulder Colo., Westview Press.
Presvelou, C. (1975) 'The invisible woman', *Ceres*, March/April.
Tinker, I. (1981) 'Food and related activities: an equity strategy', in Dauber and Cain, *Women and Technological Change*.

Related Items

1, 2, 3, 9, 13, 15, 17, 18, 22, 23, 25, 26, 29, 42, 53, 54, 55, 59, 61.

58

Of Virtuous Peasants?

Henry Bernstein

Peasants are often viewed as the representative victims of the modern world. At the same time, widely held images depict them variously as expert ecologists and agricultural innovators, exemplars of a benevolent small-scale production, militants of the 'moral economy', the driving force of liberation struggles. In different ways these images resonate deep ideological opposition to the generalization of commodity production (i.e. capitalism), to the brutalities of both its historical formation and its everyday reproduction in the contemporary Third World.

This opposition rests on potent conceptions of *family* and *community* as principles of social organization. The values attributed to family economy (self-reliance and independence through the use of household resources and labour) and to the community (cooperation, reciprocity, solidarity) inform one kind of critique of the possessive individualism of the market and the inevitable divisions and inequalities of capitalism. The appeal of such virtuous construction of peasants and peasant societies is reinforced by another pervasive motif of resistance to urban industrial civilization and its discontents, that of a direct relation with nature in securing a livelihood from the land.

Thus peasant life comes to represent a world we have lost. Apart from nostalgia for a golden past, it is argued that peasants can adapt to modern conditions and make major contributions to economic and social development, even though they are generally prevented from doing so. This is because of economic exploitation: the terms on which peasants obtain land and credit, sell their crops and buy means of production and consumption; and because of political and ideological oppression: peasants are dispossessed of any effective political voice and influence, their ways of life are denigrated in stereotypes of rural 'backwardness' held by those who concentrate economic, political and cultural power.

An original paper.

In particular these negative stereotypes are intrinsic to the practice of 'developmental' states, whose vision of 'modernization' is urban-industrial in inspiration, justifying in the name of progress the exploitation and oppression of peasants that the state organizes or otherwise colludes in.

Current emphasis on the viciousness of states is so powerful because it encompasses the regimes of capitalism, state capitalism and socialism, providing a common terrain in which diverse ideological currents converge. For radicals the colonial state was as central to initially and forcibly integrating peasants in (international) capitalist economy as contemporary developmental states of different political complexions are to squeezing peasants in the name of industrial accumulation. 'Free-market' ideologues deplore the economic activity of states which, to reap a bureaucratic rent from the exchange of commodities, distort prices and incentives and thereby stifle the energies of the small farmer as economic man (*sic*).

One may ask: are peasants uniformly so virtuous (and embattled), states necessarily so vicious? Or is reality more contradictory and complex than the dualism of either family/community versus state/capital or market versus state suggests?

An alternative position is that as peasants are petty commodity producers within capitalism, the contradictions of capitalism are as much part of, that is *internal* to, peasant economy as they are of its location within wider divisions of labour. In principle, the most widespread manifestations of the contradictions of capitalism – the divisions, exploitation and oppression of class and gender relations – are no less constitutive of peasant families and communities than they are of other spheres of productive activity in capitalist societies.

Peasant households combine the contradictory class places of capital and labour: peasants are (petty) capitalists who employ, and thus exploit, themselves. Self-exploitation is not necessarily evenly distributed, however. Commonly patriarchy structures the appropriation of surplus labour from women and children by male household heads, possibly enabling them to accumulate. Class differentiation between households, as well as within them, is to be expected, providing a similarly critical perspective on persisting notions of the egalitarian peasant community.

This is not to say that class differentiation occurs everywhere, in the same way, and with the same results. Its extent, character and stability are always the outcome of specific conditions of competition and struggle amongst peasants, and between peasants and others. The latter may overshadow the former, generating solidary ideologies of community, 'tradition', custom, etc., as means of defence against the depredations of landlords, or merchants, or the state itself.

The purpose of these observations is to jettison the morally charged dualism of peasant virtue and state viciousness, *and* the theoretical conceptions called into its service. Moving beyond 'actually existing capitalism' requires transformation of the peasantries as well as the state regimes that it contains. The contradictions of their existence mean that peasants themselves, in alliance with the political struggles of other social classes, may play a central role in hindering or advancing this revolutionary process. The supposedly 'anti-peasant' socialist Karl Marx, in his 'Eighteenth Brumaire of Louis Bonaparte', was careful therefore to distinguish the 'conservative peasant' clinging to the conditions of private production and 'the (revolutionary) peasant that strikes out beyond the condition of his social existence, the small holding . . . the country folk who, linked up with the towns, want to overthrow the old order through their own energies'.

Related Items

21, 28, 30, 33, 38, 42, 48, 49, 55, 56, 59, 62.

59

Development as a Threat: The Struggle for Rural Mexico

Gustavo Esteva

The majority of Mexican society was, and still is, *campesino*. Social consensus is inconceivable if it excludes or subordinates peasantry which makes up half the total population, and which at the beginning of the century embraced all areas of society. Both the *campesinos'* admission to and their exclusion from the Mexican state and its government necessarily imply some kind of rupture. To include them explicitly with full rights means giving them the strength and mobility to oppose the interests of other social classes radically – be these permanent or transitory, tactical or strategic. This would obviously make impossible the social consensus necessary for government. A direct decision to exclude them explicitly would also make the government's task impossible; and violence would be the only way to enforce this kind of exclusion. This situation may help to explain the little significance of *explicit* positions which go beyond mere rhetoric. The reactions they evoke – both at verbal and real levels – mean they are soon blocked. Hence an *implicit* definition of the issue tends to be maintained, while a deep, quiet struggle evolves round the dialectics of admission/exclusion, which varies according to the continuously changing circumstances.

Because of the original sin of the 'polarizing dynamics' of society, the existence of two sectors in the agrarian structure is taken for granted: one modern and dynamic, the other backward and stagnant. Even though some say the crisis is a result of the loss of dynamism of the former sector, analytical studies tend to concentrate on the cause of the latter's backwardness as a way of also explaining the loss of dynamism of the former. This line of thought leads some to look for the problem in the backward sector by using static comparisons: they detect the 'missing elements' which hinder development. Obviously, it is impossible to *see* a missing element; however, since this is a comparative exercise, the idea is to highlight what is missing in the backward

An original paper.

sector by comparing it to the advanced sector: capital, education, technology, business-mindedness, etc. Then, according to this kind of reasoning, the solution would merely be to inject the missing elements in order to stimulate development. Another point of view, along these same lines, simply describes it within the framework of a linear process of development, where the backward sector is merely at an earlier stage and its 'natural' or artificially accelerated evolution will lead it to the developed stages of the modern sector. Finally, some simply say tautologically that the crisis is related to the rupture of the post-war expansion model which had led to a boom, especially in the 1950s and the first half of the 1960s. The real problem lies in looking for the cause of this rupture. Theories which talk of missing elements, necessary stages, or the exhaustion of the model, rapidly exhaust themselves.

Mexican peasants are *still* people born in a space, physical, cultural and social – to which they belong and which belongs to them.

In 1938, at the height of the agrarian reform (under the Cardenas government) the Confederacion Nacional Campesina (CNC) was founded. It soon became a powerful and well-rooted peasant organization, perhaps the largest and strongest that ever existed on the American continent. In the post-war era, however, at the service of the development dream, it became a tool for control and manipulation of the peasantry. This function weakened it, as the peasants lost control of its direction and practices, and the national balance of forces became mostly adverse to peasant interests. As the green revolution progressed, destroying both peasant economy and culture, the peasants tried to replace CNC with other national, class-oriented organizations which enjoyed short periods of success, regional rather than national, before joining the CNC in its brokerage function.

In the sixties, when the Mexican 'agricultural miracle' started to fall apart, the peasants tried again to advance their interests through all forms of political struggle, including revolts and guerrilla activities, and, concurrently, they broadened their claims. In the seventies, the populist regime of Luis Echeverria tried to federate all 'national' peasant organizations, and submitted the peasants to a form of permanent mobilization from the top down, which produced much ado about nothing, insofar as their basic claims were concerned, while, at the same time, it opened for them new spaces and opportunities.

By the early 1970s, the green revolution had lost its charm, but the conventional modernizing ethos still prevailed, frustrating peasant aspirations step by step. After 1976, a vigorous modernizing push was launched by the Mexican government supported by the World Bank and other international institutions. That orientation, stubbornly maintained, precipitated a disastrous agricultural year in 1979 which intensified peasant unrest. In reaction, the government launched, in 1980, a new and ambitious food strategy: for the first time in forty

years, the official policy focused on food self-sufficiency and recognized the
key role of the peasantry in achieving that goal. This jettisoned the conventional orientation, which was religiously attached to the idea of 'comparative advantages', following the World Bank's catechism. Oil and debt money gave the government the opportunity to give effect to the new strategy by generous subsidies to the peasants, without abandoning its clientele in the 'modern sector'. The impressive results of the strategy in terms of production were not enough to give this policy a long life. In 1982, when the new administration took office, in the midst of the so-called crisis of the Mexican economy, the conventional policies of the past were implemented again, now linked to the reduced budgets of the 'adjustment process' prescribed by the IMF for countries like Mexico.

In 1978 the peasants made one more and possibly the last attempt to build a new 'national' organization to replace those weakened, corrupted or co-opted. The limited success of this effort corresponds not only to the prevailing mood of Mexican society and the present balance of political forces, but to a change in the orientation of the peasant movements. After 1975, the peasants concentrated on the regeneration of local and regional organizations, effectively controlled by the peasants themselves, and no longer on 'national' bodies. These local organizations are constantly multiplying and intensifying their horizontal contacts, relationships and alliances, but carefully avoid the temptation to federate themselves in bigger, 'national' organizations. Some of them follow the conventional lines of class struggle, or make economic and political claims, and are usually linked to political parties. They struggle for a larger piece of the economic pie, and look toward the goods and services associated with 'development'. But many others are no longer paralysed by this vision. More and more they subordinate conventional economic struggle to the recovery and regeneration of their own social space.

In the peasant world, for a long time now, 'development' has been recognized as a threat. Most peasants are aware that it has undermined their subsistence on the basis of centuries-old diversified crops. For some time, through the 'Mexican Agricultural Miracle', or the oil boom, this threat was masked by illusions. The so-called crisis has laid the threat bare. In Mexico, you must be very stupid or very rich to fail to notice that 'development' stinks. The damage to persons, the corruption of politics and the degradation of nature which till recently were only implicit in 'development', can now be seen, touched and smelled. The causal connection between the loss of environment and the loss of solidarity, both of which hitherto had been taken for granted mainly by the poorest, have now been documented by experts. The so-called crisis in Mexico has enabled the peasants and others to dismantle the goal of 'development'.

After 1982, the Mexican Rural Development Bank no longer had enough funds to force the peasants to plant sorghum for animal feed. As a result, many places return to the traditional inter-cropping of corn and beans, which improve the diet, but also restore some of the traditional village solidarity, facilitating wider distribution of costs.

The destruction of the peasant economy and culture, a by-product of the green revolution, forced many peasants to emigrate. In the cities, already congested by the demographic explosion (also created by 'development'), they could hardly find a promised land. Very few of them were able to secure a livelihood, atomized as they were, and placed in the lowest rank of the homogenized and hierarchical world of this urban life. They became the true 'marginals' to everything. As a survival strategy, many of them, however, resorted to tradition. They re-created, in the city, physical and cultural village spaces, the *barrios*, and maintained links with their original communities. And so they were able to resist the permanent threat of urban development, which attempts to replace the *barrios* – living and lively social entities – by homogenized and specialized spaces whose functions are to sleep, work, to buy or use free time, and which are intertwined by the speedways conceived for cars and no longer for men and women. For a long time, slum-dwellers knew that development had made their skills redundant, and their education inadequate for the jobs that were created. The truly marginal groups know very well how painfully 'development' has forced them, in ever new ways, into the cash economy. With the so-called crisis, however, many of them enjoy a new opportunity. Production cooperatives are springing up in the very heart of Mexico City, and they thrive thanks to the decreasing purchasing power of those formerly employed. A phenomenal increase of next-door catering has been observed in many places. Street stands and tiny markets have returned to the corners from where they disappeared years ago. As some rural communities start to flourish again, some rural-urban 'marginals' are also recovering the space to which they belong.

During the seventies, when the peasants made an effort to recover their local spaces after their disenchantment with the 'national' organizations, people coming from the other educational extreme began joining them. They also were disenchanted with 'development' and its institutions, with political parties and bureaucratic or academic careers. As a result new and diversified forms of social institutions began to flourish. Decentralized webs of heterogeneous organizations proliferated. An expanding circle of ex-economists and erstwhile sociologists or industrial managers finds it increasingly difficult to make their peers grasp what they themselves learned from the grassroots: no indicator can reflect the pain caused by the loss of local self-reliance, dignity and solidarity, which are the inevitable by-products of 'measurable' progress. Similarly, no indicators tell about the human joy people find in a more hospitable world.

Trust and friendship, linking groups of peasants, urban 'marginals', as well as de-professionalized intellectuals, and providing for the successful circulation of ideas or goods among them, look to many observers like a utopian, romantic fantasy. To them these ingenuous tools cannot operate in the 'real' economic world, but are limited to marginal spaces. In contrast, for the people, these webs are not a mere survival strategy but a promising, joyful and pragmatic way of life. It is to base their lives on the promises of 'development' or dependence, on the 'market forces' or on public institutions for the making of a living which seem not only a foolish fantasy but a dead-end. They know very well that they have but very limited access to the goods and services associated with 'developments'. More and more, with the so-called crisis, they can see that they are themselves dispensable in the economic and official world. Yet it is this world which is, in turn, falling apart.

The physical, cultural and social space originally defining the peasant world was *localized* – located in a specific place, but *unlimited* – without defined limits. The outer space was perceived as a horizon, not as a frontier. Under such conditions, hospitality defines basic attitudes towards others. Modern Mexican peasants are thus inclined, whether in their rural communities or in the cities, to redefine some rules of hospitality, and how to host foreign ideas, tools, goods and practices of people who ignore hospitality but impose on others what they have (and assume to be of universal value). By hosting the Spaniards, the people were colonized. By hosting other gods, their own gods were destroyed. By hosting 'development', their environment and livelihood were seriously damaged. By hosting 'improved' seeds, for example, they have been losing the genetic richness of their centuries-old selection of seeds, able to respond to the constant variation of their micro-climates. It seems like a miracle that after all these experiences Mexican peasants still retain hospitality and solidarity as a defining trait. Since the complete failure of this monstrous experiment can now be recognized, beyond 'development', they are successfully trying to regenerate a hospitable world, following traditional paths now enriched with the experience, good and bad, of modernity. *Homo sapiens* and *homo ludens* are beginning to move out of the nightmare created by the impossible attempt to replace them on earth by the *homo oeconomicus*.

Bibliographic Clues

For a general view of rural Mexico, see Gustavo Esteva (1983) *The Struggle for Rural Mexico* (Massachusetts, Bergin & Garvey Publishers) from which the introductory section of the paper was taken.

For a detailed account of the consequences of the green revolution, see Cynthia Hewitt de Alcantara (1974) *Modernizing Mexican Agriculture* (Global II Project on Social and Economic Implications of the Introduction of New Varieties of Foodgrains, Geneva, UNDP/UNRISD).

For a systematic argument against 'development' and its new forms, see Gustavo Esteva (1986) 'A new call for celebration', *Development*, Rome, SID, June.

Related Items

1, 2, 3, 4, 7, 8, 9, 10, 18, 19, 20, 21, 23, 25, 26, 29, 33, 34, 35, 37, 42, 47, 48, 49, 53, 54, 55, 56, 57, 58, 60, 61, 62.

60

Ecological Particularities and Rural Populism

Paul Richards

Most scientists would subscribe to the view that science deals in universals: principles that are true for all times and places. They would say that it makes sense to talk of Yoruba music, Islamic art, Marxist history, but less sense to regard the laws of physics and chemistry in the same way. There are, so it would be argued, no Marxist laws of soil erosion or Yoruba principles of rainfall. Science has its unique power to transform the world precisely because it is not confined to the particularities of time, place and special interests.

One of the justifications once advanced in favour of colonialism was that it brought Africa under the 'rule of law'. This was meant, I think, in two senses. First that British or French principles of jurisprudence were beneficial to Africa because they were based on 'universal' notions of human rights, and second, that colonialism connected Africa to the global march of progress by bringing scientific principles to bear on development problems.

The first argument has been widely, and rightly, contested. If there are universal principles of jurisprudence these are not located in the surface layers of legal systems, but by analogy with a term used by linguists, in their 'deep structures'. Looked at in this light there are as many universals in African law as in European. Assessed at the level of 'deep structure' it would be difficult to claim the innate superiority of European legal codes over African. At the surface level, European codes were often quite manifestly unsuited to African conditions.

Would a similar argument be true of the sciences? Did colonial scientific and technical departments see themselves as bringing the 'anarchy' of the African environment under the rule of scientific law? And were these laws as beneficial as the protagonists hoped?

John Ford (1971), surveying the lessons to be learned from attempts by the colonial scientific services to solve the 'tsetse fly problem', argues that

Excerpts from Paul Richards, *Indigenous Agricultural Revolution*, Hutchinson, 1985.

inflexible commitment to universalist assumptions of this sort fundamentally misdirected trypanosomiasis research for a generation or more. Drawing on many years of experience as an entomologist working for the colonial sleeping sickness services, Ford arrived at the conclusion that the spread of tsetse flies and sleeping sickness in the early colonial period was a direct consequence of disruptions brought about by colonial conquest. Colonial administrators found it difficult to appreciate that they themselves were partly the cause of the problem they were struggling to solve. So the erroneous idea became firmly established that the spread of the tsetse fly hazard was due to the 'outmoded' and 'wasteful' cultivation practices of African farmers.

African environment management practices reflected sets of conditions and constraints with which scientists trained in Europe were unfamiliar. Africa was a lightly populated continent. Many of the key issues in the ecology of development derived from the zone of contact between the wilderness and the settled domain. The African trypanosomiases, Ford argues, were characteristic of the diseases that have to be overcome when settlements and wildlife ecosystems come into contact. French, Belgian and British scientists in Africa came from densely settled countries where the problem of 'wilderness diseases' had been overcome many centuries earlier. Many African communities, however, were still engaged upon the work of taming the wilderness at the time of colonial conquest, in part due to depopulation caused by earlier contact with Europe. Russian ecologists, confronting the problems posed by a major wilderness settlement frontier in Siberia, had elaborated theories much more relevant to African conditions (so Ford argues), but Russia was never a colonial power in Africa. French, Belgian and British colonialists, convinced of their own intellectual and cultural superiority, failed to understand both how particular and place-bound were their own principles of environmental resource management, and the extent to which many of the characteristic practices of African farmers and pastoralists were effective responses to the highly specific challenges posed by the African environment.

After several decades of failure to control the trypanosomiasis problem in colonial Africa scientists eventually concluded that many of their 'solutions' made the problem worse and not better, and that it might be advisable to reassess indigenous management strategies. Ford concludes by reversing previous judgements. Far from being a cause of the tsetse problem, African farming methods offered many useful pointers to an effective solution. He suggests, therefore, that especial attention should be paid to the particularities of ecological relationships in the African environment. This is not to dismiss universals in the ecological sciences altogether. Still less is it support for the notion that science is 'a central villain in the exhaustion and despoliation of man's own environment' (Ley and Samuel, 1978, p. 1). What Ford's work suggests, however, is that in ecological and agricultural studies the universals often lie on deeper levels than hitherto has been suspected.

My own argument may be summed up as follows. Intellectuals, development agencies and governments have all pursued environmental management problems at too high a level of abstraction and generalization. Many environmental problems are, in fact, localized and specific, and require local, ecologically particular, responses. The issue then becomes how to stimulate such situation-specific responses. One of the answers explored below is through mobilizing and building upon existing local skills and initiatives. Everything should be done – so the argument runs – to stimulate vigorous 'indigenous science' and 'indigenous technology'.

... The notion of 'people's science' relates to a broader set of arguments about agricultural change sometimes termed 'agrarian populism'.... Debates concerning agrarian populism were important among Russian socialists in the late nineteenth century. In contradistinction to the views of many orthodox Marxists, the populists rejected 'evolutionist' interpretations of agrarian change, arguing instead that it would be possible to pass from feudalism to socialism without capitalist agriculture as an intervening 'stage'. Translated into action, the populist approach sought to transform Russian agriculture through appeal to peasant economic interests and cultural values, and through the improvement of existing peasant institutions and systems of production.

After the revolution the agricultural economist Chayanov developed an influential theory of peasant economy, derived from detailed studies of peasant farming systems, in which emphasis was placed on both the durability of the peasantry as a social grouping and 'non-capitalist' rationality of many peasant decision-making procedures. These notions ran contrary to the Leninist argument that the peasantry was undergoing rapid differentiation into a class of capitalist farmers and a mass of landless labourers. A pro-peasant development programme was worked out in detail by Chayanov and colleagues during the 1920s. Further experiments on populist lines, however, were terminated by the drive towards collectivization and 'industrial' methods of production in Soviet agriculture under Stalin.

Populism was also a significant force in late nineteenth-century agriculture in the United States. American populism was a political movement (directed in particular against urban-based financial speculators) organized by small and medium-scale farmers themselves. Populism was a strong force among 'family farmers' in the cotton belt and the prairie wheat lands, many of whom, despite a fine record for commercial and technical enterprise, found themselves threatened by especially poor prices and high credit charges during the last quarter of the nineteenth century.

In addition to the direct political significance of American populism (e.g. the activities of the Popular Party in the 1980s) populist attitudes had a profound influence on educational and agricultural research institutions. In some measure, both the Land Grant College movements and the organization of state agricultural extension services came to reflect this populist heritage. American extension agents were seen, initially, as employees of the farming community, not agents of a centralized scientific bureaucracy (in many countries – in Britain for example – extension workers are counted as civil servants, with the implication that their loyalty lies to the state, not the farming community). A priority for a number of early extension services in the United States was to communicate farmers' needs to researchers, not to disseminate scientific findings to potential users. Under a populist rubric extension workers were truly 'agents' (professionals charged with the representation of their clients' interests) rather than the 'educators', 'communicators', even 'salesmen', they have since become.

In Africa, the term populism has been used to describe peasant resistance movements directed against colonial and capitalist penetration and to characterize a number of idioms of 'nationalist' politics. The term has also been used in a programmatic sense as a rallying call for pro-rural, pro-peasant, development strategies. A revived interest in agrarian populism in this second sense reflects the depth of the current food production crisis in Africa, and the apparent ineffectiveness of orthodox initiatives for dealing with this problem.

My own view draws much of its inspiration from populist arguments of the following kinds:

1   Whereas much of Africa's rural population is scattered and poor it is also inventively self-reliant. The degree of isolation and poverty is in many cases such as to foredoom to failure attempts to copy agricultural development strategies attempted in Europe and Asia. On the other hand, inventive self-reliance is one of Africa's most precious resources. Development initiatives should aim to maximize the utilization of this resource.

2   Small-scale farmers are capable of making changes in their own interest which are potentially of benefit to society as a whole. The most effective and rapid rates of agricultural change will occur when state resources are used to back changes that small-scale farmers are already keen to make. (Such support will not be applied indiscriminately to all peasant interests, of course, but will inevitably reflect wider societal goals and priorities.)

3   Although rural development programmes of the last 10–15 years have placed the interests of small-scale farmers high on their agenda, the results have so far failed to come up to expectations because of a failure seriously to address questions of popular participation in project design and the development of new technologies. This results either in inappropriate innovations or in support for the least appropriate groups in the farming community. Typically, project inputs fail to work as intended or they end up in the hands of non-farmers (merchants, transporters, civil-servants, politicians) and those most anxious to quit farming for town.

Politics, sociology and economics of agrarian populism are not my main concern here. My main concern is with ecological aspects of the populist case; more specifically, with the possibility that the populist approach is a good, and perhaps the most effective, way to foster the resource-management and biological skills upon which an African agricultural revolution might rest.

References

Ford, J. (1971) *The Role of Trypanosomiasis in African Ecology*, Clarendon Press.
Ley, D. and Samuel, M. (1978) *Humanistic Geography: Prospects and Problems*, Croom Helm.

Related Items

18, 19, 20, 21, 25, 29, 33, 37, 53, 54, 56, 57, 59, 61.

61

The Pueblos Carry Out a Revolution: 'Hanging on tight to the tail of our jefe Zapata's horse'

John Womack

Zapata had already rebuked military chiefs who interfered in village affairs. When he himself took part in settling local troubles, as he did more than once, he limited his involvement to enforcing decisions the villagers reached on their own. When, for instance, during the agrarian reform it came to time to mark the boundaries between Yautepec and Anenecuilco fields, he accompanied the district agrarian commission into the countryside to a tecorral, a stone fence, where the representatives of both communities had gathered. The oldest men around had come along as experts. For years these elders had struggled in their neighbours' defence, and Zapata listened to their judgements 'with particular deference', recalled a young member of the commission. As Anenecuilco's president and as the Liberating Army's commander-in-chief, he then instructed the agronomists who would do the surveying. 'The pueblos say that this tecorral is their boundary,' he told them, 'and that's where you are going to trace me your marks. You engineers sometimes get stuck on straight lines, but the boundary is going to be the stone fence, even if you have to work six months measuring all the ins and outs. . . .' Significantly, Zapata never organized a state police: law enforcement, such as it was, remained the province of village councils.

. . . The authority reconstituted in the villages provided the ground for the state's agrarian reform. And the reform in turn reinforced the villages by concentrating in them control over agricultural property. As Palafox declared in September 1914, the 'repartition of lands will be carried out in conformity with the customs and usages of each pueblo. . . . that is, if a certain pueblo wants the communal system, so it will be executed, and if another pueblo wants the division of land in order to admit small [individual] property, so it will be

Excerpts from John Womack, *Zapata and the Mexican Revolution*, Knopf, 1968, pp. 227–230, 241.

done'. Thus emerging as the sources of power and livelihood were the most traditional agencies of local society.

This resort to the past was different from the Carrancista agrarian reform. On 6 January 1915 Carranza signed a decree according to which state authorities would control the provisional allotment of lands to claimants. And because of the war, state authorities might be military as well as civil, natives of their zone of command or not, ignorant of its local 'custom and usages' or not. Carranza expressly noted that the reform was not 'to revive the old communities nor to create others like them but only to give ... land to the miserable rural population which today lacks it. . . .' He further specified that 'the property of the lands will not belong to the pueblo in common but is to be divided in pleno dominio – fee simple. . . .' In practice those who took charge of expropriations and redistributions were enterprising generals contemptuous of old ways and intent on success in the new. And the graft was wondrous. So firm a grip did these Carrancista chiefs fasten on the benefits of the reform that a year later in another decree Carranza had to proclaim that the military were to intervene 'only when the action of the political authorities might be difficult', and even then only on special instructions from the chief executive, for a limited purpose and a temporary period. But in the Carrancista areas the entrepreneurs remained in charge. As they managed it, agrarian reform was to help create a new, national economy in which they could flourish. For the Zapatistas, it was the discharge of a national duty to uphold the dignity of local life. The regime that would form in Morelos would come about not only through the orders of bureaucrats or generals but through the cooperation of village leaders.

. . . Within days Palafox became secretary of agriculture in the Conventionist cabinet, the ranking Zapatista in the government. And to the reporter who asked him on the day of his appointment if he meant now, like officials before him, 'to study the agrarian question', he replied, 'No, señor, I'll not dedicate myself to that. The agrarian question I've got amply studied. I'll dedicate myself to carrying [reform] into the field of practice. . . .'

Immediately the American agents singled him out as a troublemaker. When one agent asked him for safe-conduct passes to visit an American-owned hacienda in a Zapatista zone, 'he told me,' the agent reported, 'that he could not give them, as all of these estates were to be divided up, and the land distributed to the poor'. The agent explained that this property was American. Palafox's answer was scandalous: 'He replied, that it did not make any difference whether it was American or any other foreign property; that these estates were to be divided up. . . .' The agent promised his superiors further reports on Palafox. 'I can foresee,' he wrote 'that he will be an element destined to give the Minister of Foreign Affairs a great deal of avoidable work.' By late December, identifying Palafox as the one who would divide properties 'whether they belonged to Americans or Chinamen', the agent filed a conclusive judgement on him. 'He is impossible,' the agent had decided, 'and his rabid socialist ideas could never be of any help in solving the problems in a beneficial manner for his country.' Gloatingly the agent then anticipated how Villa would 'attend to' Palafox when Villa and Zapata split.

... these metropolitan intrigues did not really interest Zapata, which was why they went on and on. And they did not carry into Morelos. These people were moving on their own course, in no need of outside sponsors or patrons. And there in full force the revolution continued.

In the spring harvests began, the first fruit to mature from this progress of the pueblos. The crops the farmers now brought in were not the planters' cane or rice but the traditional foodstuffs, corn and beans. As the rainy season came on, Governor Vázquez distributed among the municipal governments 500,000 pesos – a loan from the Convention – which were to go to local farmers as credit for seed and tools. By mid-June reporters found all the fields in the state under cultivation again mainly in corn.

... Zapata himself urged villagers to quit growing vegetables and instead produce a cash-crop. 'If you keep on growing chile peppers, onions, and tomatoes,' he told Villa de Ayala farmers, 'you'll never get out of the state of poverty you've always lived in. That's why, as I advise you, you have to grow cane. . . .' Through conditional gifts of money and seed, he did persuade some villagers to resume the cultivation of cane.

But most families went on truck farming. Rather than rehabilitate the *hacienda*, they obviously preferred to work and trade in foodstuffs that had always seemed the mainstay of the pueblo. And during the summer they restocked Morelos's district markets with the familiar beans, corn, chickpeas, tomatoes, onions, chile peppers, even chickens. While Mexico City was on the verge of starvation at this time, common folk in Morelos evidently had more to eat than in 1910 – and at lower real prices. So profuse was the production of food that despite the constant infusion of Conventionist currency into the state's economy, there was little sign of inflation. In the fondas, the crude country inns where revolutionary officers, local officials, and metropolitan refugees ate, the young agrarian commissioners got by easily on four pesos a day.

In such clear relief the character of revolutionary Morelos emerged: in the very crops people liked to grow, they revealed the kind of community they liked to dwell in. They had no taste for the style of individuals on the make, the life of perpetual achievement and acquisition, of chance and change and moving on. Rather, they wanted life they could control, a modest, familial prosperity in the company of other modestly prosperous families whom they knew, and all in one place. An experiment, for instance, they would try only after they were certain it would work – after, that is, it was no longer experimental. And profits they appreciated only if they had an orthodox use for them.

Related Items

18, 19, 20, 21, 25, 26, 31, 37, 53, 55, 56, 58, 59, 61, 62.

62

Short Historical Outline of Peasant Studies

Teodor Shanin

The literate attitude to peasants in the pre-industrial world combined hostility with silence. This massive majority of all people produced the wealth of the wealthy, provided for the culture of the cultured, while their numbers, when under control, defined the might of the powerful. Peasants had to be subjugated 'to deliver the goods'. It seems that they had also to be nullified or dehumanized in the consciousness of those who held dominion over arms, bureaucracies and the written word. It is easier to grind into dust some humans, and see this as eternal, if we do not admit that the enslavement of beings like ourselves lies at the root of our good fortune. More simple was to see 'them' as beyond the pale of humanity. It was even better to forget 'them' altogether. Medieval writings are full of kings and wars, of philosophy, poetry, law and astrology, with some lives of saints and sages thrown in for good measure. They are mostly silent about peasants. When peasants were recognized, usually in connection with some man-made disasters (be it a new tax, law of enserfment or a rebellion of the brutalized), hostility and contempt for the peasants burst through. The *Declinatio Rustico* of the thirteenth century defined 'the six declensions of the word peasant' as 'villain, rustic, devil, robber, brigand and looter, and in plural wretches, beggars, liars, rogues, trash and infidels' (Le Goff, 1977, p. 71). The usages of language tell us much the same. In early Russian the term peasant was *smerd*, from the verb *smerdet'*, 'to stink'. The Polish term *cham* indicated crudity, mythically rooted in different racial origins from the nobles 'nation'. In eighteenth-century English a 'peasant' meant a brute and an illiterate while the verb 'to peasant' meant to subjugate and enslave (*Oxford English Dictionary*, 1933, vol. VII, p. 594).

Modernity and capitalism came to Europe with the triple revolution of industrialization, of citizenship within a nation state, and of the spread of

An original paper developing further the theme of Teodor Shanin, 'The conceptual reappearance of peasantry in Ango-Saxon social science', in Ernest Gellner (ed.), *Soviet and Western Anthropology*, Duckworth, 1980.

secular, mathematics-bound science of practical application. In its most fundamental self-images this was a world without peasants, indeed de-peasantization became a major index of modernization. 'Modernity' was due to transform completely the life of humanity, make it progress from the dark ages of poverty, oppression and prejudice into the realm of plenty, freedom and wisdom. In the nineteenth century the past hostility towards peasants by those who drew their living from peasant sweat was being supplemented by detached pity, a shrug of the shoulders over the irrationality and brutality of the past and the cheerful assumption of it rapidly coming to an end. It was less vicious but as dismissive. Peasants were treated as an anachronism and thereby as an irrelevance by scholars and politicians alike.

Under the surface of literate public opinion all this was in fact somewhat less straightforward. Anachronistic or not in the face of the growing manufacturing industries, peasants were still the majority of Europeans, let alone of mankind at large. Also, their decline was less evident or at least less rapid than the first predictions would have it. The newly created social sciences and the organizers of popular political movements were beginning to react to that. Their reactions differed, owing to diverse ideological assumptions, political goals, social interest and schools of thought. But apart from these determinations and impacts, the way peasants were approached in scholarly endeavour can be meaningfully divided into three global regions, even though, of course, there was no absolute matching of geography and intellectual tendencies.

First, the popular and scholarly consciousness of the industrial West, of which those who wrote in English provided a major component, was dominated by the fundamental arch-model of evolutionist theory. This meant a historiography-cum-typology dividing the social world into 'modern' and 'backward'. The assumption of decomposition and necessary disappearance of all things backward was part of it. On such an intellectual map the actual peasants disappeared even more effectively than in the olden days. They were now a conceptually unspecific part of the mixed bag of 'remainders of the past' (together with slaves and feudals, caravans and pirates, astrology and witch-craft). The one unifying characteristic of the whole category was its necessarily declining significance.

A somewhat closer examination of the body of social sciences shows that even then the non-peasant/peasant division, charged with mixed emotions, did not quite disappear from the consciousness of the West. In particular, much of sociology, itself a product of modernity, has its origins in a sequence of taxonomies with dual types at their core. Tönnies's 'community' versus 'society', Durkheim's 'mechanical' versus 'organic' solidarity, Cooley's 'primary' versus 'secondary' relations, de Coulange's 'individualism' versus 'collectivism', all share a polarized model in which on the one side appear the characteristics of 'us', that is the evident or the anticipated modern society – role-centred, individualistic and bureaucratic. That much is explicit, but what is often missed is that in terms of the actual and direct experience of 'men in the street' in the pre-TV Europe, the opposite conceptual box of 'non-us' was filled mostly by the contemporary peasants or by what passed as the knowledge of them. From behind the social theory the physiognomy of the peasant could be thereby glimpsed, to surface more clearly when past societies were looked at historically. It was also recovered at times in a novel searching out of un-alienated personalities. Yet, even there, the message seemed clear. Peasants were condemned by history to rapid oblivion and thereby to irrelevance. When at the turn of the century rural sociology emerged, first in the USA, as a sub-discipline in its own right (Galeski, 1972), it was focused on farming as an occupation but not on peasants as a social entity.

The polar opposite of 'the West' with its modernity, power and plenty were in those days the 'Colonies' and the 'Orient'. There, life seems to have trickled more slowly, the hand of state was heavier and modern science more sparse, imported or imposed as it was from the West. The fact that more than nine-tenths of the population was peasant mattered little to the local *literati*. To the extent this was discussed at all, it was done not unlike in the European Middle Ages, or else under the direct impact of the European theories of progress and as dismissive of the issue. There were several exceptions to it, both foreign and native, e.g. the studies of China by Tawney and Fei (Tawney, 1931; Fei, 1939). But exceptions they were.

It was the third region, *Eastern and Central Europe*, where the studies of peasantry first blossomed to become a major component of the social sciences and of political debate. In those countries a highly sophisticated intelligentsia, politically committed to nationalism and/or modernization, to liberalism, populism or socialism, faced massive peasantry – the poorest and most oppressed segment of their people. The ideologies and politics of reforms or of revolution necessarily related to the peasant majorities as the major object, the possible carrier or the main bottleneck of the necessary advance. On the eve of the First World War the intellectual and political attempts to look at and to activate peasantries were being increasingly matched by the peasants' own efforts to establish viable political movements in defence of their own interest (in Poland, Romania, Bulgaria, Russia of 1905–6, etc.). Farther to the West, German academic culture offered a possible case of marginality-induced analytical advance. West European in its impetus, East European in some of its rural experience, it produced some inspired writing about peasants and the rural scene, present and past: Marx and Weber, Sombart and Kautsky, Rodbertus Buchner and Oppenheimer. And it was Denmark which became for a time the prime example of a successful cooperative movement and self-generated innovation of peasant smallholders. From the North Sea to the Black Sea and the Urals, studies of peasantry flourished on both empirical and theoretical levels. Much of this work and of its methods are still unsurpassed.

The blossoming of peasant studies in Eastern and Central Europe and some measure of their cross-fertilizing impact elsewhere came to an end during the 1920s/30s. Rapidly spreading military dictatorships destroyed or crippled most of the peasant parties which initiated the Green International. Nazism and similar pests demolished the academic heritage which played a central role in the advancement of the studies of peasant societies. Stalin's collectivization and 'purge' brought a great silence into the USSR as both its Marxist and non-Marxist analysts of peasantry went under. The build-up towards and the World War focused intellectual and political attention elsewhere. With few exceptions (e.g. Warriner, 1939) peasant studies passed into an oblivion which lasted for thirty years.

They were to re-emerge *en masse* into a very different world. The World War and following rapid decolonization changed the global map and its power balance. The United Nations provided a major international stage where the case of the global underdogs came to be presented in national terms, as an issue of 'underdevelopment'. For a time a global theory of progress, the modernization theory, was to define the prevailing images, self-images and plans: independence, education and the world markets, with a dash of economic planning, were to secure that the 'backward societies' of the world, especially its ex-colonies, would rapidly catch up with the industrial West. The failure of this prediction and strategies, the 'growing gap' of wealth and power, came eventually to be theorized by new images and models which were well represented by Myrdal's concept of 'cumulation of advancement and backwardness' and Paul Baran's simultaneously appearing 'political economy of backwardness' (Myrdal, 1957; Baran, 1957). The 'developing societies' became synonymous with the world's worst slum and global crises. Social scientists, politicians and planners were made to turn their attention from the purely economic indices and curves of 'up and up' to the social structures of the 'developing societies'. The majority there were peasants. Simultaneously, a 'critique by arms – an assault against corrupt regimes of the Third World was increasingly being mounted by guerrilla movements taught by Mao that their success is subject to their link with the rural people. The majority of them were peasants. Right and left, scholars, politicians and revolutionaries, were turning their attention to peasants and peasant societies. The explosion of peasant studies in the late 1960s/early 1970s was part of a new political situation, a major conceptual refocusing and reformulation which reached their symbolic peak in the heady days of 1968.

When it came, general knowledge of the (re)discovered subject matter and, especially, its analytical and theoretical components was remarkably thin. Yet the appetite for it broke all bounds. A new theoretical armoury was rapidly set up consisting of some of the old and partly forgotten texts or chapters by Znaniecki, Redfield, Marx, Lenin, Sorokin, etc. (see the Further Reading list). Those were now supplemented and integrated with a number of major new works (new, that is, to the Anglo-Saxon leading academic tradition of the West) which received outstanding attention. Of those, particularly dramatic was the impact of Chayanov and of Marx's newly discovered *Grundrisse*, first published in 1966 and 1964 respectively (Chayanov, 1966; Marx, 1964). This linked with a number of integrative works in different disciplines, both manuscripts (by Wolf, Galeski and Schultz) and Readers (by Shanin, Dalton and Foster), which mapped out the subject matter. A concept and a field of studies were established. The continuous debate which followed and its applications within social planning made the field and its analysts grow in sophistication and factionalize along lines representing diversity of goals and assumptions as well as different disciplinary perspectives and regional traditions.

Of the schools of thought which offered the initial bricks from which the theoretical structure of the discipline was being constructed, four stood out in impact: the class theory, the 'specific economy' typology, the ethnographic cultural tradition and the Durkheimian taxonomy as developed by Kroeber. The Marxist tradition of class analysis has approached peasantry in terms of exploitative power-relations, i.e. as the characteristic producers of the feudal mode of production. Contemporary peasantry appears accordingly as a leftover of this earlier social structure, 'frozen' by remaining at the bottom of the power structure in societies of belated development. The second tradition viewed peasant social organization as rooted in a specific type of economy, the crux of which lies in the way a family farm operates. This approach, too, can be traced to Marx but also to the German 'historical economists' and Russian 'rural statisticians' of 1880s to 1920s. It was brought into focus in the Anglo-Saxon literature of 1960s/70s with the debate which followed the publication of Chayanov's 1926 study.[1] The third tradition, which stems from European ethnography linked to traditional Western anthropology, tended to approach peasants as the representatives of an earlier national tradition preserved by a 'cultural lag', i.e. of inertia typical of peasant societies.[2] The fourth tradition originated from Durkheim's basic dualism dividing societies into 'traditional' (segmented/'mechanical solidarity') and modern (integrated, of 'organic solidarity'). It was developed further by Kroeber through placing peasant societies in the intermediate position as 'part-societies with part-cultures', i.e. as partly open segments in a town-centred society (Durkheim, 1960; Kroeber, 1948). Peasant 'part-segments' were turned by Redfield into the cornerstone of a conceptualization accepted for a time by a major part of American anthropologists.

The full scope of the 1960s/70s grand decade of 'peasantology' presents too large an issue to be discussed here. The *Further Reading* list will partly substitute for it but much of it remains still to be written. Only the chapter headings of this 'event' and process will be mentioned here. We have already spoken of its context, expressed as much in major political and economic processes symbolized by the Vietnam War, the 'developing societies', economic disasters and spreading 'military regimes' as by the intellectual eclipse of the Modernization Theory and the 'taken for granted' optimism concerning global futures. General analysis confined to political decisions, economicist extrapolations and gung-ho optimism was being increasingly replaced by more complex and realistic considerations of different aspects of social structure and the dynamics of contradiction. One can say it was being 'sociologized', given some new historical depth and charged with dialectics. In this framework the blossoming of peasant studies resulted in new attention given and much work done concerning the actual operation of the family farm, the social context of rural productivity and capital formation, multi-generational mobility and the political and cultural resistance of the rural communities as well as to guerrilla, counter-guerrilla and peasant political action. Those issues found their further extension in the analysis of rural labour *vis-à-vis* migration, issues of urbanization and of the new 'cities of peasants', of peasant-workers and of peasants' sons as phenomena of extensive social significance. There was a massive output of studies, empirical and theoretical, relevant to all these problems.

For a time the subject matter became a fashion, with the particular dynamics of academic fashions taking over – the term being overused and made less clear by excessive application while the intellectual product became more thin in content and repetitious. Quite often, old orthodoxies which made peasants disappear were replaced by new oversimplifications in which peasants came to be treated as unrelated to broader society, unchanging and/or necessarily wise or virtuous in contradistinction to anybody else. Yet, while the actual analytical achievement of those days was of mixed quality, much of it was very substantial. Extensive data and important analytical insights were gathered. The methods applied did improve. The criticism of the concept, especially of its naive applications, served the analytical advance of the field.

We are now in the period following the 1960s/70s peak period of peasant studies. The dynamics of fashion has eased off. As intellectual treasure-hunters have moved elsewhere in the pursuit of easily saleable commodities, the substantive group of analysts of solid achievement which was established continues its work. On the base of the achievements of the 1960s/70s a number of excellent studies emerged in the 1980s. They tackled anew some of the topics developed earlier and added or re-accentuated a number of issues. More work was done and new critique and ideas offered concerning land reform and state intervention aiming at modernization and collectivization. The new or re-accentuated topics were those of peasant consciousness, of famine and international food regimes, of peasant 'subsumption' by agribusiness, increasingly multinational, of the analytical relations between peasantry and broader concepts of 'family economy', informal economy and 'subaltern classes'. New and important work was done by historians and sociologists looking at the past on peasant resistance and its long-term impact, and on pre-capitalist non-peasant agriculture in Europe, etc. Information was gathered and analysed concerning contemporary and past peasant day-to-day life and consciousness in different countries and regions, expanding the field and its comparative potentials.

At the conceptual level it has been a period when the fundamental debate about peasantry's conceptual existence has come back to the fore. Up to a point this represented the logical consequence of the swing of an intellectual fashion – an over-use of a phrase and a concept followed by dismay and a move to drop (and to 'demystify') old pets. It must also be read in the context of a general disarray and doubts within the field of 'development theories'. But the issue itself is serious and goes to the very root of social sciences. It also has considerable implications for theory and action. Should we drop the concept and the assumption of qualitative and structural particularity of peasants to return to an analysis in which peasants do not exist conceptually speaking, i.e. are but a section or an epiphenomenon of other structures or groups (capital? agriculture? farming population? petite bourgeoisie?). In such an outlook the 'data' gathered could be reconsidered via different sets of concepts like 'rural poverty', 'backwardness', 'modern farming', 'petit bourgeois production', etc.

The Introduction to this volume has already touched on this argument. A systematic answer to it is given elsewhere.[3] Put at its shortest, to demystify contemporary peasants out of existence seems mistaken and counterproductive when advance of knowledge and increase in human welfare and liberty are concerned. It is mistaken because it usually uses the unrealistic logic of total exclusion, i.e. either peasants or capitalism, either market or family farming, etc. The fact that contradictory characteristics persist side by side should not lead to their intellectual reduction but to more realistic models and to more sophisticated analysis which treats them for what they are, i.e. a social reality, rich in complexity and historical connotations. It is mistaken because it disregards considerable achievements of the analysts who focused on peasantry's particularity by illuminating comparatively the dynamics of contemporary society. It is mistaken also because the analysis of peasants has broader significance for a number of other contemporary problems, especially those concerning family economies, from capitalist family-farming in the US to the 'second economy' of contemporary Italy or Hungary. It is most substantively mistaken because peasants are still half of mankind, and if we add the peasants' sons, a large majority of the population of the globe. Analytically the abolition of peasants is dangerous because it facilitates 'deductivism', i.e. an approach in which out of a chosen general principle an actuality is deduced, with all humans in general and peasants in particular treated as carriers only of the total logic of the system adopted. It therefore develops or condones lack of appetite for actual research and restricts understanding of actual complexity of social reality. Finally, it is politically dangerous for it can be used and often was used to disregard the destitution, oppression and inequality of the poorest of the poor in the name of abstract future principles and corrupt immediate practices, code-named 'progress'. The contributions above described some of such mixtures of repression, miscomprehension and lies.

The criticism of peasant studies as a project and a practice has often been apt and sometimes useful. The emotional undercurrent and ideological pressures in it are, as in the past, remarkably strong and colour every debate. Further advance will have to guard against supra-substantive assumptions by which peasants can be understood on their own, unrelated to society at large, and against the rural sentimentalism of those who fail to see how vicious such life experience can be. But intellectual subsumptions of peasants which write them out of existence are not an effective response to that. The response must be found in the realism of accepting the complex and contradictory nature of social life, its changeability and the necessity of parallel models and intellectual styles which are irreducible to each other, but must combine analytically to match the riches of social experience. In the final resort it is not a question of logic but one of understanding real social relations which concepts must serve. Within the traditions of struggle for the betterment of human existence, one must add here a commitment to define the dimensions of oppression of humans by other humans and of the ways to combat it and change it. During the last two decades the concept of peasantry has performed all these services well enough. This capacity is not yet spent.[4]

Notes

1 For discussion see Introductions to the new edition of Chayanov's *Theory of Peasant Economy*, Wisconsin University Press, 1986.
2 A particular caricature-like dimension of it were the 'folkist' fashions and peasantist-cult promoted by German reactionary romanticism (with high-bred ladies of Nazi sympathies resolving the us/them dilemmas by dressing up in peasant fashion).
3 Some of it has been considered in the Introduction. For further discussion of the relevant 'rules for the retiring of sociological concepts' when peasants are concerned, see Shanin (1982).
4 The last sentences intentionally follow the text mentioned earlier (Shanin, 1982).

References

Baran, P. (1957) *The Political Economy of Growth*, MR Press.
Chayanov, A. (1986) *The Theory of Peasant Economy*, Wisconsin University Press (1st edition, 1966).
Durkheim, E. (1960) *The Division of Labour in Society*, Free Press.
Galeski, B. (1972) *Basic Concepts of Rural Sociology*, Manchester University Press.
Fei Hsiao Tung (1939) *Peasant Life in China*, Dutton.
Kroeber A. F. (1948), *Anthropology*, Harcourt.
Le Goff, J. (1977) 'The town as an agent of civilisation', in C. M. Cipolla, *The Fontana Economic History of Europe: The Middle Ages*, Penguin.
Marx, K. (1964) *Pre-Capitalist Economic Formations*, Lawrence & Wishart.
Myrdal, G. (1957) *Economic Theory and Underdeveloped Regions*, Methuen.
Oxford English Dictionary (1933) Clarendon Press.
Shanin, T. (1985) *Russia as a 'Developing Society'*, Macmillan.
Shanin, T. (1982) 'Defining peasants: conceptualisations and de-conceptualisations', *Sociological Review*, vol. 30, no. 1.

Wolf, E. R. (1966) *Peasants*, Prentice-Hall.
Tawney, R. H. (1931) *Land and Labour in Chile*, Allen & Unwin.
Warriner, D. (1939) *Economics of Peasant Farming*, Oxford University Press.

Related Items

1, 7, 8, 9, 10, 16, 17, 19, 21, 25, 26, 29, 35, 37, 45, 46, 48.

Further Reading
Hussain Zillur Rahman

The division of references corresponds closely but not exactly to the part titles in the Reader. Only English-language sources are included.

1   Systematic Text-books

E. R. Wolf, 1966, *Peasants*, Prentice-Hall.
B. Galeski, 1972, *Basic Concepts in Rural Sociology*, Manchester University Press.

2   General Readers and Edited Collections

H. Alavi and T. Shanin (eds), 1982, *Introduction to the Sociology of Developing Societies*, Macmillan.
Philip K. Bock (ed.), 1969, *Peasants in the Modern World*, University of New Mexico Press.
G. Dalton (ed.), 1967, *Tribal and Peasant Economics*, Natural History Press.
J. Harriss (ed.), 1982, *Rural Development: Theories of Peasant Economy and Agrarian Change*, Hutchinson University Library.
E. J. Hobsbawm, W. Kula, A. Mitra, K. N. Raj and I. Sachs (eds), 1980, *Peasants in History: Essays in Honour of Daniel Thorner*, Oxford University Press.
J. M. Potter, M. N. Diaz and G. M. Foster (eds), 1967, *Peasant Society: A Reader*, Little, Brown.
T. Shanin, 1988, *Defining Peasants: Essays concerning Rural Societies and Peasant Studies*, Basil Blackwell.
P. A. Sorokin, F. F. Zinnerman and C. J. Golpin (eds), 1965, *Systematic Source Books in Rural Sociology*, Russell & Russell.

3 Journals and Abstracts of Specific Relevance

Sociologia Ruralis, the Journal of the European Society for Rural Sociology, published quarterly, Van Gorcum, Assen, Netherlands.
The Journal of Peasant Studies, published quarterly, Frank Cass, London.
Peasant Studies, published quarterly at the University of Utah, USA.
Agriculture and Human Values, published quarterly by the Humanities of Agriculture Programme, University of Florida.
World Agricultural Economics and Rural Sociology Abstracts, published monthly by the Commonwealth Bureau of Agricultural Economics, Oxford.

Much relevant material can also be found in journals devoted to particular regions, e.g. *Economic and Political Weekly* (Bombay; in particular the quarterly Review of Agriculture), *Review of African Political Economy* (London), MERIP Reports on Middle East (Washington), *Journal of Contemporary Asia* (Stockholm), *Latin American Perspectives* (California), also *Comparative Studies in Society and History* (Ann Arbor), *Past and Present* (Oxford), *American Ethnologist* (Washington DC), *Ethnologia Europaia* (Odenza), *Economic Development and Cultural Change* (Chicago).

4 Theoretical Perspectives and Debate

A major development in the discussion of peasantry within the contemporary English-speaking world took place over the late sixties and early seventies (see item 62). This section has accordingly been organized into three sub-sections so as to bring into sharper focus the specific developments of the field. Part A covers the 'classical' sources, i.e. the writings which have both shaped the field and constituted the point of departure for the developments of the late sixties and early seventies. Part B covers the latter contributions while part C takes account of developments since.

Part A

I. H. Boeke, 1953, *Economics and Economic Policy of Dual Societies*, Institute of Pacific Relations. A discussion of peasantry with a particular emphasis on peasant economy and in the framework of colonial and post-colonial society.
R. Firth and B. S. Yamey (eds), 1964, *Capital, Saving and Credit in Peasant Societies*, Allen & Unwin. A statement of views that the peasant economy is essentially similar to the capitalist one and is to be treated in the same conceptual framework.
C. Geertz, 1963, *Agricultural Involution*, California University Press. Discussion of the social and ecological dimensions of rural pauperization which does not result in proletarization.
V. I. Lenin, 1967, *The Development of Capitalism in Russia*, Progress Publishers.
K. Marx, *Capital*, 1976: vol. I (chapters on primitive accumulation); and 1981: vol. III (chapters on rent), Penguin.
Ashok Mitra, 1957, 'The concept of subsistence', *Economic and Political Weekly*, March 25.
R. Redfield, 1956, *Peasant Society and Culture*, University of Chicago Press.

Sorokin et al. (section 2).

W. I. Thomas and F. Znaniecki, 1958, *The Polish Peasant in Europe and America*, Dover Publications.

D. Warriner, 1939, *Economics of Peasant Farming*, Oxford University Press.

K. A. Wittfogel, 1957, *Oriental Despotism*, Yale University Press.

Part B

H. Alavi, 1973, 'Peasant classes and primordial loyalties', *Journal of Peasant Studies*, vol. 1, no. 1.

J. Banaji, 1976, 'A summary of Kautsky's "The Agrarian Question"', *Economy and Society*, vol. 5, no. 1.

A. V. Chayanov, 1966, *The Theory of Peasant Economy*, D. Thorner, R. E. F. Smith and B. Kerblay (eds), *The major statement of thought and theory of the school which treats peasant economy as qualitatively specific*. New edition 1987, Wisconsin University Press, introduced by Teodor Shanin.

G. M. Foster, 1965, 'The peasants and the image of limited good', *American Anthropologist*, vol. 62, no. 2.

Galeski (section 1).

M. Lipton, 1968, 'The theory of the optimising peasant', *Journal of Development Studies*, April issue.

H. H. Mann, 1967, *The Social Framework of Agriculture: India, the Middle East, England*, Verry.

K. Marx, 1964, *Pre-Capitalist Economic Formations*, Lawrence & Wishart. Introduced by E. J. Hobsbawm.

M. Nash, 1966, *Primitive and Peasant Economic Systems*, Chandler Publishing.

R. E. Pahl, 1966, 'The rural–urban continuum', *Sociologia Ruralis*, vol. 6, pp. 299–330. See also the follow-up debate in vol. 7.

A. Pearse, 1970, *The Latin American Peasant*, Pall Mall Press.

T. W. Schultz, 1965, *Transforming Traditional Agriculture*, Yale University Press.

A. Sen, 1966, 'Peasants and dualism with or without surplus labour', *Journal of Political Economy*.

T. Shanin, 1971, 'Peasantry: delineation of a sociological concept and a field of study', *European Journal of Sociology*, vol. 12.

T. Shanin (ed.), 1971, *Peasants and Peasant Societies*, Penguin.

T. Shanin, 1972, *The Awkward Class: Political Sociology of Peasantry in a Developing Society: Russia, 1910–1925*, Clarendon Press.

Wolf (section 1).

P. Worsley, 1984, *The Three Worlds*, Weidenfeld & Nicholson. See in particular section II for a review of the main schools of analysis of peasantry and their significance for contemporary Third World societies.

Also Shanin 1973/4 (section 6), Skinner (section 6), Alavi (section 8), Moore (section 8), Shanin, 1966 (section 8).

Part C

H. Alavi, 1975, 'India and the colonial mode of production', *Socialist Register*, Merlin Press.

H. Bernstein, 1979, 'African peasantries: towards a theoretical framework', *Journal of Peasant Studies*, vol. 8, no. 4, pp. 421–43.

A. Bhaduri, 1984, *The Economic Structure of Agricultural Backwardness*, Academic Press. An important contribution on the contemporary significance of antediluvian forms of capital on the social dynamics of agrarian society.

Krishna Bharadwaj, 1985, 'A view of commercialisation in Indian agriculture and the development of capitalism', *Journal of Peasant Studies*, vol. 12, no. 4, pp. 7–25.

Jacques M. Chevalier, 1983, 'There is nothing simple about simple commodity production', *Journal of Peasant Studies*, vol. 10, no. 4, pp. 153–86.

C. D. Deere and A. de Janvry, 1979, 'A conceptual framework for the empirical analysis of peasants', *American Journal of Agricultural Economics*, vol. 61, no. 4, pp. 601–11.

G. Djurfeldt, 1981, 'What happened to the agrarian bourgeoisie and the rural proletariat under monopoly capitalism', *Acta Sociologica*, Scandinavian Review of Sociology, vol. 24, no. 3, pp. 167–91.

J. Ennew, P. Hirst and K. Tribe, 1977, '"Peasantry" as an economic category', *Journal of Peasant Studies*, vol. 4, no. 4, pp. 295–322.

Joshua B. Forrest, 1982, 'Defining African peasants', *Peasant Studies*, vol. 9. no. 4.

Harriet Friedmann, 1978, 'Simple commodity production and wage labour in the American plains', *Journal of Peasant Studies*, vol. 6, no. 1, pp. 71–100.

Harriet Friedmann, 1980, 'Household production and the national economy: concepts for the analysis of agrarian formations', *Journal of Peasant Studies*, vol. 7, no. 2, pp. 158–84.

M. Harrison, 1977, 'Resource allocation and agrarian class formation', *Journal of Peasant Studies*, vol. 4, no. 3, pp. 127–61. Republished in *Sociological Review*, 1982, vol. 30. no. 3.

A. Hussain and K. Tribe, 1981, *Marxism and the Agrarian Question*, Macmillan. Part I covers German social democracy and the peasantry 1890–1907; part II covers Russian Marxism and the peasantry 1861–1930.

Journal of Peasant Studies, 1983, vol. 10, nos 2 and 3. Special issue on share-cropping.

K. Kautsky, 1987, *The Agrarian Question*, Manchester University Press and Wisconsin University Press. First appearance in English. Introduction by H. Alavi and T. Shanin.

E. Le Roy Ladurie, 1980, 'Peasants', *The Cambridge Modern History*, vol. 13, appendix 7, Cambridge University Press.

R. Manchin and I. Szelenyi, 1978, 'Theories of family agricultural production in collectivized economies', *Sociologia Ruralis*, vol. 18, pp. 248–69.

N. Mouzelis, 1976, 'Capitalism and the development of agriculture', *Journal of Peasant Studies*, vol. 3, no. 4, pp. 483–92.

U. Patnaik, 1976, 'Class differentiation within the peasantry', *Economic and Political Weekly*, Review of Agriculture, September.

J. M. Scott, 1976, *The Moral Economy of the Peasant: Rebellion and Subsistence in Southeast Asia*, Yale University Press.

T. Shanin, 1977, 'Measuring peasant capitalism: the operationalization of political economy: Russia 1920s and India 1970s', *Economic and Political Weekly*, November.

T. Shanin, 1979, 'Defining peasants: conceptualizations and de-conceptualizations – old and new in a Marxist debate', *Peasant Studies*, vol. 8, no. 4, pp. 38–60.

T. Shanin, 1984, *Late Marx and the Russian Road: Marx and the 'Peripheries of Capitalism'*, Routledge & Kegan Paul.

Sociologia Ruralis, 1984, vol. 24, no. 2. Special theme – 'Family farm: corporatism, the state and survival strategies'. A discussion on East Europe.

K. Vergopoulous, 1978, 'Capitalism and peasant productivity', *Journal of Peasant Studies*, vol. 5, no. 4, pp. 446–81. Also reply by Mouzelis to Vergopoulous in the same journal in 1979.

H. Wolpe, 1975, 'The theory of internal colonialism: the South African case', in I. Oxaal, T. Barnett and D. Booth (eds), *Beyond the Sociology of Development: Economy and Society in Latin America and Africa*, Routledge & Kegan Paul.

Also Brenner (section 5), Popkin (section 5), Shanin (section 5), Hart (section 6), Terence (section 6), Sen (section 6), Bergen (section 7), Stockpol (section 8), Tilly (1977) (section 8), de Janvry (section 9).

5 Peasants: Structure and Change, Past and Present

Andrew Abelson, 1978, 'Inheritance and population control in a Basque Valley before 1900', *Sociologia Ruralis*, vol. 7, no. 1, pp. 11–28.

Herman Bebel, 1983, *Peasant Classes: the Bureaucratisation of Property and Family Relations under Early Hapsburg Absolutism 1511–1636*, Princeton University Press.

A. Béteille, 1975. *Studies in Agrarian Social Structure*, Oxford University Press.

Marc Bloch, 1966, *French Rural History*, California University Press.

J. Blum, 1971, 'The European village as community: origins and functions', *Agricultural History*, vol. 45, no. 3, pp. 157–78.

J. Blum, 1978, *The End of the Old Order in Rural Europe*, Princeton University Press.

M. Boserup, 1963, 'Agrarian structure and the take-off', in W. Rostow (ed.), *The Economics of Take-off into Sustained Growth*, Macmillan. A useful analysis of the diversity of 'models' in the agrarian transition in Europe.

R. Brenner, 1976, 'Agrarian class structure and economic development in pre-industrial Europe', *Past and Present*, no. 70.

Colin Bundy, 1979, *The Rise and Fall of the South African Peasantry*, Heinemann.

Manuel V. Cabral, 1978, 'Agrarian structures and recent movements in Portugal', *Journal of Peasant Studies*, vol. 5, no. 4, pp. 411–45.

W. Cole and E. R. Wolf, 1974, *The Hidden Frontier: Ecology and Ethnicity in Alpine Valley*, Academic Press.

M. von Freyhold, 1979, *Ujamaa Villages in Tanzania*, Heinemann.

René Gallissot, 1975, 'Precolonial Algeria', *Economy and Society*, vol. 4, no. 4, pp. 418–45.

C. Geertz, 1963, *Agricultural Involution: The Processes of Ecological Change in Indonesia*, University of California Press.

Leela Gulati, 1978, 'Profile of a female agricultural labourer', *Economic and Political Weekly*, Review of Agriculture, March.

Irfan Habib, 1963, *The Agrarian System of Mughal India*, Asia Publishing House.

P. D. A. Harvey, 1985, *The Peasant Land Market in Medieval England*, Clarendon Press.

Polly Hill, 1970, *The Migrant Cocoa-farmers of Southern Ghana*, Cambridge University Press.

R. H. Hilton, 1973, *Bondmen Made Free: Medieval Peasant Movements and the English Uprising of 1381*, Temple Smith.

Philip C. C. Huang, 1985, *The Peasant Economy and Social Change in North China*, Stanford

University Press. An important analysis of the origins and nature of the agrarian crisis which gripped the North China Plain in the two centuries before the Revolution.

C. Keyder, 1983, 'Small peasant ownership in Turkey: historical formation and present structure', *Review*, vol. 7, no. 1, pp. 53–107.

T. G. Kessinger, 1974, *Vilayatpur 1848–1968: Social and Economic Change in a North Indian Village*, University of California Press. A good case study on social mobility within a peasant society.

A. M. Khazanov, 1983, *Nomads and the Outside World*, Cambridge University Press.

M. A. Klein (ed.), 1980, *Peasants in Africa: Historical and Contemporary Perspectives*, Sage Publications.

W. Kula, 1976, *The Economic Theory of the Feudal System*, New Left Books.

Alan Macfarlane, 1978, *The Origins of English Individualism: The Family, Property and Social Transition*, Cambridge University Press.

M. Marriot (ed.), 1955, *Village India: Studies in the Little Community*, University of Chicago Press.

J. Martinez-Alier, 1971, *Labourers and Landowners in Southern Spain*, Rowman & Littlefield.

A. Plakans, 1975, 'Peasant farmsteads and households in the Baltic littoral, 1797', *Comparative Studies in Society and History*, vol. 17, no. 1, pp. 2–35.

Samuel L. Popkin, 1979, *The Rational Peasant: The Political Economy of Rural Society in Vietnam*, University of California Press.

Peter H. Prindle, 1985, 'Peasant–worker households and community-based organizations in rural Japan', *Modern Asian Studies*, vol. 19, no. 2, pp. 279–97.

T. Shanin, 1986, *Russia as a Developing Society*, Macmillan.

Henri H. Stahl, 1980, *Traditional Romanian Village Communities: The Transition from the Communal to the Capitalist Mode of Production in the Danube Region*, Cambridge University Press.

R. Stavenhagen, 1964, 'Changing functions of the community in underdeveloped countries', *Sociologia Ruralis*, vol. 4, nos 3 and 4.

E. Stokes, 1978, *The Peasant and the Raj: Studies on Agrarian Society and Peasant Rebellions in Colonial India*, Cambridge University Press.

John Thirsk (ed.), 1967, *The Agrarian History of England and Wales, Vol. IV, 1500—1640*, Cambridge University Press. Excellent discussion on the structure of medieval society.

E. A. Wilkening and B. Galeski (eds), 1987, *Family Farming in Europe and America*, Westview Press.

E. R. Wolf, 1955, 'Types of Latin American peasantry', *American Anthropolgist*, vol. 58.

E. R. Wolf and S. W. Miatz, 1950, An analysis of ritual co-peasanthood' "Compedrzgo", *South West Journal of Anthropology*, vol. 6.

K. Young et al. (eds), 1981, *Of Marriage and the Market: Women's Subordination in International Perspective*, CSE Books.

6   Capital, Peasantry, Economy

M. Abdel-Fadil, 1975, *Development, Income Distribution and Social Change in Rural Egypt (1952–1970): A Study in the Political Economy of Agrarian Transition*, Cambridge University Press.

C. H. de Alcantra, 1976, *Modernizing Mexican Agriculture: Socio-economic Implications of Technological Change 1940–70*, UNRISD Publications, Geneva.

Shahid Amin, 1984, *Sugarcane and Sugar in Gorakhpur: An Enquiry into Peasant Production for Capitalist Enterprise in Colonial India*, Oxford University Press.

Lourdez Arizpe, 1982, 'Relay migration and the survival of the peasant household', in Helen I. Safa (ed.), *Towards a Political Economy of Urbanization in the Third World*, Oxford University Press.

J. Banaji, 1977, 'Capitalist domination and the small peasantry: Deccan districts in the late nineteenth century', *Economic and Political Weekly*, vol. 12, nos 33 and 34, pp. 1375–404.

R. H. Bates, 1981, *Markets and States in Tropical Africa*, University of California Press.

L. Beneria, 1979, 'Reproduction, production and the sexual division of labour', *Cambridge Journal of Economics*, vol. 3.

Bhaduri (section 4C).

A. Bhaduri, Hussain Z. Rahman and L. Arn, 1986, 'Persistence and polarization: a study in the dynamics of agrarian contradictions', *Journal of Peasant Studies*, vol. 13, no. 3, pp. 82–9.

Krishna Bharadwaj, 1974, *Production Conditions in Indian Agriculture*, Occasional Paper no. 33, Department of Applied Economics, University of Cambridge.

Bharadwaj (section 4C).

E. Boserup, 1970, *Women's Role in Economic Development*, St Martin's Press.

Roger Burbach and Patricia Flynn, 1980, *Agribusiness in the Americas*, Monthly Review Press.

T. J. Byres, 1981, 'The new technology, class formation and class practice in the Indian countryside', *Journal of Peasant Studies*, vol. 8, no. 4, pp. 405–54.

M. Cernea, 1978, 'Macrosocial change, feminization of agriculture and peasant women's threefold economic role', *Sociologia Ruralis*, vol. 18, pp. 107–25.

Chayanov (section 4B).

L. Cliffe and R. Moorsom, 1979, 'Rural class formation and ecological collapse in Botswana', *Review of African Political Economy*, vol. 15, no. 16.

R. Dauber and M. L. Cain (eds), 1981, *Women and Technological Change in Developing Countries*, Westview Press.

C. D. Deere, 1976, 'Rural women's subsistence production in the capitalist periphery', *Review of Radical Political Economy*, vol. 8, no. 1, pp. 9–17.

C. D. Deere, 1978, 'The differentiation of the peasantry and the family structure: a Peruvian case study', *Journal of Family History*, vol. 3, no. 4, pp. 422–38.

P. Durrenberg (ed.), 1984, *Chayanov, Peasants and Economic Anthropology*, Academic Press.

E. Feder, 1976, 'The new World Bank programme for the self-liquidation of the Third World peasantry', *Journal of Peasant Studies*, vol. 3, no. 3, pp. 343–54.

J. Foweraker, 1981, *The Struggle for Land: A Political Economy of the Pioneer Frontier in Brazil from 1930 to the Present*, Cambridge University Press.

F. R. Frankel and K. Van Vorys, 1972, *The Political Challenge of the Green Revolution:*

Shifting Patterns of Peasant Participation in India and Pakistan, Policy Memorandum No. 38, Center for International Studies, Princeton.

H. Friedmann, 1978, 'World market, state and family farm: social bases of household production in the era of wage labour', *Comparative Studies in Society and History*, vol. 20, no. 4, pp. 545–86.

H. Friedmann, 1987, *The Political Economy of Food*, Verso.

Susan George, 1976, *How the Other Half Dies: The Real Reasons for World Hunger*, Penguin.

Lim Teck Ghee, 1977, *Peasants and their Agricultural Economy in Colonial Malaya 1874–1941*, Oxford University Press.

J. Gjerde, 1985, *From Peasants to Farmers: The Migration from Balestrad, Norway to the Upper Middle West*, Cambridge University Press.

P. Ghorayshi, 1986, 'the identification of capitalist farms', *Sociologia Ruralis*, vol. 24, no 2.

Kathy and Pandeli Glavanis, 1983, 'The sociology of agrarian relations in the Middle East: the persistence of household production', *Current Sociology*, vol. 31, no. 2. See in particular section 3, which makes a useful application of the major theoretical positions to the experience of contemporary Egypt.

D. Goodman and M. R. Redclift, 1982, *From Peasant to Proletarian: Capitalist Development and Agrarian Transitions*, St Martin's Press.

Barbara Harriss, 1981, *Transitional Trade and Rural Development: The Nature and Role of Agricultural Trade in a South Indian District*, Vikas.

John Harriss, 1982, *Capitalism and Peasant Farming: Agrarian Structure and Ideology in Northern Tamil Nadu*, Oxford University Press.

K. Hart, 1982, *The Political Economy of West African Agriculture*, Cambridge University Press.

U. Haymi, V. W. Ruttan, 1985, *Agricultural Development*, Johns Hopkins University Press.

Deniz Kandyoti, 1985, *Women in Rural Production Systems: Problems and Policies*, UNESCO.

Kautsky (section 4C).

C. Keyder, 1983, 'Paths of rural transformation in Turkey', *Journal of Peasant Studies*, vol. 11, no. 1, pp. 34–49.

Francis M. Lappe and Joseph Collins, 1982, *World Hunger: 10 Myths*, Institute of Food and Development Policy, San Francisco.

Lenin (section 4A).

Norman Long, 1984, *Family and Work in Rural Societies*, Tavistock.

Marx (section 4A).

S. Mintz, 1960, 'Peasant markets', *Scientific American*, vol. 203, no. 2, pp. 112–18.

S. W. Mintz, 1979, 'Slavery and the rise of peasantries', *Historical Reflections*, vol. 6, no. 1. A discussion on the Caribbean region.

R. Munting, 1976, 'Outside earnings in the Russian peasant farm: Tula province 1900–1917', *Journal of Peasant Studies*, vol. 3, no. 4, pp. 428–46.

C. Murray, 1980, 'Migrant labour and changing family structure in the rural periphery of southern Africa', *Journal of Southern African Studies*, vol. 6, no. 2, pp. 139–56.

J. S. Nalson, 1968, *Mobility of Farm Families*, Manchester University Press.

H. Newby and P. Utting, 1984, 'Agrobusiness in UK and social and political implications', in G. N. Barody and G. Geisler, *Social Consequences and Challenges of New Agricultural Technology*, Westview Press.

A. L. Njonjo, 1981, 'The Kenyan peasantry: a re-assessment', *Review of African Political Economy*, vol. 20, pp. 27–40.

Andrew Pearse, 1980, *Seeds of Plenty, Seeds of Want: Social and Economic Implications of the Green Revolution*, UNRISD Publications, Clarendon Press. The result of a world-wide survey.

B. Paolucci, O. A. Hall and W. Axuin, 1977, *Family Decision-Making: An Ecosystem Approach*, John Wiley and Sons.

Paul Richards, 1985, *Indigenous Agricultural Revolution*, Hutchinson.

A. Sen, 1981, *Poverty and Famines: An Essay on Entitlement and Deprivation*, Clarendon Press.

T. Shanin, 1973–4, 'The nature and logic of peasant economies', *Journal of Peasant Studies*, vol. 1, nos 1 and 2.

T. Shanin, 1978, 'The peasants are coming: migrants who labour, peasants who travel and Marxists who write', *Race and Class*.

G. W. Skinner, 1964, 'Marketing and social structure in rural China', *Journal of Asian Studies*, vol. 24.

R. Stavenhagen, 1979, 'Capitalism and the peasantry in Mexico', *Latin American Perspectives*, vol. 5, no. 3, pp. 27–37.

N. Swain, 1985, *Collective Farms Which Work?*, Cambridge University Press.

E. Taylor, 1984, 'Peasants or proletarians? The transformation of agrarian production relations in Egypt', in B. Munslow and H. Finch (eds), *Proletarianisation in the Third World*, Croom Helm.

M. Taussig, 1978, 'Peasant economics and the development of capitalist agriculture in the Cauca valley, Colombia', *Latin American Perspectives*, vol. 4, no. 3, pp. 62–90.

Octavio G. Velho, 1973, 'Modes of Capitalist Development, Peasantry and the Moving Frontier', unpublished Ph.D. thesis, Sociology Department, University of Manchester.

A. R. Waters, 1973, 'Migration, remittances and the cash constraints in African small-holder economic development', *Oxford Economic Papers*, vol. 25, no. 3, pp. 435–54.

C. R. Wharton (ed.), 1969, *Subsistence Agriculture and Economic Development*, Frank Cass.

Gavin Wright, 1978, *The Political Economy of Cotton South*, Norton.

K. Young, 1978, 'Modes of appropriation of the sexual division of labour: a case study from Oaxaca, Mexico', in A. Kuhn and A. M. Wolpe (eds), *Feminism and Material-ism*, Routledge & Kegan Paul.

7 Peasant Culture and Consciousness

Janus M. Bak and Gerhard Benecke, 1984, *Religion and Rural Revolt*, Manchester University Press.

E. C. Banfield, 1958, *The Moral Basis of a Backward Society*, Free Press. A discussion on southern Italian peasant society. For a critique, Sydel Silverman, 1968, 'Agricultural organization, social structure and values in Italy: amoral familism reconsidered', *American Anthropologist*, vol. 70, no. 1.

J. D. Berger, 1978, 'Towards understanding peasant experience', *Race and Class*, vol. 11, no. 4, pp. 345–59.

A. Blok, 1972, 'The peasant and the brigand: social banditry reconsidered', *Comparative Studies in Society and History*, vol. 14, no. 4, pp. 494–503. A critique of Hobsbawm arguing that not all social banditry is an expression of 'primitive rebellion'.

Palle Ove Christiansen, 1983, 'The paradox of capitalist farmers and peasant ideology', *Proceedings of the XIIth European Congress of Rural Sociology*, Budapest. An analysis of the highly capitalized Danish agriculture which underlines the continuing significance of the family farm as a socio-occupational life-choice.

Frantz Fanon, 1965, *The Wretched of the Earth*, MacGibbon & Kee.

Foster (section 4B). See also the follow-up articles, 'Foster's reply to Kaplan, Saler and Bennet', *American Anthropologist*, vol. 68, no. 1 (1966) and 'A second look at limited good', *Anthropological Quarterly*, vol. 45, no. 2 (1972).

E. K. L. Francis, 1945, 'The personality types of the peasant according to Hesiod's Works and Days', *Rural Sociology*, vol. 10, pp. 275–95.

P. Greenough, 1983, *Prosperity and Misery in Modern Bengal*, Oxford University Press.

R. Guha, 1983, *Elementary Aspects of Peasant Insurgency*, Oxford University Press. See also the various volumes of *Subaltern Studies*, Oxford University Press.

E. J. Hobsbawm, 1959, *Primitive Rebels: Studies in Archaic Forms of Social Movements in the 19th and 20th Centuries*, Manchester University Press.

Narahari Kaviraj, 1982, *Wahabi and Farazi Rebels of Bengal*, People's Publishing House, New Delhi. Two cases of peasant struggle conducted under a religious idiom.

E. Le Roy Ladurie, 1980, *Montaillou: Cathars and Catholics in a French Village 1294—1324*, Penguin.

Oscar Lewis, 1964, *Pedro Martinez: A Mexican Peasant and His Family*, Secker & Warburg.

D. Mitrany, 1961, *Marx Against the Peasant*, Collier.

T. Ranger, 1985, *Peasant Consciousness and Guerrilla War in Zimbabwe*, James Currey.

R. Redfield, 1955, *The Little Community*, University of Chicago Press.

Scott (section 4B).

J. C. Scott and B. J. T. Kerkvliet, 1986, 'Everyday forms of peasant resistance in South-East Asia', special issue of *Journal of Peasant Studies*, vol. 13, no. 2.

J. C. Scott, 1986, *Weapons of the Weak: Everyday Forms of Peasant Resistance*, Yale University Press.

Bjarne Stoklund, 1979–80, 'On interpreting peasant diaries: material life in collective consciousness', *Ethnologia Europea*, vol. 11, no. 2.

Charles Tilly, 1982, 'Proletarianization and rural collective action in East Anglia and elsewhere', *Peasant Studies*, vol. 10, no. 1, pp. 5–35.

Andrew Turton and Shigeharu Tanabe (eds), 1984, *History and Peasant Consciousness in South-East Asia*, Senri Ethnological Studies No. 13, National Museum of Ethnology, Osaka.

8 Peasant Political Action

H. Alavi, 1965, 'Peasants and revolution', *Socialist Register*, Merlin Press.

H. Alavi, 1971, 'The politics of dependence: a village in west Punjab', *South Asian Review*, vol. 4, no. 2, pp. 112–18.

Alavi (section 4B).

Giorgi Alberti, 1972, 'The breakdown of provincial urban power structure and the rise of peasant movements', *Sociologia Ruralis*, vol. 12, pp. 315–34.

M. Banton (ed.), 1965, *Political Systems and the Distribution of Power*, Tavistock Publications.

John D. Bell, 1977, *Peasants in Power: Alexander Stomboliski and the Bulgarian Agrarian National Union 1899—1923*, Princeton University Press.

Herbert P. Bix, 1986, *Peasant Protest in Japan, 1590—1884*, Yale University Press.

A. Blok, 1974, *The Mafia of a Sicilian Village: A Study of Violent Peasant Entrepreneurs*, Basil Blackwell.

Amilcar Cabral, 1969, *Revolution in Guinea*, Stage 1.

Basil Davidson, 1974, 'African peasants and revolution', *Journal of Peasant Studies*, vol. 1, no. 3, pp. 269–90.

D. N. Dhanagare, 1982, *Peasant Movements in India 1920—1950*, Oxford University Press.

P. G. Eidelberg, 1974, *The Great Rumanian Peasant Revolt of 1907*, Brill.

F. Engels, 1956, *The Peasant War in Germany*, Progress Publishers.

David Hardiman, 1981, *Peasant Nationalists of Gujarat: Kheda District, 1917—1934*, Oxford University Press.

W. Hinton, 1966, *Fanshen: A Documentary of Revolution in a Chinese Village*, Monthly Review Press.

E. J. Hobsbawm, 1965, 'Vietnam and the dynamics of guerilla warfare', *New Left Review*, vol. 17.

E. J. Hobsbawm, 1967, 'Peasants and rural migrants in politics', in C. Veliz (ed.), *The Politics of Conformity in Latin America*, Oxford University Press.

G. Huizer, 1973, *Peasant Rebellion in Latin America*, Penguin.

B. J. Kerkvilet, 1977, *The Huk Rebellion: A Study of Peasant Revolt in the Philippines*, University of California Press.

Geoff Lamb, 1974, *Peasant Politics*, Julian Friedman Publishers. A district-level case-study on Kenya.

H. Landsberger and C. H. de Alcantra, 1971, 'From violence to pressure-group politics and co-operation: a Mexican case-study', in P. Worsley (ed.), *Two Blades of Grass*, Manchester University Press.

Colin Leys, 1971, 'Politics in Kenya: the development of peasant society', *British Journal of Political Science*, vol. 1, no. 3, pp. 307–37.

M. Mamdani, 1986, 'Peasants and democracy in Africa', *New Left Review*, no. 156.

K. Marx, 1973, 'The eighteenth Brumaire of Louis Bonaparte', in *Surveys From Exile*. Political writings vol. 2, Penguin.

Anne Mayhew, 1972, 'A reappraisal of the causes of farm protest in the United States 1870–1900', *Journal of Economic History*, no. 30.

MERIP Reports No. 87, May 1980, *Iran's Revolution: The Rural Dimension*.

D. B. Miller, 1979, *Peasants and Politics: Grass Roots Reaction to Change in Asia*, St Martin's Press.

Swasti Mitter, 1977, *Peasant Movements in West Bengal: Their Impact on Agrarian Class Relations Since 1967*, Department of Land Economy, Occasional Paper No. 8, University of Cambridge. Interesting look at dynamics of peasant struggle in a region which has had periods of elected communist government.

Barrington Moore, 1969, *Social Origins of Dictatorship and Democracy*, Penguin. An illuminating discussion of the impact of power relations in the countryside on the political making of the contemporary world.

Nicos Mouzelis, 1976, 'Greek and Bulgarian peasants: aspects of their socio-political situation during the inter-war period', *Comparative Studies in Society and History*, vol. 18.

J. Petras and M. Zeitlin, 1968, 'Agrarian radicalism in Chile', *British Journal of Sociology*, vol. 19, no. 3, pp. 254–70. A comparative analysis of legal political action in rural society.

S. W. Schmidt, J. C. Scott, C. Lande and L. Guesti (eds), 1977, *Friends, Followers and Factions*, University of California Press. A useful reader.

Scott (section 7).

Shanin (section 4B).

T. Shanin, 1986, *Russia 1905—07: Revolution as a Moment of Truth*, Macmillan.

K. E. Sharpe, 1977, *Peasant Politics: Struggle in a Dominican Village*, Johns Hopkins University Press.

R. Stavenhagen (ed.), 1970, *Agrarian Problems and Peasant Movements in Latin America*, Doubleday.

Sydney M. Tarrow, 1967, *Peasant Communism in Southern Italy*, Yale University Press.

C. Tilly, 1964, *The Vendée*, Harvard University Press.

C. Tilly, 1977, 'Town and country in revolution', in J. Lewis (ed.), *Peasant Revolution and Communist Revolution in Asia*, Stanford University Press.

R. Waterbury, 1975, 'Non-revolutionary peasants: Oaxaca compared to Morelos in the Mexican Revolution', *Comparative Studies in Society and History*, vol. 17, no. 4.

R. P. Weller and S. E. Guggenheim (eds), 1982, *Power and Protest in the Countryside*, Duke University Press. (Especially Theda Skocpol, 'What makes peasant revolutionary'.)

E. R. Wolf, 1969, *Peasant Wars of the Twentieth Century*, Harper & Row.

L. Zamosc, 1986, *The Agrarian Question and the Peasant Movement in Colombia: Struggles of the National Peasant Association 1967—81*, Cambridge University Press.

9 State, Peasantry, Reforms

H. Alavi, R. D. Stevens and P. Bertocci, 1972, *Rural Development in Bangladesh and Pakistan*, Michigan University Press.

D. Atkinson, 1983, *The End of the Russian Land-Commune*, Stanford University Press.

H. Bernstein, 1981, 'Notes on state and peasantry: the Tanzanian case', *Review of African Political Economy*, vol. 21, pp. 4–62.

J. Collins, with F. M. Lappe, N. Allen and P. Rice, 1985, *What Difference Could a Revolution Make? Food and Farming in the New Nicaragua*, Institute for Food and Development Policy, San Francisco.

R. P. Dore, 1959, *Land Reform in Japan*, Oxford University Press.

F. Ellis, 1983, 'Agricultural marketing and peasant–state transfers in Tanzania', *Journal of Peasant Studies*, vol. 10, no. 4, pp. 214–42.

C. Erasmus, 1967, 'The upper limits of peasantry and agrarian reform: Bolivia, Venezuela and Mexico compared', *Ethnology*, vol. 6, no. 4.

C. M. Hann, 1980, *Tazlav: A Village in Hungary*, Cambridge University Press. A good discussion of the nature of the state's political presence at the local level.

Judith Heyer, Pepe Roberts and Gavin Williams (eds), 1981, *Rural Development in Tropical Africa*, Macmillan.

Marida Hollos and Bela C. Maday (eds), *New Hungarian Peasants: An East European Experience with Collectivization*, Social Science Monographs, Brooklyn College Press.

G. Huizer, 1969, 'Community development, land reform and political participation', *American Journal of Economic Sociology*, vol. 28, no. 2.

Alain de Janvry, 1981, *The Agrarian Question and Reformism in Latin America*, Johns Hopkins University Press.

A. K. S. Lambton, 1969, *The Persian Land Reform 1962—66*, Clarendon Press.

John Lonsdale, 1981, 'State and peasantry in colonial Africa', in R. Samuel (ed.), *People's History and Socialist Theory*, Routledge & Kegan Paul.

M. R. Redclift, 1976, 'Agrarian reform and peasant organization in Guayas Basin, Ecuador', *Inter-American Affairs*, vol. 30, no. 1, pp. 3–27.

E. H. Tuma, 1979, 'Agrarian reform in historical perspective revisited', *Comparative Studies in Society and History*, vol. 21, no. 1, pp. 3–29.

K. E. Wadekin, 1982, *Agression Policies in Communist Europe*, Allanheld, Osmun. Includes extensive bibliography of the issue.

D. Warriner, 1969, *Land Reform in Principle and Practice*, Clarendon Press.

K. Westergaard, 1985, *State and Rural Society in Bangladesh*, Curzon Press.

P. Worsley, 1971, *Two Blades of Grass: Rural Co-operatives in Agricultural Modernization Societies*, Manchester University Press.

10 Selected Monographs on Specific Peasant Societies

H. Ammar, 1954, *Growing up in an Egyptian Village*, Routledge & Kegan Paul.

C. M. Arensberg, 1937, *The Irish Countrymen*, Macmillan.

G. Dallas, 1982, *The Imperfect Peasant Economy: The Loire Country 1800—1914*, Cambridge University Press.

G. Djurfeldt and S. Lindberg, 1975, *Behind Poverty: The Social Formation in a Tamil Village*, Scandinavian Institute of Asian Studies Monograph Series No. 22, Curzon Press.

G. Esteva, 1983, *The Struggle for Rural Mexico*, Bergin & Garvey.

Orlando Fals-Borda, 1962, *Peasant Society in the Colombian Andes: A Sociological Study of Saucio*, University of Florida Press.

E. Fel and T. Hofer, 1969, *Proper Peasants: Traditional Life in a Hungarian Village*, Viking Fund Publications in Anthropology No. 46, New York.

Betsy Hartman and James Boyce, 1983, *A Quiet Violence: View from a Bangladesh Village*, Zed Press/Oxford University Press.

Polly Hill, 1972, *Rural Hausa: A Village and a Setting*, Cambridge University Press.

W. G. Hoskins, 1957, *The Midland Peasant: The Economic and Social History of a Leicestershire Village*, Macmillan.

Jan Myrdal, 1967, *Report from a Chinese Village*, Penguin.

G. T. Robinson, 1949, *Rural Russia under the Old Regime: A History of Landlord—peasant World and a Prologue to the Peasant Revolution of 1907*, California University Press.

D. Seddon, 1981, *Moroccan Peasants: A Century of Change in the Eastern Rif, 1870—1970*, Dawson.

T. C. Smith, 1959, *The Agrarian Origins of Modern Japan*, Stanford University Press.

Sol Tax, 1953, *Penny Capitalism: A Guatemalan Indian Economy*, Smithsonian Institution.

M. K. Whyte and P. L. William, 1978, *Village and Family in Contemporary China*, Chicago University Press.

E. Wolf, 1959, *Sons of the Shaking Earth* (Peru), University of Chicago Press.

C. K. Yang, 1959, *A Chinese Village in Early Communist Transition*, Massachusetts Institute of Technology Press.

11 Novels, Memoirs, Films about Peasant Life
(This section with the help of Tim Allen)

Chinou Achebe, *Arrow of God*, Heinemann, African Writers Series (Nigeria).
J. D. Berger, 1985, *Pig Earth*, Chatto & Windus/The Hogarth Press (France).
Pearl S. Buck, *The Good Earth* (China).
Knut Hamsun, *Growth of the Soil* (Norway).
Thomas Hardy, *Far From the Madding Crowd* (England).
Euclides da Kunha, 1970, *Rebellion in the Backlands*, University of Chicago Press.
Le Roy Ladurie (section 7) (France).
Joan Rockwell, 1981, *Evald Tang Kristensen: A Lifelong Adventure in Folklore*, Aalborg University Press (Denmark).
Salvattore Samperi, *Padre Padrone* (Italy).
M. Sholokhov, *And Quiet Flows the Don* (USSR).
V. Shukshin, 1978, *Snowball, Beny Road and Other Stones*, Ardin (USSR).
John Steinbeck, *The Grapes of Wrath* (USA).
Ngugi Wa Thiongo, *The River Between*, Heinemann, African Writers Series (Kenya).
Thomas and Znaniecki (section 4A) (Poland).
Émile Zola, *Earth* (France).

The Apu Trilogy (Bengal). Films directed by Satayjit Ray, based on the novels of Bibhuti Bhusan Bandopadhay.
Kaos (Italy). Film, directed by the Taviani brothers.
The Tree of Wooden Clogs (Italy). Film, directed by the Taviani brothers.

Index

Index

Index by Mandy Crook